Celebrating Peanuts 65 Years

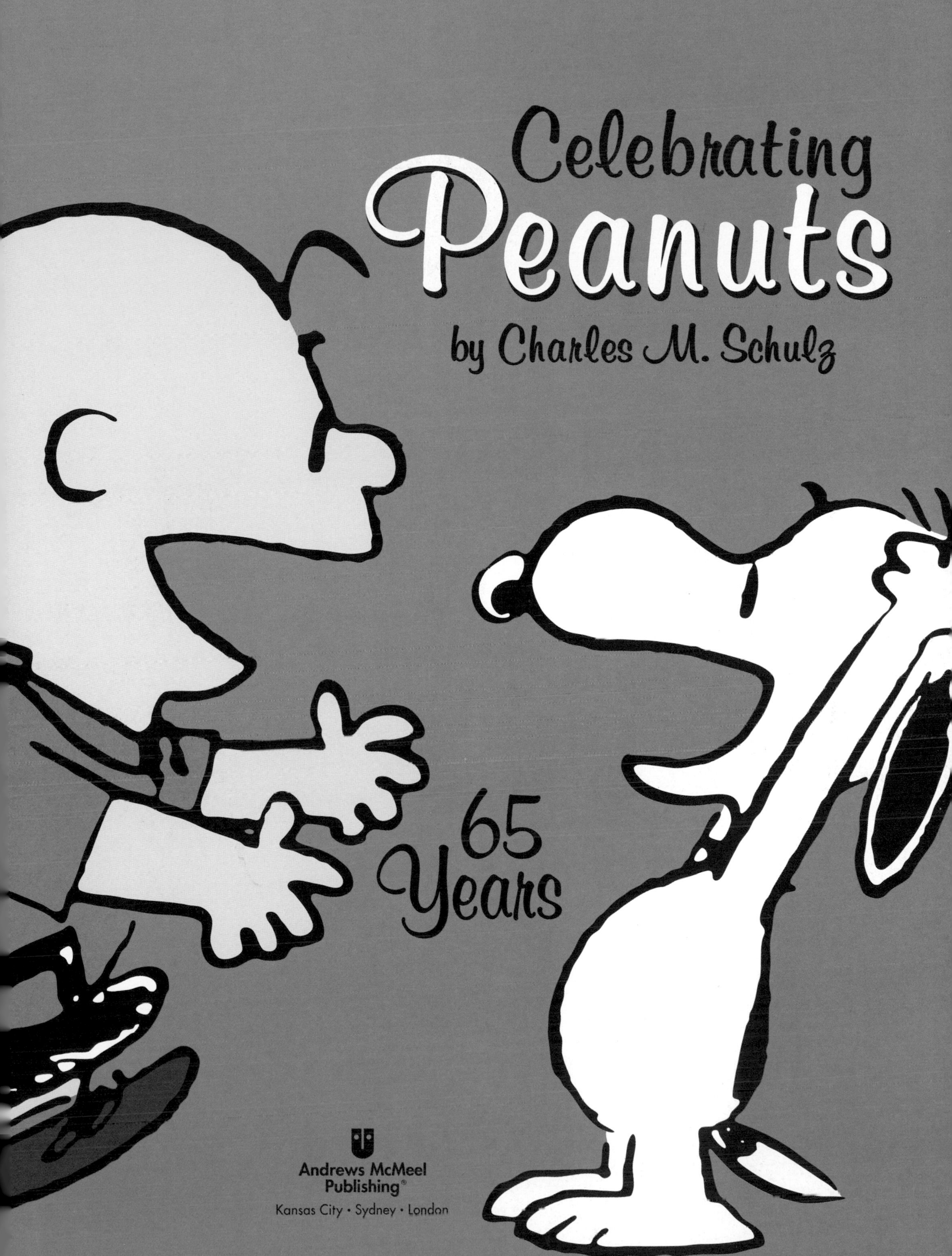

Celebrating Peanuts

by Charles M. Schulz

65 Years

Andrews McMeel Publishing®
Kansas City • Sydney • London

Peanuts is distributed internationally by Universal Uclick.

Peanuts is a registered trademark of Peanuts Worldwide, Inc.

Andrews McMeel Publishing, LLC
an Andrews McMeel Universal company
1130 Walnut Street, Kansas City, Missouri 64106

www.andrewsmcmeel.com

peanuts.com

15 16 17 18 19 POA 10 9 8 7 6 5 4 3 2

ISBN: 978-1-4494-7182-8

Library of Congress Control Number: 2015936611

This book was originally published as *Celebrating Peanuts: 60 Years* in a hardcover slipcased edition in 2009.

Produced by Lionheart Books Ltd.
3522 Ashford Dunwoody Rd. N.E. #229
Atlanta, Georgia 30319

Editors: Paige Braddock and Alexis E. Fajardo

Book design by Michael Reagan

Assistant Editors:
1950s—Paige Braddock
1960s—Stephan Pastis
1970s—Alexis Fajardo
1980s—Justin Thompson
1990s and 2000—Erin Samuels

Production Assistant: Janis Fein

Slipcase and chapter openers design by Ridge Rooms

Art Assists and Sunday Page Color:
Chris Bracco, Paige Braddock, Meggin Chinkel, Jessica Dasher, Alexis Fajardo, Janis Fein, Daniel Paz, Ridge Rooms, Erin Samuels, Justin Thompson, and Brian Whitmer.

Era FAQs compiled and written by Jane O'Cain, Lisa Monhoff, and Gretchen Emmert.

Thanks to Helene Gordon, April Heeren, Josh Kislevitz, Amy Lago, Allison Mak, Jean Sagendorph, and Kim Towner.

Printed in China
through Asia Pacific Offset

Contents

Foreword

I grew up, I'm sure like most of you reading this, spending many a rainy day poring over *Peanuts* books. In fact, I pored over them on sunny days as well. I read them over and over, memorizing every gag and pose. I drew copies of my favorite strips. I knew I didn't want to be a comic strip artist (there was something rather daunting about coming up with ideas for a strip every single day), but I was obsessed.

More than anything, I wanted to be able to draw expressions like Schulz did. A few simple lines and he'd capture these incredibly strong, specific emotions. And they were funny! They showed so clearly what was going on inside those characters' minds, and to me that was absolutely magical.

Schulz's work has definitely had a strong impact on me and what I do. And I'm not the only one. It's not uncommon to hear *Peanuts* shorthand spoken around the building at Pixar. "All I want is what's coming to me. All I want is my fair share." "You're right—needs more crayons." "I was going to say I saw a ducky and a horsie, but I changed my mind." If you can't picture the strips that these quotes come from, you've got some studying to do!

Rain or shine, open this book and get cracking.

Pete

Pete Docter, director of *Monsters, Inc.* and *Up*
Pixar Animation Studios

Introduction

"If you want to be a cartoonist, draw every day."

This was the advice Charles Schulz gave to aspiring cartoonists, and this is exactly what he did almost every day of his life for as long as he could remember.

Charles Schulz was known as Sparky to his family and friends. The nickname came from Spark Plug, the racehorse in the *Barney Google and Snuffy Smith* comic strip. Sparky said it seemed as if he was born to be a cartoonist, and the comic strip nickname given to him when he was just a few days old proved prophetic. As a small boy he drew, and as a teenager he worked on his comic strips. All of this drawing was coming from inside of him. No one was showing him how—he just copied and copied the comic strips he loved. During seventy-three years of drawing, Sparky perfected his craft so that he could whip out a drawing for a fan or a reporter from a newspaper, TV show, or magazine, in ten seconds. This facility made drawing the comic strip seem deceptively easy to others.

It wasn't until the daily strip ceased that people, and I count myself among them, began to explore what we had all taken for granted since we first became fans of *Peanuts*.

At the Charles M. Schulz Museum and Research Center, which opened in August 2002 in Santa Rosa, California, we are fortunate to pore over 7,500 original strips as we select the ones to display in our strip gallery. As we prepare the strips for display, we note all the discrepancies, while the cartoonist in our review team explains how the change in a line or a perspective affects the artwork. Seeing the daily strips and Sunday pages in their original size, laid out on a table without a frame or case to interfere, one can often see a faint pencil line underneath and see how Sparky changed a line for a more dramatic effect. He didn't draw in pencil and then "ink in" over the pencil lines. He made only the faintest of markings so he could see how much space the dialogue would take and then just the lightest line to indicate the size of the character. That way, his drawing was spontaneous. Sparky said he could feel the emotion he was drawing. How fortunate we are to be able to see his amazing craftsmanship up close and unfettered.

In the strip gallery, visitors can also see what an amazing repertoire Sparky had, from the expressions he coined in the comic strip—"security blanket," "Good grief!" and "Aaugh!"—to the endless variety of themes, such as Lucy and the football, the Great Pumpkin, baseball, Schroeder and his piano, and the Kite-Eating Tree. Every *Peanuts* fan has a favorite and can name many more. I call the strip gallery the heart and soul of the museum.

"In cartooning the first thing is to develop patience." This is one of Sparky's quotes, which is painted on the wall of the museum's education room; patience, because a cartoon doesn't appear full blown and fully formed. Ideas are everywhere, and if you develop your own unique sense of humor and embrace the absurdity of life, you can pluck these ideas and become a comedian. Everything is grist for the mill, but a comic strip requires a cohesive story, shoehorned into a specific space and timing. It takes a craftsman as well as an artist and a writer. *Peanuts* strips have a unique pacing: statement, complication, the denouement, and then the signature *Peanuts* punch line (1/23/63, page 134).

Even when Sparky knew the subject he wanted to write about, say the ubiquitous Tiny Tots concerts featuring Peter and the Wolf (which Sparky narrated once with the San Jose Symphony), it could take him months to come up with the strip (3/5/85, page 390). And then, of course, one idea might lead to another (7/10/85, page 393). The rainout of a spring baseball game, a memory Sparky brought with him from Minnesota, took him weeks to get just the right *Peanuts* ending (4/9/72, page 235). The next spring, he created a fresh take on the same theme. Sparky said it took twenty-one years before it dawned on him how to use a memory from 1950 (6/13/71, page 225).

When asked if he got many ideas from his five children, Sparky answered that they had given him sixteen ideas in twenty years, hardly enough to keep him going. He credited them publicly with "Am I buttering too loud for you?" (5/28/61, page 122) and "If you hold your hands upside down, you get the opposite of what you pray for" (4/3/68, page 185).

Sparky's first son, Monte, and his World War I airplane models inspired Sparky to create one of his most popular Snoopy personas; and watching Craig, his second son, who loved riding dirt bikes, brought forth a series about motocross (2/18/75, page 267). I claim the expressions "Sweet Babboo" and "Poor, Sweet Baby." Yet, none of us would have known how to use these ideas, with which character, or in which circumstance. I was amazed to discover my Powder Puff Derby race of June 1975 turned into an adventure for Peppermint Patty and Marcie (and, of course, Snoopy). How did Sparky conceive of this configuration of characters for this series? It works because he knew his cast of characters intimately. It works just as the complete silliness works (12/10/73, page 254), because it all came from within Sparky.

The ten years since Sparky's death have given us perspective on his fifty years of drawing and storytelling visible in this anniversary edition. We realize how much each of the characters evolved, from kids doing kid things, albeit with a certain sauciness (3/9/53, page 30), to kids becoming spokespeople for all our hopes, fears, anxieties, obsessions, and small joys. Snoopy evolved from a puppy hiding behind a tree to escape a ball, to the most multifaceted dog on the planet (and the moon) (3/14/69, page 195). The *Peanuts* gang evolved from children making mud pies and snowmen (2/22/53, page 30) to commenting on the latest popular psychology (12/5/93, page 465).

Most literary works are based on a certain arc. The comic strip and its daily insertion into our lives is an anomaly. It must be familiar and the characters instantly recognizable (thus Charlie Brown's iconic zigzag T-shirt). It must work for the occasional reader and for the dedicated reader. And to hold readers' interest for fifty years, it must grow, but not outpace its readers.

In *Peanuts*, character evolution and story evolution went hand in hand. With the Sunday pages leading the way, gradually the strip moved from a gag-a-day to story lines. One of the first was the Charlotte Braun story line (11/30/54, page 47). This was followed by a series of daily strips where Linus miraculously blew square balloons, showing that square-balloon ideas overflowed in Sparky's own head (12/20/54, page 49).

Perhaps most surprising was the story line in April 1956, when Charlie Brown's kite got caught in a tree. For eight days, Charlie Brown stood by the tree, holding the kite string, while Violet, Lucy, Patty, and Shermy came by to comment. The static nature of these strips caused some editors to question the wisdom of such a tack.

The storyteller must continue to push the envelope and try something new. Often Sparky would begin a story idea and then realize he didn't know where to go with it, or perhaps he would just lose the inspiration to take it any further. Notice the story when Linus and Lucy's father is transferred to another city. For twelve days in May of 1966, Sparky kept his readers in suspense as the story moved along. Two of the most poignant moments in this story happen when Linus bequeaths his beloved blanket to Charlie Brown (5/13/66, page 166), and the day when even Beethoven can't assuage Schroeder's guilty feelings (5/18/66, page 167). The story ends abruptly with the simple explanation, "Dad . . . didn't like the new job."

The complications of a story line are many. It can only progress in the daily strips, because many people don't read the paper on the weekend. At the same time, each daily strip must stand alone for the episodic reader. Look carefully at any ongoing story and you will see that each daily component works on its own.

One of Sparky's quotes is something of a conundrum. He said it frequently in slightly different ways. We have this quote written prominently, over Sparky's photograph, in the museum's Great Hall: "A cartoonist is someone who draws the same thing day after day without repeating himself." And because Sparky did just that, three generations of fans grew to know and love the *Peanuts* characters.

Nick Meglin, former editor of *MAD* magazine and writer of several popular books and articles on drawing, said it best when he related a question-and-answer session with Sparky at one of the yearly National Cartoonists Society's Reuben Awards weekends. Nick recalled, "When asked if he ever thought about giving up drawing the *Peanuts* feature, Sparky responded, 'I would only do that if the feeling and sound of the pen gliding over the page no longer excites me. It still does as much today as it did when I first started the strip.' It was obvious Sparky never anticipated the silence that followed. Every artist turned to his neighbor, acknowledging the moment in his own way—smiling, nodding, and shrugging in disbelief at the eloquence of those words."

Following emergency surgery for an aortic aneurysm on November 15, 1999, Sparky spent two weeks in the hospital. After that he never went back to his drawing board except to create, with Paige Braddock, his final Sunday page saying good-bye to his readers.

He died peacefully in his sleep the night before his good-bye appeared in the Sunday papers.

—Jean Schulz, October 2009
Santa Rosa, California

The creation of any book requires the talents and work of many people. But the level of care, commitment, and attention on the part of so many people who made this book happen surely exceeds anyone's expectations. It is truly a tribute to Charles Schulz's legacy that so many people were inspired to celebrate *Peanuts*'s 60th anniversary by contributing so much to this book.

A special thank-you goes to Jean Schulz for generously sharing the resources of the Schulz Museum and Creative Associates to create the content for this book, and also for her heartfelt introduction to the book.

Editor's Note

All the quotes that appear throughout the book are directly from Charles M. Schulz, either in print or in interviews. References to each one's origin are cited on page 534.

Because of varied production methods over the fifty years of *Peanuts*, the Sunday cartoons included in this book appear in a range of presentations. Some are the black line only, some are scanned from newspaper tearsheets, some are the original Sunday color, and some have been colored for this book.

Celebrate 1950s

"I was a product of the times. You see, the comic strips were very important when I was growing up, which was during the thirties. Radio shows, Saturday afternoon movies, and the comics were the real thing. And, of course, I could draw. I could never draw real well—I could never paint or do anything like that—but I could draw."

—Charles M. Schulz

TICKLE
TICKLE
TIC...

1950–1959

Peanuts debuted on October 2, 1950, with a strip featuring Charlie Brown, Shermy, and Patty. Throughout the 1950s, many of *Peanuts*'s most beloved, and some of its least remembered, characters were introduced. Snoopy first appeared on October 4, 1950, and Schroeder, Linus, and Sally were subsequently added to the cast as babies. Lucy and Pig-Pen also joined the gang during the decade. Violet first appeared on February 7, 1951, but she, along with the original Patty, is a little-remembered early character.

Many of Schulz's most recognizable themes that would make *Peanuts* an outstanding strip were introduced before the decade's end:

- Charlie Brown appeared in his trademark zigzag shirt for the first time on December 21, 1950. "I first drew Charlie Brown just wearing a little white T-shirt," Schulz remarked, "but he didn't bounce off the page. So I gave him that little jagged stripe. . . . The stripe sets Charlie Brown apart."

- Schroeder received his first piano in September 1951 and revealed his love for Beethoven in the November 26, 1951, strip. Schulz said that although Brahms was his favorite composer, he chose Beethoven as the object of Schroeder's affection simply because the name "Beethoven" sounded funnier.

- Charlie Brown first attempted to fly a kite on March 21, 1952; his struggles with kites and the dreaded Kite-Eating Tree would reach epic proportions over the next five decades. At times, Charlie Brown would have to flee in terror as his kite literally turned on him and attempted to chase him down.

- Charlie Brown's ill-fated baseball games mirror some of Schulz's boyhood games. Schulz's team did, in fact, once lose a baseball game by a score of 40 to 0. The March 23, 1952, strip is the first *Peanuts* Sunday strip to feature the all-American sport.

- In what would become a much-anticipated fall strip, Lucy holds the football for Charlie Brown to kick for the first time on November 16, 1952. As the years went by, Lucy devised ever more devious and cunning arguments to convince Charlie Brown to kick the football, and Charlie Brown, trusting and gullible to a fault, always made the attempt. Schulz created this fall classic thirty-six times, but each year he doubted if he could think of another scenario for this strip.

- On June 1, 1954, Linus is first seen with his security blanket. Schulz's children were toddlers during the early 1950s and he wrote that Linus's blanket was "inspired" by the blankets that his first three children "dragged around the house." Schulz commented that he thought the security blanket was his "best idea," as "it suddenly made security blankets and thumb-sucking okay all around the world." He hoped, finally, that it might have made "parents a little less worried about their kids."

- Snoopy first appeared upright on his two hind legs on January 9, 1956; later in the year, he did his first "happy dance." Snoopy's walking upright changed the comic strip in profound ways, as it freed Snoopy to explore an increasingly more complex fantasy life.

- The Cat Who Lives Next Door, Snoopy's worthy, but never seen opponent, was introduced November 23, 1958. Over the years, the cat would destroy many of Snoopy's doghouses with his well-aimed slashes.

- As *Peanuts* became less realistic, Snoopy no longer inhabited his doghouse like a normal dog would (and what other dog has a Van Gogh or a pool table in his doghouse anyway?); he first attempted to sleep on top of his doghouse on December 12, 1958.

- Lucy first appeared in an early "proto" psychiatrist's booth on March 27, 1959. It wasn't until May 1961 that Lucy's booth took on the more recognizable form with sides and a top.

- The Great Pumpkin, a hallmark of the strip, was introduced by Linus on October 26, 1959. Linus's yearly preoccupation with the Great Pumpkin was a source of endless frustration to the rest of the gang.

October 2, 1950

WELL! HERE COMES OL' CHARLIE BROWN!
GOOD OL' CHARLIE BROWN....YES, SIR!
GOOD OL' CHARLIE BROWN...
HOW I HATE HIM!
SCHULZ

"Not one of the characters in Peanuts *is modeled after anyone I know. But the names mostly come from friends. Charlie Brown, for instance, is named after a man I worked with at an art school in Minneapolis."*

October 4, 1950—First appearance of Snoopy.

?
SCHULZ

October 7, 1950

WATCH OUT FOR CHILDREN
WATCH OUT FOR CHILDREN
WATCH OUT FOR CHILDREN
LET'S LEAVE... I DON'T THINK ANY ARE COMING!
SCHULZ

October 10, 1950

?
KLUNK!
SCHULZ

October 13, 1950

SCHULZ

October 18, 1950

ROOT BEER
FOR SALE

FLOWERS
FOR SALE

LEMONADE
FOR SALE

BONES
FOR SALE
10-18
SCHULZ

October 26, 1950

IS PATTY HOME?
NO...I'M HER AUNT AGNES

OH, WELL, I'LL GO VISIT THAT PRETTY LITTLE GIRL IN THE NEXT BLOCK!
?

WAIT! I'M HOME!!

I COULD HAVE FOOLED YOU IF I WEREN'T SO JEALOUS!
10/26
SCHULZ

October 28, 1950

C'MON, GIMME A BITE!

PHOOIE!!

WHAT KIND OF ICE CREAM IS THAT?!
I DIDN'T SAY IT WAS ICE CREAM

IT'S MASHED POTATO!
10/28
SCHULZ

November 3, 1950

READ THE BOTTOM LINE, PLEASE!
?

I CAN'T MAKE IT OUT

TRY THE OTHER TWO LINES

ONLY FOUR YEARS OLD, AND ALREADY I NEED GLASSES!
SCHULZ

November 9, 1950

THE FUTURE FRIGHTENS ME!

I DON'T SEE WHY...YOU'RE YOUNG AND FULL OF LIFE...

YOU'LL PROBABLY LIVE FOR ANOTHER SIXTY YEARS!

THAT'S WHAT FRIGHTENS ME!
11/9
SCHULZ

November 25, 1950

"PEANUTS"
SO LONG, OL' PAL...I'M GONNA MISS YOU...

BUT DON'T BE SAD...TRY TO KEEP YOUR CHIN UP!

IT WON'T BE FOR LONG...

IN FACT, I'LL SEE YOU IN THE MORNING!
11-25
SCHULZ

December 6, 1950

"PEANUTS"
?

!

YOU'RE THE MOST INCONSIDERATE PERSON I'VE EVER KNOWN!
12-6
SCHULZ

December 7, 1950

"PEANUTS"
YOUR MOTHER IS A GIRL!

YOUR GRANDMOTHER IS A GIRL! YOUR WIFE WILL BE A GIRL!

AND ALL YOUR DAUGHTERS WILL BE GIRLS, TOO!! SO THERE!

WOW!
12-7
SCHULZ

December 18, 1950

"PEANUTS"
HELLO, SHERMY
HELLO, CHARLIE BROWN

LOOKS LIKE IT MAY GET A LITTLE COLDER..
YES, IT LOOKS THAT WAY...

WELL, DON'T TAKE ANY WOODEN NICKELS!
DON'T DO ANYTHING I WOULDN'T DO!

NOW THERE WAS A REAL ADULT CONVERSATION!
SCHULZ 12-18

December 21, 1950—First appearance of Charlie Brown's zigzag shirt.

CHARLIE BROWN, SEE WHAT TIME IT IS, PLEASE?

?

TEN MINUTES TO THREE? ALL RIGHT, THANK YOU
12-21
SCHULZ

"For the first two weeks of the strip, Charlie Brown wore a plain white T-shirt. But then I realized the strip needed more color, so I drew the [zigzag] shirt."

January 10, 1951

"PEANUTS"
BOY, IT'S HOT IN HERE!

ARE YOU REALLY HOT, PATTY?
I'LL SAY I AM!

YOU DON'T LOOK SO HOT TO ME!
!

I GET MY LAUGHS!
SCHULZ
1/10

February 7, 1951—First appearance of Violet.

WELL, HELLO, THERE!
?

YOU DON'T KNOW ME, DO YOU? MY NAME IS "VIOLET"
AHEM

YOU'RE REAL CUTE...
AHEM!!

WELL, WHY DIDN'T YOU INTRODUCE ME?!
2-7
SCHULZ

February 26, 1951

"PEANUTS"
LET'S PLAY HOUSE, CHARLIE BROWN

I'LL BE THE MOTHER AND YOU BE THE FATHER

YOU'LL HAVE TO DO EVERYTHING I TELL YOU!

DO WE HAVE TO BE SO REALISTIC?
2/26
SCHULZ

April 9, 1951

"PEANUTS"
FORTY-EIGHT, FORTY-NINE, FIFTY! HERE I COME, READY, OR NOT!

HA!! I SEE CHARLIE BROWN!

?

RATS! HOW DID SHE EVER SEE ME HERE?!
4/9
SCHULZ

April 11, 1951

"PEANUTS"
SAY, I JUST SAW SOMEONE ELSE WITH A SHIRT LIKE YOURS

YOU MUST HAVE BEEN MISTAKEN... THIS IS AN EXCLUSIVE NUMBER!

OH, YEAH? LOOK WHO'S COMING...

4/11
SCHULZ

April 17, 1951

"PEANUTS"

?

!!!

4/17
SCHULZ

May 15, 1951

"PEANUTS"
SOMETIMES I GET SO MAD AT YOU!

DO YOU KNOW WHAT YOU ARE? YOU'RE NOTHING BUT AN OL' CHARLIE BROWN!!!
!

NOW HOLD ON! THAT'S GOING TOO FAR!!
HMM!

BOY, ALL THIS MAKES ME FEEL GREAT!!
5/15
SCHULZ

May 22, 1951

"PEANUTS"
SNOOPY!! HERE, SNOOPY!

C'MON, BOY! HERE, SNOOPY! C'MON, BOY!

IT'S SUPPERTIME!!

5/22 SCHULZ

"Schroeder was named after a young boy with whom I used to caddy at a golf course in St. Paul. I don't recall ever knowing his first name, but just Schroeder seemed right for the character in the strip even before he became the great musician."

May 30, 1951—First appearance of Schroeder.

"PEANUTS"
HAVE YOU MET SCHROEDER YET, CHARLIE BROWN?

SCHROEDER?! WHO'S HE?
HE LIVES NEXT DOOR... C'MON, I'LL INTRODUCE YOU

HERE HE IS! SAY SOMETHING TO HIM
I DON'T KNOW WHAT TO SAY...
SCHULZ
5/30

I ALWAYS FEEL SO UNCOMFORTABLE NEAR CHILDREN!

August 16, 1951

"PEANUTS"
I DON'T CARE WHAT YOU CALL ME, CHARLIE BROWN

"STICKS AND STONES MAY BREAK MY BONES, BUT NAMES CAN NEVER HURT ME !!!"

YOU BLOCKHEAD!
8/16
SCHULZ

August 24, 1951

"PEANUTS"

A BALL ?! WHAT DO Y'MEAN ?! THAT WAS RIGHT OVER THE PLATE !!
SCHULZ
8/24

August 29, 1951

"PEANUTS"
GEE, THIS IS A SWELL LITTLE POOL!

?
OW!

A SHARK!! A SHARK!! I'VE BEEN BITTEN BY A SHARK!

8/29 SCHULZ

September 4, 1951

I SHOULD MOW THE GRASS AROUND HIS HOUSE?!

LET HIM MOW HIS OWN GRASS! WHAT DO YOU MEAN, HE CAN'T?!

OH..

FOR YOU, SNOOPY, I'LL DO IT!
9/4
SCHULZ

September 8, 1951

"PEANUTS"
SLIDE!!

SLIDE, CHARLIE BROWN!

SLIDE!!!

THAT'S THE WAY!
9/8
SCHULZ

September 13, 1951

"PEANUTS"
THERE'S CHARLIE BROWN ON HIS NEW BIKE...
HEY, CHARLIE BROWN!

WILL YOU GIVE ME A RIDE ON THE HANDLE BARS ?....PLEASE?

IT'S AGAINST THE LAW FOR TWO TO RIDE AT ONCE...
THAT'S WHAT I FIGURED!

9/13
SCHULZ

November 5, 1951

PEANUTS
?

SAY, YOU'VE BEEN STANDING IN THE SAME SPOT FOR THE LAST HALF HOUR...WHAT'S WRONG?

IT'S THESE NEW COWBOY BOOTS...

I CAN'T BEND MY KNEES!
11-5
SCHULZ

November 7, 1951

"PEANUTS"
BANG!
BANG!! BANG!

BANG BANG
BANG!
Copr. 1951 by United Feature Syndicate, Inc.

PING
"PING"?!
11/7
SCHULZ

WHAT DID I TELL YOU ?! GIRLS JUST AREN'T CUT OUT FOR THIS SORT OF THING!

November 8, 1951

"PEANUTS"
ff

!

PLAYING YOUR TOY PIANO, EH, SCHROEDER ? THAT'S A NICE BOY...
PLINK PLINK PLINK
I'LL LEAVE SO AS NOT TO BOTHER YOU

marcendo
ff
11/8
SCHULZ

November 13, 1951

"PEANUTS"
A PARTY? WHY, YES, I THINK I CAN COME...

WHO ELSE IS GOING TO BE THERE?

WILL YOU BE SERVING ICE CREAM?

SHE HUNG UP!
11-13
SCHULZ

November 14, 1951

"PEANUTS"
HE'LL KICK MY HAND! I JUST KNOW HE WILL!

I CAN'T GO THROUGH WITH IT!

?

YOU DIDN'T KICK THE BALL, CHARLIE BROWN... WHY DIDN'T YOU KICK IT?
11/14 SCHULZ

November 17, 1951

"PEANUTS"
?
THAT SNOOPY IS A VERY SMART DOG!

I'LL SAY HE IS...

WHY, I DON'T BELIEVE THERE'S A SMARTER DOG ALIVE!

!
YES, SIR, SOMETIMES YOU'D THINK HE'S ALMOST HUMAN!
11/17 SCHULZ

November 19, 1951

"PEANUTS"
EVERYBODY'S BUYING TELEVISION SETS THESE DAYS

EVERYBODY?

SNOOPY

UH HUH....EVERYBODY!
11/19 SCHULZ

November 26, 1951

I GOT IT, SCHROEDER!

BUT, BOY, IS IT EVER HEAVY...

WHERE DO YOU WANT IT? ON TOP OF YOUR PIANO?

BEETHOVEN!!!
☆SIGH☆
BEETHOVEN
11/26 SCHULZ

December 5, 1951

"PEANUTS"
JUST A MINUTE... I'LL HAVE TO FIND OUT...

MOM SAID THAT YOU CAN COME IN, CHARLIE BROWN....
12-5 SCHULZ

BUT YOUR FRIEND WILL HAVE TO WAIT OUTSIDE!

December 14, 1951

"PEANUTS"

?
PLOP!

12-14
SCHULZ

YOU WOULDN'T LOOK SO SMUG IF I COULD THROW FARTHER!
PLOP!

December 15, 1951

"PEANUTS"
YOU'RE GOING TO FIX THE ROOF?!

BUT THAT'S DANGEROUS, CHARLIE BROWN...WHAT IF YOU FALL?

WHAT HAS TO BE DONE, HAS TO BE DONE!
OH, MY!
12-15
SCHULZ

SNOOPY

"My interest in cartooning came from my father when I was a child. Dad liked reading me the funnies and I liked listening and looking at the funny pictures. The first indication that I had any drawing talent was in kindergarten. I drew a picture, and the teacher said to me, 'Someday, Charles, you're going to be an artist.'"

January 6, 1952

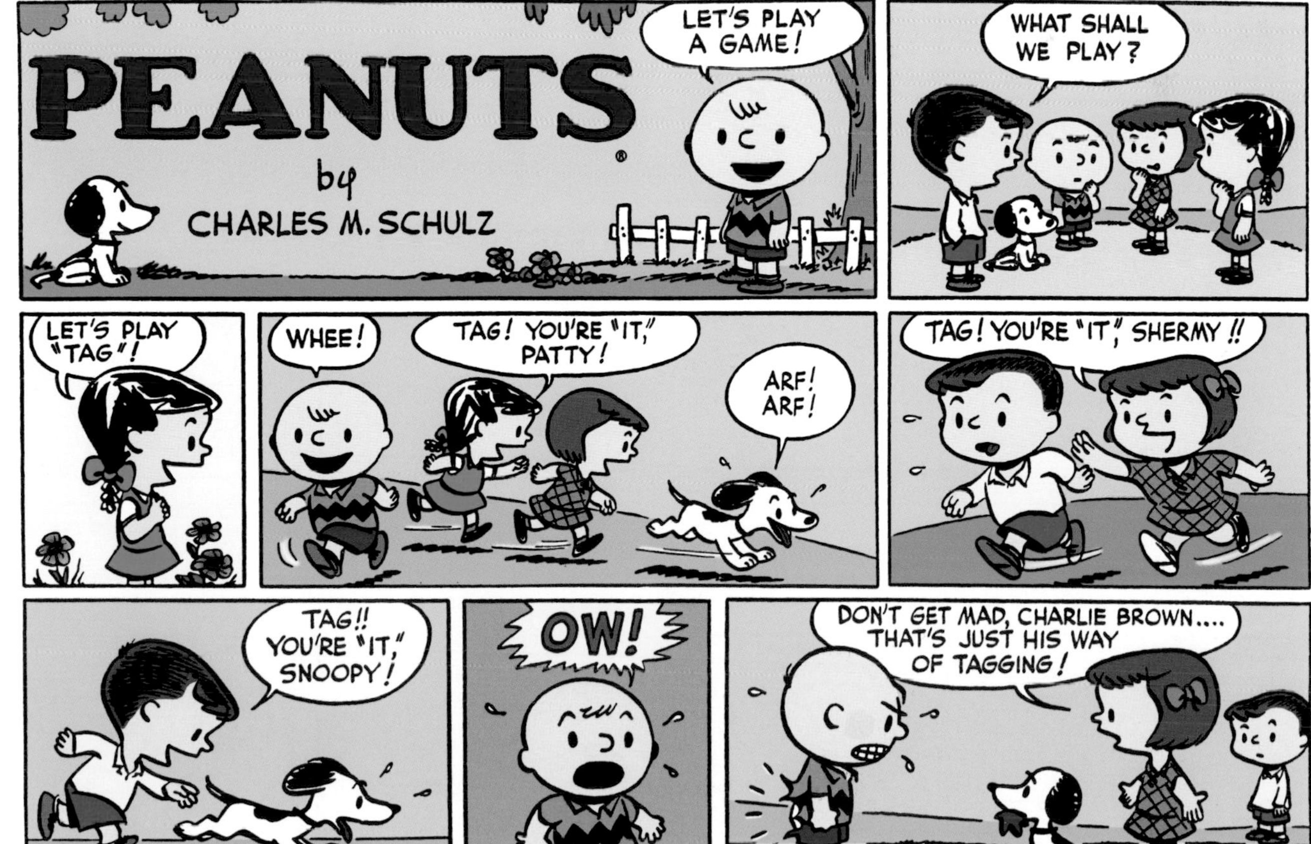
PEANUTS
by
CHARLES M. SCHULZ
LET'S PLAY A GAME!
WHAT SHALL WE PLAY?
LET'S PLAY "TAG"!
WHEE!
TAG! YOU'RE "IT," PATTY!
ARF! ARF!
TAG! YOU'RE "IT," SHERMY!!
TAG!! YOU'RE "IT," SNOOPY!
OW!
DON'T GET MAD, CHARLIE BROWN.... THAT'S JUST HIS WAY OF TAGGING!
1-6
SCHULZ

December 31, 1951

"PEANUTS"
I'M READY IF YOU ARE...

THIS IS HARDER THAN IT LOOKS

DON'T WORRY, PATTY...I THINK IT'LL BE EASIER GOING ONCE WE GET OUT IN THE COUNTRY
12-31
SCHULZ

WELL, I HOPE SO!

January 7, 1952

"PEANUTS"

HIC
BANG!
I GOT YOU, CHARLIE BROWN!
SCHULZ 1-7

YOU WOULDN'T HAVE IF I HADN'T HICCUPED!

January 12, 1952

"PEANUTS"
PUTT
PUTT
PUTT
CHARLIE BROWN

WELL, WHAT DO YOU THINK OF IT?
IT'S SENSATIONAL! AND WHAT A SWEET-SOUNDING MOTOR!!
CHARLIE BROWN
PUTT
PUTT
PUTT

MAY I LOOK AT IT?
BY ALL MEANS! JUST LIFT UP THE HOOD...
PUTT
PUTT

SCHULZ 1-12
PUTT PUTT PUTT

January 18, 1952

"PEANUTS"
LOOK! SCHROEDER JUST DROPPED HIS WALLET!

BEFORE WE RETURN IT, LET'S SEE IF HE CARRIES ANY PICTURES OF US!
GEE, DO YOU THINK HE DOES?

HERE'S A SNAPSHOT...
WHO IS IT? YOU OR ME?

BEETHOVEN!
1-18
SCHULZ

January 23, 1952

"PEANUTS"
Allegro
ff

SAY, THAT'S SENSATIONAL, SCHROEDER ... WHAT IS IT?

"Grosse Sonata für das Hammer-Klavier"
?

SOMETIMES I FEEL LIKE I DON'T BELONG AROUND HERE!
Schulz 1-23

January 31, 1952

"PEANUTS"
GEE, EVERYBODY CAN SKATE BETTER THAN I CAN...

EVEN PATTY AND VIOLET...LOOK AT THEM GO...IT'S SO DISCOURAGING

!

THAT DID IT!
1-31
SCHULZ

February 8, 1952

"PEANUTS"
OUR NEXT REQUEST WAS SENT IN BY A LISTENER NAMED SCHROEDER...

SIGH
HE WANTED TO HEAR BEETHOVEN'S PIANO SONATA NUMBER TWENTY-NINE...

?
I'M SORRY, MR. SCHROEDER, BUT WE DO NOT HAVE THAT RECORD...

HOWEVER, AS A SUBSTITUTE, WE HAVE A LITTLE ACCORDION NUMBER HERE, AND...
2-8
SCHULZ

February 12, 1952

"PEANUTS"
LET'S MAKE THIS THE BIGGEST SKATING RINK IN TOWN!

WE'LL TEAR DOWN THOSE TWO FENCES, AND COVER ALL THREE OF THESE LOTS!
IT'LL BE THE BIGGEST RINK IN THE WHOLE STATE!

I'M GETTING TIRED...
THIS SNOW IS HEAVY

IF YOU MAKE A RINK TOO LARGE, IT'S HARD TO KEEP CLEAN
2-12
SCHULZ

February 20, 1952

"PEANUTS"
PATTY, YOU'LL BE RIGHT WING...

VIOLET WILL BE LEFT WING, AND OLSEN WILL BE GOALIE

OLSEN?!
UH, HUH

2-20
SCHULZ

February 25, 1952

"PEANUTS"
FAMILY BARBER SHOP

YES, SIR, "IT PAYS TO LOOK WELL"
FAMILY BARBER SHOP

HMM...THIS STARTED OUT TO BE MERELY A SHAMPOO...
FAMILY BARBER SHOP

BUT WITH A CUSTOMER LIKE THIS IT'S HARD TO KNOW WHERE TO STOP!
FAMILY BARBER SHOP
2-25 SCHULZ

February 17, 1952

PEANUTS
by
CHARLES M. SCHULZ
LET'S BUILD A TREE-HOUSE, CHARLIE BROWN!
WE'LL USE THIS TREE ... IT'S PERFECT!
THIS WILL BE THE BEST TREE-HOUSE EVER MADE!
YOU HAVE SPOKEN A TRUISM!
WE'LL ISOLATE OURSELVES FROM THE CARES OF THIS OLD WORLD....
WE'LL BE REGULAR HERMANS!
YOU MEAN HERMITS...
I KNEW YOU'D GET THE IDEA!
THAT'S THE BEST PART OF IT ALL... NO ONE WILL BE ABLE TO BOTHER US BECAUSE NOBODY ELSE CAN GET UP HERE!
LET'S GO GET OUR PROVISIONS
JUST THINK OF IT... OUR OWN PRIVATE TREE-HOUSE!
I CAN'T GET OVER IT... A PLACE THAT NO ONE ELSE CAN GET TO!
2-17-52
!
SCHULZ

"After high school, I had a job delivering packages, and I used to enjoy walking by the windows of the St. Paul Pioneer Press *and watching the Sunday comics as they came rolling off the presses. It was my dream, of course, that one day my own comic strip would be included."*

February 27, 1952

"PEANUTS"
AND THEN I DREAMED I WAS CLIMBING A STAIRWAY...
BUT SUDDENLY I BEGAN TO FALL...
I CAN'T STAND PEOPLE WHO TELL ME THEIR DREAMS!
AND THEN, BEFORE I KNEW IT, I WAS IN THIS GARDEN...
WHY DO THEY ALWAYS HAVE TO GO INTO DETAIL?
2-27
DO YOU SUPPOSE ALL THAT MEANS ANYTHING, CHARLIE BROWN?
ABSOLUTELY! IT MEANS YOU WERE ASLEEP!
SCHULZ

March 1, 1952

"PEANUTS"
LET'S RING CHARLIE BROWN'S DOORBELL, AND THEN RUN...
WHEE!
WHOM, ARE WE HIDING FROM?
3-1
SCHULZ

March 3, 1952—First appearance of Lucy.

"PEANUTS"
ONE, ONE, ONE,
?

ONE, ONE, ONE,

TWO, LUCY! TWO!

TWO, TWO, TWO...
3-3
SCHULZ

March 5, 1952

"PEANUTS"
WHY ARE YOU MAD AT CHARLIE BROWN, VIOLET ?

BECAUSE!

BECAUSE WHY ?
JUST BECAUSE!
3-5
SCHULZ

I UNDERSTAND...AND HERE HE TOLD ME THAT YOU HAD NO REASON!

"After World War II, when I came home, Krazy Kat *became my hero. I had never seen* Krazy Kat *up until then . . . but it became my ambition to draw a strip that would have as much life and meaning and subtlety to it as* Krazy Kat *had."*

March 23, 1952—First Sunday baseball strip.

PEANUTS®
by
CHARLES M. SCHULZ
THROW IT IN HERE! I'LL HIT IT A MILE!
LET HIM HIT IT...WE'VE GOT AN AIRTIGHT INFIELD!
A BASE HIT!
POW
?
TAG HIM, SNOOPY! DON'T LET HIM GET TO FIRST!
TAG HIM, SNOOPY!
DON'T LET HIM GET TO SECOND!
DON'T LET HIM GET TO THIRD!
DON'T LET HIM GET HOME!
TAG HIM!
3-23
YOU'RE OUT!
SCHULZ

March 21, 1952

"PEANUTS"

THAT'S THE LOWEST-FLYING KITE I'VE EVER SEEN!
I DON'T BELIEVE IN TAKING CHANCES

WHAT ARE YOU AFRAID OF?

AIRPLANES!
3-21
SCHULZ

March 22, 1952

"PEANUTS"
DO YOU LIKE HAVING ME WITH YOU, CHARLIE BROWN?

OF COURSE... WHY?
I JUST WONDERED... YOU DO LOOK HAPPY

IT DOESN'T TAKE MUCH TO MAKE ME HAPPY
!
3-22
SCHULZ

I ALWAYS SAY THE WRONG THING...

March 28, 1952

"PEANUTS"
NITE-NITE, DADDY

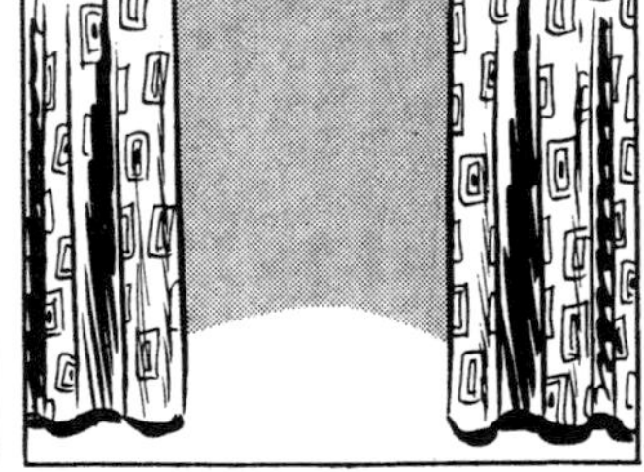

DADDY..... I'M NOT SLEEPY
SCHULZ
3-28

April 1, 1952

"PEANUTS"
HE WANTS TO KNOW IF HE CAN BRING A FRIEND...

ASK HIM IF HIS FRIEND IS CUTE
VIOLET WANTS TO KNOW IF HE'S CUTE...

HE IS? O.K., WE'LL TAKE YOUR WORD FOR IT... SEE YOU SOON, SCHROEDER
OH, BOY!

SCHULZ
4-1
BEETHOVEN

April 4, 1952

"PEANUTS"
SPEAK!
ARF! ARF!!

SIT UP!

CHASE IT! BRING IT BACK!

HEY, SNOOPY! WAKE UP!! I WANT YOU TO PULL ME IN THE WAGON!
SCHULZ 4-4

April 9, 1952

"PEANUTS"
♪

PAPER BOY!!
FIRE AWAY!

♪
4-9
SCHULZ

April 14, 1952

"PEANUTS"

Allegro
ff
Ped
4-14
SCHULZ

April 16, 1952

"PEANUTS"
GIDDYAP, HORSIE!

GIDDYAP!
GIDDYAP!
GIDDYAP!

CHARLIE BROWN! COME QUICK! THERE'S A GREAT BIG KITE UP IN THE SKY!
4-16

POOR LUCY!
SCHULZ

April 25, 1952

"PEANUTS"
I'LL GET THIS KITE UP IN THE AIR IF IT'S THE LAST THING I EVER DO!

?

OOF!!

SCHULZ
4-25

May 6, 1952

"PEANUTS"
"A" IS FOR APPLE
"B" IS FOR BOAT

"C" IS FOR CHARLIE BROWN...
HUH?

REALLY? REALLY? DOES IT SAY THAT? HUH? REALLY?

5-6
SCHULZ

May 11, 1952

ALL RIGHT, CHARLIE BROWN... WE'RE READY... START THE CONCERT
PEANUTS
by
CHARLES M. SCHULZ
HALF THE SUCCESS OF A CONCERT LIES IN A DIGNIFIED ENTRANCE!
SCHROEDER AND I WILL NOW PLAY THE "CHROMATIC FANTASIA AND FUGUE" BY BACH...THE LOVELY TONE OF MY VIOLIN IS DUE TO ITS FORMERLY CONTAINING FIFTY-CENT CIGARS!
SQUEAK SQUAWK SQUEAK
SQUEAK RASP AAK SQUAWK SQUEAK
THAT'S THE WORST VIOLIN PLAYING I'VE EVER HEARD!
IT SOUNDS LIKE HE FORGOT TO TAKE THE CIGARS OUT OF THE BOX!
BOO! BOO!!
THAT'S AWFUL! LET HIM PLAY BY HIMSELF!!
WELL, I'LL BE! I NEVER EXPECTED ANYTHING LIKE THIS...
5-11
I'M SORRY, SCHROEDER, BUT I GUESS THEY WANT ME TO PLAY A SOLO!
SCHULZ

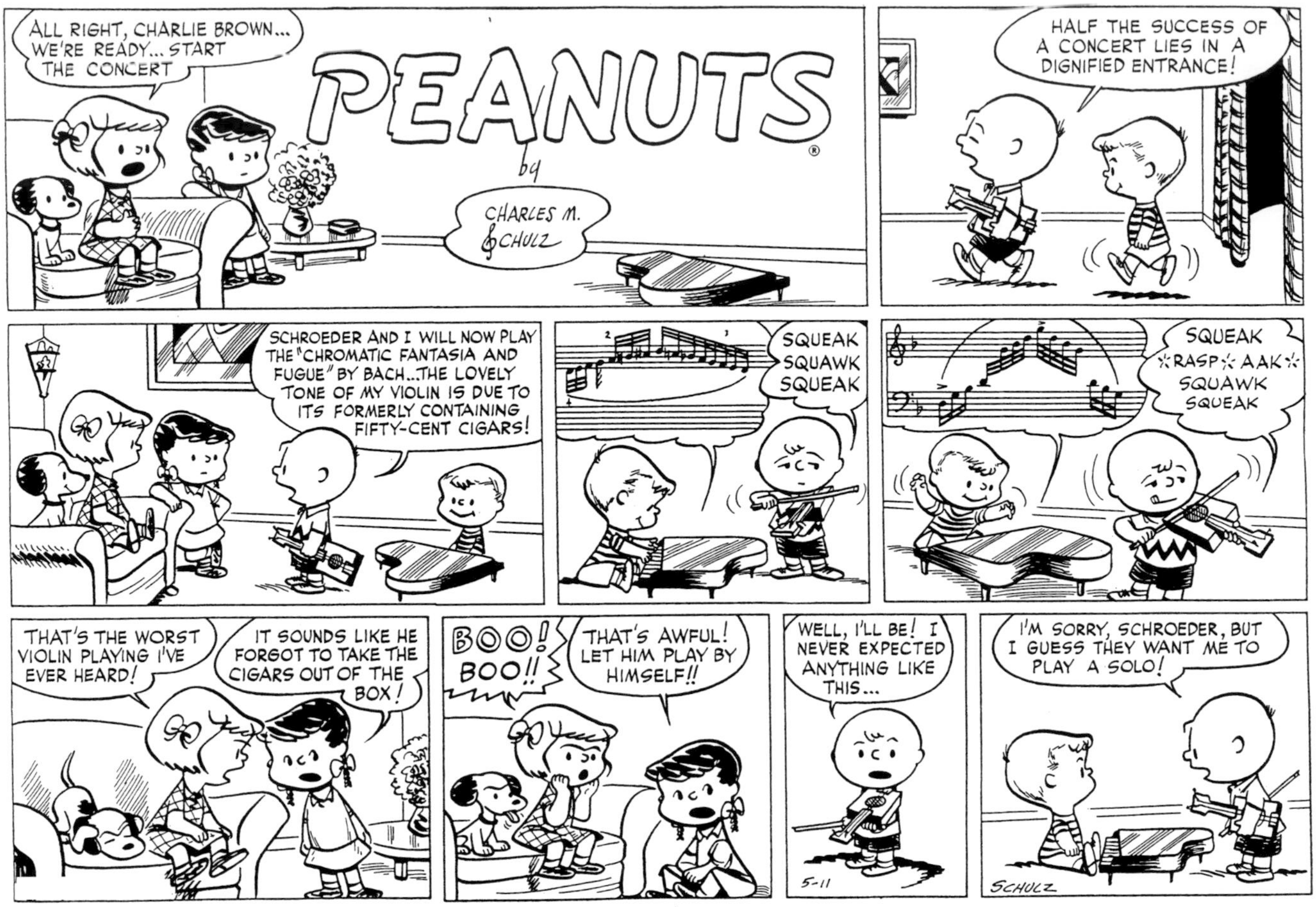

"To me it was not a matter of how I became a cartoonist but a matter of when. I am quite sure if I had not sold Peanuts *at the time I did, then I would have sold something eventually. Even if I had not, I would continue to draw because I had to."*

May 22, 1952

DADDY!! I'M ALL THROUGH!
5 22
SCHULZ

May 27, 1952—Snoopy's first thought balloon.

KIND OF WARM OUT TODAY FOR EAR MUFFS, ISN'T IT?
WHY DO I HAVE TO SUFFER SUCH INDIGNITIES!?
5/27
SCHULZ

May 28, 1952

"PEANUTS"

YOU REALIZE THAT THE SCORE IS SIXTY TO NOTHING, DON'T YOU?

UH, HUH

WELL, DON'T WORRY ABOUT IT...WE'LL GET 'EM BACK IN THE SECOND INNING!
5/28
SCHULZ

June 3, 1952

"PEANUTS"

6-3
SCHULZ

June 4, 1952

"PEANUTS"
TWINKLE TWINKLE LITTLE STAR

THIS SONG ALWAYS DEPRESSES ME... IT MAKES ME FEEL REAL SAD...

I CAN'T EXPLAIN IT

IT JUST SORT OF GETS ME RIGHT HERE...YOU KNOW WHAT I MEAN?
6-4
SCHULZ

June 9, 1952

"PEANUTS"
I'LL BE THE GOOD GUY!

ALL RIGHT,...AND I'LL BE THE BAD GUY!

WHAT ARE YOU GOING TO BE, CHARLIE BROWN ?
I'LL BE SORT OF IN-BETWEEN

I'LL BE A HYPOCRITE!
6/9
SCHULZ

June 13, 1952

"PEANUTS"

AH, HA!

HEH, HEH, HEH, HEH, HEH

I JUST CAUGHT A CONFIRMED BEETHOVEN MAN PLAYING AND ENJOYING TSCHAIKOWSKY!
6/13
SCHULZ

June 25, 1952

"PEANUTS"
RATS!

WHAT DID YOU GET, CHARLIE BROWN?
THIRTY-THREE!

BOY, IS THAT EVER DISGUSTING!

I ALMOST ALWAYS CAN GET A TWENTY ON THAT HOLE!
6-25
SCHULZ

June 22, 1952

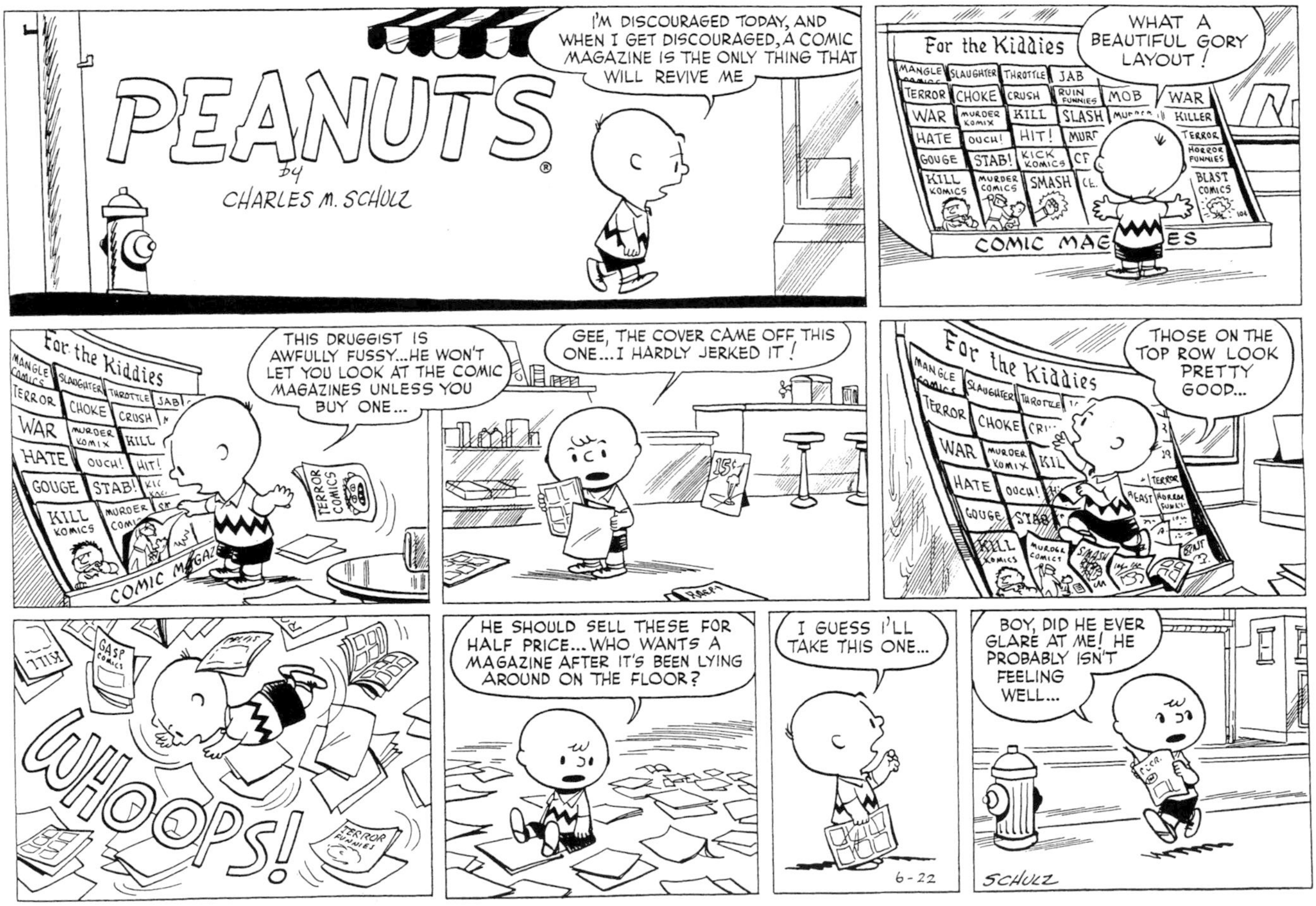

PEANUTS

by CHARLES M. SCHULZ

I'M DISCOURAGED TODAY, AND WHEN I GET DISCOURAGED, A COMIC MAGAZINE IS THE ONLY THING THAT WILL REVIVE ME

For the Kiddies

WHAT A BEAUTIFUL GORY LAYOUT!

MANGLE COMICS, SLAUGHTER, THROTTLE, JAB, TERROR, CHOKE, CRUSH, RUIN FUNNIES, MOB, WAR, MURDER KOMIX, KILL, SLASH, KILLER, HATE, OUCH!, HIT!, TERROR, HORROR FUNNIES, GOUGE, STAB!, KICK KOMICS, KILL KOMICS, MURDER COMICS, SMASH, BLAST COMICS

COMIC MAGAZINES

THIS DRUGGIST IS AWFULLY FUSSY...HE WON'T LET YOU LOOK AT THE COMIC MAGAZINES UNLESS YOU BUY ONE...

TERROR COMICS

GEE, THE COVER CAME OFF THIS ONE...I HARDLY JERKED IT!

15¢

THOSE ON THE TOP ROW LOOK PRETTY GOOD...

WHOOPS!

GASP COMICS

TERROR FUNNIES

HE SHOULD SELL THESE FOR HALF PRICE...WHO WANTS A MAGAZINE AFTER IT'S BEEN LYING AROUND ON THE FLOOR?

I GUESS I'LL TAKE THIS ONE...

6-22

BOY, DID HE EVER GLARE AT ME! HE PROBABLY ISN'T FEELING WELL...

SCHULZ

July 2, 1952

"PEANUTS"
WE CAN'T PLAY HERE...

LET'S FIND SOMEPLACE WHERE THE GRASS IS SMOOTH, AND WE CAN SIT DOWN...
HOW ABOUT OVER THERE?

SAY, THAT LOOKS SWELL!

DO YOU HEAR SOMEONE YELLING?
5
7-2
SCHULZ

July 14, 1952—First mention of Lucy Van Pelt's brother, Linus.

"PEANUTS"
I'LL TELL YOU WHAT, CHARLIE BROWN...

I'VE GOT A BABY BROTHER AT HOME...I'LL TRADE YOU HIM FOR YOUR TRICYCLE!

ABSOLUTELY NOT! WHAT GOOD WOULD A BABY BROTHER DO ME?
I KNEW YOU'D SAY THAT, AND I DON'T BLAME YOU AT ALL...

HE'S NO GOOD TO ME, EITHER!
SCHULZ

July 13, 1952

FORE!
PEANUTS
by CHARLES M. SCHULZ
GOOD SHOT, CHARLIE BROWN!

THE GREENS ON THIS COURSE ARE KIND OF BUMPY...
MAYBE YOU WANT ME TO VACUUM THE RUG!?

THIS IS AN EASY HOLE... WAIT 'TIL YOU SEE THE NEXT ONE

I DREAD THE DAY WHEN I'LL BEGIN PLAYING THIS GAME JUST FOR THE EXERCISE!

NOW ON THIS HOLE YOU SHOOT PAST THAT RED CHAIR, OVER THE BOOKCASE AND DOWN THE HALLWAY....

DO YOU THINK I SHOULD TAKE A FULL SWING?
SURE, HIT IT AS HARD AS YOU CAN!

CRASH!

CANCEL MY CLUB MEMBERSHIP!
7-13
SCHULZ

July 30, 1952

"PEANUTS"
SLUP-SLUP! LAP-LAP! SLUP!

SLURP-SLURP!

CHOMP, SLUP SLURP
I GUESS I'LL HAVE TO MOVE TO THE COUNTRY...
7-30
SCHULZ

I HATE THE SOUNDS OF THE CITY DURING THE SUMMER!

July 31, 1952

"PEANUTS"
DOCTOR! DOCTOR!! YOU'VE GOT TO SAVE MY DOLLY!

HER LEG CAME OFF!
SO I SEE...HMM... WE'LL GET AT THIS RIGHT AWAY BEFORE SHE LOSES TOO MUCH SAWDUST

THERE YOU ARE, MISS...SHE'S AS GOOD AS NEW!
WHAT DID YOU USE, DOCTOR...PENICILLIN? AUREOMYCIN?

GLUE!
SCHULZ
7/31

August 7, 1952

"PEANUTS"
sempre pp

WELL, SCHROEDER, OL' PAL! I SEE YOU'RE "BACH"!

WHERE HAVE YOU BEEN "HAYDN"?

NOBODY APPRECIATES GOOD HUMOR THESE DAYS...
SCHULZ
8-7

"I have been told an uncle came in and looked at me and said, 'By golly, we're going to call him Spark Plug.' So, I've been called Sparky since the day after I was born—named after a comic strip character."

August 24, 1952

PEANUTS
by CHARLES M. SCHULZ
IT'S GONE!
OF ALL THE NERVE!
LUCY'S TAKEN MY BASEBALL GLOVE AGAIN!
JUST BECAUSE I LEAVE IT ON THE FRONT SIDEWALK EVERY NIGHT, SHE THINKS IT'S PUBLIC PROPERTY!
I'M GOING TO SETTLE THIS ONCE AND FOR ALL...
HEY, YOU!!
THUMP!
?
!
KLOP!
PLUNK!
CLUMP!
OH, DO YOU WANT YOUR GLOVE BACK, CHARLIE BROWN?
NO, YOU MIGHT AS WELL KEEP IT, LUCY.... I'LL PROBABLY NEVER HAVE ANY USE FOR IT AGAIN!
8-24
SCHULZ

August 16, 1952

"PEANUTS"
HOW ABOUT A GAME OF MARBLES, CHARLIE BROWN?

THAT WOULD BE FINE...IF I COULD WIN....BUT I'D PROBABLY LOSE.... THEN I'D GET DEPRESSED...

THEN I'D BE REAL GRUMPY, AND WOULDN'T TALK TO ANYONE, AND I'D HATE MYSELF...
8-16
SCHULZ

THANKS, ANYWAY

September 29, 1952—Introduction of Linus by name.

"PEANUTS"

SCHROEDER CERTAINLY SEEMS FASCINATED BY YOUR BABY BROTHER

I GUESS HE THINKS LINUS IS REAL CUTE
IT'S NOT THAT AT ALL...

LINUS REMINDS HIM OF BEETHOVEN!
9-29
SCHULZ

"Linus came from a drawing that I made one day of a face almost like the one he now has. I experimented with some wild hair, and I showed the sketch to a friend of mine [Linus Maurer] who sat near me at the correspondence school. . . . He thought it was kind of funny, and we both agreed that it might make a good new character for the strip."

August 31, 1952

PEANUTS
by
CHARLES M. SCHULZ
IT'S FUNNY...EVERYTIME THE THERMOMETER GOES WAY UP, IT GETS REAL HOT OUTSIDE
WHEN IT'S AS HOT AS IT IS TODAY, THERE'S NOTHING BETTER THAN SITTING IN A POOL OF COOL WATER
I'LL GO PUT MY SWIMMING TRUNKS ON NOW, AND THEN I'LL RELAX
HEY! GET OUT OF THERE!!
OF ALL THE CRAZY DOGS!!
!
NOW I HAVE TO EMPTY THIS, AND START ALL OVER!
THERE! IT'S FULL AGAIN...BUT WHAT A JOB THAT WAS!
NOW, I'LL GO TURN OFF THE WATER,..
AND GET RIGHT BACK BEFORE...
SCHULZ
8-31

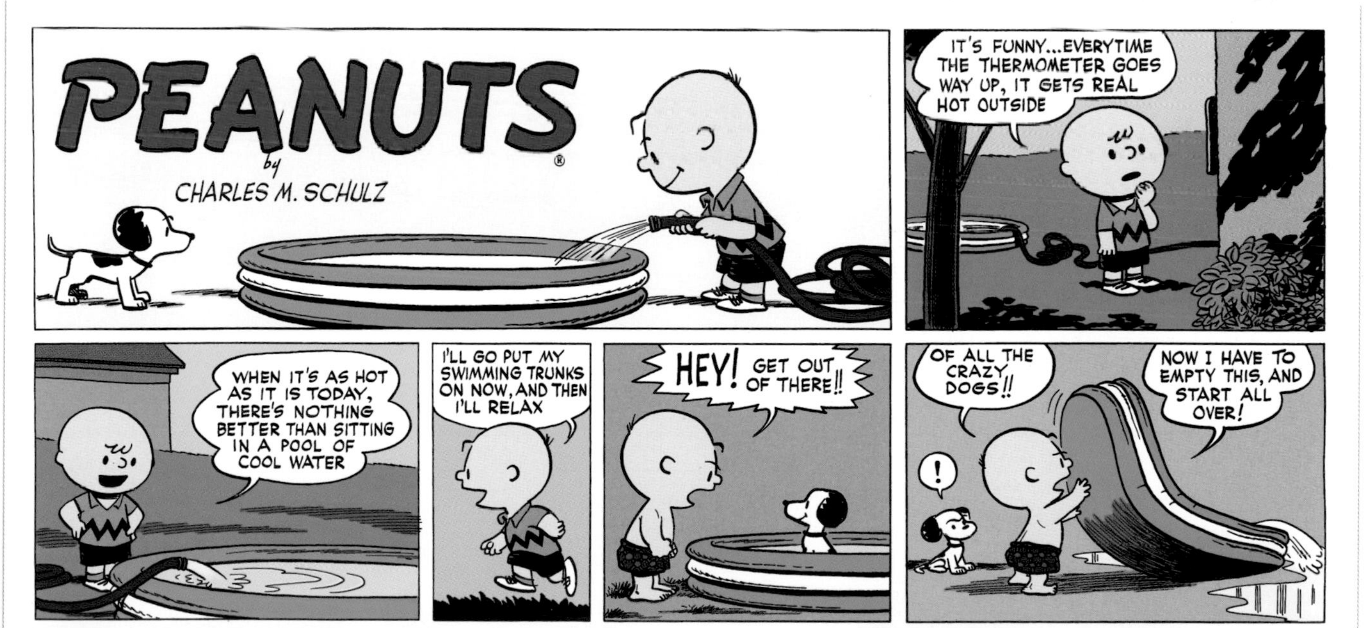

October 1, 1952

"PEANUTS"
HMMMM

HEY, CHARLIE BROWN! I'VE GOT "PERFECT PITCH"!!

YOU MEAN "A PERFECT PITCH"... BESIDES, WHO CARES? THE BASEBALL SEASON IS OVER!

SCHULZ 10-1
SOMETIMES I THINK I SHOULD PUT IN FOR A TRANSFER TO A NEW COMIC STRIP!

October 26, 1952

PEANUTS by CHARLES M. SCHULZ

READY?

LET'S GO...

BOO!

BOO!!

BOO!

SIGH

SIGH

SIGH

SCHULZ 10-26

BOO!

!

!

!

November 5, 1952

"PEANUTS"
HOW WOULD YOU LIKE TO READ A COMIC STRIP I JUST DREW?

SEE? THIS FELLOW PULLS UP IN FRONT OF THE ZOO WITH THIS TRUCK FULL OF ANIMALS, AND SAYS, "GOT GNUS FOR YOU!"

GET IT?

WHEN IT COMES RIGHT DOWN TO IT, MY TYPE OF HUMOR IS TOO SUBTLE FOR THE COMIC STRIPS...
SCHULZ 11-5

November 7, 1952

"PEANUTS"
MY MOTHER THINKS I'M WONDERFUL!

I IMAGINE SHE DOES, LUCY...
SHE THINKS I'LL BE A CINCH TO WIN THE TITLE...

WHAT TITLE?
"MISS FUSS-BUDGET OF 1952"

YOUR MOTHER IS A SHREWD JUDGE OF CHARACTER, LUCY
SHE THINKS I'M WONDERFUL
11-7
SCHULZ

November 16, 1952

PEANUTS
by
CHARLES M. SCHULZ
ALL YOU HAVE TO DO IS HOLD THE BALL, LUCY... THEN I'LL COME RUNNING UP, AND KICK IT...

I DON'T KNOW IF THIS IS SUCH A GOOD IDEA

?
!

WHOMP

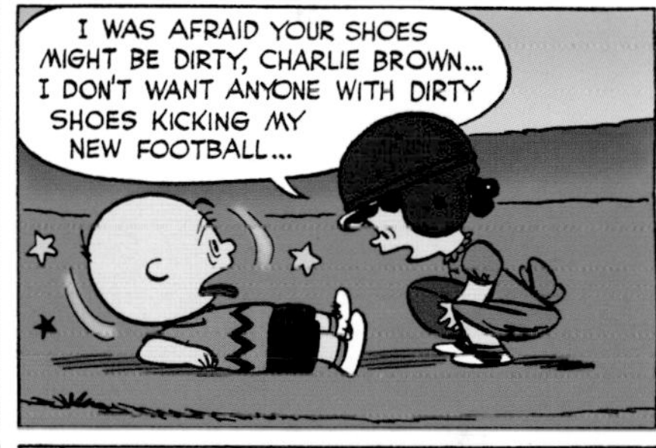
I WAS AFRAID YOUR SHOES MIGHT BE DIRTY, CHARLIE BROWN... I DON'T WANT ANYONE WITH DIRTY SHOES KICKING MY NEW FOOTBALL...

DON'T EVER DO THAT AGAIN! DO YOU WANT TO KILL ME?! THIS TIME HOLD IT TIGHT!

HERE WE GO!

?
!
THUMP

I HELD IT REAL TIGHT, CHARLIE BROWN...
I'M NOT GOING TO GET UP.... I'M GOING TO LIE HERE FOR THE REST OF THE DAY...
11-16
SCHULZ

November 15, 1952

"PEANUTS"
RING!!!

HELLO?....WHO?

THE HEAD OF THE HOUSEHOLD?

SPEAKING!
11
15
SCHULZ

November 24, 1952

"PEANUTS"
!
SLURP SLURP SLUP

FOOD!
SLUP SLURP

SLURP SLURP
11-24
SCHULZ

December 8, 1952

"PEANUTS"
IS THAT THE ONLY T-SHIRT YOU OWN?!

WHY? WHAT'S THE MATTER WITH IT?
IT'S THAT STRIPE! I'M TIRED OF SEEING IT!!

I'M SORRY...I DIDN'T KNOW IT BOTHERED YOU... I'LL GO HOME, AND CHANGE....

HOW'S THIS?
12-8
SCHULZ

December 31, 1952

"PEANUTS"
I'LL NEVER BE ABLE TO GET TO VIOLET'S PARTY ON TIME..

MAYBE I'D BETTER PHONE, AND TELL HER I'LL BE LATE...

OH, AREN'T YOU HERE YET, CHARLIE BROWN? WE HADN'T EVEN NOTICED!
12-31

THAT'S THE WAY IT GOES...
SCHULZ

January 7, 1953

"PEANUTS"
HOW HUMILIATING!

WHAT'S THE MATTER WITH YOU?
I'VE BEEN DISGRACED FOR LIFE!

THEY SAY IT'S NEVER HAPPENED TO ANYONE BEFORE

I'VE JUST BEEN EXPELLED FROM NURSERY SCHOOL!
SCHULZ
1-7

January 15, 1953

"PEANUTS"
OLD-FASHIONED! NO IMAGINATION!

TRITE! VERY TRITE!

I DON'T KNOW WHAT'S WRONG WITH THE KIDS IN THIS NEIGHBORHOOD...

1-15
SCHULZ

January 22, 1953

"PEANUTS"
Charlie Brown

Charlie Brown

SCHULZ

Schroeder
1-22

January 23, 1953

"PEANUTS"
CAN YOU COME TO OUR PARTY ON MONDAY, CHARLIE BROWN?

MONDAY? SURE, I CAN BE THERE MONDAY
HOW ABOUT IF WE HAD IT TUESDAY?

NO, I COULDN'T BE THERE IF YOU HAD IT TUESDAY
THAT SETTLES IT THEN...

WE'LL HAVE OUR PARTY ON TUESDAY!
1-23
SCHULZ

January 30, 1953

"PEANUTS"
HOW DO YOU LIKE MY NEW DOLL, CHARLIE BROWN?

I'VE NAMED HIM AFTER YOU
REALLY? THAT'S VERY FLATTERING

YES, SIR... THAT'S VERY FLATTERING

TAKE THAT, CHARLIE BROWN!
!
1-30
SCHULZ

February 3, 1953

"PEANUTS"
CHARLIE BROWN, DO YOU CARE IF I HIT YOU WITH THIS SNOWBALL?

GO RIGHT AHEAD...I'VE NEVER SEEN A GIRL YET WHO COULD THROW VERY HARD...MOST GIRLS JUST...

POW

I'VE BEEN PRACTICING!
2-3
SCHULZ

February 14, 1953

"PEANUTS"
NOBODY LOVES ME...EVERYBODY HATES ME!
I DIDN'T GET A SINGLE VALENTINE! NOT ONE!!

THAT'S AWFUL, CHARLIE BROWN.. HERE...HOW DO YOU LIKE THIS?
FOR ME? OH, BOY! WOW!

THIS IS SOMETHING! A REAL VALENTINE!
DON'T TAKE IT TOO SERIOUSLY...
SCHULZ

2-14
I'M JUST LOANING IT TO YOU SO YOU WON'T FEEL BAD

February 21, 1953

"PEANUTS"

SCHULZ
2-21

February 22, 1953

PEANUTS
WHEW I HAVEN'T WORKED THIS HARD IN YEARS...
I LIKE TO SEE A YOUNG MAN WORKING HARD..
IT'S A SIGN THAT HE'S AMBITIOUS, AND SOMEDAY WILL MAKE A GOOD HUSBAND!
THAT'S GOING TO BE A SLICK SNOWMAN, CHARLIE BROWN...
I GUESS MAYBE YOU'RE WHAT THEY CALL A PERFECTIONIST, HUH ?
YES, I GUESS MAYBE I AM
BUT SOMETIMES I THINK I'M EVEN MORE THAN THAT..
WHAT DO YOU MEAN?
!
I'M THE KIND OF PERSON THAT OVERDOES THINGS!
SCHULZ
2-22

March 9, 1953

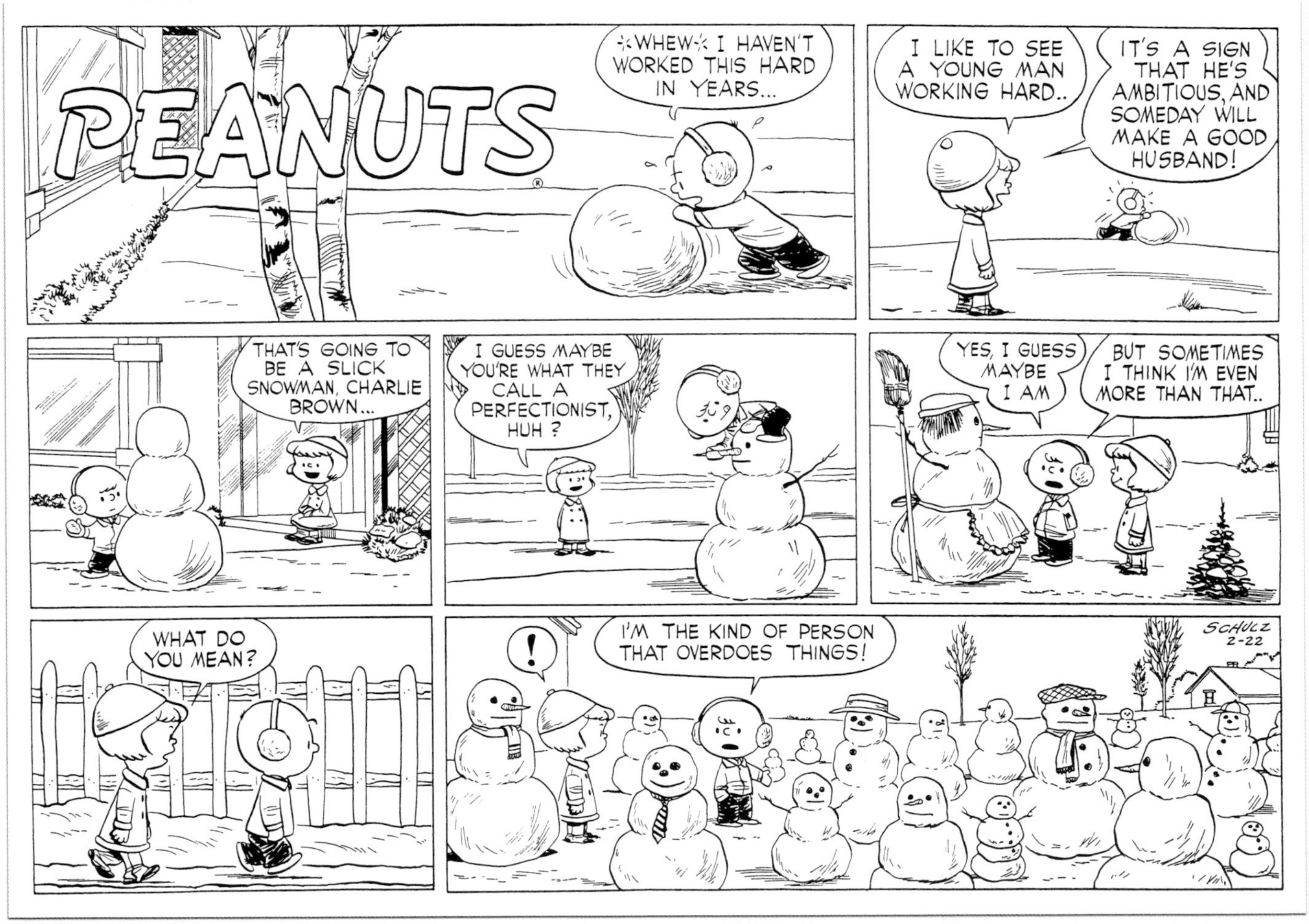

"PEANUTS"
EVERYBODY'S BEEN TEASING ME, CHARLIE BROWN..
WHY?

THEY SAY THAT YOU'RE MY BOY FRIEND...ISN'T THAT FUNNY?
OH, YES... THAT'S A RIOT

DO YOU THINK WE'LL EVER GET MARRIED?
NOT UNLESS I LOSE MY MIND!

WELL, AT LEAST THERE'S **SOME** HOPE...
3-9
SCHULZ

April 3, 1953

"PEANUTS"
WE CAN'T DECIDE WHAT COLOR TO PAINT SNOOPY'S HOUSE...

WHAT DO YOU THINK, CHARLIE BROWN...SHOULD WE USE RED OR YELLOW?
SNOOP

WELL...I'M VERY FLATTERED THAT YOU HAVE ASKED FOR MY OPINION.. I THINK THE COLOR SHOULD BE RED

THAT SETTLES IT...WE'LL PAINT IT YELLOW!
4-3
SCHULZ

March 1, 1953

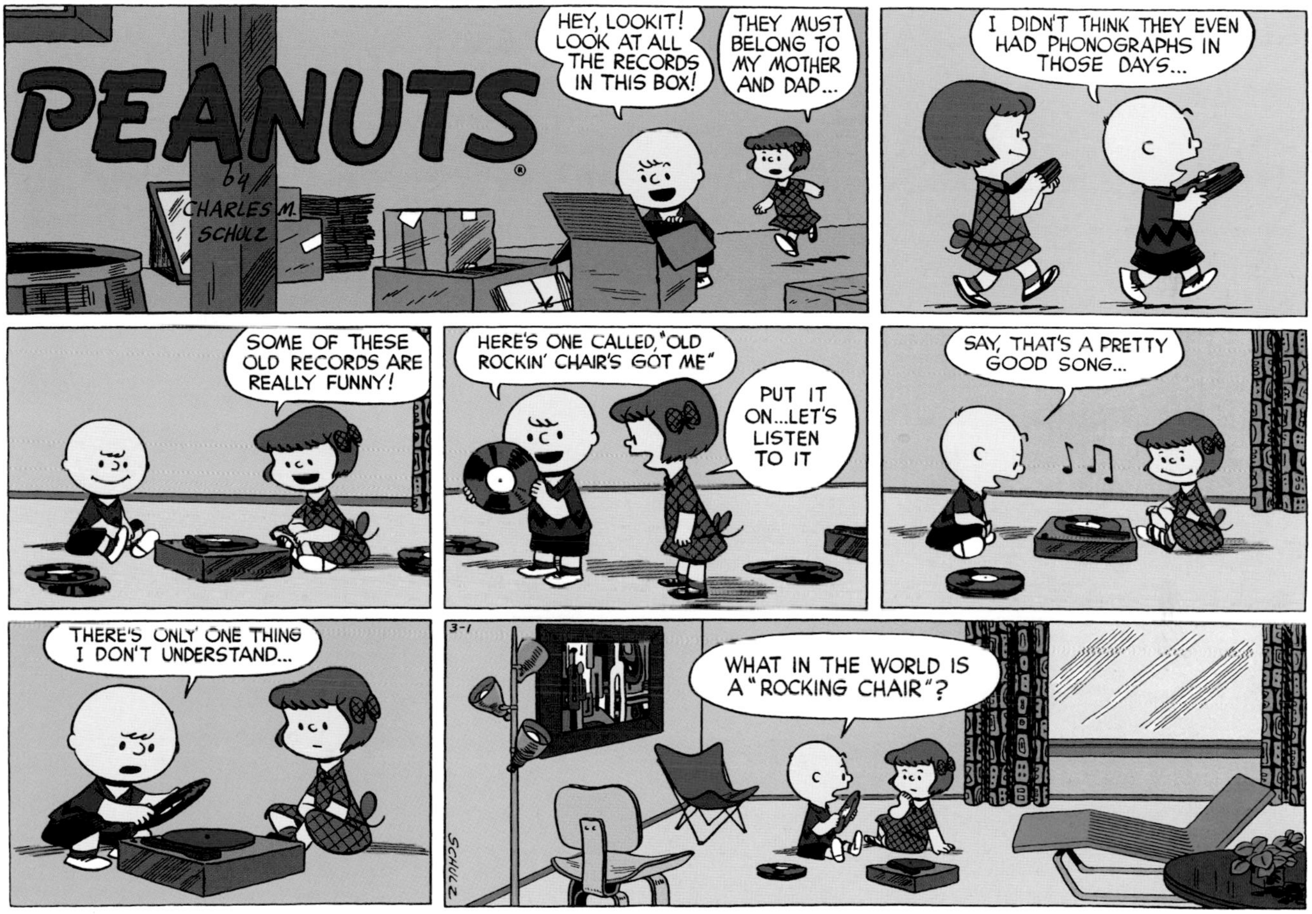

PEANUTS by CHARLES M. SCHULZ

HEY, LOOKIT! LOOK AT ALL THE RECORDS IN THIS BOX!

THEY MUST BELONG TO MY MOTHER AND DAD...

I DIDN'T THINK THEY EVEN HAD PHONOGRAPHS IN THOSE DAYS...

SOME OF THESE OLD RECORDS ARE REALLY FUNNY!

HERE'S ONE CALLED, "OLD ROCKIN' CHAIR'S GOT ME"

PUT IT ON...LET'S LISTEN TO IT

SAY, THAT'S A PRETTY GOOD SONG...

THERE'S ONLY ONE THING I DON'T UNDERSTAND...

3-1

WHAT IN THE WORLD IS A "ROCKING CHAIR"?

SCHULZ

April 17, 1953

"PEANUTS"
ALL RIGHT, MEN! ON TO MARS!!

THE BOYS CERTAINLY SEEM ENVIOUS OF YOUR NEW SPACE-SUIT, LUCY...

YOU WON'T TELL THEM, WILL YOU?
TELL THEM WHAT?

THESE ARE MY SLEEPERS!
SCHULZ

May 12, 1953

"PEANUTS"
SNOOPY HAD TO MOVE OUT OF HIS HOUSE..

REALLY? WHERE'S HE LIVING NOW?
IN A DUPLEX

A DUPLEX ?!
UH, HUH..

SCHULZ
5-12

May 13, 1953

"PEANUTS"
WHAT A BLOCKHEAD THAT CHARLIE BROWN IS!

I WONDER WHO EVER TOLD HIM HE COULD PITCH?! HE GETS WORSE EVERY INNING!

YOU'RE DOING GREAT, OL' PAL!! KEEP UP THE GOOD WORK!

WHAT A BLOCKHEAD THAT CHARLIE BROWN IS!
5-13
SCHULZ

May 15, 1953

"PEANUTS"
NOBODY LOVES ME.. EVERYBODY HATES ME...

SOMETIMES I GET SO DEPRESSED..

BUT ALL IT TAKES TO CHEER ME UP IS A SMILE FROM A DOG...
5-15
SCHULZ

May 21, 1953

"PEANUTS"
WE'VE BUILT A PITCHER'S MOUND FOR YOU, CHARLIE BROWN...
REALLY?

WE THOUGHT IT MIGHT HELP YOUR DELIVERY...
BOY, I'LL SAY IT WILL!

GEE, A REAL MOUND.. THIS WILL IMPROVE MY PITCHING A HUNDRED PERCENT...
5-21

I'M AFRAID TO MOVE!
SCHULZ

May 30, 1953

"PEANUTS"

AHEM

!

HE NOTICED ME! HE NOTICED ME!! I'VE NEVER BEEN SO HAPPY IN ALL MY LIFE!
5-30
SCHULZ

June 29, 1953

"PEANUTS"
LUCY, WE'RE GOING TO LET YOU PLAY CENTER FIELD..
SWELL!

?

I THOUGHT YOU WERE OUT IN CENTER FIELD?!
I WAS..

6-29
BUT I GOT LONESOME..
SCHULZ

June 14, 1953

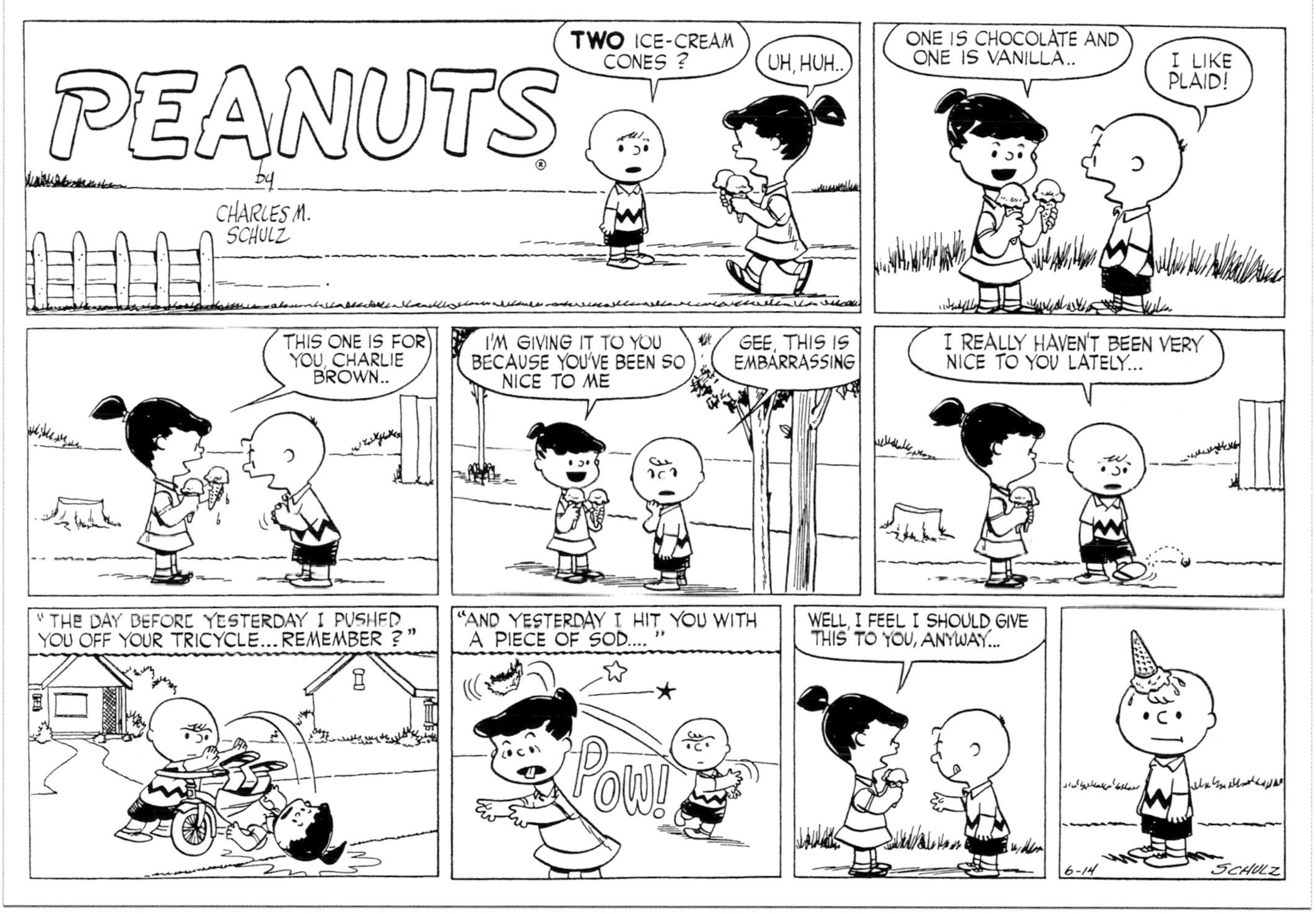

PEANUTS
by
CHARLES M. SCHULZ
TWO ICE-CREAM CONES ?
UH, HUH..
ONE IS CHOCOLATE AND ONE IS VANILLA..
I LIKE PLAID!
THIS ONE IS FOR YOU, CHARLIE BROWN..
I'M GIVING IT TO YOU BECAUSE YOU'VE BEEN SO NICE TO ME
GEE, THIS IS EMBARRASSING
I REALLY HAVEN'T BEEN VERY NICE TO YOU LATELY...
"THE DAY BEFORE YESTERDAY I PUSHED YOU OFF YOUR TRICYCLE... REMEMBER ?"
"AND YESTERDAY I HIT YOU WITH A PIECE OF SOD...."
POW!
WELL, I FEEL I SHOULD GIVE THIS TO YOU, ANYWAY...
6-14
SCHULZ

July 1, 1953

"PEANUTS"
WE'RE GOING TO LET YOU PLAY CENTER FIELD AGAIN TODAY, LUCY...
GOOD

HEY, LUCY! C'MON IN... THE INNING'S OVER..

WHAT ?! I JUST GOT OUT HERE!
SCHULZ
7-1

July 24, 1953

"PEANUTS"
SIGH

WHAT'S THE MATTER, CHARLIE BROWN?
I'M A LONESOME COWBOY

WHY ARE YOU SO LONESOME?

ALL THE OTHER KIDS ARE PLAYING "SPACEMAN"
7-24
SCHULZ

August 5, 1953

"PEANUTS"
marcando
ff
p

SCHROEDER, HOW DO YOU MANAGE TO PLAY ALL THOSE GREAT PIECES ON A TOY PIANO?

8-5
YOU GOTTA GET THE BREAKS!
SCHULZ

August 22, 1953

"PEANUTS"

!
8-22
SCHULZ

August 27, 1953

HEY, PATTY!

HOW ABOUT GIVING ME A PUSH?

BONK!

THAT WAS A STRANGE THING TO ASK FOR.. ??
SCHULZ
8-27

September 28, 1953

"PEANUTS"
WELL! YOU TWO LOOK LIKE YOU'RE HAVING A GOOD TIME..

WE ARE... WE'RE MAKING FUN OF THIS PICTURE IN THE PAPER..

WHY ARE YOU MAKING FUN OF IT?

9-28
BECAUSE WE DON'T UNDERSTAND IT..
SCHULZ

October 4, 1953

PEANUTS
!
GRRRRR...
ARF!
ARF!!
ARF!!
ARF! ARF!
ARF! ARF! ARF!
WHEW! GASP!
PANT PANT
?
WHEW
YAWN
SIGH
10-4
SCHULZ

"I patterned Snoopy in appearance after a dog I had when I was about thirteen years old. His name was Spike, and he looked a little bit like the original Snoopy. But Snoopy didn't start off being a beagle. It's just that 'beagle' is a funny word."

October 7, 1953

"PEANUTS"

10-7
SCHULZ

October 9, 1953

"PEANUTS"
RATS!

IT'S NO USE... I GIVE UP!

WELL, DON'T FEEL SO BADLY ABOUT IT, CHARLIE BROWN.... AFTER ALL..

..MOST COLLEGE PLAYERS ARE BIGGER THAN US!
10-9
SCHULZ

October 13, 1953

"PEANUTS"
GO AHEAD! MAKE FUN OF ME! YOU JUST WAIT..

SOMEDAY I'LL GET TO BE PRESIDENT, AND THEN YOU'LL ALL BE SORRY!

I'LL SAY WE WILL..

SOMEHOW THAT DIDN'T COME OUT RIGHT..
10-13
SCHULZ

October 28, 1953

"PEANUTS"

BOO!

SCHULZ
10-28
BOO!

November 7, 1953

"PEANUTS"

ALL RIGHT.. PUT 'EM UP!

SCHULZ
11-7

November 12, 1953

"PEANUTS"

?

I'VE GOT TO ADMIT THAT THERE'S NOTHING LIKE THE 'POLKA' WHEN DANCED BY AN EXPERT..
11/12
SCHULZ

December 9, 1953

"PEANUTS"
HEY!! LET'S GO!

SAY, ISN'T LINUS COMING OUTSIDE?
NO, IT'S TOO COLD FOR HIM TODAY...

HE'S GOING TO WATCH US THROUGH THE FRONT DOOR..

12-9

December 13, 1953

PEANUTS
by
CHARLES M.
SCHULZ
I REALLY APPRECIATE YOUR GIVING ME THIS OPPORTUNITY, VIOLET, BUT..
WHAT'S THE MATTER?
I CAN'T DO IT.. I'VE LOST MY NERVE..
I'M GOING HOME!
OH, COME ON, SCHROEDER... MOTHER WON'T CARE..
WELL,....IT'S NOT AS IF I'M GOING TO **RUIN** HER PIANO, IS IT?
OF COURSE NOT.. NOW, COME ON..
THIS IS GOING TO BE THE BIGGEST THRILL OF MY LIFE...
SCHULZ
12-13

January 25, 1954

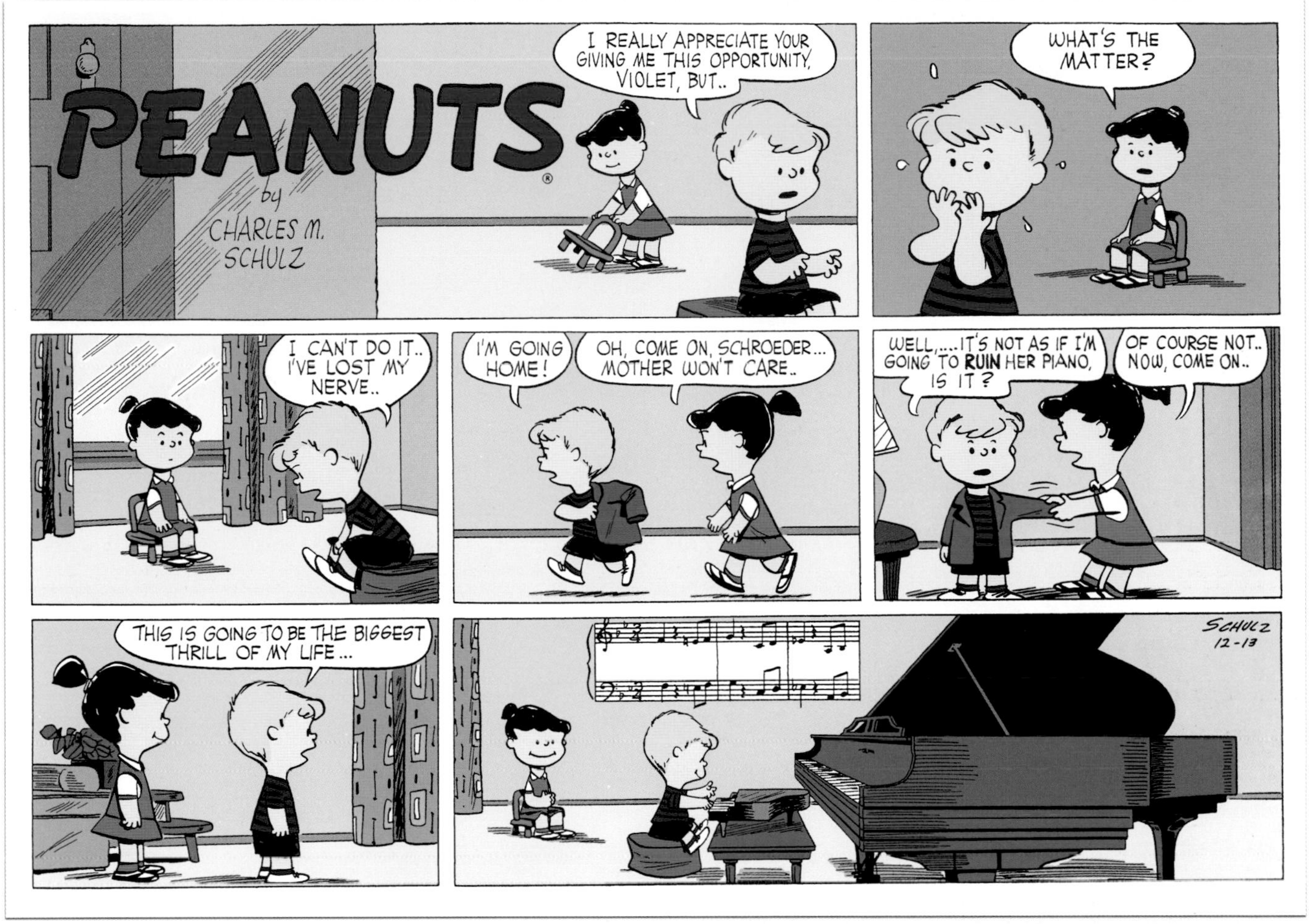

"PEANUTS"
EVERYBODY THAT I KNOW HAS SEEN THAT NEW 3-D MOVIE
EVERYBODY?
UH, HUH...EVERYBODY
1-25
SCHULZ

January 26, 1954

"PEANUTS"
WELL, YOU LOOK WARM, CHARLIE BROWN...

OH, I AM...YES, SIR..I BELIEVE IN BEING PREPARED FOR COLD WEATHER

THERE'S ONLY ONE THING WRONG..
WHAT'S THAT?

1-26
SCHULZ
I CAN'T MOVE!

January 24, 1954

THAT'S WHAT I THINK OF YOUR BOX OF COOKIES!
PEANUTS
by CHARLES M. SCHULZ
COOKIES
THAT'S WHAT I THINK OF YOUR OL' PIANO!
?
THAT'S WHAT I THINK OF YOUR OL' STAMP COLLECTION!
AND THAT'S WHAT I THINK OF YOUR OL' PICTURE PUZZLE!
AND THAT'S WHAT I THINK OF YOUR STUPID OL' MARBLES!
AND THAT'S WHAT I THINK OF YOUR SILLY OL' COLOR CRAYONS!
SCHULZ 1-24
I'M FRUSTRATED AND INHIBITED, AND NOBODY UNDERSTANDS ME..

January 28, 1954

"PEANUTS"
1-28
SCHULZ

January 29, 1954

"PEANUTS"
WE'RE GOING TO HAVE A PARTY AND WE'RE NOT GOING TO INVITE YOU!!
THAT'S A GOOD IDEA...I THINK YOU'RE DOING THE RIGHT THING...
IF I HAVE THE TYPE OF PERSONALITY THAT ANNOYS YOU, IT WOULD BE SILLY TO INVITE ME..
SCHULZ
1-29

February 1, 1954

"PEANUTS"

SCHULZ
2-1

February 24, 1954

"PEANUTS"
THIS IS A WONDERFUL PICTURE OF YOU, CHARLIE BROWN

I THINK SO, TOO...IT'S THE BEST YOU'VE EVER HAD TAKEN

IT'S A WONDERFUL PICTURE! ABSOLUTELY WONDERFUL!
UH, HUH..

2-24
IT DOESN'T LOOK A BIT LIKE YOU!
SCHULZ

January 31, 1954

PEANUTS
by
CHARLES M. SCHULZ

WHAT IN THE WORLD IS GOING ON OVER THERE?

?

SNOOPY

?

HEY! IS THERE ROOM FOR ONE MORE?
SURE.. COME ON IN!
1-31

THE HOUSE ITSELF ISN'T SO BIG, BUT YOU OUGHT TO SEE THE RECREATION ROOM!
SCHULZ

March 30, 1954

"PEANUTS"
GET 'WAY OUT!! 'WAY OUT! GO ON! 'WAY OUT!

SCHULZ
3-30
WELL? WHERE WERE YOU ON THAT ONE?

April 1, 1954

NEW CHEST PROTECTOR?
UH HUH..

OOF!!

4/1
I DIDN'T THINK IT LOOKED VERY STURDY..
SCHULZ

March 21, 1954

PEANUTS
by
CHARLES M. SCHULZ
POW!
WHEE!
STOMP!
STOMP
STOMP!
3-21
SCHULZ
SIGH

April 11, 1954

PEANUTS
by
CHARLES M. SCHULZ
I THINK WE'D BETTER QUIT
I DO, TOO
IT'S GOING TO CLEAR UP...
YOU'RE OUT OF YOUR MIND, CHARLIE BROWN!
I THINK IT'S GOING TO CLEAR UP..
WE'RE GOING HOME!
BUT IT'S GOING TO CLEAR UP!
IT'S GOING TO CLEAR UP...
IT'S GOING TO CLEAR UP..
IT'S GOING TO CLEAR UP!
SCHULZ
4/11
IT'S GOING TO CLEAR UP....

"I have found drawing with pen and ink to be very challenging as well as gratifying. I feel that it is possible to achieve something near to what fine artists call 'paint quality' when working with the pen."

April 21, 1954

ONE FINGER WILL MEAN AN 'OUT-CURVE'..
RIGHT
TWO FINGERS WILL MEAN AN 'OUT-CURVE UP-SHOOT,' THREE FINGERS WILL MEAN AN 'IN-CURVE SLIDER'..
RIGHT.. RIGHT..
FOUR FINGERS WILL MEAN AN 'OUT-CURVE SLIDER UP-SHOOT,' AND FIVE FINGERS WILL MEAN A 'DROP'
HOLD IT!
4-21
YOU KNOW I CAN'T THROW A 'DROP'!
SCHULZ

April 24, 1954

"PEANUTS"
"MARY WORE HER RED DRESS, RED DRESS, RED DRESS...MARY WORE HER RED DRESS ALL DAY LONG..
"MARY WORE A RED HAT, RED HAT, RED HAT... MARY WORE A RED HAT ALL DAY LONG...
"MARY WORE HER RED SHOES, RED SHOES, RED SHOES.... MARY WORE HER RED SHOES ALL DAY LONG..."
SCHULZ
4-24
THAT POOR GIRL WAS OUT OF HER MIND!

May 4, 1954

"PEANUTS"

?

WHAT IN THE WORLD DO YOU THINK YOU'RE DOING?

I WAS LISTENING TO THE OCEAN ROAR!
5-4
SCHULZ

May 12, 1954

"PEANUTS"

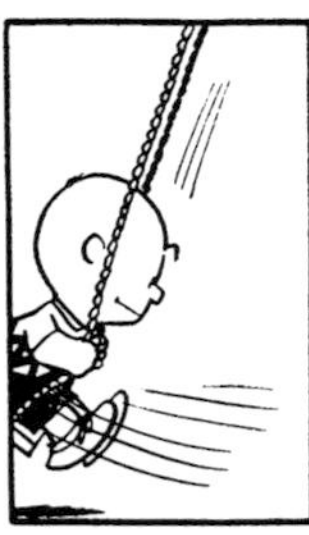

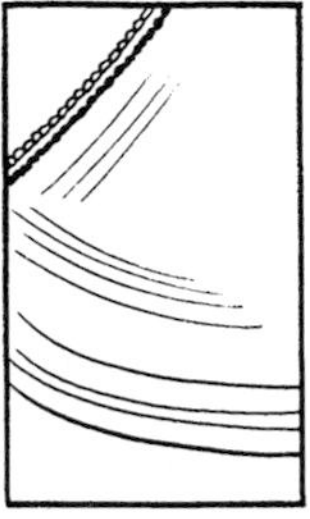

THUMP
5-12

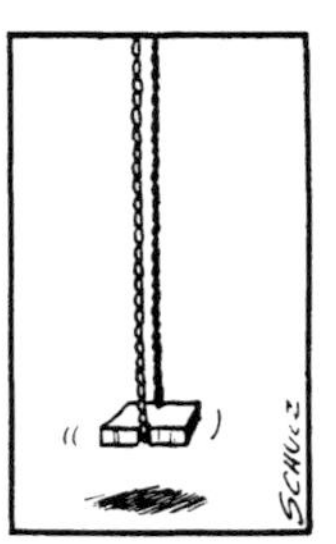
SCHULZ

"At one point, I drew a whole bunch of adults in a gallery where Lucy was playing in a golf tournament, which is something I never should have done. But it was an experiment. . . . and then I used to have off-stage voices, which again was simply because I didn't know how to handle it. Now, the strip has become so abstract that the introduction of an adult would destroy it."

May 16, 1954

PEANUTS by CHARLES M. SCHULZ

WELL, I PAID YOUR ENTRY FEE, LUCY....BUT IT SURE EMPTIED THAT OL' PIGGY BANK..

I GUESS IT'S TOO LATE TO BACK OUT NOW, ISN'T IT?

I'M SO NERVOUS, CHARLIE BROWN... I'VE NEVER PLAYED IN A GOLF TOURNAMENT BEFORE..

WHAT CHANCE HAVE I GOT AGAINST SAM SNEAD AND BEN HOGAN AND 'IKE'?

DON'T BE SILLY! THIS IS A WOMEN'S TOURNAMENT..THOSE GUYS DON'T PLAY IN WOMEN'S TOURNAMENTS!

LUCILLE VAN PELT ON THE FIRST TEE, PLEASE

SCHULZ

I FEEL LIKE I'M WALKING THE 'LAST MILE'...

DON'T WORRY... YOU'RE AN UNKNOWN.. NOBODY WILL EVEN BE WATCHING YOU...

To the First tee

CONTINUED 5-16

June 1, 1954

"PEANUTS"
WHY DOES LINUS HOLD HIS BLANKET LIKE THAT?
A B

I'M NOT SURE...I THINK MAYBE IT GIVES HIM A FEELING OF SECURITY..

?
6-1

IT DOESN'T WORK...I FEEL LIKE AN IDIOT!
SCHULZ

June 16, 1954

"PEANUTS"
BANG BANG! BANG! BANG!
BANG BANG! BANG
BANG BANG BANG BANG BANG BANG!

BANG! BANG BANG BANG!
BANG BANG! BANG BANG
BANG! BANG
BANG BANG BANG BANG!

RELOAD!
CLICK-CLICK

BANG! BANG! BANG! BANG
BANG! BANG! BANG! BANG BANG!
BANG! BANG! BANG!
BANG BANG BANG!
6/16
SCHULZ

"I have never been a very successful kite flyer and have used the excuse that I never lived where there were good areas to fly kites. When I was growing up, we always lived in residential areas which had too many trees and too many telephone wires. Recollections of those handicaps inspired Charlie Brown's troubles with kite flying."

June 13, 1954

PEANUTS
by
CHARLES M. SCHULZ
THUMP THUMP THUMP THUMP
RIP!
CRASH!
SNAP! TEAR!
BONK!
SMASH!
6-13
?
SCHULZ

June 18, 1954

"PEANUTS"
WE'RE PLAYING "H-BOMB" TEST...

BWHAM!
6-18
SCHULZ

July 3, 1954

"PEANUTS"
HAVE YOU SEEN CHARLIE BROWN'S NEW T-SHIRT?

NO! DON'T TELL ME HE FINALLY TOOK THE HINT?!

I WAS GETTING SO SICK OF THAT SILLY BLACK STRIPE..
OH? WELL, PREPARE YOURSELF FOR A BLOW..

SCHULZ
7-3
!

July 13, 1954—First appearance of Pig-Pen.

"PEANUTS"
HELLO, THERE.. WHAT'S YOUR NAME?

I HAVEN'T GOT A NAME..PEOPLE JUST CALL ME THINGS..REAL INSULTING THINGS...

WHAT DO THEY CALL YOU MOST OF THE TIME?
I'LL TELL YOU IF YOU WON'T LAUGH...

'PIG-PEN'
7-13
SCHULZ

July 14, 1954

"PEANUTS"
CHARLIE BROWN, HAVE YOU MET LITTLE 'PIG-PEN'?

'PIG-PEN,' THIS IS GOOD OL' CHARLIE BROWN..
HI, KID...

ISN'T HE A MESS? LOOK AT HIS HANDS AND FACE...AND THOSE OVERALLS...

7-14
I GOT CLEAN THOUGHTS!
SCHULZ

July 21, 1954

"PEANUTS"

!

A SHARK! A SHARK!

SCHULZ
7-21

July 23, 1954

"PEANUTS"
LUCY I'D LIKE TO HAVE YOU MEET 'PIG-PEN'...

BOY!! YOU ARE WELL NAMED, AREN'T YOU? BUT WHO AM I TO BE CRITICAL? WELCOME TO THE GANG

WHACK!
7-23

EVERYBODY STAND STILL UNTIL THE DUST SETTLES!
SCHULZ

August 3, 1954

"PEANUTS"
I'M GOING TO TEACH YOU A NEW CARD GAME, LINUS...

FIRST I'D BETTER GET A PENCIL SO WE CAN KEEP SCORE..

!
SCHULZ 8-3

August 17, 1954

"PEANUTS"
PSST...LINUS...I THINK YOU'D BETTER WAKE UP
Z

I THINK YOU'D BETTER WAKE UP, LITTLE BROTHER..
Z

I THINK YOU'D BETTER WAKE UP BECAUSE IT'S ALMOST TIME FOR..
Z

SUPPER!
SCHULZ
8-17

August 18, 1954

"PEANUTS"
'PIG-PEN', YOU'RE A MESS!

YOU'RE A MESS WHEN YOU EAT, A MESS WHEN YOU PLAY AND A MESS WHEN YOU'RE JUST STANDING STILL..

WELL, YOU'LL HAVE TO ADMIT ONE THING..

I'M CONSISTENT!
8-18
SCHULZ

September 16, 1954

"PEANUTS"
GET 'WAY OUT, I TELL YOU! 'WAY OUT! DO YOU WANT TO GET MURDERED?

ALL RIGHT! STAND THERE, THEN! GET YOUR HEAD KNOCKED OFF!! HERE IT COMES!!

POW!

SCHULZ 9-16

October 4, 1954

"PEANUTS"
I'M WAITING TO SEE THE ECLIPSE

THE ECLIPSE? GOOD GRIEF!! THAT'S BEEN OVER FOR **MONTHS**!!!

WELL, DON'T YOU THINK I KNOW THAT, CHARLIE BROWN? I'M NOT STUPID, YOU KNOW..

I JUST THOUGHT THAT BY THIS TIME IT MIGHT BE SHOWING IN **SUBURBAN** AREAS..
10-4
SCHULZ

September 12, 1954

PEANUTS
by
CHARLES M. SCHULZ
JOKER
JOKER
WATCH ME, LINUS, AND I'LL SHOW YOU HOW TO BUILD A HOUSE OF CARDS...
IT'S KIND OF HARD AT FIRST, BUT AFTER YOU CATCH ON, IT... **RATS!**
C'MON! STAND UP, THERE.. RATS! C'MON, NOW... THAT'S THE WAY.. **RATS! RATS! RATS!**
STEADY... STEADDY.. STEAAAADDDDY...
There! HOW'S THAT!?
!
I CAN'T STAND SMART-ALECKY KIDS!
SCHULZ
9-12

October 14, 1954

"PEANUTS"
IT SAYS HERE THAT BRAHMS AN' FRANZ LISZT NEVER GOT ALONG WELL..
DID BRAHMS EVER **HIT** HIM?
NO...NO,...I DON'T THINK SO..
DID LISZT EVER HIT BRAHMS?
I'VE NEVER READ THAT HE DID...
HUH...YOU'D THINK SOMEBODY WOULD HAVE HIT SOMEBODY!
10-14
SCHULZ

October 29, 1954

"PEANUTS"
THIS IS THE OUTFIT I'M GOING TO WEAR ON HALLOWEEN..

IT MIGHT BE KIND OF CHILLY THAT NIGHT..

I CAN ALWAYS PUT ON A JACKET..

SOMEHOW THAT SEEMS TO SPOIL THE EFFECT
SCHULZ 10-29

November 21, 1954

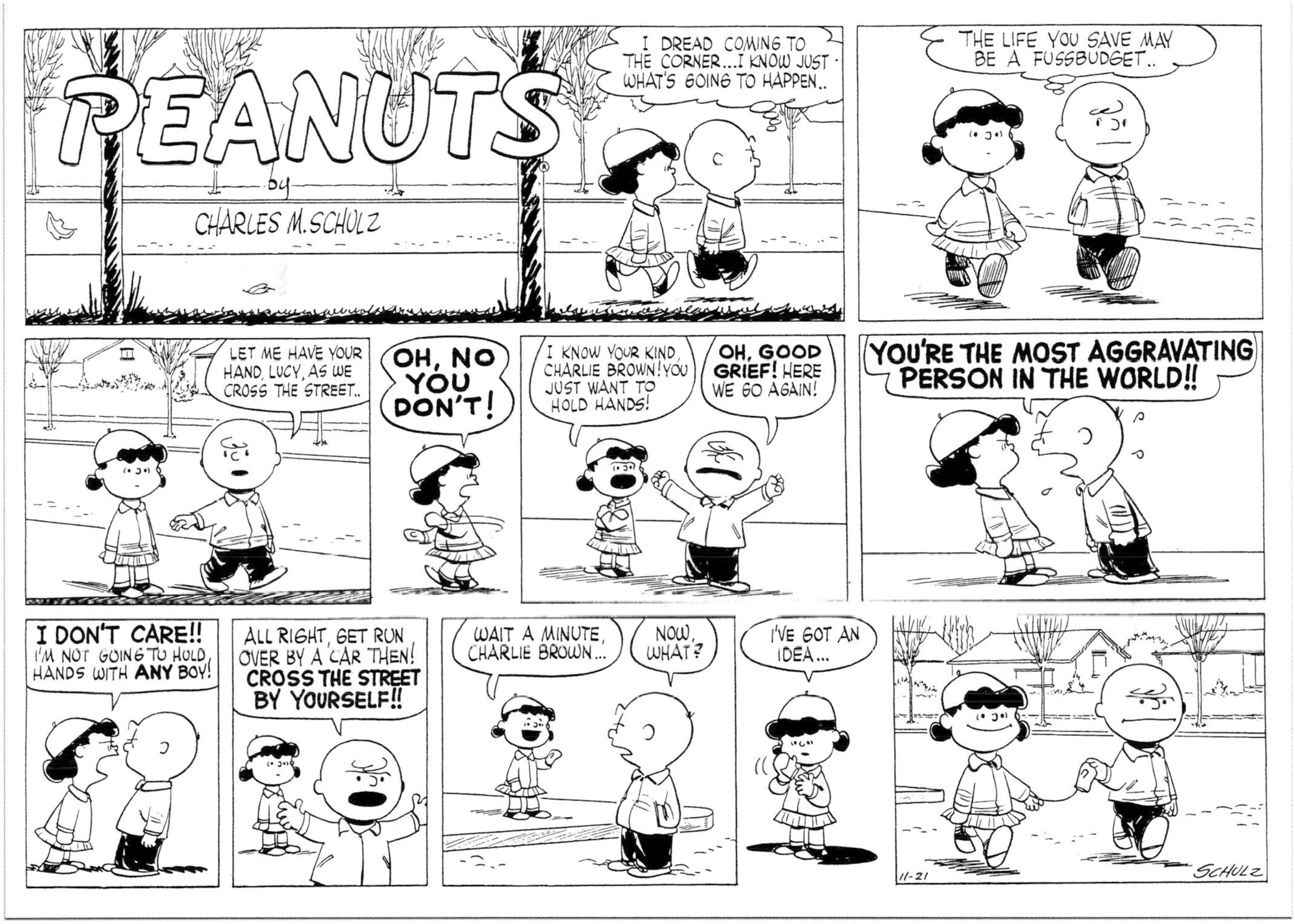

PEANUTS by CHARLES M. SCHULZ

I DREAD COMING TO THE CORNER...I KNOW JUST WHAT'S GOING TO HAPPEN..

THE LIFE YOU SAVE MAY BE A FUSSBUDGET..

LET ME HAVE YOUR HAND, LUCY, AS WE CROSS THE STREET..

OH, NO YOU DON'T!

I KNOW YOUR KIND, CHARLIE BROWN! YOU JUST WANT TO HOLD HANDS!

OH, GOOD GRIEF! HERE WE GO AGAIN!

YOU'RE THE MOST AGGRAVATING PERSON IN THE WORLD!!

I DON'T CARE!! I'M NOT GOING TO HOLD HANDS WITH ANY BOY!

ALL RIGHT, GET RUN OVER BY A CAR THEN! CROSS THE STREET BY YOURSELF!!

WAIT A MINUTE, CHARLIE BROWN...

NOW, WHAT?

I'VE GOT AN IDEA...

11-21 SCHULZ

November 30, 1954

AHEM! YOU'RE NEW AROUND HERE, AREN'T YOU?

MY NAME IS CHARLIE BROWN.. ALL MY FRIENDS REFER TO ME AS 'GOOD OL' CHARLIE BROWN'..

THAT'S WHAT MY FRIENDS CALL ME, TOO..
HUH?

GOOD OL' CHARLOTTE BRAUN!
OH, NO...
11-30
SCHULZ

December 12, 1954

PEANUTS
by CHARLES M. SCHULZ
Pat Pat Pat
AH! THE FIRST SNOWBALL OF THE YEAR!
I LIKE TO BEGIN EACH WINTER BY HITTING CHARLIE BROWN RIGHT ON THE HEAD!
I CAN'T DO IT... I CAN'T DO IT...
IT'S NO USE...I JUST CAN'T DO IT...OH, BOO, HOO, HOO...HE'S SO INNOCENT...I JUST CAN'T DO IT..
SOB SOB SOB
?
I WAS GOING TO HIT YOU WITH THIS SNOWBALL, CHARLIE BROWN, BUT I'M TOO SOFT-HEARTED...
WELL, I'M GLAD YOU CHANGED YOUR MIND, LUCY...YOU'RE A GOOD GIRL..
WHAT AM I DOING? I'VE GOT TO GET HOLD OF MYSELF!
POW!
OH, IT'S GOING TO BE A GREAT WINTER!
12-12
SCHULZ

"Nothing in life ends with a 'pow!' And aren't all kids egotists? And brutal? Children are caricatures of adults . . . maybe I have the cruelest strip going."

December 14, 1954

"PEANUTS"
Dear Santa, I feel good tonight.
I like everybody. Everybody is my friend.
I don't hate anybody. Oh, by the way...
don't make the mistake you made last year, and bring that no good Shermy all the best toys. Yours, Charles Brown
12-14
SCHULZ

December 15, 1954

"PEANUTS"
WOULD YOU LIKE TO READ THIS BEFORE I MAIL IT OFF?
'DEAR SANTA CLAUS, I DON'T THINK I WANT ANY TOYS THIS YEAR..
I WOULD MUCH RATHER HAVE A PHOTOGRAPH OF YOURSELF TO HANG ON THE WALL OF MY ROOM'
PSYCHOLOGY!
12-15
SCHULZ

December 18, 1954

"PEANUTS"
HEY, PATTY!! LOOK!

SANTA CLAUS HAS ANSWERED ONE OF MY LETTERS!
WELL, OPEN IT UP...LET'S SEE WHAT HE WROTE

RATS!
WHAT IS IT?

A FORM REJECTION SLIP!
12-18
SCHULZ

December 20, 1954

"PEANUTS"
WATCH, LINUS... I'LL SHOW YOU HOW TO BLOW UP A BALLOON..

THERE! HOW'S THAT?

NOW, LET'S SEE YOU DO IT...

12-20
SCHULZ
?

January 4, 1955

"PEANUTS"
LINUS! YOU GIVE ME THAT BLANKET!

LET GO OF IT! LET GO, I SAY!

SCHULZ
1-4

January 13, 1955

"PEANUTS"
IT WAS THE STRANGEST FEELING, CHARLIE BROWN... I COULDN'T HEAR A THING..

I WAS SLIDING DOWN THIS HILL, SEE, GOING REAL FAST, AND YET EVERYTHING SEEMED SO QUIET..

NO WONDER..YOU'VE GOT YOUR EARMUFFS TOO TIGHT.
WAS THAT IT? RATS! WHAT A DISAPPOINTMENT..

I THOUGHT I HAD BROKEN THROUGH THE SOUND BARRIER!
SCHULZ
1-13

February 23, 1955

"PEANUTS"
THERE'S NOTHING MORE STUPID THAN SOMEONE TRYING TO BE SOMETHING THEY AREN'T!

THAT DUMB SNOOPY THINKS HE'S A RHINOCEROS, AND HE'S TOO LITTLE...

WHOOPS!!

..TO BUMP ANYBODY...
2-23
SCHULZ

March 4, 1955

"PEANUTS"
HE SAYS HE'S FROM MARS... I DON'T BELIEVE HIM

OH, I DO...
YOU DO?

I'M SURE HE'S TELLING THE TRUTH..

NOBODY ON EARTH HAS A HEAD THAT ROUND!
3-4
SCHULZ

March 22, 1955

"PEANUTS"

3-22
SCHULZ

"It was the way I drew the characters; they filled up the strip and I drew them from the side view. The type of humor that I was using did not call for camera angles. I liked drawing the characters from the same view all the way through because the ideas were very brief and I didn't want anything in the drawing to interrupt the flow of what the characters were either saying or doing. So there became no room for adults in the strip."

April 10, 1955

OH, OH..
PEANUTS by CHARLES M. SCHULZ
C'MON.. LET'S HAVE THE BALL..
ON WITH THE GAME!
HEY! WHERE'S EVERYBODY GOING?
YOU'RE NOT GOING TO LET A LITTLE RAIN BOTHER YOU, ARE YOU?!
COME ON BACK! IT'S GOING TO CLEAR UP!
COME ON BACK!
COWARDS! QUITTERS!
RATS!
SCHULZ 4-10

April 14, 1955

"PEANUTS"
C'MON! HIT ONE OUT HERE!!!

WHAT'S THE MATTER? CAN'T YA HIT 'EM THIS FAR? ARE Y'WEAK, OR SOMETHING ?

WHAT DO Y'THINK I'M STANDIN' OUT HERE FOR, MY HEALTH? C'MON! HIT ONE! WHAT DO...

SCHULZ
4-14

April 27, 1955

"PEANUTS"
'PIG-PEN,' WHY ARE YOU SO MESSY?

DO YOU SUPPOSE IT'S HEREDITARY, OR IS IT YOUR ENVIRONMENT?

IT MUST BE MY ENVIRONMENT...

I'M COVERED WITH IT!
4-27
SCHULZ

April 28, 1955

"PEANUTS"
JUST LOOK AT THAT 'PIG-PEN'..
?

ISN'T HE AWFUL?
TERRIBLE .. JUST TERRIBLE!

A REAL 'GOOD-FOR-NOTHING'..
I'LL SAY... A COMPLETE FLOP!

I'M WELL-READ!
4-28
SCHULZ

May 21, 1955

"PEANUTS"

5-21
SCHULZ

May 31, 1955

PEANUTS
?

AARGH
!

HERE IT IS, LINUS! ALL FLUFFY AN' CLEAN!

SIGH
LINUS REALLY SUFFERS ON THE DAY HIS BLANKET IS BEING WASHED..
5-31
SCHULZ

May 22, 1955

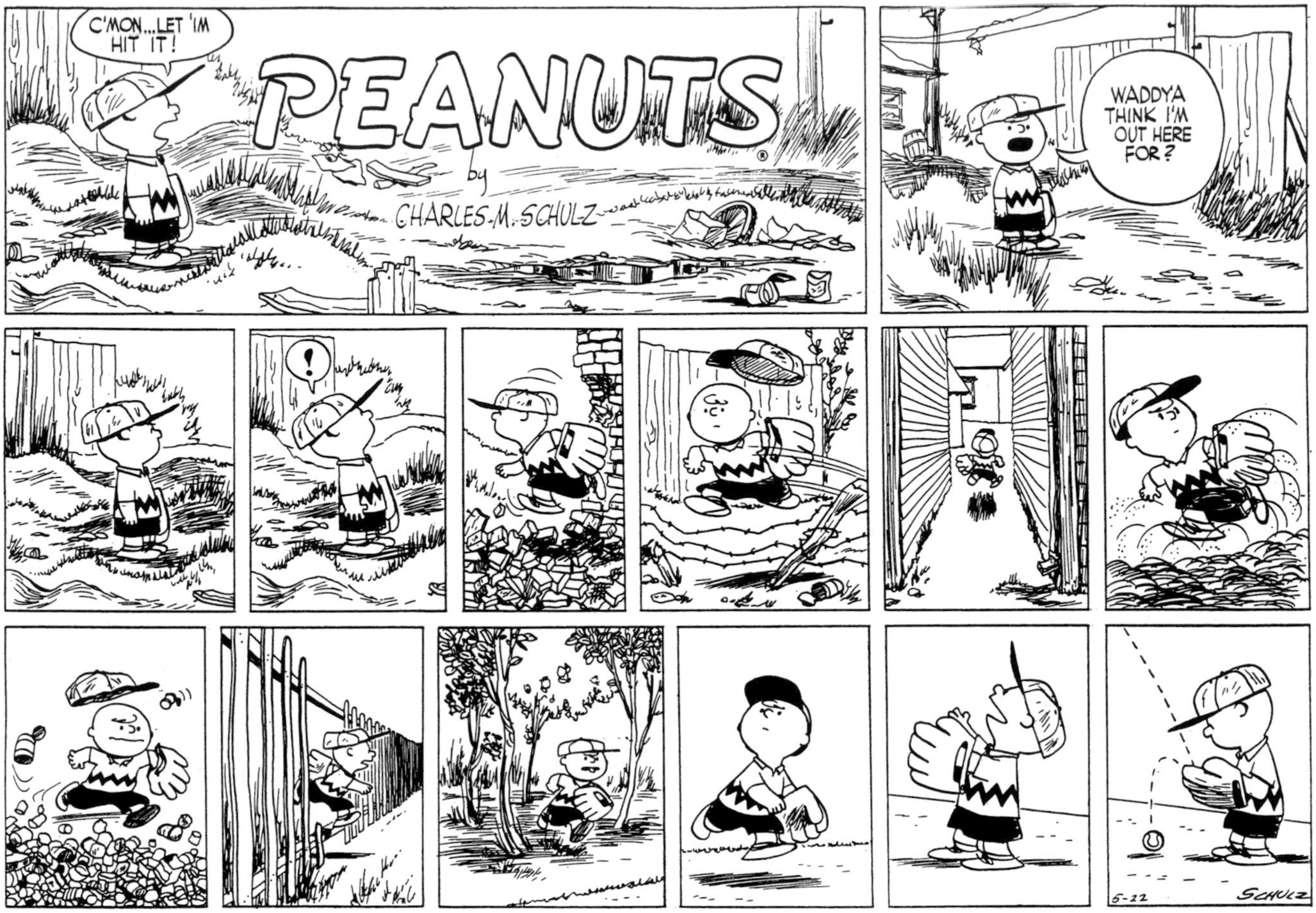

C'MON...LET 'IM HIT IT!

PEANUTS

by CHARLES M. SCHULZ

WADDYA THINK I'M OUT HERE FOR?

5-22

SCHULZ

June 7, 1955

"PEANUTS"
DAVY CROCKETT ALWAYS WORE A COONSKIN CAP...
I'LL BET BEETHOVEN NEVER HAD A COONSKIN CAP!
OH?
6-7
SCHULZ

June 29, 1955

"PEANUTS"
YOU'D BETTER HANG ON TO ME, LINUS, WHILE WE CROSS THE STREET...
6-29
SCHULZ

May 29, 1955

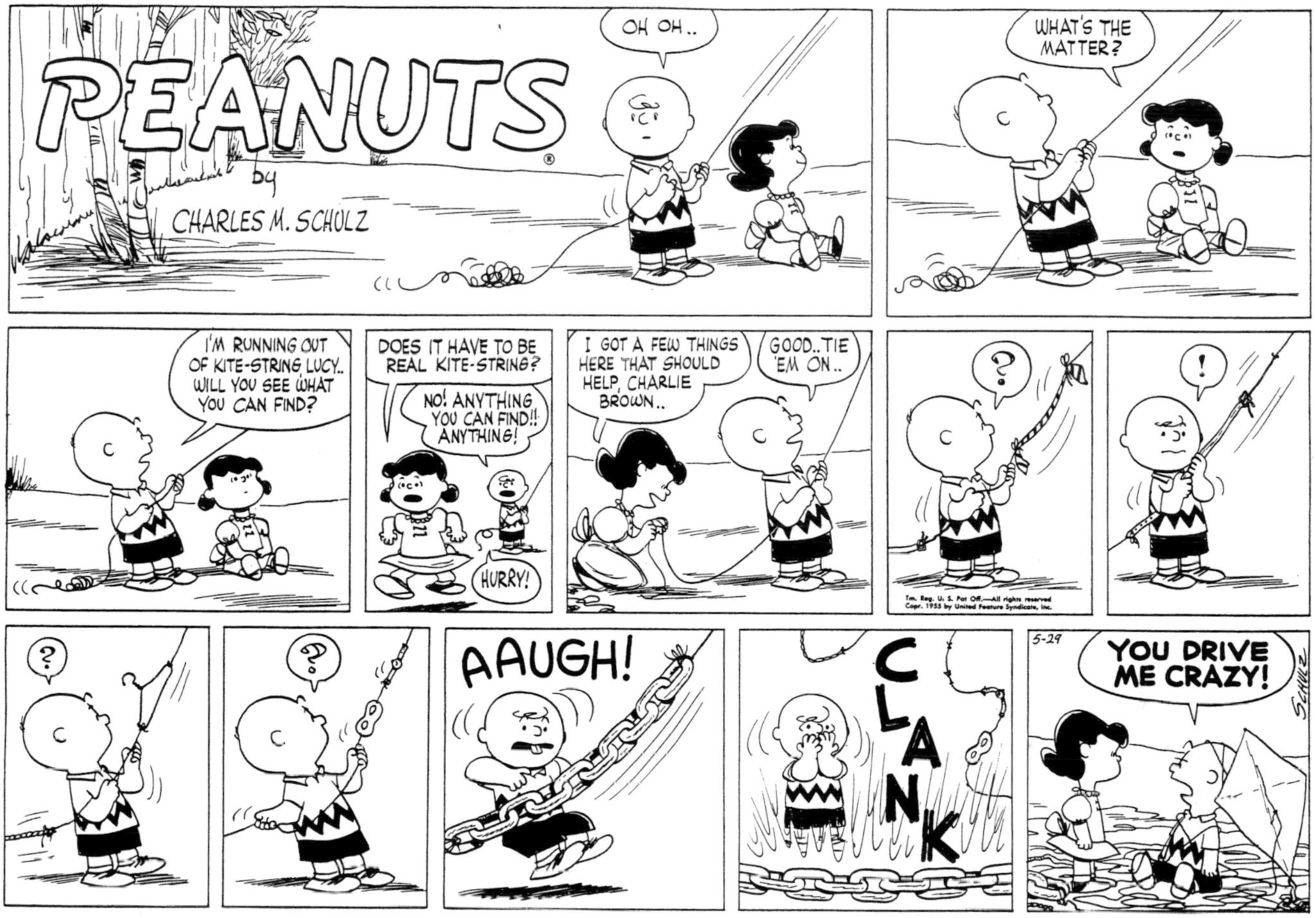

PEANUTS®
by
CHARLES M. SCHULZ

OH OH..

WHAT'S THE MATTER?

I'M RUNNING OUT OF KITE-STRING LUCY.. WILL YOU SEE WHAT YOU CAN FIND?

DOES IT HAVE TO BE REAL KITE-STRING?

NO! ANYTHING YOU CAN FIND!! ANYTHING!

HURRY!

I GOT A FEW THINGS HERE THAT SHOULD HELP, CHARLIE BROWN..

GOOD..TIE 'EM ON..

?

!

?

?

AAUGH!

CLANK

5-29

YOU DRIVE ME CRAZY!

SCHULZ

June 30, 1955

"PEANUTS"
6-30
SCHULZ

July 1, 1955

"PEANUTS"
DON'T TELL ME YOU'RE BURYING YOUR COONSKIN CAP?!

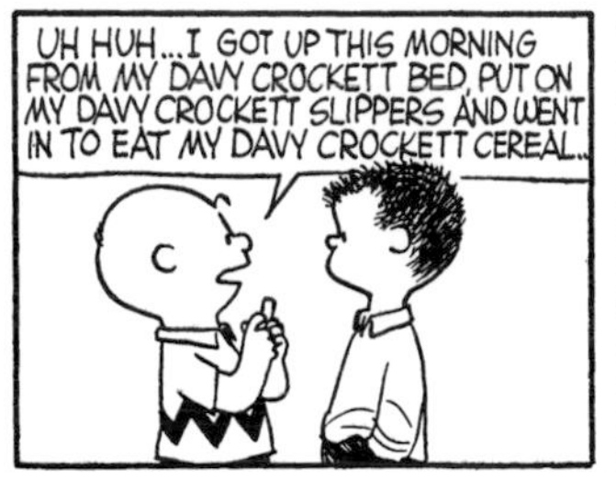
UH HUH...I GOT UP THIS MORNING FROM MY DAVY CROCKETT BED, PUT ON MY DAVY CROCKETT SLIPPERS AND WENT IN TO EAT MY DAVY CROCKETT CEREAL..

I'M SITTING THERE IN A DAVY CROCKETT CHAIR EATING WITH A DAVY CROCKETT SPOON OUT OF A DAVY CROCKETT BOWL.. SUDDENLY IT HITS ME!....

WHERE WILL IT ALL END?
7-1
SCHULZ

July 2, 1955

"PEANUTS"
IT'S VERY STRANGE...

SOMETIMES I THINK THAT I LIKE BEETHOVEN THE BEST, BUT OTHER TIMES I THINK THAT I LIKE BRAHMS THE BEST...

I KNOW **EXACTLY** WHAT YOU MEAN, SCHROEDER..

I FEEL THE SAME WAY ABOUT WILLIE MAYS AND DUKE SNIDER!
SCHULZ
7-2

July 6, 1955

"PEANUTS"
YOU ALWAYS CAN TELL WHICH WAY IS NORTH, LINUS BY LOOKING AT THE SUN...

YOU SEE, IT COMES UP EVERY MORNING IN THE NORTH...

AND THEN EVERY EVENING IT SETS IN THE SOUTH!

GEE...I'M REAL LUCKY TO HAVE A SISTER WHO'LL TEACH ME ALL THESE THINGS...
SCHULZ
7-6

July 8, 1955

"PEANUTS"
LINUS...MOMMY SAYS COME ON IN AND EAT LUNCH..

SHE SAYS IF YOU DON'T, YOU'LL NEVER GROW UP TO BE A BIG BOY...

Huh!

7-8
FIVE HUNDRED YEARS FROM NOW, WHO'LL KNOW THE DIFFERENCE?
SCHULZ

July 9, 1955

"PEANUTS"
DO YOU KNOW THAT THERE ARE OVER TWO BILLION PEOPLE IN THE WORLD?

AND NOT **ONE** OF THEM LIKES ME! NOT **ONE**!!

AND DO YOU KNOW WHAT MAKES IT EVEN WORSE?
7-9

THE WAY THE POPULATION IS RISING, I'M GETTING MORE UNPOPULAR EVERY DAY!
SCHULZ

July 11, 1955

"PEANUTS"

SIGH

7-11
SCHULZ

July 23, 1955

"PEANUTS"
HI, 'PIG-PEN'... WHERE YOU GOIN' ALL DRESSED UP?

I'M NOT 'GOING'...I'M COMING...I'VE BEEN TO A BIRTHDAY PARTY...
OH? WAS IT FUN?

NOT FOR ME... I NEVER GOT INSIDE THE HOUSE...

THEY DIDN'T RECOGNIZE ME!
7-23
SCHULZ

July 31, 1955

SWING, 'PIG-PEN'! SWING!
PEANUTS
by CHARLES M. SCHULZ
KLOP
!
GIMME THAT BALL!! HE'S GONNA SCORE! GIMME IT, I SAY!!!
BY GOLLY, I'M NOT GONNA FOOL AROUND WITH YOU!
?
HOME! HOME! GET 'IM AT HOME!
I'M SAFE!
OH, GOOD GRIEF!
YOU DRIVE ME CRAZY!
SCHULZ
7-31

August 3, 1955

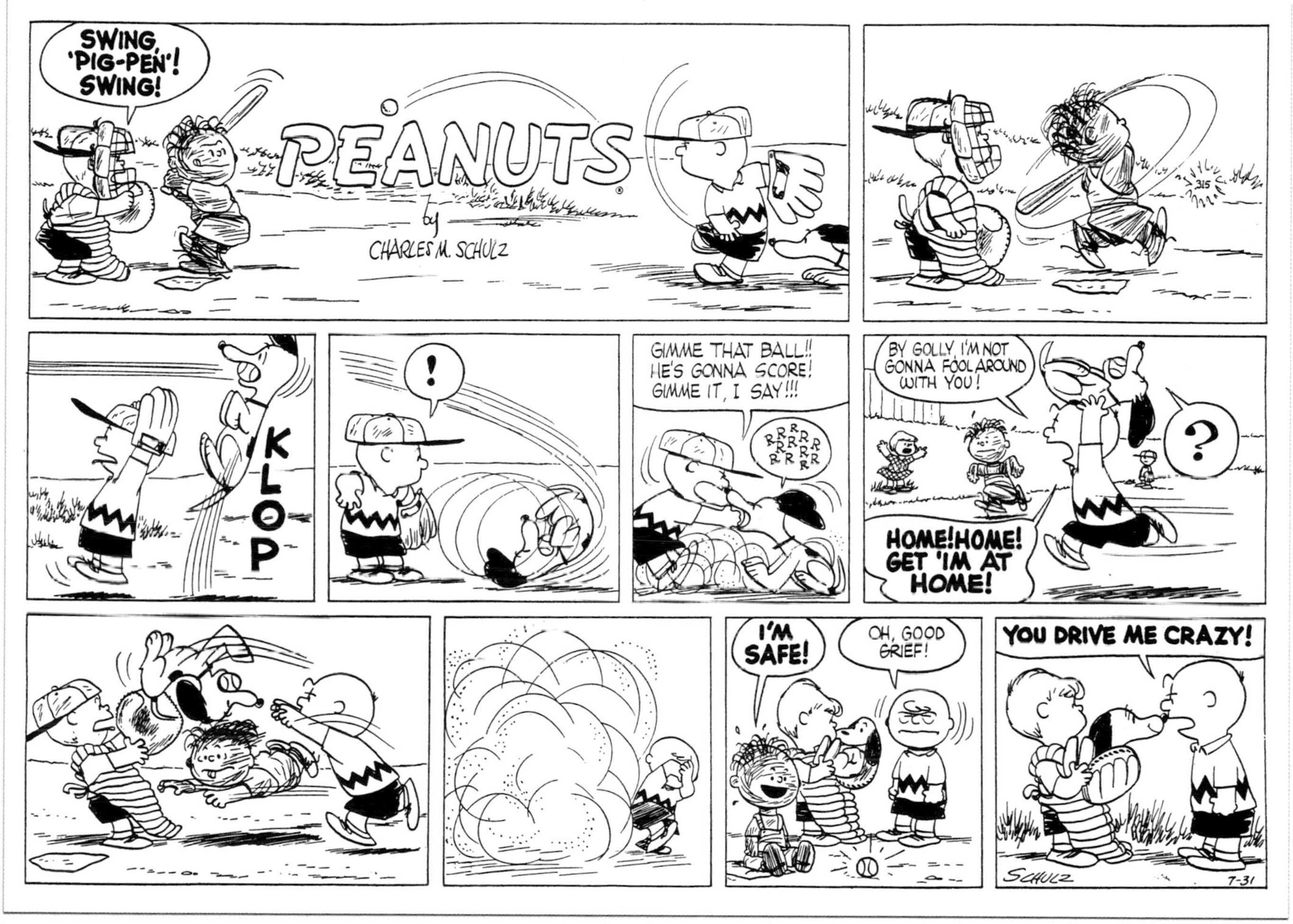

"PEANUTS"
AREN'T THE STARS BEAUTIFUL CHARLIE BROWN?
UH, HUH

LET'S GO INSIDE AND WATCH TELEVISION...

I'M BEGINNING TO FEEL INSIGNIFICANT..
8-3
SCHULZ

August 10, 1955

"PEANUTS"
ALL YOU HAVE TO DO, SNOOPY, IS LIFT YOUR PAW LIKE THIS...SEE?

NOW, LET'S SEE IF YOU CAN DO IT........READY?.....SHAKE

SCHULZ 8-10
IT'S NO FUN TEACHING YOU ANYTHING!

August 14, 1955

PEANUTS®
by CHARLES M. SCHULZ
YOU WANT ME TO 'BREAK'?
SURE, GO AHEAD.. LADIES FIRST..
WHERE'S THE CHALK?
WHAT HAPPENS IF I CLEAR THE TABLE?
THEN YOU WIN, OF COURSE..
'CLEAR THE TABLE'.. WHAT A LAUGH!
?!
!
WHAM!!
I CLEARED THE TABLE! I CLEARED THE TABLE! I WON!! I WON!
GOOD GRIEF! WHAT HAPPENED?
I THINK SHE CLEARED THE TABLE...
SCHULZ 8-14
DON'T GET TOO UPSET, CHARLIE BROWN...MAYBE NEXT WINTER YOU CAN USE IT FOR A SLED!

August 13, 1955

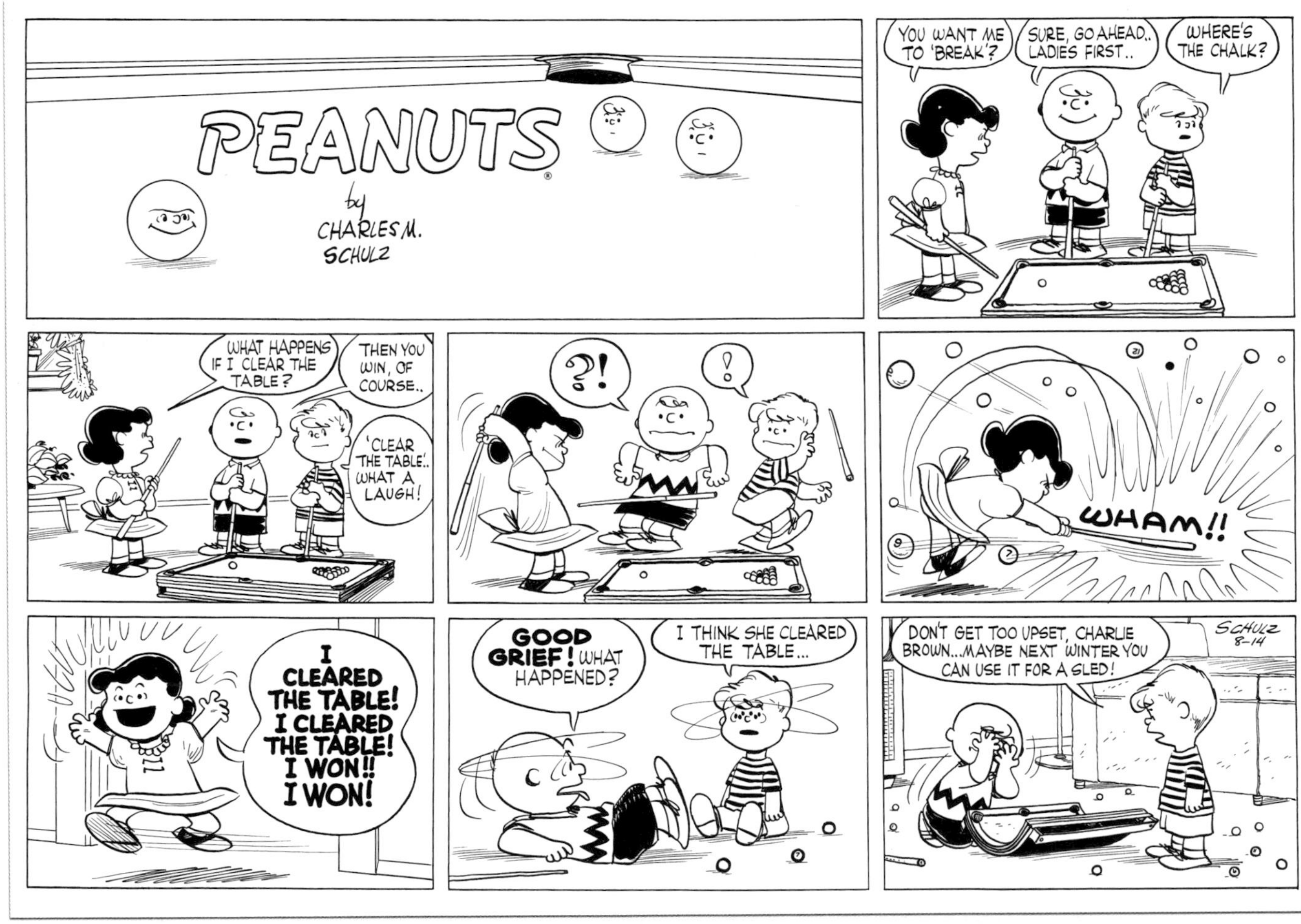

"PEANUTS"
GO ON HOME, CHARLIE BROWN! I DON'T EVER WANT TO SEE YOU AGAIN!

SCHULZ 8-13

August 16, 1955

"PEANUTS"
YOUR BLANKET?

I THINK MOMMY JUST WASHED IT, LINUS...I'LL BET IT'S HANGING OUT ON THE CLOTHESLINE..

8-16
SCHULZ

August 17, 1955

"PEANUTS"
I FEEL SORRY FOR LINUS...IN A FEW YEARS THEY'LL TAKE THAT BLANKET AWAY FROM HIM...

THEN HE'LL HAVE NO MORE SECURITY.. THERE'LL BE NOTHING TO TURN TO... HE'LL BE LONESOME, FRIGHTENED, AND

LIKE YOU, CHARLIE BROWN?

SCHULZ
8-17

August 26, 1955

"PEANUTS"
YOU'LL NEVER BE GOOD AT ANYTHING, CHARLIE BROWN!

YOU'LL ALWAYS BE MEDIOCRE! DO YOU HEAR ME? JUST PLAIN MEDIOCRE!

I DON'T CARE...WHY SHOULD I CARE?

8-26
JUST SO I'M ABOVE AVERAGE!
SCHULZ

September 28, 1955

"PEANUTS"
A BLANKET CAN BE A REAL SOURCE OF COMFORT, CHARLIE BROWN..

WHEN LIFE BECOMES UNBEARABLE, IT GIVES YOU SOMETHING TO CLING TO..

OH, I TELL YOU, NOTHING ELSE CAN GIVE YOU SUCH A FEELING OF SECURITY...

AND THEN, OF COURSE, IF THE GOING GETS REALLY TOUGH, YOU CAN ALWAYS SELL IT!
9-28
SCHULZ

October 25, 1955

"PEANUTS"
SHH...

I'M LISTENING TO BEETHOVEN'S NINTH...

IN AN OVERCOAT?

THE FIRST MOVEMENT WAS SO BEAUTIFUL IT GAVE ME THE CHILLS!
10-25
SCHULZ

October 26, 1955

"PEANUTS"
'FINALLY THE DAY CAME FOR THE REHEARSAL OF BEETHOVEN'S NEW SYMPHONY...'

'ONE OF THE SOLOISTS COMPLAINED ABOUT THE DIFFICULTY OF HER PART..'

'SHE ASKED THE COMPOSER IF HE WOULD MAKE A FEW CHANGES...'

DON'T DO IT, BEETHOVEN!
10-26
SCHULZ

October 31, 1955

"PEANUTS"
NOW, THE AREA WHICH I'VE OUTLINED IN BLACK IS OURS..

IF WE GET STARTED EARLY ENOUGH, WE SHOULD COVER THE ENTIRE COUNTY... HERE ARE YOUR MIMEOGRAPHED ORDERS.

WE'LL PUSH OFF AT FIVE O'CLOCK... COMMUNICATION WILL BE BY HAND AND ARM SIGNALS... ANY QUESTIONS?

THIS SHOULD BE THE BIGGEST NIGHT OF 'TRICKS OR TREATS' WE'VE EVER HAD
10-31
SCHULZ

November 3, 1955

"PEANUTS"
BOY, AM I EVER DISGUSTED!

THEY WON'T LET DOGS RUN LOOSE ANY MORE... ALL THE DOGS IN THE CITY HAVE TO BE KEPT TIED UP!

HAVE YOU TIED UP SNOOPY?
OF COURSE... WHAT ELSE COULD I DO?

11-3
SCHULZ

November 26, 1955

"PEANUTS"
WHO DID YOU SAY HE WAS GOING TO IMITATE?

MSSSP MSSSPE
WOW!

O.K., SNOOPY... GO AHEAD...

FRIGHTENING, ISN'T IT?
SCHULZ
11-26

November 28, 1955

"PEANUTS"

YOU FASCINATE ME!
11-28
SCHULZ

December 3, 1955

"PEANUTS"
TRY TO CATCH THE SNOWFLAKES ON YOUR TONGUE, LINUS...

HMM...SMACK-SMACK..

NEEDS SUGAR!
SCHULZ
12-3

"I knew that little kids live a life that is different from the adults. I always had this feeling that little kids are trapped on playgrounds or in other places, and in order to get away you have to learn how to work your way around. It's tough to be a little kid."

November 27, 1955

December 24, 1955

"PEANUTS"
HAVE YOU HUNG YOUR CHRISTMAS STOCKING YET, CHARLIE BROWN?

I SURE HAVE...GO IN, AND SEE IT WHILE I PUT AWAY YOUR COAT..

HEY! YOU'VE GOT A PRESENT ALREADY!

OH, GOOD GRIEF!

December 29, 1955

"PEANUTS"
"Jack fell down, and broke his crown, and Jill came tumbling after."

MAY I USE ONE OF YOUR PENCILS, CHARLIE BROWN?

THANK YOU..
12-29

I ALWAYS LIKE TO UNDERLINE PARTICULARLY SIGNIFICANT PASSAGES..
SCHULZ

December 11, 1955

PEANUTS® by CHARLES M. SCHULZ

WHEW

WHAT A MASTERPIECE!

I WISH THERE WERE SOMEONE HERE TO SEE IT..

I THINK I'LL GO GET LINUS, AND SHOW IT TO HIM...

A LITTLE KID LIKE LINUS HAS PROBABLY NEVER EVEN SEEN A SNOWMAN..

!

?

THIS IS GOING TO BE A LONG WINTER...

12-11 SCHULZ

January 9, 1956

"PEANUTS"

1-9
SCHULZ

January 18, 1956

"PEANUTS"
WILL YOU BE MY FRIEND, CHARLIE BROWN?

WHY, SURE, LINUS...I'D BE GLAD TO BE YOUR FRIEND!

LUCY TOLD ME IT WAS ABOUT TIME I MADE A FEW FRIENDS..

SO I FIGURED I'D BETTER START RIGHT AT THE BOTTOM...
1-18
SCHULZ

January 8, 1956

PEANUTS
by
CHARLES M. SCHULZ

THIS LOOKS LIKE A GOOD SPOT..

YOU BUILD YOUR SNOW FORT 'WAY OVER THERE LINUS, AND I'LL BUILD MINE HERE..

LET ME KNOW WHEN YOU'RE READY, AND WE'LL HAVE A BIG BATTLE..

AH! AN IMPREGNABLE FORTRESS OF SNOW!

THAT POOR LITTLE KID WILL BE SICK WITH JEALOUSY WHEN HE SEES WHAT I'VE BUILT...

I'M NOT READY..
1-8
SCHULZ

January 26, 1956

"PEANUTS"
HUMANS ARE INFINITELY SUPERIOR TO DOGS!
!

WHO DISCOVERED AMERICA? A HUMAN, THAT'S WHO! WHO DISCOVERED ELECTRICITY? A HUMAN, THAT'S WHO!

THUD!

I ALWAYS KNOW WHEN I'VE GOT HIM OUTARGUED... HE HAS TO RESORT TO VIOLENCE!
1-26
SCHULZ

February 1, 1956

"PEANUTS"
CAN'T A PERSON HAVE SECURITY WITHOUT HOLDING ON TO A BLANKET?

SURE...BUT MOST PEOPLE FIND SECURITY IN ONLY ONE OR TWO PLACES...

HERE WE HAVE SOMETHING INFINITELY GREATER...

PORTABLE SECURITY!
SCHULZ
2-1

February 3, 1956

"PEANUTS"
I'M STUBBORN!! I'M THE MOST STUBBORN PERSON IN THE WORLD!

I BELIEVE THAT A PERSON WITH CONVICTIONS HAS TO BE STUBBORN!

OH? I DIDN'T KNOW THAT YOU HAD CONVICTIONS, LINUS...

I DON'T, BUT IF I EVER GET SOME, I'LL BE PLENTY STUBBORN!
2-3
SCHULZ

February 14, 1956

"PEANUTS"
I THINK I'LL SIT HERE UNTIL THE MAILMAN COMES BY WITH ALL MY VALENTINES..

WELL, THAT'S THE WAY IT GOES..
SCHULZ
2-14

February 16, 1956

"PEANUTS"
DON'T YOU THINK RIN-TIN-TIN AND LASSIE ARE WONDERFUL?

I DON'T THINK THERE'S ANOTHER DOG IN THE WHOLE WORLD THAT CAN COMPARE WITH THEM!

I DON'T THINK SO, EITHER...

2-16
SCHULZ

March 6, 1956

"PEANUTS"
SEE THAT TINY SCAR?

I GOT THAT LAST SUMMER WHEN I FELL OFF MY TRICYCLE...

DO YOU HAVE ANY SCARS, CHARLIE BROWN?
LOTS OF THEM..

BUT THEY'RE ALL MENTAL!
3-6
SCHULZ

March 9, 1956

"PEANUTS"
I WISH I KNEW WHY PEOPLE DON'T LIKE ME...I WISH I KNEW THE REASONS..

DO YOU HAVE A PIECE OF PAPER?
I CAN GET ONE..

ALL RIGHT...NOW DIVIDE THE PAPER INTO TEN COLUMNS...THEN PUT NUMBERS DOWN THE LEFT SIDE FROM ONE TO A HUNDRED...
!

MAYBE YOU'D BETTER CALL THIS FIRST SHEET "A" IN CASE WE RUN OUT OF ROOM, AND HAVE TO USE MORE PAPER...
SIGH
3-9
SCHULZ

March 14, 1956

"PEANUTS"
I'M READING ABOUT 'LITTLE RED RIDING HOOD'..

I THOUGHT YOU'D READ THAT ALREADY, LUCY...

OH, I HAVE, BUT YOU SEE, THIS IS A NEW TRANSLATION...

IT MAKES CLEAR A LOT OF FORMERLY DIFFICULT PASSAGES!
3-14
SCHULZ

March 27, 1956

THERE'S TOO MUCH INSECURITY IN THE WORLD TODAY..

EVERYBODY'S NERVOUS...AND EVERYBODY'S FRUSTRATED..

MAYBE THE GOVERNMENT SHOULD PASS OUT BLANKETS..
3-27
SCHULZ

April 7, 1956

"PEANUTS"

4-7

EXCUSE ME..I THINK SOMEBODY'S HUNGRY...
SCHULZ

April 10, 1956

"PEANUTS"
LOOKING AT 'PETER RABBIT,' EH, LINUS?
PETER RABBIT

THERE'S A LOT OF SYMBOLISM IN THAT STORY...I'VE ALWAYS FELT THAT THE HOE CARRIED BY THE FARMER REPRESENTED PARENTAL AUTHORITY

YOU GO AHEAD, THOUGH, AND LOOK AT IT YOURSELF...I'LL BE ANXIOUS TO SEE WHAT CONCLUSIONS YOU DRAW..
PETER RABBIT

I MUST BE STUPID.. I THOUGHT IT WAS JUST A STORY...
4-10
SCHULZ

April 12, 1956

"PEANUTS"
KITE CAUGHT IN THE TREE?
YUP!

CAN'T GET IT DOWN, HUH?
NOPE!

WHAT ARE YOU GOING TO DO ABOUT IT?
NOTHING..

I'M SO MAD I'M JUST GOING TO STAND HERE FOR THE REST OF MY LIFE!
4-12
SCHULZ

April 13, 1956

"PEANUTS"
KITE STILL UP IN THE TREE, CHARLIE BROWN?
YUP!

GOING TO STAND HERE THE REST OF YOUR LIFE, HUH?
YUP!

WELL, I'LL SEE YOU AROUND...

I'LL BE HERE..
4-13
SCHULZ

April 14, 1956

"PEANUTS"
IF I HAD A KITE CAUGHT UP IN A TREE, I'D YELL AT IT..
OH?

DO YOU WANT ME TO YELL AT IT, CHARLIE BROWN?
NO, THANK YOU, LUCY..

IF I HAD A KITE CAUGHT UP IN A TREE, I'D YELL AT IT..
4-14
SCHULZ

April 20, 1956

"PEANUTS"
CHARLIE BROWN! IT'S RAINING! YOU'RE GOING TO GET DRENCHED!

IS THAT STUPID KITE GETTING WET, TOO?

IT'S SOAKED!!

4-20
SCHULZ

April 23, 1956

"PEANUTS"
BANG!

I GOT YOU, LINUS! YOU'RE DEAD! YOU'RE OUT OF THE GAME!

4-23
SCHULZ

May 1, 1956

YOU NEVER PAY ANY ATTENTION TO ME, SCHROEDER..

ALL YOU EVER THINK OF IS THAT STUPID BEETHOVEN, AND THAT STUPID PIANO, AND THAT STUPID CLASSICAL MUSIC, AND THAT..
!

KLUNK

NEVER FALL IN LOVE WITH A MUSICIAN..
SCHULZ
5-1

May 18, 1956

NOW LOOK HERE, LINUS...I'M **NOT** GOING TO BE SEEN WALKING DOWN THE STREET WITH ANY BOY WHO'S HOLDING ON TO A STUPID BLANKET!

5-18
HOW'S THAT?
SCHULZ

July 15, 1956

PEANUTS
by
CHARLES M. SCHULZ
C'MON! HIT ONE OUT HERE!

PLUCK

GREATEST CATCH I'VE EVER SEEN!
7-15
SCHULZ

May 19, 1956

YOU KNOW THE KIND OF PERSON I MEAN..THEY'RE SORT OF....

WELL, TAKE CHARLIE BROWN,HERE, HE'S A PERFECT EXAMPLE...
?

OH, YES, NOW I KNOW EXACTLY WHAT YOU MEAN..

SIGH
5-19
SCHULZ

May 29, 1956

I'M GOING TO ASK YOU A QUESTION, SCHROEDER, AND I WANT A STRAIGHT ANSWER...

DO YOU THINK YOU AND I WILL GET MARRIED SOMEDAY?

NEVER!! NEVER IN TEN THOUSAND MILLION BILLION YEARS!
SCHULZ

I CAN'T STAND THOSE STRAIGHT ANSWERS...
5-29

"The first Reuben Award that I got from the National Cartoonists Society means the most. It really was a surprise. I never dreamed that I would win anything like that so quickly."

July 29, 1956

PEANUTS by CHARLES M. SCHULZ

LOOK AT THAT SMUG EXPRESSION...

HA! I GOT IT!

I'LL TEACH YOU TO BE SO SMUG! I'M GONNA TEAR THIS BLANKET TO SHREDS!

I'M GONNA TEAR IT INTO A MILLION PIECES!!

THERE! NOW WHAT ARE YOU GOING TO DO, SMARTY?

THAT WASN'T MY BLANKET... THAT WAS YOURS!

NO, NO, NO, NO, NO, NO!

7-29

SCHULZ

May 31, 1956

ARE YOU OUT OF YOUR MIND? YOU'RE SUPPOSED TO BE PLAYING RIGHT FIELD! YOU LET THAT BALL GO RIGHT BY YOU!

OF ALL THE STUPID THINGS! GOOD GRIEF!!

A WISE MANAGER NEVER SHOUTS AT HIS PLAYERS..
SCHULZ
5-31

July 21, 1956

..MORE PATIENCE, AND MORE REAL UNDERSTANDING AND...AND....

..AND SNIF ...AND.. SNIF SNIF
?

SOB
7-21

EXCUSE ME...I WAS CARRIED AWAY BY MY OWN ORATORY...
SCHULZ

August 10, 1956

YOU SURE SEE A LOT OF AIR CONDITIONERS AROUND THESE DAYS..

ALMOST ALL THE STORES AND OFFICES HAVE THEM..

AND EVEN QUITE A FEW HOMES, TOO..

UH HUH..
SNOOPY
SCHULZ
8-10

August 31, 1956

GULP!

AAK!! PHOOEY!

I THOUGHT HE HAD DROPPED A POTATO-CHIP!
8-31
SCHULZ

September 18, 1956

"PIG-PEN," WHY ARE YOU ALWAYS SO DIRTY?

WHEN IN THE WORLD ARE YOU GOING TO CLEAN UP?

I HAVE AFFIXED TO ME THE DIRT AND DUST OF COUNTLESS AGES..

WHO AM I TO DISTURB HISTORY?
9-18
SCHULZ

September 21, 1956

I'M GOING TO MY GRAMPA'S TO SPEND THE WEEK-END!

DO YOU THINK YOU MAY GET A LITTLE LONESOME?

I'VE CONSIDERED THAT SO I'M GOING TO TAKE ALONG MY FUZZY ELEPHANT, MY TEDDY-BEAR, MY LITTLE PILLOW AND MY BLANKET..

9-21
HOW SECURE CAN YOU GET?
SCHULZ

August 26, 1956

PEANUTS
by CHARLES M. SCHULZ
WHAT'S GOING ON HERE?
WHOOSH
ZOOM
8-26.
I GUESS I KNEW I'D NEVER GET AWAY WITH IT.
SCHULZ

September 28, 1956

!

I THOUGHT I TOLD YOU TO STOP THAT DANCING?! YOU HAVE NO RIGHT TO BE SO HAPPY!!! NOW, STOP IT! DO YOU HEAR ME?!

SCHULZ
9-28

October 12, 1956

SMACK!

YOU NEVER KNOW HOW CHOPIN IS GOING TO AFFECT SOMEONE..
10-12
SCHULZ

September 16, 1956

PEANUTS
by
CHARLES M. SCHULZ

HOW'S THAT, CHARLIE BROWN ?

I WORKED ALL MORNING PILING UP THOSE LEAVES..

I'LL BET THEY'RE AS SOFT AS A FEATHER-BED..

YAHOO!

WHAM!

WHY DO YOU BELIEVE EVERYTHING I TELL YOU?
9-16
SCHULZ

October 17, 1956

SEE, LINUS? YOU TAKE A PIECE OF PAPER...FOLD A LITTLE HERE...

..TEAR A LITTLE THERE, AND BEHOLD! YOU HAVE A BOAT!

?

10-17
SCHULZ

October 19, 1956

THE TEACHER SAID I DID REAL WELL TODAY..

SHE SAID I WAS THE BEST PUPIL IN HER WHOLE CLASS!

WELL! THAT SHOULD MAKE YOU HAPPY, CHARLIE BROWN..

UH, HUH...IT'S ALWAYS THRILLING TO BE RECOGNIZED IN ONE'S OWN LIFETIME!
10-19
SCHULZ

October 28, 1956

PEANUTS®
by
CHARLES M. SCHULZ
10-28
SIGH
SCHULZ

October 31, 1956

IS THAT YOU, LUCY?

UH, HUH... LINUS WILL BE ALONG IN A MINUTE...

HE WAS HAVING A LITTLE TROUBLE WITH HIS COSTUME..
?

HE'S NOT VERY GOOD YET WITH A SCISSORS!
10-31
SCHULZ

November 5, 1956

I WAS JUST TRYING TO TALK WITH THAT LITTLE GIRL UP THE STREET...

BUT I COULDN'T SAY A WORD... I JUST **STOOD** THERE ALL EMBARRASSED AND CONFUSED

I GOT SO SELF-CONSCIOUS I DIDN'T KNOW WHAT TO DO..

SO I **HIT** HER!!
11-5
SCHULZ

December 16, 1956

PEANUTS
CHARLES M. SCHULZ
NO!
OH, COME ON, CHARLIE BROWN..

I'LL HOLD IT REAL STEADY...

NO!

PLEASE?

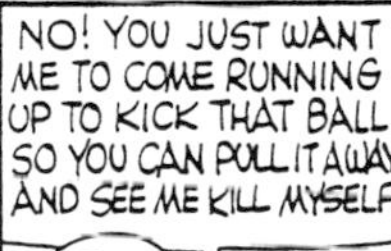
NO! YOU JUST WANT ME TO COME RUNNING UP TO KICK THAT BALL SO YOU CAN PULL IT AWAY AND SEE ME KILL MYSELF!

LOOK...JUST TO SHOW YOU I'M SINCERE, I'LL GIVE YOU A MILLION DOLLARS IF I PULL THE BALL AWAY!

IN FACT, I'LL GIVE YOU A **HUNDRED** MILLION DOLLARS!!

I MUST BE OUT OF MY MIND, BUT I CAN'T RESIST KICKING FOOTBALLS..

HA!

WHAM

HERE'S YOUR MONEY, CHARLIE BROWN!

HEE HEE HEE HEE HEE HEE

I THINK I'LL JUST LIE HERE UNTIL THE FIRST SNOW COMES AND COVERS ME UP...
12-16
SCHULZ

November 16, 1956

DID YOU KNOW THAT SCHOLARS DISAGREE ON WHY YOU GET SECURITY FROM A BLANKET?

SOME SCHOLARS FEEL THAT IT ALL DEPENDS ON THE QUALITY OF THE MATERIAL...OTHERS SAY IT DEPENDS MORE ON SIZE, COLOR OR CERTAIN...

OH, I'M SORRY, CHARLIE BROWN...I MUST BE BORING YOU...

YOU KNOW HOW IT IS WHEN A PERSON GETS TALKING ABOUT HIS FAVORITE SUBJECT..
11-16
SCHULZ

December 4, 1956

?
THERE'S A STRANGE LEGEND, LINUS, THAT SAYS NO TWO SNOWFLAKES ARE ALIKE..

THAT'S NO LEGEND, LUCY..IT'S THE TRUTH! OUT OF THE BILLIONS OF SNOWFLAKES THAT FALL EACH WINTER, NO TWO ARE ALIKE!

12-4

THERE'S A STRANGE LEGEND, LINUS, THAT SAYS NO TWO SNOWFLAKES ARE ALIKE..
SCHULZ

December 12, 1956

YOU KNOW WHAT IS A FRIGHTENING THOUGHT?

NO, WHAT?
12-12

ONLY ONE YARD OF OUTING FLANNEL STANDS BETWEEN ME AND A NERVOUS BREAKDOWN!
SCHULZ

December 30, 1956

PEANUTS
by
CHARLES M. SCHULZ
BEAUTIFUL! BEAUTIFUL!

MMMMMMMM

MMMMM

?

!

12-30
SCHULZ
SIGH

January 20, 1957

PEANUTS

by

CHARLES M. SCHULZ

MY BLANKET IS IN THE DRYER..HOW LONG DO YOU THINK IT'LL TAKE TO GET DRY?

HOW IN THE WORLD SHOULD I KNOW?

I GOTTA HAVE THAT BLANKET..

SIGH

THIS IS A LONELY VIGIL...

1-20

SCHULZ

January 2, 1957

I'D LIKE TO BE ABLE TO FEEL THAT I'M NEEDED..
DON'T FORGET, CHARLIE BROWN, THAT PEOPLE WHO ARE REALLY NEEDED ARE ASKED TO DO A LOT OF DIFFERENT THINGS...
UH, HUH...
WELL, I'D LIKE TO FEEL NEEDED, AND YET NOT HAVE TO DO ANYTHING
1-2
SCHULZ

January 21, 1957

WHAT'S LINUS CRYING ABOUT?

OH, HIS BALLOON BROKE FROM THE COLD...

THAT'S STRANGE... I DIDN'T KNOW THAT A BALLOON WOULD BREAK FROM THE COLD...

THIS ONE SURE DID... I STUCK IT WITH AN ICICLE!
1-21
SCHULZ

January 22, 1957

EVERY TIME I GO OUTSIDE WITH MY HEAVY COAT ON, I FALL DOWN ON THE ICE...

THEN I CAN'T GET UP, AND I HAVE TO LIE THERE UNTIL I FREEZE TO DEATH..
BOY, THAT'S DISGUSTING!

I KNOW HOW YOU FEEL, CHARLIE BROWN...EVERY TIME I GO IN SWIMMING, I DROWN..

THAT CAN GET SO ANNOYING!
1-22
SCHULZ

January 27, 1957

PEANUTS
by
CHARLES M. SCHULZ

?
POW!

!
WHAM!

?
POW!

I FEEL TORN BETWEEN THE DESIRE TO CREATE AND THE DESIRE TO DESTROY..
1-27
SCHULZ

January 31, 1957

HI, CHARLIE BROWN..
HI, GIRLS..

GOOD OL' CHARLIE BROWN

GEE..I HEARD ONE OF THEM SAY, "GOOD OL' CHARLIE BROWN.." MAYBE THOSE GIRLS DON'T THINK I'M SO BAD AFTER ALL...

GOOD OL' WISHY-WASHY CHARLIE BROWN!
1-31
SCHULZ

February 6, 1957

LOOK, LUCY... LOOK HOW NICE I COLORED IN MY COLOR-BOOK..

ARE YOU CRAZY? DO YOU WANT TO BE FRUSTRATED AND INHIBITED FOR THE REST OF YOUR LIFE? GOOD GRIEF!!

DON'T YOU KNOW THAT IF YOU COLOR INSIDE THE LINES IN A COLOR-BOOK, YOU'LL BECOME INHIBITED?!

WORSE YET, YOU'RE LIABLE TO BECOME GOOD AT IT, AND END UP AS A COMMERCIAL ARTIST!
HORRORS!
SCHULZ 2-6

February 9, 1957

HERE COMES THE BIG POLAR BEAR STALKING ACROSS THE SNOW!

I'LL BET REAL POLAR BEARS NEVER GET COLD!
SCHULZ 2-9

February 16, 1957

AS A FUSSBUDGET, MY RISE WAS METEORIC!

FIRST THE COUNTY CHAMPIONSHIP, THEN THE STATE, THEN THE FAMOUS WESTERN OPEN, THE NORTH-SOUTH INVITATIONAL, THE EASTERN OPEN..

TITLE AFTER TITLE! AWARD AFTER AWARD!!

AS ONE NEWSPAPER EDITOR PUT IT, 'THIS GIRL WAS BORN TO FUSS!'
2-16 SCHULZ

February 23, 1957

I'M HAVING A BIG PARTY, CHARLIE BROWN, BUT I'M NOT GOING TO INVITE YOU!

RATS! I REALLY LIKE PARTIES, TOO...YES, SIR, THERE'S NOTHING LIKE A GOOD PARTY!

I LIKE PARTIES... I'VE ALWAYS LIKED PARTIES...THERE'S JUST SOMETHING ABOUT ME, I GUESS... I'VE ALWAYS LIKED PARTIES...

AT LEAST, I THINK I DO...I'VE NEVER BEEN INVITED TO ONE!
2-23 SCHULZ

March 1, 1957

I'M ALL SET TO FLY MY KITE, CHARLIE BROWN.. WHAT SHOULD I DO FIRST?

WELL, THE FIRST THING TO DO IS FIND OUT WHICH WAY THE WIND IS BLOWING..

ALL RIGHT...THEN WHAT?
3-1 SCHULZ

March 9, 1957

I'M A GREAT BELIEVER IN EDUCATION..

I INTEND TO BE THE MOST EDUCATED PERSON IN THIS PART OF THE CITY..

I INTEND TO BE THE MOST EDUCATED PERSON IN THE WHOLE WORLD..

I'LL NEVER BE SATISFIED UNTIL I'M TOO SMART FOR MY OWN GOOD!
3-9
SCHULZ

March 19, 1957

THIS IS GOING TO BE A LONG SUMMER..
3-19
SCHULZ

March 20, 1957

CLOUDS ARE VERY PECULIAR, LINUS.. SOMETIMES THEY SEEM TO FORM ACTUAL WORDS..
?

THOSE AREN'T CLOUDS... THAT'S SKY-WRITING!

CLOUDS ARE VERY PECULIAR, LINUS...SOMETIMES THEY SEEM TO FORM ACTUAL WORDS..
SCHULZ
3-20

April 11, 1957

WHAT'S THE MATTER WITH YOU, SCHROEDER?

THAT'S THE THIRD GROUND BALL YOU'VE MISSED TODAY!

I SUPPOSE YOU'RE GONNA SAY IT TOOK A BAD BOUNCE AGAIN, HUH?!

YES, I AM!!
4-11
SCHULZ

April 17, 1957

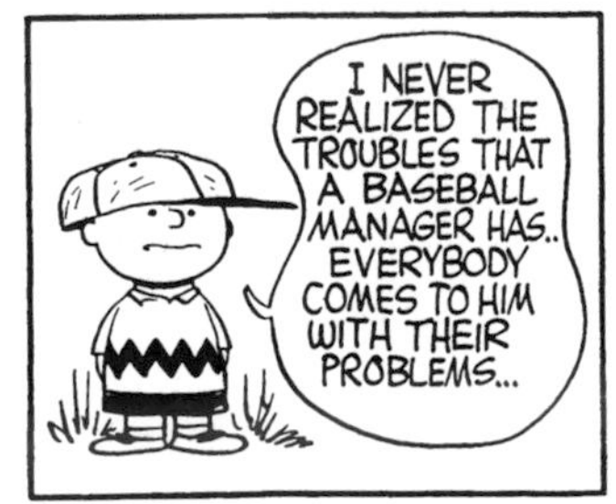
I NEVER REALIZED THE TROUBLES THAT A BASEBALL MANAGER HAS.. EVERYBODY COMES TO HIM WITH THEIR PROBLEMS...

HEY, MANAGER... TIE MY SHOE!
SURE

4-17
!

GET OUT OF HERE!!
SCHULZ

April 18, 1957

HEY, AREN'T WE SHORT ONE MAN? WHERE'S 'PIG-PEN'?

HE'S RIGHT WHERE YOU PUT HIM...AT SECOND BASE..

OH, YES, SO HE IS..

HE'S HARD TO SEE BECAUSE HE BLENDS IN WITH THE DIRT ON THE INFIELD!
4-18
SCHULZ

April 26, 1957

YOU KNOW WHAT BOTHERS ME THE MOST?

I FEEL THAT I'VE LET DOWN YOU PLAYERS WHO HAD FAITH IN ME AS YOUR MANAGER..

OH, WELL, IF THAT'S WHAT'S BOTHERING YOU, CHARLIE BROWN, JUST FORGET IT..
4-26

WE NEVER REALLY **HAD** ANY FAITH IN YOU!
SCHULZ

April 28, 1957

PEANUTS
by
CHARLES M. SCHULZ
HEY! WHERE'S EVERYBODY GOING?
YOU'RE NOT GONNA LET A LITTLE RAIN BOTHER YOU, ARE YA?!
C'MON BACK! IT'S GONNA LET UP! C'MON BACK!!
?

QUITTERS! THAT'S WHAT YOU ARE!! YOU'RE ALL A BUNCH OF QUITTERS!

SIGH
4-28
SCHULZ

May 8, 1957

CAN YOU REALLY GET SECURITY FROM A BLANKET LIKE THAT?

APPARENTLY SOME PEOPLE CAN... OTHERS CAN'T..

OF COURSE, YOU HAVE TO REALIZE THAT SECURITY DOES NOT JUST COME TO A PERSON..

SOMETIMES IT HAS TO BE PURSUED!
5-8

May 9, 1957

WELL, I WARNED HIM!

HE'S BEEN TAGGING AFTER ME ALL MORNING! EVERY TIME I'D TURN AROUND, THERE HE'D BE!

I COULDN'T STAND IT ANY LONGER...

SCHULZ
5-9

May 17, 1957

THE WAY I SEE IT, "THE COW JUMPED OVER THE MOON" INDICATES A RISE IN FARM PRICES...

THE PART ABOUT THE DISH RUNNING AWAY WITH THE SPOON MUST REFER TO THE CONSUMER..

DO YOU AGREE WITH ME, CHARLIE BROWN?
I CAN'T SAY...

I DON'T PRETEND TO BE A STUDENT OF PROPHETIC LITERATURE!
SCHULZ
5-17

May 30, 1957

"PIG-PEN" NEVER SAYS VERY MUCH, DOES HE?

HE'S AFRAID TO... WHENEVER HE TALKS, THE DIRT ON HIS FACE FLAKES OFF, AND FALLS ON THE GROUND BY HIS FEET..

THAT'S NOT TRUE!!

5-30
SCHULZ

June 3, 1957

LOOK, SCHROEDER.. I FOUND YOU A NEW BUST OF BEETHOVEN!

THIS ISN'T BEETHOVEN..THIS IS GEORGE WASHINGTON!
IT IS?

WELL, I'LL BE!

I NEVER COULD TELL ONE COMPOSER FROM THE OTHER!
SCHULZ
6-3

June 7, 1957

YOU HAVE TO KNOW A LOT OF THINGS BEFORE YOU CAN ENTER KINDER-GARTEN, LINUS..

YOU HAVE TO BE ABLE TO USE A HANDKERCHIEF, GET A DRINK OF WATER ALONE, PUT ON YOUR OWN COAT AND CUT WITH SCISSORS!

WOW!
6-7

I NEVER REALIZED THE REQUIREMENTS WERE SO RIGID!
SCHULZ

June 28, 1957

STAND UP, SNOOPY.. I'LL TEACH YOU TO WALK ON YOUR HIND LEGS..

IT'S NO FUN TEACHING **YOU** ANYTHING!!
6-28
SCHULZ

"I believe Snoopy was the first to think conversationally, in bubbles, while standing on his hind legs. Quite a few cartoon animals have learnt the trick now."

July 4, 1957

NEVER WORRY ABOUT TOMORROW CHARLIE BROWN..

TOMORROW WILL SOON BE TODAY, AND BEFORE YOU KNOW IT TODAY WILL BE YESTERDAY

I ALWAYS WORRY ABOUT THE DAY **AFTER** TOMORROW!
SCHULZ
7-4

July 13, 1957

7-13

SLACKER!!!
SCHULZ

July 15, 1957

7-15
SCHULZ

July 26, 1957

GOOD HOT DOGS, HUH, CHARLIE BROWN?

FAIR, I GUESS...

A HOT DOG JUST DOESN'T TASTE RIGHT WITHOUT A BALL GAME IN FRONT OF IT..
7-26
SCHULZ

August 12, 1957

SIGH
8-12
SCHULZ

"The name Peanuts *has no dignity. I don't even like the word. It's not even a nice word. The syndicate didn't realize that I was going to draw a strip that I think has dignity. I think it has class. But, of course, when a young person goes into the president's office, what that syndicate president is buying is the potential of this young person. He's not even buying the work that he is looking at, he's buying the potential ten, twenty years down the road, and how does he know? They didn't know when I walked in there that here was a fanatic. Here was a kid totally dedicated to what he was going to do. And to label something that was going to be [my] life's work with a name like* Peanuts *was really insulting."*

August 13, 1957

RATS!

IF I DON'T FIND THAT BLANKET OF MINE PRETTY SOON, I'M AFRAID I'LL CRACK UP...

THIS IS AN EMERGENCY..

SCHULZ
8-13

August 17, 1957

OUR FAMILY IS **FILLED** WITH IMPORTANT PEOPLE!

DOCTORS AND LAWYERS AND BARBERS AND EVERYTHING!

AND THAT'S NOT **ALL**..

WE EVEN HAVE A MAN WHO IS A VETERAN OF WORLD WAR **II**!
OH, GOOD GRIEF!
8-17
SCHULZ

September 12, 1957

THIS IS MY ROOM AND THESE ARE MY TOYS!

NOW, GET OUT OF HERE!!

SCHULZ 9-12
SLAM!

September 22, 1957

PEANUTS
by CHARLES M. SCHULZ
NO!

ABSOLUTELY NOT!

YOU MUST THINK I'M CRAZY!

YOU SAY YOU'LL HOLD THE BALL, BUT YOU WON'T! YOU'LL PULL IT AWAY, AND I'LL BREAK MY NECK!
WHY, CHARLIE BROWN.. HOW YOU TALK...

I WOULDN'T THINK OF SUCH A THING! I'M A CHANGED PERSON! LOOK...ISN'T THIS A FACE YOU CAN TRUST?

ALL RIGHT...YOU HOLD THE BALL, AND I'LL COME RUNNING UP, AND KICK IT...

SHE DID IT AGAIN!!

WUMP!

SCHULZ 9-22
I ADMIRE YOU, CHARLIE BROWN... YOU HAVE SUCH FAITH IN HUMAN NATURE..

"If Peanuts *chronicles defeat it is probably because defeat is a lot funnier than victory. Most of us know what it is like to lose some kind of contest, and we can identify with the loser."*

September 25, 1951

molto rall.

?

9-25
DID BEETHOVEN EVER WRITE ANYTHING FOR PIANO AND ELECTRIC GUITAR?
SCHULZ

October 27, 1957

NOW'S THE TIME FOR A GOOD PASS PLAY!
PEANUTS
by CHARLES M. SCHULZ
ALL RIGHT, MEN, LET'S GET IN THERE THIS TIME, AND SMEAR 'EM!
NOW, LISTEN CAREFULLY
SCHROEDER HIKES THE BALL TO YOU, LINUS, AND YOU FADE BACK, AND THROW ME A LONG PASS..
NOW, ARE YOU SURE YOU UNDERSTAND?
OF COURSE, I UNDERSTAND!
WELL, I HOPE SO..
SIGNALS! THIRTY-THREE! EIGHTEEN! FORTY-NINE!
HIKE!
PASS IT!
10-27
SCHULZ

October 14, 1957

YOU AND THAT STUPID BLANKET! YOU'LL BE CARRYING IT AROUND FOR THE REST OF YOUR LIFE!
THAT'S NOT TRUE! I HAVE TREMENDOUS WILL POWER! WHY, I COULD GIVE UP THIS BLANKET RIGHT TODAY IF I HAD TO!
ALL RIGHT! LET'S SEE YOU GIVE IT UP TODAY!
?
GOOD GRIEF! WHAT HAVE I DONE?!
10-14
SCHULZ

October 16, 1957

WHERE DID YOU PUT MY BLANKET?
I PUT IT IN THIS CLOSET, AND LOCKED THE DOOR! NOW, WE'LL SEE IF YOU CAN DO WITHOUT IT FOR TWO WEEKS!
TWO WEEKS? IS THAT ALL? WHY, OF COURSE, I CAN! TWO WEEKS! HA! ONLY TWO WEEKS! IT'LL BE A CINCH! TWO WEEKS!
10-16
HOW LONG IS TWO WEEKS?
SCHULZ

October 21, 1957

WELL, LINUS, YOU'VE GONE WITHOUT YOUR BLANKET FOR A WHOLE WEEK..

I'LL NEVER LAST ANOTHER WEEK! I HAVE HOT AND COLD FLASHES..MY EYES WON'T FOCUS..

I GOTTA HAVE THAT BLANKET!!

I'M CRACKING UP AND NOBODY CARES! NOBODY! NOBODY! NOBODY!
10-21
SCHULZ

January 4, 1958

REAL PENGUINS DON'T GET COLD FEET!
1-4
SCHULZ

January 5, 1958

PEANUTS
by
CHARLES M. SCHULZ

!

IT'S HAPPENING, CHARLIE BROWN! IT'S HAPPENING JUST LIKE THEY SAID IT WOULD!!

OF COURSE, IT'S HAPPENING.. IT'S SNOWING..WHAT ELSE DID YOU EXPECT THIS TIME OF YEAR?

SNOWING?

GOOD GRIEF..I THOUGHT IT WAS THE FALLOUT!
1-5
SCHULZ

January 13, 1958

MY DAD SAID THAT SOMEDAY I MIGHT BE ABLE TO RUN FOR PRESIDENT!

REALLY, CHARLIE BROWN? HE CERTAINLY MUST THINK HIGHLY OF YOU..

WELL, I DON'T KNOW..

HE ALSO SAID THAT HE DIDN'T THINK HE'D VOTE FOR ME!
1-13
SCHULZ

January 27, 1958

THREE TIMES A DAY.

DAY AFTER DAY, WEEK AFTER WEEK, HE EATS THE SAME THING!

1-27
WHAT'S THAT?

PIZZA!
SIGH
SCHULZ

"I don't know where the Peanuts *kids live. I think that, originally, I thought of them as living in these little veterans' developments, where Joyce and I first lived when we got married out in Colorado Springs. Now I don't think about it at all. My strip has become so abstract and such a fantasy that I think it would be a mistake to point out a place for them to live."*

January 26, 1958

PEANUTS
by CHARLES M. SCHULZ
WHAT ARE YOU MAKING?
THESE ARE SNOW-BUNNIES
THEY LOOK REAL CUTE..
CAN I HELP YOU, LUCY?
NO, YOU CAN'T HELP ME! GET OUT OF HERE! MAKE YOUR OWN THINGS!!
AND DON'T BOTHER ME ANY MORE! DO YOU HEAR ME?
LITTLE BROTHERS CAN SURE BE A NUISANCE SOMETIMES!
SCHULZ
1-26

February 10, 1958

YOU AND THAT STUPID BLANKET!

YOU'LL STILL BE HANGING ON TO THAT THING WHEN YOU'RE TWENTY YEARS OLD!

SO WHAT IF I AM?

2-10
I'LL NEVER BE DRAFTED!
SCHULZ

February 11, 1958

BLANKETS ARE THE OPIATE OF THE HOPELESSLY IMMATURE!

2-11

INSULTS! ALWAYS INSULTS!
SCHULZ

February 14, 1958

DID YOU GIVE CHARLIE BROWN A VALENTINE?

OH YES..I FINALLY GAVE HIM ONE OF THOSE REAL CHEAP ONES..
2-14

WAS HE HAPPY WITH IT?
SURE

WHEN YOU'RE A CHARLIE BROWN, YOU REALLY DON'T EXPECT TOO MUCH.
SCHULZ

March 3, 1958

3-3

SCHULZ

March 4, 1958

3-4

WITH CHARLIE BROWN, FLYING A KITE IS AN EMOTIONAL EXPERIENCE
SCHULZ

March 2, 1958

!
PEANUTS
by
CHARLES M. SCHULZ
YAWN!
CLOMP!
AND THERE HE GOES!
WHOOSH!
3-2
I'M THE FIRST DOG EVER TO LAUNCH A HUMAN BEING!
SCHULZ

March 22, 1958

I WISH I COULD BITE SOMEBODY... I NEED A RELEASE FROM MY INNER TENSIONS..
OF COURSE, IF I EVER DID BITE SOMEBODY, I CAN JUST IMAGINE WHAT WOULD HAPPEN..
THERE'D BE YELLING AND SCREAMING, AND PEOPLE CHASING ME, AND THROWING THINGS... I DON'T THINK I COULD STAND THAT..
I GUESS I'D BE BETTER OFF JUST LEARNING TO LIVE WITH MY INNER TENSIONS.
3-22
SCHULZ

April 4, 1958

4-4
IT ALWAYS RAINS ON THE UNLOVED!
SCHULZ

April 11, 1958

WHAT SORT OF GIRL WOULD YOU LIKE TO MARRY, SCHROEDER?

WELL, I'D LIKE HER TO HAVE BLONDE HAIR...AND HAVE AN EVEN DISPOSITION...
4-11

AND I THINK SHE SHOULD BE FOND OF CLASSICAL MUSIC..

STRIKE THREE!!!!
SCHULZ

April 17, 1958

A PITCHER AND HIS CATCHER NEED A GOOD SET OF SIGNALS...

ONE FINGER WILL MEAN A HIGH BALL...
4-17

TWO FINGERS WILL MEAN A LOW BALL...

AND THREE FINGERS WILL MEAN THE BROAD AREA IN-BETWEEN!
SCHULZ

"Sometimes it gets a little embarrassing to realize that, every day, a hundred million people read about the dumb things I did as a kid."

March 30, 1958

OH, OH!
PEANUTS
by CHARLES M. SCHULZ
HERE IT COMES!
HEY! WHERE'S EVERYBODY GOING?
HOME! IT'S RAINING YOU BLOCKHEAD!
COME BACK HERE!
THIS IS ONLY A SPRING SHOWER!
QUITTERS!
ARE YOU AFRAID OF A LITTLE WATER?
QUITTERS!
QUITTERS!
QUITTERS!
QUITTERS!
WELL, AT LEAST LINUS, MY FAITHFUL RIGHT-FIELDER, HASN'T DESERTED ME....HE'S STILL..
3-30
SCHULZ

April 19, 1958

WHAT LEAGUE ARE WE IN, CHARLIE BROWN?

WELL, YOU'VE HEARD OF THE MAJOR LEAGUES, THE MINOR LEAGUES AND THE BUSH LEAGUES, HAVEN'T YOU?

OH, YES, I'VE HEARD OF THEM..
WELL, HAVE YOU HEARD OF THE "LITTLE LEAGUE"?
4-19

OH, YES..
WELL, WE'RE ABOUT THREE LEAGUES BELOW THAT!
SCHULZ

"There was no Little League at that time, so all of our baseball games were between neighborhood teams. We would make up our own teams and challenge another neighborhood. We literally did lose a game once 40 to 0, which is where I got the idea for Charlie Brown's string of losses."

May 4, 1958

PEANUTS
by
CHARLES M. SCHULZ

DID YOU GET THAT KITE UP ALL BY YOURSELF, LINUS?
YUP!
DID YOU HAVE ANY TROUBLE?
NOPE!
DIDN'T YOUR KITE GET TANGLED UP IN ANY TREES OR AROUND SOME TELEPHONE WIRES OR EVEN GO DOWN A SEWER?
NOPE!
SIGH
SCHULZ 5-4
I DIDN'T THINK IT WOULD BE RIGHT TO LET A LITTLE KID LIKE HIM SEE ME CRY..

May 3, 1958

SO LONG, LUCY.. I'LL SEE YOU TOMORROW..
OKAY

GOOD OL' CHARLIE BROWN... SIGH

YOU BLOCKHEAD
5-3

THERE'S A VERY FINE LINE BETWEEN LOVE AND HATE..
SCHULZ

May 5, 1958

"TO LIVE IS TO DANCE.."

5-5
"TO DANCE IS TO LIVE!"
SCHULZ

May 6, 1958

THAT KID IN SCHOOL SURE SAID SOME MEAN THINGS ABOUT YOU TODAY..

HOW COME YOU DIDN'T HIT HIM?

I HAVE OBSERVED THAT WHENEVER YOU TRY TO HIT SOMEBODY, THERE IS A TENDENCY FOR THEM TO TRY TO HIT YOU BACK

YOU ARE A SHREWD JUDGE OF HUMAN NATURE, CHARLIE BROWN
SCHULZ
5-6

May 7, 1958

I FEEL ON EDGE TODAY..

I FEEL ALL NERVOUS AND TENSE!

PSYCHIATRISTS WILL TELL YOU THAT THERE'S NO BETTER WAY TO RELAX THAN TO LIE WITH YOUR HEAD IN YOUR WATER DISH!
5-7
SCHULZ

May 13, 1958

I'M SCARED TO PLAY ANY MORE, CHARLIE BROWN..

THERE'S A VULTURE SITTING ON THE CROQUET STAKE..

A VULTURE?
5-13

OH, GOOD GRIEF!
SCHULZ

June 5, 1958

SOME DOGS ARE BORN TO BE HUNTING DOGS...

AND SOME DOGS ARE BORN TO BE WATCHDOGS..

HE'S CRAZY!
6-5

DOGS ARE BORN TO SLEEP IN THE SUN!
SCHULZ

June 7, 1958

I AM A FRIEND OF ALL NATURE!

I LOVE PEOPLE, AND I LOVE BIRDS, AND I LOVE FISH, AND I LOVE ANIMALS AND I LOVE PLANT LIFE!

I LOVE WITHOUT RESERVATION! I LOVE WITHOUT QUALIFICATION!

I LOVE WITHOUT EVEN THINKING!
6-7
SCHULZ

July 4, 1958

GOOD GRIEF! I THINK I'VE FOUNDED A NEW MOVEMENT!!
7-4
SCHULZ

July 17, 1958

LISTEN TO THIS, VIOLET..

THERE ARE NEARLY A QUARTER OF A MILLION DOGS AND CATS BORN IN THIS COUNTRY EVERY DAY!

THAT'S FANTASTIC!

FANTASTIC?! IT'S DISGUSTING! THEY SHOULD DO SOMETHING ABOUT ALL THOSE CATS!
7-17
SCHULZ

August 25, 1958

DEAR PEN-PAL
RATS!

DEAR PEN
RATS!

DE
RATS!
8-25

DEAR PENCIL-PAL,
SCHULZ

August 29, 1958

DEAR PENCIL-PAL,

YOU ARE MY ONLY FRIEND. NOT COUNTING YOU I AM FRIENDLESS. I HAVE NO OTHER FRIENDS.
YOUR FRIEND,
CHARLIE BROWN

P.S. EVERYBODY HATES ME
8-29
SCHULZ

August 30, 1958

HOW LONG DO YOU THINK IT WILL TAKE FOR YOUR LETTER TO GET TO YOUR PENCIL-PAL?

I DON'T KNOW.. A FEW DAYS I SUPPOSE..
WHAT KIND OF STAMP DID YOU PUT ON IT?

STAMP?

8-30
SCHULZ

September 21, 1958

PEANUTS
by
CHARLES M. SCHULZ

YOU SHOULD TRY SOME 'PLACE-KICKS'...

WHY DON'T YOU LET ME HOLD THE BALL FOR YOU, CHARLIE BROWN?

DO YOU THINK I'M CRAZY? DO YOU THINK YOU CAN FOOL ME WITH THE SAME TRICK EVERY YEAR?!

OH, I WON'T PULL THE BALL AWAY, CHARLIE BROWN.. I PROMISE YOU... I GIVE YOU MY BONDED WORD!

ALL RIGHT, I'LL TRUST YOU... I HAVE AN UNDYING FAITH IN HUMAN NATURE!

I BELIEVE THAT PEOPLE WHO WANT TO CHANGE CAN DO SO, AND I BELIEVE THAT THEY SHOULD BE GIVEN A CHANCE TO PROVE THEMSELVES..
9-21

AAUGH!

WUMP!

CHARLIE BROWN, YOUR FAITH IN HUMAN NATURE IS AN INSPIRATION TO ALL YOUNG PEOPLE..
SCHULZ

September 18, 1958

BZZZZ
ZZZZ

TWACK!

DEADLY!
9-18
SCHULZ

October 6, 1958

KINDERGARTEN IS AS FAR AS I'M GOING TO GO!

AS SOON AS I'M THROUGH WITH KINDERGARTEN, I'M GOING TO DROP OUT OF SCHOOL!

10-6
AS FAR AS I'M CONCERNED, THAT'S IT!

THERE'S NOTHING THAT CAN HARM A PERSON MORE THAN TOO MUCH FORMAL EDUCATION!
SCHULZ

November 23, 1958—First mention of the Cat Who Lives Next Door.

SNOOPY!
PEANUTS by CHARLES M SCHULZ
WHERE IS THAT CRAZY DOG?
SNOOPY! SUPPERTIME!!
SNIF SNIF
GOOD GRIEF!
11-23
I'M GETTING TO BE LIKE A HOUSEWIFE... I HATE MEALTIME! I HATE IT!!
ALL RIGHT, IF YOU DON'T WANT YOUR SUPPER, I'LL GIVE IT TO THE CAT NEXT DOOR!!
SCHULZ

November 6, 1958

11-6

AUGH!

SCHULZ

December 12, 1958

Z
12-12
SNOOPY

?!
SNOOPY

WHAM!

LIFE IS FULL OF RUDE AWAKENINGS..
SCHULZ

"I'm not sure how Snoopy got on top of the doghouse, but I'm glad he did, because it opened up whole new areas of fantasy for me."

February 22, 1959

PEANUTS
by SCHULZ
WHERE DID YOU FIND IT?
HE LEFT IT AT OUR HOUSE ONE DAY LAST SUMMER WHEN WE WERE ALL PLAYING UNDER THE SPRINKLER..

CAN YOU GET IT OVER YOUR HEAD?
IF HE CAN, I CAN!
?

LUCY'S PUTTING ON ONE OF CHARLIE BROWN'S T-SHIRTS..

LOOK! I'M CHARLIE BROWN!

NOBODY LIKES ME! EVERYBODY HATES ME! POOR, POOR ME!

I WISH I HAD A FRIEND! EVERYBODY HATES ME!! NOBODY LIKES ME!
HA HA HA HA HA HA HA HA HA HA HA HA

HEY! HERE COMES CHARLIE BROWN HIMSELF! OH, BOY, JUST WAIT 'TIL HE SEES LUCY!
THIS OUGHT TO BE GOOD!
2-22

!

WELL, HELLO THERE, CHARLIE BROWN, YOU BLOCKHEAD!!

SCHULZ
SIGH
HA HA HA HA HA HA HA HA HA HA HA HA

December 18, 1958

DEAR SANTA CLAUS, WELL, IT'S THAT TIME OF YEAR AGAIN, ISN'T IT?

THERE ARE SO MANY THINGS I WOULD LIKE TO SAY TO YOU, BUT I FIND IT HARD TO PUT THEM IN WRITING.

IT WOULD BE SO MUCH EASIER IF I COULD TALK TO YOU IN PERSON.

DO YOU THINK MAYBE WE COULD HAVE LUNCH TOGETHER SOMETIME?
12-18
SCHULZ

February 6, 1959

PEANUTS
WHAT'S THE MATTER, CHARLIE BROWN?
OH, IT'S JUST SOMETHING YOUR SISTER SAID..

SHE SAID MY FACE HAS NO CHARACTER...AND SHE'S RIGHT, TOO...I'M A NOTHING!

DON'T PAY ANY ATTENTION TO LUCY, CHARLIE BROWN...WHY, IF I LISTENED TO HER, I'D HAVE BEEN A NERVOUS WRECK A LONG TIME AGO!

2-6
SCHULZ

February 21, 1959

PEANUTS
ARF
ARF
ARF

ARF ARF ARF

I GUESS I'D BETTER KEEP QUIET..

THERE'S NO SENSE IN DOING A LOT OF BARKING IF YOU DON'T REALLY HAVE ANYTHING TO SAY..
2-21
SCHULZ

February 25, 1959

PEANUTS
HOW ARE YOU DOING IN SCHOOL THESE DAYS, CHARLIE BROWN?

OH, FAIRLY WELL, I GUESS... I'M HAVING MOST OF MY TROUBLE IN ARITHMETIC..

I SHOULD THINK YOU'D LIKE ARITHMETIC...IT'S A VERY PRECISE SUBJECT..
2-25

THAT'S JUST THE TROUBLE.. I'M AT MY BEST IN SOMETHING WHERE THE ANSWERS ARE MOSTLY A MATTER OF OPINION!
SCHULZ

March 2, 1959

PEANUTS
I'VE LOST A LIBRARY BOOK..
YOU HAVE? OH, BOY! YOU'RE A DEAD DUCK!
COMIX

I'VE LOOKED ALL OVER, BUT I CAN'T FIND IT
I'D SAY YOU'RE A DEAD DUCK

I'VE LOOKED AND I'VE LOOKED AND I'VE LOOKED..
YOU KNOW WHAT, CHARLIE BROWN?
3-2

NO, WHAT?
YOU'RE A DEAD DUCK!
SCHULZ

March 4, 1959

PEANUTS
MAYBE THE LIBRARY THINKS YOU STOLE THEIR BOOK..

STOLE IT? I WOULDN'T STEAL THEIR BOOK!
WELL, HOW DO THEY KNOW THAT?

STOLE IT! GOOD GRIEF!
WELL, WHAT DO YOU EXPECT THEM TO THINK?

3-4
LIBRARIES ARE HUMAN, TOO, YOU KNOW!
SCHULZ

March 9, 1959

PEANUTS
I THINK I'LL JUST CALL UP THE LIBRARY, AND TELL THEM I'VE LOST THEIR BOOK!
3-9

I THINK I'LL GO RIGHT OVER TO THE PHONE, AND CALL THEM UP!

I THINK I'LL JUST PICK UP THE PHONE, CALL THE LIBRARY AND TELL THEM THAT I'VE LOST THEIR BOOK..

SCHULZ
I THINK I'LL DROP DEAD..

March 12, 1959

PEANUTS
DEAR LIBRARY,
I HAVE LOST YOUR BOOK.

I CAN NOT FIND IT ANYWHERE.

I WILL COME TO THE LIBRARY AND TURN MYSELF IN.

PLEASE DO NOT HARM MY MOTHER AND FATHER.
3-12
SCHULZ

March 13, 1959

PEANUTS
I FOUND IT
3-13

I FOUND MY LIBRARY BOOK! I LOOKED IN THE REFRIGERATOR AND THERE IT WAS! I FOUND IT!!!
THAT'S GREAT, CHARLIE BROWN..

I FOUND IT! I FOUND IT!! HA HA HA HA HA HA I FOUND IT! I FOUND IT! HEE HEE HEE HEE HEE I FOUND IT! I FOUND IT!!

IN ALL THIS WORLD THERE IS NOTHING MORE INSPIRING THAN THE SIGHT OF SOMEONE WHO HAS JUST BEEN TAKEN OFF THE HOOK!
SCHULZ

March 27, 1959—First appearance of Lucy's psychiatric booth.

PEANUTS
PSYCHIATRIC HELP 5¢

I HAVE DEEP FEELINGS OF DEPRESSION...

WHAT CAN I DO ABOUT THIS?
3-27

SNAP OUT OF IT! FIVE CENTS, PLEASE.
SCHULZ

"Everyone is a lay psychiatrist, so I keep up with the latest on neuroses and phobias."

April 2, 1959

PEANUTS
WOULDN'T IT BE WONDERFUL IF THERE WERE NO HATRED?

WOULDN'T IT BE WONDERFUL IF THERE WERE NO HATRED IN THE WHOLE WORLD?
4-2

WHY DOES THIS INTEREST YOU SO MUCH, CHARLIE BROWN?

THEN NOBODY WOULD HATE **ME**!
SCHULZ

April 7, 1959

PEANUTS
SNOOPY

!
SNOOPY

ARF!
SNOOPY

CRAZY SALESMEN!
SNOOPY
SCHULZ
4-7

March 22, 1959

PEANUTS

THERE'S A LESSON TO BE LEARNED HERE SOMEWHERE, BUT I DON'T KNOW WHAT IT IS...

SCHULZ

May 9, 1959

PEANUTS

5-9

I'VE BEEN FEELING KIND OF DEPRESSED ALL WEEK..
SCHULZ

May 12, 1959

PEANUTS
I'M BUILDING UP A PRETTY GOOD COLLECTION OF DISHES..
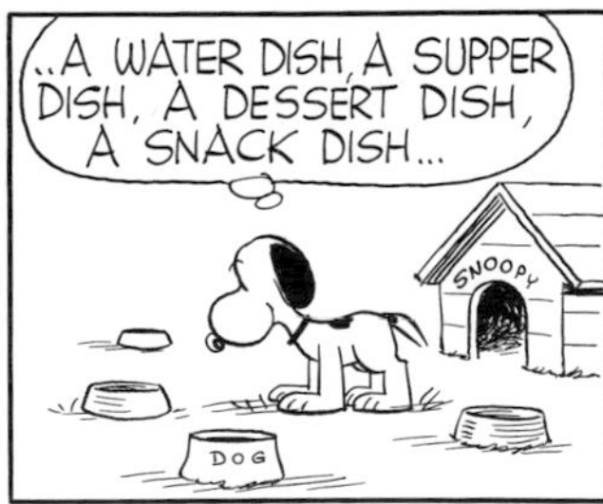
..A WATER DISH, A SUPPER DISH, A DESSERT DISH, A SNACK DISH...
SNOOPY
DOG

..AND OVER HERE IS MY FAVORITE OF ALL...
5-12

A SPECIAL PLATE FOR TWENTY-SIX-INCH PIZZA!
SCHULZ

May 18, 1959

PEANUTS
THAT'S PRETTY GOOD...

BUT I DON'T THINK IT'S GOOD ENOUGH..
5-18

THEY GOT THIRTY-TWO IN...

YEAH, BUT JUST REMEMBER... A TELEPHONE BOOTH IS A LOT BIGGER!
SCHULZ

May 26, 1959—First mention of Charlie Brown's sister, Sally.

PEANUTS
A BABY SISTER?

I'M A FATHER!

I MEAN MY DAD'S A FATHER! I'M A BROTHER! I HAVE A BABY SISTER!! I'M A BROTHER!

5-26
YOU DIDN'T ACT LIKE THAT WHEN I WAS BORN!
SCHULZ

May 30, 1959

PEANUTS
HEY, C'MON!

CHARLIE BROWN HAD A BABY SISTER! HE'S HANDING OUT CHOCOLATE CIGARS!

CONGRATULATIONS, CHARLIE BROWN!
THANK YOU, 'PIG-PEN'..
5-30

NOT BAD...THIS SHOULD HAPPEN MORE OFTEN!
SCHULZ

June 2, 1959

PEANUTS
HAVE THEY DECIDED ON A NAME FOR YOUR SISTER YET, CHARLIE BROWN?

YES, HER NAME IS GOING TO BE SALLY!
SALLY?

SALLY... SALLY BROWN... GOOD OL' SALLY BROWN!
6-2

IT FIGURES!
SCHULZ

June 9, 1959

PEANUTS
Hey, Violet!
6-9

WAIT UNTIL YOU SEE THE PAIR OF SLEEPERS I BOUGHT FOR LITTLE SALLY..

YOU CERTAINLY ARE A DEVOTED BROTHER, CHARLIE BROWN
WELL, I'M TRYING TO BE

SCHULZ

June 11, 1959

PEANUTS
THIS HAVING A BABY SISTER MAY DO A LOT FOR CHARLIE BROWN..

IT'S JUST LIABLE TO MAKE HIM INTO A NEW PERSON!

THAT'S A FRIGHTENING THOUGHT...

I CAN THINK OF NOTHING IN ALL THIS WORLD MORE OBNOXIOUS THAN A WELL-ADJUSTED CHARLIE BROWN!
6-11
SCHULZ

June 24, 1959

PEANUTS
THAT'S NOT A REAL BABY! THAT'S JUST A DOG DRESSED UP LIKE A BABY!

GOO!
SCHULZ
6-24

July 6, 1959

PEANUTS
THIS ROCKET BUSINESS IS FASCINATING

EVERY DAY THEY SEEM TO COME UP WITH SOMETHING NEW

FOR AWHILE THEY WERE SENDING UP DOGS... NOW THEY'RE SENDING UP MICE..

THAT'S A VERY HEALTHY TREND!
SCHULZ
7-6

July 9, 1959

PEANUTS
DID ANYONE EVER TELL YOU THAT YOU HAVE PRETTY EYES, SCHROEDER?

7-9

MUSICIANS GET UNNERVED WHEN YOU TELL THEM THAT THEY HAVE PRETTY EYES
SCHULZ

July 12, 1959

PEANUTS
by SCHULZ
BOY, I CAN HARDLY WAIT TO GET INTO THAT WADING POOL!
LOOK OUT, GIRLS! HERE I COME!
STAY RIGHT WHERE YOU ARE, CHARLIE BROWN!
THERE'S NOT ENOUGH ROOM FOR YOU!
GO FIND YOUR OWN POOL!
THAT'S WHAT I SAY! GO FIND YOUR OWN POOL!
7-12
SIGH
SCHULZ

July 20, 1959

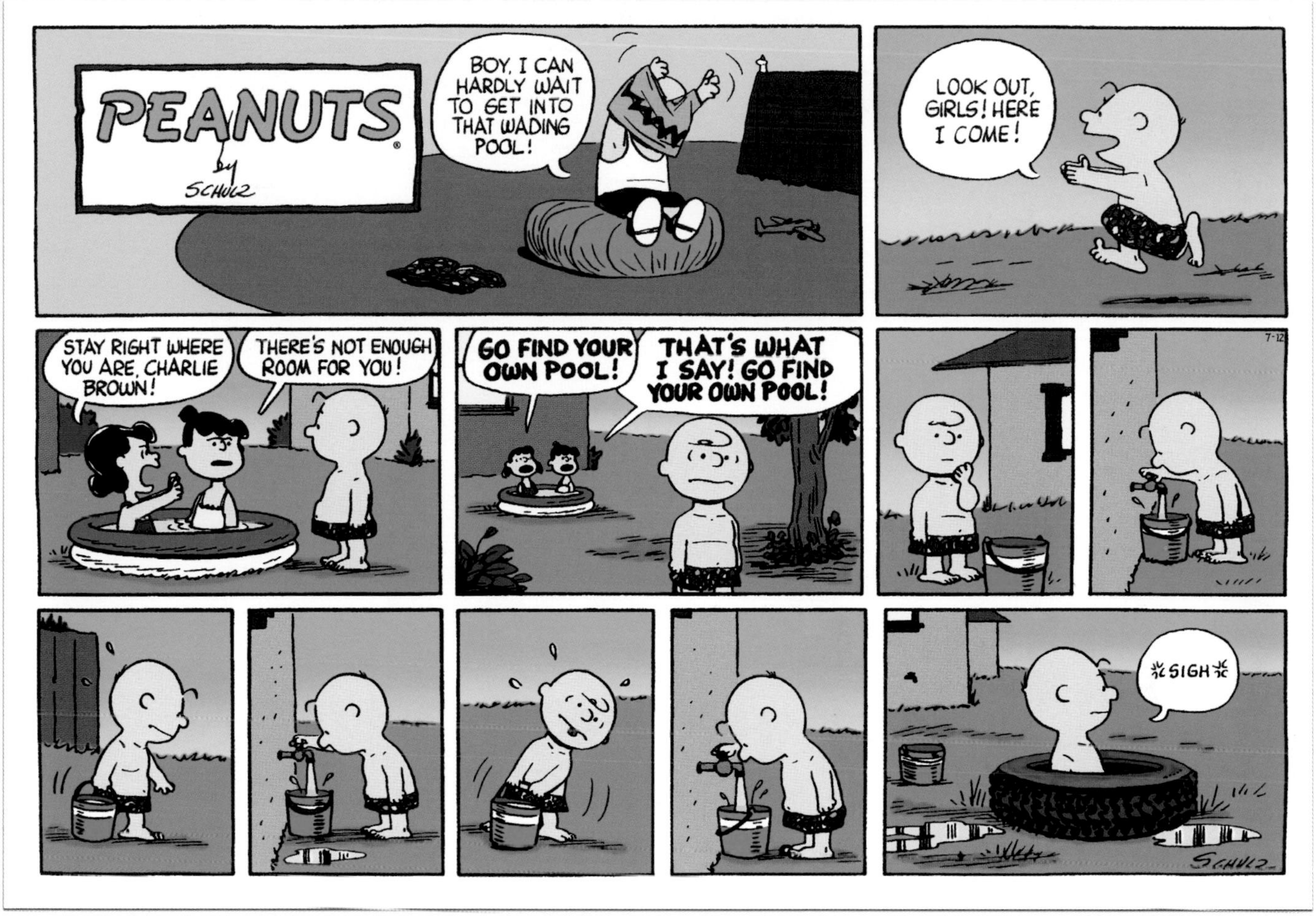

PEANUTS
7-20
SCHULZ

August 17, 1959

PEANUTS
THESE ROCKS ARE A RELEASE FOR MY PENT-UP EMOTIONS.

WHEN I FEEL ALL TIED UP INSIDE, I JUST STAND HERE AND THROW ROCKS INTO THAT VACANT LOT!

HELLO, CHARLIE BROWN, YOU BLOCKHEAD!

SOMETIMES I THINK I'M KIND OF A VACANT LOT MYSELF...
8-17
SCHULZ

July 26, 1959

PEANUTS
by
SCHULZ

CLOMP

!
?

SCHULZ

August 24, 1959—First appearance of Sally Brown.

PEANUTS
THERE'S NO USE ARGUING ABOUT IT! I'D LIKE TO PLAY, BUT I CAN'T!
MY MOTHER TOLD ME TO PUSH SALLY AROUND IN HER STROLLER, AND THAT'S WHAT I'M GOING TO DO! IT'S WHAT I HAVE TO DO!
WELL, YOU'VE GOT TO ADMIT THAT IT'S THAT KIND OF DEVOTION THAT BUILDS CHARACTER...
8-24
...AND LOSES BALL GAMES!
SCHULZ

August 26, 1959

PEANUTS
I HOPE SHE'S SATISFIED!
DEPRIVING US OF A MANAGER JUST BEFORE OUR LAST AND MOST CRUCIAL GAME!
8-26
ALL BECAUSE SHE HAS TO RIDE AROUND IN HER OL' STROLLER! WELL, I JUST HOPE SHE'S SATISFIED!
MY FIRST YEAR IN THIS WORLD, AND ALREADY I HAVE GUILT FEELINGS!
SCHULZ

October 2, 1959

PEANUTS

10-2

SCHULZ

October 16, 1959

PEANUTS

10-16

SUDDENLY I FEEL LIKE THE PIED PIPER!
SCHULZ

August 30, 1959

PEANUTS
by
SCHULZ

I SURE LIKE CHARLIE BROWN'S LITTLE SISTER..

SOMEHOW I FEEL THAT SHE AND I HAVE SOMETHING IN COMMON..

I JUST CAN'T FIGURE OUT WHAT IT IS, THOUGH...

THAT'S IT!

SHE'S THE ONLY OTHER ONE AROUND HERE WHO KNOWS HOW TO WALK ON FOUR FEET!
SCHULZ

October 22, 1959

PEANUTS

10-22

SCHULZ

October 25, 1959

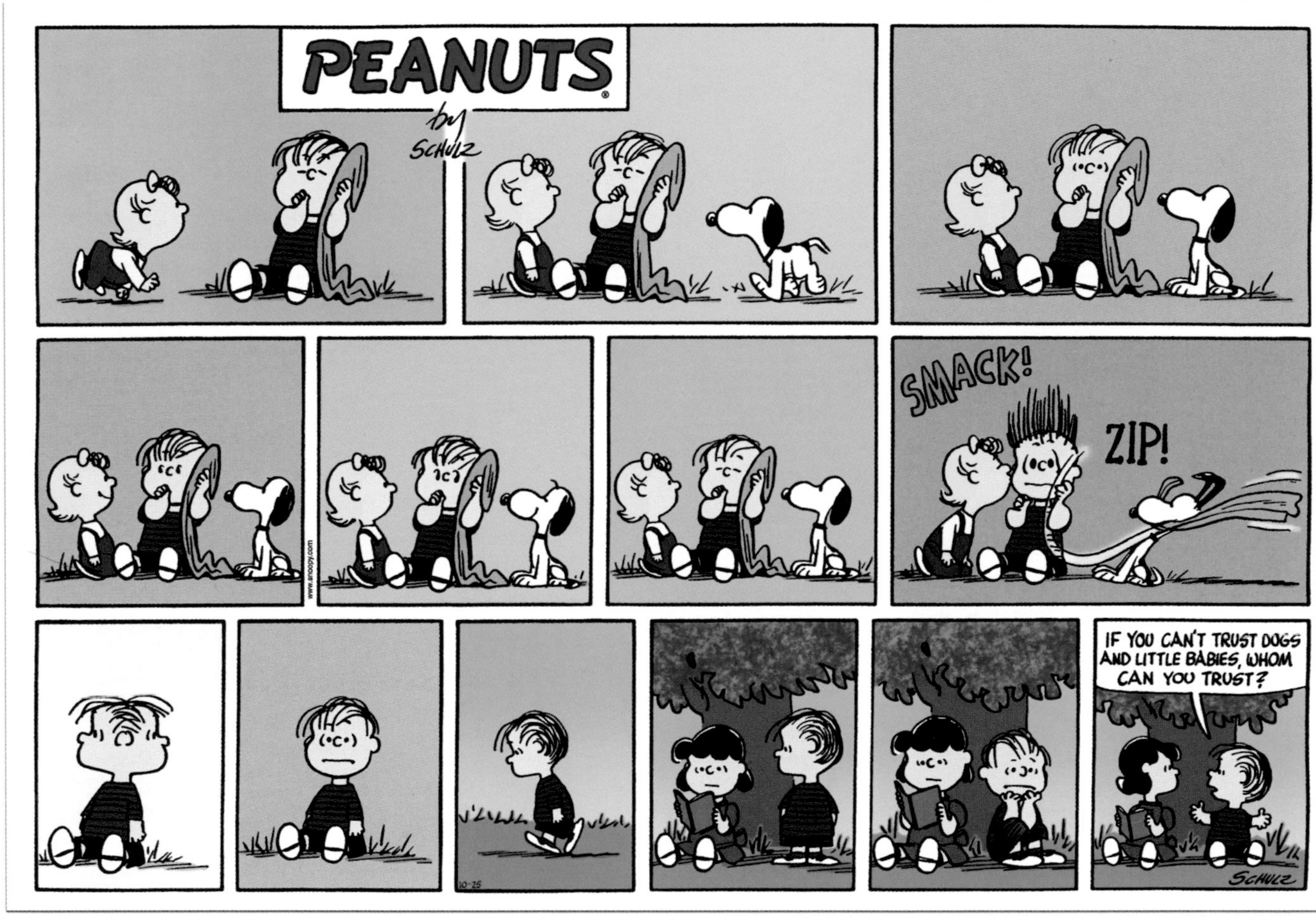

PEANUTS

by SCHULZ

SMACK!

ZIP!

IF YOU CAN'T TRUST DOGS AND LITTLE BABIES, WHOM CAN YOU TRUST?

SCHULZ

"I was drawing some Halloween strips about Linus, who is bright but very innocent, and he was confusing Halloween with Christmas because he was one holiday ahead of himself. Now the whole thing has become a parody of Christmas, and Linus gives the Great Pumpkin those qualities Santa Claus is supposed to have."

October 26, 1959—First mention of the Great Pumpkin.

PEANUTS
10-26
WHAT IN THE WORLD ARE YOU DOING?
DON'T YOU KNOW?

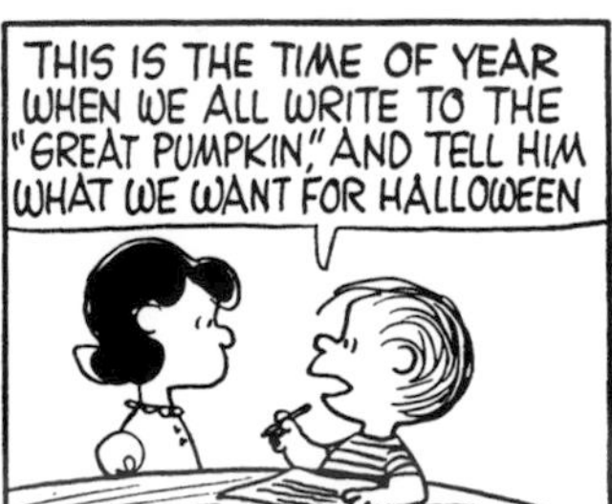
THIS IS THE TIME OF YEAR WHEN WE ALL WRITE TO THE "GREAT PUMPKIN," AND TELL HIM WHAT WE WANT FOR HALLOWEEN

THE "GREAT PUMPKIN" LOVES LITTLE CHILDREN

I CAN SEE HIM NOW RISING UP OUT OF THE PUMPKIN PATCH WITH HIS BIG BAG OF TOYS!
SCHULZ

October 29, 1959

PEANUTS
...AND THEN ON HALLOWEEN NIGHT THE "GREAT PUMPKIN" RISES UP OUT OF THE PUMPKIN PATCH...

..AND HE BRINGS TOYS TO ALL THE GOOD LITTLE CHILDREN IN THE WORLD!
YOU'RE CRAZY!

ALL RIGHT, SO YOU BELIEVE IN SANTA CLAUS, AND I'LL BELIEVE IN THE "GREAT PUMPKIN"..
10-29

THE WAY I SEE IT, IT DOESN'T MATTER WHAT YOU BELIEVE, JUST SO YOU'RE SINCERE!
SCHULZ

November 2, 1959

PEANUTS
WELL, HALLOWEEN HAS COME AND GONE...

SO IT HAS

DID THE "GREAT PUMPKIN" BRING YOU LOTS OF NICE PRESENTS?

OH, SHUT UP!
11-2
SCHULZ

November 3, 1959

PEANUTS
LOOK AT ME.. I'M THE "GREAT PUMPKIN"!

I RISE UP OUT OF THE PUMPKIN PATCH, AND BRING TOYS TO ALL THE CHILDREN ON HALLOWEEN!

HEY, LINUS! HOW MANY TOYS DID HE BRING YOU?!!
HAHAHAHA!!!

I WAS A VICTIM OF FALSE DOCTRINE..
11-3
SCHULZ

November 26, 1959

PEANUTS
DID IT EVER OCCUR TO YOU THAT "PIG-PEN" MIGHT BE CARRYING THE DIRT AND DUST OF SOME PAST CIVILIZATION?
11-26

NOTICE HOW THE DUST CLINGS TO HIM...

HE COULD HAVE ON HIM SOME OF THE SOIL OF ANCIENT BABYLON

SORT OF MAKES YOU WANT TO TREAT ME WITH MORE RESPECT, DOESN'T IT?
SCHULZ

November 28, 1959

PEANUTS
POOR OL' "PIG-PEN"

THEY SAY HE CARRIES ON HIM THE DIRT AND DUST OF ANCIENT CIVILIZATIONS...

11-28

HISTORY IS PASSING BEFORE MY EYES!
SCHULZ

Celebrate
1960s

"Actually, I've never liked the word 'artist.' I always qualify it by calling myself a comic strip artist. But to me, the words don't really mean anything. No matter what I do and how well I do it, I don't think I will ever be able to attain the stature of an artist like Rembrandt or Picasso— even though more people know Snoopy than anything Picasso and other great painters have done."

—*Charles M. Schulz*

SMAK!

1960–1969

In the 1960s, the *Peanuts* gang ventured beyond the comic pages and became icons of popular culture in the United States. The first *Peanuts* animated TV special, *A Charlie Brown Christmas*, debuted in 1965 (and won an Emmy and a Peabody award!). That same year, the gang was featured on the cover of *Time* magazine. In 1967, the play *You're a Good Man, Charlie Brown* opened in New York off Broadway, and in 1969 the gang went to the movies in *A Boy Named Charlie Brown*.

This decade also saw the introduction of some of the comic strip's most memorable characters (and personas!):

- Frieda, who debuted on March 6, 1961, was a secondary character known mostly for her "naturally curly hair" and for being the owner of Faron the cat. Schulz considered Faron to be one of his least successful ideas, believing that he did not draw cats very well. Schulz also worried that the presence of a cat in the strip would force Snoopy to act more like a real dog, taking the strip in a direction that he did not wish to take it.
- The Little Red-Haired Girl was another character that never appeared in the strip (except in silhouette). Charlie Brown's unrequited love for her is revealed for the first time on November 19, 1961. Schulz had great affection for a little red-haired girl when he was a young man and never forgot the sting of her rejection.
- On April 6, 1963, after yet another crushing defeat on the baseball field, Charlie Brown uttered a statement that resonated with readers everywhere: "How can we lose when we're so sincere?"
- Snoopy first appeared as the World War I Flying Ace, one of the most popular of his more than one hundred alter egos, on October 10, 1965. Snoopy's epic battles with the never-seen Red Baron became a pop culture phenomenon; in 1966 the Royal Guardsmen released their hit song "Snoopy vs. the Red Baron."

CURSE YOU, RED BARON!

- Peppermint Patty, who would become an important character in *Peanuts*, first appeared in the August 22, 1966, strip. Peppermint Patty was a multidimensional character who excelled in sports but was a lackluster student. And, unlike most other *Peanuts* characters, we get a glimpse of her home life when we learn that she is being raised by her father in a single-parent home. Schulz once remarked about Peppermint Patty, "I think she could almost carry another strip by herself."

- A bird (who wouldn't get his official name until 1970) "flitter-fluttered" into the public's heart on April 4, 1967. Snoopy and his little sidekick would prove to be one of the great duos in comic strip history.

- In the summer of 1968, after the assassinations of Martin Luther King, Jr. in April and Robert Kennedy in June, a great admirer of *Peanuts* encouraged Schulz to introduce a black character. Franklin debuted on July 31, 1968.

- On August 29, 1968, Charlie Brown learned the shocking truth that he was not Snoopy's first owner. This series of strips became the basis of a 1972 feature-length movie, *Snoopy, Come Home*.
- Snoopy the World-Famous Astronaut blasted off for the moon on March 10, 1969, beating the United States' *Apollo 11* by several months. Schulz was given a special honor by the crew of *Apollo 10* when, in May 1969, they named their command and lunar modules *Charlie Brown* and *Snoopy*, respectively.

January 4, 1960

PEANUTS
I FEEL SORRY FOR LITTLE BABIES..

WHEN A LITTLE BABY IS BORN INTO THIS COLD WORLD, HE'S CONFUSED! HE'S FRIGHTENED!
1-4

HE NEEDS SOMETHING TO CHEER HIM UP...

THE WAY I SEE IT, AS SOON AS A BABY IS BORN, HE SHOULD BE ISSUED A BANJO!
SCHULZ

"I think that has been one of the secrets to whatever success I've had. Everything that I cartoon or write about is done with authenticity. The notes in Schroeder's music are actually notes from different piano works, and I copy them out very carefully. . . . So when I do things about medicine, or historical things from World War I, where Snoopy is over in France, it's all very authentic. I think it's important to try to break beneath the surface in everything you are doing, rather than just drawing surface cartoons."

January 7, 1960

PEANUTS
THAT'S RIDICULOUS!

OH?
1-7

WELL, MAYBE SO...

ALL I KNOW IS IT GIVES US A BETTER PICTURE!
SCHULZ

January 18, 1960

PEANUTS
SNOOPY, HAVE YOU EVER FELT THAT YOU WERE A BORE?

HAVE YOU EVER FELT THAT PEOPLE WERE BORED BY EVERYTHING YOU SAID?

HAVE YOU EVER FELT THAT THEY WEREN'T THE LEAST BIT INTERESTED IN ANYTHING YOU..

1-18
SCHULZ
Z

February 9, 1960

PEANUTS
GOOD GRIEF! TRAPPED IN A DOGHOUSE BY AN ICICLE!
SNOOPY

I'LL BET IF I MAKE JUST THE SLIGHTEST MOVE, IT'LL CRASH DOWN AND KILL ME!
SNOOPY

I DON'T WANT TO DIE! I'M TOO YOUNG TO DIE! I'M TOO NICE TO DIE!
SNOOPY

2-9
SCHULZ
I'M TOO ME TO DIE!!

January 24, 1960

PEANUTS
by SCHULZ
JANUARY ISN'T OVER YET...ACTUALLY, NINETEEN-SIXTY HAS JUST BEGUN!
I'VE GOT TO CONVINCE HIM! I'VE GOT TO!
LINUS, THERE'S STILL TIME FOR YOU TO MAKE A NEW YEAR'S RESOLUTION TO GIVE UP THAT BLANKET...
YOU KNOW, I THINK YOU'RE RIGHT! I THINK IF I'M EVER GOING TO GET RID OF IT, NOW IS THE TIME!
SO I'LL JUST THROW IT AWAY, AND BE DONE WITH IT ONCE AND FOR ALL!
1-24
NEVER BELIEVE ANYTHING I SAY!
SCHULZ

February 10, 1960

PEANUTS
IT'S SILLY TO BE TRAPPED IN A DOGHOUSE BY AN ICICLE!
SNOOPY
I THINK I'LL JUST MAKE A RUN FOR IT! I THINK I'LL JUST ZOOM OUT OF HERE!
2-10
I THINK I'LL JUST LEAP UP AND ZOOM RIGHT OUT!
SCHULZ
I THINK I'LL JUST LIE HERE FOR THE REST OF MY LIFE!

February 11, 1960

PEANUTS
2-11
LOOKS BAD, DOESN'T IT?
TERRIBLE!
SNOOPY
YOU KNOW WHAT I'VE HEARD?
NO, WHAT HAVE YOU HEARD?
I'VE HEARD THAT LOUD NOISES WILL SOMETIMES CAUSE AN ICICLE TO FALL...
IS THAT RIGHT?
SCHULZ

February 12, 1960

PEANUTS
I'M DOOMED!
SNOOPY

HELLO, HUMANE SOCIETY? WE NEED YOUR ADVICE...HOW DO YOU GET A DOG OUT OF A DOGHOUSE BEFORE AN ICICLE FALLS ON HIM?

HE SAID TO TRY COAXING HIM OUT WITH HIS FAVORITE FOOD... SOMETHING HE JUST CAN'T RESIST...
2-12

WHAT'S THE NUMBER OF "VILLELLA'S TAKE-OUT PIZZA PARLOR"?
SCHULZ

February 13, 1960

PEANUTS
I'M DOING JUST WHAT THE MAN FROM THE HUMANE SOCIETY SAID TO DO...
2-13

SNIF? SNIF? SNIF?
?
SNOOPY

ZOOM
WHAM!

SAVED BY A PIZZA!
GOOD GRIEF!
SCHULZ

February 22, 1960

PEANUTS
YOU'RE WEAK! YOU'RE A REAL JELLYFISH!

YOU'RE DUMB, YOU'RE STUPID YOU'RE IGNORANT AND YOU HAVE A SILLY FACE!

POOR CHARLIE BROWN... I SEE THE CATS HAVE BEEN USING YOU TO SHARPEN THEIR CLAWS AGAIN, HUH?

YEAH, I'M SORT OF A SPIRITUAL SCRATCHING POST!
2/22
SCHULZ

March 3, 1960

PEANUTS
SNOOPY! SUPPERTIME!
3-3

ALL RIGHT, IF YOU DON'T WANT YOUR SUPPER, I'LL GIVE IT TO THE CAT NEXT DOOR!

THAT USUALLY DOES IT!
SCHULZ

March 4, 1960

PEANUTS
WHEN I GROW UP, I'D LIKE TO STUDY ABOUT PEOPLE...

PEOPLE INTEREST ME... I'D LIKE TO GO TO SOME BIG UNIVERSITY, AND STUDY ALL ABOUT PEOPLE..

I SEE...YOU WANT TO LEARN ABOUT PEOPLE SO THAT WITH YOUR KNOWLEDGE YOU WILL BE EQUIPPED TO HELP THEM...

NO, I'M JUST NOSY!
SCHULZ
3-4

March 5, 1960

PEANUTS
CHARLIE BROWN, WHAT WOULD BE YOUR REACTION IF SOMEONE SAID YOU COULD HAVE YOUR LIFE OVER AGAIN?

YOU MEAN EXACTLY AS I'VE LIVED IT? NO CHANGES? EVERYTHING HAPPENING JUST THE WAY IT DID BEFORE?

UH HUH...WHAT WOULD BE YOUR REACTION?
3/5

AAAUGHH!
SCHULZ

March 11, 1960

PEANUTS
I SEE WHERE THE PRICE OF HAIRCUTS MAY GO UP AGAIN..

MY DAD SAYS HE'S GOING TO BUY A PAIR OF CLIPPERS, AND CUT MY HAIR HIMSELF...

I HOPE HE CUTS YOUR EARS OFF!

3-11
I KEEP FORGETTING THAT CHARLIE BROWN'S DAD IS A BARBER!
SCHULZ

"My dad was a barber. I always admired him for the fact that both he and my mother had only third-grade educations and, from what I remembered hearing in conversations, he worked pitching hay in Nebraska one summer to earn enough money to go to barber school, got himself a couple of jobs, and eventually bought his own barber shop."

March 13, 1960

RUN, BOY! RUN!
PEANUTS
SCHULZ
KEEP THOSE FEET MOVING!
LET OUT SOME MORE STRING!
YOU GOT IT UP, CHARLIE BROWN! YOU GOT IT UP!

KEEP GOING! KEEP GOING!

IT'S FLYING! IT'S FLYING!

IT'S...

BOOM!

THAT'S THE FIRST TIME I'VE EVER SEEN A KITE EXPLODE!
SCHULZ

March 20, 1960

PEANUTS
by SCHULZ
HOLD THE BLANKET IN YOUR LEFT HAND...THAT'S THE WAY...
NOW THE THUMB...
WHAT IN THE WORLD IS GOING ON HERE?!
LOOK, LINUS, YOU'RE NOT GONNA TEACH ANY SISTER OF MINE TO SIT AROUND HOLDING A BLANKET!
JUST BECAUSE YOU NEED A CRUTCH, IT DOESN'T MEAN SHE DOES!
OF ALL THE STUPID HABITS, THAT BLANKET IS THE STUPIDEST! AND THAT'S ALL IT IS, JUST A HABIT! A STUPID HABIT!!

YOU'RE NOT GOING TO TEACH HER TO USE A BLANKET FOR SECURITY OR FOR HAPPINESS OR FOR ANYTHING! SALLY IS GOING TO USE HER OWN WILL-POWER TO GROW FROM A BABY TO A WELL-ADJUSTED CHILD !!!!

LIKE HER BROTHER?

SIGH
SCHULZ

April 2, 1960

PEANUTS
DEAR PENCIL-PAL,
HOW HAVE YOU BEEN?
I HAVE BEEN FINE. WE HAVE HAD NICE WEATHER HERE.

YESTERDAY IT WAS WARM ALL DAY. THIS MORNING IT WAS A LITTLE CHILLY, BUT BY NOON IT WAS NICE.

AM I BORING YOU?
SCHULZ
4-2

April 25, 1960

PEANUTS

PAT
PAT PAT

MMMMM!

4-25
HAPPINESS IS A WARM PUPPY..
SCHULZ

May 16, 1960

PEANUTS
I CAN'T LOOK!
THE SCORE IS THREE TO TWO IN THE LAST OF THE NINTH!

BUT WE HAVE TWO OUTS!
BUT CHARLIE BROWN IS ON THIRD! AND OUR BEST HITTER IS COMING UP!

SAY, YOU DON'T THINK CHARLIE BROWN WILL TRY TO STEAL HOME, DO YOU?
NEVER! NOT EVEN CHARLIE BROWN WOULD DO ANYTHING THAT STUPID!

I WONDER IF I SHOULD TRY TO STEAL HOME !?
SCHULZ
5-16

May 17, 1960

PEANUTS
THIS IS MY BIG CHANCE TO BE A HERO!

IF I COULD STEAL HOME, THE GAME WOULD BE ALL TIED UP, AND I'D BE THE HERO!

5-17

SCHULZ
I HAVEN'T GOT THE NERVE!

May 19, 1960

PEANUTS
I GOTTA TRY IT!
IF I'M GONNA BE A HERO, I GOTTA TRY TO STEAL HOME!

FIRST I'LL DANCE AROUND A LITTLE ON THE BASELINE TO CONFUSE THEIR PITCHER...

5-19
...AND THEN I'LL...

TAKE OFF!
SCHULZ

May 20, 1960

PEANUTS
CHARLIE BROWN IS TRYING TO STEAL HOME!!

SLIDE, CHARLIE BROWN! SLIDE!

OH, YOU BLOCKHEAD!
SCHULZ
5-20

May 21, 1960

PEANUTS
WHAAAH! WE LOST THE GAME ALL BECAUSE OF CHARLIE BROWN WHHAAAAHHH!!

WAS I OUT?
OUT?! WHY, YOU BLOCKHEAD, YOU DIDN'T EVEN GET HALF WAY HOME!

RATS!
SCHULZ
5-21

May 24, 1960

PEANUTS
WHY DIDN'T I JUST WAIT ON THIRD BASE? WHY DID I HAVE TO TRY TO STEAL HOME?!
WHY? WHY? WHY? WHY?

CHARLIE BROWN?

I HAVE BEEN ASKED TO TELL YOU THAT YOUR CRIES OF ANGUISH ARE KEEPING THE WHOLE NEIGHBORHOOD AWAKE!

WHY? WHY? WHY? WHY?

May 26, 1960

PEANUTS
ALL I WANTED TO DO WAS BE A HERO...

BUT DO I EVER GET TO BE A HERO? NO! ALL I EVER GET TO BE IS THE STUPID GOAT!

DON'T BE DISCOURAGED, CHARLIE BROWN... IN THIS LIFE WE LIVE, THERE ARE ALWAYS SOME BITTER PILLS TO BE SWALLOWED..

IF IT'S ALL THE SAME WITH YOU, I'D RATHER NOT RENEW MY PRESCRIPTION!

May 27, 1960

PEANUTS
DEAR TEAMMATES,

I HAVE BEEN THINKING OF RESIGNING MY JOB AS YOUR MANAGER, AND I

WE ACCEPT!

WAIT 'TIL I FINISH THE LETTER

May 31, 1960

PEANUTS
NO, BY GOLLY! NO!!

OH, ALL RIGHT.. HAVE IT YOUR OWN WAY!

WHAT'S WRONG WITH WANTING TO EAT ON THE TERRACE?

June 15, 1960

PEANUTS
YOU KNOW WHAT WE'RE GOING TO DO TOMORROW?

PATTY AND VIOLET AND I ARE GOING ON A PICNIC!

I JUST HOPE TO GOODNESS THAT IT DOESN'T RAIN...

"HOPING TO GOODNESS" IS NOT THEOLOGICALLY SOUND!

June 21, 1960

PEANUTS
!

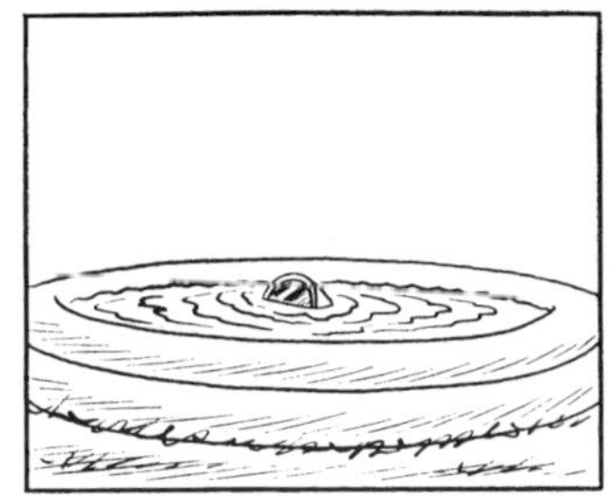

6-21
SCHULZ

June 24, 1960

PEANUTS
DRAWING WITH CHALK ON THE SIDEWALK IS LOTS OF FUN
6-24

IT'S REALLY A WONDERFUL MEDIUM...YOU CAN GET SOME VERY NICE EFFECTS...

I THINK IT RANKS RIGHT ALONGSIDE TEMPERA AND OIL AS AN ARTISTIC MEDIUM

OF COURSE, IT HAS ITS DRAWBACKS, TOO
SCHULZ

July 5, 1960

PEANUTS
THE PEOPLE OF THIS WORLD HAVE GONE MAD!

I'M GOING TO STAND ON MY HEAD AS A PUBLIC PROTEST!

I WILL BECOME SYMBOLIC OF THE "LITTLE MAN" CRYING OUT IN ANGUISH AGAINST THE WORLD'S MADNESS...
SNIF? SNIF?
?

...AFTER SUPPER..
SCHULZ
7-5

July 14, 1960

PEANUTS
I'VE JUST DRAWN A CARTOON.. LOOK AT IT, AND LAUGH!

I DON'T THINK IT'S VERY FUNNY...
I SAID, LOOK AT IT, AND LAUGH!

HE HE HE HE HE HE

THAT'S THE TROUBLE WITH CARTOONISTS TODAY...THEY DON'T MAKE PEOPLE LAUGH!
7-14
SCHULZ

July 15, 1960

PEANUTS
I'VE DECIDED TO GO INTO POLITICAL CARTOONING..

I'M GOING TO RIDICULE EVERYTHING!

I UNDERSTAND, LUCY...BY THE USE OF RIDICULE YOU HOPE TO POINT UP OUR FAULTS IN GOVERNMENT, AND THUS IMPROVE OUR WAY OF LIFE...
7-15

NO, I JUST WANT TO RIDICULE EVERYTHING!
SCHULZ

August 14, 1960

AREN'T THE CLOUDS BEAUTIFUL? THEY LOOK LIKE BIG BALLS OF COTTON...
PEANUTS
by SCHULZ
I COULD JUST LIE HERE ALL DAY, AND WATCH THEM DRIFT BY...
IF YOU USE YOUR IMAGINATION, YOU CAN SEE LOTS OF THINGS IN THE CLOUD FORMATIONS... WHAT DO YOU THINK YOU SEE, LINUS?
WELL, THOSE CLOUDS UP THERE LOOK TO ME LIKE THE MAP OF THE BRITISH HONDURAS ON THE CARIBBEAN..
THAT CLOUD UP THERE LOOKS A LITTLE LIKE THE PROFILE OF THOMAS EAKINS, THE FAMOUS PAINTER AND SCULPTOR...
AND THAT GROUP OF CLOUDS OVER THERE GIVES ME THE IMPRESSION OF THE STONING OF STEPHEN...I CAN SEE THE APOSTLE PAUL STANDING THERE TO ONE SIDE...
UH HUH...THAT'S VERY GOOD... WHAT DO YOU SEE IN THE CLOUDS, CHARLIE BROWN?
WELL, I WAS GOING TO SAY I SAW A DUCKY AND A HORSIE, BUT I CHANGED MY MIND!
SCHULZ

October 11, 1960

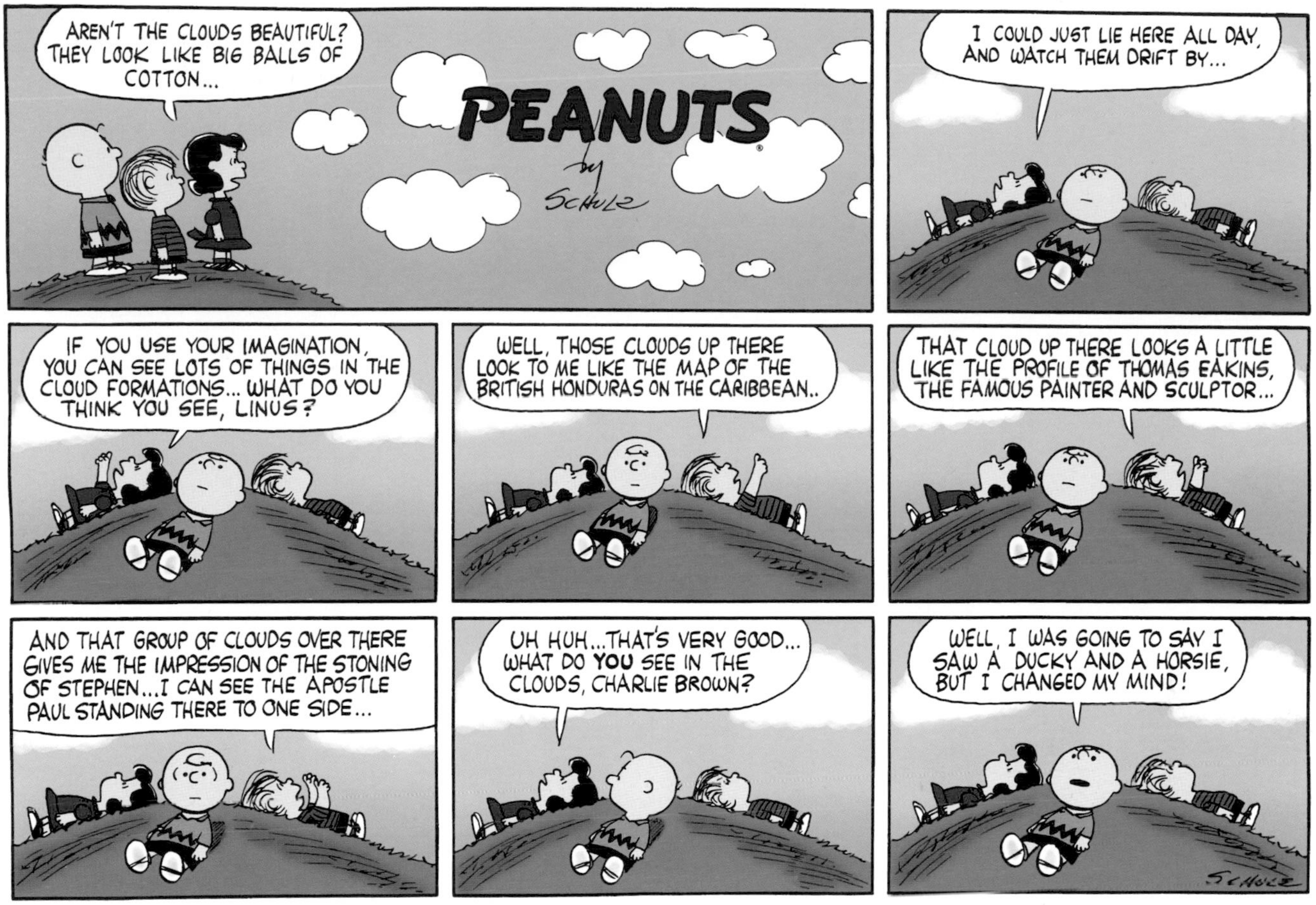

PEANUTS
I'M DEPRESSED! I'M COMPLETELY DEPRESSED!
I AM FIRMLY CONVINCED THAT THERE IS NO ONE IN THIS WORLD WHO REALLY LIKES ME!
SO WHAT ELSE IS NEW?
SCHULZ
10-11

October 13, 1960

PEANUTS
THIS IS MY "DEPRESSED STANCE"

WHEN YOU'RE DEPRESSED, IT MAKES A LOT OF DIFFERENCE HOW YOU STAND...

10-13

THE WORST THING YOU CAN DO IS STRAIGHTEN UP AND HOLD YOUR HEAD HIGH BECAUSE THEN YOU'LL START TO FEEL BETTER..

IF YOU'RE GOING TO GET ANY JOY OUT OF BEING DEPRESSED, YOU'VE GOT TO STAND LIKE THIS..
SCHULZ

October 9, 1960

PEANUTS
by
SCHULZ
WHAT'S THAT?

WHAT'S WHAT?

I THOUGHT I HEARD A CAR DOOR SLAM!

IT'S DAD! HE'S BACKING THE CAR OUT OF THE GARAGE!

HEY, DAD! ARE YOU GOING TO THE STORE? WILL YOU BRING ME SOMETHING?

TELL HIM I WANT A COMIC BOOK!
LUCY WANTS A COMIC BOOK! AND I WANT A CANDY BAR!

I WANT A CANDY BAR, TOO!!
LUCY WANTS A CANDY BAR, TOO! AND I WANT A COMIC BOOK, TOO! AND CAN I HAVE A BOAT?

WILL YOU BRING ME A BOAT? OR A FOOTBALL?

WILL YOU BRING ME A CANDY BAR AND A COMIC BOOK AND A BOAT AND...

OH...

HE WAS JUST BACKING THE CAR INTO THE DRIVEWAY TO WASH IT!
SCHULZ

"Linus is strong enough to carry a strip by himself. His biggest weakness, of course, is the blanket. But he's very bright. If I want to quote the Bible or say something profound, it comes best from Linus. But he's not a little intellectual. Linus's problem is that he's under the thumb of this dominating sister and a mother who puts notes in his lunch telling him to study harder. As Charlie Brown says, 'No wonder he carries that blanket.' I like to work with Linus. He's a neat character."

October 29, 1960

PEANUTS
SANTA CLAUS IS TWICE THE MAN THE GREAT PUMPKIN IS!

YOU'RE CRAZY!
THE GREAT PUMPKIN DOESN'T EVEN EXIST!

WHY DON'T YOU KEEP QUIET? YOU DON'T EVEN KNOW WHAT YOU'RE TALKING ABOUT!
WELL, YOU'RE SO STUPID, YOU BELIEVE ANYTHING!

I'M ALWAYS DISTURBED BY DENOMINATIONAL SQUABBLING
10-29
SCHULZ

November 22, 1960

PEANUTS
DEAR SNICKER SNACK CEREAL COMPANY,
SNICKER SNACKS

I APPRECIATE YOUR OFFER OF ONE HUNDRED REVOLUTIONARY WAR SOLDIERS FOR FIFTEEN CENTS.

HOWEVER, BEING AGAINST VIOLENCE, I AM NOT SURE I WANT THEM.

INSTEAD, COULD I PLEASE HAVE A SET OF PEACE-TIME CIVILIANS?
11-22
SCHULZ

January 2, 1961

PEANUTS
THIS IS THE BEGINNING OF A NEW YEAR, RIGHT? RIGHT!

BAD HABITS ARE BEST DESTROYED AT THE BEGINNING OF A NEW YEAR, RIGHT? RIGHT! THAT STUPID BLANKET YOU'RE HOLDING IS A BAD HABIT, RIGHT? RIGHT!
1-2

NOW, LISTEN CAREFULLY... I HAVE A SUGGESTION....

SUDDENLY I FEEL VERY COLD...
SCHULZ

January 3, 1961

PEANUTS
THIS IS IT!

1-3

WELL, THAT'S THAT! A JOB WELL DONE!

I BURIED YOUR BLANKET!
SCHULZ

January 4, 1961

YOU BURIED MY BLANKET?

YOU CAN'T DO THAT! I'LL DIE WITHOUT THAT BLANKET! I'LL BE LIKE A FISH OUT OF WATER! I'LL DIE! I'LL DIE!

TELL ME WHERE YOU BURIED IT! TELL ME!

SCHULZ
TELL ME! TELL ME! TELL ME! TELL ME! OH, TELL ME!

January 6, 1961

LINUS TELLS ME YOU'VE BURIED HIS BLANKET..

ARE YOU SURE THAT WAS THE RIGHT THING TO DO?
OF COURSE, I'M SURE! I'M ALWAYS SURE OF EVERYTHING I DO!
SCHULZ

WHERE ARE YOU GOING?
LINUS ASKED ME TO SIT UP WITH HIM TONIGHT..

THIS FIRST NIGHT WITHOUT THE BLANKET IS GOING TO BE THE HARDEST!

January 9, 1961

PEANUTS
IS IT MORNING YET?
NO, IT'S ONLY TEN O'CLOCK.

TEN O'CLOCK?! GOOD GRIEF! THIS NIGHT IS GOING TO LAST FOREVER! I'LL NEVER MAKE IT! WHY DID LUCY HAVE TO BURY MY BLANKET? WHY?

ANYWAY, CHARLIE BROWN, IT'S NICE OF YOU TO SIT UP WITH ME THIS FIRST NIGHT..
THIS IS WHAT FRIENDS ARE FOR...

GOOD OL' CHARLIE BROWN!
1-9
SCHULZ

January 10, 1961

PEANUTS
HE'S FINALLY GONE TO SLEEP...
1-10

MAYBE IF HE CAN MAKE IT THROUGH THE NIGHT WITHOUT HIS BLANKET, HE'LL BE ALL RIGHT..

SLEEP IS WHAT HE NEEDS... IF HE CAN JUST SLEEP FOR...
SCHULZ

WELL, HOW'S HE DOING?!

January 12, 1961

PEANUTS
YOU THINK I'M BEING MEAN TO LINUS BECAUSE I BURIED HIS BLANKET, DON'T YOU?

WELL, I'M NOT! I'M REALLY DOING HIM A FAVOR! HE'S TOO WEAK EVER TO BREAK THE HABIT BY HIMSELF! HE'S AS WEAK AS... AS... WHY, HE'S AS WEAK AS YOU ARE, CHARLIE BROWN!

1-12
THAT'S A DISTURBING COMPARISON!
SCHULZ

January 13, 1961

PEANUTS
I HAVE A SUGGESTION, LINUS...

WHY DON'T YOU LET ME TRY TO FIND SOME SORT OF SUBSTITUTE FOR YOUR BLANKET?
1/13

MAYBE I COULD GET YOU A DISHTOWEL OR SOMETHING...

WOULD YOU GIVE A STARVING DOG A RUBBER BONE?
SCHULZ

January 14, 1961

PEANUTS
YOU THINK I'M BEATEN, DON'T YOU?

WELL, I'M NOT! I'M GONNA FIND THAT BLANKET IF I HAVE TO DIG UP THE WHOLE NEIGHBORHOOD!

I'LL FIND IT! DO YOU HEAR ME? I'LL FIND IT! I'LL FIND IT!!!

SCHULZ 1-14
PLEASE TELL ME WHERE IT IS!

January 17, 1961

PEANUTS
I'VE GOTTA FIND THAT BLANKET, CHARLIE BROWN!

LUCY WON'T TELL ME WHERE SHE BURIED IT SO I'VE GOTTA DIG 'TIL I FIND IT!

I'VE JUST GOTTA DIG AN' DIG AN' DIG UNTIL I FIND IT!

SCHULZ 1-17
GOOD LUCK!

January 19, 1961

PEANUTS
1-19

MY BLANKET!

OH, SNOOPY! YOU FOUND IT!! YOU FOUND IT! YOU FOUND IT! YOU FOUND IT! YOU FOUND IT!

EVERY NOW AND THEN I FEEL THAT MY EXISTENCE IS JUSTIFIED!
SCHULZ

January 21, 1961

PEANUTS
MY BLANKET! I GOT IT BACK! I CAN'T BELIEVE IT! MY GOOD OL' BLANKET!

FOR TWO WEEKS IT'S BEEN BURIED BENEATH THE GROUND..

IT'S DIRTY, IT'S RAGGED, IT'S TORN...IT'S EVEN A LITTLE MOLDY...

SCHULZ
1-21
BUT IT'S MY BLANKET!
SIGH

January 28, 1961

PEANUTS
PSYCHIATRIC HELP 5¢
5¢

I'VE BEEN VERY NERVOUS LATELY...
5¢
1-28

EVERYTHING SEEMS TO UPSET ME..I'M NERVOUS ALL THE TIME...
5¢

LEARN TO RELAX.... FIVE CENTS, PLEASE!
5¢
SCHULZ

February 2, 1961

PEANUTS

2-2

THAT WAS TOO BAD...HE SEEMED LIKE SUCH A DECENT SORT...
SCHULZ

February 8, 1961

PEANUTS
DO THEY ALWAYS BRING THE COWS IN FROM THE PASTURE AT NIGHT?

OF COURSE, YOU BLOCKHEAD! IF THEY LEAVE THEM OUT OVER NIGHT, THEY GET PASTEURIZED!!
2-8

I NEVER REALIZED THAT

I GUESS I'D MAKE A LOUSY FARMER!
SCHULZ

February 9, 1961

PEANUTS
EXERCISE, THAT'S WHAT WE NEED!

EVERYONE SHOULD START THE DAY WITH THIRTY PUSH-UPS!

HE'S RIGHT...
2-9

BUT HOW CAN YOU DO PUSH-UPS WHEN YOUR NOSE GETS IN THE WAY?
SCHULZ

February 10, 1961

PEANUTS
CAN YOU SEE ANYTHING?
UH HUH...HERE.. YOU TAKE A LOOK...

SOME OF THOSE STARS UP THERE ARE TWENTY-FIVE BILLION YEARS OLD!
2/10

THAT'S PRETTY OLD..

WHY DON'T WE TRY LOOKING AT SOME NEW ONES?
SCHULZ

February 14, 1961

PEANUTS
HERE COMES THE MAILMAN WITH ALL THE VALENTINES SENT TO ME BY MY FRIENDS..

I'LL JUST STAND HERE AND LET HIM GIVE THEM TO ME, AND THEN I'LL TAKE THE WHOLE ARMFUL INTO THE HOUSE...
2-14

..THEN I'LL OPEN THEM ONE BY ONE, AND.... AND... AND....

SIGH
SCHULZ

February 22, 1961

PEANUTS
I ALWAYS ENJOY READING THE LITTLE NOTES MY MOTHER PUTS IN MY LUNCH..
2-22

HMM...SO NOW SHE'S A COMEDIENNE...

WHY? WHAT DOES SHE SAY?

"HELP! I'M BEING HELD PRISONER IN A SCHOOL LUNCH FACTORY!"
SCHULZ

February 25, 1961

PEANUTS
"BEWARE OF THE FROG!".. WHAT DOES THAT MEAN?
BEWARE OF THE DOG

IT DIDN'T SAY, "FROG" YOU BLOCKHEAD, IT SAID, "DOG"!
WARE OF THE DOG

OH..

GOOD GRIEF!
2-25
BEWARE OF THE DOG
SCHULZ

March 2, 1961

PEANUTS
DID YOU EVER STOP TO THINK WHAT THE WORLD WOULD BE LIKE IF THERE WERE NO SUN?

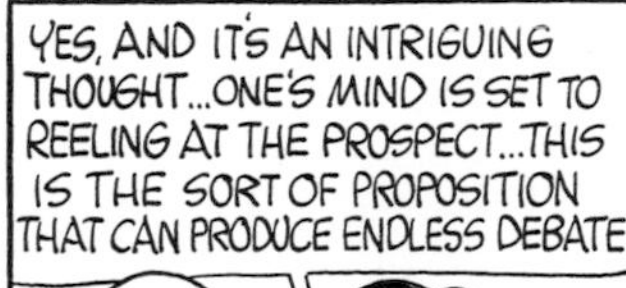
YES, AND IT'S AN INTRIGUING THOUGHT...ONE'S MIND IS SET TO REELING AT THE PROSPECT...THIS IS THE SORT OF PROPOSITION THAT CAN PRODUCE ENDLESS DEBATE

WHAT ARE **YOUR** VIEWS ON THE SUBJECT?
3-2

IT WOULD BE DARK!
SCHULZ

"I want to get the humor from the personalities of the characters, to get people to know them. It's a mistake to try to please all the readers every day. It's unreasonable to think someone should be able to pick up the paper for the first time and enjoy Peanuts. *We have to tease the reader along from day to day."*

March 6, 1961—First appearance of Frieda.

PEANUTS
?
CHARLIE BROWN, I WOULD LIKE VERY MUCH TO HAVE YOU MEET FRIEDA!

HOW DO YOU DO, FRIEDA..
HOW DO YOU DO, CHARLIE BROWN... I HAVE NATURALLY CURLY HAIR!

DO YOU FEEL THAT SPRING WILL BE HERE SOON? I BELONG TO TWELVE RECORD CLUBS! NOW THAT WE'RE GETTING A GOOD PICTURE ON OUR TV, THE PROGRAMS ARE LOUSY!
3-6

FRIEDA PRIDES HERSELF ON BEING A GOOD CONVERSATIONALIST!
SCHULZ

April 16, 1961

PEANUTS
SCHULZ

SCHULZ

May 28, 1961

PEANUTS
by SCHULZ
JUST BEFORE THE BATTLE, MOTHERRR..
I AM THINKING OF YOOO TONIGHT!
CAN'T YOU EVER BE QUIET?!
YOU'RE THE NOISIEST PERSON WHO EVER LIVED!
IF YOU'RE NOT SINGING, YOU'RE KNOCKING THINGS OVER OR RUNNING THROUGH THE HOUSE LIKE YOU'RE CRAZY!
AND TURN THAT STUPID TV DOWN
SIGH
Bread
WHAT ARE YOU DOING NOW?
MAKING MYSELF A BREAD AND BUTTER SANDWICH..
AM I BUTTERING TOO LOUD FOR YOU?
SCHULZ

"Through the years my children have given me a total of three lines for Peanuts*. Nobody could give you all those lines I've used. They come from me. But one night Amy was talking so much at the dinner table that I said, 'Couldn't you be quiet for just a little while?' And she was very quiet for a time. Then she buttered a piece of bread and said, 'Am I buttering too loud for you?'"*

April 17, 1961

PEANUTS
SEE THAT BUILDING THERE? THAT'S THE LIBRARY
IF YOU EVER WANT TO BORROW A BOOK, ALL YOU HAVE TO DO IS GO IN THERE AND TELL THEM WHICH ONE YOU WANT, AND THEY'LL LET YOU TAKE IT HOME!
FREE?
ABSOLUTELY FREE!
SORT OF MAKES YOU WONDER WHAT THEY'RE UP TO!
SCHULZ

April 21, 1961

PEANUTS
DID YOU FILL OUT THAT PAPER FOR THE SCHOOL OFFICE?
I HAVE IT RIGHT HERE...
MY MOTHER'S NAME, MY FATHER'S NAME, OUR ADDRESS AND OUR TELEPHONE NUMBER...
WHAT DID YOU PUT DOWN UNDER "FAMILY PHYSICIAN"?
WELL, I WASN'T SURE SO I PUT DOWN "DR. SEUSS"!
SCHULZ

April 26, 1961

PEANUTS
YOU CAN'T DRIFT ALONG FOREVER...

YOU HAVE TO DIRECT YOUR THINKING... FOR INSTANCE, YOU HAVE TO DECIDE WHETHER YOU'RE GOING TO BE A LIBERAL OR A CONSERVATIVE...

YOU HAVE TO TAKE SOME SORT OF STAND...YOU HAVE TO ASSOCIATE YOURSELF WITH SOME SORT OF CAUSE...
4-26

ARE THERE ANY OPENINGS IN THE LUNATIC FRINGE?
SCHULZ

May 4, 1961

PEANUTS
REMEMBER HOW KIDS USED TO MAKE LEMONADE STANDS?

I WONDER WHY YOU DON'T SEE THEM SO MUCH ANY MORE... WHAT'S TAKEN THEIR PLACE?

PSYCHIATRIC HELP 5¢
THE DOCTOR IS IN

NOW YOU KNOW!
SCHULZ
5-4

June 17, 1961

PEANUTS
LOOK AT THIS CARTOON, LUCY, AND TELL ME IF YOU THINK IT'S FUNNY

WHO DREW IT?

I DREW IT...
THEN I DON'T THINK IT'S FUNNY!

6-17
BIG SISTERS ARE THE CRAB GRASS IN THE LAWN OF LIFE!
SCHULZ

June 26, 1961

PEANUTS
I'VE JUST BEEN READING ABOUT THE DECLINE AND FALL OF THE ROMAN EMPIRE...
6-26

I'VE ALSO READ ABOUT THE DECLINE OF HOLLYWOOD, THE DECLINE OF POPULAR MUSIC, THE DECLINE OF FAMILY LIFE...

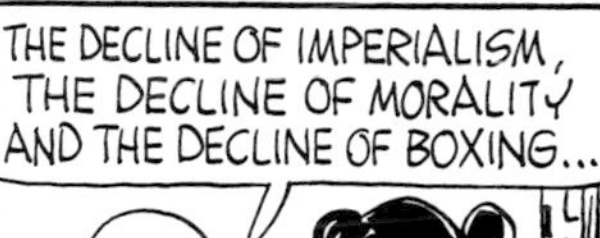
THE DECLINE OF IMPERIALISM, THE DECLINE OF MORALITY AND THE DECLINE OF BOXING...

I'VE ALWAYS BEEN FASCINATED BY FAILURE!
SCHULZ

July 5, 1961

PEANUTS
THIS IS AN INTERESTING ARTICLE
7/5

IT SAYS THAT TV IS NOT HARMFUL TO CHILDREN..

DO YOU THINK TV IS HARMFUL TO YOU, LINUS?

I DON'T KNOW...I'VE NEVER HAD ONE FALL ON ME!
SCHULZ

October 15, 1961

PEANUTS
by SCHULZ
GOOD GRIEF!
..IT WOULD TAKE YOU FOREVER TO GET THERE...
NOT NECESSARILY..
YOU'RE CONFUSED BECAUSE YOU'RE LOOKING AT A MAP WHICH IS FLAT...
COME OVER HERE..
NOW LET ME HAVE YOUR CRAYON...
TEXAS WOULD BE RIGHT ABOUT HERE ALONG THE THIRTIETH NORTH PARALLEL..
NOW, TO GET TO SINGAPORE, YOU MERELY FLY NORTH OVER THE TOP OF THE WORLD...SEE?
OH, YES, NOW I SEE... NOW, I UNDERSTAND...THAT MAKES IT A LOT MORE CLEAR...
ACTUALLY, YOU COULD GO TO ANY STORE, AND PICK UP A GOOD WORLD GLOBE FOR ABOUT TEN DOLLARS
SCHULZ

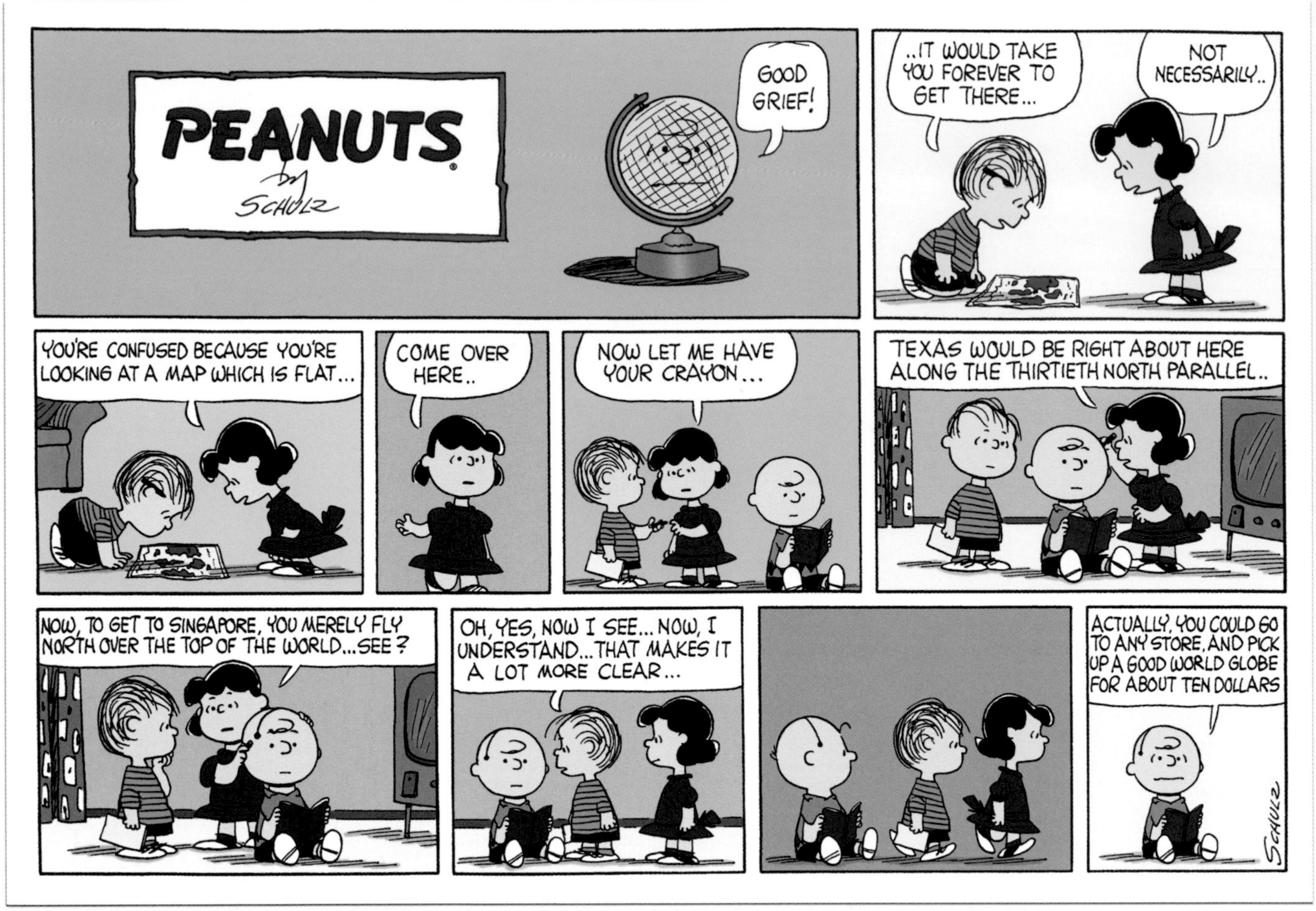

"This will come as a terrible disappointment. I've never been one much fascinated by the tools. I use simply a No. 2 pencil. I almost hate to mention the pen I use: a discontinued 914 Esterbrook Radio Pen. It's not a drawing pen, but a writing pen."

November 2, 1961

PEANUTS
DEAR PENCIL PAL,
I HAVE ALWAYS KNOWN IT WASN'T PROPER FOR ME TO WRITE TO YOU WITH PENCIL.
THEREFORE, TODAY I AM GOING TO TRY AGAIN TO WRITE TO YOU WITH
Tm. Reg. U. S. Pat. Off.—All rights reserved Copr. 1961 by United Feature Syndicate, Inc.
11-2
SIGH
SCHULZ

November 3, 1961

PEANUTS
DEAR PEN PAL,

TODAY I TAKE PEN IN HAND TO WRITE. HOW HAVE YOU BEEN?

EVERYTHING HERE IS FINE. THE WEATHER HAS BEEN WARM. PLEASE WRITE.
11-3

REGARDS, CHARLIE BROWN
SCHULZ

November 19, 1961—First mention of the Little Red-Haired Girl.

PEANUTS
by SCHULZ
SIGH!
I DON'T THINK I'D MIND SCHOOL AT ALL IF IT WEREN'T FOR THESE LUNCH HOURS...I GUESS I'LL SIT ON THIS BENCH...
I HAVE TO SIT BY MYSELF BECAUSE NOBODY ELSE EVER INVITES ME TO SIT WITH THEM...
PEANUT BUTTER AGAIN! OH, WELL, MOM DOES HER BEST...
THOSE KIDS LOOK LIKE THEY'RE HAVING A LOT OF FUN...I WISH THEY LIKED ME... NOBODY LIKES ME...
THE PTA DID A GOOD JOB PAINTING THESE BENCHES...
I'D GIVE ANYTHING IN THE WORLD IF THAT LITTLE GIRL WITH THE RED HAIR WOULD COME OVER AND SIT WITH ME..
I GET TIRED OF ALWAYS BEING ALONE...I WISH THE BELL WOULD RING...
A BANANA...RATS! MOM ALWAYS...STILL, I GUESS SHE MEANS WELL...
I BET I COULD RUN JUST AS FAST AS THOSE KIDS. THAT'S A GOOD GAME THEY'RE PLAYING...
THAT LITTLE GIRL WITH THE RED HAIR IS A GOOD RUNNER...
AH, THERE'S THE BELL! ONE MORE LUNCH HOUR OUT OF THE WAY...
TWO-THOUSAND, ONE-HUNDRED AND TWENTY TO GO!
SCHULZ

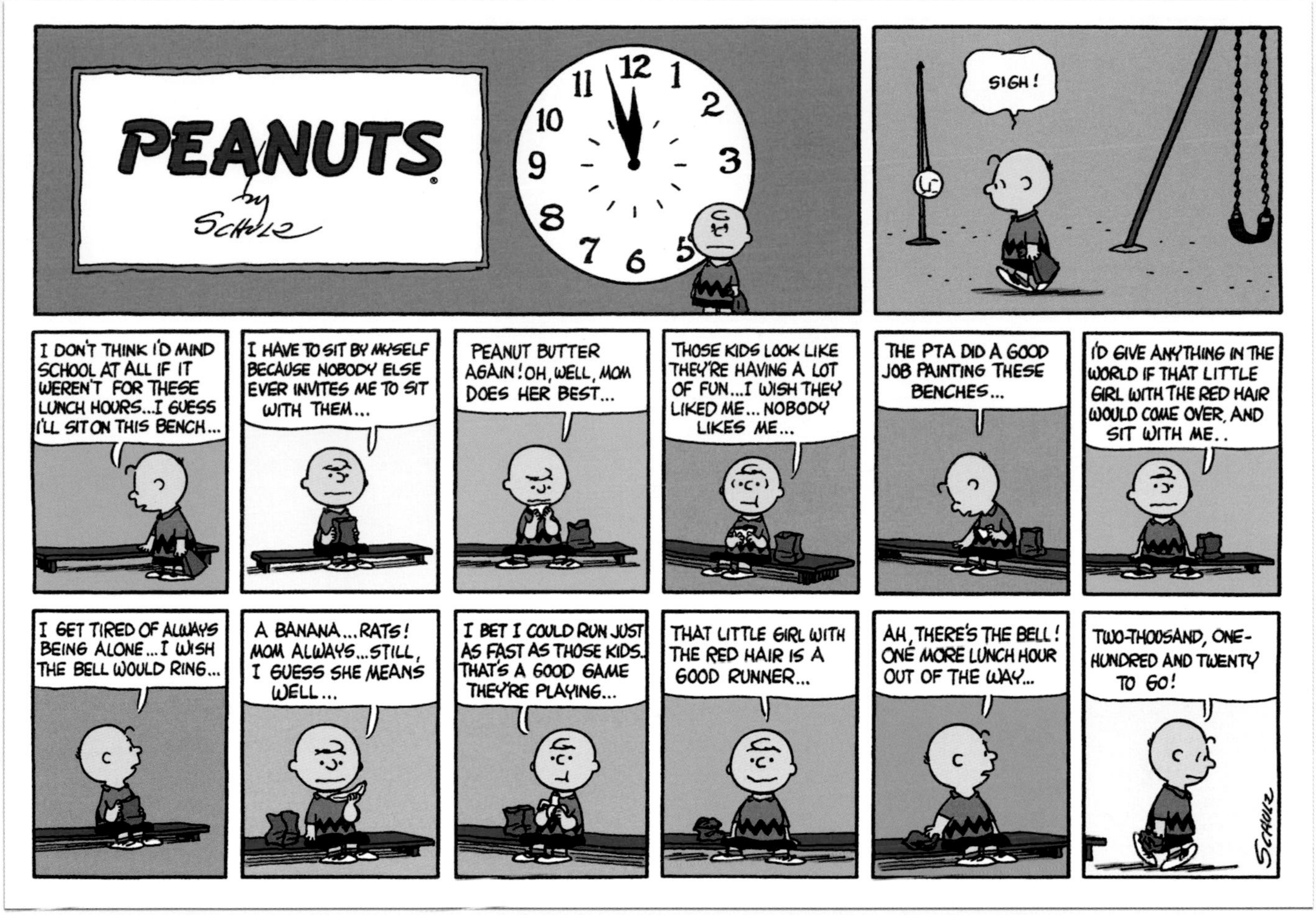

"I used to love country and western music. The whole business of Charlie Brown and the Red-Haired Girl came from listening to a Hank Williams song. I was home alone one night listening to it and it was so depressing that it occurred to me that I would do something with Charlie Brown and the Little Red-Haired Girl and that's how it all started."

November 4, 1961

PEANUTS
DEAR
RATS! I JUST CAN'T DO IT!!
YOU WANT ME TO SHOW YOU HOW TO HANDLE A PEN, CHARLIE BROWN? I'M AN EXPERT!
11-4

IT'S JUST A MATTER OF KNOWING HOW MUCH INK TO USE AND THEN BEING CAREFUL WITH THE UP-AND-DOWN STROKES...

DEAR PEN PAL
MY PROBLEM IS USUALLY MARGINS..
SCHULZ

November 6, 1961

PEANUTS
HAVE YOU EVER TRIED TO WRITE WITH A PEN, LINUS?

I'VE BEEN PRACTICING FOR A WEEK NOW, AND I THINK I'M GETTING BETTER...HERE, TRY IT..
11-6

DON'T BE WORRIED IF YOU DO POORLY AT FIRST....YOU'LL PROBABLY HAVE THE SAME TROUBLE THAT I....

Dear Pen-pal,
How are you?
SCHULZ

January 3, 1962

PEANUTS
IF I WERE YOU, I'D BE AFRAID OF WHAT THE KIDS IN SCHOOL WOULD SAY ABOUT THAT BLANKET..
DO YOU HAVE A NICKEL? TOSS IT IN THE AIR...

WHACK!
PING

THEY DON'T SAY VERY MUCH!
SCHULZ

January 30, 1962

PEANUTS
THE THOUGHT OF ANOTHER SCHOOL DAY MAKES MY STOMACH HURT!

WHEN I GET ALL THOSE ANSWERS WRONG, I GET SHARP PAINS RIGHT HERE..
1-30

THEN WHEN I SEE THE OTHER KIDS ENJOYING THEMSELVES AT LUNCH TIME WHILE I EAT ALONE, MY STOMACH STARTS TO HURT AGAIN..

MY BRAIN DOESN'T MIND SCHOOL AT ALL...IT'S MY STOMACH THAT HATES IT!
SCHULZ

February 18, 1962

PEANUTS
by SCHULZ
PLEASE TRY TO UNDERSTAND...

SIGH

YOU'RE A FINE FELLOW, BUT I CAN'T RISK YOUR FRIENDSHIP..

EVERY TIME I BECOME CLOSE FRIENDS WITH ONE OF THESE SNOWMEN, THE SUN MELTS HIM AWAY, AND I'M LEFT BROKENHEARTED

I CAN'T STAND THE AGONY...THE TERRIBLE SENSE OF LOSS...I'VE BEEN HURT TOO OFTEN...

ALTHOUGH, I WILL ADMIT YOU HAVE BEEN A GOOD NEIGHBOR...YOU LOOK QUITE HANDSOME WITH YOUR COAL EYES AND CARROT NOSE..

OH, WELL, ONE CAN'T DELIBERATELY AVOID FRIENDSHIPS, I GUESS...

YOU CAN'T KEEP TO YOURSELF JUST BECAUSE YOU'RE AFRAID OF BEING HURT, OR...

AAUGH!
SOB

POOR SNOOPY...I SEE HE'S LOST ANOTHER FRIEND.. IT'S TOO BAD.... HE'S SO SENSITIVE...
UH, HUH... BUT I NOTICE HE WASN'T TOO SENSITIVE TO EAT THE CARROT!
SCHULZ

February 5, 1962

PEANUTS
..AND SO THE OPHTHALMOLOGIST SAID I HAVE TO START WEARING GLASSES...
2-5

AT FIRST I WAS PRETTY UPSET... IT WAS A REAL EMOTIONAL BLOW.. ALL SORTS OF THINGS WENT THROUGH MY MIND...

BUT, FINALLY, ONE THOUGHT SEEMED TO STAND OUT..
WHAT WAS THAT?

IT'S KIND OF NICE TO BE ABLE TO SEE WHAT'S GOING ON!
SCHULZ

February 20, 1962

PEANUTS

ZOOM

WITH A LITTLE PRACTICE I BET I COULD GET THE SHOES, TOO!
2-20
SCHULZ

March 17, 1962

PEANUTS
EVERYWHERE YOU GO YOU SEEM TO RUN INTO PHONIES!
3-17

THE PEOPLE YOU THINK ARE SINCERE USUALLY TURN OUT NOT TO BE, AND THE PEOPLE YOU THINK **AREN'T** SINCERE USUALLY TURN OUT TO **BE** SINCERE!

THE QUESTION IS...HOW DO YOU TELL THE PHONIES FROM THE REALIES?

THE "**REALIES**"?!
SCHULZ

March 19, 1962

PEANUTS
I'VE DECIDED WE NEED A BASEBALL SCOUT!

WE NEED SOMEONE TO GO OVER, AND MINGLE WITH THE OTHER TEAM, AND FIND OUT THEIR STRENGTH AND WEAKNESSES..

IT CAN BE A VERY DANGEROUS JOB, OF COURSE, BUT IT'S A JOB THAT NEEDS TO BE DONE, AND...

I'VE FOUND YOU A VOLUNTEER!
3-19
SCHULZ

March 20, 1962

PEANUTS
YOU WANT ME TO BE A **SPY**?
NOT A SPY.. A SCOUT! A BASEBALL SCOUT!

I'LL ADMIT IT'S A DANGEROUS JOB, BUT IT HAS TO BE DONE!

NOW, I SUPPOSE THE FIRST QUESTION THAT COMES TO YOUR MIND IS, "**WHY** DOES THIS JOB HAVE TO BE DONE?"
3-20

NO, THE FIRST QUESTION THAT COMES TO MY MIND IS, "**WHY ME?**"
SCHULZ

March 21, 1962

PEANUTS
ALL RIGHT, SO I'M A BASEBALL SCOUT...WHAT DO I DO?
YOU GO, AND FIND OUT ALL YOU CAN ABOUT THEIR PITCHERS AND HITTERS..

WRITE EVERYTHING YOU FIND OUT ON THIS SQUARE OF BUBBLE GUM..IF THEY SUSPECT THAT YOU'RE SCOUTING THEM, YOU CAN JUST CHEW UP THE EVIDENCE...

WELL, GOOD LUCK, OL' BUDDY...
THANK YOU, CHARLIE BROWN..
3-21

SOMEHOW I HAVE THE FEELING OF IMPENDING DOOM!
SCHULZ

March 23, 1962

PEANUTS
WELL, I'M BACK, CHARLIE BROWN, AND I FOUND OUT EVERYTHING YOU WANTED TO KNOW..
3-23

I EVEN WROTE IT ALL DOWN ON A SQUARE OF BUBBLE GUM LIKE YOU TOLD ME SO IF THE OTHER TEAM BECAME SUSPICIOUS, I COULD CHEW IT UP, AND DESTROY THE NOTES

WELL, WHAT DID YOU FIND OUT? WHERE'S YOUR REPORT?

SCHULZ

March 24, 1962

PEANUTS
I WATCHED THIS TEAM PRACTICE, SEE? THEY WERE TERRIBLE! ANYBODY COULD BEAT THEM!

NONE OF THEIR PLAYERS CAN HIT A BALL OUT OF THE INFIELD! AND THEY HAVE THIS LOUD-MOUTHED GIRL IN CENTER FIELD WHO CAN'T CATCH A THING!
3-24

THEY ALSO HAVE SOME ANIMAL AT SECOND BASE WHO CAN'T EVEN THROW, AND THEIR PITCHER IS KIND OF A ROUND-HEADED KID WHO IS ABSOLUTELY NO GOOD AT ALL! AND..

YOU SCOUTED YOUR OWN TEAM!!!
SCHULZ

April 2, 1962

PEANUTS
BOY, LOOK AT IT RAIN!
I'VE NEVER SEEN IT RAIN SO HARD FOR SUCH A LONG TIME..
I'M JUST GLAD I'M INSIDE..

WELL, GOOD GRIEF, ONLY A REAL BLOCKHEAD WOULD BE OUT IN A RAIN LIKE THIS...

4-2
WHERE IS EVERYBODY?
SCHULZ

April 4, 1962

PEANUTS
WHEN I LOOK FORWARD TO A BALL GAME, I DON'T WANT TO BE DISAPPOINTED

I DON'T SEE WHY A LITTLE RAIN SHOULD KEEP EVERYBODY AWAY! IF I CAN SHOW UP TO PLAY, I DON'T SEE WHY THE OTHERS CAN'T!

MAYBE I'M JUST MORE DETERMINED THAN THEY ARE.. MAYBE I'M JUST MORE STUBBORN..

4-4
..MAYBE I'M JUST MORE STUPID!
SCHULZ

April 5, 1962

PEANUTS
I DON'T THINK THERE'S ANYONE IN THE WORLD WHO IS DUMBER THAN MY BROTHER!

HE IS REALLY DUMB! WHY, JUST THE OTHER DAY I WAS TELLING HIM THAT HE WAS SO DUMB, HE DIDN'T EVEN KNOW ENOUGH TO COME IN OUT OF THE...............
4-5

OH, I......I......I DIDN'T...I MEAN, I...I...

OH, WELL...IF YOU'RE GOING TO GO AROUND WATCHING EVERY WORD YOU SAY ALL THE TIME, YOU'LL NEVER GET MUCH SAID!
SIGH
SCHULZ

April 7, 1962

PEANUTS

THANK YOU!
YOU'RE WELCOME!
SCHULZ
4-7

"Some things happen in the strip simply because I enjoy drawing them. Rain is fun to draw. I pride myself on being able to make nice strokes with the point of the pen, and I also recall how disappointing a rainy day can be to a child. When I think back to those ball games that we looked forward to as teenagers, and how crushed we were if the game had to be postponed because of rain, it brings to mind emotions that can be translated into cartoon ideas."

April 22, 1962

PEANUTS
by SCHULZ
HOW CAN I PLAY BASEBALL IN THE RAIN? MY GLASSES ARE SO FOGGED UP I CAN'T EVEN SEE!
THIS IS STUPID!
YOU'RE NOT QUITTING?!
OF COURSE, I'M QUITTING! EVERYONE ELSE HAS GONE HOME! WHY SHOULDN'T I?
BUT WE NEED THE PRACTICE!
WHAT'S A LITTLE RAIN?
EVERYBODY, COME BACK! WE NEED THE PRACTICE!!
A LITTLE RAIN NEVER HURT ANYBODY!
SCHULZ

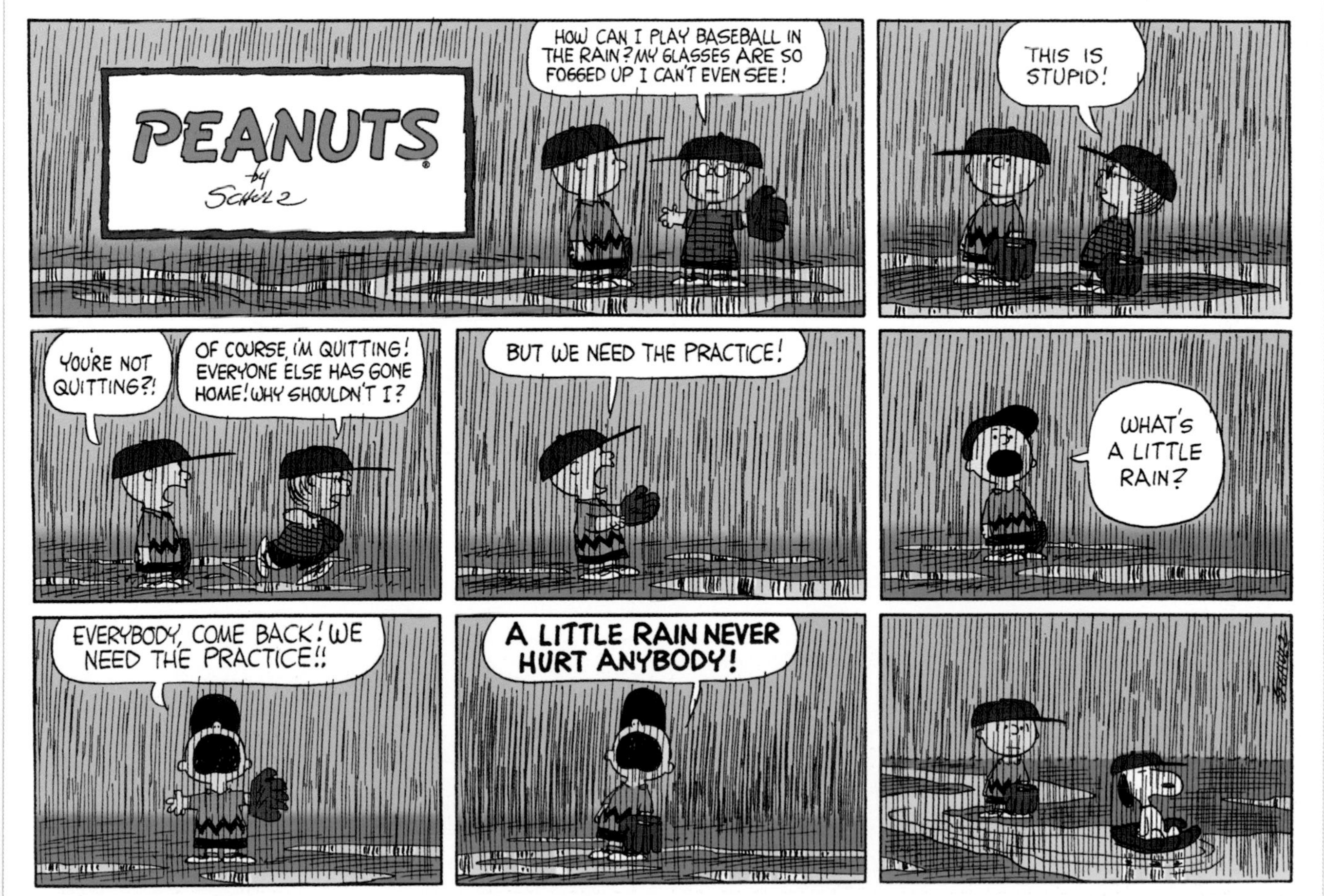

April 9, 1962

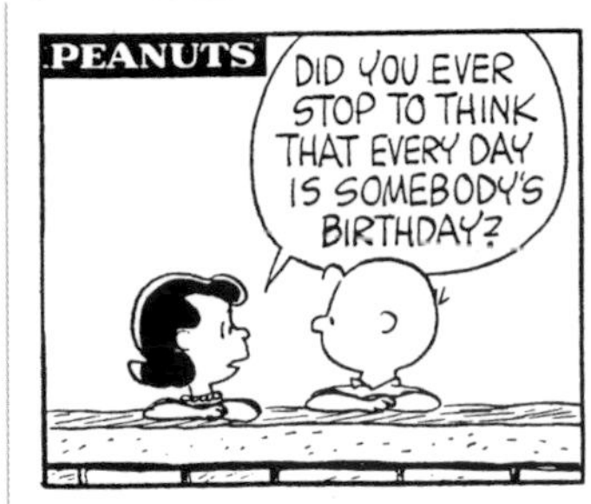
PEANUTS
DID YOU EVER STOP TO THINK THAT EVERY DAY IS SOMEBODY'S BIRTHDAY?

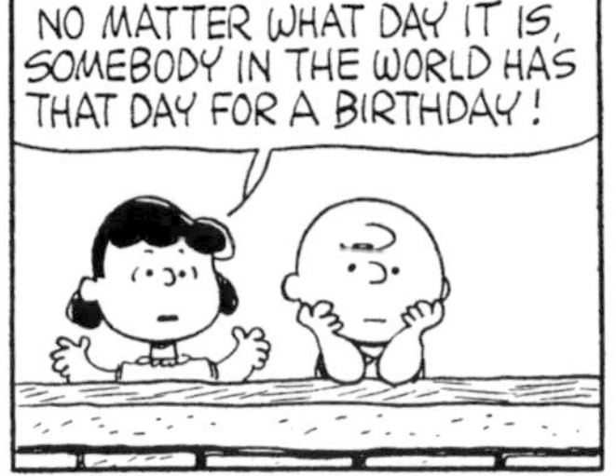
NO MATTER WHAT DAY IT IS, SOMEBODY IN THE WORLD HAS THAT DAY FOR A BIRTHDAY!

HAVE YOU EVER THOUGHT ABOUT THAT, CHARLIE BROWN?
NO, I CAN'T REALLY SAY THAT I HAVE...
4-9

YOU'RE GOING TO HAVE TROUBLE WHEN YOU GET TO COLLEGE!
SCHULZ

May 20, 1962

PEANUTS
by
SCHULZ

AAUGH!

IT'S A STORY I'VE BEEN READING CALLED "THE PIT AND THE PENDULUM" BY POE, AND IT'S ABOUT THIS MAN, SEE, WHO IS A PRISONER....

HE'S TIED TO A TABLE, AND THIS BIG PENDULUM KEEPS SWINGING BACK AND FORTH ABOVE HIM, GETTING NEARER AND NEARER...

IT SOUNDS LIKE AN EXCITING STORY.. I'LL HAVE TO READ IT..
I THINK YOU'D ENJOY IT.. I REALLY DO...

SCHULZ
THAT EDGAR ALLAN POE WAS A RIOT..

April 12, 1962

PEANUTS
DO YOU WEAR GLASSES BECAUSE YOU'RE FARSIGHTED OR NEARSIGHTED?
4-12

WHICH IS WHICH?
WELL, FARSIGHTED IS WHEN YOU CAN.. OR IS THAT NEARSIGHTED?

FARSIGHTED IS WHEN YOU CAN SEE THINGS THAT...OR IS IT THE OTHER WAY AROUND? MAYBE IT'S WHEN YOU... OR MAYBE...OR MAYBE IT'S...
SCHULZ

I WEAR GLASSES SO I CAN SEE BETTER!

May 7, 1962

PEANUTS
THIS IS A REPORT ON WHAT SORT OF MEN MAKE THE BEST HUSBANDS

DENTISTS, DRAFTSMEN, HOCKEY PLAYERS, WELL-DIGGERS AND LUMBER SALESMEN RATE THE HIGHEST...PIANO PLAYERS RATE SHOCKINGLY LOW!

WHERE DID YOU GET A REPORT LIKE THAT?

I JUST MADE IT UP!

May 27, 1962

PEANUTS
by SCHULZ
IT'S FUNNY I NEVER FIND ANY FOUR-LEAF CLOVERS OUT HERE...

YOU'D THINK THERE'D BE LOTS OF THEM OUT HERE...

HEY, FRIEDA..HOW'RE THINGS IN RIGHT FIELD?

KIND OF BORING...YOU GOING TO THE PARTY WEDNESDAY AFTERNOON?

I SURE AM..YOU SHOULD SEE WHAT MY MOTHER BOUGHT ME TO WEAR...

IT'S A WHITE PARTY DRESS WITH A HUGE SASH OF SUGAR PINK SATIN!

?
WUMP!

KEEP PITCHIN' 'EM IN THERE, CHARLIE BROWN, OL' BOY... WE'RE RIGHT BEHIND YOU!

May 10, 1962

PEANUTS
YOU WANT TO HEAR SOME **REAL** MUSIC? LISTEN TO THIS!

POLKAS, SCHOTTISHES AND WALTZES
POLKAS, SCHOTTISHES AND WALTZES

SEE? THAT'S REAL MUSIC! THAT'S THE SORT OF MUSIC THAT PEOPLE LIKE! NOT THAT OL' BEETHOVEN STUFF!

I CAN'T STAND IT! I JUST CAN'T STAND IT!
POLKAS, SCHOTTISHES AND WALTZES
POLKAS, SCHOTTISHES AND WALTZES

May 15, 1962

PEANUTS
WHAT'S THE BEST WAY TO KEEP COOL DURING WARM WEATHER?
5-15

OH, I DON'T KNOW...I CAN THINK OF SEVERAL GOOD WAYS..

I GUESS DIFFERENT PEOPLE HAVE DIFFERENT METHODS..
SCHULZ

July 5, 1962

PEANUTS
IT SAYS HERE THAT THE FORCE OF GRAVITATION IS 13% LESS TODAY THAN IT WAS 4½ BILLION YEARS AGO..
7-5

WHOSE FAULT IS THAT?
WHOSE FAULT IS IT? IT'S NOBODY'S FAULT...

WHAT DO YOU MEAN, NOBODY'S FAULT! IT HAS TO BE SOMEBODY'S FAULT! SOMEBODY'S GOT TO TAKE THE BLAME!

FIND A SCAPEGOAT!!
SCHULZ

July 16, 1962

PEANUTS
7-16

SO WHAT'S SO MUCH FUN ABOUT A BALLOON?
SCHULZ

August 10, 1962

PEANUTS
I CAN SWIM! I CAN SWIM!!

I JUST LEARNED HOW TO SWIM! I CAN SWIM FOUR FEET!

WELL, I'M GLAD TO HEAR THAT, LINUS...CONGRATULATIONS..
8-10

YES, SIR...IF I'M EVER ABOARD AN OCEAN LINER, AND IT SINKS FOUR FEET FROM SHORE, I WON'T HAVE A THING TO WORRY ABOUT!
SCHULZ

August 11, 1962

PEANUTS
HERE'S SOMETHING I THINK ABOUT QUITE OFTEN..

I'M SITTING IN THE STANDS AT THE BALL GAME, SEE...SUDDENLY A LINE DRIVE IS HIT MY WAY..EVERYBODY DUCKS, BUT I STICK UP MY HAND, AND MAKE A GREAT CATCH!

8-11

THE MANAGER OF THE HOME TEAM SEES ME, AND YELLS, "SIGN THAT KID UP!"

HAVE YOU EVER HEARD OF ANYONE ELSE HAVING THAT DREAM?
ONLY ABOUT THIRTY BILLION OTHER KIDS!
SCHULZ

October 17, 1962

PEANUTS
SOMETIMES I GET DISCOURAGED
WELL, LUCY, LIFE DOES HAVE ITS UPS AND DOWNS, YOU KNOW...
10-17

BUT WHY? WHY SHOULD IT?! WHY CAN'T MY LIFE BE ALL "UPS"? IF I WANT ALL "UPS," WHY CAN'T I HAVE THEM?

WHY CAN'T I JUST MOVE FROM ONE "UP" TO ANOTHER "UP"? WHY CAN'T I JUST GO FROM AN "UP" TO AN "UPPER-UP"?

I DON'T WANT ANY "DOWNS"! I JUST WANT "UPS" AND "UPS" AND "UPS"!
I CAN'T STAND IT...
SCHULZ

October 22, 1962

PEANUTS
YOU'RE SO CRABBY ALL THE TIME YOU'VE FORGOTTEN HOW TO SMILE!

WHO'S FORGOTTEN HOW TO SMILE?
YOU HAVE! LET'S SEE YOU SMILE! I'LL BET YOU CAN'T!

THERE! SEE? A SMILE GOES UP, NOT DOWN! YOU'VE FORGOTTEN HOW TO SMILE! SEE?!
10-22

HOW HUMILIATING!
SCHULZ

October 31, 1962

PEANUTS
ALL RIGHT, SALLY...YOU WANT PROOF...YOU'RE GOING TO GET IT...
10-31

WE'LL JUST SIT HERE IN THIS PUMPKIN PATCH, AND YOU'LL SEE THE "GREAT PUMPKIN" WITH YOUR OWN EYES!

IF YOU TRY TO HOLD MY HAND, I'LL SLUG YOU!!
SCHULZ

December 3, 1962

PEANUTS

!

MY MOTHER DIDN'T RAISE ME TO BE A SKI-SLOPE!
12-3
SCHULZ

December 10, 1962

PEANUTS
HERE'S YOUR CRAYONS...THANKS FOR LETTING ME USE THEM!

12-10

IT'S HARD TO GET MAD AT SOMEONE WHO RETURNS THINGS SO PROMPTLY...
SCHULZ

December 27, 1962

PEANUTS
THANK YOU FOR THE CHRISTMAS CARD YOU SENT ME, LUCY

I NEVER SENT YOU ANY CHRISTMAS CARD, CHARLIE BROWN

DON'T YOU KNOW SARCASM WHEN YOU HEAR IT?!
SCHULZ
12-27

January 20, 1963

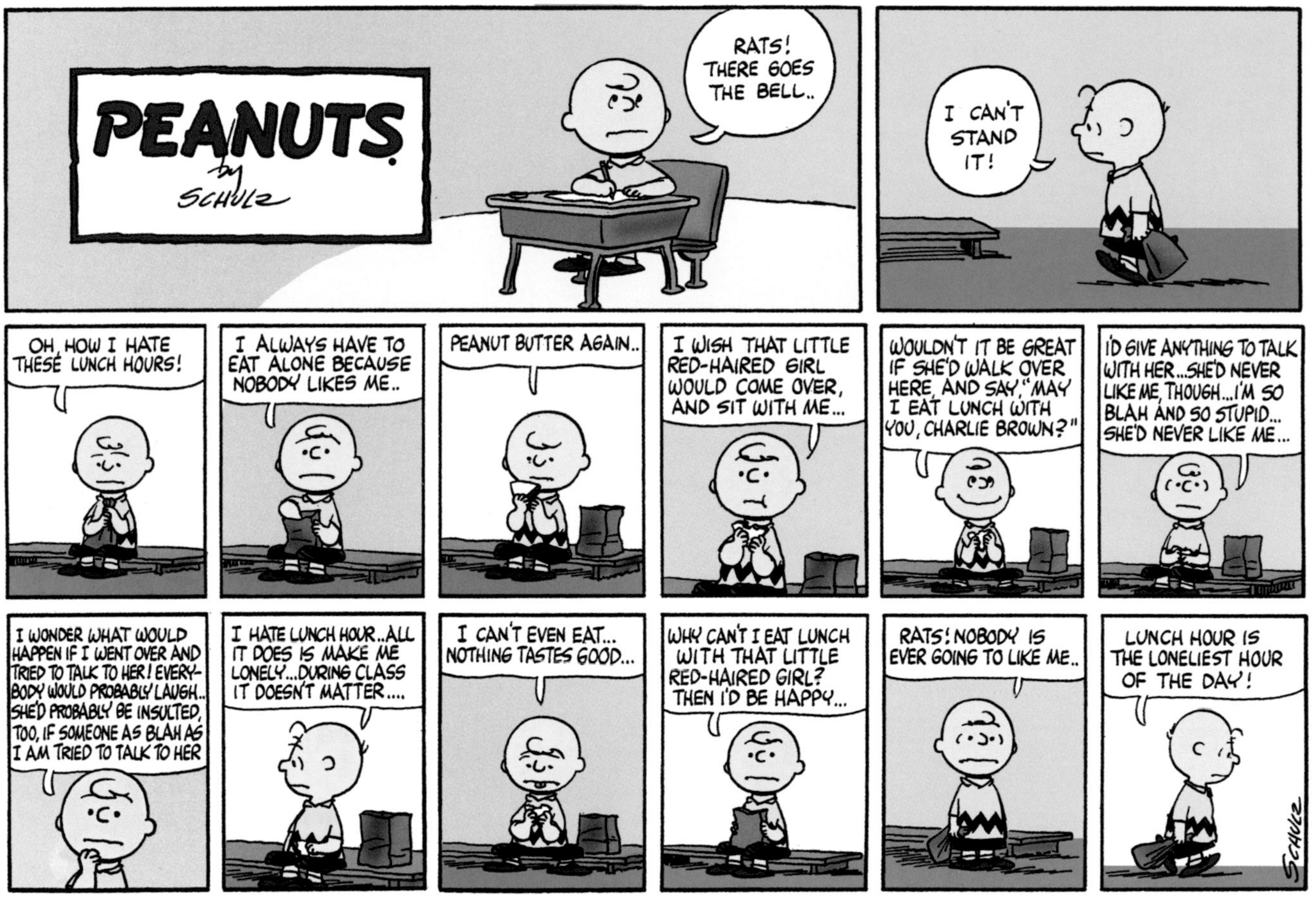

PEANUTS by SCHULZ

RATS! THERE GOES THE BELL..

I CAN'T STAND IT!

OH, HOW I HATE THESE LUNCH HOURS!

I ALWAYS HAVE TO EAT ALONE BECAUSE NOBODY LIKES ME..

PEANUT BUTTER AGAIN..

I WISH THAT LITTLE RED-HAIRED GIRL WOULD COME OVER, AND SIT WITH ME...

WOULDN'T IT BE GREAT IF SHE'D WALK OVER HERE, AND SAY, "MAY I EAT LUNCH WITH YOU, CHARLIE BROWN?"

I'D GIVE ANYTHING TO TALK WITH HER...SHE'D NEVER LIKE ME, THOUGH...I'M SO BLAH AND SO STUPID... SHE'D NEVER LIKE ME...

I WONDER WHAT WOULD HAPPEN IF I WENT OVER AND TRIED TO TALK TO HER! EVERYBODY WOULD PROBABLY LAUGH.. SHE'D PROBABLY BE INSULTED, TOO, IF SOMEONE AS BLAH AS I AM TRIED TO TALK TO HER

I HATE LUNCH HOUR..ALL IT DOES IS MAKE ME LONELY...DURING CLASS IT DOESN'T MATTER....

I CAN'T EVEN EAT... NOTHING TASTES GOOD...

WHY CAN'T I EAT LUNCH WITH THAT LITTLE RED-HAIRED GIRL? THEN I'D BE HAPPY...

RATS! NOBODY IS EVER GOING TO LIKE ME..

LUNCH HOUR IS THE LONELIEST HOUR OF THE DAY!

"Well, I know about loneliness. I won't talk about it, but I was very lonely after the war. I know what it feels like to spend a whole weekend all by yourself and no one wants you at all."

January 23, 1963

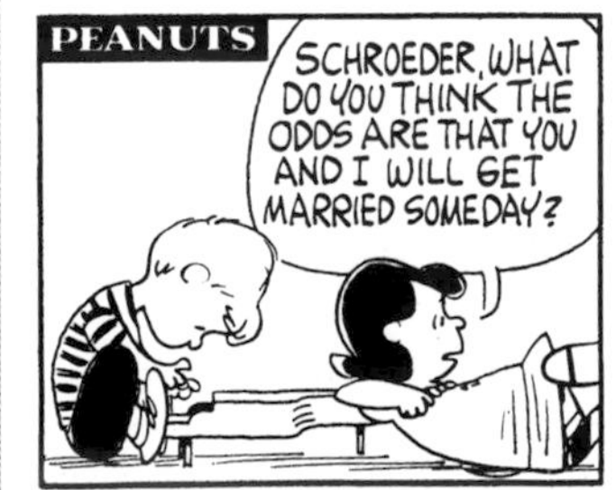
PEANUTS
SCHROEDER, WHAT DO YOU THINK THE ODDS ARE THAT YOU AND I WILL GET MARRIED SOMEDAY?

OH, I'D SAY ABOUT "GOOGOL" TO ONE
HOW MUCH IS A "GOOGOL"?

10,000,000,000,000,000,000,000,000,000,000,000,000,000,000,000,000,000,000,000,000,000,000,000,000,000,000,000,000,000,000,000,000,000,000
1/23

SCHULZ
SIGH

February 8, 1963

PEANUTS
"HERE'S THE CHURCH...
2-8

..HERE'S THE STEEPLE... OPEN THE DOOR...

...AND SEE ALL THE PEOPLE!"

IT LOOKS LIKE A RATHER SMALL CONGREGATION!
SCHULZ

March 24, 1963

PEANUTS by SCHULZ

AND I'VE GOT LINUS DOWN FOR RIGHT-FIELD..

LINUS?

RIGHT-FIELD? ARE YOU SURE?

OF COURSE, I'M SURE..

WATCH..

3-24

WHAP

PLUNK

ALL RIGHT... WHO YOU GOT DOWN FOR **LEFT** FIELD?

SCHULZ

February 23, 1963

PEANUTS
I'D LIKE TO MAKE A LOT OF MONEY, BUT I'D HATE TO BE A SNOB..

I'VE GIVEN THIS A LOT OF THOUGHT
SO WHAT HAVE YOU DECIDED?

SO I'VE DECIDED TO BE A VERY RICH AND FAMOUS PERSON WHO DOESN'T REALLY CARE ABOUT MONEY, AND WHO IS VERY HUMBLE BUT WHO STILL MAKES A LOT OF MONEY AND IS VERY FAMOUS, BUT IS VERY HUMBLE AND RICH AND FAMOUS..

GOOD LUCK!
SCHULZ
2-23

February 28, 1963

PEANUTS
WHAT IF EVERYONE WAS LIKE YOU?

WHAT IF WE ALL RAN AWAY FROM OUR PROBLEMS? HUH? WHAT THEN?

WHAT IF EVERYONE IN THE WHOLE WORLD SUDDENLY DECIDED TO RUN AWAY FROM HIS PROBLEMS?
2-28

WELL, AT LEAST WE'D ALL BE RUNNING IN THE SAME DIRECTION!
SCHULZ

April 6, 1963

PEANUTS
GOOD GRIEF!
4-6

ONE HUNDRED AND EIGHTY-FOUR TO NOTHING!

I DON'T UNDERSTAND IT...

HOW CAN WE LOSE WHEN WE'RE SO SINCERE?!
SCHULZ

April 10, 1963

PEANUTS
"SOON HANSEL AND GRETEL CAME TO A LITTLE COTTAGE"

"WHEN THEY GOT QUITE NEAR, THEY SAW THAT THE LITTLE HOUSE WAS MADE OF BREAD AND ROOFED WITH CAKE"
4-10

"THE WINDOWS WERE TRANSPARENT SUGAR"

THERE MUST NOT HAVE BEEN A VERY STRICT BUILDING CODE..
SCHULZ

April 16, 1963

PEANUTS
I JUST DON'T FEEL VERY WELL TODAY...

MAYBE I'D BETTER NOT PLAY..
THAT'S A GOOD IDEA, CHARLIE BROWN...STAY HOME, AND REST..
4-16

YOU'VE BEEN STRIKING OUT EVERY TIME YOU GOT UP ANYWAY... IT'LL BE BEST IF YOU STAY HOME..

DON'T LET YOUR TEAM DOWN BY SHOWING UP!
SCHULZ

May 22, 1963

PEANUTS
WHAT'S THE MATTER WITH YOU?

MY FINGERS HURT...
5-22

MAYBE YOUR FINGERNAILS ARE TOO TIGHT...

I NEVER EVEN KNEW THEY WERE ADJUSTABLE!
SCHULZ

May 19, 1963

PEANUTS
by SCHULZ
EMPTY! AND I'M DYING OF THIRST!
5-19
THAT'S ONE I'M GOING TO HAVE TO THINK ABOUT FOR AWHILE!
SCHULZ

June 5, 1963

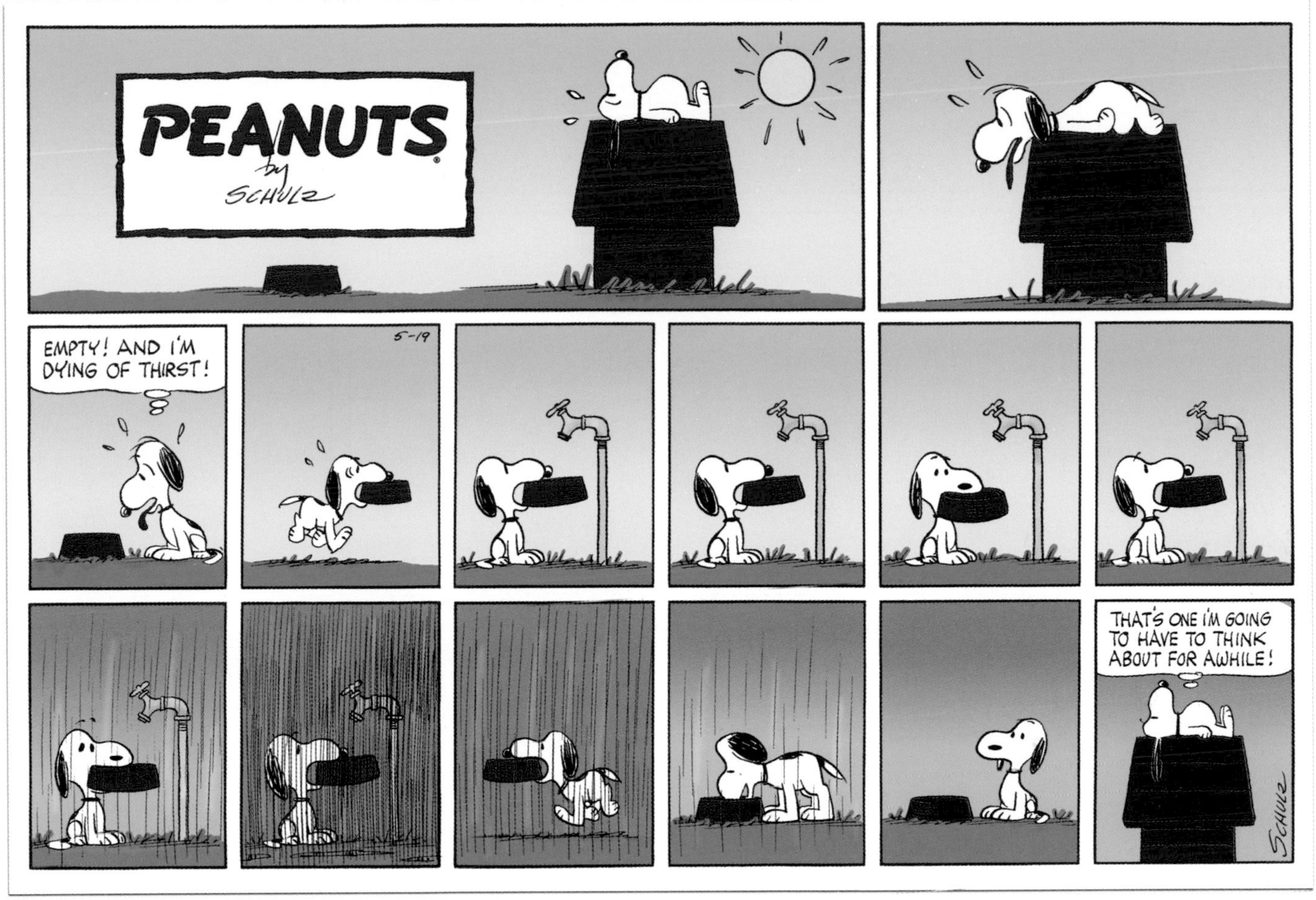

PEANUTS
SNOOPY, SCHROEDER CAN'T BE WITH US TODAY...
HOW ABOUT YOU BEING OUR CATCHER? ACTUALLY, YOU'RE THE BEST PLAYER I HAVE..
HERE...TRY ON THIS MASK AND CHEST PROTECTOR SO WE CAN SEE HOW YOU LOOK..
6-5
MMM...PERHAPS WE'D BETTER ASK SOMEONE ELSE
SCHULZ

June 6, 1963

PEANUTS
YOU WANT **ME** TO BE CATCHER?
YES, SCHROEDER CAN'T MAKE IT TODAY..
6-6

DO I HAVE TO WEAR ALL **THIS**?
OF COURSE... IT'S FOR YOUR OWN GOOD..

I FEEL LIKE I'M IN A BIRD CAGE...

TWEET TWEET CHIRP CHIRP ♪ ♪ ♪ ♪
ALL RIGHT, WE CAN DO WITHOUT THAT!
SCHULZ

June 11, 1963

PEANUTS
LITTLE GIRLS NEED BIG BROTHERS..
6-11

BIG BROTHERS ARE STRONG, AND WHEN YOU'RE WALKING ALONG THE STREET THEY MAKE YOU FEEL SECURE

SORT OF!
SCHULZ

July 18, 1963

PEANUTS
HAS LINUS TOLD YOU ABOUT THE DANGERS OF LOOKING AT THE ECLIPSE?

YES, HE'S TOLD ME ALL ABOUT IT...
I'M HEEDING HIS WARNING...I DON'T WANT TO DO ANYTHING THAT MIGHT HARM MY BEAUTIFUL EYES...
7-18

DO YOU THINK MY EYES ARE BEAUTIFUL, CHARLIE BROWN?

YES, THEY LOOK LIKE LITTLE ROUND DOTS OF INDIA INK!
SCHULZ

July 20, 1963

PEANUTS
7-20

SO HOW'S THE ECLIPSE?

July 30, 1963

PEANUTS
IF I CAN HOLD THESE GUYS FOR ONE MORE INNING, OUR TEAM WILL WIN THE CHAMPIONSHIP

WELL, IF THEY'RE GOING TO BEAT US, THEY'RE REALLY GOING TO HAVE TO TRY!

POW!

I HATE IT WHEN THEY TRY!
7-30
SCHULZ

July 31, 1963

PEANUTS
ALL RIGHT, SO THEY HAVE A MAN ON FIRST... I'M NOT GOING TO LET THAT BOTHER ME..

SMACK!

7-31
ALL RIGHT, SO THEY HAVE MEN ON FIRST AND SECOND.. I'M NOT GOING TO LET THAT BOTHER ME..
SCHULZ

"Baseball is the ideal sport for the kind of humor I've used in the strip. There is the contemplative quality of the baseball player—of the pitcher standing still there on the mound, rubbing the ball, and there are two out and men on second and third and it's the last half of the ninth. Then someone walks up to the mound and what does he say? You have the suspense right before you. It works perfectly for Charlie Brown."

August 2, 1963

PEANUTS
8-2
"BALL FOUR"

GOOD GRIEF! I'VE LOADED THE BASES!

ONE RUN WILL TIE UP THE GAME, AND ANOTHER RUN WILL LOSE US THE CHAMPIONSHIP...

MY STOMACH HURTS!
SCHULZ

August 5, 1963

PEANUTS
BALK!!
?
!

HE BALKED IN THE TYING RUN!
OH, NO!

OH, NO! OH, NO! OH, NO!

OWOOOOOOOO!
8-5
SCHULZ

August 7, 1963

PEANUTS
DON'T SAY ANYTHING TO ME!

DON'T ANYONE SAY ANYTHING TO ME! I KNOW I LOST US THE CHAMPIONSHIP!
8-7

NOBODY HAS TO TELL ME I'M A BLOCKHEAD! I KNOW I'M A BLOCKHEAD! NOBODY HAS TO TELL ME!

YOU BLOCKHEAD!
SCHULZ

August 8, 1963

PEANUTS
ALL RIGHT, MOM...ALL RIGHT...

WHEN OTHER PITCHERS LOSE BALL GAMES, THEY GET SENT TO THE SHOWERS...

WHEN I LOSE A BALL GAME, DO I GET SENT TO THE SHOWERS? NO!
8-8

I HAVE TO TAKE A BATH!
SCHULZ

August 23, 1963

PEANUTS
8-23

SCHULZ

September 2, 1963

PEANUTS
WHY DON'T YOU EVER CALL ME "CUTIE"?

WHAT?
WHY DON'T YOU EVER COME UP TO ME, AND SAY, "HI, CUTIE"?
9/2

BECAUSE I DON'T THINK YOU'RE VERY CUTE

I HATE REASONS!
SCHULZ

September 6, 1963

PEANUTS
SCHOOL STARTS MONDAY...

NOT FOR ME!
9-6

WHAT DO YOU MEAN, NOT FOR YOU?

I WENT LAST YEAR!
SCHULZ

September 11, 1963

PEANUTS
"I PLEDGE ALLEGIANCE TO THE FLAG OF THE UNITED STATES OF AMERICA..
9-11

..AND TO THE REPUBLIC FOR WHICH IT STANDS, ONE NATION UNDER GOD, INDIVISIBLE, WITH LIBERTY AND JUSTICE FOR ALL"

AMEN!
SCHULZ

September 19, 1963

PEANUTS
HOW WOULD YOU LIKE TO GO FOR A WALK, SNOOPY?
9-19

HA! I KNEW YOU WOULD!

ALL DOGS LIKE TO GO FOR WALKS...

THIS ISN'T EXACTLY WHAT I HAD IN MIND...
SCHULZ

September 23, 1963

PEANUTS
DID YOUR DAD TAKE YOU TO MANY BALL GAMES THIS YEAR?
9-23

OH, YES...WE WENT TO QUITE A FEW

I THINK HE LIKES HAVING A SON TO TAKE TO THE BALL GAME...

I'M SORT OF A BUILT-IN FRIEND!
SCHULZ

September 22, 1963

PEANUTS
by SCHULZ
I'M IN SAD SHAPE..

GOOD MORNING, SIR.. SIT RIGHT DOWN..
FINE...I WAS AFRAID I MIGHT NEED AN APPOINTMENT..
THE DOCTOR IS IN

PSYCHIATRIC HELP 5¢
WHAT CAN YOU DO WHEN YOU DON'T FIT IN?
THE DOCTOR IS IN
9-22

WHAT CAN YOU DO WHEN LIFE SEEMS TO BE PASSING YOU BY?

FOLLOW ME..I WANT TO SHOW YOU SOMETHING..

SEE THE HORIZON OVER THERE? SEE HOW BIG THIS WORLD IS? SEE HOW MUCH ROOM THERE IS FOR EVERYBODY?

HAVE YOU EVER SEEN ANY OTHER WORLDS?
NO

AS FAR AS YOU KNOW THIS IS THE ONLY WORLD THERE IS.... RIGHT?
RIGHT

THERE ARE NO OTHER WORLDS FOR YOU TO LIVE IN...RIGHT?
RIGHT

YOU WERE BORN TO LIVE IN THIS WORLD...RIGHT?
RIGHT

WELL, LIVE IN IT, THEN!

FIVE CENTS, PLEASE..
SCHULZ

October 10, 1963

PEANUTS
MY MOTHER HAS MADE ARRANGEMENTS FOR ME TO TAKE PIANO LESSONS...

I WON'T BE PLAYING ON A TOY PIANO EITHER...I'LL BE PLAYING ON A **REAL** PIANO!

10-10
YOU'RE CUTE WHEN YOU GET MAD...
SCHULZ

October 22, 1963

PEANUTS

WHOP!

10-22
I LOVE TOUCH FOOTBALL!
SCHULZ

November 12, 1963

PEANUTS
I ALWAYS HAVE TO EAT LUNCH ALONE
I'D SURE LIKE TO EAT LUNCH WITH THAT LITTLE RED-HAIRED GIRL..

I WONDER WHAT WOULD HAPPEN IF I WALKED OVER, AND ASKED HER TO EAT LUNCH WITH ME...
11-12

SHE'D PROBABLY LAUGH RIGHT IN MY FACE..

IT'S HARD ON A FACE WHEN IT GETS LAUGHED IN
SCHULZ

November 18, 1963

PEANUTS
I WISH I HAD A STICK-HORSE..

EVERYBODY'S GOT A STICK-HORSE EXCEPT ME..
11-18

EVERYBODY!!
SCHULZ

November 19, 1963

PEANUTS
I HEAR THE PRICE OF HAIRCUTS MAY GO UP AGAIN..

YES, ISN'T THAT GREAT?! THEN MY DAD CAN BUY FOUR NEW CARS, A SWIMMING POOL AND A STABLE OF RIDING HORSES!
11-19

WE CAN EAT STEAK EVERY NIGHT, AND SPEND ALL OUR WINTERS ON THE RIVIERA!

I NEVER KNEW A BARBER'S SON COULD BE SO SARCASTIC..
SCHULZ

November 20, 1963

PEANUTS
MY DAD IS STILL WORRIED ABOUT THE PRICE OF HAIRCUTS..

HE'S THREATENING AGAIN TO BUY ONE OF THOSE KITS, AND CUT MY HAIR HIMSELF
THAT'S A GOOD IDEA... AND WHILE YOU'RE AT IT, WHY DON'T YOU WRITE YOUR OWN BOOKS, PAINT YOUR OWN PAINTINGS AND COMPOSE YOUR OWN MUSIC?
11-20

I NEVER REALIZED THAT BARBERS' SONS WERE SO SENSITIVE...
SCHULZ

December 22, 1963

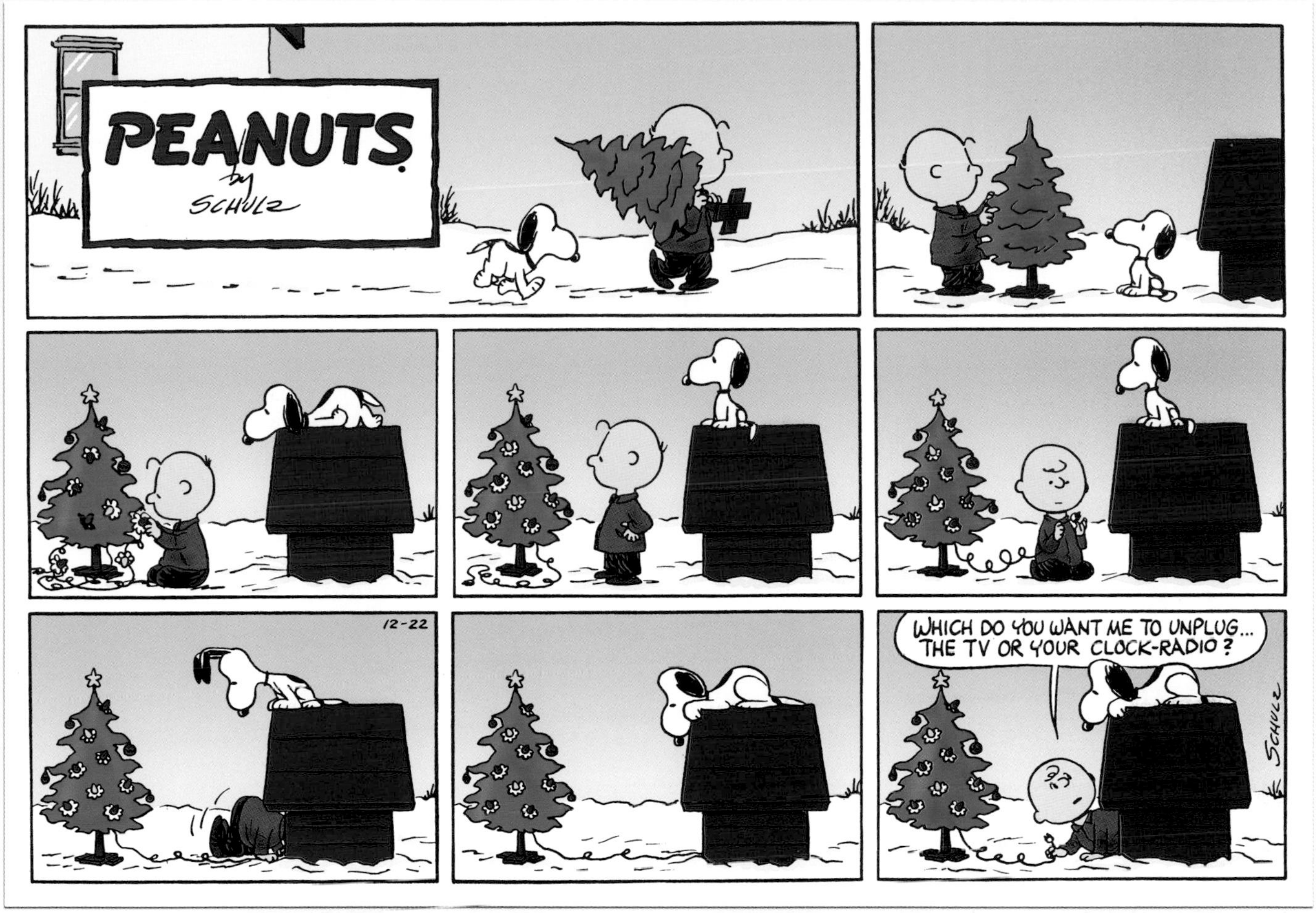

PEANUTS
by SCHULZ

12-22

WHICH DO YOU WANT ME TO UNPLUG... THE TV OR YOUR CLOCK-RADIO?

SCHULZ

"Well, I draw for myself, which is who I think we all draw for. We draw for ourselves and hope that people like it. But the licenses keep driving it down for little kids. We did the first television show, A Charlie Brown Christmas; *we did the best show we could do and what happens? We win an Emmy for the best children's animated show of the year. We didn't draw it for kids. We drew it for grown-ups. I just draw for myself and draw it as well as I can."*

December 16, 1963

PEANUTS
HERE..HAPPY BEETHOVEN'S BIRTHDAY!
WELL! THANK YOU!

THIS IS A PICTURE OF JOHANN STRAUSS...

I KNOW... THEY WERE ALL OUT OF BEETHOVEN...
12/16

DOES IT MAKE A DIFFERENCE?
SCHULZ

January 10, 1964

PEANUTS
1-10

MAIL

I GUESS SOMEBODY'S GETTING HUNGRY!
SCHULZ

January 22, 1964

PEANUTS
THIS IS A STEEP HILL, SNOOPY..

BUT WE'RE NOT AFRAID, ARE WE?

WE KNOW THAT NO MATTER WHAT DANGERS LIE AHEAD, WE CAN FACE THEM IF WE STICK TOGETHER..
1-22

SCHULZ

January 5, 1964

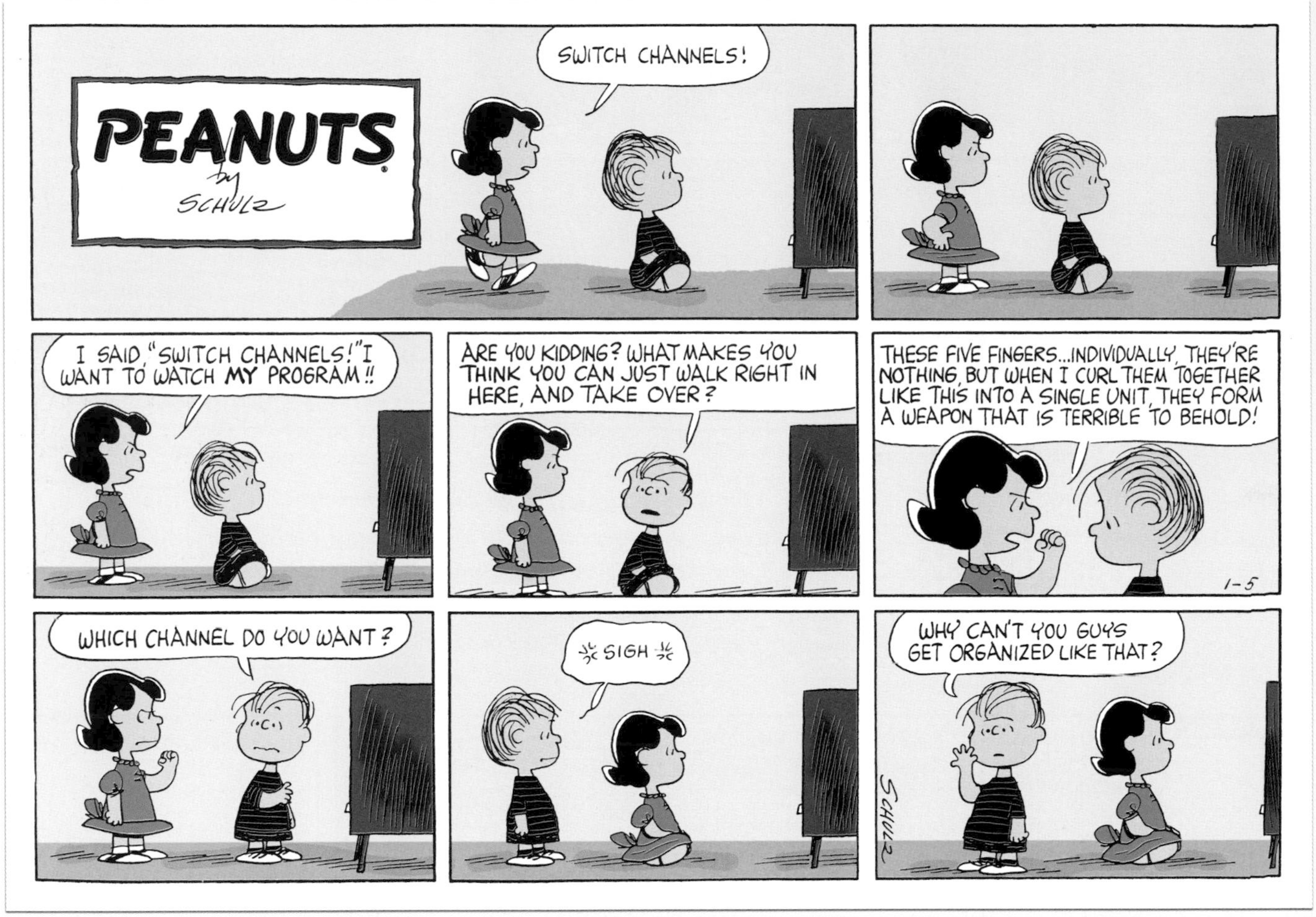

PEANUTS
by SCHULZ

SWITCH CHANNELS!

I SAID, "SWITCH CHANNELS!" I WANT TO WATCH **MY** PROGRAM!!

ARE YOU KIDDING? WHAT MAKES YOU THINK YOU CAN JUST WALK RIGHT IN HERE, AND TAKE OVER?

THESE FIVE FINGERS...INDIVIDUALLY, THEY'RE NOTHING, BUT WHEN I CURL THEM TOGETHER LIKE THIS INTO A SINGLE UNIT, THEY FORM A WEAPON THAT IS TERRIBLE TO BEHOLD!

1-5

WHICH CHANNEL DO YOU WANT?

SIGH

WHY CAN'T YOU GUYS GET ORGANIZED LIKE THAT?

SCHULZ

"Lucy comes from that part of me that's capable of saying mean and sarcastic things, which is not a good trait to have, so Lucy gives me a good outlet."

January 23, 1964

PEANUTS
YOU KNOW WHAT THE WHOLE TROUBLE WITH YOU IS, CHARLIE BROWN?
1-23

NO, AND I DON'T WANT TO KNOW! LEAVE ME ALONE!

THE WHOLE TROUBLE WITH YOU IS YOU WON'T LISTEN TO WHAT THE WHOLE TROUBLE WITH YOU IS!
SCHULZ

January 24, 1964

PEANUTS
YOU NEED ME TO POINT OUT YOUR FAULTS, CHARLIE BROWN...IT'S FOR YOUR OWN GOOD...
1-24
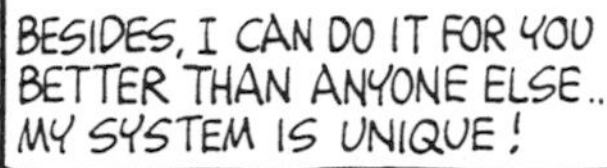
BESIDES, I CAN DO IT FOR YOU BETTER THAN ANYONE ELSE... MY SYSTEM IS UNIQUE!

WHAT'S SO UNIQUE ABOUT IT?

I'VE PUT ALL YOUR FAULTS ON SLIDES SO WE CAN PROJECT THEM ON A SCREEN!
OH, GOOD GRIEF!
SCHULZ

January 27, 1964

PEANUTS
OKAY..TURN OFF THE LIGHTS...
1-27

NOW, THIS AFTERNOON, CHARLIE BROWN, WE'RE GOING TO BE LOOKING AT SLIDES WHICH DEAL WITH YOUR MANY PERSONALITY FAULTS... SOME OF THEM ARE QUITE SHOCKING! TAKE THIS ONE FOR INSTANCE...

AAUGH!
EASY..EASY.. THIS IS ONLY THE BEGINNING..

January 29, 1964

PEANUTS
WHAT WE'RE VIEWING TODAY, CHARLIE BROWN, ARE SLIDES OF YOUR INHERITED FAULTS..

IN OTHER WORDS, THESE ARE FAULTS OVER WHICH YOU HAD NO REAL CONTROL...THESE TAKE ABOUT AN HOUR TO SHOW...
1-29
SCHULZ

IF IT'S ANY CONSOLATION TO YOU, YOU RANK ABOUT AVERAGE IN INHERITED FAULTS..

I STAND CONSOLED!

January 31, 1964

PEANUTS
TODAY WE'RE REALLY GOING TO GET DOWN TO BUSINESS, CHARLIE BROWN..
1-31

THESE SLIDES SHOW YOUR BIGGEST AND MOST DAMAGING FAULTS...
SCHULZ

BECAUSE OF THEIR IMPORTANCE, THEY WILL BE SHOWN IN COLOR

WHICH IS WORSE, A GREEN FAULT, A BLUE FAULT OR A PINK FAULT?

February 1, 1964

PEANUTS
AUGH! TURN IT OFF!!

I CAN'T STAND IT ANY LONGER! I CAN'T STAND IT!

I'VE NEVER GONE THROUGH ANYTHING LIKE THAT IN MY LIFE! I NEVER KNEW I HAD SO MANY FAULTS! I'VE NEVER FELT SO COMPLETELY MISERABLE
2-1
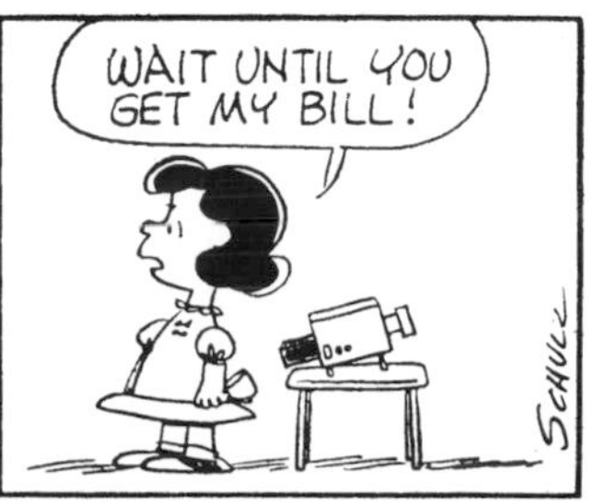
WAIT UNTIL YOU GET MY BILL!
SCHULZ

February 20, 1964

PEANUTS
I SEE YOU FOUND YOUR BLANKET..

YES, THERE WAS A LITTLE MIX-UP IN THE KITCHEN..
2-20

LUCY WAS USING MY BLANKET TO DRY THE DISHES...

WE NOW HAVE VERY SECURE DISHES!
SCHULZ

February 22, 1964

PEANUTS
2-22

SCHULZ

February 24, 1964

PEANUTS
2-24

SEE IF IT'S STILL RAINING...

I CAN'T TELL..MY ARMS ARE TOO SHORT!
SCHULZ

February 25, 1964

PEANUTS
2-25

THE FLOOD WATERS ARE RISING

RATS!

MY CARPETING WILL BE RUINED!
SCHULZ

February 27, 1964

PEANUTS
WHEN IS IT GOING TO STOP RAINING?

I DON'T KNOW..IT'S BEEN COMING DOWN FOR DAYS...EVERYTHING'S FLOODED, AND...GOOD GRIEF!
2-27

SNOOPY!

THIS IS THE END! I'M CROSSING THAT OL' RIVER JORDAN!
SCHULZ

February 28, 1964

PEANUTS
YOU CAN'T GO OUT IN THIS RAIN!

I'VE GOT TO! SNOOPY'S OUT THERE STRANDED ON TOP OF HIS DOGHOUSE! HE NEEDS HELP!

2-28

WAIT! DON'T BOTHER...

SCHULZ

February 29, 1964

PEANUTS
I'LL CHECK TO SEE IF THE WATER HURT ANY OF YOUR THINGS, SNOOPY..

I DON'T THINK THERE WAS TOO MUCH DAMAGE..THE TV STILL WORKS..EVERYTHING SEEMS OKAY
2/29

OH, AND HERE'S GOOD NEWS FOR YOU...

YOUR VAN GOGH WASN'T HARMED A BIT!
WHAT A RELIEF!
SCHULZ

March 1, 1964

PEANUTS
by SCHULZ
I SHOULDN'T BE HERE..
ONE, PLEASE

I SHOULD GET OUT OF LINE AND GO HOME..

I FEEL GUILTY ABOUT GOING TO THE SHOW TODAY...I SHOULD BE HOME HELPING MY MOTHER..
ONE, PLEASE

I HAVE SCHOOLWORK TO DO, TOO...I HAVE A BOOK REPORT TO WRITE AND ABOUT TEN PAGES OF ARITHMETIC...
ONE, PLEASE

I REALLY SHOULDN'T BE GOING TO THE SHOW..I FEEL AWFULLY GUILTY ABOUT IT...I SHOULD GO HOME..
ONE, PLEASE

I CAN'T REALLY ENJOY A SHOW WHEN I FEEL GUILTY ABOUT GOING TO IT...I SHOULD JUST GET OUT OF LINE, AND GO BACK HOME..
ONE, PLEASE

3-1
ONE, PLEASE

GOOD OL' WISHY-WASHY CHARLIE BROWN..ONE, PLEASE..

April 1, 1964

PEANUTS
CHARLIE BROWN, THAT LITTLE RED-HAIRED GIRL WANTS YOU TO COME OVER, AND EAT LUNCH WITH HER..

APRIL FOOL!
4-1
SCHULZ

April 7, 1964

PEANUTS
4-7

I DON'T **WANT** ANOTHER RABIES SHOT!
SCHULZ

April 30, 1964

PEANUTS
ARE YOU READY FOR THE PARTY, LINUS?
4-30

YES...I'M JUST COMBING MY HAIR...I'M SOAKING IT DOWN WITH LOTS OF WATER...

I'M AFRAID, THOUGH, OF WHAT WILL HAPPEN WHEN I GET OUT IN THE...

...SUNSHINE!
SCHULZ

May 12, 1964

PEANUTS
CHARLIE BROWN, I WANT TO ASK YOU SOMETHING..
5-12

DO YOU THINK I'M A CRABBY PERSON?

YES, I THINK YOU'RE A VERY CRABBY PERSON

WELL, WHO CARES WHAT YOU THINK?!
SCHULZ

May 13, 1964

PEANUTS
LINUS, DO YOU THINK I'M A VERY CRABBY PERSON?

STAND RIGHT THERE... DON'T MOVE!

5-13

YES, I THINK YOU'RE A VERY CRABBY PERSON!
SCHULZ

May 3, 1964

PEANUTS
by
SCHULZ
TRUTH

WHAT'S THIS?

IT'S A PROJECT FOR SCHOOL...WE'RE SUPPOSED TO DRAW SOMEONE IN OUR FAMILY...

I NOTICE YOU HAVEN'T PUT IN THE MOUTH YET..

WELL, UH...THERE'S NO REAL HURRY...IT DOESN'T HAVE TO BE FINISHED TODAY...IN FACT, I WAS JUST THINKING OF QUITTING...
PUT IN THE MOUTH..I WANT TO WATCH YOU..

NO, I THINK I'LL WAIT...IT'S WRONG TO RUSH A WORK OF ART..THERE'S NO REAL HURRY ANYWAY...I THINK I'LL JUST WAIT...
PUT IN THE MOUTH!

POW!

IT'S HARD TO DRAW WELL WHEN YOUR HAND IS SHAKING!
SCHULZ
5-3

"I still think drawing is the most important aspect of cartooning. The words, the ideas are important, but weren't Chaplin, say, or Laurel and Hardy funny just by their appearance. Weren't they basically cartoons of people? Good cartooning is at heart good design. If a character looks good to you, it's because he's been well designed, well placed in nice shapes within the four panels you have to work with. Keeping it simple is the key."

May 14, 1964

PEANUTS
MAYBE I AM TOO CRABBY...

MAYBE I SHOULD TRY TO BE NICER TO PEOPLE...

I SUPPOSE I COULD IF I REALLY TRIED..
5/14

OH, HOW I HATE TO GIVE THE REST OF THE WORLD THAT SATISFACTION!
SCHULZ

May 15, 1964

I'M ON A NEW CAMPAIGN TO BE NICE TO PEOPLE..
5-15

WHILE I'M AT IT, I SUPPOSE I MIGHT AS WELL INCLUDE DOGS..

HERE'S A NICE PAT ON THE HEAD..

THRILLSVILLE!
SCHULZ

June 20, 1964

PEANUTS

6-20

WHAT'S SO HAPPY ABOUT A WARM PUPPY ?
SCHULZ

June 21, 1964

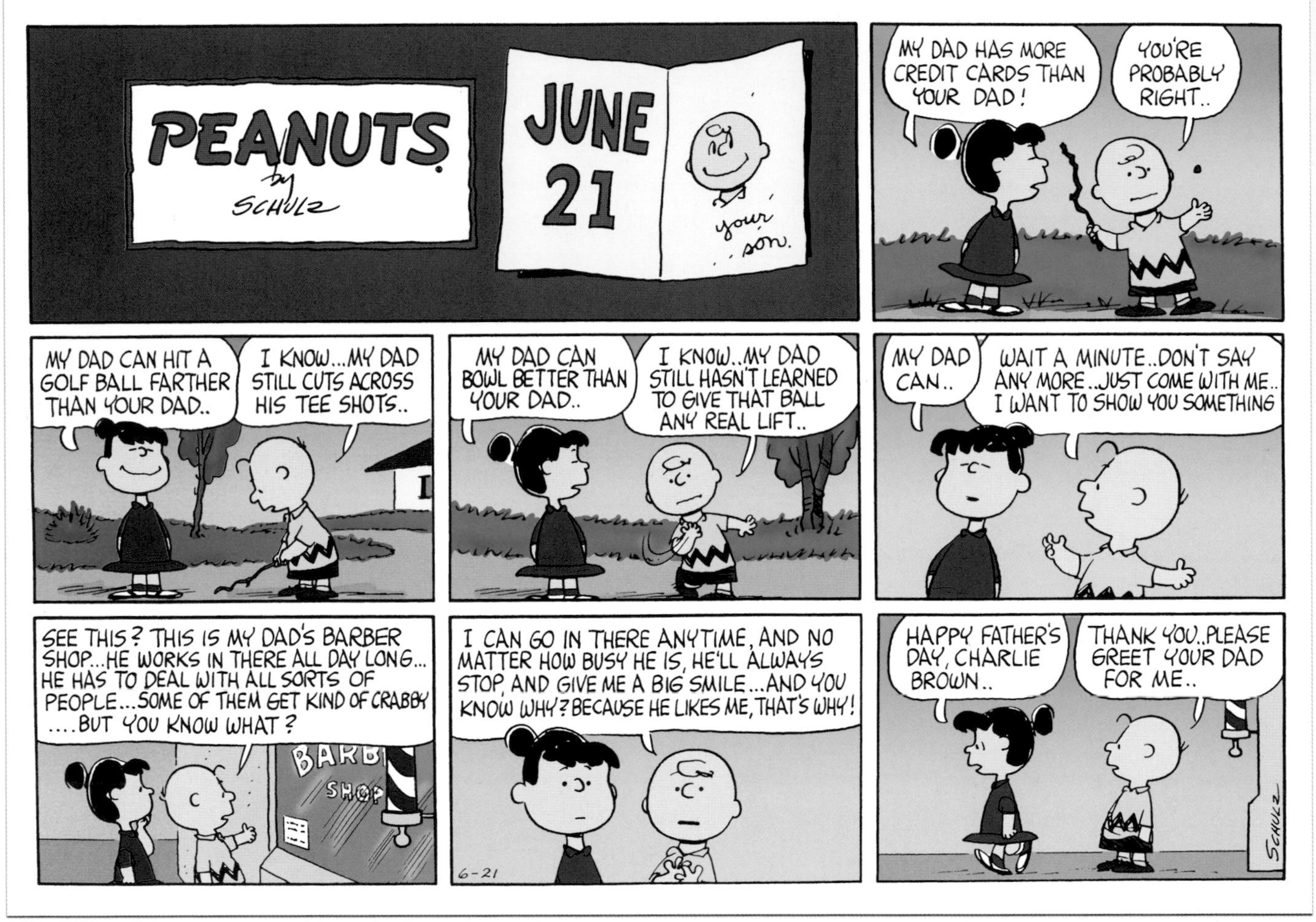

PEANUTS by SCHULZ
JUNE 21
your son.

MY DAD HAS MORE CREDIT CARDS THAN YOUR DAD!
YOU'RE PROBABLY RIGHT..

MY DAD CAN HIT A GOLF BALL FARTHER THAN YOUR DAD..
I KNOW...MY DAD STILL CUTS ACROSS HIS TEE SHOTS..

MY DAD CAN BOWL BETTER THAN YOUR DAD..
I KNOW..MY DAD STILL HASN'T LEARNED TO GIVE THAT BALL ANY REAL LIFT..

MY DAD CAN..
WAIT A MINUTE..DON'T SAY ANY MORE..JUST COME WITH ME.. I WANT TO SHOW YOU SOMETHING

SEE THIS? THIS IS MY DAD'S BARBER SHOP...HE WORKS IN THERE ALL DAY LONG... HE HAS TO DEAL WITH ALL SORTS OF PEOPLE...SOME OF THEM GET KIND OF CRABBY ....BUT YOU KNOW WHAT?
BARB SHOP

I CAN GO IN THERE ANYTIME, AND NO MATTER HOW BUSY HE IS, HE'LL ALWAYS STOP, AND GIVE ME A BIG SMILE...AND YOU KNOW WHY? BECAUSE HE LIKES ME, THAT'S WHY!
6-21

HAPPY FATHER'S DAY, CHARLIE BROWN..
THANK YOU..PLEASE GREET YOUR DAD FOR ME..
SCHULZ

"Some of the offstage characters reach a point where they could never be drawn. I think the Little Red-Haired Girl is a lot like the inside of Snoopy's doghouse. Each of us can imagine what she must look like much better than I could ever draw her, and I am sure that every reader sees a different doghouse interior and would be a little disappointed if I were to attempt to draw it in detail."

June 22, 1964

PEANUTS
SNOOPY, I HAVE A SURPRISE FOR YOU...

SOME OF YOUR FRIENDS HAVE AGREED TO GET TOGETHER, AND GIVE YOUR HOUSE A REAL GOOD CLEANING...

WE'LL BE STARTING TOMORROW.. I JUST THOUGHT YOU'D LIKE TO KNOW...

JUST SO THEY DON'T DAMAGE MY VAN GOGH OR TEAR THE CLOTH ON MY POOL TABLE!
6-22
SCHULZ

June 23, 1964

PEANUTS
I BROUGHT A BROOM, CHARLIE BROWN
GOOD...SCHROEDER SAID HE'D BRING A DUST PAN..

I BROUGHT A PAIL OF WATER, CHARLIE BROWN, AND VIOLET HAS SOME DUST RAGS...
GREAT

BE CAREFUL GOING DOWN THE STAIRS...TRY NOT TO SPILL WATER ON THE CARPET...

I FEEL LIKE I SHOULD BE DOING SOMETHING TO HELP..
6-23
SCHULZ

June 24, 1964

PEANUTS
?
OKAY.. EASY NOW..

WATCH OUT... THERE'S A TURN HERE IN THE STAIRWAY..

6-24
DON'T DROP THEM, OR WE'LL HAVE GLASS ALL OVER EVERYTHING

DON'T YOU EVER RETURN ANY OF YOUR EMPTY POP BOTTLES?!
HOW EMBARRASSING!
SCHULZ

June 25, 1964

PEANUTS
GOT IT ROLLED UP? OKAY, BRING IT OUT..

GOOD WORK

WE'RE SENDING THE CARPET OUT TO BE CLEANED

WHO'S GOING TO PAY FOR ALL THIS?
6-25
SCHULZ

June 26, 1964

PEANUTS
LOOK AT ALL THE STUFF IN THESE CLOSETS!

6-26
AND WHAT ABOUT THIS?
DON'T THROW IT AWAY... HE MIGHT WANT TO SAVE IT..

LOOK AT THIS!
AND THIS! ISN'T THIS SOMETHING?
WHY WOULD HE WANT SOMETHING LIKE THAT?

I DON'T KNOW IF I'M HAVING MY HOUSE CLEANED OR BEING PSYCHOANALYZED!
SCHULZ

June 29, 1964

PEANUTS
6-29
WE'RE ALL DONE, CHARLIE BROWN...

THE FLOORS ARE POLISHED
WE STRAIGHTENED UP ALL THE CLOSETS..
AND CLEANED OFF ALL THE COUNTER TOPS

WE EVEN VACUUMED THE TOP OF THE POOL TABLE
HE NOW HAS THE CLEANEST HOUSE IN THE WHOLE NEIGHBORHOOD

ISN'T IT NICE TO HAVE FRIENDS?
SCHULZ

July 6, 1964

PEANUTS
WHAT IF WE WERE REAL POOR?

WHAT IF YOU AND I HAD TO GET JOBS TO HELP SUPPORT MOM AND DAD?

I COULD WORK... I COULD EARN MONEY...
WHAT COULD YOU DO?

I COULD MAKE MY BED!
SCHULZ
7-6

August 20, 1964

PEANUTS
DON'T LET HIM HIT IT, CHARLIE BROWN! DON'T LET HIM HIT IT!
8-20

POW!

YOU LET HIM HIT IT!
SCHULZ

December 15, 1964

PEANUTS
THAT LITTLE RED-HAIRED GIRL IS SURE CUTE..

I'D GIVE ANYTHING IN THE WORLD TO BE SITTING THERE NEXT TO HER EATING LUNCH..

12-15
BLEAH!

NOTHING TAKES THE TASTE OUT OF PEANUT BUTTER LIKE UNREQUITED LOVE!
SCHULZ

December 17, 1964

PEANUTS
WHY DON'T I GO OVER AND TALK TO THAT LITTLE RED-HAIRED GIRL?

I CAN'T... I JUST CAN'T...

I HATE MYSELF FOR NOT HAVING ENOUGH NERVE TO TALK TO HER!
12-17

WELL, THAT ISN'T EXACTLY TRUE... I HATE MYSELF FOR A LOT OF OTHER REASONS, TOO...
SCHULZ

January 22, 1965

PEANUTS
1-22

RATS!

IT'S LONELY SKATING BY YOURSELF AT NIGHT..
SCHULZ

March 2, 1965

PEANUTS
WHAT BALANCE!
3-2

I SHOULD HAVE BEEN A GREAT TRAPEZE ARTIST

ONE HUNDRED FEET IN THE AIR WITHOUT USING A..

SCHULZ
NET!

August 23, 1964

PEANUTS by SCHULZ
THEY'RE IN THE TREE AGAIN..
BY THIS TIME YOU'D THINK THEY'D KNOW BETTER!
MOM SAYS FOR YOU GUYS TO GET DOWN FROM THAT TREE RIGHT NOW!
8-23
STUPID KIDS!
SHE SAYS, "WHAT ARE YOU TRYING TO DO...BREAK YOUR NECKS?"
THAT MEANS YOU, TOO!
SCHULZ

April 1, 1965

PEANUTS
MY HEART IS FULL ON THE DAY I FIRST GO OUT TO THE OL' BALL FIELD...

I LOVE THE SMELL OF THE HORSEHIDE, THE GRASSY OUTFIELD AND THE DUSTY INFIELD...I LOVE THE MEMORIES..THE HOPES...AND THE DREAMS FOR THE NEW SEASON..
4-1

AH! THERE IT IS! MY PITCHER'S MOUND...COVERED WITH TRADITION..

AND DANDELIONS!
SCHULZ

April 2, 1965

PEANUTS
THIS PITCHER'S MOUND IS COVERED WITH DANDELIONS
DON'T TOUCH THEM, CHARLIE BROWN!

DON'T YOU DARE HURT ALL THOSE INNOCENT DANDELIONS! THEY'RE BEAUTIFUL! DON'T YOU DARE CUT THEM DOWN!

BESIDES, YOU MAY NOT KNOW IT, BUT YOU LOOK KIND OF CUTE STANDING THERE SURROUNDED BY DANDELIONS..

I DON'T WANT TO LOOK CUTE!!

April 3, 1965

PEANUTS
HERE WE GO... THE FIRST PITCH OF THE SEASON..

POW!

IT'S KIND OF PEACEFUL LYING HERE AMONG THE DANDELIONS..

April 5, 1965

PEANUTS
WHAT IN THE WORLD ARE ALL THESE DANDELIONS DOING ON THE PITCHER'S MOUND?

THEY GREW THERE! AND MY STUPID GIRL-OUTFIELDERS WON'T LET ME CUT THEM DOWN! THEY SAY THEY'RE PRETTY, AND I LOOK CUTE STANDING HERE AMONG THEM!

THEY'RE RIGHT...YOU DO LOOK KIND OF CUTE STANDING THERE..

April 6, 1965

PEANUTS
HOLD YOUR CHIN UP, CHARLIE BROWN..

I'M GOING TO TICKLE YOU WITH THIS DANDELION..IF YOUR CHIN TURNS YELLOW, IT MEANS YOU LIKE BUTTER..
?

HEY, LOOK! CHARLIE BROWN LIKES BUTTER!

I WONDER IF MY FONDNESS FOR DAIRY PRODUCTS WILL HELP US WIN BALL GAMES

April 7, 1965

PEANUTS
WHY, CHARLIE BROWN! YOU CUT DOWN ALL THE DANDELIONS!

YES, I CUT DOWN ALL THE DANDELIONS! THIS IS A PITCHER'S MOUND, NOT A FLOWER GARDEN!

SPEAKING OF FLOWER GARDENS, I'LL BET A CIRCLE OF DAFFODILS WOULD LOOK NICE AROUND THIS MOUND, DON'T YOU THINK SO?

OH, YES, VERY NICE...OR EVEN SOME MARIGOLDS..
I CAN'T STAND IT!

April 11, 1965

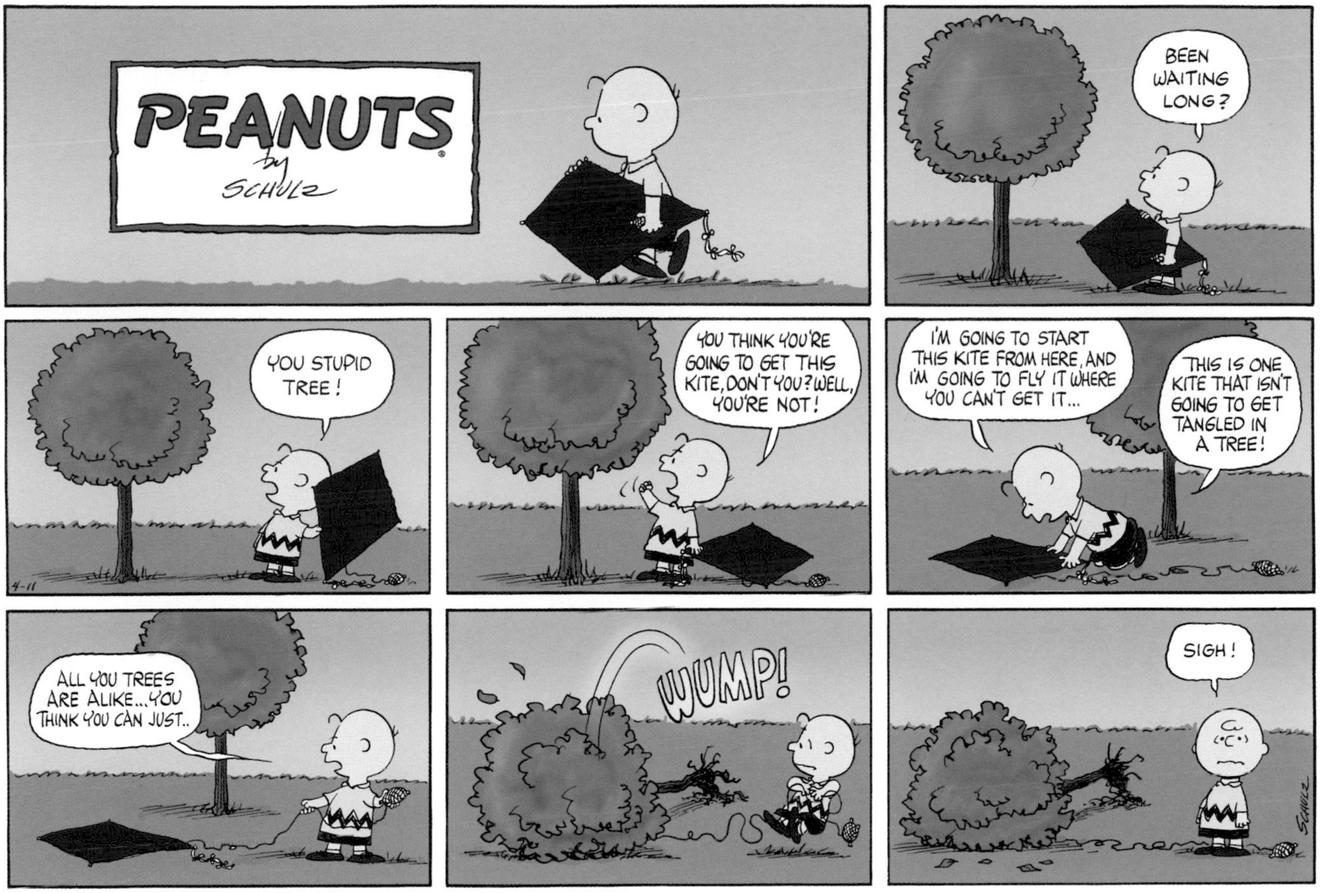

PEANUTS by SCHULZ

BEEN WAITING LONG?

YOU STUPID TREE!

YOU THINK YOU'RE GOING TO GET THIS KITE, DON'T YOU? WELL, YOU'RE NOT!

I'M GOING TO START THIS KITE FROM HERE, AND I'M GOING TO FLY IT WHERE YOU CAN'T GET IT...

THIS IS ONE KITE THAT ISN'T GOING TO GET TANGLED IN A TREE!

ALL YOU TREES ARE ALIKE...YOU THINK YOU CAN JUST..

WUMP!

SIGH!

April 24, 1965

PEANUTS
4-24
YOU THINK BEING AVERAGE IS ENOUGH, DON'T YOU?

WELL, IT ISN'T!

WHAT SHAPE WOULD THE WORLD BE IN TODAY IF EVERYONE SETTLED FOR BEING AVERAGE?

WHAT SHAPE IS THE WORLD IN TODAY?
SCHULZ

May 1, 1965

PEANUTS
5-1

PTUI!

I MUST ADMIT I HAVE THE MOST UNIQUE DOUBLE-PLAY COMBINATION IN BASEBALL!
SCHULZ

May 5, 1965—First mention of the Daisy Hill Puppy Farm.

PEANUTS
I WONDER WHAT HAPPENED TO ALL MY BROTHERS AND SISTERS...

WE USED TO HAVE A PRETTY GOOD TIME THERE AT THE OL' "DAISY HILL PUPPY FARM"
5-5

MAYBE I CAN GET IN TOUCH WITH THEM..

I NEVER THOUGHT I'D END UP BEING A MALE SECRETARY TO A BEAGLE!
SCHULZ

April 18, 1965

PEANUTS by SCHULZ
WAIT!
HMM...
?
BRUSH THIS GUY BACK, CHARLIE BROWN! GIVE 'IM THE OL' BEAN-BALL!
NO, I CAN'T DO THAT... IT WOULDN'T BE RIGHT...
IT WOULDN'T BE RIGHT?!
LISTEN TO WHO'S GONE MORAL ON US ALL OF A SUDDEN! OL' WISHY-WASHY HERE IS TOO MORAL TO THROW A BEAN-BALL!
?
WHAT ABOUT THE WAY THE EARLY SETTLERS TREATED THE INDIANS? WAS THAT MORAL? HOW ABOUT THE CHILDREN'S CRUSADE? WAS THAT MORAL?
YEAH, AND HOW ABOUT THOSE AWFUL MOVIE ADS YOU SEE NOWADAYS?
DO YOU CALL THOSE MORAL, CHARLIE BROWN?
DO YOU THINK THAT INCIDENT AT HARPER'S FERRY WAS CONSISTENT WITH MORALITY?
DEFINE MORALITY!
OUR WHOLE SYSTEM OF FREEWAYS IS A PERFECT EXAMPLE OF WHAT I'M TRYING TO SAY!
HAVE YOU LISTENED TO RADIO LATELY?
HOW ABOUT THIS WHOLE CONSERVATION SITUATION?
WE NEVER WIN ANY BALL GAMES, BUT WE HAVE SOME INTERESTING DISCUSSIONS!
SCHULZ

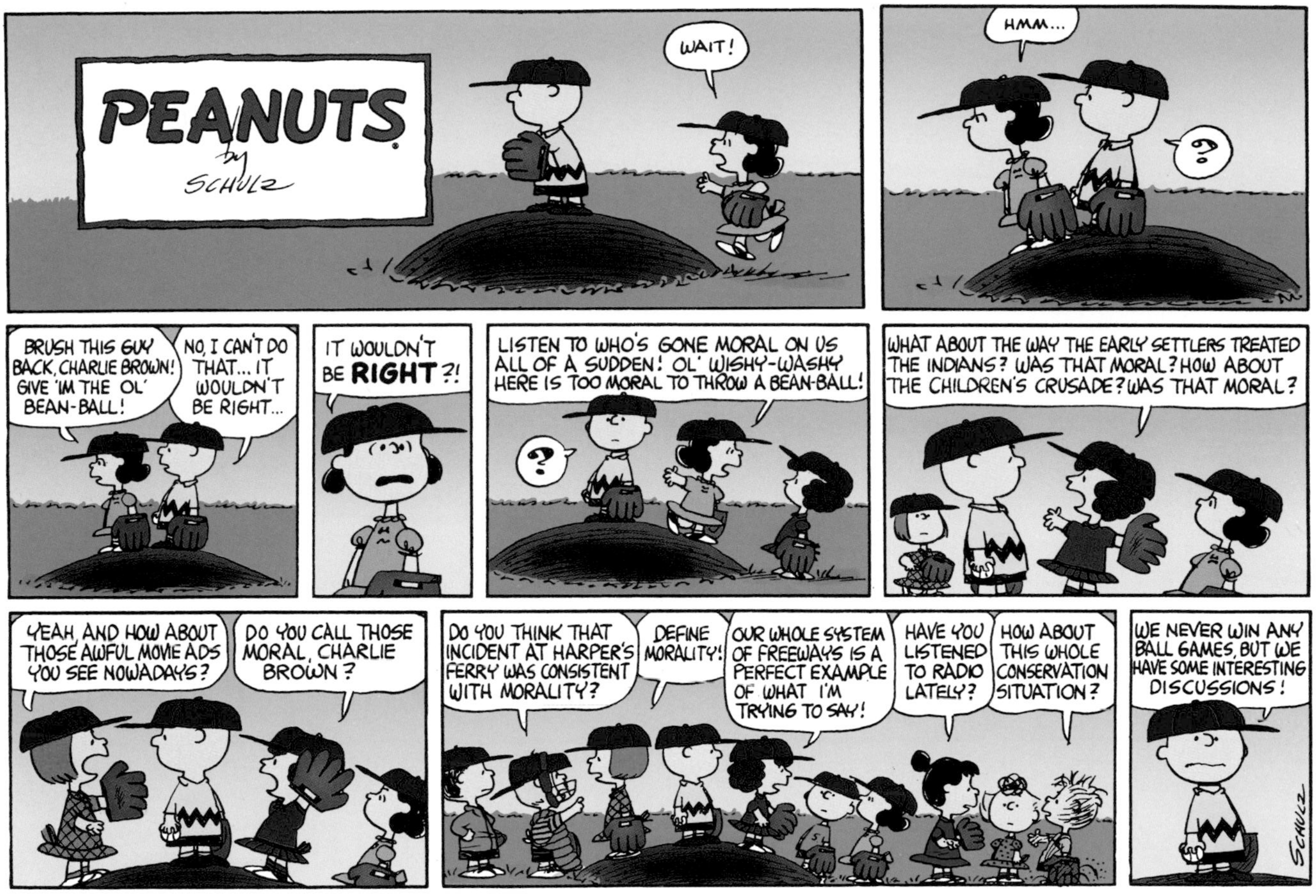

"Who are all these little people? They have become so real to so many people it's frightening. Am I controlling them or are they controlling me?"

May 17, 1965

PEANUTS
5-17

YOU'RE GETTING PRETTY GOOD ON THAT SKATEBOARD, LINUS!

BUT HE CAN'T DO "WHEELIES"!
SCHULZ

May 24, 1965

PEANUTS
I FEEL MEAN!
I HATE THE WHOLE WORLD!

BY GOLLY, NOBODY BETTER GET IN MY WAY TODAY!

5-24

I'M GONNA GET SLAUGHTERED, BUT I CAN'T RESIST THE CHALLENGE!
SCHULZ

May 25, 1965

PEANUTS
FIGHT! FIGHT!
5-25

LUCY AND SNOOPY ARE HAVING A FIGHT!
!

GOOD GRIEF!

STAND STILL, AND FIGHT LIKE A MAN!!
SCHULZ

May 26, 1965

PEANUTS
SWISH!

SLURP SLURP SLURP SLURP

SWISH!
5-26

SLURP! SLURP! SLURP!
WHAT IN THE WORLD KIND OF STUPID FIGHT IS THIS?!
SCHULZ

May 27, 1965

PEANUTS
HERE, NOW! YOU TWO STOP THAT FIGHTING! STOP IT, I SAY!
5-27

SLURP! SLURP! SLURP!
WHO'S FIGHTING? I SURRENDER!

I SAID, I SURRENDER! STOP IT! I SURRENDER! I SURRENDER!

I SAID, I SURRENDER!!!
SCHULZ

May 29, 1965

PEANUTS
I HAVE MIXED EMOTIONS ABOUT THAT FIGHT..

I HATE BRAWLING, BUT I HAVE TO ADMIT THAT I ADMIRE THE WAY YOU STOOD UP TO LUCY
5-29

I'D EVEN LIKE TO SHAKE YOUR HAND, BUT I'M AFRAID SHE MIGHT SEE ME..

HOW WISHY-WASHY CAN YOU GET?
SCHULZ

June 25, 1965

PEANUTS
AREN'T YOU GOING TO BE IN YOUR PSYCHIATRIC BOOTH TODAY?

NOPE! THIS IS MY DAY OFF... IF YOU HAVE A PROBLEM, GO SEE MY ASSISTANT...

6-25

PSYCHIATR
HELP 5¢
THE DOCTOR IS IN
I THINK I'D FEEL A LITTLE LESS RIDICULOUS IF HE WEREN'T MY OWN DOG...
SCHULZ

June 28, 1965

PEANUTS
ALL RIGHT, SNOOPY, THIS IS THE LAST OF THE NINTH...WE NEED ONE RUN TO TIE UP THE GAME..
6-28

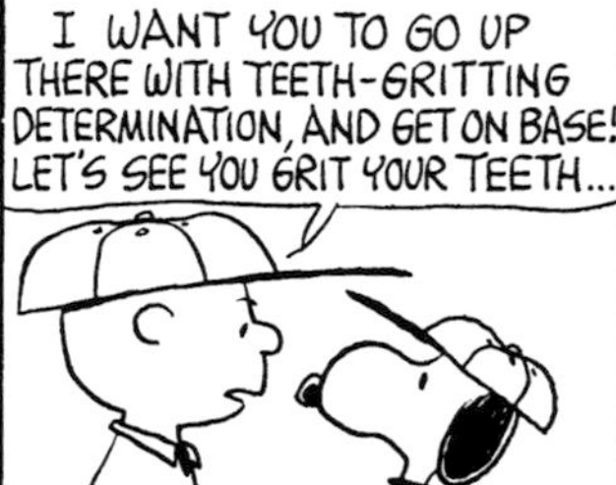
I WANT YOU TO GO UP THERE WITH TEETH-GRITTING DETERMINATION, AND GET ON BASE! LET'S SEE YOU GRIT YOUR TEETH...

THAT'S FINE...KEEP GRITTING YOUR TEETH, AND YOU'LL GET A HIT!

I FEEL LIKE A FOOL...
SCHULZ

July 12, 1965—First appearance of Snoopy as an author.

PEANUTS

7-12

It was a dark and stormy night.
SCHULZ

July 13, 1965

PEANUTS
IT'S FOR YOU, SNOOPY...DO YOU WANT ME TO READ IT?

"DEAR SIR, WE ARE PLEASED TO INFORM YOU THAT YOUR STORY HAS BEEN ACCEPTED FOR PUBLICATION. ENCLOSED IS OUR CHECK FOR $50.00"
7-13

"IF YOU WOULD CARE TO SUBMIT OTHER STORIES, WE WOULD BE VERY HAPPY TO SEE THEM."

It was a dark and stormy night.
SCHULZ

July 14, 1965

PEANUTS
"DEAR SIR, WE ARE PLEASED TO ACCEPT YOUR STORY FOR PUBLICATION."
7-14

"ENCLOSED IS OUR CHECK FOR $75.00"

SOME GOT IT, AND SOME HAVEN'T!

It was a dark and stormy night.
SCHULZ

July 15, 1965

PEANUTS
THIS WAS A GOOD BOOK, CHARLIE BROWN...

I LIKE AN AUTHOR WHO IS VERSATILE
I KNOW WHAT YOU MEAN..

OF COURSE, SOME AUTHORS BECOME SUCCESSFUL SIMPLY BY DEVELOPING A FORMULA..ALL THEIR STORIES FOLLOW A CERTAIN PATTERN
7-15

It was a dark and stormy night.
SCHULZ

July 16, 1965

PEANUTS
"DEAR SIR, WE ARE RETURNING YOUR LATEST MANUSCRIPT.."

"IT DOES NOT SEEM TO BE UP TO YOUR PREVIOUS EFFORTS"
!

THUS ENDETH THE WRITING CAREER...

I CAN'T STAND CRITICISM!
7-16
SCHULZ

"I'd like to try writing, but I don't know if I could do it. I don't think I'm very good with words, only in my own medium, which uses words sparingly. I don't consider myself having a very good vocabulary and I just don't know if I could do it. And, I don't know how anyone can write anything when John Updike is around. He makes you feel so inferior. It's like playing the piano when Beethoven is standing in the other room. . . . I like comic strips and I like to draw them."

July 25, 1965

PEANUTS by SCHULZ
WHAT ARE YOU DOING?
WHAT DO YOU MEAN, WHAT AM I DOING?

I'M WALKING...WHAT DID YOU EXPECT TO SEE ME DOING?

AREN'T YOU GOING TO BE IN YOUR PSYCHIATRY BOOTH TODAY? I HAVE A PROBLEM..

SORRY...TODAY'S MY DAY OFF... GO SEE MY ASSISTANT..

PSYCHIATRIC HELP 5¢
THE DOCTOR IS IN

PSYCHIATRIC HELP 5¢
WELL, MY PROBLEM IS MAINLY ONE OF INSECURITY, I GUESS..I JUST DON'T SEEM TO BE ABLE TO..
THE DOCTOR IS IN

Z
PSYCHIATRIC HELP 5¢
!
THE DOCTOR IS IN

WHAT IN THE WORLD KIND OF ASSISTANT DO YOU HAVE ANYWAY? HE FELL ASLEEP WHILE I WAS TALKING TO HIM

REALLY? GEE, I'M SORRY. I APOLOGIZE..MAYBE I CAN HELP YOU...WHAT IS YOUR PROBLEM?

WELL, I WAS TELLING HIM ABOUT THIS INSECURE FEELING I HAVE, AND...

Z
SCHULZ

August 5, 1965

PEANUTS
MAYBE FRIEDA IS RIGHT..MAYBE I SHOULD GET OUT AND DO MORE
8-5

I'LL DO IT!

I'LL DO SOMETHING REALLY CONSTRUCTIVE

SURF'S UP!
SCHULZ

August 6, 1965

PEANUTS
THIS IS THE LIFE! THE BEACH, THE WARM SUN, MY SURFBOARD AND...

IT'S HER! MY OLD SKATING GIRL FRIEND!
A BEAGLE IN A BIKINI!

I CAN'T STAND TO HAVE MY HEART BROKEN AGAIN..
I'M NOT EVEN GOING TO LOOK AT HER..
8-6

SHE'S BEAUTIFUL!
SCHULZ

August 7, 1965

PEANUTS
THERE SHE IS... MY OLD SKATING GIRL FRIEND..
8-7

I REMEMBER HOW SHE AND I USED TO ICE-SKATE EVERY NIGHT DOWN AT THE POND... THOSE WERE HAPPY TIMES...BUT HER FATHER DIDN'T APPROVE OF ME...

I'D BETTER GO ON HOME BEFORE I DO SOMETHING FOOLISH..I CAN'T AFFORD ANOTHER BROKEN HEART...

WHO AM I KIDDING? I CAN'T RESIST THAT BEACH-BEAGLE..
YOO HOO!
SCHULZ

August 9, 1965

PEANUTS
I'VE GOT TO SHOW THAT BEACH-BEAGLE WHAT A GREAT SURFER I AM!

I'LL PROVE TO HER I'M NO HODAD... I'LL IMPRESS HER WITH SOME FAST TURNS AND HOTDOGGING..

COWABUNGA!

ISN'T THAT YOUR DOG OUT THERE, CHARLIE BROWN? I THINK HE'S LOST HIS MIND!
SCHULZ
8-9

August 10, 1965

PEANUTS
LOOK AT THAT CRAZY DOG...HE'S GOING TO....

WIPE OUT!
8-10

GOOD GRIEF!
SCHULZ

August 11, 1965

PEANUTS
8-11

PUT HIM DOWN FOR A MINUTE, CHARLIE BROWN...HE'S STARTING TO GURGLE AGAIN...

WHAT HAPPENED?
STUPID DOG!
SCHULZ

August 12, 1965

PEANUTS
OF ALL THE DUMB TRICKS!

DO YOU REALIZE YOU ALMOST DROWNED WHILE YOU WERE OUT THERE HOTDOGGING A SURFBOARD JUST TO IMPRESS THAT GIRL BEAGLE?

WHAT DO YOU HAVE TO SAY FOR YOURSELF?!
8-12

SCHULZ

August 13, 1965

PEANUTS
I WANT YOU TO KNOW SOMETHING...I WANT YOU TO KNOW IT FOR YOUR OWN GOOD!

YOU ALMOST DROWNED YOUR SILLY SELF OUT THERE HOTDOGGING THAT SURFBOARD FOR A BEACH-BEAGLE WHO DIDN'T EVEN CARE

8-13
THE LAST TIME I SAW HER SHE WAS RUNNING DOWN THE BEACH WITH A GOLDEN RETRIEVER!

WAAH!
OH, GOOD GRIEF!
SCHULZ

August 27, 1965

PEANUTS

WHY DID YOU WRITE, "CHARLIE BROWN IS A BLOCKHEAD" ON THE SIDEWALK?

BECAUSE I SINCERELY BELIEVE YOU **ARE** A BLOCKHEAD! I HAVE TO WRITE WHAT I BELIEVE IS TRUE.. IT'S MY MORAL RESPONSIBILITY!
8-27

DEEP DOWN I ADMIRE HER INTEGRITY..
SCHULZ

October 21, 1965

PEANUTS
I THINK I'LL GO OVER AND INTRODUCE MYSELF TO THAT LITTLE RED-HAIRED GIRL

I THINK I'LL INTRODUCE MYSELF, AND THEN ASK HER TO COME OVER AND SIT NEXT TO ME

I THINK I'LL ASK HER TO SIT NEXT TO ME HERE, AND THEN I THINK I'LL TELL HER HOW MUCH I'VE ALWAYS ADMIRED HER...
10-21

I THINK I'LL FLAP MY ARMS, AND FLY TO THE MOON
SCHULZ

October 10, 1965—First appearance of Snoopy as the World War I Flying Ace.

PEANUTS
by SCHULZ
PILOTS! EMPTY YOUR POCKETS HERE!
GOOD MORNING, GROUND CREW!
HERE'S THE WORLD WAR I FLYING ACE POSING BESIDE HIS "SOPWITH CAMEL"...
CONTACT!
IT'S THE DAWN PATROL! WE'RE OUT TO HUNT DOWN THE RED BARON!
I CROSS OVER THE ENEMY LINES...I CAN SEE THE NETWORK OF TRENCHES BELOW...
SUDDENLY A "FOKKER TRIPLANE" APPEARS OUT OF THE CLOUDS! IT'S THE RED BARON!!

DIVING DOWN OUT OF THE SUN, ANTI-AIRCRAFT FIRE EXPLODING ALL AROUND ME, I CATCH HIM IN MY SIGHTS! I...

RAT A TAT TAT TAT TAT TAT TAT!
AAUGH!

MAYBE I CAN GET A JOB WITH A GOOD COMMERCIAL AIRLINE...
SCHULZ

"My son Monte was very interested in making World War I model airplanes. And one day I was just sitting at my drawing board and he came in with his latest model plane. While we were talking about World War I planes, I just drew a little helmet on Snoopy and suddenly got the idea for it, and put him on top of the doghouse. I asked Monte to get one of his books about World War I planes he'd been reading. I thumbed through the book until we found the name—Sopwith Camel. That seemed to be the best. And that's how it all started. It really began as a parody of World War I movies."

January 13, 1966

PEANUTS

SCHULZ

January 18, 1966

PEANUTS
SHOVEL YOUR WALK?

YOU MEAN FOR MONEY?
YES, I DON'T HAVE ANY USE FOR BEADS!

SLAM!

I GUESS A GOOD BUSINESSMAN CAN'T AFFORD TO BE SARCASTIC...
SCHULZ

January 20, 1966

PEANUTS
ASK YOUR MOTHER IF SHE WANTS HER SIDEWALK SHOVELED

TELL HER I'LL DO IT FOR ONLY EIGHTY-FIVE DOLLARS!

SHE SAYS SHE'LL GIVE YOU FIFTY CENTS...
IT'S A DEAL!
1-20

I'M NOT MUCH FOR HAGGLING..
SCHULZ

January 21, 1966

PEANUTS
1-21

WELL, DON'T JUST STAND THERE... GO GET A SHOVEL, AND HELP ME!

SCHULZ

"Snoopy is a very contradictory character. In a way he's quite selfish. He likes to think of himself as independent, and he has dreams of doing great things. Without Charlie Brown he couldn't survive, but Snoopy won't even give Charlie Brown the love and affection he deserves. That's part of the humor."

February 6, 1966

PEANUTS by SCHULZ
SO LONG, CHAPS!

CONTACT!

HERE'S THE WORLD WAR I PILOT TAKING OFF FROM A FIELD SOMEWHERE IN ENGLAND...

DRAT THIS FOG! IT'S BAD ENOUGH HAVING TO FIGHT THE RED BARON WITHOUT FIGHTING THE FOG, TOO!

HEADQUARTERS EXPECTS TOO MUCH OF US...WHEN I GET BACK, I THINK I'LL WRITE A LETTER TO PRESIDENT WILSON

IT'S THE "RED BARON"! HE'S GOT ME AGAIN!

CURSE YOU, RED BARON!

I'VE GOT TO MAKE A FORCED LANDING BEHIND THE TRENCHES...

BRUISED AND BATTERED I CRAWL OUT OF MY WRECKED SOPWITH CAMEL... I'M TRAPPED IN THE MIDDLE OF NO-MAN'S LAND! SLOWLY I CREEP FORWARD...

SUDDENLY, THERE IT IS.... BARBED WIRE!!! I'VE GOT TO GET THROUGH IT BEFORE THE MACHINE GUNNERS SEE ME..

? ? ?
2-6

WHAT WAS THAT?
I THINK IT WAS A WORLD WAR I PILOT GOING THROUGH SOME BARBED WIRE, BUT I'M NOT SURE...
SCHULZ

January 29, 1966

PEANUTS
LISTEN..

DON'T YOU THINK SOME NICE MUSIC IN THE MORNING IS A GOOD WAY TO START THE DAY?

I NEVER WORRY ABOUT HOW I START THE DAY...

IT'S HOW IT ENDS UP THAT BOTHERS ME!

February 20, 1966

PEANUTS by SCHULZ
SIGH
I LIKE YOU, LINUS... I LIKE YOU, AND I ADMIRE YOU, BUT I COULD LIKE YOU EVEN MORE IF YOU'D GIVE UP THAT BLANKET...
I DON'T REALLY CARE IF YOU LIKE ME OR NOT...
I LOOK FORWARD TO THE DAY WHEN I'LL UNDERSTAND GIRLS..

March 10, 1966

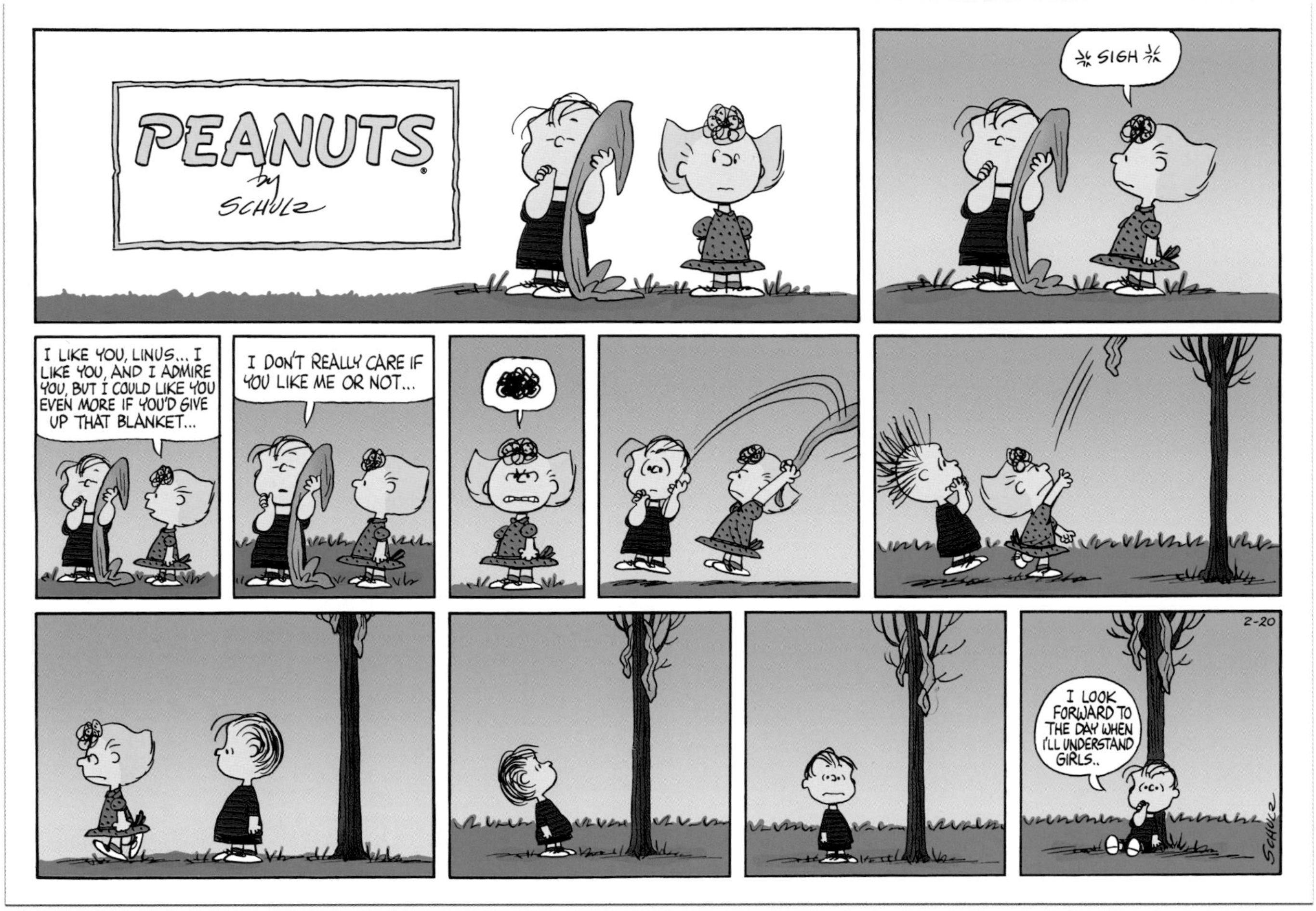

PEANUTS
WE LEARNED IN SCHOOL TODAY THAT THERE ARE SIXTEEN OZZES IN A LIB..
WE'VE BEEN STUDYING PINTS AND QUARTS, AND FEET AND INCHES AND OZZES AND LIBS...
I GET KIND OF CONFUSED ON QUARTS AND FEET, BUT I'M GOOD ON OZZES AND LIBS..
DID YOU KNOW THERE ARE SIXTEEN OZZES IN A LIB?
I NEVER KNOW HOW TO ANSWER A QUESTION LIKE THAT..

March 21, 1966

PEANUTS
I THOUGHT I HAD A CLEAN WHITE HANDKERCHIEF IN HERE...

THERE'S A BLUE ONE... A GREEN ONE..ANOTHER BLUE ONE...
3-21

WHAT IN THE WORLD HAPPENED TO MY WHITE HANDKERCHIEF?

THERE IT IS, MEN... FORT ZINDERNEUF !!
SCHULZ

March 13, 1966

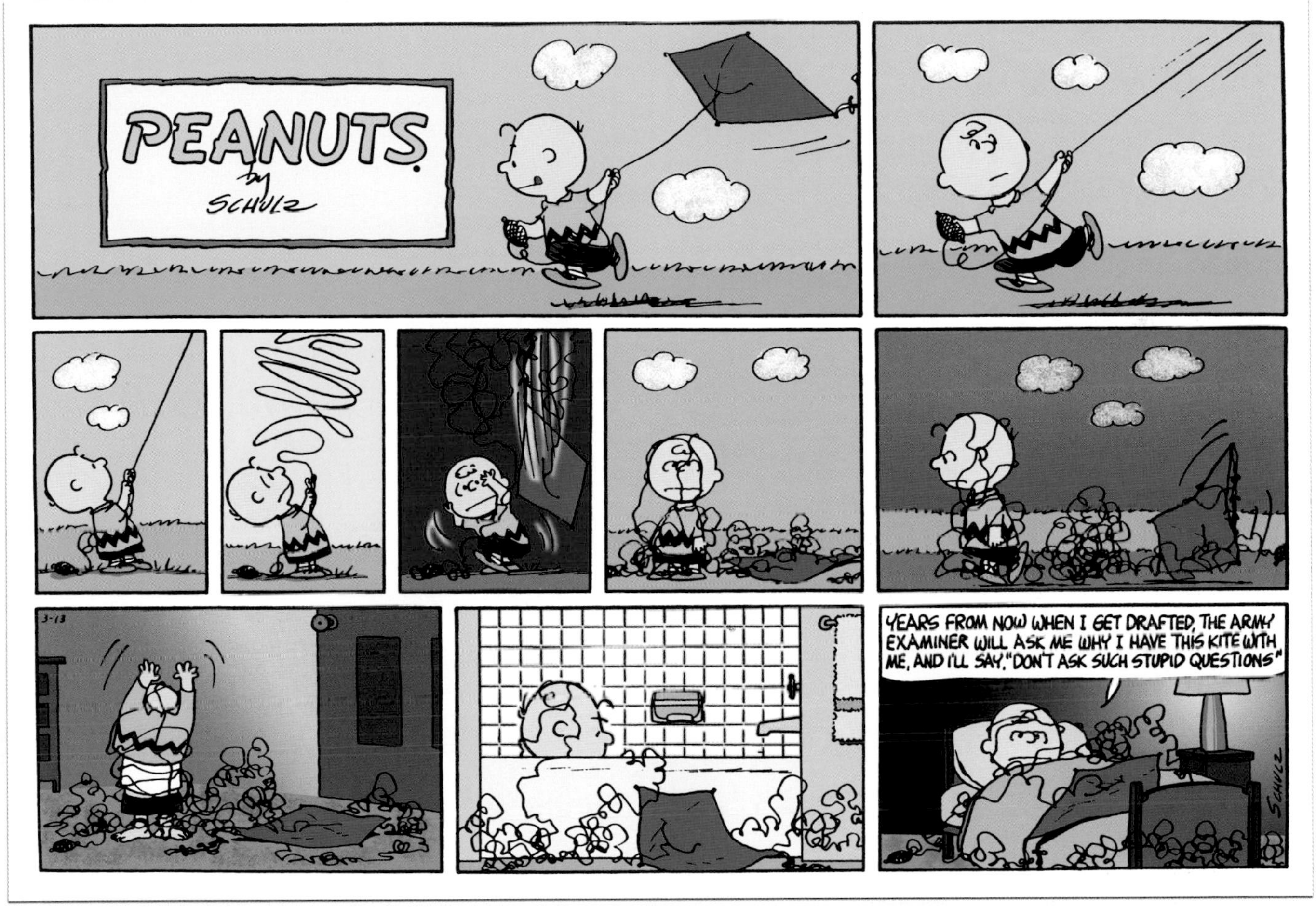

PEANUTS by SCHULZ

3-13

YEARS FROM NOW WHEN I GET DRAFTED, THE ARMY EXAMINER WILL ASK ME WHY I HAVE THIS KITE WITH ME, AND I'LL SAY, "DON'T ASK SUCH STUPID QUESTIONS"

SCHULZ

April 12, 1966

PEANUTS
HERE'S THE GRIM SOLDIER OF THE FRENCH FOREIGN LEGION STANDING AT HIS POST..

OUR COMPANY IS STATIONED AT FORT ZINDERNEUF ON THE EDGE OF NOWHERE..
4-12

AND I? I HAVE A TRAGIC PAST, AND I HAVE JOINED THIS "LEGION OF LOST SOULS" TO FORGET!

I WONDER WHAT IT WOULD BE LIKE TO HAVE A PLAIN OL' "DOG" DOG..
SCHULZ

May 9, 1966

PEANUTS
!
5-9

TRY TO STAY CALM....
I HAVE TERRIBLE NEWS!

DAD'S BEEN TRANSFERRED!
WE'RE MOVING TO A NEW CITY!

AAUGH!
SCHULZ

May 10, 1966

PEANUTS
THIS MAY BE MY LAST GAME, CHARLIE BROWN

MY DAD'S BEEN TRANSFERRED... WE'RE MOVING TO A NEW CITY... I'LL PROBABLY NEVER SEE YOU AGAIN...
5-10

UNLESS, OF COURSE, WE HAPPEN TO GO TO THE SAME COLLEGE.. WHAT COLLEGE DO YOU THINK YOU'LL BE GOING TO?

IT'S KIND OF HARD TO DECIDE IN THE LAST HALF OF THE NINTH INNING
SCHULZ

May 11, 1966

PEANUTS
WHAT WOULD YOU SAY IF I TOLD YOU THAT I WAS MOVING AWAY?

WOULD YOU MISS MY SMILING FACE?
5-11

I COULD STAND IT
OH, I KNOW YOU COULD STAND IT

BUT WOULD YOU MISS MY SMILING FACE?!
SCHULZ

May 12, 1966

PEANUTS
BEFORE WE GO, I THINK I'D BETTER SAY GOOD-BYE TO SNOOPY...

HERE I AM IN MY SOPWITH CAMEL LOOKING FOR..

..THE RED BARON!
5-12

SO LONG, OL' PAL... I'M GOING TO MISS YOU..
SCHULZ

May 13, 1966

PEANUTS
GOOD-BYE, CHARLIE BROWN.. IT'S BEEN NICE KNOWING YOU..
THIS IS REALLY HAPPENING! I CAN'T BELIEVE IT!

SO LONG, YOU OL' BLOCKHEAD... IT'S BEEN NICE KNOWING YOU..
I DON'T KNOW WHAT TO SAY.. I CAN'T BELIEVE IT... I....I.....
5-13

HERE, CHARLIE BROWN... I WANT YOU TO HAVE THIS...
YOUR BLANKET!

SCHULZ

May 14, 1966

PEANUTS
WHAT DO YOU MEAN, LINUS IS GONE?
HE'S GONE! HE AND LUCY HAVE MOVED AWAY...THEIR WHOLE FAMILY JUST PLAIN MOVED AWAY....

THAT'S RIDICULOUS! HE CAN'T MOVE AWAY! I LIKED HIM! I REALLY LIKED HIM!
5-14

THINGS LIKE THIS JUST DON'T HAPPEN!

HOW CAN I LOSE LINUS AND HAVE AMBLYOPIA BOTH IN ONE YEAR?!
SCHULZ

May 17, 1966

PEANUTS
LOOK! A POST CARD FROM LINUS!

"DEAR CHARLIE BROWN, THIS IS THE MOTEL WE STAYED IN THE FIRST NIGHT...IT HAD A SWIMMING POOL, BUT WE DIDN'T GO SWIMMING..

LUCY HAS BEEN CRABBY ALL DAY... I HAVE TO RIDE IN THE BACK SEAT WITH HER...THIS LOOKS LIKE IT'S GOING TO BE A LONG TRIP...YOUR FRIEND, LINUS... P.S. TELL SNOOPY I HOPE HE GETS THE RED BARON"
5-17

THAT'S THE SADDEST POST CARD I'VE EVER READ!
SCHULZ

May 18, 1966

PEANUTS

DON'T TELL ME I'VE GROWN ACCUSTOMED TO THAT FACE!
5-18
SCHULZ

May 19, 1966

PEANUTS
5-19

CLOMP
HEY!

YOU GOT THE WRONG GUY! I'M NOT LINUS! LINUS HAS MOVED AWAY! HE JUST LEFT ME HIS BLANKET! STOP! STOP, I SAY!

MY APOLOGIES
STUPID DOG!!
SCHULZ

May 20, 1966

PEANUTS
YOU'RE BACK!?!
MY DAD CHANGED HIS MIND... HE DIDN'T LIKE THE NEW JOB...
5-20

WHAT KIND OF A NEIGHBORHOOD IS THIS? IT DIDN'T CHANGE A BIT WHILE WE WERE GONE!

DON'T PEOPLE EVER PROGRESS AROUND HERE? WHAT A STUPID NEIGHBORHOOD!!

SHE'S BACK, TOO...
SCHULZ

May 21, 1966

PEANUTS
5-21

YOUR SWEETIE IS BACK!
SCHULZ

August 2, 1966

PEANUTS
BONK
8-2

WHAT HAPPENED?
CHARLIE BROWN GOT HIT WITH A LINE-DRIVE!

DOES ANYONE HERE KNOW ANYTHING ABOUT FIRST-AID?

IT'S PROBABLY NOT SERIOUS.. SECOND OR THIRD-AID WILL DO
SCHULZ

"Anyone who is really creative does not create to bring joy to the world, they create because they have to. Cartooning is the only thing I know how to do and I would be really lost if I didn't do it. I have a good time doing it, but I have no idea of what readers' reaction will be to my strip—whether they'll think it funny or not."

July 24, 1966

PEANUTS
by SCHULZ
HERE'S THE WORLD WAR I PILOT SALUTING THE CAPTAIN

HERE I AM LEAVING COMPANY HEADQUARTERS

HERE'S THE WORLD WAR I PILOT ARRIVING IN PARIS FOR A SHORT LEAVE

AH, PARIS! WHAT A GLORIOUS SIGHT!

WHAT'S THIS? A SMALL SIDEWALK CAFE...

HOW GOOD IT IS TO BE AWAY FROM THE SOUNDS OF BATTLE... TO SIT HERE IN THE SUN...

GARÇON! A ROOT BEER, PLEASE!

PERHAPS MADEMOISELLE WOULD CARE TO JOIN ME IN A ROOT BEER?

SHE IS DAZZLED BY THE HANDSOME PILOT OF THE ALLIES... AH, THE WAR SEEMS SO FAR AWAY....

BUT THIS IS OUTRAGEOUS! I CAN'T SIT HERE WITH THIS BEAUTIFUL FRENCH GIRL WHILE MY BUDDIES ARE FIGHTING THE RED BARON!

AH, MY LITTLE ONE, YOU ARE GOING TO MISS ME, NO? BUT I MUST GO...DO NOT WEEP..... PLEASE, DO NOT HANG ONTO MY TUNIC...

THIS IS WHERE I BELONG! HIGH ABOVE THE CLOUDS SEARCHING FOR THE RED BARON!

!
7-24

I SHOULD HAVE STAYED IN PARIS...
SCHULZ

August 8, 1966

PEANUTS
LIFE IS DIFFICULT, ISN'T IT, CHARLIE BROWN?
8-8

YES, IT IS

BUT I'VE DEVELOPED A NEW PHILOSOPHY...

I ONLY DREAD ONE DAY AT A TIME!
SCHULZ

August 22, 1966—First appearance of Peppermint Patty.

PEANUTS
HI, ROY... WHO YOU WRITIN' TO?
I'M WRITING TO A LITTLE KID NAMED LINUS THAT I MET AT CAMP SEVERAL WEEKS AGO

IS HE CUTE? IF HE IS, TELL HIM YOUR VERY GOOD FRIEND, "PEPPERMINT" PATTY SAYS, "HELLO"

TELL HIM WHAT A REAL SWINGER I AM...
8-22

PUT IN A GOOD WORD FOR ME, ROY, AND THE NEXT TIME WE INDIAN WRESTLE I'LL TRY NOT TO CLOBBER YOU!
SCHULZ

"Patty has been a good addition for me, and I think could almost carry another strip by herself. A dish of candy sitting in our living room inspired her name. So in this case I created the character to fit the name, and Peppermint Patty came into being."

August 14, 1966

PEANUTS by SCHULZ

WORLD'S CHAMPION DIVER

8-14

I HATE THESE PRACTICE SESSIONS!

SCHULZ

September 16, 1966

PEANUTS
YOU SURE HAVE BECOME A LONER..

YOU'RE ALWAYS BY YOURSELF!

I CAN'T HELP IT...

I'VE BECOME ALLERGIC TO PEOPLE!
9-16
SCHULZ

September 4, 1966

PEANUTS
by SCHULZ

OW!
WHAT HAPPENED? WHAT'S THE MATTER?

I GOT HIT ON THE FINGER WITH A FOUL TIP...

IS IT GOING TO BE ALL RIGHT? ARE YOU GOING TO BE ABLE TO PLAY?
I'M NOT SURE.... I'LL HAVE TO FIND OUT

pp
leggiero
Tempo I

IT'S ALL RIGHT... I CAN PLAY!
9-4

THAT ISN'T EXACTLY WHAT I MEANT..
SCHULZ

September 19, 1966

PEANUTS
SNIF?
I SMELL SMOKE!
SNIF SNIF
9-19

BAM! BAM!
BAM! BAM!

WHAT IN THE WORLD.....

MY BOOKS! MY RECORDS! MY POOL TABLE! MY VAN GOGH!
GOOD GRIEF!
SOB!
SCHULZ

September 20, 1966

PEANUTS

9-20

WAAH!
SCHULZ

September 21, 1966

PEANUTS
JUST LOOK AT THAT, WILL YOU...
I WONDER HOW IT STARTED...

HE WAS PROBABLY SMOKING IN BED..
THEY SAY HE LOST EVERYTHING...
9-21

I'LL BET THAT WAS IT...I'LL BET HE WAS SMOKING IN BED...
FIRE IS A TERRIBLE THING..

EVERYTHING IS GONE... EVERYTHING!
HE WAS PROBABLY SMOKING IN BED
SCHULZ

September 22, 1966

PEANUTS
9-22

SCHULZ

September 23, 1966

PEANUTS
ACCORDING TO THIS, YOUR FIRE INSURANCE HAS LAPSED!

YOU DIDN'T KEEP UP THE PREMIUMS, SNOOPY
I DIDN'T?!

HOW COULD THAT BE?
9-23

I SENT THEM A CAN OF DOG FOOD EVERY MONTH!
SCHULZ

September 24, 1966

PEANUTS
YOU KNOW WHY YOUR DOGHOUSE BURNED DOWN? BECAUSE YOU SINNED, THAT'S WHY!

YOU'RE BEING PUNISHED FOR SOMETHING YOU DID WRONG! THAT'S THE WAY THESE THINGS ALWAYS WORK!

BLEAH!

HER KIND DESERVES TO BE BLEAHED!
SCHULZ
9-24

September 26, 1966

PEANUTS
SO YOUR HOUSE BURNED DOWN! SO WHAT?

A LITTLE TRAGEDY NOW AND THEN WILL MAKE YOU A BETTER PERSON! MAN WAS BORN TO SUFFER!
9-26

HE'S NOT A MAN...HE'S A DOG..
THE THEOLOGY IS THE SAME

I DON'T BELIEVE IT...DOGS WERE BORN TO BITE PEOPLE ON THE LEG, AND TO SLEEP IN THE SUN!
SCHULZ

September 27, 1966

PEANUTS
9-27

THIS IS RIDICULOUS!
SCHULZ

September 11, 1966

PEANUTS
by SCHULZ
Sleeping Pills
I CAN'T SLEEP!
MAYBE IF I MOVE AROUND AND TRY DIFFERENT POSITIONS...
RATS! I JUST CAN'T GET COMFORTABLE!
SNOOPY?
SNOOPY?
WHERE'D HE GO?
Z
9-11
SCHULZ

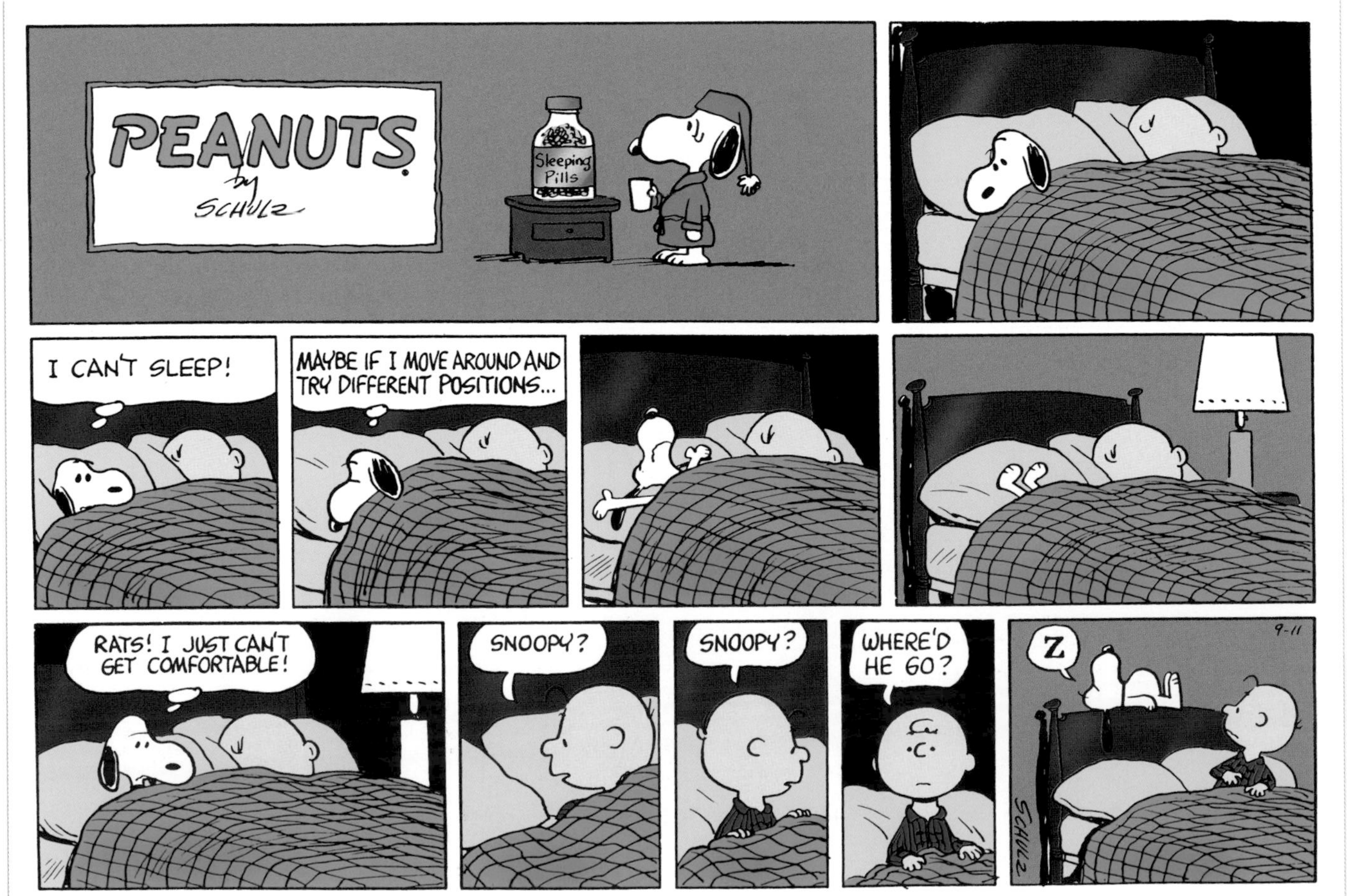

September 28, 1966

PEANUTS
WELL, HERE'S THE LIST OF ALL THE THINGS YOU LOST IN THE FIRE

ALL THE CARPETING WAS RUINED, OF COURSE, AND THE POOL TABLE IS SHOT...YOUR WHOLE LIBRARY IS GONE, AND YOUR VAN GOGH IS DESTROYED...

9-28

ACTUALLY, SNOOPY, EVERYTHING IS GONE!

EVEN MY PINKING SHEARS?!
SCHULZ

September 29, 1966

PEANUTS
HERE'S THE WORLD WAR I FLYING ACE REPORTING FOR DUTY
9-29

HIS MISSION TODAY IS TO SEARCH OUT THE RED BARON, AND BRING HIM DOWN..HE CROSSES THE FIELD TO HIS SOPWITH CAMEL..

WHAT SOPWITH CAMEL?!
SCHULZ

January 1, 1967

PEANUTS featuring "Good ol' Charlie Brown" by SCHULZ

JAN.1

RATS!

NEW YEAR'S DAY AND WHERE AM I? ALONE IN A STRANGE COUNTRY.. WHAT IRONY!

HOW MUCH LONGER CAN THIS WAR GO ON? IF IT DOESN'T END SOON, I THINK I SHALL GO MAD!

GARÇON, ANOTHER ROOT BEER, PLEASE

HOW MANY ROOT BEERS CAN A MAN DRINK? HOW MANY DOES IT TAKE TO DRIVE THE AGONY FROM YOUR BRAIN? CURSE THIS WAR! CURSE THE MUD AND THE RAIN!

AND CURSE YOU TOO, RED BARON, WHEREVER YOU ARE!

I'M GOING TO GET YOU YET! I'M GOING TO SHOOT YOU DOWN

DISTURBANCE? WHO'S CREATING A DISTURBANCE?

I'M A PILOT WITH THE ALLIES! I'M GOING TO SAVE THE WORLD!

BOOT!

YOU CAN'T DO THIS TO A FLYING-ACE! YOU'LL BE SORRY!

GRUMBLE GRUMBLE GRUMBLE GRUMBLE GRUMBLE

SIGH HAPPY NEW YEAR!

SCHULZ 1-1

January 10, 1967

PEANUTS
GOOD GRIEF!

RATS! EVERY TIME I GET A NEW SOPWITH CAMEL, THE RED BARON SHOOTS IT FULL OF HOLES!

OUR SUPPLY SERGEANT HATES ME!

January 11, 1967

PEANUTS
HERE'S THE WORLD WAR I PILOT FLYING OVER ENEMY LINES...

IF I LOSE ANOTHER SOPWITH CAMEL, OUR SUPPLY SERGEANT WILL KILL ME...

OH, NO! IT'S THE RED BARON! HE'S DIVING DOWN OUT OF THE SUN! MACHINE GUN BULLETS RIP THE SIDE OF MY PLANE!

THIS COULD RUIN MY WHOLE DAY..

January 12, 1967

PEANUTS
HERE'S THE WORLD WAR I PILOT DOWN BEHIND ENEMY LINES...

IF I'M CAPTURED, I'LL BE SHOT AT DAWN...

I'LL SNEAK BACK INTO MY DAMAGED SOPWITH CAMEL, AND PUT ON MY SPECIAL DISGUISE..

WO IST DER ROOT BEER HALL?

January 13, 1967

PEANUTS
HERE'S THE WORLD WAR I PILOT SITTING IN A LITTLE RESTAURANT BEHIND ENEMY LINES
NO ONE RECOGNIZES ME IN MY VERY CLEVER DISGUISE

WHO'S THAT AT THE NEXT TABLE? HE LOOKS FAMILIAR.... GOOD GRIEF, IT'S THE RED BARON!

HI, RED!

January 14, 1967

PEANUTS
AH, RED BARON, AT LAST WE MEET FACE TO FACE!

THERE IS RESPECT IN YOUR EYES, NO? YES, I AM THE FAMOUS PILOT WITH THE ALLIES

PERHAPS THERE IS ALSO A LITTLE FEAR IN YOUR EYES, NO?

NO!

January 16, 1967

PEANUTS
PRISON! THEY THREW ME IN PRISON!

WHY DID I HAVE TO GIVE MYSELF AWAY IN THAT RESTAURANT? WHY DID I GO OVER AND TALK TO THE RED BARON?

NOW, I'LL SPEND THE REST OF WORLD WAR I IN THIS PRISON... THEY'LL NEVER LET ME OUT! NEVER!
1-16

OWOOOOOOO
SCHULZ

January 17, 1967

PEANUTS
HERE'S THE WORLD WAR I FLYING ACE IN PRISON..

A GUARD!

I LEAP ON THE GUARD, AND WRESTLE HIM TO THE GROUND! JUDO CHOP! WHAM! WHAM! WHAM!

I'M FREE! I'M FREE! I'M FREE!
NEVER STICK YOUR HEAD INTO AN EMPTY DOG HOUSE!
SCHULZ
1-17

"Snoopy is kind of frightening because he is so uncontrollable. And he's a little selfish, too. He really isn't all he claims to be."

February 12, 1967

PEANUTS
featuring
"Good ol' Charlie Brown"
by SCHULZ
HERE YOU ARE, SNOOPY...THERE'S EVEN ONE FOR YOU...HOW ABOUT THAT? WELL! HERE'S ANOTHER ONE FOR YOU...THIS IS YOUR LUCKY DAY....

THE MAILMAN CAME!

VALENTINES!

WOW!

AND ONE MORE FOR YOU, AND ONE MORE, AND ONE MORE, AND ONE MORE, AND ONE MORE, AND..

I CAN'T STAND IT.. I JUST CAN'T STAND IT...
2-12
SCHULZ

February 9, 1967

PEANUTS
YOU THINK YOU'RE THE "ARM WRESTLING" CHAMP, DON'T YOU?

OF COURSE, I'M THE CHAMP... I'VE BEATEN EVERYBODY AROUND HERE!
NOT EVERYBODY...

YOU'RE NOT THE CHAMPION UNTIL YOU'VE BEATEN THE "MASKED MARVEL"......
2-9

OH, GOOD GRIEF!
SCHULZ

February 10, 1967

PEANUTS
I REFUSE TO "ARM WRESTLE" WITH A STUPID BEAGLE!

I'LL BREAK HIS PAW OR HIS ARM OR HIS SHANK OR WHATEVER IT'S CALLED!

YOU'RE AFRAID OF THE "MASKED MARVEL"!
I'M NOT AFRAID! I JUST DON'T WANT TO BREAK HIS ARM OR WHATEVER IT IS!
2-10

I THINK IT'S A FRONT LEG..
SCHULZ

February 11, 1967

PEANUTS
ALL RIGHT, YOU STUPID BEAGLE! YOU WANTED TO "ARM WRESTLE," LET'S "ARM WRESTLE"!

I'M GONNA SEND YOU BACK TO THE DOG POUND WHERE YOU BELONG, "MASKED MARVEL"!

I'M GONNA CLOBBER YOU! I'M GONNA RUN ROUGHSHOD OVER YOU! START PUSHING!
2-11

START? I'VE BEEN PUSHING FOR THREE MINUTES!
SCHULZ

February 14, 1967

PEANUTS
YIELD, YOU RASCAL!
SURRENDER, YOU DUMB DOG!
2-14

SUCCUMB, YOU DARK-HAIRED FIEND!
QUIT, YOU LONG-EARED MONSTER!

I CAN'T HOLD OUT ANOTHER SECOND... I'VE GOT TO DO SOMETHING!
I CAN'T HOLD OUT ANY LONGER! I THINK I'M GOING TO FAINT!

SMAK!
AUGHH!

February 15, 1967

PEANUTS
IT WASN'T A FAIR FIGHT! HE KISSED ME!
2-15

HE KISSED ME WITH HIS STUPID DOG LIPS!!
BLEAH!

I'M STILL THE "ARM WRESTLING" CHAMP OF THE NEIGHBORHOOD!

YOU LET US DOWN, "MASKED MARVEL"
SORRY, BOYS... THAT'S THE WAY IT GOES....
SCHULZ

February 28, 1967

PEANUTS
IN KITE-FLYING, THE RATIO OF WEIGHT TO SAIL-AREA IS VERY IMPORTANT
2-28

THIS RATIO IS KNOWN AS "SAIL LOADING" AND IT IS MEASURED IN OUNCES PER SQUARE FOOT..FOR EXAMPLE, A THREE-FOOT FLAT KITE WITH A SAIL AREA OF FOUR AND ONE-HALF SQUARE FEET SHOULD WEIGH ABOUT TWO OR THREE OUNCES...

YOU KNOW A LOT ABOUT KITES, DON'T YOU, CHARLIE BROWN?
YES, I THINK I CAN SAY THAT I DO...

THEN WHY IS YOUR KITE DOWN THE SEWER?
SCHULZ

February 19, 1967

PEANUTS
featuring
"Good ol' Charlie Brown"
by SCHULZ

HELLO, KITE-EATING TREE!

IT LOOKS LIKE YOU'VE PUT ON A LITTLE WEIGHT SINCE I LAST SAW YOU... YOU LOOK A LITTLE TALLER, TOO

BUT YOU HAVEN'T HAD ANY KITES LATELY, HAVE YOU?

WELL, YOU'RE NOT GOING TO GET THIS KITE, YOU DIRTY KITE-EATING TREE! I'LL FLY IT CLEAR OVER ON THE OTHER SIDE OF TOWN JUST TO SPITE YOU! YOU CAN STARVE, DO YOU HEAR?!

YOU'RE PRACTICALLY DROOLING, AREN'T YOU? YOU HAVEN'T EATEN A KITE FOR MONTHS, AND YOU'RE JUST DYING TO GET HOLD OF THIS ONE, AREN'T YOU? AREN'T YOU?

WELL, YOU'RE NOT, DO YOU HEAR ME? YOU'RE NOT!

HERE.. TAKE IT
2-19

IT'S BEEN A LONG WINTER, AND I'M VERY TENDER-HEARTED..
CHOMP! CHOMP! CHOMP!
SCHULZ

April 4, 1967—First appearance of Woodstock, though not yet named.

PEANUTS
!
flitter
flutter
flitter
flutter
flitter
flutter

whew!
GASP GASP
4-4

Z
MUST HAVE BEEN A ROUGH FLIGHT
SCHULZ

April 17, 1967

PEANUTS
THIS IS A HARD WORLD TO GET ALONG IN...

I FEEL SORRY FOR ALL THE NEW LITTLE BABIES..
BUT THEY KEEP RIGHT ON GETTING BORN...

DO YOU REALIZE THAT SOMEWHERE THIS VERY MOMENT A CHILD IS BEING BORN?

GOOD LUCK, KID, WHEREVER YOU ARE!

April 18, 1967

PEANUTS
"'ALL RIGHT,' SAID THE CAT; AND THIS TIME IT VANISHED QUITE SLOWLY...

BEGINNING WITH THE END OF THE TAIL, AND ENDING WITH THE GRIN, WHICH REMAINED SOME TIME AFTER THE REST OF IT HAD GONE."

I'VE BEEN ABLE TO DO THAT FOR YEARS!

April 26, 1967

PEANUTS
RATS!
I THINK YOU'RE TOO TENSE WHEN YOU TRY TO WRITE WITH A PEN, CHARLIE BROWN...

BEFORE YOU BEGIN, YOU SHOULD SORT OF SWIRL YOUR PEN AROUND A BIT TO LOOSEN UP

THAT'S THE WAY... MOVE YOUR WHOLE ARM AROUND... FASTER! 'ROUND AND AROUND...

THOSE WERE GOOD SWIRLS..

May 12, 1967

PEANUTS
WOULD YOU LIKE TO BE THE FIRST MAN ON THE MOON?
NO, I'M NOT THAT BRAVE

I DON'T THINK I'D EVEN LIKE TO BE THE SECOND...THE THIRD MAN WILL HAVE QUITE A BIT OF RESPONSIBILITY, TOO, AND THE FOURTH WILL HAVE TO KEEP A LOT OF RECORDS..

THE FIFTH MAN WILL HAVE A LOT TO LIVE UP TO BECAUSE OF WHAT THE OTHERS DID, AND THE SIXTH WILL HAVE TO WORK HARD AROUND THE MOON-STATION...THE SEVENTH WILL...

YOUR BROTHER IS THE ONLY PERSON I KNOW WHO WANTS TO BE THE FORTY-THIRD MAN ON THE MOON!

June 12, 1967

PEANUTS
WELL, SCHOOL'S OVER, AND HERE I AM IN A BUS GOING TO SUMMER CAMP..

SIGH

AT LEAST THIS YEAR I'M NOT HAVING TO GO ALONE...

HERE'S THE WORLD WAR I FLYING ACE RIDING ACROSS FRANCE ON A TROOP TRAIN...

June 13, 1967

PEANUTS
WELL, SNOOPY, HERE WE ARE AT SUMMER CAMP...

THE FIRST THING THEY'LL DO IS ASSIGN US TO A BARRACKS, AND THEN WE'LL HAVE LUNCH...

NOT "LUNCH"... CHOW! WE WORLD WAR I FLYING ACES ALWAYS CALL IT "CHOW"...WHAT A MISERABLE CAMP.. WE MUST BE FIFTY KILOMETERS FROM THE NEAREST VILLAGE! CURSE THIS HOT WEATHER! CURSE THIS STUPID WAR!

WE WORLD WAR I FLYING ACES DO A LOT OF GRIPING!

June 14, 1967

PEANUTS
SURPRISE!

PEPPERMINT PATTY! WHAT ARE YOU DOING HERE?
HI, CHUCK! I'M AT THE GIRLS' CAMP ACROSS THE LAKE!

HI, SNOOPY, OL' PAL... HOW'S THE SHORTSTOP?

WHAT IS IT WITH THIS KID AND THE GOGGLES, HUH, CHUCK?
VERY STRANGE GIRL...MUST BE FROM THE FRENCH COUNTRYSIDE...

June 15, 1967

PEANUTS
I WONDER WHAT WE...
THERE'S A BUG IN YOUR HAIR, CHARLIE BROWN...

WHERE? WHERE? BRUSH IT OFF!
THAT'S ALL RIGHT... IT'S GONE NOW...

THAT'S THE ONE THING I HATE ABOUT ALL THIS OUTDOOR LIVING!
WELL, DON'T WORRY...IT'S NOT IN YOUR HAIR ANY MORE..

IT FELL DOWN YOUR NECK!

June 16, 1967

PEANUTS
YOU STILL HAVEN'T TOLD ME WHAT YOU'RE DOING HERE
THE GIRLS' CAMP IS GOING TO PLAY THE BOYS' CAMP IN A BALL GAME...AREN'T YOU GOING TO PLAY?

THEY HAVEN'T ASKED ME...I DON'T THINK I'M GOOD ENOUGH..
BUT YOU LOVE BASEBALL, CHARLIE BROWN..

THIS IS A SUMMER CAMP! YOU'RE HERE TO HAVE FUN NO MATTER HOW LOUSY YOU ARE! I'LL GO SPEAK TO YOUR COUNSELOR, CHARLIE BROWN...

SO LONG, SWEETIE...
POOR, UNFORTUNATE GIRL...SHE MUST BE STARVED FOR LOVE... CURSE THIS WAR!
SMAK

June 19, 1967

PEANUTS
STRIKE THREE!

"HEY, KID, WHO TOLD YOU YOU WERE A BALL PLAYER?"
BOO!! BOO!!
"GET OFF THE FIELD, KID!"
"WE CAN DO WITHOUT YOUR KIND, KID!"

"WHERE'D YOU LEARN TO PLAY BALL, KID, IN KINDERGARTEN?!!!"
HA!HA! HA!HA!
HA!HA! HA!HA!
HA!HA!

SPRING LAKE
Summer camp
FUN! RECREATION!
COMPANIONSHIP!
SIGH

June 20, 1967

PEANUTS
HI, CHUCK... GREAT GAME YESTERDAY, WASN'T IT?

BEAUTIFUL!
SORRY I HAD TO STRIKE YOU OUT

FOR A WHILE I CONSIDERED LETTING YOU HIT ONE AND BE A HERO, BUT I KNEW YOU WOULDN'T WANT ME TO DO THAT...

OH?

June 22, 1967

PEANUTS
HEY, CHARLIE BROWN, COME QUICK! THEY'RE HAVING A CANOE RACE!

A CANOE RACE?! C'MON, SNOOPY...IF WE CAN WIN THE CANOE RACE, EVERYONE WILL FORGET ABOUT MY LOUSY BALL PLAYING...

WE'LL SHOW 'EM, SNOOPY...WE'LL GET IN THIS CANOE, WE'LL WIN THIS RACE AND WE'LL BE HEROES!

ACTUALLY, I HAD PLANNED FOR YOU TO HELP WITH THE PADDLING..

June 23, 1967

PEANUTS
WE'RE GONNA WIN THIS CANOE RACE, SNOOPY, OR DIE TRYING! I'M GONNA PADDLE AN' PADDLE AN'...

WHEW I'M EXHAUSTED! I FEEL LIKE I'VE PADDLED A HUNDRED MILES......

I WONDER IF WE WON...

NO, BUT YOU GOT FOUR FEET FROM THE DOCK!

June 24, 1967

PEANUTS
YOU'RE GOING TO ENTER THE ROPE-CLIMBING CONTEST, CHARLIE BROWN?

I'VE GOT TO! I'VE GOT TO SHOW THE KIDS IN THIS CAMP THAT I'M NOT A COMPLETE FLOP!

AARGH! CLIMB! CLIMB! CLIMB! CLIMB! UP! UP! UP! UP! UP! UP!

SIGH

June 26, 1967

PEANUTS
WELL, I'M BACK FROM CAMP!
YOU'RE WHAT?

I'M BACK! I'M BACK FROM CAMP!
FROM WHERE?

FROM CAMP! I'M BACK FROM SUMMER CAMP... I WAS AWAY FOR TWO WEEKS TO SUMMER CAMP, AND NOW I'M BACK!

SO?

July 4, 1967

PEANUTS
YOU JUST CAN'T DO ANYTHING RIGHT, CAN YOU?

YOU BLOCKHEAD!!
7-4

I SEE YOUR SISTER'S BEEN YELLING AT YOU AGAIN
SCHULZ

July 16, 1967

PEANUTS
featuring
"Good ol' CharlieBrown"
by SCHULZ

I LIKE YOUR NEW SWEATER, CHARLIE BROWN..
THANK YOU... I WAS JUST DOWN TO THE PLAYGROUND, AND...

WHAT'S THE MATTER?
A NOTE! IT FEELS LIKE SOMEONE PUT A NOTE IN MY POCKET!

I'LL BET IT WAS THAT LITTLE RED-HAIRED GIRL! I WAS SITTING NEXT TO HER IN THE SAND BOX AT THE PLAYGROUND...I'LL BET SHE SLIPPED A NOTE INTO MY POCKET...

I'LL BET SHE KNOWS HOW MUCH I ADMIRE HER AND HOW MUCH I'VE ALWAYS WANTED TO MEET HER, AND I'LL BET SHE'S WRITTEN ME A NOTE TELLING ME SOMETHING.. I'LL BET THAT'S IT...
7-16

I CAN HARDLY WAIT TO READ IT... JUST THINK.. A NOTE.... A REAL NOTE...

WELL? WHAT DOES IT SAY?

"THIS GARMENT HAS BEEN INSPECTED BY OPERATOR 23"
SCHULZ

July 10, 1967

PEANUTS
HERE'S THE WORLD WAR I FLYING ACE ABOUT TO TAKE OFF IN HIS SOPWITH CAMEL
7-10

"CONTACT!" HE SHOUTS...

?

I SEE MY MECHANIC HAS SPENT THE WEEK-END IN PARIS AGAIN
Z
SCHULZ

September 17, 1967

PEANUTS
featuring "Good ol' Charlie Brown"
by SCHULZ
NINE HOME RUNS IN A ROW!! GOOD GRIEF!
WHAT CAN I DO?!!
WE'RE GETTING SLAUGHTERED AGAIN, SCHROEDER... I DON'T KNOW WHAT TO DO..WHY DO WE HAVE TO SUFFER LIKE THIS?
"MAN IS BORN TO TROUBLE AS THE SPARKS FLY UPWARD."
WHAT?
HE'S QUOTING FROM THE 'BOOK OF JOB,' CHARLIE BROWN... SEVENTH VERSE, FIFTH CHAPTER....
9-17
ACTUALLY, THE PROBLEM OF SUFFERING IS A VERY PROFOUND ONE, AND..
IF A PERSON HAS BAD LUCK, IT'S BECAUSE HE'S DONE SOMETHING WRONG, THAT'S WHAT I ALWAYS SAY!
THAT'S WHAT JOB'S FRIENDS TOLD HIM, BUT I DOUBT IF..
WHAT ABOUT JOB'S WIFE? I DON'T THINK SHE GETS ENOUGH CREDIT!
I THINK A PERSON WHO NEVER SUFFERS, NEVER MATURES...SUFFERING IS ACTUALLY VERY IMPORTANT..
WHO WANTS TO SUFFER? DON'T BE RIDICULOUS!
BUT PAIN IS A PART OF LIFE, AND..
A PERSON WHO SPEAKS ONLY OF THE "PATIENCE" OF JOB REVEALS THAT HE KNOWS VERY LITTLE OF THE BOOK! NOW, THE WAY I SEE IT...
I DON'T HAVE A BALL TEAM..I HAVE A THEOLOGICAL SEMINARY!
SCHULZ

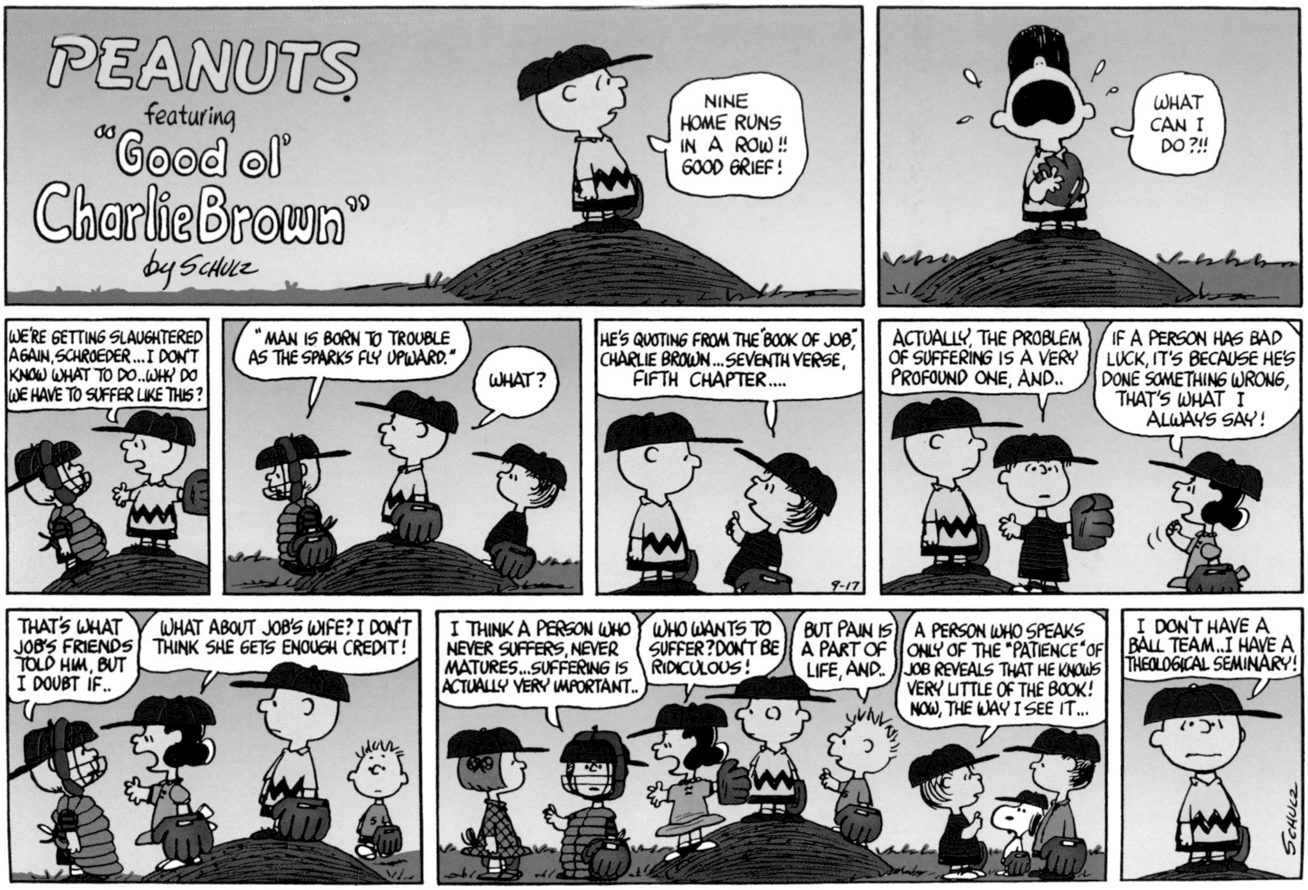

"Religion without humor is a worthless religion. Humor is part of man and man never would have survived without humor. It's the only thing that makes life palatable—if that's the word. And to say that there's no room for humor in religion is like saying there's no room for humor in life. The scriptures themselves have quite a few incidents of humor—probably more than we realize, especially if we had the ability to go back and understand the cultures which contain some of the occurrences reported in the Bible. Of course, I do believe that the scriptures are holy, but I do not believe that the Bible itself is a holy instrument to be worshiped. After all, the words are only the words which men put down under inspiration."

October 26, 1967

PEANUTS
ON HALLOWEEN NIGHT THE "GREAT PUMPKIN" RISES OUT OF THE PUMPKIN PATCH THAT HE PICKS AS THE MOST SINCERE

THEN HE FLIES THROUGH THE AIR BRINGING TOYS TO ALL THE GOOD CHILDREN IN THE WORLD!

JUST THINK, SNOOPY, IF HE PICKS THIS PUMPKIN PATCH, YOU AND I WILL BE HERE TO SEE HIM!

FRANKLY, THIS LOOKS LIKE A GOOD PLACE TO GET MUGGED!
SCHULZ

October 27, 1967

PEANUTS
I WISH YOU COULD TALK, SNOOPY...

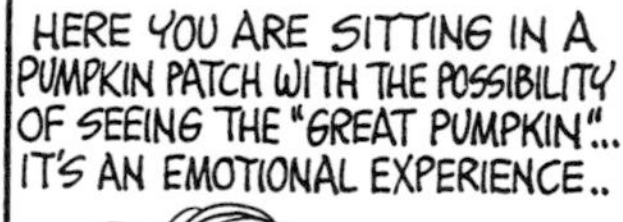
HERE YOU ARE SITTING IN A PUMPKIN PATCH WITH THE POSSIBILITY OF SEEING THE "GREAT PUMPKIN"... IT'S AN EMOTIONAL EXPERIENCE..

I'D REALLY BE INTERESTED IN KNOWING WHAT THOUGHTS ARE RUNNING THROUGH YOUR MIND...

10-27

WHEN DO WE EAT?
SCHULZ

October 28, 1967

PEANUTS
WHAT ARE YOU GUYS DOING?
WE'RE WAITING FOR THE "GREAT PUMPKIN"

IF HE SELECTS THIS PUMPKIN PATCH AS THE MOST SINCERE, WE'LL GET TO SEE HIM!

OH, BROTHER..

I THINK YOU'RE BOTH CRAZY!
WE DON'T CARE WHAT YOU THINK, DO WE, SNOOPY?

SCHULZ 10-28

October 30, 1967

PEANUTS
HALLOWEEN WILL SOON BE HERE..

AND WHAT AM I DOING? I'M SITTING IN A PUMPKIN PATCH WITH THIS STUPID KID WAITING FOR THE "GREAT PUMPKIN"

WHY?
10-30

THE ONLY CONCLUSION I CAN COME TO IS THAT I REPRESENT A DECLINE IN BEAGLE MENTALITY!

October 31, 1967

PEANUTS
THIS IS IT, SNOOPY.. THIS IS HALLOWEEN NIGHT...
10-31

IF THE "GREAT PUMPKIN" PICKS THIS PUMPKIN PATCH AS THE MOST SINCERE, WE'LL GET TO SEE HIM! NOW, I...

WHAT'S THAT?
WHAT'S WHAT?

RUSTLE RUSTLE RUSTLE
IT'S THE "GREAT PUMPKIN"! HE'S RISING OUT OF THE PUMPKIN PATCH!
I NEVER SHOULD HAVE LEFT THE DAISY HILL PUPPY FARM!
SCHULZ

November 1, 1967

PEANUTS
I CAN'T BELIEVE IT... WHAT A DISAPPOINTMENT!
11-1

I APOLOGIZE, SNOOPY... WHEN I HEARD ALL THAT RUSTLING IN THE PUMPKIN PATCH, I THOUGHT FOR SURE IT WAS THE "GREAT PUMPKIN"

AND WHO DOES IT TURN OUT TO BE?

A BIRD-HIPPIE!
SCHULZ

November 24, 1967

PEANUTS
DEAR PENCIL PAL, I AM DISTURBED.
11-24

ACCORDING TO WHAT I READ, YOUR COUNTRY HATES MY COUNTRY AND MY COUNTRY HATES YOUR COUNTRY.

I DON'T HATE YOU, AND I DON'T THINK YOU HATE ME. I THINK ABOUT THIS A LOT.

IT MAKES SLEEPING AT NIGHT VERY DIFFICULT.
SCHULZ

January 27, 1968

PEANUTS
MY DAD LIKES TO HAVE ME COME DOWN TO THE BARBER SHOP, AND WAIT FOR HIM

NO MATTER HOW BUSY HE IS, EVEN IF THE SHOP IS FULL OF CUSTOMERS, HE ALWAYS STOPS TO SAY, "HI" TO ME...
Tm. Reg. U. S. Pat. Off.—All rights reserved © 1968 by United Feature Syndicate, Inc.

I SIT HERE ON THE BENCH UNTIL SIX O'CLOCK, WHEN HE'S THROUGH, AND THEN WE RIDE HOME TOGETHER..
1-27

IT REALLY DOESN'T TAKE MUCH TO MAKE A DAD HAPPY...
SCHULZ

"There aren't many things you can say in a comic strip. It's a very restrictive medium. . . . I never say things like 'you idiot'. . . it's too literal. That's why 'blockhead' works so well. There are no people who are literal blockheads. The word 'stupid' works well. . .the characters never say to each other, 'you're stupid'; they always say, 'you stupid beagle.' There's also something funny about 'you stupid beagle.' That's why he's a beagle because the phrase is funny. 'You stupid wolfhound' or 'you stupid collie' isn't very funny. Some words really work."

February 4, 1968

PEANUTS® featuring "Good ol' Charlie Brown" by SCHULZ
WHAT ARE YOU HANGING AROUND THE HOUSE FOR?
I'M AFRAID.
AFRAID?!
I'M AFRAID TO GO OUTSIDE..THERE'S A VULTURE SITTING ON MY SNOWMAN!
SEE?
WELL, HE WON'T BE SITTING THERE VERY LONG THE WAY THE SUN IS SHINING...
2-4
STUPID BEAGLE!
WE VULTURES HAVE A HARD LIFE...
SCHULZ

February 25, 1968

PEANUTS
featuring
"Good ol' Charlie Brown"
by SCHULZ
I'M HUNGRY.. IT MUST BE SUPPERTIME..
BAM
BAM
BAM
WHAT IN THE WORLD...
YOU'RE EARLY! SUPPER WON'T BE READY FOR AN HOUR YET!
FIND YOURSELF SOMETHING TO DO
SCHULZ

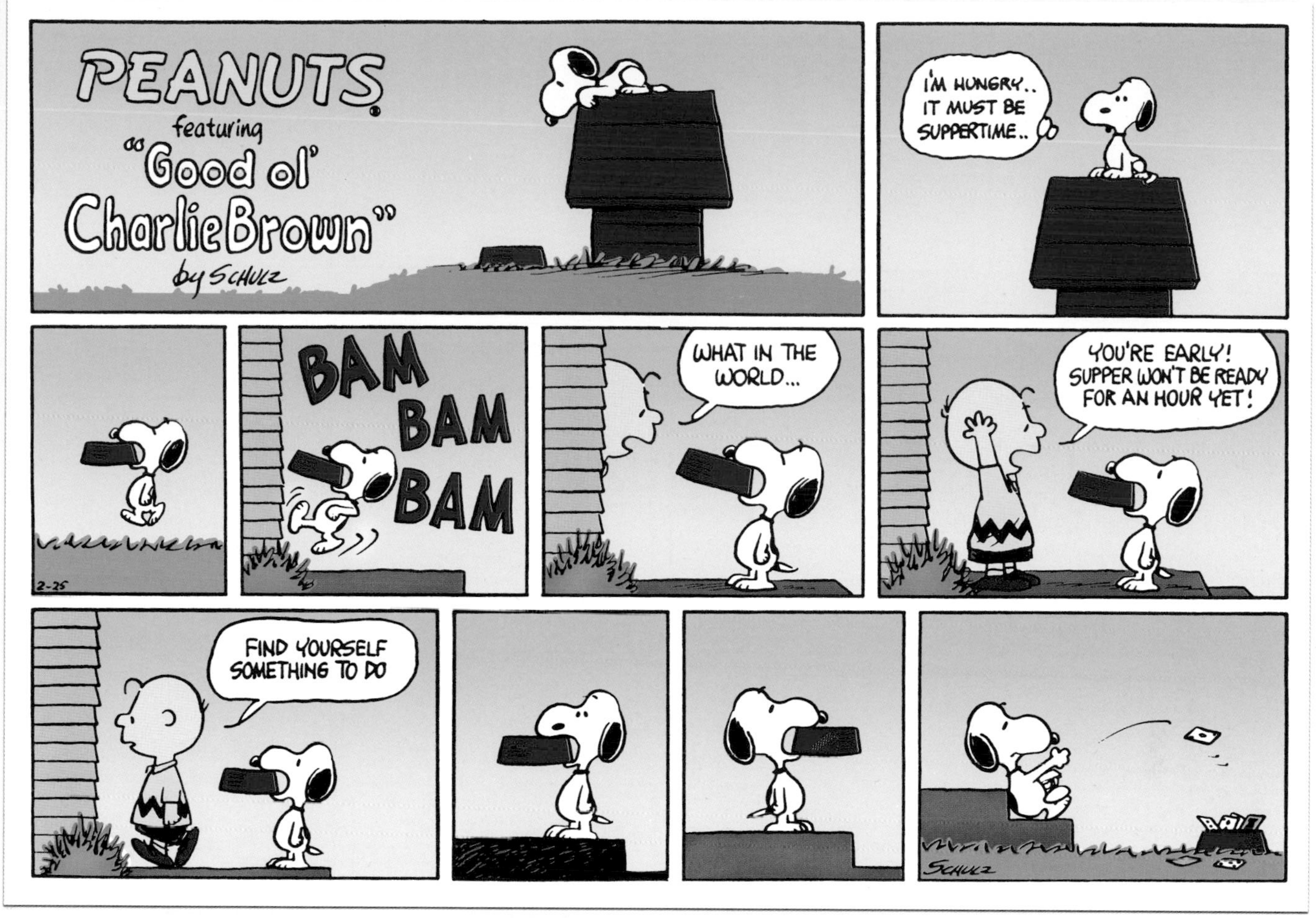

"It gives me a real buzz when people write to tell me that the strip has cheered them up when they're depressed or helped them through a time of stress. I'm proud of the way Charlie Brown has turned out; maybe he's a little less satirical than he was back in the fifties, but he's still basically the same character: a nice little guy—not into politics—trying to get along with the world."

April 3, 1968

PEANUTS

I THINK I'VE MADE A NEW THEOLOGICAL DISCOVERY...

WHAT IS IT?

IF YOU HOLD YOUR HANDS UPSIDE DOWN, YOU GET THE OPPOSITE OF WHAT YOU PRAY FOR!
SCHULZ

April 22, 1968

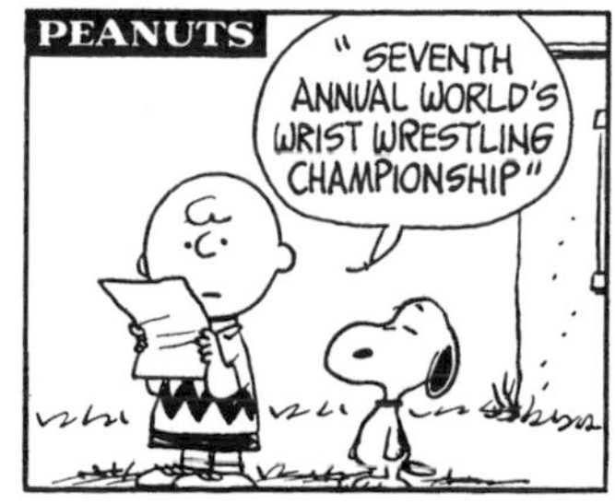
PEANUTS
"SEVENTH ANNUAL WORLD'S WRIST WRESTLING CHAMPIONSHIP"

YOU SHOULD ENTER, SNOOPY... IT'S GOING TO BE HELD ON MAY 3rd IN PETALUMA..

"PETALUMA"?

THE DEFENDING CHAMPION STANDS SIX FOOT THREE AND WEIGHS 333 POUNDS..
"PETALUMA"?!
SCHULZ

April 24, 1968

PEANUTS

HERE'S THE WORLD-FAMOUS WRIST WRESTLER TAKING PART IN A PRACTICE MATCH BEFORE HE GOES TO PETALUMA FOR THE CHAMPIONSHIPS...
4-24

WAM!

THERE'S FEAR AND TREMBLING IN PETALUMA TONIGHT!
SCHULZ

April 25, 1968

PEANUTS
4-25

KLUNK!!

WE WRIST WRESTLERS SHOW OUR OPPONENTS NO MERCY!
SCHULZ

May 1, 1968

PEANUTS
I HOPE I'M GOING THE RIGHT WAY...

AS LONG AS I STAY SOUTH OF THE 40th PARALLEL AND WEST OF THE 120th MERIDIAN, I THINK I'M ALL RIGHT...
5-1

THEY SHOULD HAVE THE MERIDIANS MARKED ALONG THE GROUND SOME PLACE...
SCHULZ

May 3, 1968

PEANUTS
WHAT ARE YOU DOING HOME? WHAT HAPPENED IN PETALUMA?
5-3

?

"OFFICIAL RULES AND REGULATIONS OF WRIST WRESTLING... THE CONTESTANTS FACE EACH OTHER GRASPING THE BASE OF EACH OTHER'S THUMB AND...

I WAS DISQUALIFIED... I DON'T HAVE A THUMB!
SCHULZ

June 3, 1968—First mention of Lila, Snoopy's first owner.

PEANUTS
6-3
A LETTER? FOR ME?

OH, I CAN'T STAND IT!

HOW CRUEL...

EVERYTIME I THINK I'VE FINALLY PUT LILA FOREVER FROM MY THOUGHTS, SHE WRITES TO ME!
SCHULZ

June 4, 1968

PEANUTS
ANOTHER LETTER FROM LILA?!

SHE'S COMING TO SEE ME! LILA'S COMING TO SEE ME!!
6-4

OH, WHY DOESN'T SHE LEAVE ME ALONE? WHY MUST SHE REOPEN OLD WOUNDS?!

NOT ONLY THAT, SHE'LL PROBABLY COME RIGHT AT SUPPERTIME!
SCHULZ

June 5, 1968

PEANUTS
OH, LILA...LILA... LILA....YOU AND I USED TO HAVE SUCH GOOD TIMES TOGETHER!

BUT YOU SAID IT COULD NEVER WORK OUT BETWEEN US SO YOU LEFT ME...AND I CRIED...
6-5

AND NOW, AFTER I'VE SPENT ALL THESE YEARS TRYING TO FORGET, YOU SAY YOU'RE COMING BACK TO SEE ME...

OH, LILA, YOU'RE GOING TO DRIVE ME CRAZY!!
BOOT!
SCHULZ

June 6, 1968

PEANUTS
LILA'S COMING TO SEE YOU?! AFTER ALL THESE YEARS?

HOW CAN SHE DO THIS TO YOU? DOESN'T SHE REALIZE THE AGONY SHE'S PUTTING YOU THROUGH? HASN'T SHE DONE ENOUGH HARM ALREADY?
SNIF!

I DON'T EVEN KNOW WHO LILA IS...
6-6
SCHULZ

June 7, 1968

PEANUTS
IT'S LILA!

LILA'S COMING! I DON'T WANT TO SEE HER! I DON'T WANT TO REVIVE OLD MEMORIES...
6-7

WHERE CAN I GO? WHERE CAN I HIDE?

UNDER THE POOL TABLE!!
SCHULZ

June 8, 1968

PEANUTS
6-8
HAS SHE LEFT?

SHE'S GONE... LILA'S GONE..

LILA'S GONE, AND I DIDN'T EVEN SEE HER... I JUST COULDN'T.... I JUST COULDN'T BEAR TO REVIVE THOSE OLD PAINFUL MEMORIES...

OH, LILA, YOU KNOW YOU MEANT MORE TO ME THAN LIFE ITSELF, AND NOW YOU'RE GONE AGAIN...OH, LILA...
I WONDER IF IT'S SUPPER-TIME?
SCHULZ

July 18, 1968

PEANUTS

BEEP!

I HAVEN'T BEEPED YOU IN A LONG TIME

I HAVEN'T MISSED IT A BIT!
7-18
SCHULZ

July 23, 1968

PEANUTS

POW!

HERE'S YOUR CAP, CHARLIE BROWN...
7-23

SIGH
SCHULZ

July 24, 1968

PEANUTS

THAT FIRST GUY GOT A HIT, CHARLIE BROWN, BUT DON'T LET IT BOTHER YOU..
I'M UPSIDE DOWN

JUST KEEP THROWIN' 'EM IN THERE!
I'M UPSIDE DOWN
7-24

I'M UPSIDE DOWN
SCHULZ

July 26, 1968

PEANUTS

7-26

SCHULZ

July 27, 1968

PEANUTS
flitter
flitter
flitter
flitter

flutter
flutter

BUMP!

THAT'S EMBARRASSING FOR BOTH OF US...
7-27
SCHULZ

June 30, 1968

PEANUTS
featuring
"Good ol' Charlie Brown"
by SCHULZ

HOW SHALL WE PITCH THIS NEXT GUY, CHARLIE BROWN?
WELL, I DON'T KNOW..
THROW HIM YOUR CURVE, CHARLIE BROWN
6-30

SAY, HAVE YOU NOTICED HOW BUILT-UP IT'S GETTING AROUND HERE? PRETTY SOON THERE WON'T BE ANY PLACE FOR US TO PLAY..LOOK AT ALL THE HOUSES...

MY GRAMPA SAYS THAT ALL OF THIS USED TO BE A BIG PASTURE..

HE SAYS HE CAN REMEMBER WHEN THEY USED TO DRIVE CATTLE RIGHT ACROSS HERE
MY DAD SAYS HE COULD HAVE MADE A LOT OF MONEY IF HE HAD BOUGHT THIS LAND TWENTY YEARS AGO

TWENTY YEARS AGO? FIVE YEARS AGO WOULD HAVE BEEN ENOUGH!
THAT'S WHAT I SAY!
OF COURSE! LAND VALUES ARE GOING UP EVERYWHERE

LOOK AT THAT PLACE WHERE THEY PUT UP THE NEW SUPER-MARKET..
THAT'S WHAT MY GRAMPA WAS TALKING ABOUT..HE SAID YOU COULD HAVE BOUGHT THAT PROPERTY FOR ALMOST NOTHING ONLY TWO YEARS AGO!

WHAT DO YOU THINK, CHARLIE BROWN?

FRANKLY, I THINK HE'D HIT A CURVE BALL...
SCHULZ

July 31, 1968—First appearance of Franklin.

PEANUTS
IS THIS YOUR BEACH BALL?

HEY! YEAH! THANK YOU VERY MUCH!
I WAS SWIMMING OUT THERE, AND IT CAME FLOATING BY..
7-31

MY SILLY SISTER THREW IT INTO THE WATER
I SEE YOU'RE MAKING A SAND CASTLE..

IT LOOKS KIND OF CROOKED
I GUESS MAYBE IT IS.. WHERE I COME FROM, I'M NOT FAMOUS FOR DOING THINGS RIGHT...
SCHULZ

"I've been thinking of how to do this for a long time, but up until recently I had always come to the conclusion that I wasn't capable of doing this thing properly. I had always thought that black people might feel I was doing it in a patronizing or condescending manner. Then, I received two letters from black fathers asking that Peanuts *be integrated. That was the turning point."*

August 1, 1968

PEANUTS
IS YOUR WHOLE FAMILY HERE AT THE BEACH, FRANKLIN?

NO, MY DAD IS OVER IN VIETNAM
MY DAD'S A BARBER.. HE WAS IN A WAR, TOO, BUT I DON'T KNOW WHICH ONE

DO YOU LIKE BASEBALL, CHARLIE BROWN?
MY PROBLEM IS I LIKE BASEBALL TOO MUCH

ARE YOU A GOOD PLAYER?
I HAVE SOME FRIENDS WHO WOULD REGARD THAT AS A GREAT TOPIC FOR A PANEL DISCUSSION
SCHULZ

August 2, 1968

PEANUTS
NOW, THERE YOU ARE, CHARLIE BROWN.. THERE'S A REAL SAND CASTLE!

IT LOOKS GREAT, FRANKLIN
I HEAR MY MOM CALLING ME.. I HATE TO GO..THIS HAS BEEN A GOOD DAY...

ASK YOUR MOTHER IF YOU CAN COME OVER SOMETIME AND SPEND THE NIGHT! WE'LL PLAY BASEBALL AND BUILD ANOTHER SAND CASTLE
8-2

YOUR BEACH BALL JUST LEFT FOR HAWAII AGAIN
OH, GOOD GRIEF!
SCHULZ

August 5, 1968

PEANUTS
8-5

OH, NO, YOU DON'T!

NOW, HOW DID I DO THAT?
SCHULZ

August 29, 1968

PEANUTS
WHAT HAPPENED?
HOW CAN I TELL YOU SOMETHING THAT WILL SHOCK YOU IF YOU PASS OUT BEFORE I CAN TELL YOU?

I'M SORRY... I'VE BEEN HYPERVENTILATING A LOT LATELY...

WELL, ANYWAY, HERE'S WHAT I FOUND OUT WHEN I CALLED THE DAISY HILL PUPPY FARM...YOU ARE NOT SNOOPY'S ORIGINAL OWNER!
8-29

KLUNK!
OH, GOOD GRIEF!
SCHULZ

August 30, 1968

PEANUTS
YOU BOUGHT SNOOPY IN THE MONTH OF OCTOBER, RIGHT?

ACCORDING TO THE RECORDS AT THE DAISY HILL PUPPY FARM, SNOOPY WAS BOUGHT BY ANOTHER FAMILY IN AUGUST...THIS FAMILY HAD A LITTLE GIRL NAMED LILA...
8-30

SNOOPY AND LILA LOVED EACH OTHER VERY MUCH, BUT THEY LIVED IN AN APARTMENT, AND THE FAMILY DECIDED THEY JUST COULDN'T KEEP SNOOPY SO THEY RETURNED HIM...

YOU GOT A USED DOG, CHARLIE BROWN!
SCHULZ

August 31, 1968

PEANUTS
NOW, I SEE WHY THOSE LETTERS FROM LILA WOULD UPSET SNOOPY SO MUCH

SURE, HE WAS TRYING TO FORGET HER, BUT WHEN HE FOUND OUT SHE WAS IN THE HOSPITAL, HE RAN OFF TO SEE HER...
8-31

I'LL BET HE WISHES HE WAS STILL HER DOG INSTEAD OF MINE...
I DOUBT IT, CHARLIE BROWN.. HE WOULDN'T HAVE BEEN HAPPY IN AN APARTMENT

HERE'S THE WORLD WAR I FLYING ACE ZOOMING THROUGH THE AIR IN HIS SOPWITH CAMEL!
SCHULZ

September 14, 1968

PEANUTS
..FOURTEEN, FIFTEEN, SIXTEEN..

TEN BILLION AND ONE, TEN BILLION AND TWO,

TEN BILLION AND THREE, TEN BILLION AND FOUR,

..TWENTY-ONE, TWENTY-TWO, TWENTY-THREE..

September 29, 1968

PEANUTS featuring "Good ol' Charlie Brown" by SCHULZ
CHARLIE BROWNNNN

I CAN'T BELIEVE IT...SHE MUST THINK I'M THE MOST STUPID PERSON ALIVE...

COME ON, CHARLIE BROWN..I'LL HOLD THE BALL, AND YOU KICK IT...
HOLD IT? HA! THAT'S A LAUGH! YOU'LL PULL IT AWAY, AND I'LL KILL MYSELF!

WHY, CHARLIE BROWN, HOW CAN YOU SAY THAT? DON'T I HAVE A FACE YOU CAN TRUST? DON'T I HAVE AN INNOCENT LOOK ABOUT ME?

LOOK AT THE INNOCENCE IN MY EYES...

SHE'S RIGHT... IF A GIRL HAS INNOCENT-LOOKING EYES, YOU SIMPLY HAVE TO TRUST HER...

THIS TIME I'M GONNA KICK THAT FOOTBALL CLEAR TO THE MOON!

AAUGH

WHAM!

WHAT YOU HAVE LEARNED HERE TODAY, CHARLIE BROWN, WILL BE OF IMMEASURABLE VALUE TO YOU FOR MANY YEARS TO COME
SIGH!

September 23, 1968

PEANUTS
PSYCHIATRIC HELP 5¢
THE DOCTOR IS IN

SYCHIATRIC HELP 5¢
THE DOCTOR IS IN

PSYCHIATRIC HELP 5¢
THE DOCTOR IS IN
FRIENDLY ADVICE 2¢
THE ADVISER IS IN

October 30, 1968

PEANUTS
TOMORROW IS HALLOWEEN, SNOOPY..

TOMORROW NIGHT I'LL BE SITTING HERE IN THIS SINCERE PUMPKIN PATCH, AND I'LL SEE THE 'GREAT PUMPKIN'! HE'LL COME FLYING THROUGH THE AIR, AND I'LL BE HERE TO SEE HIM!

ISN'T THAT EXCITING?
10-30

WHEE!
SCHULZ

November 8, 1968

PEANUTS
HERE COMES THAT LITTLE RED-HAIRED GIRL TO GET A DRINK OF WATER..

I'LL TURN THE FOUNTAIN ON FOR HER, AND IMPRESS HER WITH MY THOUGHTFULNESS
11-8

I WONDER IF I COULD GET TRANSFERRED TO ANOTHER PLANET..
SCHULZ

November 9, 1968

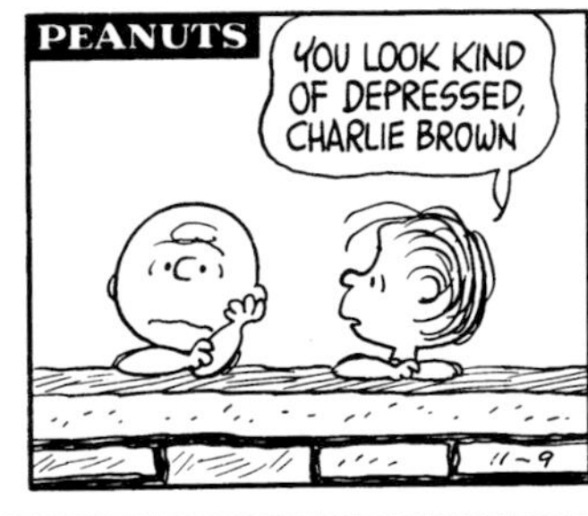
PEANUTS
YOU LOOK KIND OF DEPRESSED, CHARLIE BROWN
11-9

I WORRY ABOUT SCHOOL A LOT...

I ALSO WORRY ABOUT MY WORRYING SO MUCH ABOUT SCHOOL..

MY ANXIETIES HAVE ANXIETIES
SCHULZ

December 2, 1968

PEANUTS
HELLO, CHUCK? THIS IS PEPPERMINT PATTY...

I'M MAKING OUT MY CHRISTMAS CARD LIST, CHUCK, AND I WANTED TO KNOW YOUR ADDRESS SO I COULD SURPRISE YOU WITH A CARD...
12-2
BUT NOW THE SURPRISE IS GONE, ISN'T IT? WELL, I'LL JUST SEND YOUR CARD TO SOMEONE ELSE SO I GUESS I WON'T NEED YOUR ADDRESS.. FORGET I CALLED, CHUCK

SIGH
SCHULZ

December 10, 1968

PEANUTS
I LIKE STANDING IN THE SNOW
12-10
AS I STAND HERE WITH THE SNOW FALLING GENTLY ALL AROUND ME, I FEEL SORT OF CLOSED-OFF... I GET SORT OF A FEELING OF SECURITY

WOP!

SORT OF!
SCHULZ

December 23, 1968

PEANUTS
HERE'S THE WORLD WAR I FLYING ACE ZOOMING THROUGH THE AIR IN HIS SOPWITH CAMEL..

SUDDENLY HE SEES A SHADOW MOVE ACROSS THE GROUND..AN ANGRY SOUND FILLS THE AIR!

IT'S THE RED BARON! HE'S RIDDLING MY PLANE WITH BULLETS

THIS COULD RUIN MY WHOLE CHRISTMAS!

December 24, 1968

PEANUTS
IT'S CHRISTMAS EVE, AND THE WORLD WAR I FLYING ACE IS DOWN BEHIND ENEMY LINES..

BACK HOME EVERYONE IS OPENING PRESENTS AND HAVING A GOOD TIME...CURSE YOU, RED BARON!

IT'S ALL HIS FAULT...BUT I'LL GET EVEN WITH HIM...

NEXT YEAR I WON'T SEND HIM A CHRISTMAS CARD!

January 5, 1969

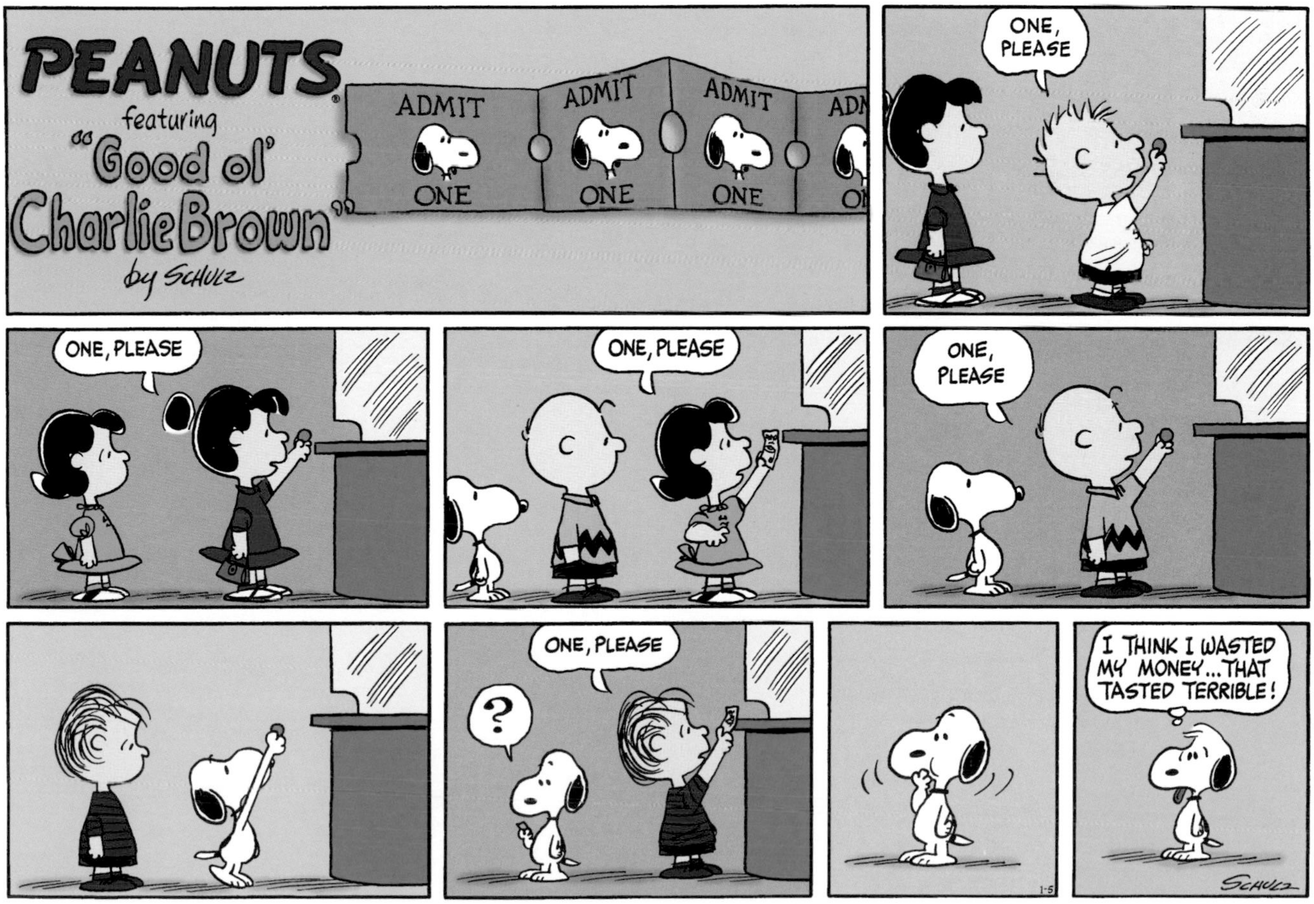

PEANUTS featuring "Good ol' Charlie Brown" by SCHULZ

ADMIT ONE ADMIT ONE ADMIT ONE

ONE, PLEASE

ONE, PLEASE

ONE, PLEASE

ONE, PLEASE

ONE, PLEASE

?

I THINK I WASTED MY MONEY...THAT TASTED TERRIBLE!

January 2, 1969

PEANUTS
THIS IS MY YEAR!

I CAN FEEL IT! I'VE BEEN WAITING FOR THIS YEAR ALL OF MY LIFE, AND I KNOW THIS IS IT!
1-2

I HEREBY DECLARE THAT THIS IS MY YEAR!!

MAYBE IF WE'RE LUCKY, SHE'LL LET US HAVE A FEW TUESDAYS...
SCHULZ

January 3, 1969

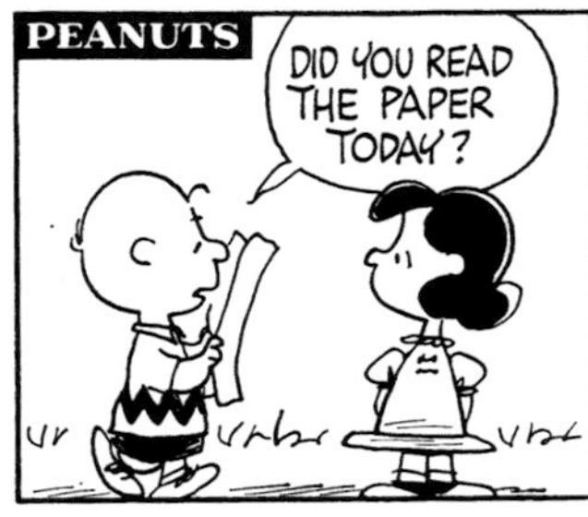
PEANUTS
DID YOU READ THE PAPER TODAY?

DID YOU READ ABOUT ALL THE TERRIBLE THINGS GOING ON IN THE WORLD?
1-3

IT'S VERY DEPRESSING

I'LL THANK YOU NOT TO CRITICIZE MY YEAR!
SCHULZ

March 8, 1969

PEANUTS
I HAVE A LOT OF PREPARATIONS TO MAKE..
3-8

THIS IS VERY SERIOUS

I'M REALLY GOING TO SURPRISE EVERYONE.. THEY'LL NEVER BELIEVE IT...

FIRST BEAGLE ON THE MOON!
SCHULZ

March 10, 1969

PEANUTS
HERE'S THE WORLD-FAMOUS ASTRONAUT TAKING OFF FOR THE MOON...
3-10

ALL SYSTEMS ARE GO! A-OK! HOW DO YOU READ? LOUD AND CLEAR!

WE HAVE LIFT OFF! THE BIRD IS BEGINNING TO MOVE....

WE HAVE A LOT OF "IN" EXPRESSIONS!
SCHULZ

March 11, 1969

PEANUTS

I'M GLAD YOU'RE GOING TO THE MOON

THAT MEANS I WON'T HAVE TO FEED YOU TONIGHT..

REPORT THAT MAN TO MISSION CONTROL!!
3-11
SCHULZ

March 12, 1969

PEANUTS
THIS IS THE WORLD-FAMOUS ASTRONAUT CALLING HOUSTON CONTROL!

COME IN, HOUSTON CONTROL... CALLING HOUSTON CONTROL..

ALL RIGHT, THEN...HOW ABOUT PETALUMA?

March 13, 1969

PEANUTS
HERE'S THE WORLD-FAMOUS ASTRONAUT APPROACHING THE MOON..

FANTASTIC!

IT LOOKS LIKE A DIRTY BEACH...

OR HAS SOMEONE ALREADY SAID THAT?

"I think that's one of the best things that's ever happened. Snoopy was the first character in comic strip history literally to land on the moon! It wasn't just a story! No, he was there! And they brought back all sorts of beautiful little lapel pins which were given as safety awards to people on the assembly line. It was a wonderful thing, very flattering."

March 14, 1969

PEANUTS
I'M ON THE MOON!

I DID IT! I'M THE FIRST BEAGLE ON THE MOON!

I BEAT THE RUSSIANS... I BEAT EVERYBODY....

I EVEN BEAT THAT STUPID CAT WHO LIVES NEXT DOOR!

March 15, 1969

PEANUTS
HERE'S THE WORLD-FAMOUS ASTRONAUT RETURNING FROM THE MOON..

TWO HUNDRED AND FORTY THOUSAND MILES THROUGH SPACE

WHAT COURAGE! WHAT FORTITUDE!

YOU CAN TELL I'M RETURNING BECAUSE I'M FACING THE OTHER WAY!

March 21, 1969

PEANUTS
POETS TELL US THAT THE ANSWERS TO LIFE CAN BE FOUND IN THE STARS...
3-21

STUPID POETS!
SCHULZ

January 12, 1969

PEANUTS
featuring "Good ol' Charlie Brown"
by SCHULZ

AH, HA!!

CAUGHT YOU IN THE ACT, DIDN'T I ?

I WANT TO SEE THAT SNOWBALL TAKEN APART SNOWFLAKE BY SNOWFLAKE, AND I WANT TO SEE IT TAKEN APART NOW!

NO CHUNKS! NO PIECES! JUST SNOWFLAKES! ONE SNOWFLAKE AT A TIME!
1-12

NO PIECES! NO CHUNKS! JUST ONE SNOWFLAKE AT A TIME!

HAVE YOU EVER TRIED TO DISMANTLE A SNOWBALL?
SCHULZ

April 8, 1969

PEANUTS
BUT YOU DON'T HAVE ANY IDEA WHERE SHE IS!
4-8

HOW WILL YOU FIND HER? WHERE WILL YOU LOOK? DON'T YOU THINK YOU SHOULD CONSIDER THIS A LITTLE MORE CAREFULLY BEFORE YOU JUST SORT OF TAKE OFF?

NO, YOUR MIND IS MADE UP, ISN'T IT? WELL, I HATE TO SEE YOU GO, BUT GOOD LUCK, OL' PAL... I HOPE YOU FIND HER...

MOM!
SCHULZ

April 9, 1969

PEANUTS
HE WHAT?
SNOOPY LEFT TO TRY TO FIND HIS MOTHER..

HE HASN'T HEARD FROM HER FOR A LONG TIME SO HE THOUGHT HE'D TRY TO FIND HER...

THAT STUPID BEAGLE! HE COULDN'T FIND ANYTHING!

MOM?

April 10, 1969

PEANUTS
IT JUST KILLS ME WHEN SNOOPY GOES OFF ON THESE TRIPS..

HE HAS NO RIGHT TO WORRY YOU LIKE THIS, CHARLIE BROWN! HE'S YOUR DOG, AND HE SHOULD STAY HOME WHERE HE BELONGS!

BUT HE WANTS TO FIND HIS MOTHER..
THAT STUPID BEAGLE SHOULDN'T BE OUT ALONE! HE'LL BUMP INTO A TREE OR SOMETHING...

BONK!!

April 11, 1969

PEANUTS
MOM?

IT'S RAINING, AND I'M LOST AND I CAN'T FIND MY MOM... I SHOULD HAVE STAYED HOME....

IF I WERE HOME, MY MASTER WOULD BE BRINGING ME MY SUPPER ABOUT NOW... WHAT WAS HIS NAME?

..THAT KID WITH THE ROUND HEAD..

April 12, 1969

PEANUTS
IF SNOOPY'S BEEN GONE FOR FIVE DAYS, CHARLIE BROWN, I THINK YOU SHOULD PUT AN AD IN THE PAPER...

BUT WE DON'T KNOW IF HE'S LOST...
WELL, MAYBE HE'S IN TROUBLE...

IT'S DANGEROUS WANDERING AROUND THE COUNTRY.. LOTS OF PECULIAR THINGS CAN HAPPEN...

GO 'WAY, YOU STUPID CAT!!

April 14, 1969

PEANUTS
I WISH I COULD FIND MY MOM...

IT'D BE GREAT TO BE ABLE TO TAKE HER HOME AND SHOW HER MY HOUSE AND HAVE HER MEET THAT ROUND-HEADED KID...

SIGH

HAVE YOU SEEN MY MOM?

April 15, 1969

PEANUTS
WHAT A BEAUTIFUL VALLEY!

AND WHAT A BEAUTIFUL FARM! WHITE FENCES..POLLED HEREFORDS, DUCKS, HORSES, A PONY.....

I WONDER IF MY MOM LIVES HERE...WOULDN'T IT BE SOMETHING IF I SAW HER, AND...

MOM!

April 16, 1969

PEANUTS
MOM

OH, EXCUSE ME! I THOUGHT YOU WERE MY MOM.....EXCUSE ME...

HOW EMBARRASSING...

ALL BEAGLES LOOK ALIKE TO ME!

April 17, 1969

PEANUTS
I'M SORRY YOU DIDN'T FIND YOUR MOTHER, SNOOPY..
SIGH

I'LL BET YOU HAD SOME INTERESTING ADVENTURES, THOUGH... MAYBE YOU SHOULD PUT THEM IN A BOOK..

THAT'S NOT A BAD IDEA...ALL I NEED IS A GOOD OPENING SENTENCE...

It was a dark and stormy night...

May 5, 1969

PEANUTS
THIS IS "BE KIND TO ANIMALS WEEK"..

PAT
PAT
PAT

YOU MEAN, THAT'S IT?

May 6, 1969

PEANUTS
I HEAR THIS IS "BE KIND TO ANIMALS WEEK"

WHAT DO YOU SUGGEST A PERSON DO?

BESIDES THAT, I MEAN..

May 10, 1969

PEANUTS
I'VE BEEN THINKING ABOUT SOMETHING...

IN THE BIG LEAGUES, WHEN A TEAM GETS A RALLY STARTED, SOMEONE BLOWS A TRUMPET AND EVERYONE YELLS, "CHARGE!!"

DO YOU THINK WE COULD DO THAT, CHARLIE BROWN?

I DON'T KNOW...WE'VE NEVER HAD A RALLY...

May 4, 1969

PEANUTS
featuring
"Good ol' CharlieBrown"
by SCHULZ
WHAT'S THAT? I THOUGHT I HEARD A NOISE..

THESE NIGHTS KILL ME..

EVERYTHING SEEMS SO HOPELESS AT NIGHT..

WHAT AM I DOING HERE? WHAT'S THE PURPOSE OF IT ALL?

WHAT'S GOING TO HAPPEN TO ME WHEN I GET OLD? WHAT IF I GET SICK? I DON'T WANT TO GET SICK..

WHAT IF I GET HIT BY A CAR SOMEDAY AND END UP IN A BODY CAST? OR MAYBE THEY'D JUST SHOOT ME LIKE AN OLD FARM HORSE! WHAT IF I LOST MY SIGHT OR MY HEARING?

Z

IT MUST BE NICE TO BE A DOG... THEY DON'T EVER HAVE ANY WORRIES...

NOT AS LONG AS THE SUN IS UP...

May 27, 1969

PEANUTS
WHAP!

POW!

WHAM!!

NOBODY BEATS ME AT "TETHER-BALL"!

May 30, 1969

PEANUTS
PSYCHIATRIC HELP 5¢
I DON'T KNOW WHAT TO DO...
THE DOCTOR IS IN
5-30

SOMETIMES I GET SO LONELY I CAN HARDLY STAND IT...

OTHER TIMES, I ACTUALLY LONG TO BE COMPLETELY ALONE...
THE DOCTOR IS IN

TRY TO LIVE IN-BETWEEN... FIVE CENTS, PLEASE!
THE DOCTOR IS IN
SCHULZ

June 8, 1969

PEANUTS
featuring
"Good ol' Charlie Brown"
by SCHULZ

Z
BONK

WELL! DID THAT NASTY OL' POP FLY AWAKEN YOU? DID IT DISTURB YOUR BEAUTY SLEEP?

I'M SORRY IF THE SOUND OF FLY BALLS LANDING BEHIND YOU IS DEPRIVING YOU OF YOUR REST!

PERHAPS WE SHOULD SOFTEN THE INFIELD SO THE BALL WON'T MAKE SO MUCH NOISE WHEN IT LANDS BEHIND YOU...

WAAH!

OH, GOOD GRIEF! NOW, I'VE HURT HIS FEELINGS...

I'M SORRY, SNOOPY.. I APOLOGIZE..I SHOULDN'T HAVE BEEN SO SARCASTIC.. I GUESS I DON'T KNOW HOW TO HANDLE PLAYERS...I'M A TERRIBLE MANAGER... I APOLOGIZE..
SNIF

SCHULZ
Z
BONK

May 31, 1969

PEANUTS
5-31

ITCHY BACK!
SCHULZ

June 2, 1969

PEANUTS
IT SAYS HERE THAT THEY'RE HAVING A DOG SHOW..

HAVE YOU EVER THOUGHT OF ENTERING A DOG SHOW?

HOW COULD I?

I DON'T EVEN **OWN** A DOG!
6-2
SCHULZ

June 11, 1969

PEANUTS
YOU'RE SURE IT'S NOT GOING TO BE ANY TROUBLE?

OF COURSE NOT! YOU GO ON YOUR VACATION, AND SNOOPY CAN STAY WITH US...
6-11

I'LL WHIP HIM INTO SHAPE! I MEAN, I'LL TAKE GOOD CARE OF HIM...

WHAT DO YOU USUALLY FEED HIM.. A FEW CRUSTS OF STALE BREAD AND SOME WATER?
AAUGH!
SCHULZ

June 14, 1969

PEANUTS

WHAT'S THIS DOG DOING IN THE HOUSE?!!!

YOU STAY OUTSIDE WHERE YOU BELONG! OUT! OUT! OUT!

RATS! I'M GONNA MISS ALL MY PROGRAMS!
SCHULZ
6-14

June 17, 1969

PEANUTS
I'LL BET SNOOPY'S GONNA MISS SLEEPING ON TOP OF HIS DOG HOUSE..
6-17

DON'T WORRY... I'VE FIXED HIM A GOOD PLACE...

I PUT HIM OUT IN THE YARD IN ONE OF MY OLD DOLL BEDS...

HE WALKS, HE TALKS, HIS ARMS MOVE...HE SAYS, "MAMA"
SCHULZ

June 18, 1969

PEANUTS
DEAR SNOOPY,
I AM WRITING FROM OUR MOTEL. WE ARE HAVING A NICE VACATION, BUT I MISS YOU.

SALLY SAYS, "HELLO"
I DIDN'T SAY "HELLO"
6-18

THIS IS TRADITIONAL VACATION POST CARD WRITING.. YOU ALWAYS WRITE THAT SOMEONE SAYS, "HELLO"... YOU JUST DON'T UNDERSTAND VACATION POST CARD WRITING...

I DON'T EVEN UNDERSTAND VACATIONS!
SCHULZ

June 20, 1969

PEANUTS
THAT WORLD WAR I ACT OF YOURS DRIVES ME CRAZY!

IF YOU WERE MY DOG, I'D STRAIGHTEN YOU OUT, BUT GOOD!
6-20

BUT I'M NOT YOUR DOG, SWEETIE!
SMAK

I THINK THIS COUNTRY LASS HAS FALLEN FOR ME.. MY KISS HAS LEFT HER SPEECHLESS!
SCHULZ

June 26, 1969

PEANUTS
HOME AT LAST!

I'VE GOT TO GO GET SNOOPY! IF THAT LUCY WAS MEAN TO HIM, I'LL NEVER FORGIVE MYSELF

I NEVER SHOULD HAVE LEFT HIM WITH HER.. WHY DID I DO IT? WHY?
6-26

IF THAT'S GENERAL PERSHING, TELL HIM I'M BUSY!
SCHULZ

October 4, 1969

PEANUTS
SOMETIMES I LIE AWAKE AT NIGHT AND THINK ABOUT THAT LITTLE RED-HAIRED GIRL...
10-4

I DON'T EVER WANT TO FORGET HER FACE, BUT IF I DON'T FORGET HER FACE, I'LL GO CRAZY...

HOW CAN I REMEMBER THE FACE I CAN'T FORGET?

SUDDENLY I'M WRITING COUNTRY WESTERN MUSIC!
SCHULZ

October 8, 1969

PEANUTS
IT'S A CRISP FALL DAY... I'LL BET THE FIELDS ARE FULL OF RABBITS!

YOU KNOW WHAT WE HAVE TO DO ON A DAY LIKE TODAY, DON'T YOU?
10-8

STATE
SCHULZ

November 8, 1969

PEANUTS
11-8
WELL, YOU WON AGAIN..

IS THAT ALL YOU'RE GOING TO SAY?

YOU'RE NO FUN TO BEAT, CHARLIE BROWN...BEATING YOU IS LIKE BEATING NOTHING!

I CAN'T EVEN LOSE RIGHT...
SCHULZ

November 30, 1969

PEANUTS
featuring
"Good ol' Charlie Brown"
by Schulz
It Was a Dark and Stormy Night by SNOOPY
all rights reserved

It was a dark and stormy night

Suddenly a shot rang out. A door slammed. The maid screamed. Suddenly a pirate ship appeared on the horizon. While millions of people were starving, the king lived in luxury.

Meanwhile, on a small farm in Kansas, a boy was growing up. End of Part I

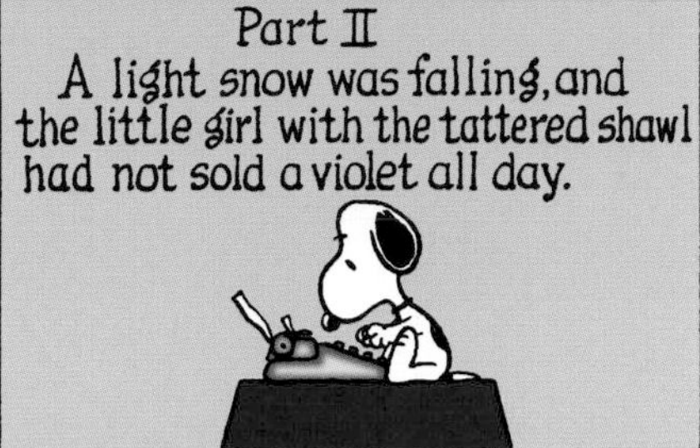
Part II
A light snow was falling, and the little girl with the tattered shawl had not sold a violet all day.

At that very moment, a young intern at City Hospital was making an important discovery.

I MAY HAVE WRITTEN MYSELF INTO A CORNER...

"In a way I suppose I'm something of a phrasemaker. Some of my things have become part of the American idiom. The most obvious is 'security blanket.' People never used to talk about security blankets, though kids have probably been dragging them around for hundreds of years. And the Red Baron and the 'Happiness is . . .' thing. Everyone is always defining happiness in some way. Even the name 'Charlie Brown' has become a phrase: 'You're the Charlie Brown type.'"

December 5, 1969

PEANUTS
YOU'RE MINE! I HAVE MADE YOU WITH MY OWN HANDS!

AND, LEST YOU FORGET, AS I CREATED YOU, I ALSO CAN DESTROY YOU!!

I'M SORRY... THAT WAS A STUPID THING TO SAY...

December 6, 1969

PEANUTS

I SHOULD HAVE STAYED HOME...

I HATE THESE PARTIES WHERE YOU JUST STAND AROUND AND NOBODY SAYS ANYTHING!

Celebrate 1970s

"To create something out of nothing is a wonderful experience. To take a blank piece of paper and draw characters that people love and worry about is extremely satisfying. I hope very much that I will be allowed to do it for another twenty-five years."

—*Charles M. Schulz*

1970–1979

In the 1970s the main characters continued to evolve—Charles Schulz wrote the following about the changes in Snoopy:

"Snoopy's appearance and personality have changed probably more than those of any of the other characters. As my drawing style loosened, Snoopy was able to do more things, and when I finally developed the formula of using his imagination to dream of being many heroic figures, the strip took on a completely new dimension."

Note Snoopy's puppylike appearance in the strips from the 1950s, and compare it to his appearance in the strips from the 1970s.

In this decade a few new characters were added to the mix, and Schulz perfected the art of the multiday story line. He wrote in *Peanuts Jubilee* (1975), "I have tried to use stories frequently. I find it a good way to think of ideas because once a story gets going all sorts of little episodes come to mind."

- From a long-running story line, the February 16, 1970, strip commemorates Snoopy's promotion to Head Beagle. Snoopy cracks under the weight of Head Beagle responsibilities and is booted from the position on March 9, 1970.
- Woodstock was officially named on June 22, 1970. The little bird, who had been gaining prominence in the strip since 1967, was cleverly named Woodstock after the most famous rock festival of the 1960s. When asked why he had named the bird after the rock festival, Schulz pithily replied, "Why not?"
- Joe Cool made his first named appearance on May 27, 1971, although a sunglasses-wearing Snoopy had been "hanging out" for almost a year before he was given his official moniker.

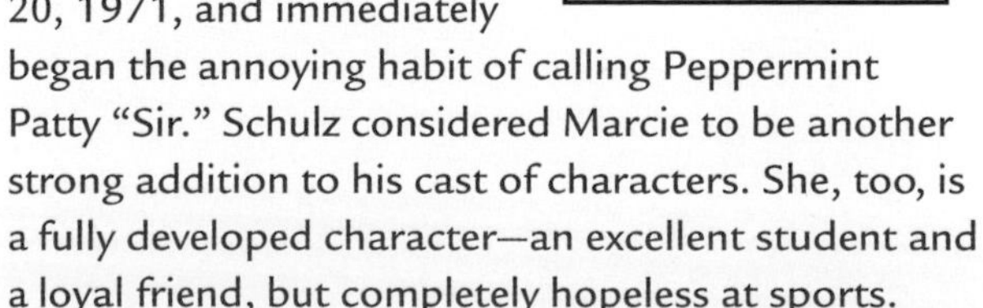

- Marcie, Peppermint Patty's great friend and confidant, debuted in the strip on July 20, 1971, and immediately began the annoying habit of calling Peppermint Patty "Sir." Schulz considered Marcie to be another strong addition to his cast of characters. She, too, is a fully developed character—an excellent student and a loyal friend, but completely hopeless at sports.
- Another character to join the cast in the 1970s was Rerun, Lucy and Linus's baby brother born on May 23, 1972. The character of Rerun grew more prominent in the strip as Schulz began to explore the grandparent/grandchild relationship in the 1990s.
- In one of Schulz's most popular story lines, Charlie Brown awakens one day to find his head covered in a rash that looks like the stitching on a baseball. Not wanting to appear at summer camp with the embarrassing rash, he wears a paper bag over his head. Much to his surprise, the bag-wearing Charlie Brown finds that he is popular and, as the June 23, 1973, cartoon details, is even elected camp president! Unfortunately, as soon as Charlie Brown removes the bag from his head, he quickly reverts back to being his same old wishy-washy self.

- Spike, Snoopy's skinny, desert-dwelling brother, made his first appearance on August 13, 1975. Spike lives in the Mojave Desert near Needles, California. That might seem like an unlikely location for a *Peanuts* character, but it was actually Schulz's boyhood home for about a year at the beginning of the Great Depression of the 1930s.
- Another of Snoopy's siblings, Belle, made her debut on June 28, 1976. Belle is a notable character in that she has a son, Snoopy's only nephew.

- A long-running gag began on January 27, 1977, when Sally called Linus her Sweet Babboo for the first time. This endearment was borrowed from Schulz's own life—it was a pet name his wife, Jean, called him!
- In a story line that ran from July 25 through August 30, 1977, Snoopy fell in love and planned his wedding. In the August 9, 1977, strip he broke the news to a bewildered Charlie Brown. As is typical in *Peanuts*, though, the course of true love did not run smoothly. His fiancée, whom the reader never sees, runs off to Needles with best man Spike before the wedding takes place. And then, fickle creature that she is, runs away from Spike with a coyote.

January 6, 1970

PEANUTS
WELL, WHO'S THE MYSTERIOUS LETTER FROM?

OOOOoo!
KLUNK!

HE FAINTED!
WHAT ELSE?

WHEN YOU RECEIVE A LETTER FROM THE HEAD BEAGLE, YOU ALWAYS FAINT!

"A comic strip also has to grow. The only way you can stay ahead of your imitators is to search out new territories. Also, what is funny in a comic strip today will not necessarily be funny the following week. A good example of this is the character of Snoopy. The mere fact that we could read Snoopy's thoughts was funny in itself when Peanuts *first began. Now, of course, it is the content of those thoughts that is important, and as he progresses in his imagination to new personalities, some of the things which he originally did as an ordinary dog would no longer be funny. Snoopy's personality in the strip has to be watched very carefully, for it can get away from me."*

January 7, 1970

PEANUTS
"GREETINGS... YOU HAVE BEEN SELECTED BY THE HEAD BEAGLE FOR A SPECIAL ASSIGNMENT"

WHEN YOU ARE SELECTED BY THE HEAD BEAGLE FOR A SPECIAL ASSIGNMENT, YOU SAY A FEW QUICK GOODBYS, AND RUSH OFF!

I'VE NEVER KNOWN ANYONE BEFORE WHO WAS SELECTED BY THE HEAD BEAGLE FOR A SPECIAL ASSIGNMENT

January 8, 1970

PEANUTS
HEY, IT'S SNOOPY, THAT FUNNY LOOKING KID WITH THE BIG NOSE!

HI, SNOOPY! HOW'S THE OL' SHORTSTOP? HOW'VE YOU BEEN?

WHEN YOU'RE SELECTED BY THE HEAD BEAGLE FOR A SPECIAL ASSIGNMENT, YOU HAVE NO TIME FOR GIRLS!

January 9, 1970

PEANUTS
HERE I AM STANDING BEFORE THE HEAD BEAGLE..

YES, SIR! YES, SIR...I'LL DO IT! YOU CAN COUNT ON ME! YES, SIR! ABSOLUTELY, SIR!

THE HEAD BEAGLE HAS SPOKEN! MY COURSE IS CLEAR! DUTY LIES AHEAD! HE HAS SPOKEN, AND I MUST OBEY!

RATS! I FORGOT TO GET HIS AUTOGRAPH...

January 14, 1970

PEANUTS
THAT'S MY BOOK YOU'RE READING!

IT IS SAID THAT ABRAHAM LINCOLN ONCE WALKED THROUGH A BLIZZARD TO RETURN A BORROWED BOOK

YOU WON'T EVEN WALK ACROSS THE ROOM!

I SHOULD HAVE LOANED MY BOOK TO ABRAHAM LINCOLN!
SCHULZ

"Linus is a lot of fun to draw. Linus is very flexible and it's fun to draw his hair. And it's fun to draw wild expressions on Linus, especially when Lucy has shouted at him, and his hair flies up in the air or he goes over backwards or something of this kind."

January 16, 1970

PEANUTS
SHOVEL YOUR WALK FOR A QUARTER?

WHAT IF IT SNOWS TOMORROW, AND COVERS UP OUR WALK AGAIN? DO WE GET OUR QUARTER BACK?

NO, BY THEN I WILL HAVE SPENT IT IN RIOTOUS LIVING...

FORGET IT!
SCHULZ

January 18, 1970

Classic
PEANUTS
featuring
"Good ol' Charlie Brown"
by SCHULZ

WHAT ARE YOU DOING HERE?

WHO WANTS TO KNOW? MAYBE I JUST LIKE MUSIC!

DO YOU LIKE BEETHOVEN?

WHAT?
IF YOU'RE GOING TO HANG AROUND HERE, YOU'VE GOT TO LIKE BEETHOVEN...

ALL RIGHT, BUT I'LL JUST HAVE A SMALL GLASS

KLUNK!

YOU BLEW IT, KID!
SCHULZ

January 23, 1970

PEANUTS
USED CAR SALE!

YES, YOU HEARD RIGHT! YOU'VE NEVER SEEN SUCH VALUES!

COME DOWN TO OUR SHOWROOM NOW!!

DON'T DELAY!! COME DOWN NOW! NOW IS THE TIME! NOW! NOW! NOW!
HELP!

February 4, 1970

PEANUTS
I WANT TO MAKE MY OWN VALENTINES THIS YEAR, BUT I CAN'T DRAW A GOOD HEART

TRY DRAWING JUST ONE SIDE, AND THEN FOLD IT OVER AND TRACE THE OTHER SIDE

FOLD IT OVER?! I HATE FOLDING THINGS OVER! WHY DOES IT HAVE TO BE SO COMPLICATED?

FOLD! CUT! CREASE! TEAR! MEASURE! TRACE! DRAW! FORGET IT! FORGET IT, I SAY! FORGET IT!!!

February 10, 1970

PEANUTS

HE'S VERY GOOD WITH A SNOW SHOVEL..

I SHOULD BE OUT OF HERE BY THE FIRST OF AUGUST!

February 16, 1970

PEANUTS
WELL, I'LL BE!

WELL, I'LL BE!

LOOK AT THIS..
WELL, I'LL BE!

WHO ELSE DO YOU KNOW WHOSE DOG HAS JUST BEEN PROMOTED TO "HEAD BEAGLE"?

February 20, 1970

PEANUTS
HERE'S THE HEAD BEAGLE AND HIS SECRETARY HARD AT WORK..
GOOD GRIEF! I NEVER REALIZED THERE'D BE SO MUCH PAPER WORK!

SIGN THIS... SIGN THAT.. SIGN THESE... SIGN THOSE... I CAN'T STAND IT!!

LET'S SEE NOW.. I'M SUPPOSED TO DIRECT SOME COLLIES TO VERMONT, SOME GOLDEN RETRIEVERS TO MINNESOTA AND SOME PEKINGESESESES TO...

I NEVER COULD PRONOUNCE THAT!

February 15, 1970

PEANUTS
featuring
"Good ol' Charlie Brown"
by SCHULZ

SNAP!

February 23, 1970

PEANUTS
A PLAYGROUND IN NEW JERSEY NEEDS A MONGREL
FOUR THOUSAND ST. BERNARDS WHERE? I CAN'T BELIEVE IT! WHO SENT ALL THOSE SHEEP DOGS TO MISSISSIPPI? WHAT ABOUT THIS CAT THING? WE DON'T HANDLE CATS!
FIFTEEN SPANIELS TO MICHIGAN.. MAKE THAT FIFTEEN HUNDRED... WHERE IS THAT PLAYGROUND IN NEW JERSEY? WHERE'S OUR MAP? WHO WANTED THOSE DACHSHUNDS?
ACTUALLY, THE LAST HEAD BEAGLE LEFT THINGS IN AN AWFUL MESS!

March 2, 1970

PEANUTS
THE WORLD IS IN TERRIBLE SHAPE!
AND DO YOU KNOW **WHY**? **IT'S ALL THE FAULT OF THE HEAD BEAGLE!**
BOOT!
MY ADMINISTRATION HATES CRITICISM!

March 5, 1970

PEANUTS
I CAN'T DO ALL THESE THINGS
r t * ? W
3-5

THIS JOB IS TOO MUCH FOR ONE BEAGLE! EVERYONE WANTS SOMETHING! EVERYONE COMPLAINS! I WORK DAY AND NIGHT AND NO ONE APPRECIATES IT!

EVEN MY POOR SECRETARY IS EXHAUSTED...
Z

I HATE BEING HEAD BEAGLE!
Z
SCHULZ

March 9, 1970

PEANUTS
HI, CHUCK! WHAT'S UP?
IS SNOOPY STILL HERE? THIS LETTER CAME FOR HIM..

IT LOOKS KIND OF OFFICIAL...

"THIS IS TO INFORM YOU THAT YOU HAVE BEEN REPLACED AS HEAD BEAGLE"

BAD NEWS, OL' PAL?
3-9
I BLEW IT!
SCHULZ

March 8, 1970

PEANUTS
featuring
"Good ol' CharlieBrown"
by SCHULZ
JOE SHLABOT

JOE SHLABOTNIK FAN CLUB NEWS
VOLUME I NO. 1
3-8

DEAR FANS OF JOE SHLABOTNIK,
WELL, HERE IT IS ALMOST SPRING AGAIN AND EVERYONE IS EXCITED ABOUT THE NEW BASEBALL SEASON.

OUR HERO WILL BE PLAYING FOR HILLCREST IN THE GREEN GRASS LEAGUE AGAIN.

I REALLY SHOULD HAVE SOME PHOTOGRAPHS IN MY FAN MAGAZINE TO GIVE IT SOME CLASS, BUT I DON'T KNOW HOW TO PRINT THEM...

LAST YEAR JOE BATTED .143 AND MADE SOME SPECTACULAR CATCHES OF ROUTINE FLY BALLS. HE ALSO THREW OUT A RUNNER WHO HAD FALLEN DOWN BETWEEN FIRST AND SECOND.

WELL, FANS, THERE IT IS. REMEMBER, THIS LITTLE OL' FAN MAGAZINE IS YOURS. WE WELCOME YOUR COMMENTS.

WHO NEEDS IT?

I SHOULDN'T HAVE WELCOMED HER COMMENTS...
SCHULZ

March 15, 1970

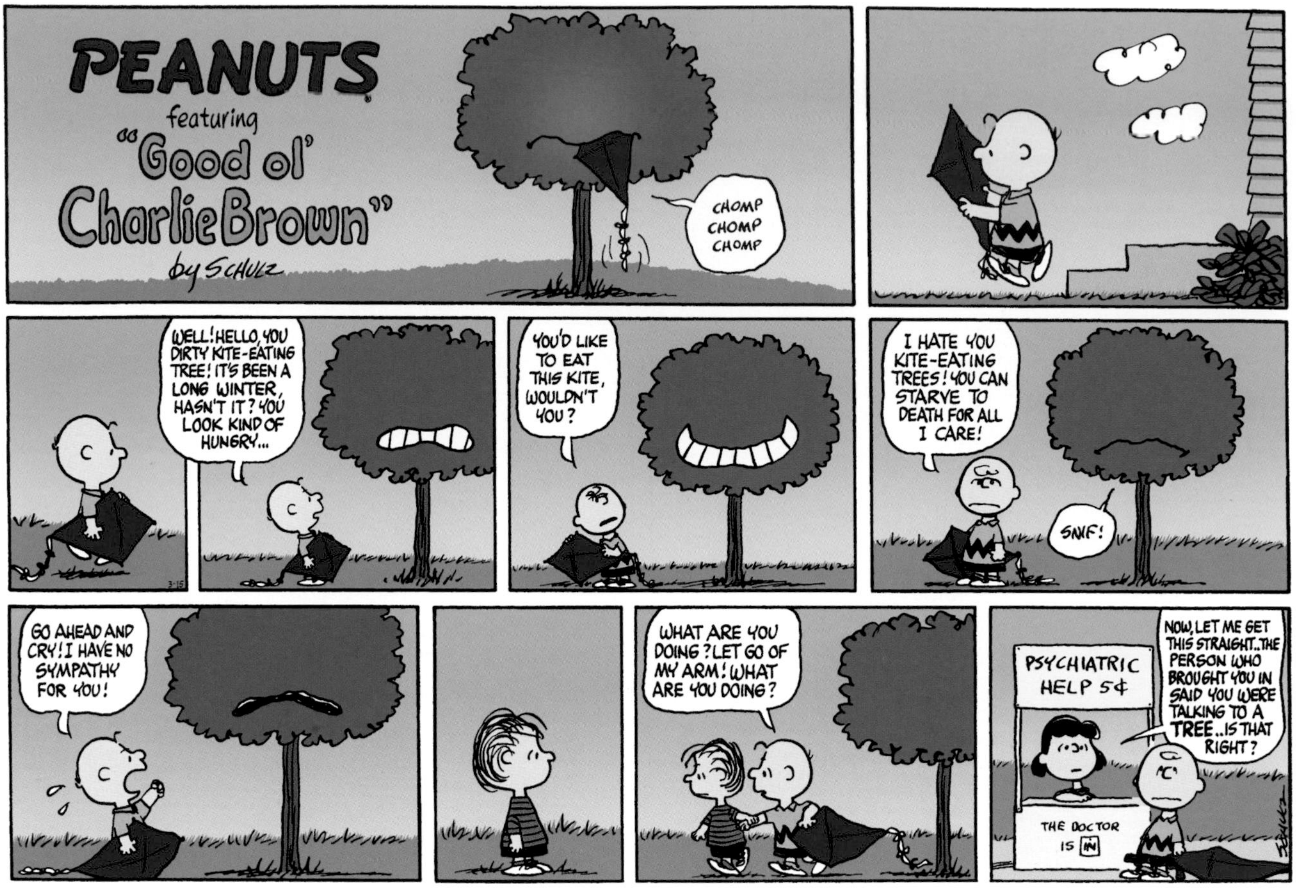

PEANUTS

featuring "Good ol' Charlie Brown"

by SCHULZ

CHOMP CHOMP CHOMP

WELL! HELLO, YOU DIRTY KITE-EATING TREE! IT'S BEEN A LONG WINTER, HASN'T IT? YOU LOOK KIND OF HUNGRY...

YOU'D LIKE TO EAT THIS KITE, WOULDN'T YOU?

I HATE YOU KITE-EATING TREES! YOU CAN STARVE TO DEATH FOR ALL I CARE!

SNIF!

GO AHEAD AND CRY! I HAVE NO SYMPATHY FOR YOU!

WHAT ARE YOU DOING? LET GO OF MY ARM! WHAT ARE YOU DOING?

PSYCHIATRIC HELP 5¢

NOW, LET ME GET THIS STRAIGHT.. THE PERSON WHO BROUGHT YOU IN SAID YOU WERE TALKING TO A TREE.. IS THAT RIGHT?

THE DOCTOR IS IN

March 19, 1970

PEANUTS
Although my early years were good, gray clouds soon appeared in my sky.
My life has been one of many hardships.
HARDSHIPS?!
WADDYAMEAN, HARDSHIPS?! I'VE TAKEN GOOD CARE OF YOU! YOU'VE NEVER HAD A HARDSHIP IN YOUR LIFE!
I HAVEN'T?
THIS COULD RUIN MY AUTOBIOGRAPHY...
SCHULZ

March 23, 1970

PEANUTS
PSYCHIATRIC HELP 5¢
Z
THE DOCTOR IS IN
PSYCHIATRIC HELP 5¢
KLUNK!!
THE DOCTOR IS IN
PSYCHIATRIC HELP 5¢
THE DOCTOR IS IN
THAT'S THE SORT OF THING THEY DON'T WARN YOU ABOUT IN MEDICAL SCHOOL...
THE DOCTOR
SCHULZ

April 19, 1970

PEANUTS
featuring
"Good ol' CharlieBrown"
by SCHULZ

THAT'S A NICE BALLOON
THANK YOU..
WHAT DOES IT DO?
IT DOESN'T DO ANYTHING EXCEPT MAYBE FLY IF I LET GO OF IT..
WHY DON'T YOU PAINT THE WORD "LOVE" ON IT, AND LET IT FLY OFF SOMEPLACE?
THIS MAY CHANGE THE LIFE OF THE PERSON WHO FINDS IT...
MAYBE SOME PERSON WHO IS DEPRESSED WILL FIND IT, AND BE ENCOURAGED TO CARRY ON
LOVE
MAYBE SOME GREAT LEADER WILL FIND IT, AND BE INSPIRED TO SEEK WORLD PEACE
GO, BALLOON! CARRY YOUR MESSAGE OF LOVE!
LOVE
LOVE
?
SCHULZ

April 1, 1970

PEANUTS
QUICK, CHARLIE BROWN, GO TO THE FRONT DOOR...
TED WILLIAMS IS THERE TO SEE YOU.. HE WANTS SOME ADVICE ON HOW TO MANAGE A BASEBALL TEAM
APRIL FOOL!
HA HA HA HA HA HA HA HA HA
4-1
IT COULD HAVE HAPPENED
SCHULZ

April 8, 1970

PEANUTS
WHAT AM I, A "NEW FEMINIST," DOING STANDING OUT HERE IN CENTER FIELD?
4-8

THIS IS A MALE-DOMINATED GAME... WHY SHOULD I TAKE ORDERS FROM THAT STUPID MANAGER? I'M JUST AS GOOD AS HE IS! WHY SHOULD I STAND OUT HERE IN CENTER FIELD? THIS IS DEGRADING, AND I RESENT IT!

WHAP!!

NOW WHAT WAS THAT ALL ABOUT?
SCHULZ

April 9, 1970

PEANUTS
WHERE ARE ALL THE GIRLS WHO PLAY OUTFIELD?
4-9

THEY SAID THEY'RE NEW FEMINISTS, AND THEY REFUSE TO PLAY BASEBALL ANY MORE.. I DON'T EVEN KNOW WHAT A NEW FEMINIST IS...

THE WORLD IS CHANGING, CHARLIE BROWN...
WHAT DOES THAT MEAN?

NO MATTER WHAT HAPPENS, I ALWAYS FEEL LIKE I'M IN THE NINTH INNING!
SCHULZ

June 14, 1970

PEANUTS featuring "Good ol' Charlie Brown" by SCHULZ

6-14

IS THIS SOMETHING UNUSUAL, OR DO ALL PITCHERS FLOAT?

SCHULZ

April 25, 1970

PEANUTS
type type type type
typetypetypetypetype type type type type type type type
HE'S NOT VERY GOOD AT MARGINS...
!
4-25
SCHULZ

May 4, 1970

PEANUTS
I HAVE A JOB FOR YOU

THERE'S BEEN A SERIES OF ROBBERIES IN THE NEIGHBORHOOD RECENTLY...

I WANT YOU TO STAY ON THE FRONT STEPS OF OUR HOUSE TONIGHT, AND LOOK REAL MEAN..

May 11, 1970

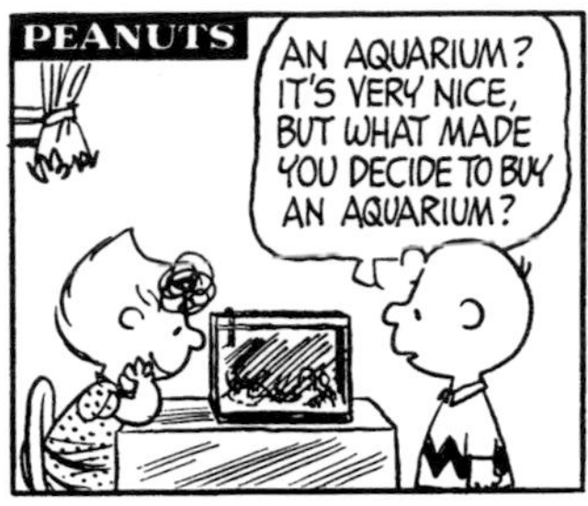
PEANUTS
AN AQUARIUM? IT'S VERY NICE, BUT WHAT MADE YOU DECIDE TO BUY AN AQUARIUM?

IT'S TIMELY! HAVEN'T YOU HEARD? THIS IS THE AGE OF AQUARIUMS!
AQUARIUS

WHAT?
FORGET IT!

BIG BROTHERS NEVER KNOW WHAT THEY'RE TALKING ABOUT

June 19, 1970

PEANUTS
I THINK I'LL DO MY SUMMER SCHOOL THEME ON JOHNNY SEBASTIAN BACH..

NOT "JOHNNY"... "JOHANN"!
THAT'S WHAT I SAID..."JOHANNY"

NOT "JOHANNY"! JOHANN!! JOHANN SEBASTIAN BACH!
WHAT ABOUT HIM?

MAYBE I'LL WRITE ABOUT BOBBY ORR...

June 20, 1970

PEANUTS

I ALWAYS HAVE TO REMIND HIM ABOUT SITTING AT LEAST SIX FEET FROM MY COLOR TV...

June 22, 1970

PEANUTS

I FINALLY FOUND OUT WHAT THAT STUPID BIRD'S NAME IS...

YOU'LL NEVER BELIEVE IT..

WOODSTOCK!

July 13, 1970

PEANUTS
HELLO? IS THIS THE DAISY HILL PUPPY FARM?

I'M CALLING FOR A FRIEND OF MINE... HE WANTS TO SPEAK TO ONE OF YOUR DOGS.. NO, HE DOESN'T KNOW HER NAME.. DESCRIBE HER?

7-13

SHE HAS VERY SOFT PAWS...
SCHULZ

July 26, 1970

PEANUTS
featuring
"Good ol' Charlie Brown"
by SCHULZ
OKAY, WHAT SHALL WE READ TONIGHT..."TREASURE ISLAND"? "HANS BRINKER"?
"THE SIX BUNNY-WUNNIES AND THEIR PONY CART"... AGAIN ?!?
I DON'T UNDERSTAND WHY YOU WANT TO READ THE SAME BOOK EVERY NIGHT... OH, WELL *SIGH* "IT WAS A WARM SPRING DAY, AND THE SIX BUNNY-WUNNIES DECIDED TO GO ON A PICNIC..."
"'I'LL FIX THE LUNCH,' SAID PAM BUNNY-WUNNIE.. 'I'LL HITCH UP OUR PONY,' SAID PETER BUNNY-WUNNY,...
Z
Z
7-26
SCHULZ

September 1, 1970

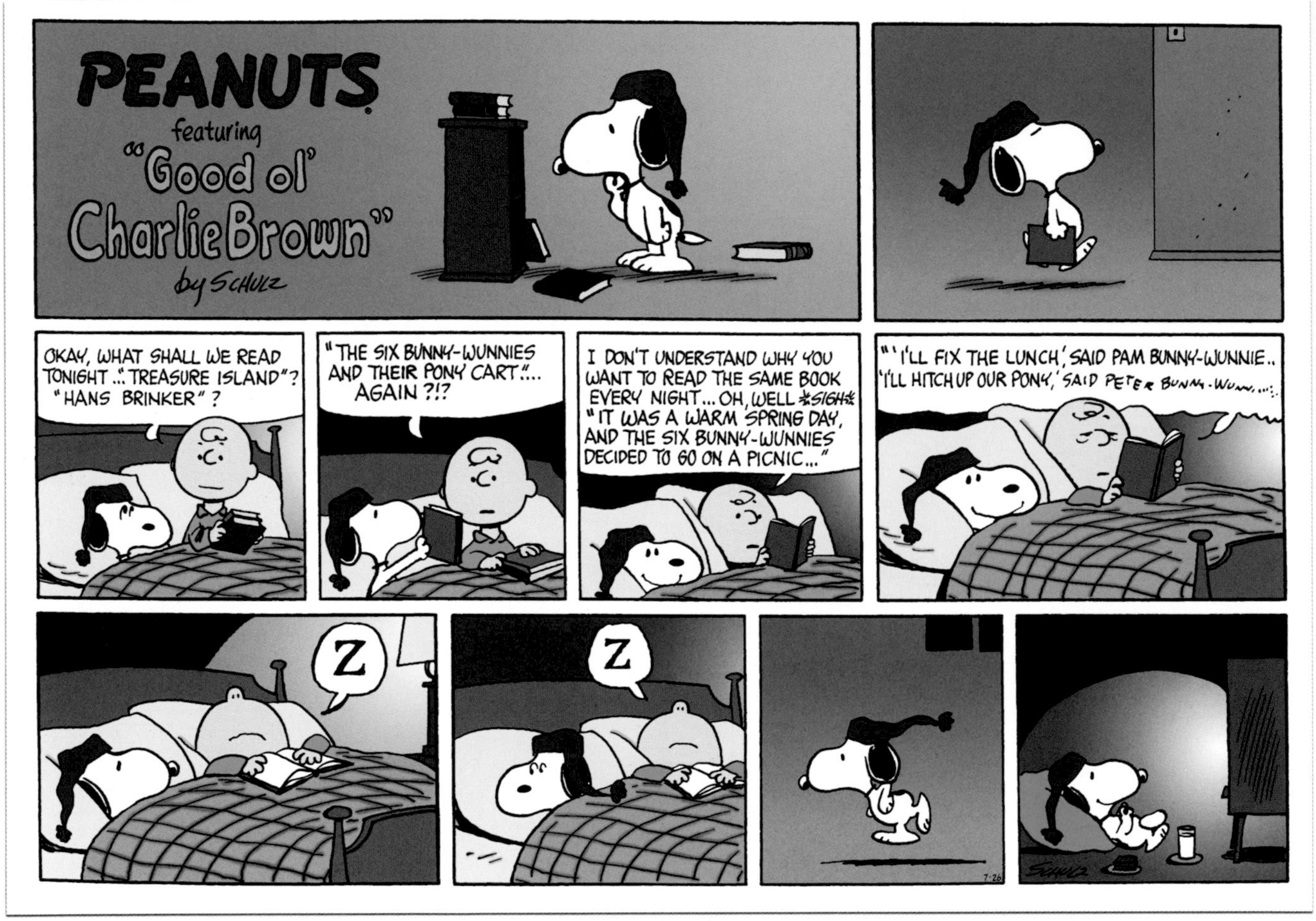

PEANUTS
WHY ARE YOU SO CRABBY ALL THE TIME?

I SUPPOSE YOU'D RATHER HAVE A SISTER WHO IS SICKENINGLY SWEET AND ALL NICEY-NICEY...

POW!

I COULD STAND IT
SCHULZ
9-1

September 8, 1970

PEANUTS
SCHOOL!

TODAY'S THE FIRST DAY OF SCHOOL! MEMORIZE THOSE CONJUNCTIONS! NAME THOSE RIVERS!

DON'T FORGET YOUR LOCKER COMBINATION!! WHAT'S THE CAPITAL OF VENEZUELA?!
9-8

I THINK THE SUMMERS ARE GETTING SHORTER..
SCHULZ

September 29, 1970

PEANUTS
English Theme
"If I Had a Pony"

If I had a pony, I'd saddle up and ride so far from this school it would make your head swim.

9-29

THAT'S A GOOD WAY TO GET A "D-MINUS"!
SCHULZ

October 8, 1970

PEANUTS
I LIKE A WALK ON A BRISK FALL DAY..

AFTERWARD, IT'S FUN TO COME HOME AND HAVE A CUP OF HOT CHOCOLATE..
10-8

AND SIT IN FRONT OF A WARM TV
SCHULZ

October 9, 1970

PEANUTS
HERE'S THE WORLD-FAMOUS HOCKEY PLAYER SKATING OUT FOR THE FIRST GAME OF THE SEASON
10-9

AH, THE NATIONAL ANTHEM!

IN A FEW SECONDS, THE GAME WILL START...THE REFEREE WILL DROP THE PUCK...

ONE MINUTE LATER I'LL BE IN THE PENALTY BOX!
SCHULZ

October 29, 1970

PEANUTS
10-29

THE GREAT PUMPKIN IS A MALE CHAUVINIST!

SIGH
SCHULZ

October 30, 1970

PEANUTS
I APPRECIATE YOUR SITTING HERE WITH ME, SNOOPY

ON HALLOWEEN NIGHT THE "GREAT PUMPKIN" WILL FLY OVER THIS PUMPKIN PATCH WITH HIS BAG OF TOYS, AND YOU AND I WILL BE REWARDED FOR OUR FAITHFULNESS...

I KNOW YOU'RE JUST AS EXCITED AS I AM... I WISH I KNEW WHAT YOU WERE THINKING...

THIS WOULD BE A TERRIBLE PLACE TO LOSE A CONTACT LENS...

November 9, 1970

PEANUTS
WOODSTOCK IS THE ONLY BIRD I KNOW WHO CAN'T FIND HIS OWN WAY SOUTH..

OH, WELL, I DON'T REALLY HAVE ANYTHING ELSE TO DO, AND I'M SORT OF ENJOYING THE TRIP

HE'S NOT AN EASY PERSON TO TRAVEL WITH, THOUGH...

FOR ONE THING, HE HATES TO EAT AT A PLACE WHERE YOU HAVE TO SIT AT A COUNTER..

November 23, 1970

PEANUTS
WHAT DID YOU WRITE FOR QUESTION NUMBER FIVE?

I SAID THAT HE WAS ONE OF OUR GREATEST PRESIDENTS AND ONE OF OUR MOST BELOVED LEADERS

DO YOU REALLY BELIEVE THAT?

NO, BUT I'VE LEARNED NEVER TO BAD-MOUTH A PRESIDENT IN A HISTORY TEST!

December 9, 1970

PEANUTS
Dear Little Red Haired Girl,
Evening is coming on.

I wish it were snowing huge white flakes, and you and I were walking along holding hands and

A LOT OF GREAT LETTERS NEVER GET MAILED

December 23, 1970

PEANUTS
WELL, DID YOU TELL SANTA CLAUS WHAT YOU WANT FOR CHRISTMAS?
Santa HERE TODAY

SURE.. I ALSO WISHED HIM A VERY HAPPY HANUKKAH...

WE DIDN'T HAVE MUCH TIME, BUT WE DISCUSSED JUDAS MACCABAEUS AND THE CLEANSING OF THE TEMPLE

IT'S NOT OFTEN THAT YOU FIND A SANTA CLAUS WHO'S INTERESTED IN RELIGION...

December 26, 1970

PEANUTS
WOODSTOCK GAVE ME A TIE FOR CHRISTMAS
12-26

I SUPPOSE HE'LL BE HURT IF HE DOESN'T SEE ME WEARING IT AT LEAST ONCE...

I THINK HE PAINTED THE PHEASANT HIMSELF..
SCHULZ

January 7, 1971

PEANUTS

DO YOU THINK THERE'S ANY TRUTH IN THE STATEMENT, "FOR EVERY SNOWFLAKE THAT FALLS A LIE IS BORN"?
1-7

I DON'T KNOW, LUCY... I'VE NEVER HEARD THAT ONE BEFORE

I JUST MADE IT UP
SCHULZ

"I'm the fastest letterer in the West. And I still do all my own lettering. Not everyone does, but there are a number of purists around. Gus Arriola, who draws Gordo*, is one. Not doing your own lettering is like Arnold Palmer having someone else hit his 9 irons for him."*

January 10, 1971

PEANUTS featuring "Good ol' Charlie Brown" by SCHULZ
AH! SAINT-POL-SUR-MER!
HERE'S THE WORLD WAR I FLYING ACE BRINGING HIS SOPWITH CAMEL IN FOR A LANDING...
I'M EXHAUSTED... THIS STUPID WAR IS TOO MUCH...
I NEED A NIGHT OF REVELRY... I NEED TO FORGET..
I SHALL GO INTO THE VILLAGE AND QUAFF A FEW ROOT BEERS..
PERHAPS SOME DARK-HAIRED LASS WILL SHARE MY TABLE..
HMM... I'LL HAVE TO WATCH WHAT I SAY TONIGHT, AND NOT BECOME TOO TALKATIVE..
1-10
SPIES!
SCHULZ

January 11, 1971

PEANUTS

THERE'S A VULTURE SITTING ON YOUR SNOWMAN...

ANY VULTURE CAUGHT SITTING ON MY SNOWMAN GETS CLOBBERED!
1-11

RATS!
SCHULZ

January 18, 1971

PEANUTS

1-18
HEE HEE HEE HEE HEE HEE

BIRDS DON'T KNOW HOW TO TELL JOKES
SCHULZ

January 28, 1971

PEANUTS

HERE'S A GENTLE REMINDER..

IF YOU THROW THAT SNOWBALL AT ME, I'LL BREAK EVERY BONE IN YOUR STUPID BODY!
1-28

SAVED BY A GENTLE REMINDER
SCHULZ

February 2, 1971

PEANUTS
ANOTHER LETTER FROM WOODSTOCK
"DEAR FRIEND OF FRIENDS"

" I ALMOST BROUGHT A GIRL HOME TO MEET YOU, BUT SHE RAN OFF WITH A STUPID ROBIN "

" IT'S HARD TO COMPETE WITH A ROBIN...NOT ONLY FROM THE STANDPOINT OF LOOKS, BUT ALSO WORMWISE "
2-2

" WORMWISE " ?!
SCHULZ

February 27, 1971

PEANUTS

2-27
SCHULZ

February 7, 1971

PEANUTS
featuring
"Good ol' Charlie Brown"
by SCHULZ

NOW SHOWING

ONE, PLEASE

ONE, PLEASE

See this MOVIE WITH SOMEONE YOU LOVE

FORGET IT!

SCHULZ

March 11, 1971

PEANUTS
I HAVE A PROBLEM, LUCILLE.. I THINK CHUCK LIKES ME..
WHY DO THINGS LIKE THIS HAPPEN? CHUCK'S A NICE GUY AND ALL THAT, BUT GOLLY...
I MEAN, HOW COULD I EVER FLIP OVER SOMEONE LIKE CHUCK?
I COULD STRIKE HIM OUT ON THREE STRAIGHT PITCHES!
SCHULZ

March 15, 1971

PEANUTS
LET'S SAY IT'S THE LAST HALF OF THE NINTH INNING..

THERE ARE TWO OUTS, AND YOU'RE UP TO BAT, CHUCK...NOW, EVEN THOUGH YOU'RE MY FRIEND, I'M STILL GOING TO HAVE TO TRY TO STRIKE YOU OUT..RIGHT?

OF COURSE...THERE'S NO OTHER WAY TO PLAY THE GAME...

YOU KIND OF LIKE ME, DON'T YOU, CHUCK?
SCHULZ

March 17, 1971

PEANUTS
Dear Friend,

I know that you like me, and in my own way, I like you, too

but only as a friend.

3-17
POOR CHUCK..
SCHULZ

March 18, 1971

PEANUTS
GOT A LETTER IN THE MAIL, EH, CHUCK?
"I KNOW THAT YOU LIKE ME, AND IN MY OWN WAY I LIKE YOU, TOO, BUT.."
3-18

I THINK IT'S FROM THAT LITTLE RED-HAIRED GIRL..SHE KNOWS I LIKE HER, AND..

THAT'S NOT FROM ANY LITTLE RED-HAIRED GIRL, CHUCK! THAT LETTER IS FROM ME! YOU LIKE ME, CHUCK!

I DO?
SCHULZ

March 21, 1971

PEANUTS
featuring
"Good ol' CharlieBrown"
by SCHULZ

LUNCH TIME AGAIN..

I REMEMBER HOW I USED TO SIT ON THIS BENCH EVERY NOON AND STARE ACROSS THE PLAYGROUND AT THAT LITTLE RED-HAIRED GIRL...

ALL I WANTED WAS TO BE ABLE TO SIT NEXT TO HER AND TALK TO HER..JUST BE WITH HER..THAT WASN'T ASKING TOO MUCH, WAS IT? BUT IT NEVER HAPPENED...

AND THEN SHE MOVED AWAY, AND NOW I DON'T EVEN KNOW WHERE SHE LIVES, AND SHE DOESN'T EVEN KNOW I EXIST, AND I SIT HERE EVERY DAY, AND I WONDER WHAT SHE'S DOING, AND I..

HI, CHARLIE BROWN..WHAT ARE YOU DOING, SITTING HERE PLANNING ANOTHER BASEBALL SEASON? THAT'S ALL YOU THINK ABOUT, ISN'T IT?

BASEBALL ISN'T THE WHOLE WORLD, YOU KNOW... THAT'S YOUR TROUBLE..YOU NEVER THINK ABOUT ANYTHING ELSE!
3-21

YOU MUST BE INSENSITIVE OR SOMETHING

SIGH
SCHULZ

April 11, 1971

PEANUTS
featuring
"Good ol' CharlieBrown"
by SCHULZ
I JUST SHOOK HANDS WITH THE EASTER BEAGLE, AND HE GAVE ME A COLORED EGG!
SMAK!
THE "EASTER BEAGLE"?

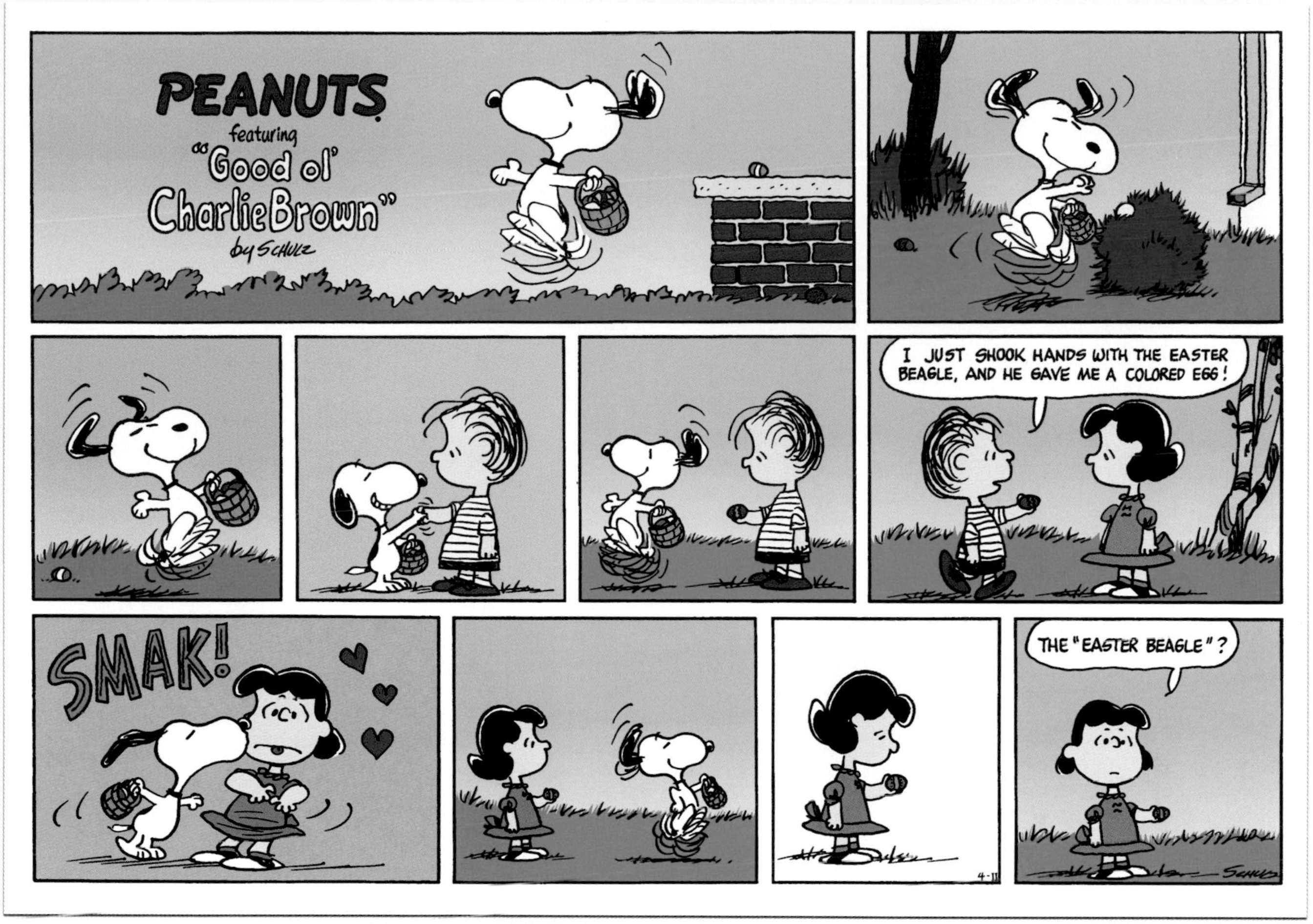

"I like the Easter Beagle. For a long while, I wouldn't do anything on Easter. I'm very sensitive to not offending anybody and I thought I shouldn't do anything with Easter. But then I thought, 'Oh, the heck with it. It's fun—the Easter Beagle.' So I did it anyway."

March 19, 1971

PEANUTS
THAT STUPID CHUCK! HE'S TOO STUPID TO EVEN KNOW WHO HE LIKES!
CAN YOU IMAGINE? HIS HEART WAS BREAKING, AND HE DIDN'T EVEN KNOW IT!!
BY GOLLY, IF I EVER HIT A DEEP DRIVE TO CENTER FIELD, AND I ROUND FIRST BASE, AND I ROUND SECOND BASE, AND I ROUND THIRD BASE AND I GO TEARING IN TO HOME LIKE A RUNAWAY FREIGHT, HE'D BETTER NOT BE IN MY WAY!

THAT'S THE LONGEST THREAT I'VE EVER HEARD!

March 31, 1971

PEANUTS

ONE FINGER WILL MEAN A STRAIGHT BALL, TWO FINGERS WILL MEAN A STRAIGHT BALL, THREE FINGERS WILL MEAN A STRAIGHT BALL AND FOUR FINGERS WILL MEAN A STRAIGHT BALL...

I HAVE A VERY SARCASTIC CATCHER

April 24, 1971

PEANUTS
I HAVE TO DO A PAPER FOR SCHOOL ON KEN AND ABEL
4-24

I'VE BEEN LOOKING ALL THROUGH THE OLD TESTAMENT, AND I'VE FOUND ABEL, BUT I CAN'T FIND KEN..

DO YOU THINK MAYBE I'M USING THE WRONG TRANSLATION?

I NEVER KNOW WHAT TO SAY...
SCHULZ

May 1, 1971

PEANUTS

5-1

IF YOU LISTEN TO WOODSTOCK LONG ENOUGH, YOUR MIND GETS ALL
SCHULZ

"Peppermint Patty is a very forthright and naive girl. There is a strong possibility of a good, long-range relationship between her and Charlie Brown. It's something I can develop over a long period of time. She's very fond of him. But Charlie Brown doesn't possess any of the characteristics she respects. He's still living deep in the past, in dreams of the Little Red-Haired Girl."

May 16, 1971

PEANUTS
featuring "Good ol' Charlie Brown"
by SCHULZ
THAT CHUCK..HE'S SOMETHING ELSE...
I DON'T KNOW WHY I EVEN THINK ABOUT HIM..
CHUCK JUST DOESN'T SEEM TO UNDERSTAND A GIRL'S EMOTIONS...
IN FACT, CHUCK DOESN'T SEEM TO UNDERSTAND GIRLS AT ALL..
CHUCK IS HARD TO TALK TO BECAUSE HE DOESN'T UNDERSTAND LIFE..
HE DOESN'T UNDERSTAND LAUGHING AND CRYING
HE DOESN'T UNDERSTAND LOVE, AND SILLY TALK, AND TOUCHING HANDS, AND THINGS LIKE THAT..
HE PLAYS A LOT OF BASEBALL, BUT I DOUBT IF HE EVEN UNDERSTANDS BASEBALL...
KNOCK KNOCK KNOCK
I DON'T THINK YOU UNDERSTAND ANYTHING, CHUCK!
I DON'T EVEN UNDERSTAND WHAT IT IS I DON'T UNDERSTAND
SCHULZ

May 27, 1971—Joe Cool makes his first named appearance.

PEANUTS
HERE'S JOE COOL HANGING AROUND THE STUDENT UNION
Tm. Reg. U.S. Pat. Off.—All rights reserved © 1971 by United Feature Syndicate, Inc.
5-27

HI, JOE.. HOW'D YOU DO IN CHEMISTRY TODAY?

THAT CHEMISTRY IS A DRAG, MAN

JOE COOL CAN'T WORRY ABOUT CHEMISTRY WHEN HE'S BUSY HANGING AROUND THE STUDENT UNION
SCHULZ

June 25, 1971

PEANUTS
I WISH I HAD A SECRET ADMIRER...
6-25

SOMEONE WHO WOULD SEND ME FLOWERS AND LITTLE NOTES AND THINGS LIKE THAT...

AND THEN, ALL OF A SUDDEN, HE WOULD TELL ME WHO HE WAS...

THEN YOU'D NEED ANOTHER SECRET ADMIRER
SCHULZ

June 13, 1971

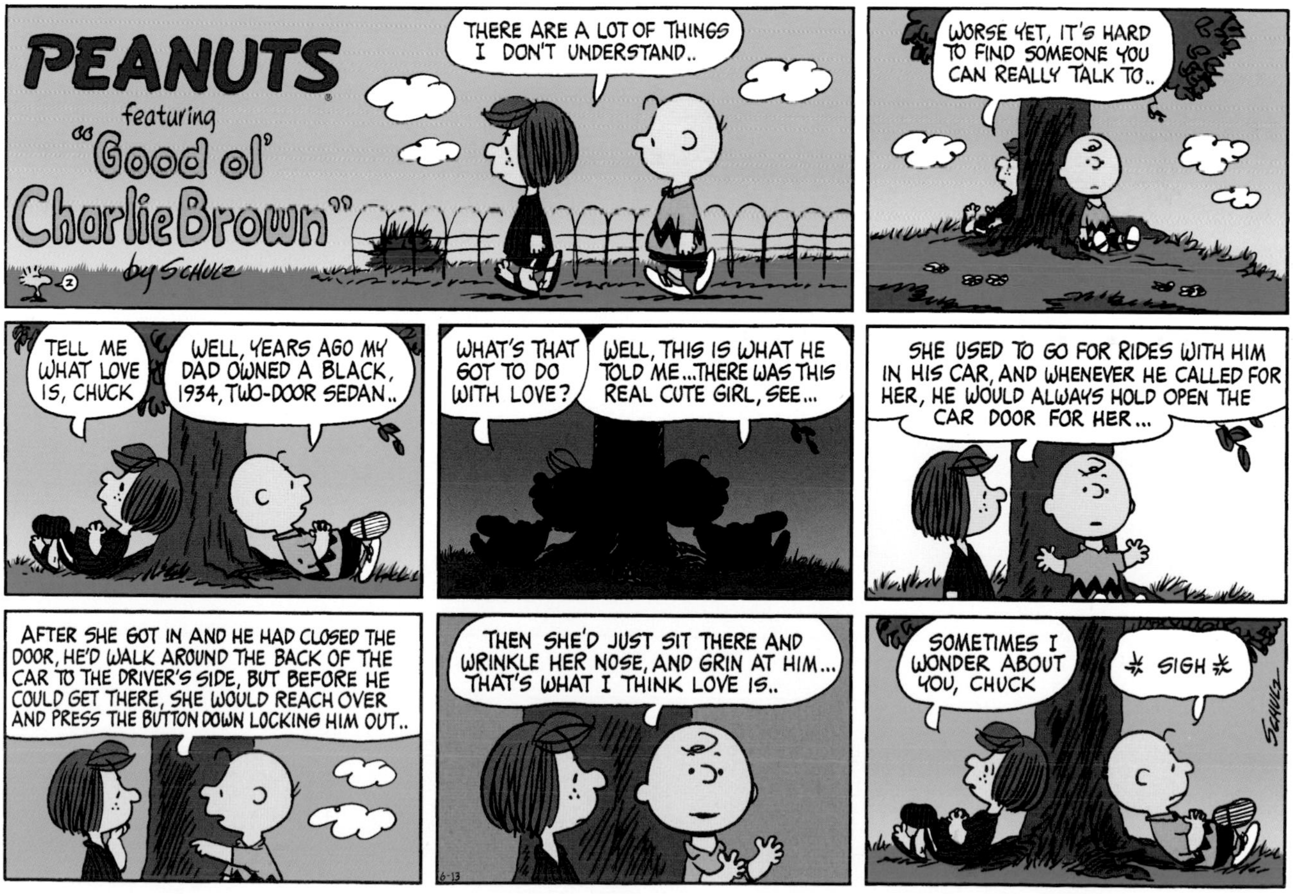

PEANUTS featuring "Good ol' Charlie Brown" by SCHULZ
THERE ARE A LOT OF THINGS I DON'T UNDERSTAND..
WORSE YET, IT'S HARD TO FIND SOMEONE YOU CAN REALLY TALK TO..
TELL ME WHAT LOVE IS, CHUCK
WELL, YEARS AGO MY DAD OWNED A BLACK, 1934, TWO-DOOR SEDAN..
WHAT'S THAT GOT TO DO WITH LOVE?
WELL, THIS IS WHAT HE TOLD ME...THERE WAS THIS REAL CUTE GIRL, SEE...
SHE USED TO GO FOR RIDES WITH HIM IN HIS CAR, AND WHENEVER HE CALLED FOR HER, HE WOULD ALWAYS HOLD OPEN THE CAR DOOR FOR HER...
AFTER SHE GOT IN AND HE HAD CLOSED THE DOOR, HE'D WALK AROUND THE BACK OF THE CAR TO THE DRIVER'S SIDE, BUT BEFORE HE COULD GET THERE, SHE WOULD REACH OVER AND PRESS THE BUTTON DOWN LOCKING HIM OUT..
THEN SHE'D JUST SIT THERE AND WRINKLE HER NOSE, AND GRIN AT HIM... THAT'S WHAT I THINK LOVE IS..
SOMETIMES I WONDER ABOUT YOU, CHUCK
SIGH
SCHULZ

June 29, 1971

PEANUTS
6-29

I DON'T KNOW WHY I LOOK AT THE MENU... I ALWAYS ORDER THE SAME THING
SCHULZ

July 1, 1971

PEANUTS
OKAY, BATTER, GET READY!
7-1

YOU'RE UP AGAINST THE WORLD'S GREATEST PITCHER HERE, AND HE'S GONNA MOW YOU DOWN!

YOU'RE GONNA LOOK SICK, DO Y'HEAR? SICK! YOU'RE GONNA WISH YOU WERE NEVER BORN! YOU'VE HAD IT!!

OKAY, YOU'RE ON YOUR OWN..
SCHULZ

July 6, 1971

PEANUTS
7-6

IT'S A LONG WAY TO...

TIPPERARY
1 Block

SIGH
SCHULZ

July 19, 1971

PEANUTS
SO HERE I AM ON A BUS GOING TO CAMP AGAIN
HERE'S THE WORLD WAR I FLYING ACE HEADING FOR THE FRONT..

I DON'T KNOW WHY I DO THIS.. I HATE GOING TO CAMP...
WE SHOULD BE GETTING NEAR VERDUN SOON...

I GUESS GOING TO CAMP IS SUPPOSED TO BE GOOD FOR YOU
I DON'T SEE ANY SIGNS..JUST A FEW BLIGHTERS WORKING IN THE FIELDS..

7-19
GOING TO CAMP PREPARES YOU FOR GETTING DRAFTED, WHICH I DON'T WANT TO DO EITHER..
CURSE THIS STUPID WAR!
SCHULZ

July 20, 1971—First appearance of Marcie.

PEANUTS
RAIN! GOOD GRIEF!

HOW CAN YOU HAVE FUN AT CAMP WITH DORKY WEATHER LIKE THIS? I WONDER HOW CHUCK IS DOING?
Tm. Reg. U.S. Pat. Off.—All rights reserved
© 1971 by United Feature Syndicate, Inc.

SIR, WHAT TIME IS LUNCH?

DON'T CALL ME "SIR"! WHAT KIND OF A DORKY KID ARE YOU?
DORKY?
7-20
SCHULZ

July 27, 1971

PEANUTS
SIR, MY STOMACH HURTS..

STOP CALLING ME "SIR," AND SCAMPER RIGHT DOWN TO THE DISPENSARY ON YOUR LITTLE BOBBY ORR LEGS!

"BOBBY ORR LEGS"?
7-27
SCHULZ

August 19, 1971

PEANUTS
Z

?

8-19

SOMETIMES THERE ARE THINGS YOU JUST CAN'T RESIST DOING..
SCHULZ

September 12, 1971

PEANUTS
featuring
"Good ol' CharlieBrown"
by SCHULZ

QUIET

CHICKS GO FOR THESE TURTLE-NECK SWEATERS..

HERE'S JOE COOL HANGING AROUND THE DORM ON A SUNDAY AFTERNOON..

MAYBE I'LL GO OVER TO THE STUDENT UNION, AND CHECK OUT THE SCENE

HERE'S JOE COOL HANGING AROUND THE STUDENT UNION LOOKING FOR ACTION..

I SEE THEY'RE SHOWING "CITIZEN KANE" AGAIN... I'VE ONLY SEEN IT TWENTY-THREE TIMES..
9-12

MAYBE I'LL GO OVER TO THE LIBRARY, AND SEE WHO'S THERE

RATS..NO CHICKS! MAYBE I SHOULD GO OVER TO THE GYM AND SHOOT A FEW BASKETS...

IF I HAD SOME WHEELS, I'D CRUISE AROUND FOR AWHILE.. MAYBE I SHOULD WALK OVER, AND LOOK AT THE GEOLOGICAL EXHIBIT...

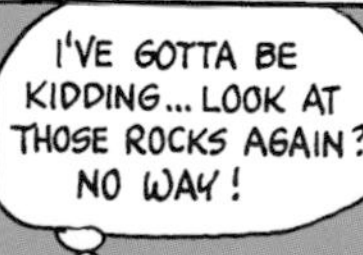
I'VE GOTTA BE KIDDING... LOOK AT THOSE ROCKS AGAIN? NO WAY!

THERE'S A GUY WITH TWO CHICKS.. HOW DOES HE DO IT?

THE LEAVES ARE BEGINNING TO FALL.. THE SUN IS WARM, BUT IT'S KIND OF CHILLY IN THE SHADE

I WONDER WHAT'S GOING ON AT HOME.. MAYBE I SHOULD GO BACK TO THE DORM AND WRITE SOME LETTERS...

SIGH JOE COOL HATES SUNDAY AFTERNOONS...
SCHULZ

September 13, 1971

PEANUTS
I'VE DECIDED SOMETHING...YOU AND I ARE THROUGH!

HOW CAN WE BE THROUGH? WE NEVER EVEN STARTED!

THAT DIDN'T EVEN COME CLOSE TO WORKING...

"Some of the ideas are rather tender about relationships, which are certainly not relationships among children. To say that this is a strip about childhood is foolish; it has nothing much to do about childhood."

September 14, 1971

PEANUTS
KNOCK
KNOCK

NOW THAT YOU AND I ARE THROUGH, SCHROEDER, WHY DON'T YOU STOP HANGING AROUND MY HOUSE?

THIS ISN'T YOUR HOUSE... THIS IS MY HOUSE!

IT'S AMAZING HOW STUPID YOU CAN BE WHEN YOU'RE IN LOVE..

September 15, 1971

PEANUTS
HELLO, SCHROEDER?

NOW THAT YOU AND I ARE THROUGH, WHY DO YOU KEEP CALLING ME ON THE PHONE?

I DIDN'T CALL YOU... YOU CALLED ME!

HOW COME YOU NEVER GET A WRONG NUMBER WHEN YOU NEED ONE?

September 16, 1971

PEANUTS
KNOCK
KNOCK

NOW THAT YOU AND I ARE THROUGH, SCHROEDER, I'M RETURNING ALL THE GIFTS I WAS GOING TO GIVE YOU...

THANK YOU

THAT DIDN'T EVEN MAKE SENSE!

September 17, 1971

PEANUTS
IF I TOLD YOU THAT WE WERE THROUGH WHEN I REALLY DIDN'T MEAN IT, WOULD WE STILL BE THROUGH?

IF I TOLD YOU THAT IT DIDN'T MATTER TO ME ONE WAY OR THE OTHER, WOULD WE STILL BE THROUGH?

WELL, IF I TOLD YOU THAT I MEANT I THOUGHT I KNEW THAT WE WERE THROUGH WHEN I SAID THAT YOU THOUGHT I KNEW I TOLD YOU WE WERE THROUGH, BUT I SAID WE...

LOVE IS NOT KNOWING WHAT YOU'RE TALKING ABOUT

September 30, 1971

PEANUTS

HERE...I FOUND THESE, AND THOUGHT YOU MIGHT LIKE TO HAVE THEM..
9-30

HOW NICE..

IF 3-D COMES BACK, I'M READY!
SCHULZ

September 19, 1971

PEANUTS
featuring
"Good ol' Charlie Brown"
by SCHULZ

HOW'S THIS ONE?
X

HOW ABOUT THIS ONE?
9-19

X!
RATS!

HOW ABOUT THIS ONE?
X!

THEN HOW ABOUT THIS ONE?
X!

IT'S IMPOSSIBLE TO GO FISHING WITH WOODSTOCK.. HE KNOWS ALL THE WORMS PERSONALLY!
SCHULZ

October 18, 1971

PEANUTS
The boy ran to the store

THIS IS FOR ENGLISH CLASS... WE'RE SUPPOSED TO DECORATE A SENTENCE..

YOU MEAN DIAGRAM

SCHULZ 10-18
SIGH

November 3, 1971

PEANUTS
I RODE IN AN ELEVATOR YESTERDAY
I GET CLAUSTROPHOBIA IN ELEVATORS

I EVEN GET CLAUSTROPHOBIA IN SMALL ROOMS..
I GET CLAUSTROPHOBIA IN STORES IF THERE ARE A LOT OF PEOPLE AROUND

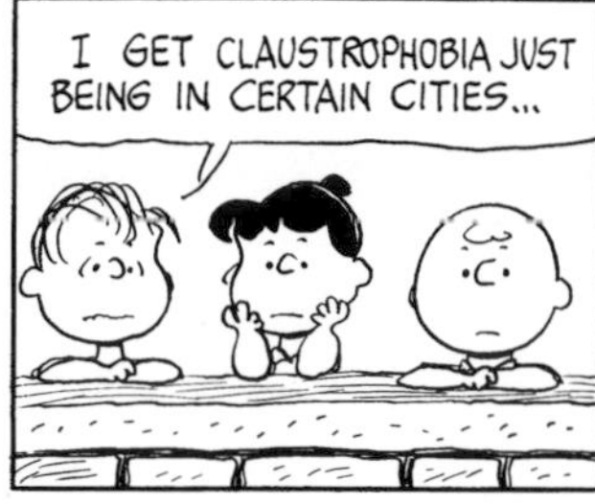
I GET CLAUSTROPHOBIA JUST BEING IN CERTAIN CITIES...

I GET CLAUSTROPHOBIA IN THE WORLD

November 5, 1971

PEANUTS
NOW LISTEN CAREFULLY, YOU STUPID BEAGLE... THIS IS WHAT I WANT YOU TO DO FOR ME..

I'M GOING TO TRY TO KICK THIS BLANKET HABIT ONCE AND FOR ALL, BUT I NEED YOUR HELP

I WANT YOU TO KEEP MY BLANKET FOR ME, AND DON'T GIVE IT BACK NO MATTER HOW MUCH I PLEAD... NO MATTER HOW MUCH I BEG.. NO MATTER HOW DESPERATE I BECOME..

THIS IS GOING TO BE FUN!
AND THIS ISN'T GOING TO BE FUN!

November 9, 1971

PEANUTS
YOU STUPID BEAGLE, I KNOW YOU'RE IN THERE!

COME OUT, AND BRING THAT BLANKET WITH YOU! DO YOU HERE ME? COME OUT!!

!

MY BLANKET! YOU HAD IT MADE INTO A SPORT COAT!!
I PREFER TO THINK OF IT AS ONE OF THE NEW DOUBLE-KNITS..

November 12, 1971

PEANUTS
IT'S ALL YOUR FAULT, CHARLIE BROWN, BECAUSE YOU OWN SUCH A STUPID BEAGLE!

DO YOU KNOW WHAT I JUST READ IN A MEDICAL JOURNAL?

IT SAID THAT A PERSON WHO IS DEPRIVED OF HIS BLANKET BY A STUPID BEAGLE WHO HAS IT MADE INTO A SPORT COAT CANNOT SURVIVE FOR MORE THAN FORTY-EIGHT HOURS!

THAT MUST BE AN INTERESTING MEDICAL JOURNAL..

November 15, 1971

PEANUTS
?????? MY HANDS AREN'T SHAKING ??!!??

I'M NOT DIZZY ANY MORE... MY STOMACH DOESN'T HURT.. I'M ACTUALLY HUNGRY!

I MADE IT THROUGH THE WEEKEND WITHOUT MY BLANKET! I DID IT! I DID IT!

AND I DID IT MY WAY!!

November 17, 1971

PEANUTS
LINUS! I HAVE A SURPRISE FOR YOU!
I HAVE A SURPRISE FOR YOU, TOO, CHARLIE BROWN... GUESS WHAT.. I'VE...
11-17

I FELT RESPONSIBLE FOR YOUR LOSING YOUR BLANKET SO I BOUGHT YOU A NEW ONE..
AAUGH!

I HAD IT LICKED, AND NOW I'M HOOKED AGAIN!

I THOUGHT I WAS DOING THE RIGHT THING...
SCHULZ
Tm. Reg. U. S. Pat. Off.—All rights reserved © 1971 by United Feature Syndicate, Inc.

November 24, 1971

PEANUTS
11-24
JOE COOL

JOE COOL

JOE COOL

NO ONE EVER INVITES JOE COOL HOME FOR THANKSGIVING...
SCHULZ

December 4, 1971

PEANUTS
WE NEVER NEEDED YOU, YOU KNOW!

OUR FAMILY WAS DOING FINE WITHOUT YOU! WE DIDN'T NEED ANOTHER CHILD!

12-4

I FEEL LIKE AN EXPANSION CLUB
SCHULZ

December 23, 1971

PEANUTS
I SUPPOSE IT'S KIND OF SILLY TO HANG AROUND THE MAILBOX WAITING FOR CHRISTMAS PACKAGES
12-23

MOST PEOPLE WOULDN'T CHECK EVERY FIVE MINUTES TO SEE IF ANY PACKAGES HAVE COME...

I SUPPOSE MOST PEOPLE WOULD THINK IT'S RIDICULOUS..

NOT AT ALL!
SCHULZ

December 31, 1971

PEANUTS
HAPPY NEW YEAR TO EVERYONE!
12-31

EVERYONE EXCEPT YOU, YOU STUPID CAT WHO LIVES NEXT DOOR!! I HOPE YOU HAVE A TERRIBLE YEAR!

THAT WASN'T VERY NICE, WAS IT?

HAPPY NEW YEAR, YOU STUPID CAT!
SCHULZ

January 12, 1972—First appearance of Snoopy as an attorney.

PEANUTS
PRINCIPAL
YES, SIR!

YES, SIR, I ADMIT THAT I HAVE DELIBERATELY CHOSEN TO DEFY THE SCHOOL DRESS CODE..

I KNEW THAT I'D PROBABLY BE SENT TO YOUR OFFICE..IN FACT, I WAS PREPARED FOR IT...

I BROUGHT MY ATTORNEY!

January 15, 1972

PEANUTS
MY NAME IS PATRICIA REICHARDT, AND I AM REPORTING TO THE STUDENT COUNCIL AS REQUESTED

I HAVE ALSO BROUGHT MY ATTORNEY WHO WILL BE ADVISING ME..
WHERE'S JOHN DOE AND RICHARD ROE? I THOUGHT THEY WERE GOING TO BE HERE..

YES, I'M PREPARED TO ANSWER ALL QUESTIONS
I THINK I SHOULD OPEN WITH AN IMPASSIONED PLEA AGAINST THE STAMP ACT

MY ATTORNEY WILL ADVISE ME OF MY RIGHTS...
"LET THE BUYER BEWARE!"

January 19, 1972

PEANUTS
THEY'RE DECIDING MY CASE NOW, SNOOPY...

WITHOUT YOUR HELP, I DOUBT IF I WOULD HAVE HAD A CHANCE
I REMEMBER MY MOST FAMOUS CASE.. JOHN DOE VERSUS RICHARD ROE! THAT RICHARD ROE WAS QUITE A GUY...

ACTUALLY, I'M VERY CONFIDENT...I HAVE FAITH IN THE JUDGMENT OF MY FELLOW HUMAN BEINGS, AND I'M SURE THAT WITH YOUR HANDLING OF MY CASE I'LL BE FOUND...

GUILTY!!

February 3, 1972

PEANUTS
MY PEN PAL HASN'T ANSWERED MY LETTER

WHAT DO YOU THINK I SHOULD DO?
WELL, YOU COULD WRITE A NICE TACTFUL LETTER ASKING IF ANYTHING IS WRONG..

Dear Stupid Pen Pal,

NOW FOR THE TACTFUL PART..

February 7, 1972

PEANUTS

I SHOULD THINK YOU'D GET BORED JUST SITTING ON A DOGHOUSE ALL DAY..

ON THE CONTRARY..

WHO COULD GET BORED FLYING THE STAR SHIP "ENTERPRISE"?

January 23, 1972

PEANUTS
featuring
"Good ol' Charlie Brown"
by SCHULZ
HERE SHE COMES..
OKAY, CHUCK, I'M ALL SET FOR THE HOCKEY GAME...HOW DO WE PLAY?
WELL, YOU AND I WILL BE CENTERS... WE'LL FACE-OFF HERE IN THE MIDDLE..
LINUS AND SCHROEDER WILL BE WINGS..
THE IDEA IS TO SHOOT THE PUCK BETWEEN THOSE CHUNKS OF SNOW...THE GOALIE, OF COURSE, WILL TRY TO STOP YOU...
WHICH ONE IS THE GOALIE?
THE GOALIE IS THE ONE WEARING THOSE PADS...
SCHULZ

"Hockey, for me, is the greatest game going. There's just nothing comparable to the exhilarating feeling of breaking down the ice with the puck, heading in on the goal. You really have a chance to go. I've also played baseball, tennis, and golf, but there's just nothing quite like ice hockey."

March 2, 1972

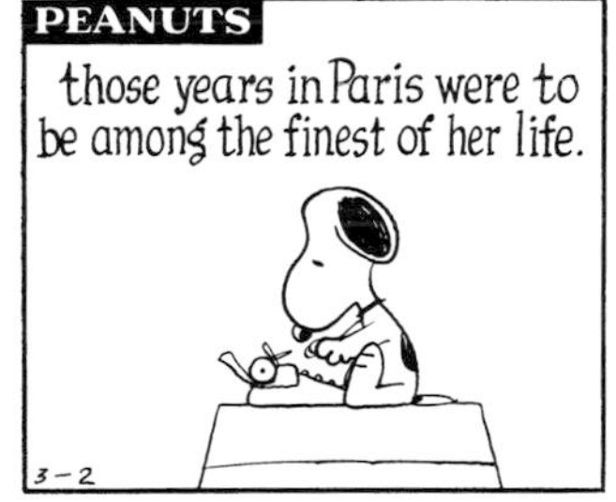
PEANUTS
those years in Paris were to be among the finest of her life.

Looking back, she once remarked, "Those years in Paris were among the finest of my life." That was what she said when she looked back upon those years in Paris

where she spent some of the finest years of her life.

I THINK THIS IS GOING TO NEED A LITTLE EDITING...
SCHULZ

March 7, 1972

PEANUTS
I JUST READ SOMETHING THAT AMAZED ME..

DID YOU KNOW THAT WE SPEND ONE-THIRD OF OUR LIVES SLEEPING?

SOME TYPES SPEND NINE-TENTHS OF THEIR LIVES SLEEPING...

I'M GOING TO PRETEND I DIDN'T HEAR THAT!
SCHULZ

March 12, 1972

PEANUTS
featuring
"Good ol' Charlie Brown"
by SCHULZ

SEVEN O'CLOCK, SALLY... TIME TO GET UP!

GOOD GRIEF... I'VE GOT TO HURRY...

The Incas

The Incas were people who lived a long time ago in Incaland.

They had a highly developed civilization.

They would still be here today, but they lacked motel facilities.

SOME OF MY BEST TERM PAPERS HAVE BEEN WRITTEN BEFORE BREAKFAST!
SCHULZ

March 15, 1972

PEANUTS
WE NEED A RUN! WE NEED A RUN!
HEY, MANAGER, WHAT'LL YOU GIVE ME IF I HIT A HOME RUN?

A HOME RUN? YOU'VE NEVER HIT THE BALL OUT OF THE INFIELD IN YOUR LIFE!

IF I HIT A HOME RUN, WILL YOU GIVE ME A KISS?
IF YOU HIT A HOME RUN, I'LL MEET YOU AT HOME PLATE, AND GIVE YOU THE BIGGEST KISS YOU'VE EVER HAD!!

INCENTIVE!!!
SCHULZ

March 17, 1972

PEANUTS
POW!

SHE DID IT! SHE HIT A HOME RUN!

AND YOU'RE GOING TO HAVE TO STAND OUT BY HOME PLATE, AND KISS HER! YOU PROMISED!!

SHE'S ROUNDING FIRST... SHE'S ROUNDING SECOND.. SHE'S ROUNDING THIRD.. SHE'S HEADING FOR HOME! IT'S KISSING TIME!
LA DE DA DE DA DE DA DE DA
SCHULZ

March 18, 1972

PEANUTS
LUCY HIT A HOME RUN!
OKAY, SCHROEDER, THIS IS IT! YOU PROMISED TO KISS HER..

A PROMISE IS A PROMISE...

FORGET IT! IF THAT'S THE ONLY WAY I'LL EVER GET YOU TO KISS ME, FORGET IT!

ANOTHER TRIUMPH FOR WOMEN'S LIB!
SCHULZ
3-18

March 21, 1972

PEANUTS
HOW ABOUT A GAME OF MARBLES AFTER SCHOOL, FRANKLIN?

I CAN'T..I HAVE A GUITAR LESSON AT THREE-THIRTY...

RIGHT AFTER THAT I HAVE LITTLE LEAGUE, AND THEN SWIM CLUB, AND THEN DINNER AND THEN A '4 H' MEETING
3-21

I LEAD A VERY ACTIVE TUESDAY!
SCHULZ

April 9, 1972

PEANUTS
featuring
"Good ol' CharlieBrown"
by SCHULZ
THIS IS RIDICULOUS
STUPID IS THE WORD!
IT'S NEVER GOING TO STOP RAINING! I'M GOING HOME!
BUT WHAT ABOUT THE GAME?
IT'LL PROBABLY CLEAR UP ANY MINUTE NOW... I THINK I SEE THE SUN..
WHERE'S EVERYONE GOING? DON'T GO! WE HAVE A GAME TO PLAY! COME BACK!!
YOU'RE OUT OF YOUR MIND, CHARLIE BROWN! ANYONE WHO WOULD STAND OUT IN THIS RAIN SHOULD SEE A PSYCHIATRIST!
MAYBE SHE'S RIGHT...
WELL, HELLO, THERE. WHAT CAN I DO FOR YOU?
PSYCHIATRIC HELP 5¢
THE DOCTOR IS IN
I THINK THERE MUST BE SOMETHING WRONG WITH ME..I DON'T SEEM TO KNOW ENOUGH TO GET IN OUT OF THE RAIN..
THAT'S VERY INTERESTING..
I JUST GET SO INVOLVED IN THESE BASEBALL GAMES I JUST SORT OF FORGET EVERYTHING ELSE, AND I JUST KIND OF LOSE TRACK OF EVERYTHING AND..
YOU KNOW WHAT?
WHAT?
THE DOCTOR IS IN
I'M GETTING WET!
SCHULZ
THE DOCTOR

March 29, 1972

PEANUTS
"'SO'"

YOU'RE READING "WAR AND PEACE" AND YOU'RE READING ONLY ONE WORD A DAY? I ALWAYS KNEW YOU WERE OUT OF YOUR MIND!
3-29

WHY ALL THE FUSS? I'M ON THE THIRD WORD ALREADY..

IT'S GOING FASTER THAN I THOUGHT
SCHULZ

May 7, 1972

PEANUTS
featuring
"Good ol' Charlie Brown"
by SCHULZ

HEY, MANAGER!

OH, NO...NOW WHAT?

AS SOON AS I HEAR HER SAY, "HEY, MANAGER," MY STOMACH STARTS TO HURT...

AS SOON AS SHE SAYS, "HEY, MANAGER," I GET THIS BURNING IN MY STOMACH BECAUSE I KNOW SHE'S GOING TO COME UP WITH SOME STUPID SUGGESTION, OR SOME SARCASTIC REMARK OR SOME SORT OF DUMB...

5-7

HEY, MANAGER, I JUST WANT TO WISH YOU LUCK IN TODAY'S GAME...

HOW'S YOUR STOMACH?!
SCHULZ

May 5, 1972

PEANUTS
WHO WAS THE FATHER OF HENRY IV?

I COULD NOT POSSIBLY CARE LESS!
5-5

I'M SORRY... I APOLOGIZE..

THAT WAS JUST A GUT REACTION
SCHULZ

May 12, 1972

PEANUTS
KICKED OUT OF MY OWN HOME BY MY OWN SISTER.. I CAN'T BELIEVE IT...
5-12

HERE'S JOE COOL HANGING AROUND THE DORM...
KICKED OUT... NO PLACE TO GO...

HI, JOE... MIND IF I STAY HERE FOR AWHILE?

OUR DORM SEEMS TO GET ALL THE WEIRDOS!
SCHULZ

May 14, 1972

PEANUTS
featuring
"Good ol' Charlie Brown"
by SCHULZ
MOM?

SIGH

I'VE NEVER REALLY THOUGHT OF MYSELF AS A MOTHER-SUBSTITUTE...
SCHULZ

May 16, 1972

PEANUTS
♡ HI, ♡ SWEETIE!

HI, JOE... WHO'S YOUR FRIEND WITH THE BLANKET?

THAT'S A GOOD QUESTION..
5-16

OUR DORM GETS ALL THE STRANGE ONES!
SCHULZ

May 20, 1972

PEANUTS
SAY, JOE, I'VE BEEN WANTING TO ASK YOU..
5-20

HOW COME YOU NEVER GO TO ANY CLASSES?

CLASSES ?!

THOSE CLASSES CAN RUIN YOUR GRADE AVERAGE!
SCHULZ

May 23, 1972

PEANUTS
WHAT I DON'T UNDERSTAND IS WHY YOUR MOTHER WOULD ALLOW LUCY TO THROW YOU OUT OF THE HOUSE...

MOM ISN'T HOME...SHE WENT TO THE HOSPITAL YESTERDAY
!

IS SHE ALL RIGHT?
I DON'T KNOW.. NOBODY EVER TELLS ME ANYTHING...

A NEW BABY BROTHER?!! BUT I JUST GOT RID OF THE OLD ONE!!!
5-23
SCHULZ

July 9, 1972

PEANUTS
featuring
"Good ol' CharlieBrown"
by SCHULZ

I SAW A MOVIE RECENTLY ABOUT A BOY AND HIS DOG

THEY WERE STANDING BY A LAKE AS WE ARE, AND THE BOY PICKED UP A STICK AND THREW IT INTO THE WATER, AND THE DOG SWAM OUT AFTER IT AND BROUGHT IT BACK..

7-9

I'M GOING TO HAVE TO STOP WATCHING THOSE MOVIES
SCHULZ

May 31, 1972

PEANUTS
AT FIRST, I WANTED TO BE AN ONLY CHILD
5-31

YOU SPOILED THAT! THEN I THOUGHT MAYBE IT WOULD BE KIND OF NICE TO HAVE A SISTER.. SO WHAT HAPPENS? I GET ANOTHER BROTHER..A RERUN!

THAT'S IT!

WE'LL CALL HIM "RERUN"!
"RERUN" VAN PELT... GOOD GRIEF!
SCHULZ

June 30, 1972

PEANUTS
WELL, THAT'S IT....

TOMORROW IS THE FIRST OF JULY...

RATS!
6-30

ANOTHER JUNE HAS PASSED, AND I DIDN'T GET ANY HONORARY DEGREES!
SCHULZ

July 23, 1972

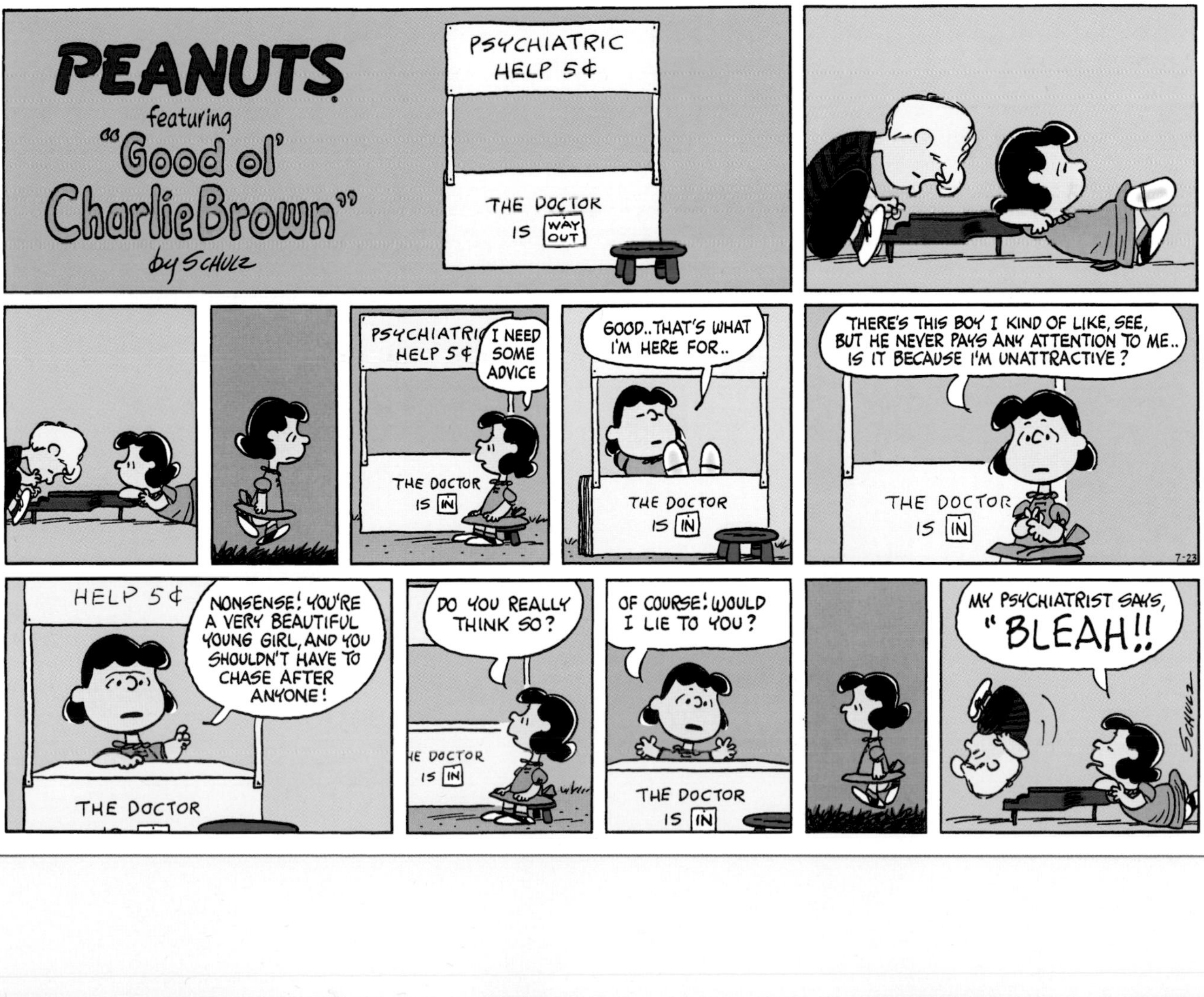

PEANUTS featuring "Good ol' Charlie Brown" by SCHULZ

PSYCHIATRIC HELP 5¢

THE DOCTOR IS WAY OUT

PSYCHIATRIC HELP 5¢

I NEED SOME ADVICE

THE DOCTOR IS IN

GOOD..THAT'S WHAT I'M HERE FOR..

THE DOCTOR IS IN

THERE'S THIS BOY I KIND OF LIKE, SEE, BUT HE NEVER PAYS ANY ATTENTION TO ME.. IS IT BECAUSE I'M UNATTRACTIVE?

THE DOCTOR IS IN

7-23

HELP 5¢

NONSENSE! YOU'RE A VERY BEAUTIFUL YOUNG GIRL, AND YOU SHOULDN'T HAVE TO CHASE AFTER ANYONE!

THE DOCTOR

DO YOU REALLY THINK SO?

E DOCTOR IS IN

OF COURSE! WOULD I LIE TO YOU?

THE DOCTOR IS IN

MY PSYCHIATRIST SAYS, "BLEAH!!"

SCHULZ

July 4, 1972

PEANUTS
Today is the Fourth of July.
7-4

This holiday is a celebration of freedom. It all began when

SCHOOL IS OUT.. YOU DON'T HAVE TO WRITE THEMES ABOUT HOLIDAYS WHEN SCHOOL IS OUT...

I'M A VICTIM OF PROGRAMMING
SCHULZ

July 26, 1972

PEANUTS
ALL RIGHT, GANG, LET'S KEEP AWAKE OUT THERE!

Z

Z
CLOMP!

ON THE OTHER HAND, FORGET I SAID ANYTHING!
SCHULZ
7-26

July 30, 1972

PEANUTS
featuring
"Good ol' Charlie Brown"
by SCHULZ
Z,z (zeta)
A Tale of Two Cities

REALLY?

Of Human Bondage
7-30
YOU'RE KIDDING!

Heart of Darkness

I CAN'T BELIEVE IT!!

I HAVE A GREAT IDEA FOR A NOVEL, BUT ALL THE GOOD TITLES ARE TAKEN!
SCHULZ

August 6, 1972

PEANUTS
featuring
"Good ol' CharlieBrown"
by SCHULZ
LATELY EVERYTHING SEEMS TO BOTHER ME...
HOW DO YOU MEAN?
WHAT DO YOU THINK SECURITY IS, CHUCK?
SECURITY?
SECURITY IS SLEEPING IN THE BACK SEAT OF THE CAR...
WHEN YOU'RE A LITTLE KID, AND YOU'VE BEEN SOMEWHERE WITH YOUR MOM AND DAD, AND IT'S NIGHT, AND YOU'RE RIDING HOME IN THE CAR, YOU CAN SLEEP IN THE BACK SEAT..
YOU DON'T HAVE TO WORRY ABOUT ANYTHING... YOUR MOM AND DAD ARE IN THE FRONT SEAT, AND THEY DO ALL THE WORRYING...THEY TAKE CARE OF EVERYTHING...
THAT'S REAL NEAT!
BUT IT DOESN'T LAST! SUDDENLY, YOU'RE GROWN UP, AND IT CAN NEVER BE THAT WAY AGAIN!
SUDDENLY, IT'S OVER, AND YOU'LL NEVER GET TO SLEEP IN THE BACK SEAT AGAIN! NEVER!
NEVER?
ABSOLUTELY NEVER!
HOLD MY HAND, CHUCK!!
SCHULZ

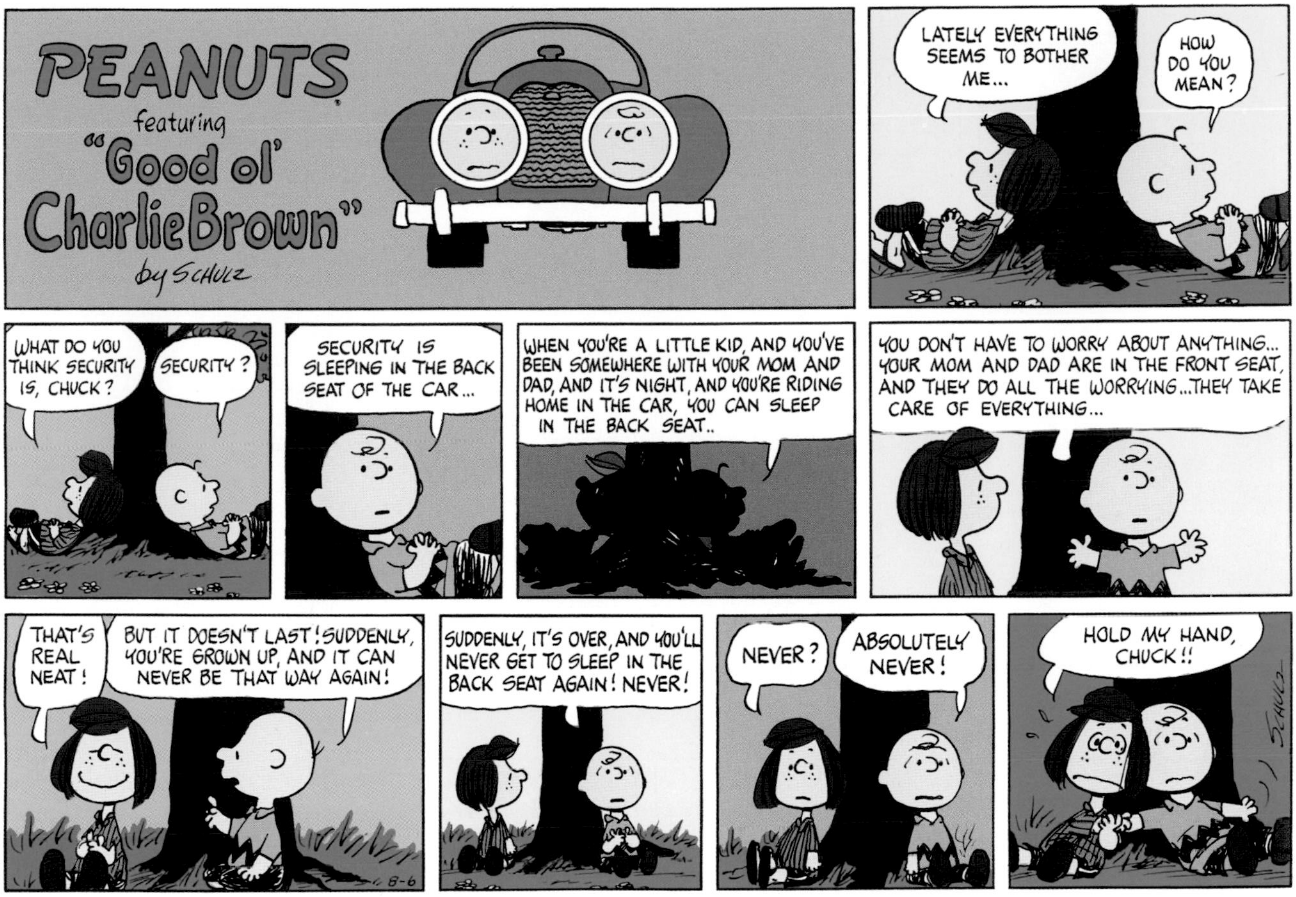

"When I first started cartoon correspondence school in St. Paul, the writing was secondary. Now it is just the opposite. Good cartooning must get away from drawing. I am a writer who keeps seeing things in terms of funny scenes. But basically what I do is dialogue—episodic things remembered from my Minnesota childhood. Like the memory of that warm, secure feeling riding home with my parents in the backseat of the car half-asleep, late at night. There comes a time when you are forced to grow up—no more backseat. That fits into a Sunday page and not many other places I can think of."

August 1, 1972

PEANUTS
YOU THREW TO THE WRONG BASE AGAIN!!

THERE WERE RUNNERS ON FIRST AND SECOND, AND YOU THREW THE BALL TO FIRST!

IN A SITUATION LIKE THAT, YOU ALWAYS THROW TO THIRD OR TO HOME!

YOU'RE DESTROYING MY CREATIVITY!!
SCHULZ

August 23, 1972

PEANUTS
MY BEACH BALL JUST FLOATED AWAY

IT PROBABLY FLOATED CLEAR ACROSS TO THE OTHER SIDE OF THE WORLD WHERE ANOTHER LITTLE KID FOUND IT, AND IS PLAYING WITH IT...

LUCKY KID!!

August 24, 1972

PEANUTS

YOU STUPID KID, WHO LIVES CLEAR ACROSS ON THE OTHER SIDE OF THE WORLD, SEND BACK MY BEACH BALL!!

WHAT ARE YOU, A COMMUNIST OR SOMETHING?!

August 25, 1972

PEANUTS
MY BEACH BALL! IT'S COMING BACK!
THAT KID ON THE OTHER SIDE OF THE WORLD SENT IT BACK! OUR NATIONS ARE IN HARMONY!

THE WIND CHANGED

TWO NATIONS, USING TWO INNOCENT CHILDREN AND A BEACH BALL, HAVE DEMONSTRATED TO THE WORLD THAT THEY CAN LIVE IN TOTAL HARMONY!

THE WIND CHANGED

September 1, 1972

PEANUTS

boot

boot boot boot boot
boot boot boot boot boot
boot boot

I'M GLAD I CAN'T HEAR WHAT HOWARD COSELL IS SAYING ABOUT THIS...

October 7, 1972

PEANUTS
ISN'T HE GOING TO SAY GOODBY?
WHEN YOU LEAVE ON AN ASSIGNMENT FOR THE HEAD BEAGLE, YOU DON'T HAVE TIME TO SAY GOODBY!
RIGHT!

"THOMPSON IS IN TROUBLE!" THAT MEANS I'VE GOT TO GET TO HIM BEFORE "THEY" DO...

THIS REMINDS ME OF THE "MOROCCAN AFFAIR"... THAT WAS A NASTY PIECE OF BUSINESS...

THAT STUPID THOMPSON... HE NEVER WANTED TO TAKE ANY ADVICE... NOW, MAYBE IT'S TOO LATE...

September 17, 1972

PEANUTS
featuring
"Good ol' Charlie Brown"
by SCHULZ
FINISH

THE YEARS ARE GOING BY..

I'M SCARED, CHUCK... WHAT IF I GROW UP, AND NO ONE EVER LOVES ME? WE PEOPLE WITH BIG NOSES ARE VERY INSECURE...

DO YOU THINK I HAVE A BIG NOSE, CHUCK? DO YOU THINK SOMEONE WILL LOVE ME SOMEDAY?
SURE

SURE?! "SURE," WHAT? "SURE" I HAVE A BIG NOSE, OR "SURE" SOMEONE WILL LOVE ME SOMEDAY?

MAYBE SOMEDAY THE REST OF YOUR FACE WILL CATCH UP WITH YOUR NOSE, AND THEN SOMEONE WILL LOVE YOU
9-17

HURRY UP, FACE!
SCHULZ

October 9, 1972

PEANUTS
THOMPSON ?
THOMPSON ?

HMM...THERE'S A LITTLE RESTAURANT THAT LOOKS FULL OF SHADY TYPES...

MAYBE THE WAITRESS KNOWS THOMPSON... I'LL GO IN, AND SLYLY STRIKE UP A CONVERSATION WITH HER...

HI, SWEETIE!
10-9
SCHULZ

October 11, 1972

PEANUTS
THAT WAITRESS SAID SHE SAW THOMPSON HEADING NORTH OF TOWN..
10-11

THAT STUPID THOMPSON! THIS IS JUST THE SORT OF THING I KNEW HE'D DO!

I SHOULD BE BACK IN THE RESTAURANT QUAFFING ROOT BEERS WITH THAT WAITRESS... I THINK SHE KIND OF LIKED ME..

NOW, IT'S RAINING, AND I'M GETTING ALL WET AND I'M PROBABLY LOST...THAT STUPID THOMPSON!!
SCHULZ

October 12, 1972

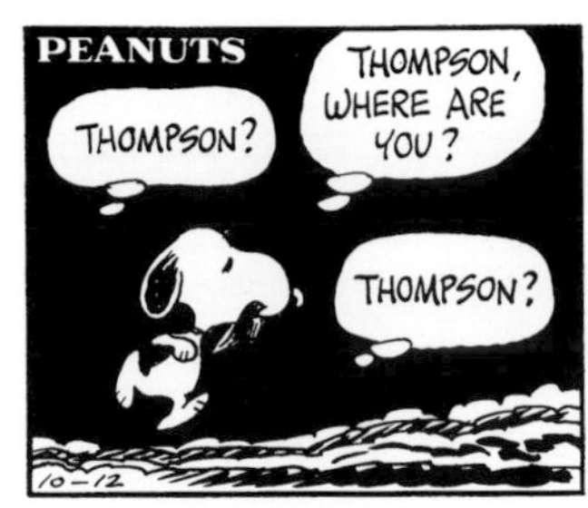
PEANUTS
THOMPSON?
THOMPSON, WHERE ARE YOU?
THOMPSON?

!

TOO LATE!

POOR THOMPSON!

October 13, 1972

PEANUTS
Report to the Head Beagle

Subject: Our Beagle in the field, Thompson.

Subject attempted to subdue ten-thousand rabbits by himself. End came quickly.

Rabbit-tat-tat, and it was all over!

October 17, 1972

PEANUTS
I GOT SIX COMPLIMENTS TODAY...

FANTASTIC!

IT'S NOT OFTEN YOU CAN GET SIX COMPLIMENTS IN ONE DAY

TWO OF THEM WERE EVEN SINCERE!

November 13, 1972

PEANUTS
SOME MORNING I'M GOING TO GET UP REAL EARLY, AND WATCH THE SUN RISE...

ACTUALLY, AS YOU PROBABLY KNOW, THE SUN DOESN'T RISE.. THE EARTH TURNS...

SOME MORNING I'M GOING TO GET UP REAL EARLY, AND WATCH THE EARTH TURN...

November 28, 1972

PEANUTS

WOODSTOCK FEELS THAT EATING BREAD CRUMBS IS KIND OF DEGRADING...

December 26, 1972

PEANUTS

I JUST WANTED TO THANK YOU AGAIN FOR THE STRING OF PEARLS YOU GAVE ME FOR CHRISTMAS...
12-26

I DID NOT GIVE YOU A STRING OF PEARLS FOR CHRISTMAS..

I'LL SAY YOU DIDN'T!
SCHULZ

December 30, 1972

PEANUTS

?
12-30

WHAT A STUPID QUESTION!

WHY WOULD I FORGET THE ROOT BEER AND THE OLIVES?
SCHULZ

January 4, 1973

PEANUTS
WHAT'S THIS, ANOTHER BILL FROM WOODSTOCK?
1-4

"THIS IS YOUR SECOND NOTICE.. YOU OWE ME SIX DOLLARS FOR WHAT YOU BROKE AT MY NEW YEAR'S PARTY!"

"DON'T TRY TO GET OUT OF PAYING, BANANA NOSE!"

BANANA NOSE?
SCHULZ

January 6, 1973

PEANUTS
FRIENDSHIPS ARE TOO IMPORTANT TO SPOIL BY BICKERING..
TRUE
1-6

I THINK YOU AND WOODSTOCK SHOULD TRY TO TALK THINGS OUT...
HA! I CAN HEAR HIM NOW...

!

I SEE WHAT YOU MEAN
THANK YOU
SCHULZ

January 15, 1973

PEANUTS
"I INVITED YOU TO MY NEW YEAR'S PARTY BECAUSE YOU ARE MY FRIEND"

"THERE WAS SOMEONE ELSE AT THE PARTY THAT I WANTED YOU TO MEET"
1-15

"SHE'S THE CUTEST LITTLE BIRD I'VE EVER KNOWN, AND YOU MONOPOLIZED HER THE WHOLE EVENING.."

"IT BROKE MY HEART.....THAT'S WHY I SENT YOU A BILL FOR SIX DOLLARS.."
SCHULZ

January 20, 1973

PEANUTS
I'LL KICK THE BALL TO YOU, AND YOU COME RUNNING DOWN THE FIELD, AND I'LL TRY TO HUG YOU
1-20

TACKLE
HUG

TACKLE
HUG

FORGET IT!
STUPID GAME!
SCHULZ

February 28, 1973

PEANUTS
"TO BE ELIGIBLE FOR THE DAISY HILL PUPPY CUP, NOMINEE MUST FILL OUT THE ENCLOSED FORM"

Name of Owner_________
?

CHARLIE BROWN !!!

2-28
HOW EMBARRASSING..
SCHULZ

January 14, 1973

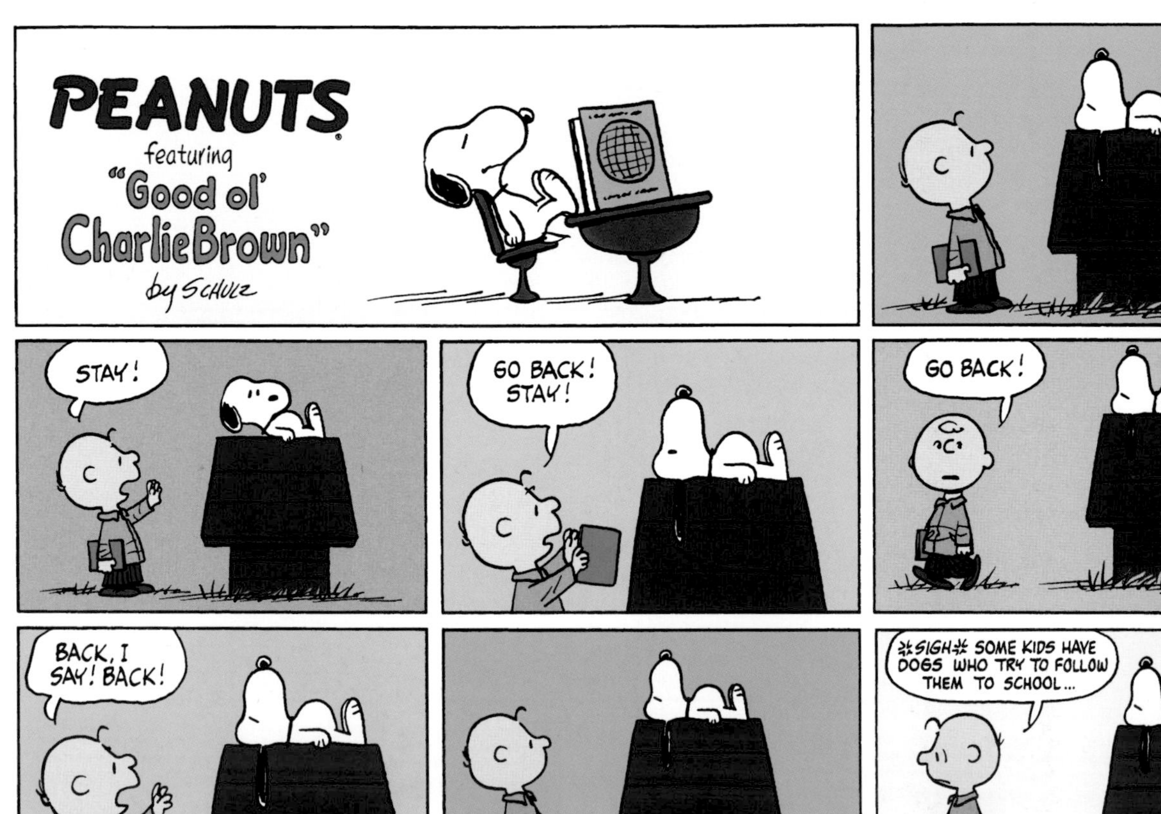
PEANUTS
featuring
"Good ol' CharlieBrown"
by SCHULZ
STAY!
GO BACK! STAY!
GO BACK!
BACK, I SAY! BACK!
SIGH SOME KIDS HAVE DOGS WHO TRY TO FOLLOW THEM TO SCHOOL...
1-14
SCHULZ

February 4, 1973

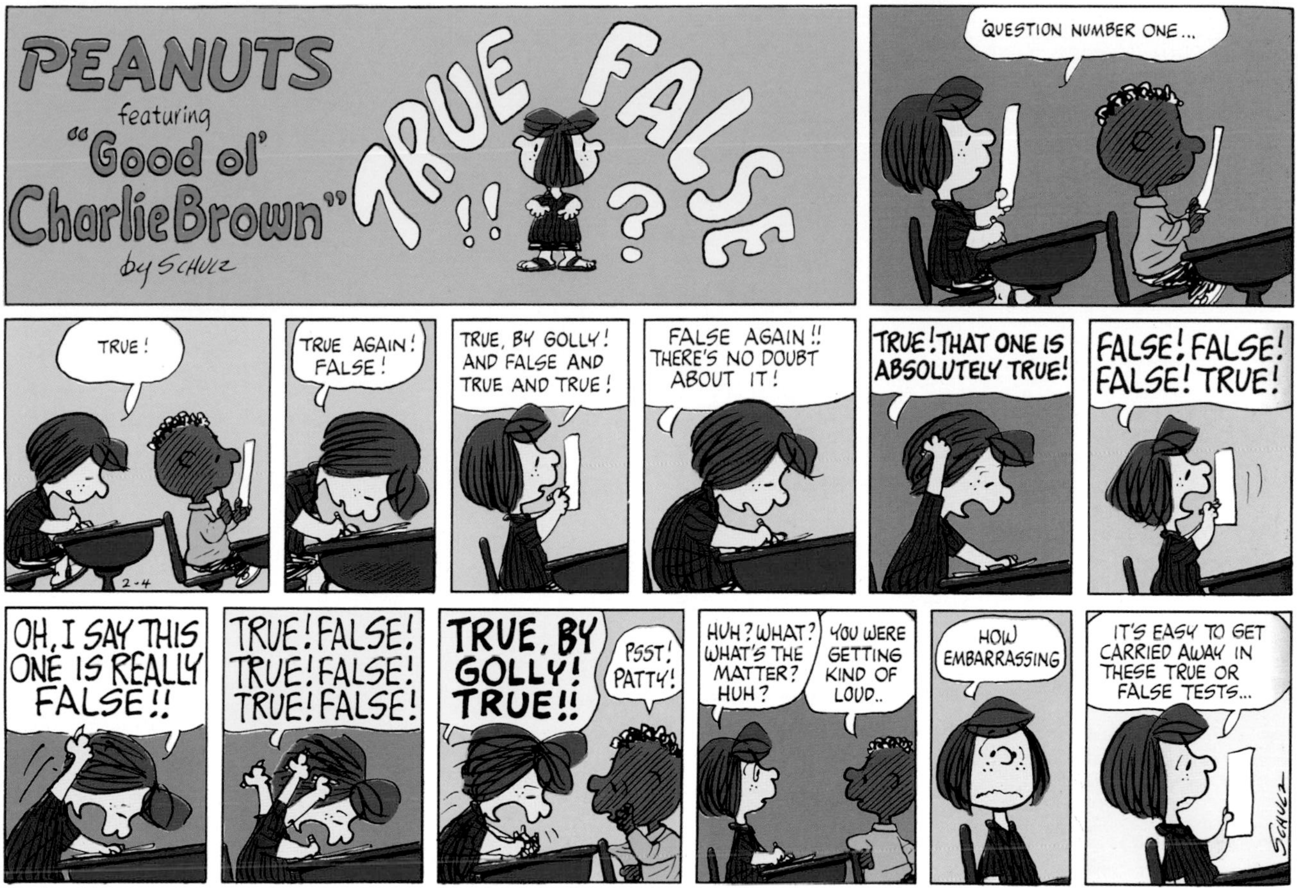

PEANUTS featuring "Good ol' Charlie Brown" by Schulz

TRUE FALSE !! ?

QUESTION NUMBER ONE...

TRUE!

TRUE AGAIN! FALSE!

TRUE, BY GOLLY! AND FALSE AND TRUE AND TRUE!

FALSE AGAIN!! THERE'S NO DOUBT ABOUT IT!

TRUE! THAT ONE IS ABSOLUTELY TRUE!

FALSE! FALSE! FALSE! TRUE!

OH, I SAY THIS ONE IS REALLY FALSE!!

TRUE! FALSE! TRUE! FALSE! TRUE! FALSE!

TRUE, BY GOLLY! TRUE!!

PSST! PATTY!

HUH? WHAT? WHAT'S THE MATTER? HUH?

YOU WERE GETTING KIND OF LOUD..

HOW EMBARRASSING

IT'S EASY TO GET CARRIED AWAY IN THESE TRUE OR FALSE TESTS...

March 26, 1973—First appearance of Rerun Van Pelt.

PEANUTS
C'MON, RERUN, I'M GOING TO TAKE YOU FOR A LITTLE WALK..

IT'S ABOUT TIME YOU GOT A LOOK AT THE OUTSIDE WORLD

WELL, WHAT DO YOU THINK?

YOU MEAN THIS IS IT?

March 28, 1973

PEANUTS
THINGS SURE AREN'T THE WAY I EXPECTED THEM TO BE..

WHEN I WAS FIRST BORN, EVERYONE FLOCKED AROUND, BUT NOW I NEVER SEE ANYONE! PEOPLE SEEMED TO LAUGH A LOT MORE IN THOSE DAYS, TOO...

SIGH

ONLY A YEAR OLD, AND ALREADY I'M LIVING IN THE PAST!

March 25, 1973

PEANUTS featuring "Good ol' Charlie Brown" by Schulz

POW!

?

?

"I think not enough cartoonists use funny drawings as well as funny ideas. There's more to comic strips than just characters standing and looking at each other. I like ideas that involve a funny expression or an outlandish pose or something wild happening. One of my favorite things to draw is the situation where a line drive goes through the box, and Charlie Brown is flipped completely over, and his shirt, socks, shoes, hat, and everything fly off. Now something like that can't happen in real life or on a television show. Only in cartooning."

April 4, 1973

PEANUTS
DO YOU REALIZE THAT WE HAVE THE LOSINGEST TEAM IN THE HISTORY OF BASEBALL?
I REFUSE TO ACCEPT THAT!
UNFORTUNATELY, YOUR REFUSAL DOES NOT ALTER THE FACT
I REFUSE TO ACCEPT THAT ALSO!
UNFORTUNATELY, YOUR REFUSAL ALSO TO ACCEPT THE FACT THAT YOUR REFUSAL DOES NOT ALTER THE FACT ALSO DOES NOT ALTER THE FACT OF OUR BEING THE LOSINGEST
I'LL ACCEPT THAT!

May 8, 1973

PEANUTS
LOVE
MENTION LOVE TO A MUSICIAN, AND YOU GET DROWNED OUT!

May 16, 1973

PEANUTS
DO YOU LIKE ME MORE THAN I LIKE YOU, CHUCK?

I DON'T KNOW...DO YOU LIKE ME MORE THAN I LIKE YOU?

LET'S NOT PLAY LOVERS' GAMES, CHUCK!
SCHULZ

May 30, 1973

PEANUTS
GOOD MORNING, PAL!

GOOD MORNING, FUZZY-FACE!

RATS!

NO ONE EVER CALLS ME "PANCHO"!
SCHULZ

"A good project is drawing from life. There's no better way to learn to draw. It doesn't have to be a real fancy art project, just using a student model in different poses. Learn how to draw shoes properly, observe how hands are shaped, how to capture an expression. And it's fun, just drawing, drawing, drawing."

April 22, 1973

PEANUTS
featuring
"Good ol' Charlie Brown"
by SCHULZ
YAWN
Z
ACTUALLY, WOODSTOCK PROBABLY SHOULDN'T HAVE A PAPER DELIVERED TO HIS HOME..
SCHULZ

June 11, 1973

PEANUTS

June 13, 1973

PEANUTS
THERE'S A FULL MOON TONIGHT, BIG BROTHER..

YOU SHOULD GO OUT, AND LOOK AT IT
MAYBE I WILL...THANK YOU..

June 14, 1973

PEANUTS
HOW ABOUT AN ICE CREAM CONE, BIG BROTHER?

THAT WOULD BE VERY NICE, THANK YOU..

ONE ICE CREAM CONE COMING UP!

June 15, 1973

PEANUTS
EVERYTHING I SEE LOOKS LIKE A BASEBALL TO ME...

AND NOW MY HEAD HAS STARTED TO ITCH...I THINK I HAVE A RASH OR SOMETHING...

TURN AROUND... LET ME LOOK..

I THINK YOU'D BETTER SEE YOUR PEDIATRICIAN, CHARLIE BROWN!

June 18, 1973

PEANUTS
I APPRECIATE YOUR SEEING ME, DOCTOR, BECAUSE I THINK I NEED A LOT OF HELP...

I HAVE THIS RASH OR SOMETHING, AND IT MAKES MY HEAD LOOK LIKE A BASEBALL...

WHY AM I WEARING THIS SACK?

SOMEONE TRIED TO AUTOGRAPH MY HEAD!

June 20, 1973

PEANUTS
WHAT ARE YOU PACKING FOR, BIG BROTHER?

MY DOCTOR SAYS I SHOULD GO TO CAMP...HE SAID I HAVE TO DO SOMETHING THAT WILL TAKE MY MIND OFF BASEBALL
6-20

I'VE SEEN YOU PLAY.. I NEVER THOUGHT YOU HAD YOUR MIND ON IT!
THANKS A LOT... I'LL SEE YOU IN TWO WEEKS...

YOU'RE GOING TO BE A BIG HIT AT CAMP CARRYING YOUR HEAD IN A SACK!!
SCHULZ

June 23, 1973

PEANUTS
CONGRATULATIONS, KID!
?

YEAH, GOOD GOING, SACK! YOU'VE JUST BEEN ELECTED CAMP PRESIDENT!

CONGRATULATIONS, SACK!!!

"SACK"?!
SCHULZ
6-23

"I was regarded by many as kind of sissified, which I resented because I really was not a sissy. I was not a tough guy, but I was good at sports. I was a good baseball player. . . . I was good at any sport where you threw things, or hit them, or caught them. . . . It wasn't until I came back from the war that I really had self-confidence, because I went into the army as a nothing person, and I came out as a staff sergeant, squad leader of a light machine gun squad. And I thought, by golly, if that isn't a man, I don't know what is. And I felt good about myself and that lasted about eight minutes, and then I went back to where I am now."

June 27, 1973

PEANUTS
Dear Mom and Dad, Guess What! I have been elected Camp President!

MR. SACK, EXCUSE ME, BUT DO YOU THINK I SHOULD SIGN UP FOR NATURE HIKE OR FOR SWIMMING?
SWIMMING, DEFINITELY!! NATURE HIKES ARE GREAT, BUT LEARNING TO SWIM IS A MUST!

THANK YOU, MR. SACK... YOU SURE ARE SMART!
6-27

Life here in camp is wonderful.
SCHULZ

June 30, 1973

PEANUTS
MR. SACK, WHICH STAR IS THE NORTH STAR?
6-30

WELL, DO YOU SEE THOSE TWO STARS THAT MAKE THE END OF THE BIG DIPPER? JUST FOLLOW THEM STRAIGHT UP SIX SPACES, AND THERE'S THE NORTH STAR...

THAT'S AMAZING! BEING WITH YOU, MR. SACK, HAS BEEN THE GREATEST EXPERIENCE OF MY LIFE!

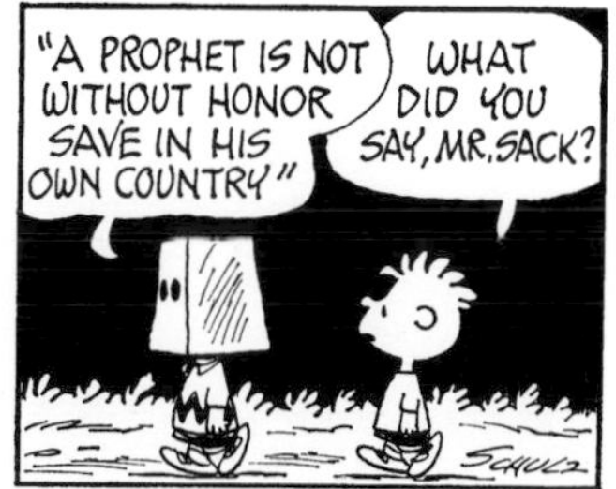
"A PROPHET IS NOT WITHOUT HONOR SAVE IN HIS OWN COUNTRY"
WHAT DID YOU SAY, MR. SACK?
SCHULZ

July 2, 1973

PEANUTS
MY HEAD DOESN'T SEEM TO ITCH ANY MORE... MAYBE MY RASH HAS GONE AWAY...

IF IT HAS, I COULD TAKE THIS STUPID GROCERY SACK OFF MY HEAD... OF COURSE, THEN I PROBABLY WOULDN'T BE CAMP PRESIDENT ANY MORE, EITHER...

ON THE OTHER HAND, I CAN'T WEAR THIS SACK FOR THE REST OF MY LIFE...

IF I EVER WENT TO A GROCERY STORE, AND THE CLERK YELLED, "CARRY OUT!" I'D END UP IN THE BACK OF SOME STATION WAGON!
7-2
SCHULZ

July 3, 1973

PEANUTS
PSST, MR. SACK... WHAT ARE YOU DOING UP SO EARLY?

I'M GOING OUT TO WATCH THE SUN RISE... IF IT'S THE SUN, I'LL KNOW I'M CURED... IF IT'S A BASEBALL, I'M STILL IN TROUBLE..

?? HE DIDN'T HAVE A SACK OVER HIS HEAD ??!??

HE IS OUR CAMP PRESIDENT ?!?
7-3
SCHULZ

July 5, 1973

PEANUTS
IT'S GETTING LIGHT... THE SUN IS COMING UP...

I CAN'T LOOK! I CAN'T STAND THE SUSPENSE! BUT I HAVE TO LOOK! I HAVE TO KNOW! WILL I SEE THE SUN, OR WILL I SEE A BASEBALL? WHAT WILL I SEE?
7-5

!

What, Me Worry?
GOOD GRIEF!
SCHULZ

August 1, 1973

PEANUTS
WHY DO YOU WEAR THOSE STUPID-LOOKING GLASSES?
8-1

GIRLS DON'T HAVE TO SEE ANYTHING! WHAT A WASTE OF MONEY SPENDING IT ON GLASSES FOR A GIRL!

YOU DON'T NEED GLASSES TO SCRUB FLOORS, DO DISHES AND MAKE BEDS!

SPEAKING OF GLASSES, MINE ARE BEGINNING TO STEAM UP!
SCHULZ

August 3, 1973

PEANUTS
NOW, LOOK HERE, YOU CEMENT-HEADED, MALE-CHAUVINIST DUMMY...

I'M GOING TO TELL YOU SOMETHING, AND I WANT YOU TO STAND STILL AND LISTEN!
8-3

IF YOU SAY ONE WORD, I'M GOING TO BELT YOU RIGHT ACROSS THE CHOPS!
OH?

THAT WAS ONE WORD!
POW!
SCHULZ

August 4, 1973

PEANUTS
NICE GOING, MARCIE... YOU DESTROYED MY SECOND BASEMAN!

I'M SORRY, SIR...I GOT CARRIED AWAY...I WAS GOING TO GIVE HIM MY LECTURE ON THE GOOD QUALITIES OF WOMEN, BUT INSTEAD I HIT HIM...

WELL, LET'S GET BACK TO THE BALL GAME
I'M NOT GOING TO PLAY ANY MORE, SIR...I HATE BASEBALL..

OKAY, BUT THE LEAST YOU COULD DO IS STOP CALLING ME "SIR"!!!...
Tm. Reg. U.S. Pat. Off.—All rights reserved © 1973 by United Feature Syndicate, Inc.

September 13, 1973

PEANUTS
TODAY FOR "SHOW AND TELL" I HAVE BROUGHT MY BROTHER'S DOG...

WHICH MAY TURN OUT TO BE THE BIGGEST MISTAKE OF MY LIFE!

September 14, 1973

PEANUTS
THE DOG IS REGARDED AS THE FRIEND OF MAN...

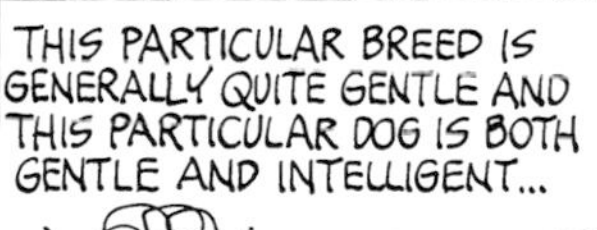
THIS PARTICULAR BREED IS GENERALLY QUITE GENTLE AND THIS PARTICULAR DOG IS BOTH GENTLE AND INTELLIGENT...

ALTHOUGH HE DOES HAVE HIS FAULTS...

SUCH AS FLIRTING WITH THE GIRL IN THE FRONT ROW!!!

September 15, 1973

PEANUTS
STUPID BEAGLE!

ALL BECAUSE OF YOU, I FAILED SHOW AN' TELL!

NOW, I'LL PROBABLY GET BAD GRADES ALL YEAR AND NEVER BE A GOOD STUDENT AND NOT GET INTO THE COLLEGE OF MY CHOICE!

SMAK!
POOR, SWEET BABY!

October 23, 1973

PEANUTS

THE RAIN FALLS ON THE JUST AND THE UNJUST

THAT'S A GOOD SYSTEM!

October 21, 1973

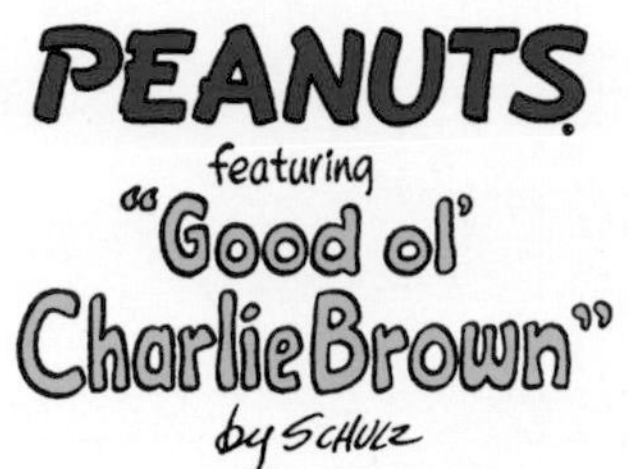
PEANUTS
featuring
"Good ol' CharlieBrown"
by SCHULZ

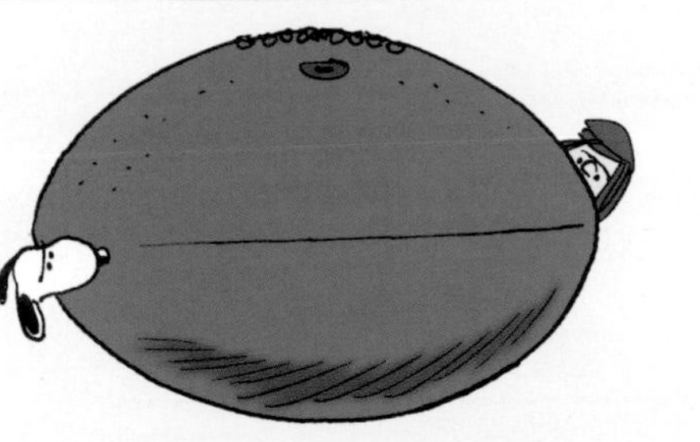

NOPE!

I'D LIKE TO HAVE YOU ON MY TEAM, CHUCK, BUT I JUST DON'T THINK YOU'RE GOOD ENOUGH...

IN FACT, I DON'T SEE ANYONE AROUND HERE WHO COULD COME UP TO MY STANDARD!

HOW ABOUT MY LINEBACKER OVER THERE? HE'S PRETTY GOOD
HIM?

OKAY, LET'S TRY HIM OUT..

HERE I COME, FELLA! STOP ME IF YOU CAN!!

FREIGHT TRAIN!!
♪
10-21

CRUNCH!
BONE-BREAKING
EAR-SPLITTING
EARTH SHATTERING
RIB-SHAKING
FLESH-TEARING
TEETH RATTLING
SMASH!
SOUND OF GLASS BREAKING

GOOD SHOT, KID! HOW WOULD YOU LIKE TO PLAY FOR A DECENT TEAM?
SIGH
KEEP TALKING, SWEETIE..
SCHULZ

November 23, 1973

PEANUTS
DO YOU THINK THAT LIFE HAS ITS PEAKS AND VALLEYS?
YES, I'M SURE THAT IT HAS

THEN, THAT MEANS THAT THERE MUST BE ONE DAY ABOVE ALL OTHERS IN EACH LIFE THAT IS THE HAPPIEST, RIGHT?
11-23

YES, I GUESS THAT'S PROBABLY TRUE...

WHAT IF YOU'VE ALREADY HAD IT?
SCHULZ

December 10, 1973

PEANUTS
They had named their Great Dane "Good Authority."
12-10

One day, she asked her husband if he had seen her new belt.

"Belt?" he said. "Oh, I'm sorry. I thought it was a dog collar. I have it on Good Authority."

Shortly thereafter, their marriage began to go downhill.
SCHULZ

November 11, 1973

Classic
PEANUTS
featuring
"Good ol' Charlie Brown"
by SCHULZ
DO YOU LIKE JOKES AND RIDDLES ?
I GUESS SO...WHY ?
I HAVE A RIDDLE FOR YOU, CHARLIE BROWN...WHAT ARE THE THREE THINGS IN LIFE THAT ARE CERTAIN ?
DEATH AND TAXES !!
THAT'S ONLY TWO...
YOU'RE RIGHT...HMM...I KNOW WHAT THE THIRD ONE IS, BUT I JUST CAN'T SEEM TO THINK... DON'T TELL ME...
RATS! I SEEM TO HAVE A MENTAL BLOCK OR SOMETHING...
♫
IT'S SO AGGRAVATING WHEN YOU'RE TRYING TO THINK OF SOMETHING, AND YOU...
NOW, I REMEMBER!
WHAM!
IT WAS SO OBVIOUS, CHARLIE BROWN!
SCHULZ

"This is the flaw in Charlie Brown's personality. He wants everyone to like him at all times, which is impossible. It's his own weaknesses that cause him his trouble and make him so vulnerable. That's why Lucy can do the things to him that she does because he's so terribly vulnerable. That's why she can fool him with the football every year. It's so easy."

December 19, 1973

PEANUTS
IF YOU'RE TYPING YOUR CHRISTMAS LIST, YOU CAN SCRATCH ME..I DON'T WANT ANY PRESENTS THIS YEAR
12-19

Sally Brown

TAP TAP TAP TAP TAP TAP TAP TAP

SCRATCHING IS ONE THING... OBLITERATING IS ANOTHER!
SCHULZ

December 20, 1973

PEANUTS
I DON'T WANT YOU TO GIVE ME ANYTHING FOR CHRISTMAS THIS YEAR, LINUS...

REALLY? THAT'S TOO BAD, BUT I CAN UNDERSTAND HOW YOU FEEL, AND I ADMIRE YOU FOR IT...
12-20

CANCEL THAT ORDER FOR THE TEN-THOUSAND DOLLAR NECKLACE!!!

AFTER THE HOLIDAYS ARE OVER AND EVERYTHING HAS QUIETED DOWN, I'M GOING TO SLUG YOU!
SCHULZ

December 24, 1973

PEANUTS
I CAN'T GO THROUGH WITH IT!!

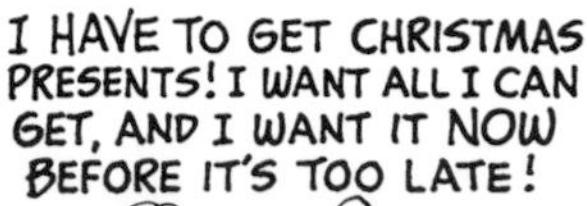
I HAVE TO GET CHRISTMAS PRESENTS! I WANT ALL I CAN GET, AND I WANT IT NOW BEFORE IT'S TOO LATE!

12-24
I WANT ALL I CAN GET BEFORE I'M TOO OLD, AND EVERYTHING IS GONE, AND THE SUN HAS DIMMED, AND THE STARS HAVE FALLEN, AND THE BIRDS ARE SILENT AND THE WHEAT IS EATEN...

"THE WHEAT IS EATEN"?
SCHULZ

January 21, 1974

PEANUTS
IS THAT YOUR BROTHER, RERUN, RIDING ON THE BACK OF YOUR MOTHER'S BICYCLE?

UH-HUH... SHE TAKES HIM WHEREVER SHE GOES...
1-21

SHE SAYS RIDING A BIKE IS SUCH GOOD EXERCISE THAT SHE'S ALREADY LOST THREE POUNDS...

AND THROUGH SHEER TERROR I'VE LOST FIVE!!
SCHULZ

December 9, 1973

PEANUTS
featuring
"Good ol' CharlieBrown"
by SCHULZ
WHAT ARE YOU WATCHING?

"CITIZEN KANE"
12-9

I'VE SEEN IT ABOUT TEN TIMES

THIS IS THE FIRST TIME I'VE EVER SEEN IT...
"ROSEBUD" WAS HIS SLED!

AAUGH!!
SCHULZ

January 24, 1974

PEANUTS
HERE WE GO AGAIN! OUT OF THE GARAGE, AND FULL SPEED AHEAD!

TODAY IT'S WELFARE LEAGUE AND A CHURCH BREAKFAST... THEN IT'S THE LEAGUE OF WOMEN VOTERS FOLLOWED BY A VISIT TO THE LIBRARY...

FROM THERE WE GO TO THE HAIRDRESSER'S AND THE SUPER-MARKET AND THEN A ROUSING MEETING OF THE PTA!

CONSIDERING I DON'T DO ANYTHING, I LEAD A VERY ACTIVE LIFE!

January 25, 1974

PEANUTS
I LIKE THE WAY YOUR MOTHER HANDLES THAT BIKE...

SEE HOW SHE WENT THROUGH THAT HEDGE INSTEAD OF INTO THE BRICK WALL?

YES, I MUST ADMIT THAT HER STEERING IS GETTING A LITTLE BETTER...

YESTERDAY WE ONLY HIT FOUR PARKED CARS!

March 17, 1974

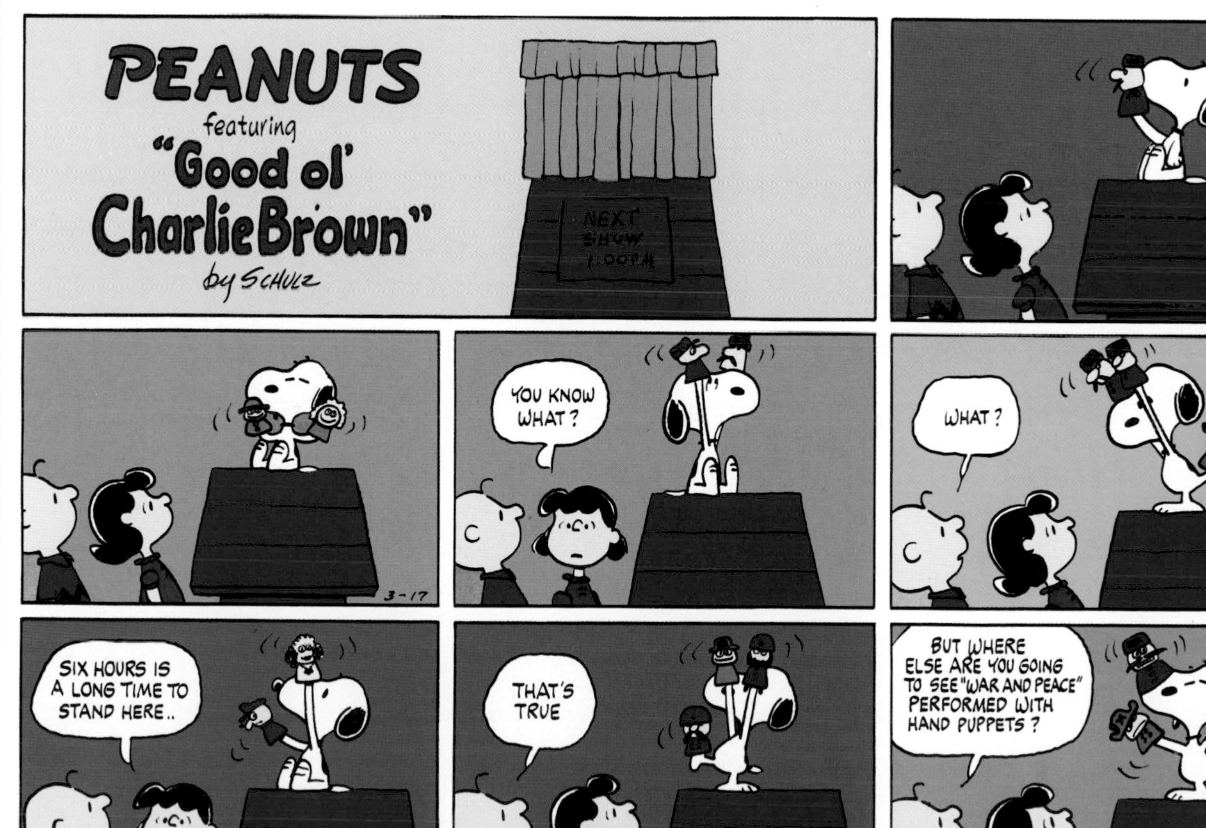
PEANUTS
featuring
"Good ol' CharlieBrown"
by SCHULZ
YOU KNOW WHAT?
WHAT?
SIX HOURS IS A LONG TIME TO STAND HERE..
THAT'S TRUE
BUT WHERE ELSE ARE YOU GOING TO SEE "WAR AND PEACE" PERFORMED WITH HAND PUPPETS?

February 4, 1974

PEANUTS
KING LOUIS THE SECOND?

WELL, IF YOU SUBTRACT KING LOUIS THE FOURTEENTH FROM KING LOUIS THE SIXTEENTH, YOU GET KING LOUIS THE SECOND!

YOU DON'T?
2-4

RATS! I THOUGHT THAT WAS A PRETTY GOOD ANSWER!
SCHULZ

April 10, 1974

PEANUTS
ABRAHAM LINCOLN USED TO DO HIS HOMEWORK ON THE BACK OF A COAL SHOVEL

ONE DAY, HIS DAD SAID TO HIM, "SORRY, SON, I HAVE TO USE THE SHOVEL," AND WIPED OUT POOR ABE'S ENGLISH REPORT!

WELL, IT COULD HAVE HAPPENED!!
SCHULZ
4-10

April 11, 1974

PEANUTS
I'M TRYING, MARCIE, BUT I'M STILL DOING LOUSY IN SCHOOL

MAYBE YOU NEED TO EAT A BETTER BREAKFAST, SIR, OR HAVE YOUR EYES CHECKED OR START GOING TO BED EARLIER

YOU'VE NEVER UNDERSTOOD, HAVE YOU, MARCIE, THAT WHEN A PERSON COMPLAINS, HE DOESN'T WANT A SOLUTION, HE WANTS SYMPATHY!!
4-11

NO, I ADMIT I'VE NEVER UNDERSTOOD THAT, SIR...
STOP CALLING ME "SIR"!
SCHULZ

April 17, 1974

PEANUTS
LOVE DOESN'T HAVE TO BE RESTRICTED TO ONE THING...
4-17

YOU CAN LOVE MUSIC, AND ALSO LOVE ANOTHER PERSON...

DID YOU KNOW THAT?
SCHULZ

April 24, 1974

PEANUTS
PRACTICE?! WHY DO WE HAVE TO PRACTICE? WE NEVER WIN ANY GAMES...
4-24

WHAT ARE WE GONNA DO, PRACTICE OUR LOSING?!

THAT WAS JUST A LITTLE JOKE!
SCHULZ

May 1, 1974

PEANUTS
History Report; Ancient Greece

Ancient Greece was ahead of its time, and before our time.

They had no TV, but they had lots of philosophers.

I, personally, would not want to sit all evening watching a philosopher.

May 26, 1974

PEANUTS
featuring
"Good ol' Charlie Brown"
by SCHULZ
CHOW

GOOD GRIEF!
ANOTHER NOTE!

"DEAR SON, I HOPE YOU ENJOY AND ALSO APPRECIATE THE LUNCH I MADE FOR YOU TODAY"

"DID YOU HAVE A NICE MORNING? DID YOU VOLUNTEER IN CLASS AS I SUGGESTED? TEACHERS ARE ALWAYS IMPRESSED BY STUDENTS WHO VOLUNTEER...IT IS A SURE WAY TO BETTER GRADES..."

"REMEMBER, BETTER GRADES NOW WILL MEAN A BETTER COLLEGE LATER ON..DID YOU EAT YOUR CARROTS? PROPER NUTRITION IS ESSENTIAL TO GOOD STUDY"

"ARE YOU SITTING IN THE SUN? I HOPE SO, FOR A LITTLE SUN IS GOOD AS LONG AS WE DON'T OVERDO IT...PERHAPS TEN MINUTES A DAY THIS TIME OF YEAR IS ABOUT RIGHT"

HI, LINUS...WHAT ARE YOU HAVING FOR LUNCH?

CARROTS, PEANUT BUTTER AND GUILT!

May 29, 1974

PEANUTS
LINUS, DO YOU THINK I SHOULD HAVE MY EARS PIERCED?

I HAVE A BETTER IDEA... WHY DON'T YOU HAVE YOUR MOUTH BOARDED UP?

POW!

THAT WAS WORTH ONE HIT... TWO HITS, NO! BUT IT WAS DEFINITELY WORTH ONE HIT!

June 29, 1974

PEANUTS
SO HERE I AM AT THE BUS STATION WAITING TO BE TAKEN TO CAMP...

HOW DO THESE THINGS HAPPEN TO ME? NO ONE ELSE I KNOW IS GOING...
6-29

MAYBE I'LL MEET A BEAUTIFUL GIRL AT CAMP, AND MAYBE WE'LL FALL IN LOVE AND BECOME CHILDHOOD SWEETHEARTS..

MAYBE I'LL SPEND THE WHOLE TWO WEEKS IN BED WITH POISON OAK!
SCHULZ

"Another reflection of my emotions are all of the summer camp ideas which I have drawn. They are a result of my having absolutely no desire as a child to be sent away to a summer camp. To me that was the equivalent of being drafted. When World War II came along, I met it with the same lack of enthusiasm."

July 1, 1974

PEANUTS
HELLO...BROWN RESIDENCE... NO, HE'S NOT HERE...HE'S AT CAMP... ME? I'M HIS SISTER...

WHAT DO YOU MEAN, HE'S NOT IN CAMP? HE LEFT SATURDAY MORNING! ARE YOU SURE HE'S NOT IN CAMP?
7-1

MAYBE YOU'D BETTER CHECK AGAIN...

MY BROTHER'S THE KIND WHO'S EASY TO OVERLOOK!
SCHULZ

July 14, 1974

PEANUTS
featuring "Good ol' CharlieBrown"
by SCHULZ
I THINK I'M AWAKE
SUDDENLY, I FEEL LIKE A TOASTED ENGLISH MUFFIN WITH GRAPE JELLY....
WAM! WAM! WAM!
I KNOW THAT KICK... THAT'S THE KICK OF SOMEONE WHO'S DECIDED AT TWO O'CLOCK IN THE MORNING THAT HE NEEDS A TOASTED ENGLISH MUFFIN WITH GRAPE JELLY...
WELL, FORGET IT!!
I'M GOING TO HAVE TO LEARN TO DISGUISE THAT KICK
7-14
SCHULZ

July 5, 1974

PEANUTS
WELL, DON'T JUST STAND THERE...START LOOKING FOR YOUR MASTER!

YOU BEAGLES ARE SUPPOSED TO HAVE GOOD NOSES...

WELL, GET THAT BEAGLE NOSE TO THE GROUND, AND FIND YOUR MISSING MASTER!

I KNOW WHAT'LL HAPPEN.. I'LL GET BITTEN BY A STUPID GROUND BUG!
7-5
SCHULZ

July 8, 1974

PEANUTS
LUCY SAID YOU KNOW WHERE MY BIG BROTHER IS
WELL, I THINK I KNOW WHERE HE IS...

THEN GO FIND HIM!
SHALL I TELL HIM YOU'VE BEEN WORRIED ABOUT HIM?
7-8

NO, DON'T TELL HIM THAT! JUST FIND OUT IF HE'S EVER COMING HOME...

IF HE'S NOT COMING HOME, ASK HIM IF I CAN HAVE HIS LAMP AND DRESSER!!
SCHULZ

July 10, 1974

PEANUTS
THIS IS WHERE YOU'VE BEEN? SITTING ON THIS STUPID PITCHER'S MOUND?!!

IF YOU WERE GOING TO RUN AWAY, WHY DIDN'T YOU GO UP TO CANADA?
7-10

WHAT A FAILURE YOU ARE! CAN'T EVEN RUN AWAY RIGHT!!

ACTUALLY, I DID CONSIDER GOING TO CANADA, BUT I WAS AFRAID I'D GET HIT WITH A HOCKEY PUCK...
SCHULZ

August 5, 1974

PEANUTS
YOU KNOW WHAT MY GRANDFATHER SAYS?
HAPPY BIRTHDAY, AMY!

HE SAYS EVERY CHILD SHOULD HAVE A DOG...

HE SAYS THAT A CHILD WHO DOES NOT HAVE A DOG IS LIKE A CHILD DEPRIVED
8-5

THE ACTUAL TERM IS "LIVING WITHOUT BENEFIT OF BEAGLE"
SCHULZ

August 6, 1974

PEANUTS
Z

RING!!

8-6
CLOMP!!

HOW DO YOU SET THE ALARM FOR A FLY BALL?
SCHULZ

August 24, 1974

PEANUTS
8-24

SUDDENLY, I JUST FELT VERY VERY RIDICULOUS!
SCHULZ

September 2, 1974

PEANUTS
STUPID SCHOOL!
9-2

YOU'RE JUST WAITING FOR TOMORROW, AREN'T YOU, SO YOU CAN TORTURE A BUNCH OF INNOCENT KIDS ?!

WELL, YOU WON'T GET AWAY WITH IT FOREVER!

SOMEBODY GET THIS KID AWAY FROM ME!
SCHULZ

September 4, 1974

PEANUTS
JUST BECAUSE YOU'RE A SCHOOL, DON'T THINK YOU'RE BEYOND CRITICISM!

ON THE CONTRARY!

I SAY THAT IT'S TIME WE ALL TAKE A CLOSER LOOK AT SOME OF OUR CHERISHED INSTITUTIONS!
9-4

LOOK CLOSER, KID, AND I'LL DROP A BRICK ON YOU!!
SCHULZ

September 6, 1974

PEANUTS
9-6

YOUR BRICKS ARE COOL

SCHULZ

September 10, 1974

PEANUTS
DID YOU TELL THE SCHOOL I WAS SICK TODAY, BIG BROTHER?
9-10

YES, I TOLD YOUR TEACHER YOU WEREN'T FEELING WELL
WHO CARES ABOUT MY TEACHER?! YOU GO BACK THERE AND TELL THE SCHOOL WHERE I WAS TODAY!
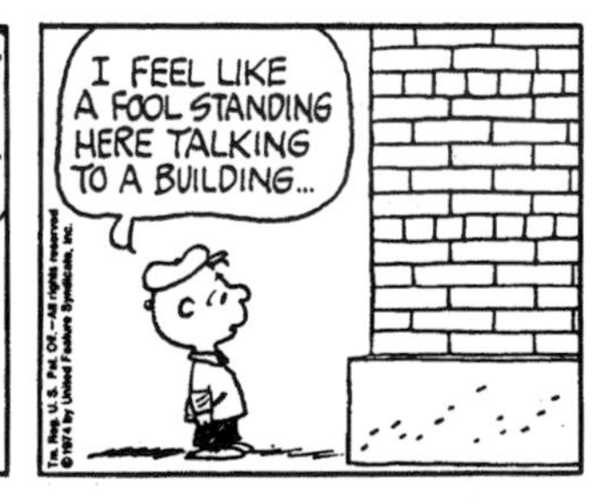
I FEEL LIKE A FOOL STANDING HERE TALKING TO A BUILDING...

THIS IS NOT THE BIGGEST THRILL OF MY LIFE, EITHER, KID!
SCHULZ

September 11, 1974

PEANUTS
THE REASON I'M HERE IS I HAVE A MESSAGE FOR YOU..

MY LITTLE SISTER WASN'T FEELING WELL SO SHE DIDN'T GO TO SCHOOL TODAY...AS YOU KNOW...YOU BEING THE SCHOOL

ANYWAY, THAT'S THE MESSAGE.. I HOPE I HAVEN'T BOTHERED YOU OR ANYTHING... I'LL PROBABLY SEE YOU TOMORROW...

I'LL BE HERE

September 19, 1974

PEANUTS

AH!

THIS IS GOING TO BE A GOOD DAY...

I GOT THE NEW CAN OF BALLS OPEN WITHOUT CUTTING MYSELF!

September 23, 1974

PEANUTS
DO YOU WANT TO HEAR SOME BASEBALL STATISTICS, CHARLIE BROWN?

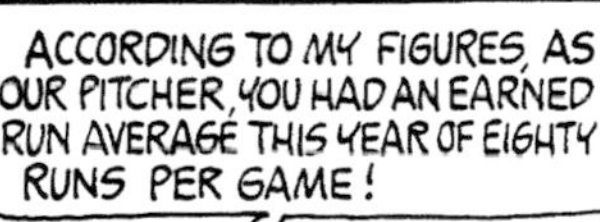
ACCORDING TO MY FIGURES, AS OUR PITCHER, YOU HAD AN EARNED RUN AVERAGE THIS YEAR OF EIGHTY RUNS PER GAME!

STATISTICS DON'T LIE, CHARLIE BROWN

NO, BUT THEY SURE SHOOT OFF THEIR MOUTH A LOT!

September 24, 1974

PEANUTS
AS OFFICIAL TEAM STATISTICIAN, I HAVE A FEW FIGURES TO REPORT..

DURING THIS PAST SEASON, WHILE YOU WERE IN RIGHT FIELD, NINETY EIGHT FLY BALLS BOUNCED OVER YOUR HEAD...

SEVENTY-SIX GROUND BALLS ROLLED THROUGH YOUR LEGS AND YOU DROPPED TWO HUNDRED FLY BALLS...YOUR FIELDING AVERAGE FOR THE SEASON WAS .000

THE SUN WAS IN MY EYES!

September 25, 1974

PEANUTS
HERE ARE A FEW STATISTICS FOR YOU, SNOOPY...

DURING THIS PAST SEASON, YOU CONSUMED TWENTY-FOUR PRE-GAME MEALS, NINETEEN MID-GAME MEALS AND FIFTY-FOUR POST-GAME MEALS

OH, YES... AND THREE HUNDRED PACKS OF BUBBLE GUM!

September 26, 1974

PEANUTS
ALL RIGHT, WE'VE HEARD THE REPORT FROM OUR STATISTICIAN..

BOTH OUR HITTING AND OUR FIELDING AVERAGES WERE DOWN THIS YEAR...

SO YOU ALL KNOW WHAT WE HAVE TO DO NEXT SEASON

GET A NEW STATISTICIAN!!!

October 2, 1974

PEANUTS
THIS PIANO IS TOO MUCH COMPETITION FOR ME...

SO YOU KNOW WHAT I'M GOING TO DO? I'M GOING TO SNATCH IT AWAY, AND THROW IT DOWN THE SEWER!

HEY!
IT'S WOMAN AGAINST PIANO!

WOMAN IS WINNING!! WOMAN IS WINNING!!!

October 4, 1974

PEANUTS
WHY WOULD LUCY THROW YOUR PIANO DOWN THE SEWER?

IS THIS WHERE SHE THREW IT DOWN? CAN YOU SEE IT?

DID YOU FIND IT?

October 8, 1974

PEANUTS
YOU THINK MY PIANO WAS WASHED INTO THE RIVER, CHARLIE BROWN?

IT MUST HAVE BEEN! BUT MAYBE WE CAN GET TO IT BEFORE IT COMES OUT OF THE STORM DRAIN...

THERE IT GOES!
GOOD GRIEF!

I'LL BET BEETHOVEN NEVER HAD TO PUT UP WITH ANYTHING LIKE THIS!

October 10, 1974

PEANUTS
COULDN'T FIND YOUR PIANO, HUH?

DOWN THE SEWER, AND OUT INTO THE RIVER, HUH?

OH, WELL, IF YOU WERE TO PLAY IT NOW, YOU'D PROBABLY JUST STRIKE A SEWER NOTE! HA! HA! HA! HA! HA!

AFTER YOU LEARN TO LOVE ME, SWEETIE, YOU'LL APPRECIATE MY HUMOR!

October 12, 1974

PEANUTS
THE SECRET TO LOVE IS REMOVAL OF THE COMPETITION
10-12

THAT'S ALL THERE IS TO IT...REMOVE THE COMPETITION, AND THE OTHER PERSON WILL LOVE YOU!

I THREW SCHROEDER'S PIANO DOWN THE SEWER...NOW, IT'S JUST A MATTER OF TIME UNTIL HE LOVES ME...

LIKE MAYBE FIVE HUNDRED YEARS!
SCHULZ

December 17, 1974

PEANUTS
I WONDER WHAT WOULD HAPPEN IF I TRIED TO MAKE FRIENDS WITH THAT STUPID CAT NEXT DOOR...

I COULD SHOW HIM MY GOOD WILL BY EXTENDING MY PAW IN FRIENDSHIP...
12-17

BY GOLLY, I'LL DO IT!

SCHULZ

October 27, 1974

PEANUTS
featuring
"Good ol' CharlieBrown"
by SCHULZ

10-27

!
3
SCHULZ

December 28, 1974

PEANUTS
I ORDERED A TOY BICYCLE FOR YOUR DOLL SET, BUT IT NEVER CAME...

I HAVE A FEELING IT WAS PROBABLY DELIVERED TO THE WRONG ADDRESS...

WELL, I HOPE WHOEVER GOT IT, ENJOYS IT!!
12-28

WHEELIES, YET! GOOD GRIEF!
SCHULZ

December 29, 1974

PEANUTS featuring "Good ol' Charlie Brown" by SCHULZ

12-29

SNOOPY! WHY DON'T YOU COME INTO THE HOUSE, AND I'LL FEED YOU HERE? IT'S A LOT WARMER!

HOW NICE... AN INVITATION TO DINNER..

TAP TAP TAP

WHY DOES HE HAVE TO MAKE A BIG DEAL OUT OF EVERYTHING?

SCHULZ

January 4, 1975

PEANUTS
1-4
SUPPERTIME!

CHOMP CHOMP
CHOMP

I WONDER HOW HE DID THAT!
SCHULZ

January 7, 1975

PEANUTS
YOUR SNOWMAN SEEMS TO LIKE TO READ...
1-7

YES, HE'S VERY FOND OF POETRY

ROBERT FROST ?

YOU SAID IT... I DIDN'T!
SCHULZ

February 8, 1975

PEANUTS

2-8
Z

SCHULZ

"I have frequently referred to the comic strip as a sidewalk medium. By this I mean that the comic strip appeals to just plain people. However, if it is handled in the proper manner, a comic strip can burst these traditional bounds and appeal also to people who are better educated and are fortunate enough to have a more cultured background. To do this, the cartoonist himself need not be extremely educated or cultured but he must possess that rarest of all commodities—plain common sense."

February 18, 1975

PEANUTS
HERE'S JOE MOTOCROSS GOING OUT TO START HIS BIKE...
2-18

VAROOM!

RIP! RIP! RIP!
RIP! RIP! RIP!
POOOOOOOSHHH!

THE NEIGHBORS HATE ME!
SCHULZ

February 22, 1975

PEANUTS
WHY DON'T YOU SURPRISE ME SOMETIME, AND SEND ME SOME ROSES?

WHY DON'T YOU SURPRISE ME SOMETIME, AND LEAVE ME ALONE?
2-22

SOME SURPRISES ARE BETTER THAN OTHERS
SCHULZ

March 9, 1975

PEANUTS
featuring
"Good ol' Charlie Brown"
by Schulz
I HATE PLAYING ON A WINDY DAY!!
SCHULZ

"It's fun to draw the tennis stuff with Snoopy in all his poses. It's much more fun than Lucy and Schroeder at the piano, where they're in pretty much the same poses in all the panels. . . . The racket is hard to draw [because] there are so many ellipses that have to be right. You have to get the perspective and be careful on those vertical and horizontal strings . . . the string lines on the paper can run together when they're wet, and you have to be very careful drawing that . . . [the net is] very difficult to draw, I usually don't draw the net in."

February 28, 1975

PEANUTS
LOOK OUT FOR THE TREE!
2-28
LOOK OUT FOR THE FENCE! LOOK OUT FOR THE TRUCK!
LOOK OUT FOR THE BRICK WALL! LOOK OUT FOR THE CAR!
LOOK OUT FOR YOUR POOR, INNOCENT SON WHO WANTS TO GROW UP AND HAVE A LIFE OF HIS OWN!!
SCHULZ

March 5, 1975

PEANUTS
HOW COME WE ONLY WATCH THE PROGRAMS THAT YOU WANT TO WATCH?
BECAUSE I CAN HIT HARDER THAN YOU!
3-5
THIS IS A GOOD PROGRAM!
SCHULZ

March 31, 1975

PEANUTS
I SAID, IF YOU FIND ANYTHING, JUST REMEMBER THAT YOU'RE DIGGING ON **OUR** PROPERTY!
3-31

ACTUALLY, THIS IS MY GRANDFATHER'S FARM...

GEE, I APOLOGIZE... I DIDN'T EVEN THINK ABOUT TRESPASSING.. WE'RE HUNTING FOR TRUFFLES...
WELL, YOU FOUND ONE

SCHULZ
WE DID?
THAT'S MY NAME... TRUFFLES!
OH, GOOD GRIEF!

April 7, 1975

PEANUTS
Dear Truffles,
"TRUFFLES"?

IT'S A GIRL'S NAME, CHARLIE BROWN... I MET THE NEATEST LITTLE GIRL LAST WEEK!
4-7

WELL, YOU'D BETTER BE CAREFUL...

YOU'VE LEFT YOUR HEADLIGHTS ON!
SCHULZ

May 25, 1975

PEANUTS
featuring
"Good ol' Charlie Brown"
by SCHULZ
TIME OUT!

YOU KNOW WHAT YOU NEED, CHARLIE BROWN? YOU NEED A NICKNAME!

WE CAN'T KEEP SHOUTING, "PITCH IT TO 'EM, CHARLIE BROWN!" THAT'S NOT COLORFUL ENOUGH.. YOU NEED A NICKNAME

YOU SHOULD BE CALLED CATFISH, OR BABE, OR LEFTY, OR DUTCH, OR SPEED, OR DOC OR SOMETHING...

I THINK I'D LIKE THAT.. IF YOU COME UP WITH ANYTHING, JUST SHOUT IT RIGHT OUT..
GOOD!

5-25

THROW IT IN THERE, CEMENTHEAD!
SCHULZ

June 19, 1975

PEANUTS
WE'RE GONNA DO IT, MARCIE!! IT'S ALL ARRANGED!

YOU AND I ARE GOING TO FLY IN THE TWENTY-EIGHTH ANNUAL POWDER PUFF DERBY!

WHERE ARE WE GOING TO GET AN AIRPLANE, SIR?
I'VE ALREADY RENTED ONE, MARCIE..
6-19

A SOPWITH CAMEL!
SCHULZ

June 21, 1975

PEANUTS
EXPLAIN THIS POWDER PUFF DERBY TO ME, WILL YOU, SIR?
6-21

ACTUALLY, IT'S THE "ALL-WOMAN TRANSCONTINENTAL AIR RACE," MARCIE... WE TAKE OFF FROM RIVERSIDE, CALIFORNIA, JULY 4th AND FLY TO BOYNE FALLS, MICHIGAN

YOU'LL BE THE NAVIGATOR, MARCIE.. IT'LL BE YOUR JOB TO SEE THAT WE DON'T GET LOST

I'VE BEEN LOST ALL MY LIFE, SIR
STOP CALLING ME "SIR"
SCHULZ

July 4, 1975

PEANUTS
THERE'S THE STARTER'S FLAG, MARCIE!

WE'RE OFF IN THE TWENTY-EIGHTH ANNUAL POWDER PUFF DERBY!!

I FORGOT THE MAPS, SIR! I FORGOT THE STOP WATCH! I FORGOT THE SANDWICHES! I FORGOT MY TOOTHBRUSH! I FORGOT MY SHOWER CAP! I FORGOT MY CAMERA!
7-4

I FORGOT TO LEAVE YOU HOME, MARCIE!
SCHULZ

July 5, 1975

PEANUTS
WELL, WE MADE IT TO TULSA!

I'M EXHAUSTED, MARCIE... FLYING AN AIRPLANE ALL DAY IS HARD WORK... LET'S FIND A NICE MOTEL AND GET A GOOD NIGHT'S REST...
7-5

THAT LOOKS LIKE A NICE PLACE, SIR...

VACANCY
Motel
POOL
DINING
DANCING
SCHULZ

July 7, 1975

PEANUTS
THIS IS THE LAST LEG OF THE POWDER PUFF, MARCIE..

TODAY WE FLY UP TO BOYNE FALLS, MICHIGAN, WHERE WE FINISH THE RACE, AND THEN JOIN EVERYONE FOR A GREAT DINNER!

HEY! WHAT ARE YOU DOING ON OUR PLANE?!
HERE'S THE WORLD WAR I FLYING ACE ON A SPECIAL MISSION..

GET OFF OUR PLANE! WE HAVE TO LEAVE!
SOME OF THESE COUNTRY LASSES GET VERY EXCITED WHEN THEY SEE A REAL FLYING ACE

July 12, 1975

PEANUTS
MARCIE AND I ALMOST WON THE POWDER PUFF DERBY, CHUCK

BUT YOU KNOW WHAT HE DID? HE TOOK BACK HIS AIRPLANE, AND WE COULDN'T FINISH THE RACE...

I PAID HIM A DOLLAR TO RENT HIS PLANE, AND I CAN'T EVEN GET MY DOLLAR BACK BECAUSE HE SPENT IT ALL ON COOKIES...

SCARF CITY!

August 12, 1975

PEANUTS
SPIKE'S HERE!!

HE GOT IN LATE LAST NIGHT.. I HAVEN'T EVEN SEEN HIM...
Z

HEY, SPIKE! WAKE UP!! WE WANT TO SEE WHAT YOU LOOK LIKE!

I NOTICE A SIMILARITY ALREADY..
THE FAMILY NOSE!

August 13, 1975—First appearance of Spike.

PEANUTS
MY BROTHER HAS ARISEN!

EGGS BENEDICT FOR MY BROTHER, SPIKE!

I THINK YOU'D BETTER MAKE THAT TEN POUNDS OF BUFFALO STEAK...

August 15, 1975

PEANUTS
HEY, WHERE ARE YOU GOING WITH SPIKE?
THIS DOG NEEDS TO BE FATTENED UP!

IF IT'S ALL RIGHT WITH YOU, CHARLIE BROWN, I'LL TAKE HIM HOME, AND DO JUST THAT

SPIKE SURE LOOKS THIN, DOESN'T HE? I HOPE THIS MAKES YOU APPRECIATE THE GOOD LIFE YOU'VE HAD...
8-15

I WAS WONDERING HOW LONG IT WOULD BE BEFORE SOMEONE SAID THAT...
SCHULZ

August 22, 1975

PEANUTS
HEY, STUPID CAT WHO LIVES NEXT DOOR...
8-22

MY BROTHER SPIKE HAS BEEN LIVING WITH THE COYOTES! PRETTY SOON, I'M GONNA SEND HIM OVER TO PUNCH YOU OUT!! WHAT DO YOU THINK OF THAT?

RIP!!

MAYBE I SHOULD SEND OVER THE COYOTES
SCHULZ

August 27, 1975

PEANUTS
YOU STUPID CAT!
8-27

YOU SCARED MY BROTHER HALF TO DEATH! NOW, HE'S GONE BACK TO NEEDLES, AND I'LL NEVER SEE HIM AGAIN!!

AND LOOK WHAT THAT CAT DID TO MY HOUSE...

MAYBE I SHOULD DO LIKE MY BROTHER..MAYBE I SHOULD GO LIVE WITH THE COYOTES...
SCHULZ

August 30, 1975

PEANUTS

8-30

SCHULZ

September 2, 1975

PEANUTS
"HOW I SPENT MY SUMMER"
9-2

MY PLANS FOR THE SUMMER WERE AMBITIOUS...

STUDY FRENCH, LISTEN TO BARTOK QUARTETS, READ "WAR AND PEACE" AND START MY OWN VEGETABLE GARDEN...

ACTUALLY, I SPENT THE WHOLE SUMMER WATCHING GAME SHOWS ON TV!
SCHULZ

September 21, 1975

PEANUTS featuring "Good ol' Charlie Brown" by SCHULZ

9-21

CITY LIMITS

Z Z Z Z

THUS ENDETH THE HIKE..

SCHULZ

September 11, 1975

PEANUTS

9-11

I FEEL SORRY FOR SOMEONE WHO HAS TO WIN AT EVERYTHING!
SCHULZ

September 27, 1975

PEANUTS

UNFORTUNATELY, I'D SAY THERE'S ALMOST NO MARKET AT ALL FOR LEAF IMITATIONS

October 8, 1975

PEANUTS
History Test

Explain World War II

EXPLAIN WORLD WAR II ?!

Use both sides of the paper if necessary.

October 24, 1975

PEANUTS
HELLO, LINUS? THIS IS MARCIE.. YOU'RE NOT GONNA BELIEVE THIS...

GUESS WHO'S OUTSIDE SITTING IN A PUMPKIN PATCH... PEPPERMINT PATTY! YOU'VE FINALLY GOT ONE, LINUS...

"GOT ONE"? GOT ONE WHAT?

A DISCIPLE!

October 29, 1975

PEANUTS
LINUS, ARE YOU AND I THE ONLY ONES WHO BELIEVE IN THE "GREAT PUMPKIN"?

NOT FOR LONG! SOMEDAY OUR NUMBERS WILL INCREASE!

SOMEDAY WE MAY EVEN BECOME A GREAT ORGANIZATION OF BELIEVERS

IF WE HAVE FUND RAISINGS, I'M NOT GONNA WASH CARS!

October 30, 1975

PEANUTS
TOMORROW IS HALLOWEEN
TOMORROW I GET MY BASEBALL GLOVE!

YOUR WHAT?
MY BASEBALL GLOVE! I ASKED THE "GREAT PUMPKIN" TO BRING ME A NEW GLOVE..

YOU DON'T ASK THE "GREAT PUMPKIN" FOR A PRESENT! YOU WAIT FOR WHATEVER HE BRINGS YOU! DON'T YOU KNOW HOW SENSITIVE HE IS?!

YOU'VE DONE THE WORST THING A PERSON CAN DO! YOU'VE OFFENDED THE "GREAT PUMPKIN"!!!

October 31, 1975

PEANUTS
YOU ASKED THE "GREAT PUMPKIN" TO BRING YOU A BASEBALL GLOVE?!!

WHAT DO YOU THINK HE IS, SOME KIND OF SANTA CLAUS?!

YOU'VE DISGRACED YOURSELF! YOU'VE OFFENDED THE "GREAT PUMPKIN" AND THE SPIRIT OF HALLOWEEN!!!

BANISHED FROM THE PUMPKIN PATCH! SIGH

November 1, 1975

PEANUTS
DO YOU KNOW WHAT HAPPENED TO ME?

I WENT "TRICK OR TREATING" LAST NIGHT, AND ALL I GOT IN MY BAG WAS A ROCK!

I SAT IN A PUMPKIN PATCH FOR A WEEK, AND I DIDN'T GET ANYTHING!

DO YOU WANT MY ROCK?

November 7, 1975

PEANUTS
I HOPE YOU ENJOYED YOUR DINNER, SIR

THIS EVENING WE HAVE THREE CHOICES FOR DESSERT... NOTHING, NOTHING, AND NOTHING!

HA HA HA HA HA

BONK!

November 23, 1975

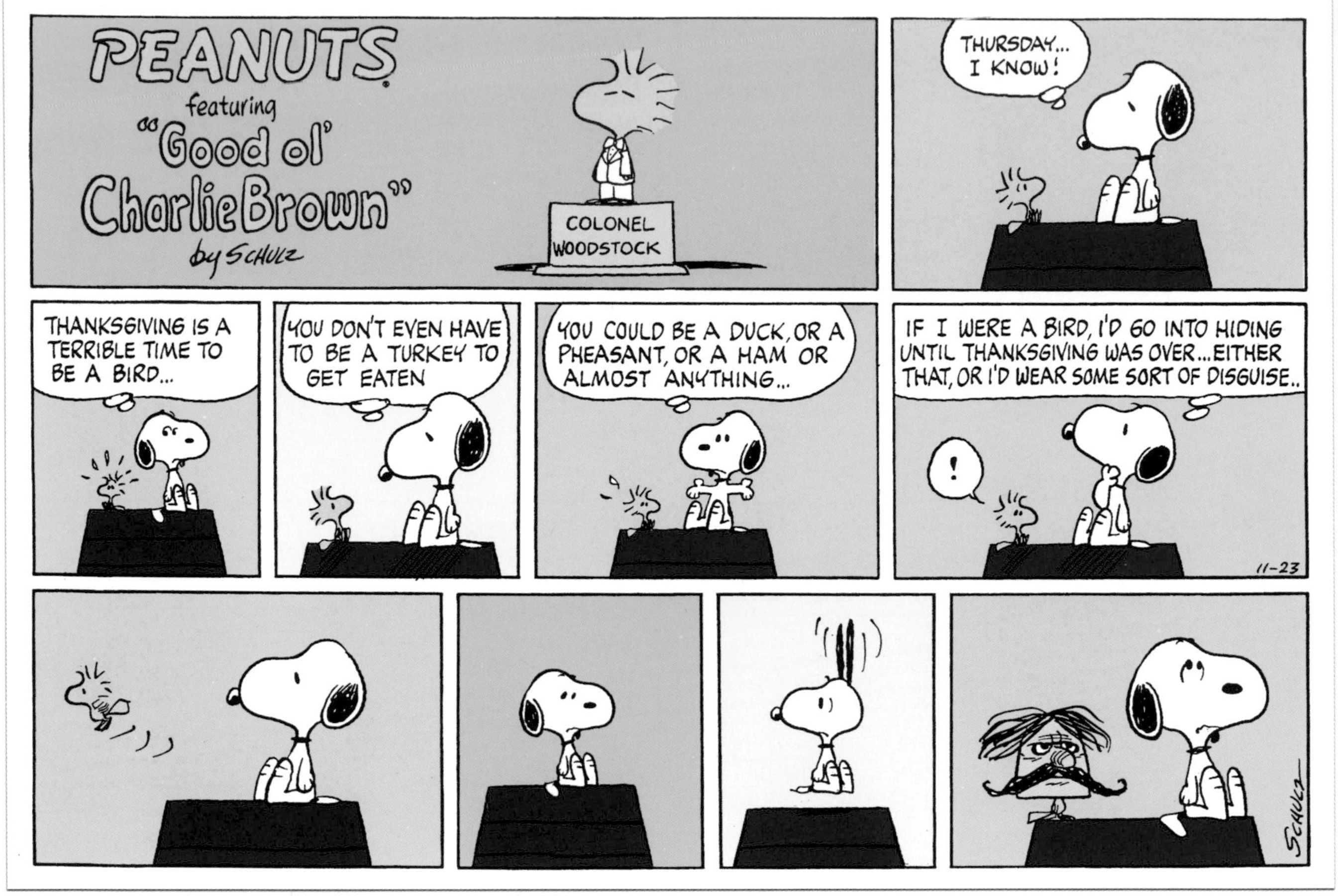

PEANUTS
featuring
"Good ol' Charlie Brown"
by Schulz

COLONEL WOODSTOCK

THURSDAY... I KNOW!

THANKSGIVING IS A TERRIBLE TIME TO BE A BIRD...

YOU DON'T EVEN HAVE TO BE A TURKEY TO GET EATEN

YOU COULD BE A DUCK, OR A PHEASANT, OR A HAM OR ALMOST ANYTHING...

IF I WERE A BIRD, I'D GO INTO HIDING UNTIL THANKSGIVING WAS OVER...EITHER THAT, OR I'D WEAR SOME SORT OF DISGUISE..

!

11-23

SCHULZ

December 10, 1975

PEANUTS
WHAT IF I KICK IT OVER YOUR HEAD, SIR?
12-10
WHAT IF SOME MAJOR LEAGUE SCOUT SPOTS ME, AND HIRES ME FOR HIS TEAM, AND I HAVE TO GO TO THE SUPER BOWL? WHAT WOULD I DO ABOUT SCHOOL?
JUST SHUT UP, MARCIE, AND KICK THE BALL!
DON'T BE IMPATIENT WITH ME, SIR...
SCHULZ

December 16, 1975

PEANUTS
HAPPY BEETHOVEN'S BIRTHDAY!
12-16
I BROUGHT YOU A LITTLE PRESENT...
WELL, THANK YOU...JUST WHAT I'VE ALWAYS WANTED
SCHULZ
ELTON JOHN GLASSES!

December 30, 1975

PEANUTS
English Report - "Familiar Quotations"
Tm. Reg. U.S. Pat. Off.—All rights reserved
©1975 by United Feature Syndicate, Inc.
12-30

My favorite "Familiar Quotation" is "Drop Dead!"

It is a very useful quotation. It can be used for almost any occasion.

GOOD GRIEF!
DROP DEAD!!
SCHULZ

January 3, 1976

PEANUTS
1-3
FIFTY-FOUR ROOT BEERS?

YOU WENT TO WOODSTOCK'S NEW YEAR'S PARTY, AND DRANK FIFTY-FOUR ROOT BEERS?

"DRANK" ISN'T QUITE THE WORD...THERE'S ANOTHER TERM THEY USE...

OH, YES... CHUG-A-LUG!
SCHULZ

January 4, 1976

PEANUTS
featuring
"Good ol' CharlieBrown"
by SCHULZ

WHY DOESN'T SOMEBODY JUST SHOOT ME, AND GET IT OVER WITH?

Bleh!

OH, WHY DO I GO TO WOODSTOCK'S NEW YEAR'S PARTIES? I FEEL AWFUL!

!!!!!!

NOW I HAVE TO LIE HERE, AND LISTEN TO MY STOMACH COMPLAIN...SO I ATE THIRTY PIZZAS! IS THAT SO MANY?

!?!?!?!
OW! NOW MY HEAD IS COMPLAINING!
WHAT'S SO BAD ABOUT DRINKING FIFTY-FOUR ROOT BEERS?

I KNEW MY FEET WOULD BE NEXT...

I ONLY DANCED UNTIL FIVE IN THE MORNING..
1-4

COMPLAIN, COMPLAIN, COMPLAIN!

THE NEXT TIME I GO SOMEPLACE, I'LL LEAVE YOU ALL HOME!
SCHULZ

January 5, 1976

PEANUTS
I HATE BEING A NOBODY
I WISH I WERE A BIG TV STAR
IF I WERE A TV STAR, I WOULDN'T HAVE TO GO TO SCHOOL
I'D LIKE TO BE THE SISTINE CHAPEL, TOO, KID, BUT I'M NOT!
1-5
SCHULZ

February 1, 1976

PEANUTS featuring "Good ol' Charlie Brown" by SCHULZ

HI, LUCY... I WAS WONDERING IF YOU'RE GOING TO BE IN YOUR PSYCHIATRIC BOOTH TODAY..

ARE YOU KIDDING? IT'S FREEZING OUT!

WELL, WHAT AM I GOING TO DO?

GO SEE MY ASSISTANT

YOUR ASSISTANT?

HE DOESN'T MIND THE COLD

SLAM!

WELL, I'VE BEEN FEELING SORT OF DEPRESSED LATELY, AND...

PSYCHIATRIC HELP 7¢

THE DOCTOR IS IN

SCHULZ

February 16, 1976

PEANUTS
LIFE IS GOING BY TOO FAST FOR ME
I'M NOT ACCOMPLISHING ANYTHING... I'M NOT GETTING ANYWHERE...
I'M NOT EVEN LEARNING ANYTHING...
STOP THE CLOCK!
2-16
SCHULZ

February 20, 1976

PEANUTS
?

WHAT KIND OF A REPORT CARD DO YOU CALL THIS?

I DIDN'T EVEN GET ANY GRADES...
2-20

ALL IT SAYS IS, "GOOD HUSTLE!"
SCHULZ

March 21, 1976

PEANUTS
featuring "Good ol' Charlie Brown"
by SCHULZ
OKAY, CHARLIE BROWN...THIS IS IT!

ONE FINGER WILL MEAN A FAST BALL, AND TWO FINGERS WILL MEAN A CURVE
TELL YOUR CATCHER THAT I THINK HE'S KIND OF CUTE

DID YOU GET THAT?
WHAT?
TELL YOUR CATCHER THAT I THINK HE'S KIND OF CUTE

I SAID, ONE FINGER WILL MEAN A FAST BALL, AND TWO FINGERS WILL MEAN A CURVE
SHE SAYS TO TELL YOU SHE THINKS YOU'RE KIND OF CUTE

WHAT?
ONE FINGER WILL MEAN A FAST BALL, AND TWO FINGERS WILL MEAN A CURVE
3-21

WHAT?

HEY! AREN'T WE GONNA HAVE ANY SIGNALS?
SCHULZ

February 24, 1976

PEANUTS
GOOD GRIEF! WHAT HAPPENED TO YOU?
2-24

WELL, THERE WERE THESE THREE AIRLINE STEWARDESSES, SEE, AND THEY WERE ON RUNAWAY HORSES, SEE, AND I HAD TO SAVE THEM...

I HEARD YOU TRIPPED OVER YOUR SUPPER DISH...

AS SOON AS I GET MY CRUTCHES, I'M GOING TO START HITTING PEOPLE!
SCHULZ

May 6, 1976

PEANUTS
COME BACK, EVERYBODY! WE CAN STILL PLAY!

A LITTLE WATER DOESN'T HURT!

THE WAVES AREN'T THAT HIGH!

THERE AREN'T EVEN ANY WHITE CAPS!
SCHULZ

May 8, 1976

PEANUTS
THIS IS RIDICULOUS!

I'M FLOATING OUT TO SEA ON A PITCHER'S MOUND!

HELP!!

THERE'S NEVER AN UMPIRE AROUND WHEN YOU NEED ONE
SCHULZ

"I can think of baseball ideas almost at will, and anytime I go out to a hockey game or ball game or anything like that, or if I go out on the tennis court or play golf, I will almost always be able to think of a cartoon idea while I'm doing that."

May 11, 1976

PEANUTS
FLOATING OUT TO SEA ON A PITCHER'S MOUND...I CAN'T BELIEVE IT!

CHARLIE BROWN'S IN TROUBLE, SNOOPY... WE SHOULD DO SOMETHING...
THAT'S TRUE!

IF HE'S NOT GOING TO BE AROUND TO FEED ME ANY MORE, MAYBE I SHOULD PLANT A GARDEN...

LET'S SEE, I COULD PUT SOME TOMATOES HERE, AND SOME CORN OVER THERE AND MAYBE SOME RADISHES HERE..
SCHULZ

May 13, 1976

PEANUTS
WHAT ARE **YOU** DOING HOME?

I THOUGHT YOU HAD FLOATED OUT TO SEA...

NO, I GUESS NOT...I ENDED UP IN AN ALLEY BEHIND A SUPERMARKET...IT WAS A TERRIBLE EXPERIENCE...

I SUPPOSE YOU'RE GOING TO WANT YOUR ROOM BACK..
SCHULZ

May 24, 1976

PEANUTS
This is my report on Dick Moby.

THAT'S WRONG, YOU KNOW

5-24

HOW ABOUT RICHARD MOBY?
SCHULZ

June 1, 1976

PEANUTS
"Light"
6-1

Light travels at a speed of 186,000 miles per second.

So why are the afternoons so long?
SCHULZ

June 3, 1976

PEANUTS
6-3
HEY, MANAGER!

THE TEAM TRAINER SAYS YOUR CATCHER NEEDS A BACK RUB!

WE DON'T HAVE A TEAM TRAINER...

I VOLUNTEER!!
SCHULZ

June 22, 1976

PEANUTS
"DEAR ROUND-HEADED KID..."

"TODAY I ARRIVED IN KANSAS CITY... WHILE I'M HERE, I'M GOING TO TRY TO SEE BELLE"

BELLE?!!
WHO IN THE WORLD IS BELLE?
6-22

"P.S. SAY HELLO TO WOODSTOCK FOR ME"
DO YOU KNOW WHO BELLE IS?
?
SCHULZ

June 25, 1976

PEANUTS
BELLE? BELLE?
HOW AM I EVER GOING TO FIND BELLE?

THE LAST I HEARD SHE HAS A TEEN-AGE SON, AND THAT WORTHLESS HOUND SHE MARRIED RAN OFF!

"I GUESS I FORGOT TO TELL YOU THAT BELLE IS MY SISTER...IF IT TURNS OUT THAT SHE NEEDS HELP, WILL YOU SEND SOME MONEY?"

MONEY? I DON'T HAVE ANY MONEY!
HE'S YOUR DOG, CHARLIE BROWN!

June 28, 1976—First appearance of Belle.

PEANUTS
?
HEY! THIS DOG LOOKS LIKE BELLE!

BELLE? YOU KNOW BELLE?
SEE? HE LOOKS JUST LIKE THAT BEAGLE IN THE NEXT BLOCK...

BEAGLE?

BELLE!!!

June 29, 1976

PEANUTS
ANOTHER LETTER FROM SNOOPY?
"DEAR ROUND-HEADED KID... GUESS WHAT HAPPENED!"

"I FOUND MY SISTER BELLE... AND WHAT A REUNION WE'RE HAVING! BELLE IS JUST AS BEAUTIFUL AS EVER"

"UNFORTUNATELY, I CAN'T SAY MUCH FOR HER TEEN-AGE SON"

July 2, 1976

PEANUTS
"BY THE TIME YOU RECEIVE THIS LETTER, I WILL BE ON A TRAIN HEADING FOR HOME"

"I GUESS I WON'T BE PLAYING AT WIMBLEDON AFTER ALL...I JUST HEARD THAT THEY STARTED WITHOUT ME"

ALL RIGHT FOR YOU GUYS!!

July 4, 1976

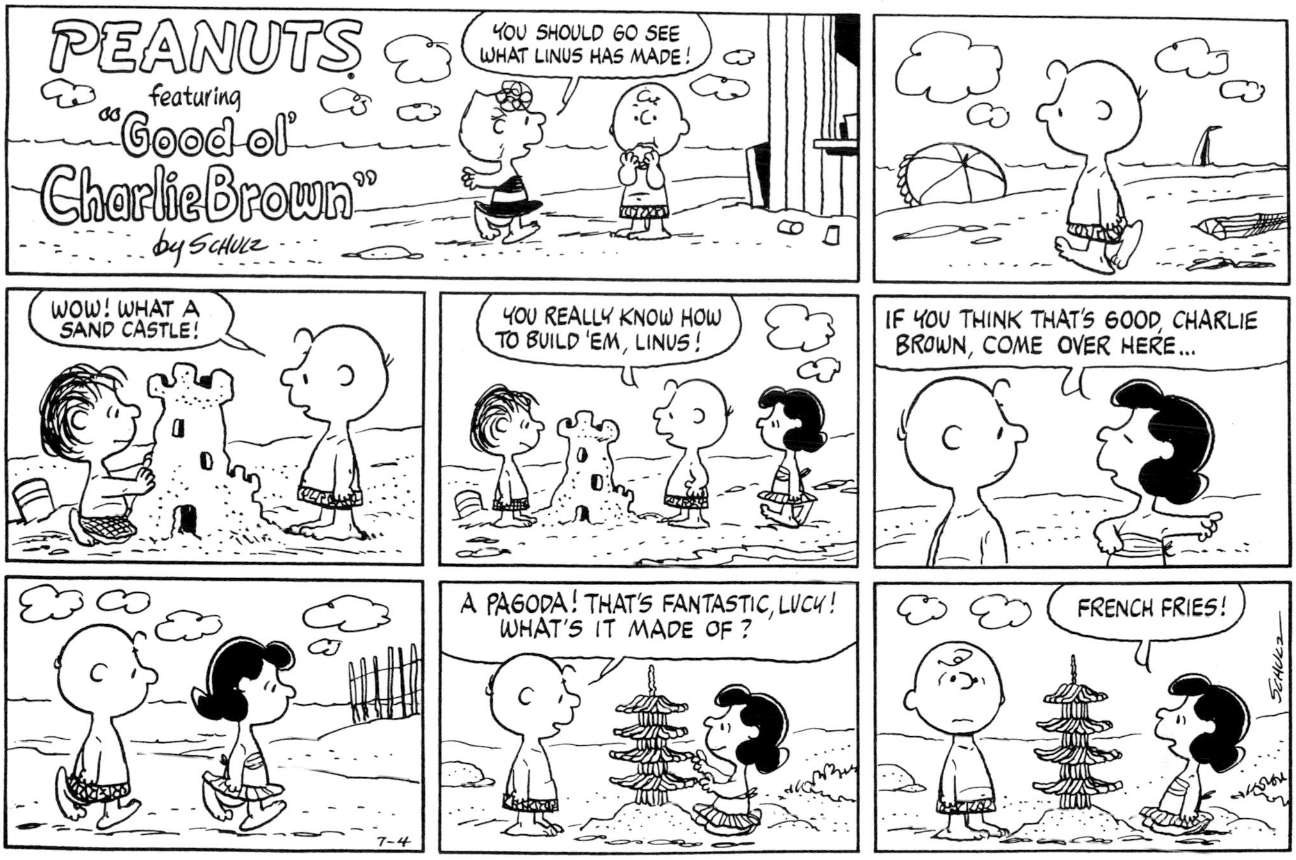

PEANUTS featuring "Good ol' Charlie Brown" by SCHULZ

YOU SHOULD GO SEE WHAT LINUS HAS MADE!

WOW! WHAT A SAND CASTLE!

YOU REALLY KNOW HOW TO BUILD 'EM, LINUS!

IF YOU THINK THAT'S GOOD, CHARLIE BROWN, COME OVER HERE...

7-4

A PAGODA! THAT'S FANTASTIC, LUCY! WHAT'S IT MADE OF?

FRENCH FRIES!

SCHULZ

July 5, 1976

PEANUTS
ARE YOU GOING TO SPEND YOUR WHOLE SUMMER WATCHING TV?
NO, I'VE DECIDED TO GO OVER TO OUR LOCAL LIBRARY, AND SIGN UP FOR A COURSE IN FRENCH LITERATURE!
HAHAHAHA!!
7-5
NOW, MY STOMACH IS GOING TO HURT FOR THE REST OF THE DAY...
SCHULZ

July 9, 1976

PEANUTS
AS LONG AS I'VE LIVED HERE, I'VE NEVER HAD WOODSTOCK OVER FOR TEA AND CAKE...
7-9
I'M NOT SURE IF WOODSTOCK EVEN LIKES TEA AND CAKE...
I REFUSE TO HAVE SOMEONE OVER FOR TEA AND WORMS!
SCHULZ

July 10, 1976

PEANUTS
I SHOULD HAVE WON TODAY...

I GUESS THE TENNIS GODS WERE AGAINST ME

7-10

THAT STUPID WOODSTOCK... HE DOESN'T BELIEVE THERE ARE SUCH THINGS AS TENNIS GODS!
SCHULZ

August 14, 1976

PEANUTS
YOU'LL NEVER BE A GOOD THEOLOGIAN

YOU'RE TOO DOGMATIC!
HAHAHAHA!
8-14

BONK!

I HATE JOKES LIKE THAT!
SCHULZ

September 1, 1976

PEANUTS
WELL, MOUND, THAT'S IT FOR ANOTHER YEAR

I GUESS IT WASN'T MUCH OF A SEASON FOR EITHER OF US...

MAYBE SOMEDAY WE'LL DO BETTER
9-1

MY MOTHER THINKS I'M IN YANKEE STADIUM
SCHULZ

September 20, 1976

PEANUTS
SNOOPY, I HAVE A PROBLEM...

MY DAD IS WILLING TO SEND ME TO A PRIVATE SCHOOL, BUT THEY ALL COST FOUR OR FIVE THOUSAND DOLLARS
9-20

I CAN'T ASK HIM TO SPEND THAT MUCH MONEY ON ME... WHAT SHOULD I DO?

"ACE OBEDIENCE SCHOOL... COMPLETE TRAINING.... TWENTY-FIVE DOLLARS"
SCHULZ

September 23, 1976

PEANUTS
IS THIS THE "ACE OBEDIENCE SCHOOL"?

IT IS? GOOD! I'M HERE TO ENROLL! DOG? NO, MA'AM, I DIDN'T BRING A DOG...

I NOTICE THAT A LOT OF YOUR STUDENTS DO HAVE DOGS, DON'T THEY?

IS THIS ONE OF THOSE PROGRESSIVE SCHOOLS?

September 27, 1976

PEANUTS
HOW WAS YOUR FIRST DAY AT PRIVATE SCHOOL, SIR?

WAS THE "ACE OBEDIENCE SCHOOL" ALL YOU EXPECTED?

MORE, MARCIE, A LOT MORE! THEY REALLY STRESS MANNERS AND SOCIAL GRACES...

WE SPENT THE WHOLE FIRST DAY JUST LEARNING HOW TO SIT!

"Peppermint Patty, the tomboy, is forthright, doggedly loyal, with a devastating singleness of purpose, the part of us that goes through life with blinders on. This can be wonderful at times but also disastrous. Patty was never very smart. Then one day Marcie appeared. Marcie is devoted to her, calls her 'Sir' and doesn't mind following her around, which is deceptive. Marcie is one up on Patty in every way. She sees the truth of things, where it invariably escapes Patty. I like Marcie."

October 1, 1976

PEANUTS
DOING YOUR HOMEWORK, EH, MARCIE?

AT THE "ACE OBEDIENCE SCHOOL" WE DON'T HAVE HOMEWORK...

OF COURSE, WE PRIVATE SCHOOL STUDENTS DESERVE A FEW PRIVILEGES, I GUESS... AFTER ALL, WE DO PAY EXTRA MONEY, AND WE ARE SPECIAL AND WE...

HEEL, SIR!!
WHAT?

October 7, 1976

PEANUTS
OUR TEACHER ASKED ME ABOUT YOU TODAY, SIR...
Tm. Reg. U.S. Pat. Off.—All rights reserved © 1976 by United Feature Syndicate, Inc.

SHE WANTED TO KNOW WHY YOU HAVEN'T BEEN TO SCHOOL... I TOLD HER THAT YOU GRADUATED, BUT I DON'T THINK SHE BELIEVED ME

COULD YOU SHOW HER YOUR DIPLOMA, SIR?
WELL, I SUPPOSE I COULD...

I JUST HATE TO TAKE IT OUT OF THE FRAME

October 11, 1976

PEANUTS
THERE'S SOMETHING I'VE ALWAYS WONDERED ABOUT...

DO YOU ATTORNEYS FIND IT VERY DIFFICULT TO PREPARE FOR A TRIAL?
10-11

THE HARDEST PART IS TRYING TO DECIDE WHAT TO PUT IN YOUR BRIEFCASE...

THE LAST TIME I WAS IN COURT I FORGOT MY HAIR SPRAY!

November 1, 1976

PEANUTS
RIDING TO THE LIBRARY ON THE BACK OF MOM'S BIKE IS SCARY...
11-1

THAT STUPID GERMAN SHEPHERD ALWAYS CHASES US!

GOING HOME ISN'T SO BAD...

"ANNA KARENINA" USUALLY TAKES CARE OF HIM!
BONK!
SCHULZ

November 6, 1976

PEANUTS
I WONDER IF WOODSTOCK PLANS TO FLY SOUTH FOR THE WINTER
11-6

I THINK HE SHOULD....

IF HE COMES BY TODAY, I THINK I'LL JUST TELL HIM THAT HE'S NOT REALLY PREPARED FOR FREEZING WEATHER, AND THAT HE...

SCHULZ

November 22, 1976

PEANUTS
AND ON THANKSGIVING, PEOPLE EAT TURKEYS!
11-22

THEY ALSO EAT CHICKENS, AND DUCKS, AND QUAIL AND PHEASANT!

THANKSGIVING IS A BAD TIME TO BE A BIRD...

WOOF!
SCHULZ

November 30, 1976

PEANUTS
Napoleon was ready to leave for Moscow.

He kissed his wife, and whispered farewell.

As he rode off to battle, she shouted, "Don't get blown apart, Bonapart!"
11-30

WELL, SHE MIGHT HAVE SAID IT!
SCHULZ

December 1, 1976

PEANUTS
WHAT AM I DOING? I'M ADDRESSING CHRISTMAS CARDS!

AREN'T THEY CUTE?

EACH ONE HAS A LITTLE BUNNY ON IT DRESSED UP LIKE A SHEPHERD...

DON'T SAY I'M NOT RELIGIOUS!!
12-1
SCHULZ

December 6, 1976

PEANUTS
HEY, STUPID CAT... PUTTING ON A LITTLE WEIGHT, AREN'T YOU?

YOU SHOULD TAKE UP TENNIS... YOU ALREADY HAVE THE GUT!

SLASH!
12-6

AND A WICKED FOREHAND!
SCHULZ

"The cat is so outrageous that you could not draw him. It's easier to make the reader ask what kind of cat is so ferocious that he could slash a doghouse totally in half. If you were to draw him, he would not come up to this standard."

December 11, 1976

PEANUTS
I ALWAYS ENJOY LOOKING UP AT THE STARS
12-11

I'VE NEVER PAID MUCH ATTENTION TO THEM MYSELF

I MEAN, WHY SHOULD I?

WHAT DID THEY EVER DO FOR ME?
SCHULZ

December 16, 1976

PEANUTS
HAPPY BEETHOVEN'S BIRTHDAY!
12-16

HOW NICE! WHAT IS IT?
IT'S A BEETHOVEN LUNCH BOX!

THE SALESMAN SAID IT'S JUST THE KIND BEETHOVEN USED WHEN HE SAT IN THE PARK, AND WROTE ALL THOSE STRAUSS WALTZES

THAT MUST HAVE BEEN SOME SALESMAN
HE SAID TO WISH YOU A HAPPY BEETHOVEN'S BIRTHDAY...
SCHULZ

December 20, 1976

PEANUTS
GUESS WHAT, CHUCK! DISASTER TIME!

OUR TEACHER WANTS US TO READ A BOOK DURING CHRISTMAS VACATION... GOT ANY SUGGESTIONS?
12-20

ON WHAT BOOK TO READ?

NO, ON HOW TO GET OUT OF IT!
SCHULZ

December 28, 1976

PEANUTS
YOU SHOULDN'T BE OUT HERE SKATING, SIR...

YOU SHOULD BE HOME READING YOUR BOOK
WHAT ARE YOU, MARCIE, MY CONSCIENCE?
12-28

IF I WERE YOUR CONSCIENCE, SIR, I'D WHIP YOU INTO SHAPE!

IF YOU WERE MY CONSCIENCE, MARCIE, I'D HAVE YOU TRANSFERRED!
SCHULZ

December 30, 1976

PEANUTS
ARE YOU READING YOUR BOOK, SIR?
12-30

NO, I'M WATCHING TV, MARCIE...

HOMEWORK IS HOMEWORK, SIR... WE'LL ALWAYS HAVE IT WITH US...

STOP BUGGING ME, MARCIE!
DEATH AND TAXES, SIR!
SCHULZ

January 9, 1977

PEANUTS
featuring
"Good ol' Charlie Brown"
by SCHULZ

THEN SHE HEARD SOMEONE TALKING..

AND WHEN ALICE LOOKED UP, THERE WAS THE CHESHIRE CAT!

YOU'VE NEVER SEEN ME DO MY CHESHIRE BEAGLE TRICK, HAVE YOU?

WATCH THIS...

WELL, I NEVER SAID IT WOULD MAKE A WEEKLY SERIES!

January 21, 1977

PEANUTS
OH, HOW I HATE THESE FIELD TRIPS!

WHEN ARE WE GETTING BACK ON THE BUS?
THAT BARN...

NOW, I REMEMBER!

TRUFFLES!
LINUS!

January 22, 1977

PEANUTS
TRUFFLES!
LINUS! WHAT ARE YOU DOING HERE?

OUR CLASS IS ON A FIELD TRIP... WHAT ARE YOU DOING HERE?

VISITING MY GRAMPA, AS USUAL... I WAS JUST...

WHAT'S GOING ON HERE?!

January 24, 1977

PEANUTS
WHAT'S GOING ON HERE? THE BUS IS LEAVING!! WHO ARE YOU?

WHAT ARE YOU DOING IN THIS BARN WITH MY BOY FRIEND?
THIS IS MY GRANDFATHER'S BARN! I CAN BE HERE IF I WANT TO!
1-24

AND I'M NOT YOUR BOY FRIEND!
YOU ARE, TOO!
HE IS NOT!

LINUS LIKES ME BETTER THAN HE LIKES YOU!
HE DOES NOT!
THIS IS A FIELD TRIP?
SCHULZ

January 26, 1977

PEANUTS
SWEETHEART! WHAT ARE YOU DOING ON THE ROOF OF THE BARN?
1-26

I'M NOT YOUR SWEETHEART! AND I'M NOT COMING DOWN UNTIL YOU GIRLS STOP FIGHTING!

GOOD GRIEF! THE BUS IS LEAVING!
LINUS, THIS IS TRUFFLES! COME DOWN BEFORE YOU FALL!

HEY! HOLD THE BUS! MY SWEETHEART IS ON TOP OF THE ROOF!!
I'M NOT YOUR SWEETHEART!
SCHULZ

January 27, 1977

PEANUTS
BE CAREFUL, LINUS...YOU'RE GOING TO FALL!
1-27

I DON'T THINK I CAN GET DOWN...IT'S TOO SLIPPERY...

I'M LEAVING ON THE SCHOOL BUS, LINUS, BUT DON'T WORRY! I'LL SEND A HELICOPTER FOR YOU! BE BRAVE, MY SWEET BABBOO!

HELICOPTER?
"SWEET BABBOO"?
SCHULZ

January 31, 1977

PEANUTS
ARE YOU THE HELICOPTER PILOT?!

OKAY, THIS IS WHERE YOU GO...HE'S ON A BARN ROOF... YOUR JOB IS TO GET HIM OFF, AND BRING HIM BACK!

$
1-31

I DON'T CARE HOW MUCH IT COSTS! BRING HIM BACK!
$ $ $
SCHULZ

February 1, 1977

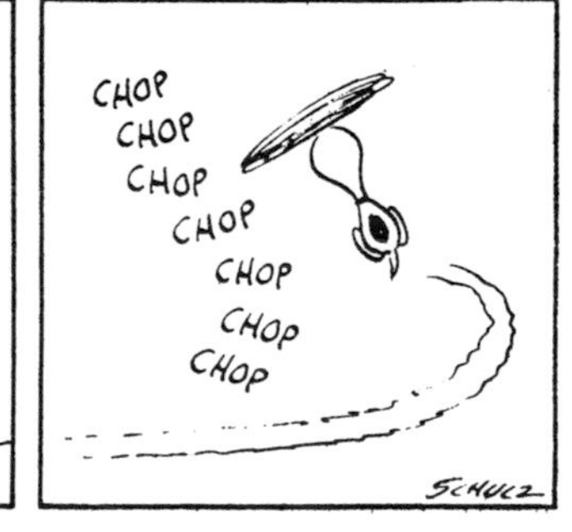

February 3, 1977

February 4, 1977

February 5, 1977

February 20, 1977

PEANUTS
featuring
"Good ol' CharlieBrown"
by SCHULZ
COME, AND SEE!

YOU'RE REALLY GONNA BE IMPRESSED...

WELL, WHAT DO YOU THINK?
WHO IS IT?

WHO IS IT?! IT'S GEORGE WASHINGTON! I MADE IT IN HONOR OF HIS BIRTHDAY! IT'S A MASTERPIECE!
2-20

YOU'RE JUST JEALOUS BECAUSE YOU COULDN'T DO ONE AS GOOD, AND BECAUSE YOU DIDN'T THINK OF IT FIRST!

WELL, ACTUALLY, I DID DO A LITTLE SOMETHING KIND OF SIMILAR...

I COULDN'T TELL A LIE!
SCHULZ

March 15, 1977

WHERE AM I?
RIGHT THERE!

WE WERE PRACTICING, AND YOUR HEAD GOT IN THE WAY OF OUR BALL...

WE'RE LOOKING FOR AN OLDER PERSON TO COACH OUR TEAM...DO YOU KNOW ANYTHING ABOUT BASEBALL?

3-15
SCHULZ

March 18, 1977

CHARLES?

MY NAME IS MILO, AND I NEED SOME HELP WITH MY HITTING
3-18

OKAY, MILO, YOU WANT HELP WITH YOUR STANCE, OR YOUR SWING, OR YOUR GRIP OR WHAT?

JUST HELP ME LIFT THE BAT!
SCHULZ

March 26, 1977

OKAY, AUSTIN... THIS IS THE PITCHER'S MOUND...

THIS IS WHERE YOU'LL STAND WHEN YOU PITCH THE BALL TO THE BATTERS

3-26

HOW DO I GET DOWN?
SCHULZ

April 1, 1977

YOU'RE THE COACH OF THIS STUPID TEAM?!

WE CAN'T PLAY **THEM**!! THEY'RE TOO LITTLE! WE'D **STEP** ON THEM!!

ARE THESE PEOPLE YOUR FRIENDS, CHARLES?
I GUESS SO...
4-1

THEIR RUDENESS MATCHES THEIR SIZE!
WHAT DID HE SAY?
SCHULZ

April 2, 1977

YOU SHOULD COME HOME, CHARLIE BROWN..

THAT KITE-EATING TREE FELL OVER DURING THE STORM..THE ENVIRONMENTAL PROTECTION AGENCY HAS NO EVIDENCE AGAINST YOU
4-2

ARE YOU AN ESCAPED CRIMINAL, CHARLES?
NO, NOT REALLY, MILO...

WHEN I GROW UP, I WANT TO BE LIKE YOU, CHARLES!
DID EVERYONE HEAR THAT?
SCHULZ

April 8, 1977

I WONDER HOW MANY YARDS IT IS TO THE GREEN...

4-8

TWO HUNDRED AND FIFTY-ONE YARDS!
SCHULZ

April 13, 1977

IS READING IMPORTANT? YES!

IF YOU DIDN'T KNOW HOW TO READ, HOW COULD YOU READ "WAR AND PEACE"?

IF YOU DON'T READ "WAR AND PEACE," LEO TOLSTOY WILL HATE YOU!

DO YOU WANT TO BE HATED BY LEO TOLSTOY?

April 26, 1977

"Molly Volley is at once an offshoot of my own recent involvement in tennis and a caricature of human behavior on the court. She is one tough cookie who embodies the widely held American belief that the only thing that matters is winning."

May 9, 1977

HI, I'M MOLLY VOLLEY!

HI, MY NAME IS CHARLIE BROWN

THIS IS SNOOPY...HE'S GOING TO BE YOUR PARTNER IN THE TOURNAMENT

I'VE HEARD OF MIXED DOUBLES, BUT THIS IS RIDICULOUS!

May 13, 1977

MINE!!

WHAP!

GOOD TEAMWORK, PARTNER! WE'RE GONNA **WIN**!

May 16, 1977

HOW'S THE MATCH GOING?

I THINK SNOOPY AND MOLLY VOLLEY JUST WON THAT GAME...

IT WAS OUT! IT WAS OUT BY FORTY FEET! WHAT IS IT WITH YOU? CAN'T Y'SEE?!

AT LEAST THEY'VE WON ALL THE ARGUMENTS...

May 20, 1977

YOU KNOW WHERE CHAMPIONS ARE MADE?

WELL, THEY'RE NOT MADE AT WIMBLEDON OR FOREST HILLS, I'LL TELL YOU THAT!

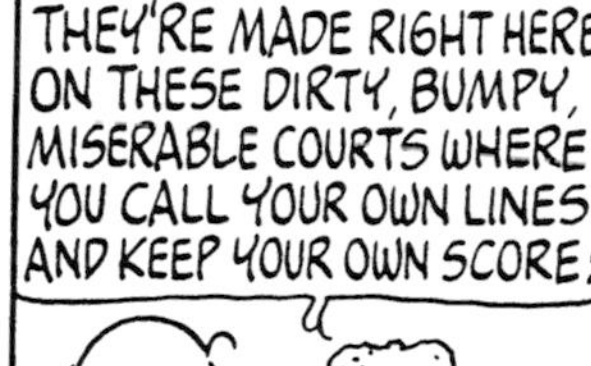
THEY'RE MADE RIGHT HERE ON THESE DIRTY, BUMPY, MISERABLE COURTS WHERE YOU CALL YOUR OWN LINES AND KEEP YOUR OWN SCORE!

YOU GET WHAT YOU GO FOR, KID!
I'D LIKE TO GO HOME, BUT I THINK SHE'D KILL ME!

May 26, 1977

YOU CALL IT, PARTNER!
WAS IT IN OR OUT? DO WE WIN OR LOSE?

IN!

SORRY, PARTNER!
SMAK!

AAUGH!!

June 3, 1977

Z

MA'AM?

OH, I'M SORRY, MA'AM.. I DIDN'T KNOW YOU WERE STILL TALKING..

I THOUGHT YOU HAD CUT AWAY FOR A STATION BREAK!

June 7, 1977

SECOND BOOK OF KINGS... CHAPTER NINE..

JEZEBEL IS SITTING THERE LOOKING OUT OF THE WINDOW, SEE...
6-7

BEFORE SHE CAN DO ANYTHING, THREE MEN PICK HER UP AND THROW HER OUT THE WINDOW!

SOUNDS LIKE A GREAT TV SERIES
SCHULZ

July 10, 1977

PEANUTS featuring "Good ol' CharlieBrown" by SCHULZ

RATS! MY TOMATO PLANTS AREN'T DOING A THING!

I KNEW YOU WERE HAVING TROUBLE SO I CALLED IN THE CROP DUSTER

CROP DUSTER?!

7-10

WHAT CROP DUSTER?

CHOP CHOP CHOP CHOP

WHOOSH!!

CHOP CHOP CHOP

CHOP CHOP

OH.....THAT CROP DUSTER...

SCHULZ

July 8, 1977

War and Punishment
7-8

Crime and Peace
SCHULZ

July 15, 1977

SIGH

WHAT'S THE MATTER? STILL HAVING TROUBLE WITH YOUR GARDEN?

MY STRING BEANS LOOK VERY UNHEALTHY
7-15

MAYBE THEY DON'T GET ENOUGH EXERCISE...
SCHULZ

July 31, 1977

PEANUTS featuring "Good ol' Charlie Brown" by SCHULZ

!

KLUNK!

7-31

SCHULZ

August 9, 1977

WEDDING INVITATIONS?
8-9

I'M GETTING MARRIED! I'VE MET THE MOST WONDERFUL GIRL IN THE WORLD!

ALL MY LIFE I'VE FELT UNSETTLED... SORT OF UP IN THE AIR...NOT ANYMORE..

SCHULZ

THE BEAGLE HAS LANDED!

August 17, 1977

HOW DO YOU INTEND TO SUPPORT A WIFE?

NOT WITH YOUR WRITING, I'M SURE
8-17

YOU COULDN'T SELL A STORY ABOUT JONAH TO A WHALING MAGAZINE!

LET ME WRITE THAT DOWN... THAT SOUNDS LIKE A GOOD IDEA...
SCHULZ

August 23, 1977

SPIKE, I'M SO GLAD YOU'RE HERE!

IT'S GOING TO BE A GREAT WEDDING, AND YOU'RE GOING TO LOVE MY BRIDE-TO-BE!
8-23

AND YOU'RE GOING TO BE MY BEST-MAN... ISN'T THIS SOMETHING?

NOW, ABOUT THAT HAT...
SCHULZ

August 25, 1977

ALL RIGHT, HERE'S THE GROOM! WHERE'S THE BRIDE AND THE BEST-MAN?

I'VE GOT SOME GOOD NEWS FOR YOU AND SOME BAD NEWS...

THE GOOD NEWS IS THAT THE BRIDE AND THE BEST-MAN ARE HERE

THE BAD NEWS IS THEY JUST RAN OFF TOGETHER!
8-25
KLUNK!
SCHULZ

August 29, 1977

HERE, YOU GOT A LETTER FROM SPIKE..

"DEAR BROTHER, WHAT CAN I SAY? I RAN OFF WITH YOUR BRIDE, AND BROKE YOUR HEART"

"BUT YOU KNOW WHAT HAPPENED? THE DAY WE GOT HERE TO NEEDLES SHE LEFT ME, AND RAN OFF WITH A COYOTE!"
8-29

"HAVE YOU SEEN ANY GOOD MOVIES LATELY? YOUR BROTHER, SPIKE"
SCHULZ

September 2, 1977

SCHOOL STARTS NEXT WEEK

I'M NOT READY TO GO BACK...
9-2

WHAT WILL IT TAKE TO GET YOU READY TO GO BACK?

BRIBERY!
SCHULZ

September 12, 1977

WATCH SNOOPY... I THINK HE'S GOING TO PULL THE OLD STATUE OF LIBERTY PLAY...

HOW DO YOU KNOW?
9-12

SOMEHOW I JUST SENSE IT...

SCHULZ

October 10, 1977

FOR MY FUTURE CAREER I HAVE DECIDED TO BE A HAIRDRESSER
10-10

MY DAD IS A BARBER, YOU SEE, AND IF I SORT OF FOLLOW IN HIS FOOTSTEPS, THAT WOULD BE SHEAR DELIGHT!

HA HA HA HA HA
© 1977 United Feature Syndicate, Inc.

JUST A LITTLE HUMOR THERE, MA'AM, BEFORE WE BREAK FOR LUNCH
SCHULZ

October 24, 1977

HEY, STUPID CAT! YOU MISSED MY BIRTHDAY AGAIN!

I KNOW HOW MUCH YOU LIKE ME..I THOUGHT MAYBE YOU'D GIVE ME A CAKE WITH SOME CANDLES ON IT...
10-24

SLASH

HOW NICE!
SCHULZ

January 4, 1978

HOW MANY SKATING TESTS ARE THERE, SIR?

EIGHT, MARCIE, AND THEY GET HARDER AND HARDER

SOMETIMES I THINK THE ONLY THING THAT KEEPS ME GOING IS THE ENCOURAGING WORDS OF MY COACH...

GROWL, SNARL, SNAP, GROWF, BARK, WOOF!

January 6, 1978

LISTEN, BEAUTIFUL, GET YOUR STUPID FIGURE SKATES OFF THE ICE! WE WANNA PLAY HOCKEY, SEE?

WE HAVE TEN HOCKEY STICKS HERE TELLING YOU TO "GET OFF THE ICE!"

OH, YEAH? COME ON AND TRY SOMETHING! ME AND MY COACH'LL TAKE YOU ALL ON!!

I THINK I'LL GO HOME.. I HAVE SOME CHAIN LETTERS TO WRITE...

January 7, 1978

THOSE HOCKEY PLAYERS ARE TRYING TO CHASE PEPPERMINT PATTY OFF THE SKATING RINK!

DON'T LET 'EM GET AWAY WITH IT, SIR!

I'LL HELP YOU

AAUGH!!

January 9, 1978

WHAT HAPPENED?
YOU FELL ON THE ICE, MARCIE...

MY HEAD HURTS..WHERE ARE MY GLASSES?

THEY FLEW OFF WHEN YOU HIT THE ICE... I DON'T KNOW WHERE THEY LANDED...

I CAN'T SEE A THING!

January 11, 1978

I DON'T EVEN REMEMBER WHAT HAPPENED, SIR...

WELL, THOSE HOCKEY PLAYERS WERE ABOUT TO GIVE ME A ROUGH TIME, AND YOU CAME RUNNING OUT TO HELP ME, MARCIE
1-11

BUT I SLIPPED AND FELL ON THE ICE, HUH?
I'LL SAY YOU DID!

LET'S GO BACK AND SHORTEN A FEW LIFE SPANS, SIR!
LATER, MARCIE, LATER
SCHULZ

January 22, 1978

PEANUTS
featuring
"Good ol' Charlie Brown"
by SCHULZ

YAWN

Z

WELL, I SUPPOSE THE FIRST THING WE SHOULD DO IS HAVE A LOOK AT YOUR HOME OWNER'S POLICY...

1-22

SCHULZ

February 6, 1978

HERE'S THE WORLD FAMOUS BEAGLE SCOUT LEADING HIS TROOP ON A HIKE

OUT TO THE WILD COUNTRY WHERE MAN HAS NEVER TROD!

BEYOND CIVILIZATION!

2-6
SCHULZ

February 7, 1978

ALL RIGHT, TROOPS... HERE'S WHERE WE CAMP FOR THE NIGHT

EACH SCOUT PITCHES HIS OWN TENT... AND THEN WE ALL GO TO SLEEP RIGHT AWAY...
2-7

JUST FOLLOW MY EXAMPLE

SCHULZ

February 10, 1978

THE WILDERNESS IS INHABITED BY MANY CREATURES

SOME ARE FRIENDLY... SOME ARE DANGEROUS...
2-10

WHAT IS THE BEST WAY TO PROTECT OURSELVES FROM SNAKES?

SCHULZ

March 12, 1978

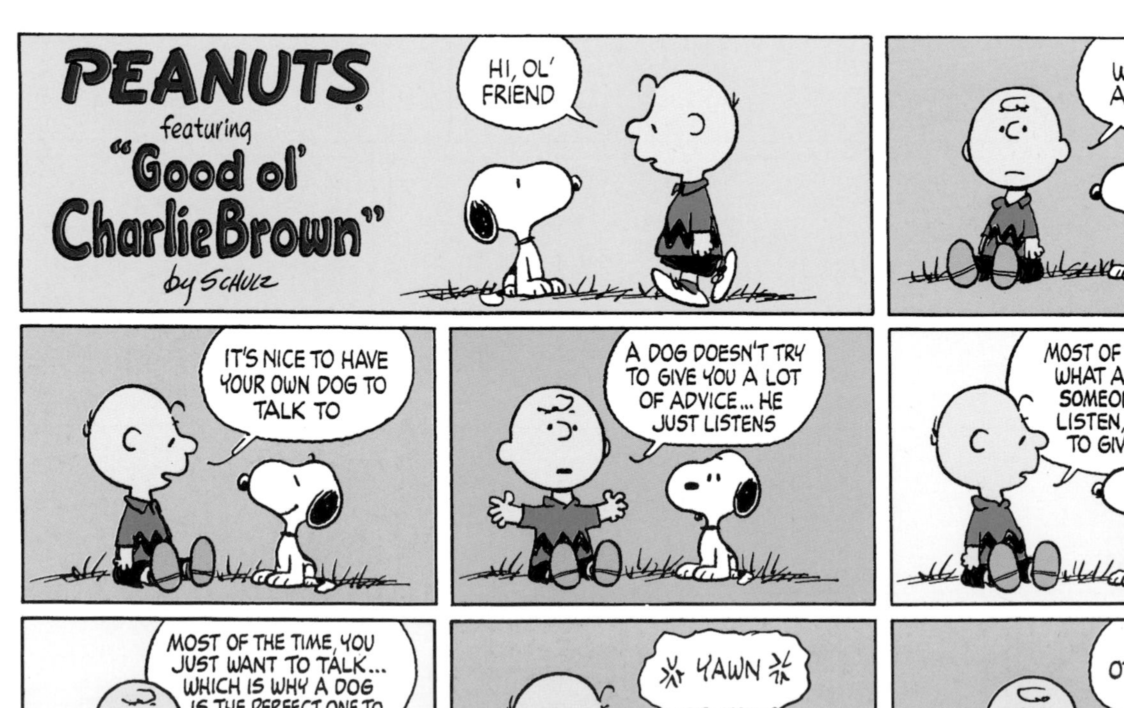
PEANUTS
featuring
"Good ol' CharlieBrown"
by SCHULZ
HI, OL' FRIEND
WHAT A DAY!
IT'S NICE TO HAVE YOUR OWN DOG TO TALK TO
A DOG DOESN'T TRY TO GIVE YOU A LOT OF ADVICE... HE JUST LISTENS
MOST OF THE TIME, THAT'S WHAT A PERSON WANTS... SOMEONE WHO WILL LISTEN, AND NOT TRY TO GIVE YOU ADVICE
MOST OF THE TIME, YOU JUST WANT TO TALK... WHICH IS WHY A DOG IS THE PERFECT ONE TO..
3-12

YAWN
ON THE OTHER HAND... SIGH
SCHULZ

February 23, 1978

2-23

WOODSTOCK ISN'T MUCH FOR DOING ANYTHING RIGHT
SCHULZ

March 4, 1978

A MOVIE, MA'AM?

THAT'S GREAT! I ALWAYS LIKE MOVIES
3-4

MOVIES IN THE CLASSROOM CAN BE ONE OF OUR BEST LEARNING TOOLS
SCHULZ

Z

March 19, 1978

PEANUTS
featuring
"Good ol' CharlieBrown"
by SCHULZ
DEUCE?! WHAT DO YOU MEAN, DEUCE?
MOLLY VOLLEY
YOU'RE SERVING TO ME!
YOU'RE WRONG! THE SCORE IS THIRTY-FORTY! IT WAS LOVE-FIFTEEN AFTER I HIT THAT BEAUTIFUL CROSSCOURT VOLLEY...
3-19
THEN, WHEN MY PARTNER HIT THAT MISERABLE BACKHAND INTO THE NET, IT WAS FIFTEEN-ALL!
© 1978 United Feature Syndicate, Inc.
THEN I HIT THAT PERFECT LOB RIGHT ON THE BASELINE TO MAKE IT FIFTEEN-THIRTY...
THEN MY PARTNER MISSED THAT COLD PUT-AWAY AT THE NET WHICH MADE IT THIRTY-ALL!
THEN I HIT A TOPSPIN BACKHAND JUST LIKE A BULLET RIGHT DOWN THE LINE! THE SCORE IS THIRTY-FORTY!
WE KNOW THE SCORE, DON'T WE PARTNER?
SIGH
SCHULZ

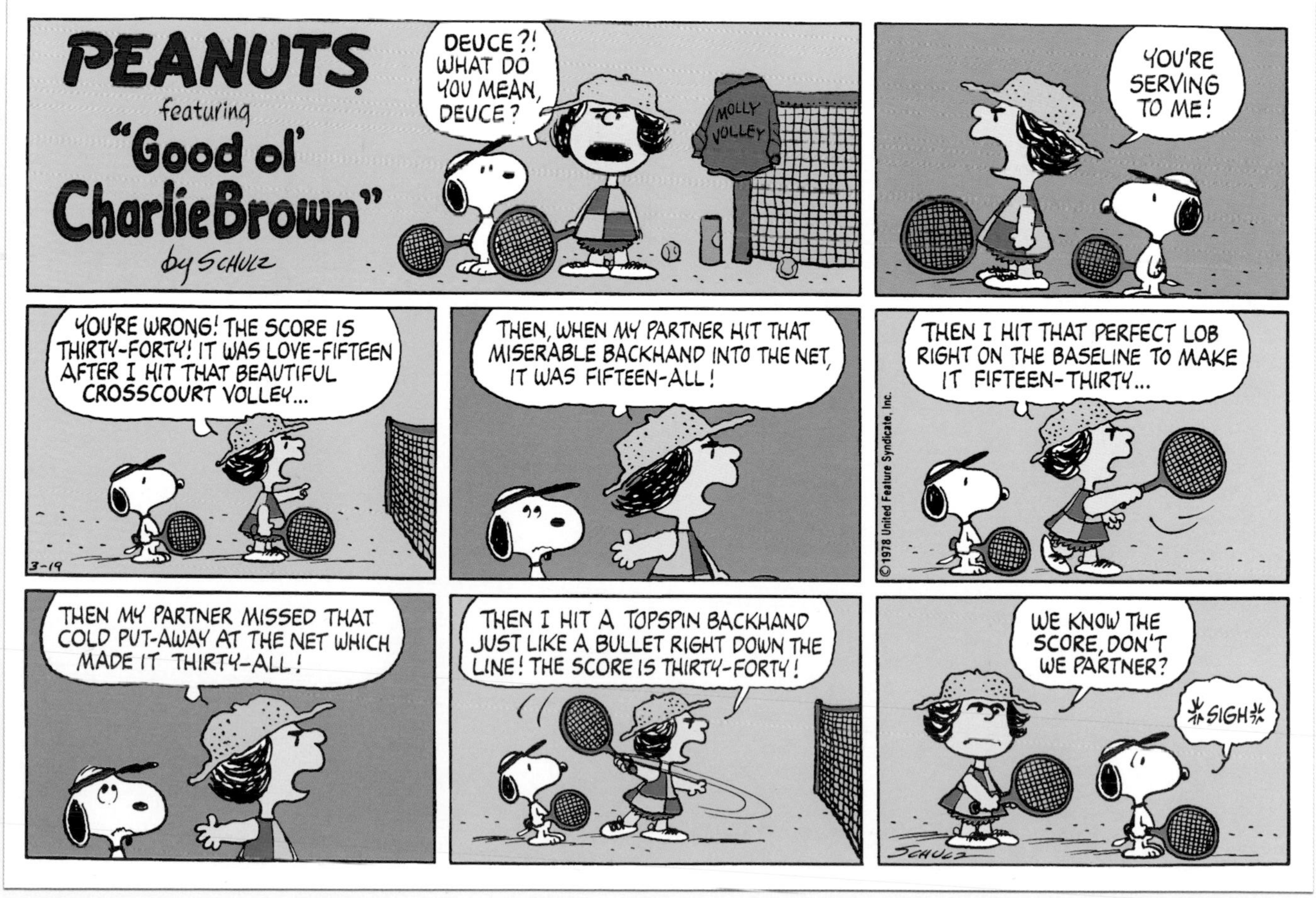

March 24, 1978

!

I ATE THE LAST PIECE OF CHEESECAKE!

April 6, 1978

Literature Quiz

When did Mark Twain write *Tom Sawyer*?

If I know him, probably in the evenings.

April 17, 1978

May 10, 1978

LUCY! WAKE UP!
Z

HOW CAN YOU FALL ASLEEP IN THE MIDDLE OF A BALL GAME?

SORRY, MANAGER... WATCHING YOUR GRACEFUL MOVES ON THE PITCHER'S MOUND LULLED ME TO SLEEP!

YES, I CAN SEE HOW THAT MIGHT HAPPEN...

May 18, 1978

HOW ABOUT THAT? I WALKED ALL THE WAY OUT HERE WITH YOUR SUPPER DISH BALANCED ON MY HEAD!
5-18

THIS IS WHAT HAPPENS WHEN YOU EAT IN THE SAME PLACE EVERY NIGHT!
SCHULZ

May 27, 1978

HOW DID I EVER END UP AS A PITCHER'S MOUND FOR A STUPID KIDS' TEAM?

"GO INTO SPORTS," MY FATHER SAID.."THAT'S WHERE THE MONEY IS!"

WHY COULDN'T I HAVE BEEN A GOLF GREEN AT PEBBLE BEACH OR A GRASS COURT AT WIMBLEDON? STILL, I GUESS IT COULD HAVE BEEN WORSE...

I COULD HAVE BEEN THE PLEXIGLASS BEHIND A HOCKEY NET!
5-27
SCHULZ

May 31, 1978

YOU FOUND IT!

HOW ABOUT THAT? YOU'RE SURE THIS IS IT, HUH?
5-31

JUST THINK...AFTER ALL THESE YEARS... YOU WERE THE ONE WHO FOUND IT...

THE LAST STRAW!
SCHULZ

June 2, 1978

YOU REALLY LIKED THAT LITTLE RED-HAIRED GIRL, DIDN'T YOU, CHUCK?
6-2

WHICH WOULD YOU RATHER DO, HIT A HOME RUN WITH THE BASES LOADED OR MARRY THE LITTLE RED-HAIRED GIRL?

WHY COULDN'T I DO BOTH?

WE LIVE IN A REAL WORLD, CHUCK!
SCHULZ

June 5, 1978

6-5

WHAT'S SO GREAT ABOUT LIFTING TWO ANGEL FOOD CAKES?
SCHULZ

June 11, 1978

PEANUTS
featuring "Good ol' Charlie Brown"
by SCHULZ
Deer
6-11
THAT SHOULD BE "DEAR"
IN THE SALUTATION OF A LETTER, THE PROPER WORD AND SPELLING OF THAT WORD IS "DEAR"
Deer are beautiful animals found in most parts of the world.

I'M SORRY... I DIDN'T REALIZE YOU WERE WRITING ABOUT DEER... I APOLOGIZE...

WELL, I SHOULD HOPE SO! IT SEEMS TO ME THAT A LOT OF THE PROBLEMS IN THIS WORLD ARE CAUSED BY PEOPLE WHO CRITICIZE OTHER PEOPLE BEFORE THEY KNOW WHAT THEY'RE TALKING ABOUT!

Dear Grandma,
SCHULZ

June 13, 1978

I HOPE I'M ON THE RIGHT BUS
© 1978 United Feature Syndicate, Inc.

I'VE NEVER BEEN TO CAMP BEFORE
6-13

YOU'LL HAVE A GREAT TIME

YOU'RE LYING, AREN'T YOU?
SCHULZ

June 15, 1978

HEY, EUDORA, WE HAVE TO GO TO THE MAIN HALL FOR ORIENTATION!

IF THEY TRY TO SHIP US TO THE ORIENT, FORGET IT!

HOW DO YOU FEEL ABOUT WASHING DISHES AND SETTING TABLES?
6-15

I'D RATHER GO TO THE ORIENT!
SCHULZ

June 20, 1978

IF WE BECAME LOST IN THE WOODS, HOW LONG COULD WE GO WITHOUT REAL FOOD?

I'LL BET WE COULD GO FOR A MONTH WITHOUT REAL FOOD

HOW ABOUT JUNK FOOD?
6-20

ELEVEN MINUTES!
SCHULZ

June 23, 1978

OKAY, EUDORA, YOU FISH IN THIS PART OF THE STREAM, AND I'LL FISH DOWN THERE IN THAT PART...

I DON'T THINK THIS IS GOING TO WORK
6-23

WHAT'S THE TROUBLE?

EITHER THE STREAM IS TOO NARROW, OR MY LINE IS TOO LONG...
SCHULZ

June 26, 1978

I CAN'T BELIEVE THAT I WAS AWAY FROM HOME FOR TWO WEEKS

I NEVER THOUGHT I'D MAKE IT... I THOUGHT I'D CRACK UP... INSTEAD, I FEEL AS THOUGH I'VE MATURED...
6-26

THERE'S YOUR MOTHER WAITING FOR YOU AT THE BUS STOP...
© 1978 United Feature Syndicate, Inc.

SO MUCH FOR MATURITY!
SCHULZ

August 2, 1978

IT'S TOO HOT TO PLAY BALL TODAY!

THE TEMPERATURE MUST BE A HUNDRED!

ABOUT THE SAME AS YOUR BATTING AVERAGE
8-2

YOU DIDN'T HAVE TO SAY THAT!
SCHULZ

August 7, 1978

STILL HITTING BALLS WITH THE GARAGE, I SEE...

IT'S GOOD PRACTICE..HE GETS EVERYTHING BACK
8-7

I WAS SURPRISED YOU DIDN'T PLAY DOUBLES AT WIMBLEDON THIS YEAR..

THE GARAGE HATES TO FLY
SCHULZ

August 13, 1978

PEANUTS
featuring
"Good ol' CharlieBrown"
by SCHULZ

SNOOPY?

I'VE DECIDED THAT YOU SHOULD DO SOMETHING TO EARN YOUR KEEP...
8-13

IT'S SORT OF TRADITIONAL FOR A DOG TO BRING IN THE NEWSPAPER SO THAT'S WHAT I WANT YOU TO DO...

THIS WILL BE YOUR JOB..YOU WAIT HERE FOR THE PAPERBOY TO COME BY, AND THEN YOU BRING IN THE PAPER...

!

I KNOW ONE THING...I'LL NEVER TRAIN HIM TO BRING IN THE GROCERIES!
SCHULZ

August 26, 1978

8-26
CLOMP!

WHY HE NEEDS AN AUTOMATIC DOOR-OPENER IS BEYOND ME
SCHULZ

"Anyone who creates a comic strip and is involved in doing it day after day works in the same manner as a novelist does. I've been doing this now for twenty-one years and if you're going to survive on a daily schedule you survive only by being able to draw on every experience and thought that you've ever had. That is, if you are going to do anything with any meaning. Of course, you can grind out daily gags but I'm not interested in simply doing gags. I'm interested in doing a strip that says something and makes some comment on the important things of life. I'm probably a little bit of Charlie Brown and a little of Lucy and Linus and all the characters. It would be impossible in this kind of strip to create any character and not be part of it yourself."

September 5, 1978

DO YOU THINK YOU HAVE A LUCKY STAR, CHARLIE BROWN?
9-5

I DON'T KNOW

I THINK YOU DO, CHARLIE BROWN...

AND THERE IT WENT!
SCHULZ

September 28, 1978

"Jogging For Everyone"
9-28

A Detailed Guide to Running

Chapter One

The Left Foot
SCHULZ

October 9, 1978

WHO'S THE KID WITH THE BLANKET?

THAT'S LINUS...HE'S MY SWEET BABBOO...
10-9

I'M NOT YOUR SWEET BABBOO!!

HE IS, BUT HE ISN'T, BUT HE IS!
SCHULZ

October 10, 1978

WHY DO YOU CARRY THAT BLANKET AROUND?
IT'S HARD TO EXPLAIN

MAY I TRY IT?
I GUESS SO
10-10

IT FEELS NICE

HOW DO I LOOK?
SCHULZ

October 11, 1978

YOU DID WHAT?
I GAVE MY BLANKET TO EUDORA!

WHAT COULD I DO? SHE SMILED AT ME!

I'M SURPRISED AT YOU! YOU USUALLY DON'T DO DUMB THINGS LIKE THAT..
10-11

IT WAS A CUTE SMILE
SCHULZ

October 14, 1978

STILL HAVE MY BLANKET, I SEE...

OH, YES...I FIND IT A GREAT SOURCE OF COMFORT AND SECURITY
10-14

THANK YOU FOR GIVING IT TO ME, SWEET BABBOO...

HE'S NOT YOUR SWEET BABBOO!!
SCHULZ

November 4, 1978

LEARN FROM YESTERDAY
11-4

LIVE FOR TODAY

LOOK TO TOMORROW

REST THIS AFTERNOON
SCHULZ

November 13, 1978

SUBTRACTION?

OH, YES, MA'AM
11-13

I CAN EXPLAIN IT

SUBTRACTION IS THE AWFUL FEELING THAT YOU KNOW LESS TODAY THAN YOU DID YESTERDAY
SCHULZ

November 20, 1978

I REMEMBER WHEN CHRISTO HUNG THE VALLEY CURTAIN IN COLORADO
11-20

I LOVED THE RUNNING FENCE IN CALIFORNIA AND THE WRAPPED WALKWAYS IN KANSAS CITY...

I WONDER WHAT HE'LL DO NEXT...

SCHULZ

November 22, 1978

11-22

NO, YOU'RE TOO SMALL TO SWING IN AN OLD TIRE LIKE THAT

YOU NEED SOMETHING MORE YOUR SIZE...

LIKE A GLAZED DOUGHNUT!
SCHULZ

November 26, 1978

PEANUTS
featuring
"Good ol' Charlie Brown"
by SCHULZ

THE WEATHER MAY GET WORSE, MEN

IS ANYONE WORRIED? DO YOU ALL KNOW HOW TO ACT IN A BLIZZARD? DOES ANYONE HAVE A QUESTION ABOUT ANYTHING?

NO, OLIVIER, I DON'T THINK THERE'S A PLACE AROUND HERE WHERE YOU CAN MAIL YOUR POST CARDS

YES, BILL, I'VE MET CHERYL TIEGS...YES, SHE'S VERY NICE..

SHOPPING DAYS? WELL, CONRAD, I'D GUESS THERE ARE ABOUT TWENTY-FOUR MORE SHOPPING DAYS UNTIL CHRISTMAS

ANY MORE QUESTIONS?

NO, WOODSTOCK, I DON'T KNOW WHY YOU'RE STANDING HERE IN A BLIZZARD WITH THESE THREE IDIOTS...

I DIDN'T THINK I WAS EVER GOING TO GET A SENSIBLE QUESTION

January 4, 1979

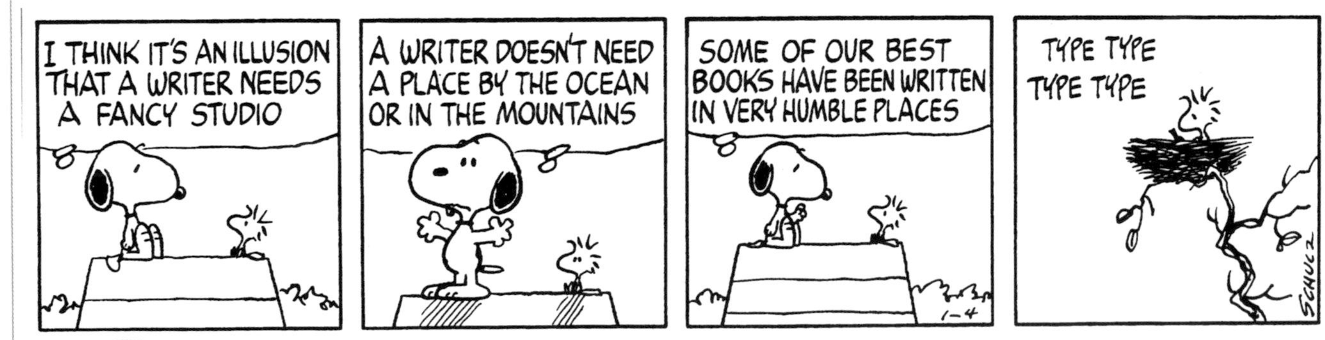

I THINK IT'S AN ILLUSION THAT A WRITER NEEDS A FANCY STUDIO
A WRITER DOESN'T NEED A PLACE BY THE OCEAN OR IN THE MOUNTAINS
SOME OF OUR BEST BOOKS HAVE BEEN WRITTEN IN VERY HUMBLE PLACES
TYPE TYPE
TYPE TYPE

January 29, 1979

HERE'S THE WORLD WAR I FLYING ACE SITTING IN A SMALL CAFE IN FRANCE

HE IS LONELY... HE IS DEPRESSED

HE REALIZES THAT HIS GIRL BACK HOME DOESN'T LOVE HIM ANY MORE..EVEN THOUGH SHE JUST SENT HIM A BOX OF COOKIES...

THEY'RE ALL FILLED WITH COCONUT!
BLEAH!
AAK!

February 1, 1979

HERE'S THE WORLD WAR I FLYING ACE WALKING ALONG A COUNTRY ROAD IN FRANCE...

HE NOTICES A BEAUTIFUL YOUNG GIRL APPROACHING FROM THE OPPOSITE DIRECTION...HE SPEAKS..
2-1

BONJOUR, SWEETIE!

SHE IS NOT IMPRESSED BY HIS FLUENT FRENCH
SCHULZ

February 5, 1979

HERE'S THE WORLD WAR I FLYING ACE BEING CHASED BY THE RED BARON...
2-5

HE HATES ME!

EVERYONE ASKS HOW I KNOW HE HATES ME...

I CAN TELL!
© 1979 United Feature Syndicate, Inc.
SCHULZ

February 9, 1979

"GOOD EVENING, MISS... BONSOIR, MADEMOISELLE"
2-9

"MAY I INVITE YOU TO DANCE? PUIS-JE VOUS INVITER À DANSER? YOU DANCE VERY WELL.. VOUS DANSEZ TRÈS BIEN"

BONSOIR, MONSIEUR

RATS! I SWALLOWED MY PHRASE BOOK!
SCHULZ

February 10, 1979

HERE'S THE WORLD WAR I FLYING ACE SITTING IN A LITTLE CAFE...ONCE AGAIN HE IS DEPRESSED...

HIS LEAVE IS OVER, AND HE HAS FAILED TO MEET THE CHARMING FRENCH LASS...

HE DECIDES TO FORGET HER BY DRINKING ROOT BEER...GARÇON! ANOTHER ROUND, S'IL VOUS PLAÎT!

UNFORTUNATELY, IT'S VERY HARD TO FORGET ANYONE BY DRINKING ROOT BEER!
SCHULZ
© 1979 United Feature Syndicate, Inc.
2-10

February 14, 1979

ANY VALENTINES IN THERE?
2-14

ANY VALENTINES IN THERE?

NOTHING ECHOES LIKE AN EMPTY MAILBOX
SCHULZ

February 18, 1979

PEANUTS featuring "Good ol' CharlieBrown" by SCHULZ

Z

2-18

SCHULZ

March 19, 1979

LET ME SEE THAT BOOK! WHAT IS IT?

PHOOEY! I WOULDN'T READ THIS FOR ANYTHING!
3-19

NOT IN A MILLION YEARS! FORGET IT! NO WAY!!

LUCY HAS NO TROUBLE JUDGING A BOOK BY ITS COVER!
SCHULZ

April 4, 1979

THAT WAS SOME LINE DRIVE, CHARLIE BROWN... IT KNOCKED YOUR SHOESIES AND YOUR SOCKIES RIGHT OFF!

MAYBE WE SHOULD COUNT TO SEE IF YOU STILL HAVE ALL YOUR TOESIES...

GET OUT OF HERE!

JUST FOR THAT, HE CAN COUNT HIS OWN TOESIES!
4-4
SCHULZ

April 25, 1979

I WANT YOU TO LEARN THE NAMES OF EVERY TREE AND PLANT THAT WE SEE...

I ALSO WANT YOU TO LEARN THEIR LATIN NAMES...GOT IT?

4-25

STOP SAYING, "HAIL, CAESAR!"
SCHULZ

May 5, 1979

DID YOU ENJOY YOUR MEAL, SIR?

NOW, DO YOU WISH TO PAY CASH OR DO YOU HAVE A CREDIT CARD?

MAY I SEE SOME KIND OF IDENTIFICATION?

5-5
SCHULZ

May 8, 1979

CHURP!
HMM..

TRY IT WITH AN UMLAUT
5-8

CHÜRP

FORGET THE UMLAUT!
SCHULZ

May 11, 1979

MAYBE YOU'RE NOT A SONGBIRD... MAYBE YOU'RE A CROW... TRY SOME "CAWS"
5-11

CAW CAW CAW CAW
NO, NO, NO! THOSE WILL NEVER DO!

THOSE ARE HOPELESS CAWSES! HEE HEE HEE!
!

I CAN'T HELP IT... I ALWAYS LAUGH!
SCHULZ

May 15, 1979

WHEN WE GET TO HIGH SCHOOL, I'M HOPING THAT WE'LL HAVE LOCKERS NEXT TO EACH OTHER
5-15

THAT WOULD BE AN ODD COMBINATION! HAHAHAHAHA!!

GET IT? LOCKERS HAVE COMBINATION LOCKS! AN ODD COMBINATION! GET IT?

MUSICIANS SHOULD NEVER TRY TO BE FUNNY
SCHULZ

May 17, 1979

THIS IS MY REPORT... I SAT UP ALL NIGHT WORKING ON IT

WELL, ACTUALLY, I DIDN'T SIT UP ALL NIGHT WORKING ON IT...
5-17

WHAT I DID WAS, I SAT UP ALL NIGHT WORRYING ABOUT IT

THERE'S A BIG DIFFERENCE!
SCHULZ

May 23, 1979

SOMEBODY GET IT! SOMEBODY GET IT!

I GOT IT! I GOT IT!

DON'T SAY YOU'VE GOT IT UNLESS YOU'RE SURE YOU'VE GOT IT!
5-23

IN MY HUMBLE OPINION, I THINK I'VE GOT IT...
SCHULZ

June 2, 1979

YOU BOUGHT A FARM? THAT'S GREAT! I'M PROUD OF YOU

AND YOU BOUGHT A TRACTOR? AND A WHEELBARROW? AND A BIG STICK?

WHAT'S THE BIG STICK FOR?
6-2

RUSTLERS
SCHULZ

June 3, 1979

PEANUTS
featuring
"Good ol' CharlieBrown"
by SCHULZ
W
N
E

YOU LOOK EXHAUSTED! RUNNING A FARM IS HARD WORK
6-3

WELL, OKAY...

I DON'T MIND HELPING OUT ON A FRIEND'S FARM ONCE IN A WHILE...

BUT I HATE BEING THE SCARECROW!
SCHULZ

June 5, 1979

YOUR TRACTOR BROKE?
!

HOW ARE YOU GOING TO FINISH YOUR PLOWING?

YOU DON'T HAVE A HORSE OR A MULE... WHAT ARE YOU GOING TO DO?
6-5

TALK ABOUT A DUMB QUESTION...

June 11, 1979

I DON'T GO INTO THAT STORE ANY MORE

I USED TO BUY ALL MY COMIC BOOKS THERE

EVERY TIME I'D BUY A COMIC BOOK, THE MAN WOULD SAY, "GOING TO DO SOME HEAVY READING TONIGHT, EH?"
6-11

I DON'T GO INTO THAT STORE ANY MORE
SCHULZ

June 14, 1979

OFF TO MARKET?

WOW! THAT MUST BE EXCITING FOR A NEW FARMER LIKE YOURSELF
6-14

GOOD LUCK!

ACTUALLY, HE SHOULDN'T HAVE ANY TROUBLE SELLING ONE RADISH...
SCHULZ

June 17, 1979

PEANUTS
featuring
"Good ol' Charlie Brown"
by SCHULZ
THAT WASN'T A BAD BREAKFAST
ANY BREAKFAST IS GOOD WHEN YOU'RE STARVING TO DEATH
DO YOU ALWAYS BRING YOUR BROTHER'S DOG TO CAMP?

NO, BUT I THOUGHT HE MIGHT ENJOY IT...
IF I THROW THIS STICK INTO THE WATER, WILL HE SWIM OUT AND BRING IT BACK?
6-17
HERE, DOGGIE.. SEE THE NICE STICK?
"DOGGIE"?

GO GET IT!

WHERE'D HE GO?
HE'S COMING..

SCHULZ

September 5, 1979

LUDWIG VAN BEAGLE!

September 7, 1979

A BEAN BAG IS A PERFECT PLACE TO SULK

YOU CAN SINK WAY DOWN DEEP, AND SULK FOR HOURS...

YOU ONLY HAVE TO STICK YOUR HEAD UP ONCE IN A WHILE...

...TO SEE IF ANYBODY CARES

September 11, 1979

SHOES? WHAT DO YOU NEED SHOES FOR?

NO, YOU'RE THINKING OF MICKEY MOUSE

DONALD DUCK DOESN'T WEAR SHOES!

September 13, 1979

HERE'S JOE COOL HANGING AROUND THE BULLETIN BOARD

THIS IS A GREAT WAY TO MEET SOME REALLY NEAT CHICKS

OF COURSE, SOME OF THEM THINK THEY'RE PRETTY SMART...

September 23, 1979

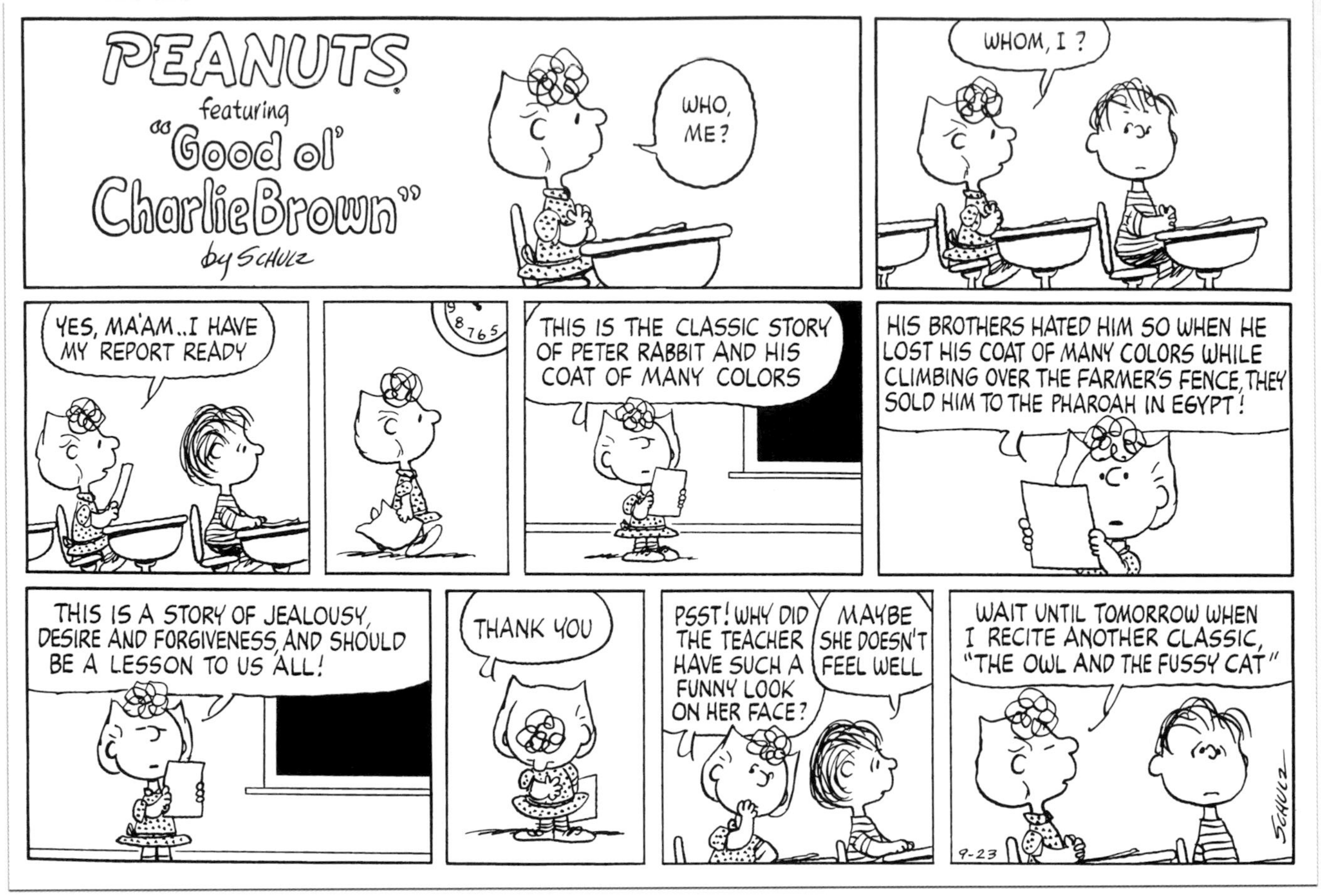

PEANUTS featuring "Good ol' Charlie Brown" by Schulz

WHO, ME?

WHOM, I?

YES, MA'AM..I HAVE MY REPORT READY

THIS IS THE CLASSIC STORY OF PETER RABBIT AND HIS COAT OF MANY COLORS

HIS BROTHERS HATED HIM SO WHEN HE LOST HIS COAT OF MANY COLORS WHILE CLIMBING OVER THE FARMER'S FENCE, THEY SOLD HIM TO THE PHAROAH IN EGYPT!

THIS IS A STORY OF JEALOUSY, DESIRE AND FORGIVENESS, AND SHOULD BE A LESSON TO US ALL!

THANK YOU

PSST! WHY DID THE TEACHER HAVE SUCH A FUNNY LOOK ON HER FACE?

MAYBE SHE DOESN'T FEEL WELL

WAIT UNTIL TOMORROW WHEN I RECITE ANOTHER CLASSIC, "THE OWL AND THE FUSSY CAT"

SCHULZ 9-23

September 24, 1979

boot!
BONK!
9-24
EXPLAIN TITLE IX TO ME AGAIN, WILL YOU?
SCHULZ

September 26, 1979

THAT'S A NEAT LOOKING BASKET-BALL, CHUCK
THE ONE THEY GAVE US GIRLS TO PLAY WITH ISN'T HALF THAT GOOD
9-26
YOU'RE NOT AGAINST WOMEN'S SPORTS ARE YOU, CHUCK?
SIGH
SCHULZ

September 28, 1979

WE'VE BEEN SILENT FOR SEVENTY YEARS ABOUT THE UNFAIR TREATMENT OF WOMEN ATHLETES, CHUCK

BUT NOW THAT UNFAIR TREATMENT IS CAUSING AN UPROAR
AN UPROAR?

UNFAIR!! UNFAIR!!

AN UPROAR, CHUCK!

September 29, 1979

WE WOMEN AREN'T GONNA KEEP QUIET ANY MORE, CHUCK! NO, SIR!

WE'RE RECRUITING ALL KINDS OF PEOPLE TO HELP US ACHIEVE EQUAL OPPORTUNITY IN ATHLETICS

LOOK WHO'S JUST JOINED OUR RANKS
LUCY? WHAT'S SHE GOING TO DO?

SPEAK OUT!!

October 6, 1979

I HAVE A VISION, CHUCK.. I CAN SEE THE DAY COMING WHEN WOMEN WILL HAVE THE SAME OPPORTUNITIES IN SPORTS AS MEN!

SPEAKING OF SPORTS, I'VE BEEN THINKING ABOUT SWITCHING TEAMS NEXT SEASON...

YOU WOULDN'T HAPPEN TO BE LOOKING FOR ANOTHER PITCHER, WOULD YOU?

YOU'RE NOT GOOD ENOUGH, CHUCK!

October 10, 1979

HERE'S THE FIERCE PYTHON SLITHERING ALONG THE GROUND...

SLOWLY HE BEGINS TO SLITHER UP A HUGE JUNGLE TREE

THAT WAS MY FAMOUS BACKWARD SLITHER

October 22, 1979

I WONDER WHAT WOULD HAPPEN IF I WALKED OVER TO THAT LITTLE RED-HAIRED GIRL, AND GAVE HER A BIG HUG...

I THINK I'LL DO IT

10-22

SURE
SCHULZ

October 26, 1979

HERE'S JOE COOL HANGING AROUND THE DORM

RING RING

RING RING RING RING
10-26

JOE COOL ONLY ANSWERS THE PHONE IF HE KNOWS IT'S FOR HIM
SCHULZ

November 3, 1979

OF ALL THE MUSICIANS WHO HAVE EVER LIVED, YOU ARE THE MOST FORTUNATE...

YOU KNOW WHY? BECAUSE YOU HAVE ME FOR AN INSPIRATION!

BONK!

11-3
WHEN YOU'RE AN INSPIRATION, YOU NEVER KNOW WHAT YOU'RE GOING TO INSPIRE...
SCHULZ

November 20, 1979

This is my new typewriter
11-20

It has many typefaces.

IT CAN ALSO cross out mistakes.

SCHULZ

November 11, 1979

PEANUTS
featuring
"Good ol' Charlie Brown"
by SCHULZ
NOVEMBER ELEVENTH
TODAY IS VETERANS DAY!
11-11
EVERY VETERANS DAY I GO OVER TO BILL MAULDIN'S HOUSE TO QUAFF A FEW ROOT BEERS
HE TELLS ME ABOUT THE TROUBLE HE HAD WITH PATTON, AND I TELL HIM ABOUT THE FUNNY THING THAT HAPPENED BETWEEN PERSHING AND ME...
?
HEY, WAIT A MINUTE! WHO ARE YOU GUYS SUPPOSED TO BE?
WILLIE AND JOE?!
SCHULZ

November 30, 1979

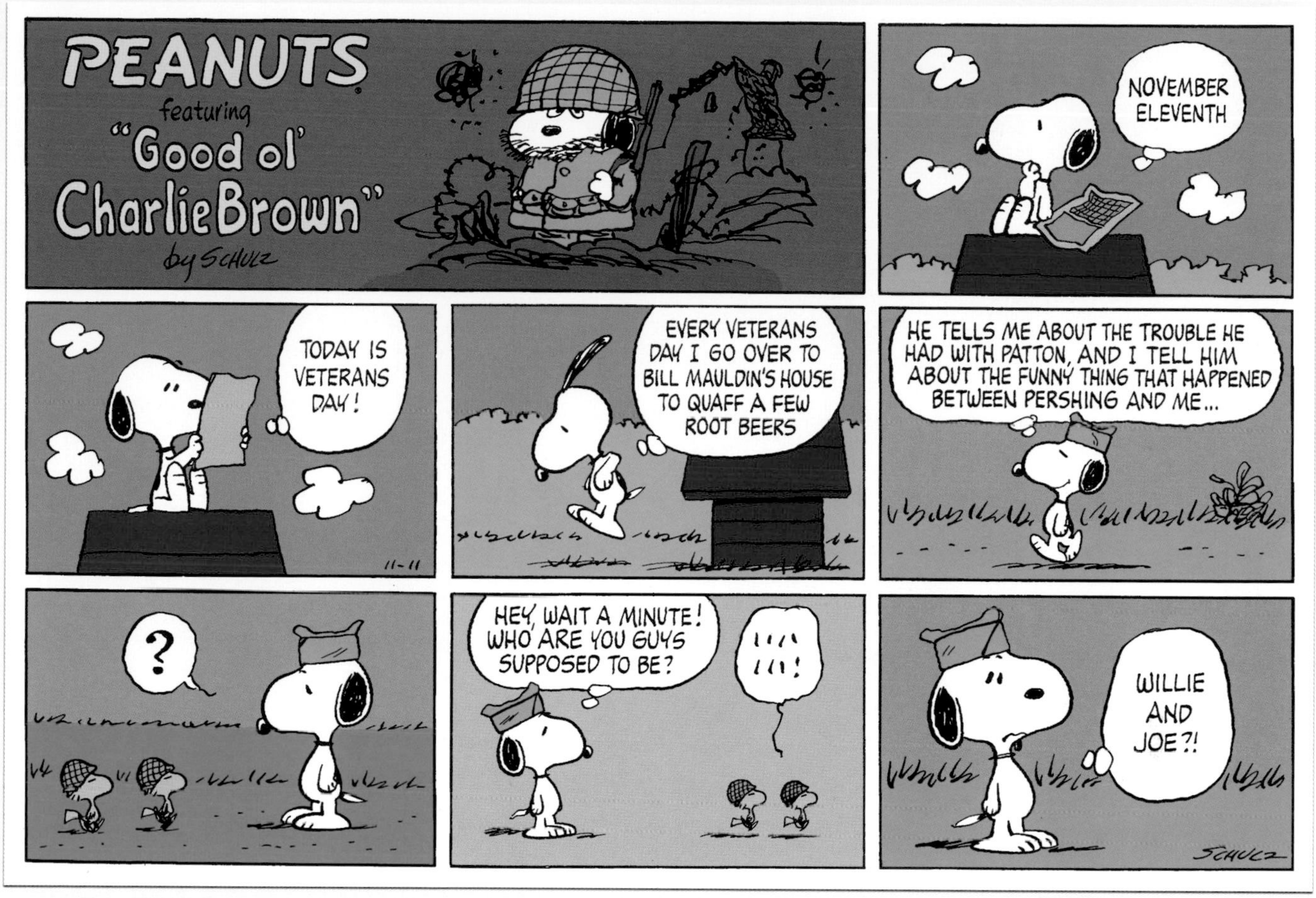

MAKES YOU WISH YOU KNEW HOW TO HANDLE A COMPASS, DOESN'T IT?
STUPID BEAGLE!
SCHULZ
11-30

December 10, 1979

THOSE ARE NICE MITTENS.. BE CAREFUL NOT TO LOSE THEM, OR YOU WON'T GET ANY PIE!
12-10

?
THE THREE LITTLE KITTENS!

HAVEN'T YOU EVER HEARD OF THE THREE LITTLE KITTENS? GOOD GRIEF!

LITERARY REFERENCES ARE WASTED ON WOODSTOCK...
SCHULZ

Celebrate 1980s

"I find that as the years have gone by, I have learned to handle the medium so that it really will accommodate every thought that comes to mind. I've discovered that every thought that occurs to me—whether it's just silly, a pun of some kind, or very serious—generally will find its way into the comic strip in one manner or other. It may not be riotously funny; it may just be smilingly funny. But somehow, the medium will accommodate it."

—Charles M. Schulz

I HOPE YOU LIKE DOUGHNUTS..

1980–1989

Something quite extraordinary happened to *Peanuts* in 1988. On February 29, *Peanuts* appeared as a three-panel strip for the first time. Until then, Schulz had been contractually obligated to draw four-panel strips. According to Schulz, the original idea for the four-panel strip was a "sales gimmick." His syndicate sold the strip to newspaper editors as a space saver, because the four panels could be run vertically, horizontally, or stacked in a square. Over time, Schulz found the four-panel strip format to be restrictive and reveled in his newfound freedom to create a three-panel, two-panel, or even a single-panel strip if he chose to do so.

- Snoopy's frequent fantasies often create havoc for the kids, as in the March 14, 1981, strip where the Flying Ace swallows secret papers that are actually Sally's term paper. Schulz commented that once he "developed the formula of using [Snoopy's] imagination to dream of being many heroic figures, the strip took on a completely new dimension."

- Schulz was an avid reader and often found a way to incorporate some of the facts he learned into *Peanuts*. The December 16, 1981, strip is a good example of this when Lucy suggests what might be ailing Charlie Brown. Note the inflation in Lucy's rate—it is ten times the original cost of five cents!
- Marbles, another of Snoopy's siblings, debuts in the strip on September 28, 1982. He appeared in only one story line that ran from September 23 through October 11, 1982.
- Schulz gave a tip of his hat to the great success of the 1983 movie musical *Flashdance* when he created the November 29, 1983, strip. The Flashbeagle character must have tickled Schulz's fancy; he went on to write *It's Flashbeagle, Charlie Brown*, an animated prime-time television special first broadcast in April 1984. He also entitled his 1985 ice show *Flashbeagle*. (Schulz produced an ice show at his Redwood Empire Ice Arena featuring well-known ice skating stars, outstanding costumes, and elaborate sets. This spectacular became an important community event in Schulz's adopted home city of Santa Rosa, California.)

- Peppermint Patty's struggles with school are legendary, but in a story line that ran from December 28, 1984, through January 17, 1985, she actually wins the All-City School Essay Contest with her simple and evocative composition "What I Did on My Christmas Vacation." (*I went outside and looked at the clouds. They formed beautiful patterns with beautiful colors. I looked at them every morning and every evening. Which is all I did on my Christmas vacation. And what's wrong with that?*). In the January 8, 1985, strip, Schulz explores one of his recurring themes—the capriciousness of grading and discipline in elementary schools.
- All of the major *Peanuts* characters evolved during the nearly fifty years that Schulz created the strip, but Sally's progression from a sweet, if naive, little girl to a rather acerbic, if no less confused, individual is one of the more humorous transformations in the strip. In the October 13, 1986, strip, Sally is promoting yet another of her "philosophies."
- Ill-starred and unrequited love is a prominent theme in *Peanuts*. In the July 13, 1987, strip, Charlie Brown finally learns that he is loved. But since Charlie Brown can never be happy, he will continue to pine for the unattainable Little Red-Haired Girl even though there is every possibility that he could find love with Marcie or Peppermint Patty.
- The health maladies that Schulz experienced were sometimes reflected in the strip. In a multiday story line, Snoopy was scheduled for knee surgery after Schulz had arthroscopic surgery on his knee due to an injury he sustained playing hockey. Snoopy narrowly averted the surgery in the December 1, 1987, strip when it was discovered that dogs don't have knees!
- Snoopy's brother Olaf waddled into the strip on January 24, 1989. With the exception of Spike, none of Snoopy's siblings played a major role in *Peanuts*.

- The October 26, 1989, strip is another case of art imitating life. In 1988, Andy, a little dog rescued from an animal shelter, became an important part of Schulz's life. Schulz wrote, "Andy spawned a series of ideas of which I was very proud." One of those ideas was something he would say to the staff at the studio as he left for the day: "Well, I'm going home now. I'm going to devote the rest of the day to making my dog happy."

January 3, 1980

WHY SHOULDN'T I BE INVITED TO A PARTY?

GO AHEAD, AND TELL ME! COME ON, TELL ME!

1-3

WHO SAYS I'M CRABBY?
SCHULZ

"Anyone involved in anything creative has to be putting a lot of himself into it. I would say all the characters are me in one form or another. It would be impossible for me to think up the sarcastic things Lucy says if I weren't sarcastic myself in the very same way. And there's a lot of Charlie Brown in me, or I should say, a lot of me in Charlie Brown."

January 10, 1980

RULERS HAVE OTHER USES, YOU KNOW

SEE? IF YOU TAKE YOUR PEN AND GO ALONG THE EDGE OF THE RULER, AND THEN LIFT IT UP, YOU'LL HAVE A NICE STRAIGHT...
1-10

...SMUDGE!
SCHULZ
© 1980 United Feature Syndicate, Inc.

January 15, 1980

SORRY, PRICES ARE GETTING TOO HIGH..WE CAN'T AFFORD TO FEED YOU ANY MORE..

YOU'RE GOING TO HAVE TO GO OUT, AND HUNT FOR YOUR OWN FOOD...
1-15

HEY! COME BACK! COME BACK!

I WAS JUST KIDDING
SCHULZ

January 23, 1980

SHOVEL YOUR WALK? ONLY TWO DOLLARS

JUST A MINUTE... I'LL ASK MY DAD
1-23

MY DAD SAYS HE USED TO CHARGE ONLY FIFTY CENTS
SCHULZ

DID THEY HAVE SIDEWALKS IN THOSE DAYS?
© 1980 United Feature Syndicate, Inc.

February 2, 1980

I THINK THEY'RE ALL AFRAID, CHUCK

OUR TEACHER'S AFRAID OF THE PRINCIPAL, THE PRINCIPAL'S AFRAID OF THE SUPERINTENDENT AND HE'S AFRAID OF THE BOARD OF EDUCATION...
2-2

WHAT ABOUT THE CUSTODIAN?

HE'S AFRAID TO GO UP ON THE ROOF!
SCHULZ

March 8, 1980

THERE'S A LOT MORE TO LIFE THAN DANCING!
3-8

SHE'S RIGHT...

THERE'S BITING!
SCHULZ

March 10, 1980

THE ROLLER SKATING SEASON IS JUST ABOUT HERE AGAIN

AND THE JUMP ROPE SEASON, TOO... AND I LOVE THE PICNIC SEASON
3-10

HOW ABOUT THE KITE SEASON?
OH, YES

THE KITE SEASON IS ALWAYS FUN
SCHULZ

March 11, 1980

EVERY TIME YOU THINK THINGS CAN'T GET ANY WORSE, THEY GET WORSE
3-11

THIS TIME, HOWEVER, I DON'T KNOW...

WHAT COULD BE WORSE THAN BEING TANGLED IN A KITE STRING AND HANGING UPSIDE DOWN FROM A TREE?

SCHULZ

March 12, 1980

MAYBE MY FAITHFUL DOG WILL RESCUE ME

MAYBE HE'LL DISCOVER THAT I'M GONE, AND COME LOOKING FOR ME
3-12

DOGS HAVE AN UNUSUAL SENSE OF LOYALTY... HE'S BOUND TO HAVE MISSED ME...

SIGH
SCHULZ

March 13, 1980

THERE I WAS, STANDING UP IN FRONT OF THE WHOLE CLASS, AND I FORGOT WHAT I WAS GOING TO SAY...

I COULD FEEL MY FACE TURNING RED.. YOU KNOW HOW IT FEELS...
3-13

IT'S LIKE WHEN YOU'RE UPSIDE DOWN, AND ALL THE BLOOD RUSHES TO YOUR HEAD

THAT'S A GOOD EXAMPLE
SCHULZ

March 14, 1980

IF YOU'RE TANGLED IN A KITE STRING AND HANGING UPSIDE DOWN FROM A TREE, IT'S NOTHING TO WORRY ABOUT

EVENTUALLY THE STRING WILL GET WET FROM THE RAIN AND DRY OUT IN THE SUN, AND THEN IT WILL WEAKEN AND BREAK..

KLUNK!

IT'S NATURE'S WAY OF PROTECTING THE KITE FLYER!
SCHULZ
3-14

March 18, 1980

I CAN UNDERSTAND HOW YOU MIGHT BECOME INFATUATED WITH ME
3-18

ONE THING I WOULDN'T WANT YOU TO DO, HOWEVER, AND THAT WOULD BE TO PUT ME ON A PEDESTAL

GOOD!
WUMP!

OF COURSE, IF I WERE ON A PEDESTAL, I COULD REALLY RUN THINGS
SCHULZ

March 22, 1980

MOM, MAY I USE YOUR DESK TO DO MY HOMEWORK? THANK YOU...

WHERE'S THE CHAIR? THERE'S NO CHAIR...

THAT'S ALL RIGHT... I'LL FIGURE OUT SOMETHING...
3-22

SCHULZ

March 27, 1980

I FIGURED IT OUT, CHARLIE BROWN

IF YOU STAY DEPRESSED FOR TWO MORE DAYS, YOU'LL MAKE IT INTO THE BOOK OF WORLD RECORDS...
3-27

WOW! THAT'S GREAT!

SCHULZ
YOU JUST BLEW IT!

April 27, 1980

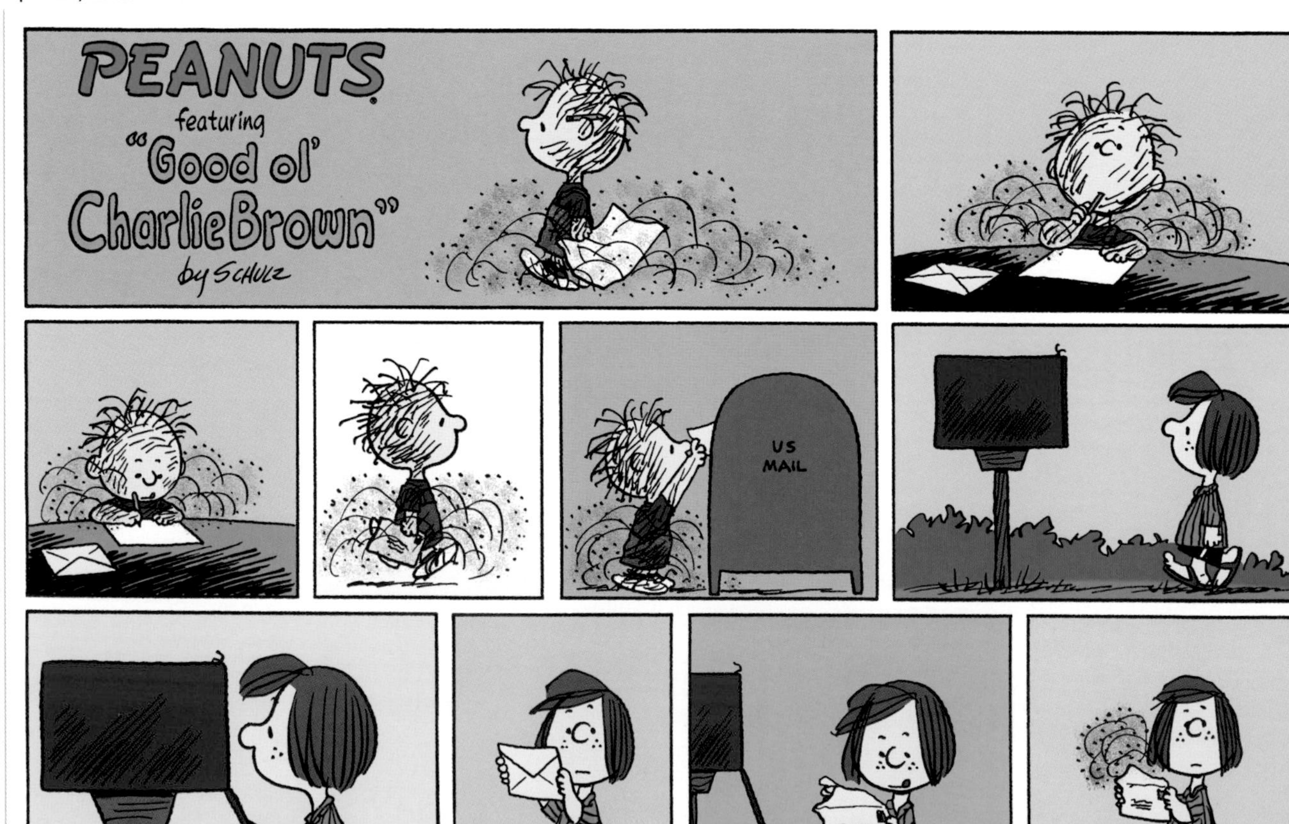
PEANUTS
featuring
"Good ol' CharlieBrown"
by SCHULZ
US MAIL
4-27
SCHULZ

May 11, 1980

PEANUTS
featuring
"Good ol' Charlie Brown"
by Schulz
THIS IS MOTHER'S DAY
MOM?
HEY, MOM, WHERE ARE YOU?
MAYBE IF YOU HAD A PHOTOGRAPH OR SOMETHING
YOU KNOW WHAT AGGRAVATES ME?
IT'S THE WHOLE SYSTEM THAT YOU BIRDS HAVE..NO WONDER YOU'RE UNHAPPY!
YOUR MOTHER AND FATHER BUILD THE NEST, YOU GUYS ARE BORN AND THEN EVERYONE LEAVES...
THAT HAS TO BE THE DUMBEST SYSTEM I'VE EVER HEARD OF!
HOW ARE YOU GOING TO FIND YOUR MOM? SHE COULD BE ALMOST ANYWHERE!
I'LL TELL YOU WHAT WE'LL DO...IF WE CAN'T FIND YOUR MOM, WHY DON'T WE AT LEAST PAY A LITTLE VISIT TO THE TREE WHERE YOU WERE BORN?
IT'S CALLED, "RETURNING TO THE OL' HOMESTEAD"
5-11
MAYBE SEEING THE TREE WHERE YOU WERE BORN WILL MAKE YOU FEEL A LITTLE BETTER...
I CAN'T STAND IT!
SCHULZ

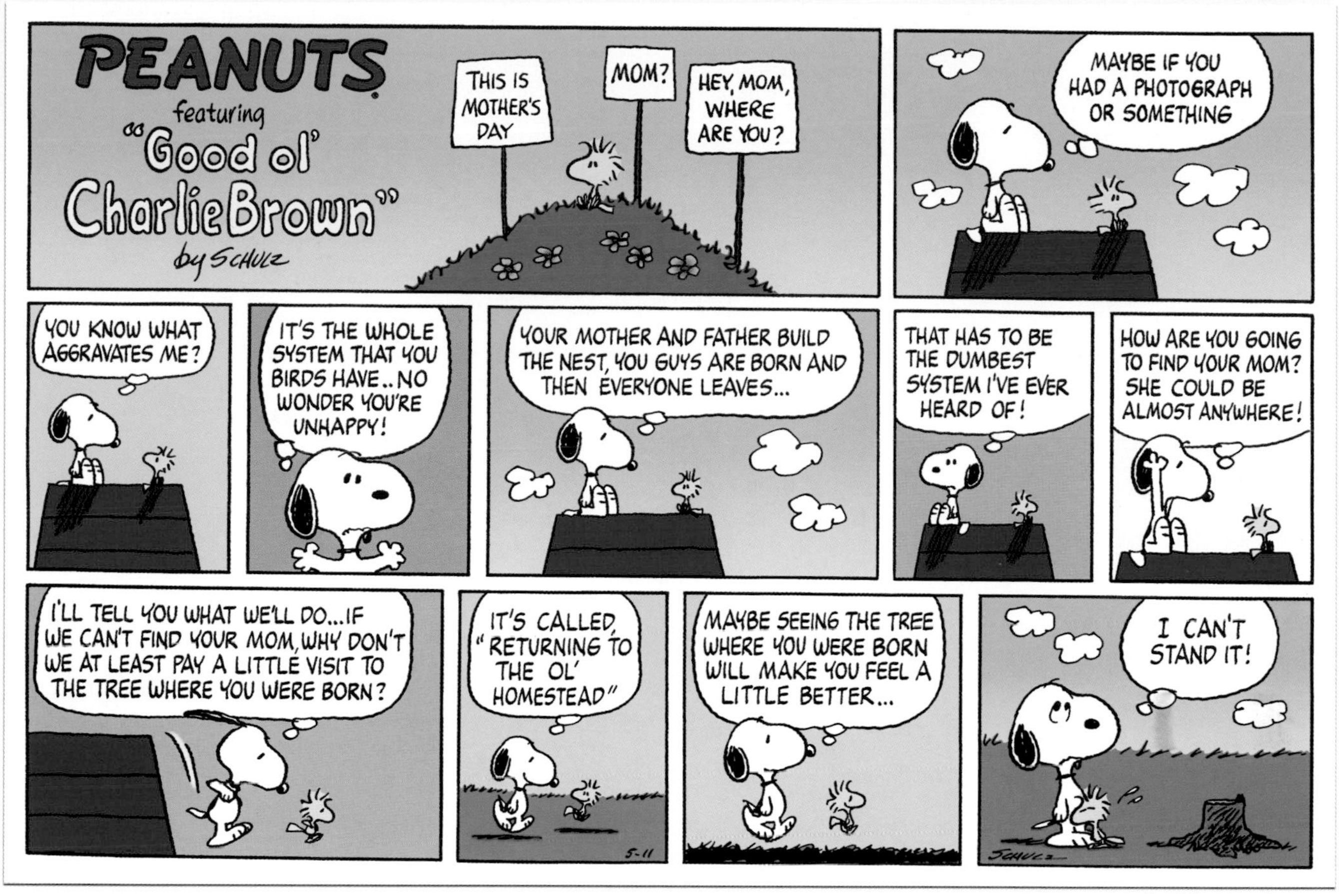

"You know, I've never been able to figure out birds. They kick the kids out of the nest and they leave, and the poor little birds have no idea where their parents went; they can never find them again. They go back to the tree, hoping that they can find the tree in which they were born and the tree is gone. Someone has cut it down."

April 16, 1980

Joe Ceremony was very short.
4-16

When he entered a room, everyone had to be warned not to stand on Ceremony.

HAHAHAHA!

I'M A GREAT ADMIRER OF MY OWN WRITING
SCHULZ

May 12, 1980

ALL RIGHT, MEN, ANSWER AS I CALL YOUR NAME... WOODSTOCK! BILL! CONRAD! OLIVIER!
5-12

!!
"HARRIET"? WHO'S HARRIET?

AND WHY, PRAY TELL, SHOULD HARRIET BE INVITED TO JOIN OUR GROUP?

RIGHT! ANYONE WHO BRINGS ALONG AN ANGEL FOOD CAKE WITH SEVEN-MINUTE FROSTING IS WELCOME!
SCHULZ

May 14, 1980

WHEN WE GET TO THE TOP OF THE HILL, WE'LL ALL EAT THE ANGEL FOOD CAKE THAT HARRIET BROUGHT

WHAT?

WHY CAN'T WE EAT THE CAKE AT THE TOP OF THE HILL?

"BECAUSE HARRIET ATE IT AT THE BOTTOM OF THE HILL!"

May 22, 1980

NAPOLEON TALKED ABOUT "TWO O'CLOCK IN THE MORNING COURAGE"

SCOTT FITZGERALD SAID, "IN A REAL DARK NIGHT OF THE SOUL IT IS ALWAYS THREE O'CLOCK IN THE MORNING"

BUT WHEN YOU HAVE TO GET UP AT SEVEN, AND YOU STILL HAVEN'T WRITTEN THE ENGLISH THEME THAT'S DUE TODAY...

SIX FIFTY-NINE IS THE WORST TIME OF DAY!

"I feel that Peanuts *reflects certain attitudes of life in our country today and perhaps some basic fears. However, I like to think of these things as part of the entire human condition and not simply something involving one generation of people in one country."*

May 23, 1980

THE ANSWER, MA'AM, IS ELEVEN MILLION, NINE HUNDRED AND SIXTY-FIVE THOUSAND, ONE HUNDRED AND FIFTY-SEVEN!

THAT'S WRONG, SIR..THE ANSWER IS "TWO"

TWO?!

CLOSE, BUT NO CIGAR, EH, MA'AM?

May 30, 1980

A PERSON SHOULDN'T HAVE TO LIVE WITH REGRETS...

IT CAN TEAR YOU APART

I KNOW ONE REGRET THAT HAS HAUNTED ME FOR YEARS...

I'VE NEVER BITTEN ANYONE!!

June 2, 1980

YOU GOT ALL A'S ? WOW! THAT'S GREAT, MARCIE! I GOT A BUNCH OF D MINUSES...

LET ME HOLD YOUR REPORT CARD, MARCIE... I'D JUST LIKE TO SEE WHAT IT'S LIKE TO HOLD A CARD WITH ALL A'S...

HERE, YOU HOLD MY CARD, AND I'LL HOLD YOURS

WELL, YOU DON'T HAVE TO HOLD IT LIKE **THAT**!

June 5, 1980

THIS IS RIDICULOUS! WHY DO WE LET THEM DO THIS TO US EVERY SUMMER?!

AS SOON AS SCHOOL IS OUT, THEY SHIP US OFF TO SOME STUPID CAMP! WE DON'T EVEN KNOW WHERE THE CAMP IS!

I'LL BET THERE ISN'T A SOUL WHO HAS ANY IDEA WHERE WE'RE GOING!

HERE'S THE WORLD WAR I FLYING ACE RIDING ACROSS NORTHERN FRANCE ON A TROOP TRAIN...

June 6, 1980

HEY, CHUCK! WELCOME TO CAMP! WE DIDN'T KNOW ALL YOU GUYS WERE COMING, TOO!

GLAD TO SEE YOU, PATTY..HOW ARE YOU, MARCIE? DO YOU KNOW WHERE WE ARE?

SEARCH ME, CHUCK..WE HAVEN'T TALKED TO ANYBODY YET WHO SEEMS TO KNOW...

THE SKY ABOVE NORMANDY IS VERY BLUE THIS TIME OF YEAR...

June 9, 1980

YOU'D BETTER PUT THAT AWAY, SALLY..THEY DON'T ALLOW COMIC BOOKS IN THIS CAMP...

YOU'RE KIDDING!
NO, THEY SAY IT'S NOT SUITABLE READING

THAT'S RIDICULOUS! HALF THE FUN OF GOING TO CAMP IS LYING ON YOUR BUNK READING COMIC BOOKS!

WHAT'S THE OTHER HALF?
SITTING UNDER A TREE READING COMIC BOOKS!

June 10, 1980

DO YOU LIKE SITTING AROUND A CAMPFIRE SINGING SONGS, SIR?
6-10

SURE, MARCIE, BUT I DON'T KNOW ANY OF THESE SONGS THEY'VE BEEN SINGING...

THEY'RE CALLED INSPIRATIONAL CHORUSES, SIR...
I'M GONNA ASK IF THEY'LL SING SOMETHING I KNOW..

I WOULDN'T SUGGEST "A HUNDRED BOTTLES OF BEER ON THE WALL," SIR
SCHULZ

June 18, 1980

I HATE THESE DISCUSSION GROUPS! I NEVER KNOW WHAT THEY'RE TALKING ABOUT! I SHOULD BE HOME WATCHING TV!

YES, SIR? YOU WANT ME TO WHAT? LEAD IN PRAYER? OUT LOUD?! ME? BUT....

GO AHEAD, SALLY... YOU CAN DO IT..
6/18

"NOW I LAY US DOWN TO SLEEP..."
SCHULZ

June 20, 1980

MAY I ASK A QUESTION, SIR? I DON'T REALLY WISH TO INTERRUPT...

I THINK I'LL LEAVE..
I ALSO DON'T WISH TO BE RUDE...

JUST AS A MATTER OF CURIOSITY, SIR...
6/20

HAS IT EVER OCCURRED TO YOU THAT YOU MIGHT BE WRONG?
SCHULZ

June 23, 1980

GOOD AFTERNOON... MY NAME IS LUCY..

I'M GOING TO BE YOUR RIGHT-FIELDER... OUR SPECIAL TODAY IS A MISJUDGED FLY-BALL

WE ALSO HAVE A NICE BOBBLED GROUND BALL AND AN EXCELLENT LATE THROW TO THE INFIELD...
6-23

I'LL BE BACK IN A MOMENT TO TAKE YOUR ORDER
SCHULZ

July 8, 1980

I DON'T KNOW WHY YOU WANTED TO "10 BRAID" YOUR HAIR, SIR...

IT'S THE "BO LOOK," MARCIE...IT'LL GIVE ME A NEW IMAGE...WHEN PEOPLE SEE ME, THEY'LL..

YIPE!

WELL, WHAT DOES A DOG KNOW?

July 9, 1980

SOMETHING SEEMS TO BE MISSING, SIR...

BEADS, MARCIE... "CORNROW" HAIR NEEDS BEADS...

I DON'T HAVE ANY PRETTY BEADS

AND TINKERTOYS DON'T QUITE DO IT!

July 14, 1980

I COULD STARE AT THE CLOUDS ALL DAY..

SOME ARE ALMOST AWESOME

SOME ARE REALLY BEAUTIFUL...

SOME OF THEM THINK THEY'RE PRETTY FUNNY!

July 16, 1980

CLOUDS ARE FASCINATING

SOME CLOUDS ARE ABSOLUTELY BEAUTIFUL...

SOME CLOUDS ARE UGLY..

...AND VERY SENSITIVE!

July 17, 1980

I'VE BEEN READING A HISTORY OF THE WORLD

I NEVER REALIZED SO MANY PEOPLE HAVE LIVED ON THE EARTH...

I FEEL SORRY FOR THEM
© 1980 United Feature Syndicate, Inc.
7-17

WHAT FUN WAS IT WITHOUT HAVING ME AROUND?
SCHULZ

July 29, 1980

I'VE HEARD THAT OUR CAPTAIN WAS A FIGHTER PILOT DURING THE WAR...
7-29

I DON'T SUPPOSE THOSE EXPERIENCES ARE EASILY FORGOTTEN...

CURSE YOU, RED BARON!

NO, I GUESS NOT
SCHULZ

July 31, 1980

OUR IN-FLIGHT MOVIE TODAY WILL BE "CITIZEN KANE"
7-31

MOVIE? WE GET TO SEE A MOVIE?

WELL, IT ISN'T EXACTLY A MOVIE..

"ROSEBUD!"
SCHULZ

August 4, 1980

LADIES AND GENTLEMEN, WE HAVE ARRIVED AT OUR DESTINATION...
CLICK
SNAP
SWITCH
8-4

PLEASE REMAIN SEATED UNTIL THE AIRCRAFT HAS COME TO A STOP...

KLUNK!

DON'T MIND HIM, SIR.. HE FAINTS AFTER EVERY LANDING!
SCHULZ

August 5, 1980

GOODBYE, SIR.. DID YOU ENJOY THE FLIGHT?
YES, THANK YOU

NO, I'M SORRY..I NEVER DATE THE PASSENGERS

I DIDN'T ASK FOR A DATE! WHERE'S "BAGGAGE RETURN"? WHERE'S MY PIANO?

BONK!!

"I am a professional. I have been drawing cartoons for thirty-five years; Peanuts *has been going for thirty-two years. I'm just like Billie Jean King or Arnold Palmer. I am a fanatic about what I do—it's my whole life. I never stop thinking about it. I'm completely devoted to the profession; I pour all my waking thoughts into this thing. I am very competitive; I want what I do to be the very best. I never think about burning out."*

August 19, 1980

NO, OUR KIND DOESN'T GET TO VOTE...WE DON'T HAVE ANYTHING TO SAY ABOUT WHAT GOES ON IN THE WORLD

SIGH

August 21, 1980

YOU AND THAT STUPID BLANKET!

AND THAT THUMB! GOOD GRIEF!!

I DON'T SEE WHY YOU WANT TO SUCK ON THAT THUMB ALL DAY...

NO CALORIES!

September 8, 1980

PSST! WAKE UP, SIR! YOU'RE MISSING THE HISTORY LESSON...
Z

9-8
WHEW!

HOW LONG DID I SLEEP, MARCIE?

FROM HENRY THE FOURTH TO HENRY THE SIXTH
SCHULZ

September 10, 1980

I'M DRAWING A COW, BUT I'M HAVING TROUBLE WITH THE HOOFSESES...

NOT "HOOFSESES"... "HOOVES"... LIKE IN "BEHOOVES"
9-10

BEES DON'T HAVE HOOVES! BEES HAVE FEET!

WHO YOU TRYIN' TO KID?
SCHULZ

September 11, 1980

THIS IS A DRAWING I MADE OF A COW IN A MEADOW CHASING MICE

WADDYA MEAN, COWS DON'T CHASE MICE?
9-11

MA'AM?

ALL RIGHT... SCRATCH THE MICE
SCHULZ

October 7, 1980

This is the

RATS!

MY PENMANSHIP IS GETTING WORSE ALL THE TIME!
10-7

MAYBE YOU SHOULD STICK TO PENCILSHIP...
SCHULZ

October 15, 1980

10-15

I GUESS IT'S HARD TO FLY WHEN YOU HAVE THE HICCUPS...
SCHULZ

October 20, 1980

ALL RIGHT, TROOPS, ANSWER AS I CALL YOUR NAMES...

BILL! CONRAD! OLIVIER! WOODSTOCK! HARRIET!
10-20

HARRIET HAS A HIGH VOICE

October 25, 1980

ALL RIGHT, GO AHEAD! GO INTO TOWN, AND DISCO ALL NIGHT!
10-25

WHAT DO I CARE IF YOU WEAR YOURSELVES OUT? YOU'LL LEARN!

AND DON'T WORRY ABOUT ME! I CAN TAKE CARE OF MYSELF...

I'LL SIT HERE BY THE FIRE, AND PORK OUT ON MARSHMALLOWS!
SCHULZ

October 27, 1980

GOOD GRIEF! WHAT HAPPENED TO YOU GUYS? I KNEW I SHOULDN'T HAVE LET YOU GO INTO TOWN...

YOU ALL LOOK TERRIBLE!
10-27

HOW ABOUT YOU, WOODSTOCK? DIDN'T YOU GET INTO IT?

SCHULZ

October 30, 1980

YES, SIR, I UNDERSTAND..

ONE OF SNOOPY'S BEAGLE SCOUTS GOT THROWN IN JAIL..I HAVE TO GO DOWN, AND GET HER OUT...

THAT STUPID DOG IS MORE TROUBLE THAN HE'S WORTH!
10-30

MOST OF US ARE
SPEAK FOR YOURSELF!
SCHULZ

November 16, 1980

PEANUTS
featuring
"Good ol' CharlieBrown"
by SCHULZ
ECCLESIASTES.. THIRD CHAPTER..

AH! JUST THE PERSON I WANTED TO SEE...

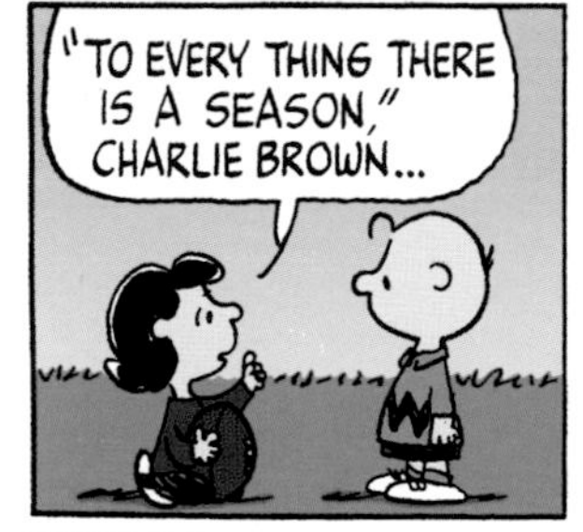
"TO EVERY THING THERE IS A SEASON," CHARLIE BROWN...

"A TIME TO BE BORN, AND A TIME TO DIE"

"A TIME TO PLANT, AND A TIME TO PLUCK UP THAT WHICH IS PLANTED"

"A TIME TO WEEP, AND A TIME TO LAUGH..A TIME TO MOURN, AND A TIME TO DANCE.."
11-16

"A TIME TO LOVE, AND A TIME TO HATE.. A TIME OF WAR, AND A TIME OF PEACE"

AAUGH!

WHAM!

AND A TIME TO PULL AWAY THE FOOTBALL
SCHULZ

November 28, 1980

LAW AND LAWYERS ARE ALWAYS WITH US

WE ALL HAVE TO DEAL WITH THE LAW FROM THE VERY DAY WE'RE BORN
11-28

THAT'S TRUE

JUST LAST WEEK I SUED A BABY!
SCHULZ

December 5, 1980

I LOVE HOCKEY GAMES

THE COACH SAID TO MAKE SURE I WAS THERE ON TIME...

WITHOUT ME, THE GAME COULDN'T BEGIN..
12-5

SCHULZ

December 8, 1980

I WOULD HAVE MADE A GOOD EVANGELIST

YOU KNOW THAT KID WHO SITS BEHIND ME AT SCHOOL?
12-8

I CONVINCED HIM THAT MY RELIGION IS BETTER THAN HIS RELIGION

HOW'D YOU DO THAT?
I HIT HIM WITH MY LUNCH BOX!
SCHULZ

December 10, 1980

WHY DOES SHE TAKE ME ON THE BACK OF HER BICYCLE WHEN SHE GOES SHOPPING?

IT'S NOT AS IF THIS IS A STATION WAGON OR A PICKUP...
12-10

THERE'S NO ROOM TO CARRY ANYTHING...

EXCEPT A FEW CHRISTMAS TREE ORNAMENTS...
SCHULZ

December 23, 1980

THERE WERE THREE WISE MEN, SEE...

THEY CAME FROM THE EAST, AND THEY WERE LOOKING FOR BETHLEHEM
12-23

YOU KNOW HOW THEY FOUND IT? THEY FOLLOWED A STAR!

WHO WAS THE STAR?
SCHULZ

January 8, 1981

THE SECOND PROBLEM, MA'AM? YES, MA'AM...

AT THE BLACKBOARD... IN FRONT OF THE WHOLE CLASS...SECOND PROBLEM..

FOR THE FIRST TIME IN MY LIFE, I BELIEVE IN SCHOOL PRAYER!

"I never even think about it [social commentary], I just draw what I think or what I hope will be funny little things. If people read more into them, that's fine. I think this is valid with any art form."

January 20, 1981

I THINK "GOOD AND EVIL" ARE VERY HARD TO DEFINE...

I HAVE MY OWN OPINION, OF COURSE, SUCH AS IT IS...

FOR INSTANCE, WHEN I'M WALKING DOWN THE STREET, I ALWAYS TRY TO AVOID STEPPING ON A BUG...

HURRAY! HURRAY! CLAP CLAP CLAP CLAP CLAP!

January 26, 1981

THIS HIGHWAY PATROLLED BY AIRCRAFT

February 2, 1981

FEBRUARY 2, "GROUNDHOG DAY"

BOY, DID I EVER GET THAT WRONG!

REMEMBER WHAT I WAS TELLING YOU ABOUT "GROUND HUG DAY"?

February 5, 1981

WELL, WHY DON'T YOU ANSWER ME ?

OH, I DIDN'T HEAR YOU... I CAN'T HEAR A THING WHEN I'M EATING TOAST BECAUSE IT ECHOES INSIDE MY HEAD...

ACTUALLY, IT'S VERY PEACEFUL

EATING TOAST IS LIKE GETTING AWAY FOR THE WEEKEND

February 9, 1981

SEE THE VALENTINE I MADE FOR LINUS ?

ON THE INSIDE I WROTE, "TO MY SWEET BABBOO"

HE SAYS HE'S NOT YOUR "SWEET BABBOO"

WHAT DOES HE KNOW ?

February 10, 1981

THESE ARE VALENTINES FOR ALL THE BOYS AT SCHOOL THAT I LIKE...

AND THIS IS A VERY SPECIAL ONE FOR MY "SWEET BABBOO"

DOES YOUR "SWEET BABBOO" KNOW WHO HE IS ?
OH, YES, HE KNOWS WHO HE IS...

I DO NOT!

February 11, 1981

ALL RIGHT, "AT EASE," OUT THERE! OUR TEACHER HAS ASKED ME TO EXPLAIN HOW THIS VALENTINE THING WILL WORK...

EACH STUDENT WILL DROP HIS OR HER VALENTINE INTO THIS BOX... PLEASE WRITE ALL NAMES CLEARLY...

SPECIAL TERMS OF ENDEARMENT LIKE "SWEET BABBOO," FOR INSTANCE, ARE PERMITTED BECAUSE THAT PERSON OBVIOUSLY KNOWS WHO HE IS...

NO, I DON'T!!

February 20, 1981

Dear Pen Pal—
How have you been?
I have been fine.
2-20

How has the weather been?

The weather here has been

IF WE EVER HAVE AN INK SHORTAGE, YOU'RE GONNA BE BLAMED!
SCHULZ

February 22, 1981

PEANUTS
featuring
"Good ol' CharlieBrown"
by SCHULZ

YOU COULD BE... WHY NOT?

I READ ONCE ABOUT AN EAGLE CARRYING OFF A SMALL CHILD...

IT'D BE A GOOD WAY FOR YOU TO FIND OUT IF YOU'RE AN EAGLE...DO YOU THINK YOU COULD CARRY AWAY A SMALL CHILD?

2-22

NO! NO! NOT LIKE THAT! YOU'RE SUPPOSED TO USE YOUR CLAWS!!

THAT'S RIGHT! YOU GOT HIM! LIFT! LIFT! UP! UP! UP!

ALL RIGHT! TELL THIS STUPID FRIEND OF YOURS TO GET LOST!

I GUESS I NEVER DID REALLY BELIEVE THOSE EAGLE STORIES...
SCHULZ

February 26, 1981

WOULDN'T IT BE SOMETHING IF THAT LITTLE RED-HAIRED GIRL CAME OVER HERE AND GAVE ME A KISS?

I'D SAY, "THANK YOU! WHAT WAS THAT FOR?" AND WOULDN'T IT BE SOMETHING IF SHE SAID, "BECAUSE I'VE ALWAYS LOVED YOU!"

2-26

THEN I'D GIVE HER A BIG HUG, AND SHE'D KISS ME AGAIN! WOULDN'T THAT BE SOMETHING?

WOULDN'T IT BE SOMETHING IF IT TURNED OUT THAT FRENCH FRIES WERE GOOD FOR YOU?
SCHULZ

March 4, 1981

YOU'VE NEVER "POOFED" A DANDELION?

YOU CAN'T SAY YOU'VE LIVED UNTIL YOU'VE "POOFED" A DANDELION...

POOF!
3-4

THAT WAS GOOD.. NOW, YOU CAN SAY YOU'VE LIVED!
SCHULZ

March 5, 1981

HERE'S ANOTHER DANDELION...GIVE IT A "POOF"

3-5
POOF!

POOF!

SORRY..I DIDN'T KNOW THEY EVER "POOFED" BACK
SCHULZ

"I'm proud of the way Snoopy looks. I think he's well drawn—not too cute in his appearance. His whole personality is a little bittersweet. But he's a very strong character. He can win or lose, be a disaster, a hero, or anything, and yet it all works out. I like the fact that when he's in real trouble, he can retreat into a fantasy and thereby escape."

March 14, 1981

HERE'S THE WORLD WAR I FLYING ACE FLEEING FROM THE ENEMY WITH THE SECRET PAPERS...

YOU STUPID BEAGLE!! COME BACK HERE WITH MY TERM PAPER!!!

KNOWING HE IS ABOUT TO BE CAUGHT, HE BECOMES DESPERATE...
3-14

HE SWALLOWS THE PAPERS!
AAUGH!
SCHULZ

April 27, 1981

Z
4-27

I THINK I JUST LEARNED SOMETHING, MARCIE

WHEN IT'S HOT IN THE ROOM, AND YOU FALL ASLEEP AT YOUR DESK...

YOUR MATH PAPER STICKS TO YOUR HEAD!
SCHULZ

April 28, 1981

THERE ARE A LOT OF TROUBLES IN THE WORLD TODAY...

PLAYING BASEBALL HELPS TO TAKE YOUR MIND OFF THEM
4-28

POW!

I THINK I'D RATHER WORRY ABOUT THE TROUBLES IN THE WORLD
SCHULZ

April 29, 1981

HERE'S THE WORLD WAR I FLYING ACE READING A LETTER FROM HOME

IT'S ABOUT MY BROTHER SPIKE..HE'S IN FRANCE! HE'S BEEN DRAFTED INTO THE INFANTRY!!
4-29

MY BROTHER SPIKE IN THE INFANTRY! WHAT A FINE FIGURE OF A SOLDIER HE MUST MAKE...

SCHULZ

May 2, 1981

HERE'S THE WORLD WAR I FLYING ACE SEARCHING NO MAN'S LAND FOR HIS BROTHER...

INTO THE SHELL HOLES, ACROSS BARBED WIRE, THROUGH THE MUD..
5-2

SPIKE! WHERE ARE YOU? SPIKE!

SPIKE?
SCHULZ

May 23, 1981

THERE'S SOMETHING LONELY ABOUT A BALL FIELD WHEN IT'S RAINING...
5-23

WHAT MAKES IT LONELY, IS BEING THE ONLY ONE DUMB ENOUGH TO BE STANDING OUT HERE...
SCHULZ

May 28, 1981

YOU KNOW WHAT OSCAR WILDE SAID, MA'AM?
5-28

HE SAID, "NOTHING THAT IS WORTH KNOWING CAN BE TAUGHT"

NOTHING PERSONAL, MA'AM...

CARRY ON
SCHULZ

March 22, 1981

PEANUTS
featuring
"Good ol' CharlieBrown"
by SCHULZ
Menu

CHOMP
CHOMP
CHOMP
CHOMP
CHOMP

YOU ROTTEN, NO-GOOD CHUNK OF WOOD!

LOOK AT THAT, WILL YOU? THAT STUPID TREE ATE EVERY BIT OF MY KITE!

ALL HE LEFT ME WAS THE STRING

WHY DON'T YOU GIVE HIM THE STRING, TOO, FOR DESSERT?

I GUESS I MIGHT AS WELL..

HERE! EAT IT ALL!! ENJOY YOURSELF!

WHAT HAPPENED?
HE DOESN'T EAT DESSERT.. HE'S AFRAID OF GETTING FAT!
SCHULZ

June 6, 1981

6-6

BEAN BAGS ARE A BOON TO SULKERS
SCHULZ

June 12, 1981

NOW!

THANK YOU

June 13, 1981

July 8, 1981

RATS...

SULKING IS SPOILED WHEN YOU CAN'T GET COMFORTABLE

July 9, 1981

ARE YOU SULKING OR ARE YOU WATCHING TV?
I'M SULKING

WELL, AS LONG AS YOU'RE JUST SULKING, WOULD YOU MIND IF I WATCHED THE TV?

YES, I'D MIND!

WHEN YOU'RE SULKING, YOU NEVER COOPERATE WITH ANYONE!

July 11, 1981

HOW ABOUT THAT?
HOW ABOUT WHAT?

I THINK YOU'VE SET A NEW RECORD...

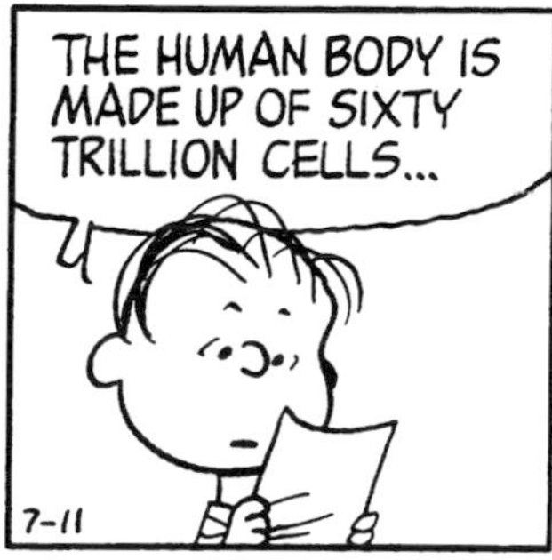
THE HUMAN BODY IS MADE UP OF SIXTY TRILLION CELLS...
7-11

YOURS ARE ALL SULKING AT THE SAME TIME!
SCHULZ

July 30, 1981

?

WHO WAS THAT?

DON'T ASK
7-30

JOE PREPPY
SCHULZ

"Snoopy's philosophy is to try to look good at a distance."

August 21, 1981

WHAT KIND OF A WATCHDOG ARE YOU?
8-21

HOW CAN YOU GUARD OUR HOUSE IF YOU'RE SITTING OUT HERE EATING PIZZA?

I DON'T KNOW WHAT YOU EXPECT US TO DO IF A BURGLAR COMES INTO OUR HOUSE...

SEND HIM OUT HERE.. I'LL BARK AT HIM!
SCHULZ

September 7, 1981

IT'S A CARRY-ON BAG...ISN'T IT NEAT?

IT'S BEAUTIFUL...ARE YOU GOING SOMEWHERE?

NO, I HATE GOING PLACES
9-7

I JUST LIKE LUGGAGE
SCHULZ

September 14, 1981

I HAVE A SLIVER IN MY FINGER, AND I CAN'T GET IT OUT

NO PROBLEM..I'LL FIND A PAIR OF TWEEZERS, AND WE'LL HAVE IT OUT IN NO TIME...
9-14

OKAY, HERE WE GO...

THAT'S CLOSE ENOUGH!!
SCHULZ

September 15, 1981

HOW CAN I GET THE SLIVER OUT OF YOUR FINGER IF YOU WON'T LET ME NEAR YOU?

I DON'T WANT YOU POKING AROUND WITH THOSE TWEEZERS!
9-15

OKAY, WISE GUY, HOW ARE YOU GONNA GET IT OUT?

IF I SHAKE MY HAND REAL HARD, MAYBE IT'LL FALL OUT!
SCHULZ

September 16, 1981

ALL RIGHT, WHICH FINGER HAS THE SLIVER? THIS ONE? GOOD...

HOLD STILL NOW WHILE I..

I SAID TO HOLD REAL STILL!
NO, YOU SAID TO HOLD STILL

"REAL STILL" IS WHEN YOU DON'T MOVE AT ALL.. THIS IS HOLDING STILL...
9-16
SCHULZ

September 17, 1981

YOU HAVE A SLIVER, TOO? LET ME SEE...

I HOPE YOU'RE NOT AS BIG A COWARD AS MY STUPID BROTHER...

HOLD REAL STILL NOW WHILE I..
IT'S GONNA HURT
9/17

WHAT DID YOU SAY THAT FOR?
SCHULZ

September 18, 1981

ALL RIGHT, YOU TWO, THIS IS RIDICULOUS! I'M NOT PERFORMING OPEN-HEART SURGERY! I'M JUST TAKING OUT TWO TINY SLIVERS!

I WANT YOU BOTH TO STAND PERFECTLY STILL, AND ACT LIKE MEN!
9-18

I'M NOT A MAN, I'M A DOG!

I'M JUST A LITTLE KID!
SCHULZ

September 26, 1981

I'VE BEEN THINKING... MAYBE YOU'RE A MOCKINGBIRD...

MOCKINGBIRDS IMITATE THE SONGS OF OTHER BIRDS...
9-26

?

NO, I'VE NEVER HEARD OF ANY COPYRIGHT PROBLEMS
SCHULZ

September 30, 1981

YOU SHOULD GO OVER AND TALK WITH THAT LITTLE RED-HAIRED GIRL, CHARLIE BROWN

ASK HER TO EAT LUNCH WITH YOU

TELL HER YOU'D BE HAPPY JUST TO BE WITH HER FOR AN HOUR OR SO
9-30

AN HOUR? I'D SETTLE FOR AN "OR SO"!
SCHULZ

October 14, 1981

MISUNDERSTANDING? ISN'T THIS THE SCHOOL FOR GIFTED CHILDREN? AREN'T YOU GONNA FILL MY BAG WITH GIFTS?

BUT I THOUGHT... I WAS SURE THAT... AREN'T YOU... I MEAN... I...
10-14

OH, NO!

IF ANYONE ASKS FOR ME, I WAS NEVER HERE!
SCHULZ

October 16, 1981

I NEED TO TALK TO SOMEONE WHO KNOWS WHAT IT'S LIKE TO FEEL LIKE A FOOL

SOMEONE WHO KNOWS WHAT IT'S LIKE TO BE HUMILIATED...

SOMEONE WHO'S BEEN DISGRACED, BEATEN AND DEGRADED.... SOMEONE WHO'S BEEN THERE...

10-16
SCHULZ

October 20, 1981

"PIGPEN"! I HAVEN'T SEEN YOU FOR A LONG TIME...

OBVIOUSLY, YOU ARE JUST AS MESSY AS EVER!
10-20

THE WORLD NEEDS MESSY PEOPLE...
© 1981 United Feature Syndicate, Inc.

OTHERWISE THE NEAT PEOPLE WOULD TAKE OVER!
SCHULZ

October 21, 1981

10-21

SCHULZ

November 10, 1981

11-10

BOING!!

SCHULZ

November 23, 1981

THIS HAS BEEN A GOOD DAY...I HAVEN'T DONE A SINGLE THING THAT WAS STUPID...

HAVE YOU DONE ANYTHING THAT WAS SMART?
© 1981 United Feature Syndicate, Inc.

11-23
SCHULZ

December 16, 1981

PSYCHIATRIC HELP 50¢
THINK ABOUT THIS, CHARLIE BROWN...
THE DOCTOR IS IN

MAYBE YOU'RE THE KIND WHO'S AFRAID TO ALLOW HIMSELF TO GET UPSET...
© 1981 United Feature Syndicate, Inc.

SOMETIMES PEOPLE ACTUALLY CATCH COLDS JUST BECAUSE OF SOME SEVERE FRUSTRATION OR DISAPPOINTMENT...

YCHIATRIC HELP 50¢
AH-CHOO!!
THE DOCTOR IS IN
SCHULZ
12/16

December 18, 1981

TELL ME WHAT YOU THINK OF THIS...

IT'S MY OWN COMPOSITION
12-18
© 1981 United Feature Syndicate, Inc.

THAT'S NICE...I LIKE CHRISTMAS MUSIC..
SCHULZ

December 30, 1981

12-30

THERE'S NO EVENT IN THE WINTER OLYMPICS CALLED "THE DOWNHILL SUPPER DISH"!

THEY'RE MISSING A GOOD BET!
SCHULZ

February 3, 1982

HERE'S THE WORLD FAMOUS HOCKEY PLAYER STANDING FOR THE NATIONAL ANTHEM

2-3

THAT'S THE LONGEST I'VE EVER GONE WITHOUT A PENALTY!
SCHULZ

February 14, 1982

PEANUTS
featuring
"Good ol' Charlie Brown"
by SCHULZ

HERE..

WHAT'S THIS?
IT'S A VALENTINE I MADE FOR THE LITTLE RED-HAIRED GIRL... I WANT YOU TO LOOK IT OVER...

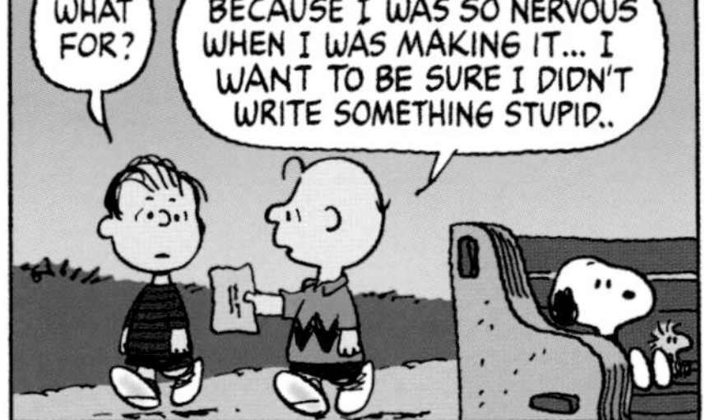
WHAT FOR?
BECAUSE I WAS SO NERVOUS WHEN I WAS MAKING IT... I WANT TO BE SURE I DIDN'T WRITE SOMETHING STUPID..

WELL, IT LOOKS FINE TO ME, CHARLIE BROWN.. YOU DREW A NICE HEART, AND YOU WROTE, "HAPPY VALENTINE'S DAY" AND YOU SIGNED IT VERY NICELY...

HOW ABOUT HER NAME ON THE ENVELOPE?
YOU GOT THAT RIGHT... WAIT A MINUTE.. WHAT'S THIS ON THE BACK?

I DON'T KNOW.. I WAS SO NERVOUS.. I CAN'T REMEMBER...
I THINK YOU'LL PROBABLY WANT TO CHANGE THIS..
2-14

" DO NOT OPEN UNTIL CHRISTMAS"
SCHULZ

February 9, 1982

I DON'T KNOW.. MAYBE I'M JUST GETTING BORED

SOMETIMES I THINK I'VE SEEN EVERYTHING

2-9

I WAS WRONG... THAT'S THE FIRST TIME I'VE EVER SEEN A BUSH PILOT!
SCHULZ

February 15, 1982

HERE'S THE WORLD FAMOUS ATTORNEY ON HIS WAY TO THE COURT HOUSE...
2-15

" FIAT JUSTITIA RUAT COELUM!"

" LET JUSTICE BE DONE THOUGH THE HEAVENS FALL!"

THAT COULD RUIN MY WHOLE CASE
SCHULZ

"Looking back, I see that the best thing my parents did for me was simply not get in my way. That's sound advice for a parent trying to encourage an artistic child. If you can provide him or her with pen, paper, colors, a table, and a place to work, you've done it all."

February 22, 1982

AS SOON AS THIS GROUND IS SPADED, I'M GOING TO ORGANIZE MY GARDEN

I'M GOING TO PLANT POTATOES, AND BEANS, AND RADISHES AND PEAS

WHY ARE YOU TELLING ME ALL THIS?
2-22

OH!
SCHULZ

February 23, 1982

YOU WANT ME TO SPADE YOUR GARDEN? I'M NOT USED TO PHYSICAL LABOR!

THEN YOU SHOULD GET USED TO IT... IT'LL BE GOOD FOR YOU!

2-23

DOES THIS THING HAVE A "FAST FORWARD"?
SCHULZ

February 24, 1982

2-24

I NEED A PUSH!
SCHULZ

February 25, 1982

I THINK I HATE GARDENING
2-25
SCHULZ

February 26, 1982

I'M EXHAUSTED.. I CAN'T MOVE

I'LL NEVER BE A FARM WORKER

I CAN'T EVEN GET UP...
2-26

JUST DUMP ME BY THE SIDE OF THE ROAD
SCHULZ

March 1, 1982

OKAY, HIRED HAND... HERE'S WHAT I WANT YOU TO DO...
3-1

I NEED THIS WHOLE YARD SPADED SO I CAN PLANT MY GARDEN..

ARE YOU SURE YOU'VE DONE THIS KIND OF WORK BEFORE?

SCHULZ

March 4, 1982

3-4

I ALWAYS WONDERED WHAT HAPPENED TO OLD WORN-OUT HIRED HANDS
SCHULZ

March 5, 1982

WHAT ARE YOU GUYS DOING?

WE'RE HELPING LUCY PLANT HER GARDEN... FIRST WE SPADED IT..NOW WE'RE PLANTING IT...
3-5

ACTUALLY, WE JUST DO WHAT WE'RE TOLD..
WELL, IT LOOKS VERY NICE... WHAT ARE YOU PLANTING?

FRENCH FRIES
SCHULZ

April 1, 1982

RATS!

WHAT COULD BE WORSE THAN THE LONG WALK HOME AFTER LOSING THE FIRST GAME OF THE SEASON?
4-1

SCHULZ

May 12, 1982

A KNIGHT?

NO, THIS ISN'T A CASTLE...THIS IS A DOG HOUSE!

NO, THAT ISN'T A MOAT... THAT'S MY WATER DISH..

5-12
I GUESS IT COULD BE A MOAT, THOUGH, COULDN'T IT?
SCHULZ

May 14, 1982

YOU'RE GOING TO ATTACK THIS CASTLE?

WELL, I DON'T THINK YOU SHOULD BECAUSE DO YOU KNOW WHO LIVES HERE?

AN UGLY GIANT!!!

THAT WAS FUN!
SCHULZ
5-14

May 20, 1982

WELL, SCHOOL, IT'S ALMOST VACATION TIME

I SUPPOSE YOU HAVE PLANS FOR THE SUMMER
5-20

I HAVE AN UNCLE IN NEW MEXICO I'D LIKE TO VISIT...THE REST OF OUR FAMILY DOESN'T CARE MUCH FOR HIM

HE'S ADOBE
SCHULZ

May 21, 1982

THEY SAY YOUR GRANDFATHER WAS A HOTEL IN PARIS... IS THAT TRUE ?

ABSOLUTELY! WHAT A GREAT LIFE HE LED... LONG LINES OF TAXIS PULLING UP IN FRONT...

BEAUTIFUL LADIES... FANCY GENTLEMEN ALL DRESSED UP...
5-21

WHAT DO I GET? SCHOOL BUSES, RAINCOATS AND RUBBER BOOTS!
SCHULZ

May 25, 1982

FISHING FOR COMPLIMENTS?

THAT'S THE DUMBEST THING I'VE EVER HEARD!!
5-25

"YOU'RE SWEET...YOU HAVE NICE EYES...YOU'RE KIND OF CUTE...YOU HAVE A GREAT BOD..."
SCHULZ

May 26, 1982

ANYONE WHO WOULD SIT BY A LAKE ALL DAY FISHING FOR COMPLIMENTS HAS TO BE CRAZY...

5-26

"YOU'RE CUTE"

TOO SMALL!
SCHULZ

May 28, 1982

I THOUGHT YOU WERE GOING TO THE LAKE TO FISH FOR COMPLIMENTS
5-28

I'VE GIVEN THAT UP...

IT TOOK ME AWHILE, BUT I FINALLY DISCOVERED SOMETHING...

YOU CAN'T EAT COMPLIMENTS!
SCHULZ

June 29, 1982

SEE WHAT I DID?

I PAINTED LITTLE FLOWERS ON THE SIDE OF YOUR SUPPER DISH

IT'S TO GIVE YOU THE ILLUSION THAT YOUR LIFE IS MORE INTERESTING THAN IT REALLY IS...
6-29

HOW THOUGHTFUL
SCHULZ

July 8, 1982

THERE'S THAT LITTLE RED-HAIRED GIRL STANDING IN THIS SAME LINE FOR THE MOVIES

GO AHEAD, AND STAND WITH HER...DON'T BE SO WISHY-WASHY...
7-8

I'LL JUST STAND HERE WITH MY SWEET BABBOO...
SCHULZ

I'M NOT YOUR SWEET BABBOO!
BUT I'M SURE WISHY-WASHY!

July 12, 1982—First appearance of Snoopy as the World-Famous Surgeon.

HERE'S THE WORLD FAMOUS SURGEON ON HIS WAY TO THE OPERATING ROOM...

DOCTOR, IT SAYS HERE THAT AFTER SURGERY, FIFTY PERCENT OF YOUR PATIENTS FEEL PRETTY GOOD FOR HALF AN HOUR

DO THOSE STATISTICS BOTHER YOU?

NO, I'M VERY EASY GOING
SCHULZ
7-12

August 11, 1982

NOW THAT WE DON'T HAVE A FIELD TO PLAY BASEBALL ON, I HAVE TO BOUNCE A GOLF BALL AGAINST THE STEPS...

IT'S NOT QUITE THE SAME, THOUGH, IS IT?

BONK!

PRETTY MUCH

August 18, 1982

I'VE ALWAYS BEEN FOND OF YOU, CHARLES... I THINK YOU'RE THE NICEST PERSON I'VE EVER KNOWN..

I HATE TO SEE YOU SUFFER ALL THE TIME

I KNOW YOU COULD NEVER LOVE SOMEONE LIKE ME WHO WEARS GLASSES SO I'LL JUST LEAVE YOU ALONE

HOW DOES HE DO THAT?

"I like drawing Charlie Brown's hat and Peppermint Patty's hair. If one line doesn't go where you want it, you can always bring it back."

August 20, 1982

I THINK I FRIGHTENED POOR CHUCK..MAYBE IT'S A MISTAKE TO TALK SO OPENLY ABOUT LOVE...

NO, MARCIE, NO! YOU WERE JUST BEING HONEST!

REALLY, SIR? I DIDN'T THINK YOU KNEW ANYTHING ABOUT LOVE
MARCIE!

I DID IT AGAIN..

August 25, 1982

I HEAR CHUCK GOT HIS BASEBALL FIELD BACK...

I GUESS SO..I HAVEN'T SEEN HIM SINCE I MADE A FOOL OF MYSELF

IS YOUR HEART BROKEN, MARCIE?

NO, BUT IT SURE IS BENT!

July 18, 1982

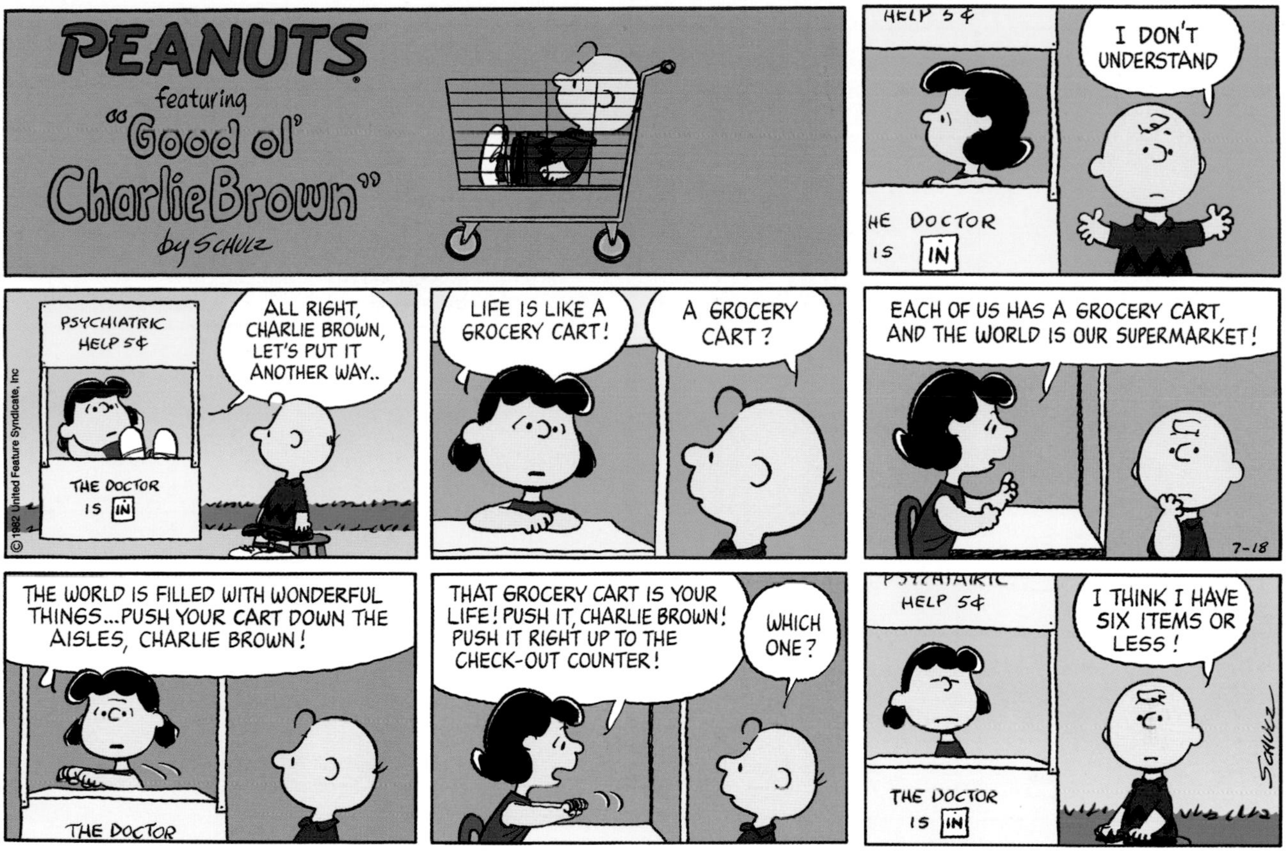

PEANUTS featuring "Good ol' Charlie Brown" by Schulz

I DON'T UNDERSTAND

ALL RIGHT, CHARLIE BROWN, LET'S PUT IT ANOTHER WAY..

LIFE IS LIKE A GROCERY CART!

A GROCERY CART?

EACH OF US HAS A GROCERY CART, AND THE WORLD IS OUR SUPERMARKET!

THE WORLD IS FILLED WITH WONDERFUL THINGS...PUSH YOUR CART DOWN THE AISLES, CHARLIE BROWN!

THAT GROCERY CART IS YOUR LIFE! PUSH IT, CHARLIE BROWN! PUSH IT RIGHT UP TO THE CHECK-OUT COUNTER!

WHICH ONE?

I THINK I HAVE SIX ITEMS OR LESS!

"Five-cent psychiatry? I can't remember when I started Lucy doing that or why. Maybe it was because in our society we all need somewhere we can go and talk to somebody for an hour for just a nickel."

August 27, 1982

DID YOU KNOW THAT MY HEART IS BENT, CHARLES?
MARCIE! I'M TRYING TO PITCH!
ALL I DID WAS TELL YOU THAT I'VE ALWAYS BEEN FOND OF YOU..IF I OFFENDED YOU, I'M SORRY.
SHUT UP! CAN'T YOU SEE WE'RE TALKING?!!
I NEVER MEANT TO OFFEND YOU, CHARLES..
I THINK I'M FALLING OVER BACKWARDS..

August 28, 1982

I GUESS ALL I REALLY WANT, CHARLES, IS FOR YOU TO TELL ME THAT YOU'RE NOT MAD AT ME...

OH, YEAH? WELL, WHO CARES ABOUT YOUR STUPID BALL GAME?!

CHARLES? CHARLES? WHERE DID YOU GO?

MAYBE I WAS WRONG... MAYBE I'M NOT SO FOND OF HIM AFTER ALL!

September 24, 1982

"DEAR SNOOPY, I HAVE LOST MY HOME...CAN YOU HELP ME? AM ARRIVING SOON...YOUR BROTHER, 'MARBLES'"

"MARBLES" IS COMING HERE? HOW CAN I FIND HIM A HOME?

I HARDLY REMEMBER HIM...

RELATIVES ARE LIKE MAIL-ORDER CATALOGS...THEY COME OUT OF NOWHERE...

September 28, 1982—First appearance of Marbles.

SO YOU'RE "MARBLES"

I KNOW YOUR WEIRD BROTHER

WELL, ANYWAY, HE AN' CHUCK ARE ON THEIR WAY OVER.. COME ON INSIDE, AND WAIT...

ANY CATS IN THERE?

September 30, 1982

SNOOPY! MARBLES!

AREN'T FAMILY REUNIONS SOMETHING, CHUCK? TWO BROTHERS, WHO HAVEN'T SEEN EACH OTHER FOR YEARS, ARE SUDDENLY REUNITED!

JUST THINK OF THE MILLIONS OF THINGS THEY HAVE TO TALK ABOUT

HOW'VE YOU BEEN?
FINE..HOW HAVE YOU BEEN?

October 1, 1982

I GUESS I'VE LIVED WITH FOUR OR FIVE DIFFERENT FAMILIES...I'M NOT SURE...

I WAS INTO RESEARCH FOR A WHILE..I SPENT WEEKS RESEARCHING WHY SOME DOGS WALK AT AN ANGLE

I DECIDED IT'S TO KEEP THEIR BACK FEET FROM HITTING THEIR FRONT FEET

THAT'S PRETTY DEEP STUFF..
SOMEONE HAD TO DO IT!

October 2, 1982

MY LIFE HERE IS SORT OF SIMPLE..I JUST HANG AROUND...

THEN EACH NIGHT, THE ROUND-HEADED KID BRINGS MY SUPPER, AND I DANCE UP AND DOWN LIKE THIS...

SUPPERTIME! SUPPERTIME! OH, IT'S SUPPERTIME!

I DON'T THINK I COULD DO THAT...
10-2
SCHULZ

October 5, 1982

MARBLES! MY CIVILIAN BROTHER! WHAT ARE YOU DOING HERE AT THE FRONT?
FRONT?

HERE'S THE WORLD WAR I FLYING ACE SHOWING HIS CIVILIAN BROTHER AROUND THE AERODROME..CAREFUL! DON'T STEP ON THAT LAND MINE!

LAND MINE ?
AND OVER HERE IS MY PLANE... MY SOPWITH CAMEL!
10-5

SOPWITH CAMEL?
IT'S OBVIOUS MY CIVILIAN BROTHER IS AWED...
SCHULZ

"There's not much room in comic strips for drastic change. All you can do is try to improve a little bit each day, or try some new directions now and then, if you can then maybe introduce a new character—but not on purpose. I think new characters should come because of some idea that you have had."

October 6, 1982

HERE'S THE WORLD WAR I FLYING ACE AND HIS CIVILIAN BROTHER WALKING OUT ONTO THE AERODROME

AERODROME?
HIS BROTHER IS IN LUCK..

THE FLYING ACE HAS AGREED TO TAKE HIM ALONG ON A MISSION

I'M IN LUCK?
CONTACT!
SCHULZ
10-6

October 7, 1982

THE RED BARON HAS BEEN SIGHTED NEAR DOUAI...OUR MISSION IS TO BRING HIM DOWN...
10-7

SUDDENLY, ANTIAIRCRAFT FIRE BURSTS AROUND US!
IT DOES?

ONLY THE SUPERB SKILL OF THE FLYING ACE KEEPS THEM UNTOUCHED

HE WAS ALWAYS THE QUIET ONE IN THE FAMILY...
SCHULZ

October 11, 1982

YOUR BROTHER LEFT TOWN THIS MORNING
MARBLES IS GONE?

I HAVE THE FEELING HE NEVER QUITE UNDERSTOOD THAT WHOLE RED BARON SOPWITH CAMEL THING...

ANYWAY, IT'S ALMOST SUPPERTIME..WHERE DO YOU WANT TO EAT TONIGHT?
10-11

RIGHT HERE AT THE OFFICER'S CLUB
SCHULZ

November 20, 1982

HOPELESS!
11-20

I'LL JUST HAVE TO WAIT UNTIL IT SNOWS...

YOU SURE CAN'T BUILD A FOG MAN!
SCHULZ

November 24, 1982

"DEAR CONTRIBUTOR.."

"THANK YOU FOR SUBMITTING YOUR STORY"

"WE REGRET THAT IT DOES NOT SUIT OUR PRESENT NEEDS"

"IF IT EVER DOES, WE'RE IN TROUBLE"
SCHULZ
11-24

December 8, 1982

WAAH!

STOP CRYING, RERUN... HAVE A COOKIE

JUST REMEMBER THIS... THE DAY IS COMING WHEN A COOKIE WON'T SOLVE ALL YOUR PROBLEMS

12-8
UNTIL THEN!
SCHULZ

December 11, 1982

WHY DO WE ALWAYS TEACH LITTLE KIDS TO WAVE "BYE-BYE"?

BECAUSE FOR THE REST OF HIS LIFE PEOPLE WILL BE LEAVING HIM

12-11

HELLO, THERE!
SCHULZ

December 14, 1982

I'M GOING TO TRY TO SELL CHRISTMAS WREATHS FROM DOOR TO DOOR
12-14

GETTING ON THE OL' COMMERCIAL BANDWAGON, EH? GOING AFTER THOSE BIG HOLIDAY BUCKS, HUH?

NEED ANY HELP?
© 1982 United Feature Syndicate, Inc.
SCHULZ

December 17, 1982

NO ONE SEEMS TO WANT TO BUY A CHRISTMAS WREATH

I THINK WE NEED BETTER PACKAGING

WE NEED A BETTER WAY TO SHOW OFF OUR PRODUCT...
© 1982 United Feature Syndicate, Inc.
12-17

GOOD MORNING! WOULD YOU LIKE TO BUY A CHRISTMAS WREATH?
SCHULZ

December 18, 1982

GOOD MORNING, MA'AM

HOW WOULD YOU LIKE TO BUY A NICE CHRISTMAS NOSE?

I MEAN "WREATH"! HOW EMBARRASSING!!

I'M GOING HOME!
© 1982 United Feature Syndicate, Inc.
SCHULZ
12-18

January 9, 1983

PEANUTS
featuring
"Good ol' CharlieBrown"
by SCHULZ

1-9

!
?

YOU KNOW WHAT I JUST SAW? A TINY BIRD JUST WALKED BY WITH FIVE HATS ON HIS HEAD, AND I THINK HE WAS CRYING..
YOU'RE WEIRD, MARCIE!
SCHULZ

January 13, 1983

CHOP
CHOP
CHOP
CHOP
1-13

CHOP CHOP CHOP
CHOP
CHOP

WHOOP!

THE TRAFFIC HELICOPTER REPORTS, "ICY SIDEWALKS"
SCHULZ

January 18, 1983

SO HERE I AM AGAIN, RIDING ON THE BACK OF MY MOTHER'S BICYCLE...

WHAT HAPPENS? SHE MEETS A FRIEND, AND WE STOP TO TALK...

IN THE MEANTIME, I'M STARVING TO DEATH
1-18

I DON'T THINK I CAN EXIST SUCKING THE JUICE FROM A WET MITTEN...
SCHULZ

January 19, 1983

Question: Why was Washington's Farewell Address important?

THIS IS A HARD ONE, ISN'T IT, SIR?

NOT IF YOU THINK ABOUT IT, MARCIE

I JUST PUT DOWN, "SO WHEN HE MOVED, THEY'D KNOW WHERE TO SEND HIS MAGAZINES"
SCHULZ
1-19

January 22, 1983

THAT'S A WEIRD-LOOKING SNOWMAN

NOT SO WEIRD...HE'S JUST COME IN FROM WORKING IN THE SNOWFIELDS

AND SEE WHAT'S IN HIS HAND?

A NICE COLD GLASS OF SNOW!
1-22
SCHULZ

January 26, 1983

DON'T YOU THINK SO?

ABSOLUTELY NOT!
1/26

BUT I CAN UNDERSTAND WHY YOU BELIEVE THAT

WHEN I WAS YOUR AGE, I WAS DUMB, TOO
SCHULZ

February 11, 1983

DID YOU SEE MY "SWEET BABBOO" STANDING THERE?

HE'S HANGING AROUND THE CANDY STORE TRYING TO DECIDE WHAT TO GET ME FOR VALENTINE'S DAY...
2-11

IT'LL PROBABLY BE A BOX OF CANDY SHAPED LIKE A BIG HEART...

ISN'T HE THE CUTEST THING?
OR A BIG **ZERO**!
SCHULZ

February 16, 1983

YOU DIDN'T SEND MY SISTER A VALENTINE... YOU BROKE HER HEART..

TECHNICALLY, I SHOULD PUNCH YOU IN THE NOSE!

I HOPE YOU DON'T

YOU'D PROBABLY MISS, AND HIT ME IN THE EYE!

February 17, 1983

WHAT COULD I DO, CHARLIE BROWN? YOUR SISTER FOLLOWS ME AROUND CALLING ME HER "SWEET BABBOO"

I NEVER SAID I WAS GOING TO GIVE HER A VALENTINE! IT WAS ALL IN HER IMAGINATION!

SO IF YOU STILL WANT TO PUNCH ME IN THE NOSE, GO RIGHT AHEAD!

WHY DON'T I JUST HOLD MY FIST OUT, AND THEN YOU WALK INTO IT?

February 18, 1983

I FEEL GRUMPY TODAY.. I DON'T WANT TO TALK TO ANYBODY OR SEE ANYBODY!

I'LL HOLD MY FIST OUT, LINUS, AND YOU WALK INTO IT...
GET OUT OF MY WAY!

BONK!

DID IT HURT?
NO, BUT IT MIGHT LATER IF WE STICK AROUND

February 19, 1983

WHAT HAPPENED?
YOU HIT ME, YOU BLOCKHEAD!

I DIDN'T HIT YOU...YOU RAN INTO MY FIST
WHAT WAS YOUR FIST DOING IN THE MIDDLE OF THE SIDEWALK?

IF YOUR BROTHER HAD GIVEN MY SISTER A VALENTINE, THIS NEVER WOULD HAVE HAPPENED...

THAT'S RIGHT! IT WAS MY SWEET BABBOO'S FAULT!
I'M NOT YOUR SWEET BABBOO!

March 20, 1983

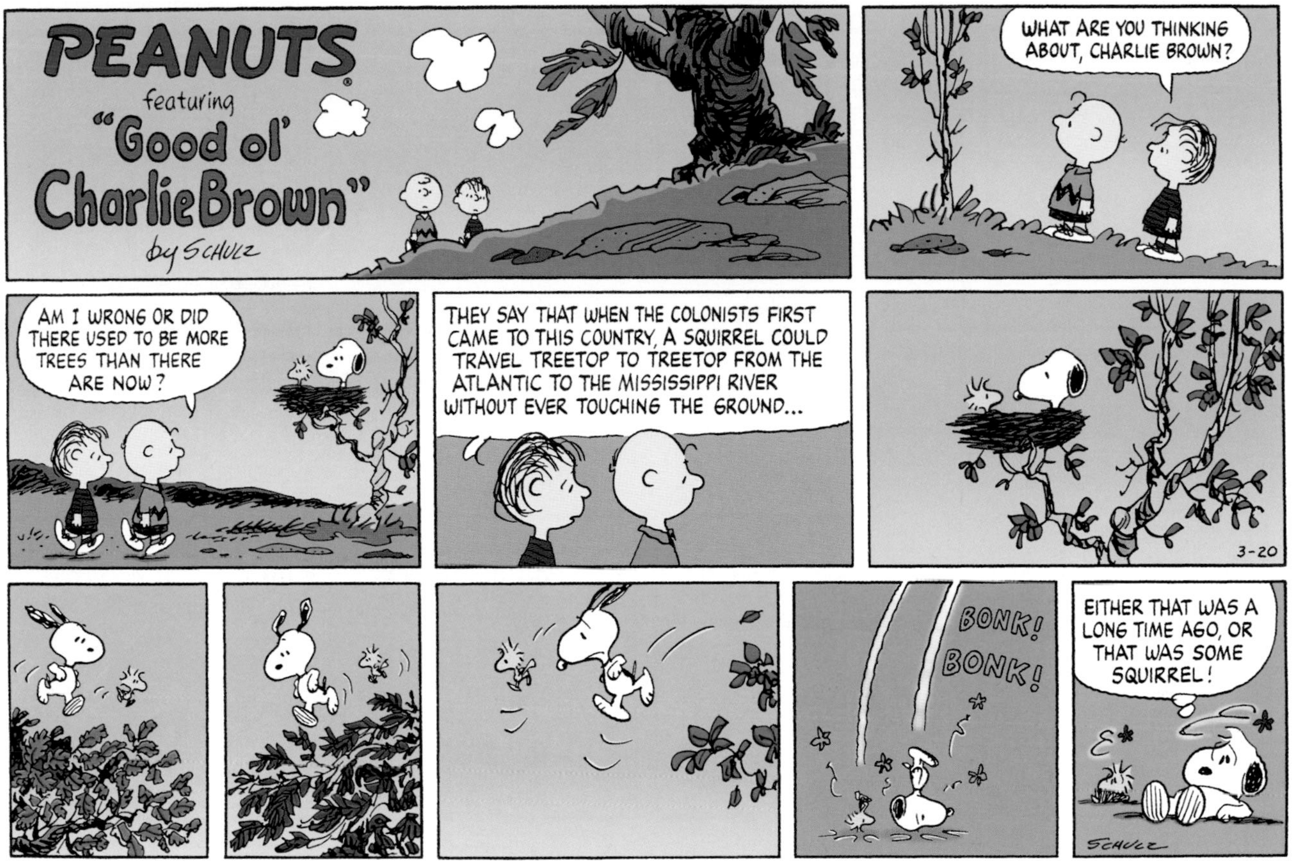

PEANUTS
featuring
"Good ol' CharlieBrown"
by SCHULZ
WHAT ARE YOU THINKING ABOUT, CHARLIE BROWN?
AM I WRONG OR DID THERE USED TO BE MORE TREES THAN THERE ARE NOW?
THEY SAY THAT WHEN THE COLONISTS FIRST CAME TO THIS COUNTRY, A SQUIRREL COULD TRAVEL TREETOP TO TREETOP FROM THE ATLANTIC TO THE MISSISSIPPI RIVER WITHOUT EVER TOUCHING THE GROUND...
3-20
BONK!
BONK!
EITHER THAT WAS A LONG TIME AGO, OR THAT WAS SOME SQUIRREL!
SCHULZ

April 11, 1983

NOTICE ANYTHING?
LIKE WHAT?
MY BLANKET IS GONE!! I'VE GIVEN IT UP! I DON'T NEED IT ANYMORE!
4-11
WHEN DID THIS HAPPEN?
SCHULZ

FOUR MINUTES AGO!

"Linus, my serious side, is the house intellectual, bright, well-informed, which, I suppose, may contribute to his feelings of insecurity."

April 15, 1983

GOOD MORNING, LITTLE GIRL.. YOU SURE ARE A CUTE LITTLE THING...I SEE YOU HAVE A SECURITY BLANKET..

WOULD YOU LIKE TO HAVE ME TELL YOU HOW I BROKE MYSELF OF THAT HABIT?
4-15

SNAP!!

STUPID KID!!!

April 18, 1983

I RAN AN AD IN THE PAPER FOR MY CLINIC
YOUR CLINIC?

I'M GOING TO TEACH LITTLE KIDS HOW TO GIVE UP THEIR BLANKETS! HUNDREDS OF KIDS WILL COME KNOCKING ON MY DOOR!

KNOCK KNOCK KNOCK KNOCK

HERE'S YOUR HUNDRED KIDS!
MY FOLKS MADE ME COME!

April 19, 1983

HI, MY NAME IS LINUS... I TAKE IT YOU'VE COME HERE TO LEARN HOW TO GIVE UP YOUR BLANKET

MY FOLKS MADE ME COME
"CAN A BLIND MAN LEAD A BLIND MAN? WILL THEY NOT BOTH FALL INTO A PIT?"

DON'T PAY ANY ATTENTION TO HER... SHE'S JUST MY SISTER

I DIDN'T COME HERE TO FALL INTO NO PIT!

April 20, 1983

YOU SAY YOUR NAME IS RANDOLPH? OKAY, RANDOLPH, LET'S GET TO WORK...

I'M GOING TO HELP YOU TO GIVE UP YOUR BLANKET... FIRST, HOWEVER, I HAVE TO ASK YOU A FEW PERSONAL QUESTIONS..

MAY I ASK WHY YOU WEAR YOUR BLANKET OVER YOUR HEAD?

SO YOU WON'T SEE THE THREE TEDDY BEARS I'M HOLDING!

April 21, 1983

I THINK THE FIRST THING WE SHOULD CONSIDER ABOUT CLINGING TO A SECURITY BLANKET IS GUILT

I DON'T FEEL GUILTY

GOOD! NOW, THERE'S ALSO EMBARRASSMENT
THAT'S NO PROBLEM, EITHER

NOW MENTION STUPIDITY!

April 22, 1983

BEFORE WE CONTINUE WITH YOUR TREATMENT, WE NEED TO DO SOMETHING..

I'M GOING TO ASK YOU TO TAKE THE BLANKET OFF YOUR HEAD...

ANYTHING YOU SAY...
4-22

IT'S ME, SWEET BABBOO!
AAUGH!
SCHULZ

April 23, 1983

4-23

I COULD HAVE GIVEN UP THIS BLANKET...

BUT I WAS DRIVEN BACK TO IT BY TREACHERY!!

NO OFFENSE...
SCHULZ

April 26, 1983

4-26

STRIKE THREE!

SCHULZ

May 2, 1983

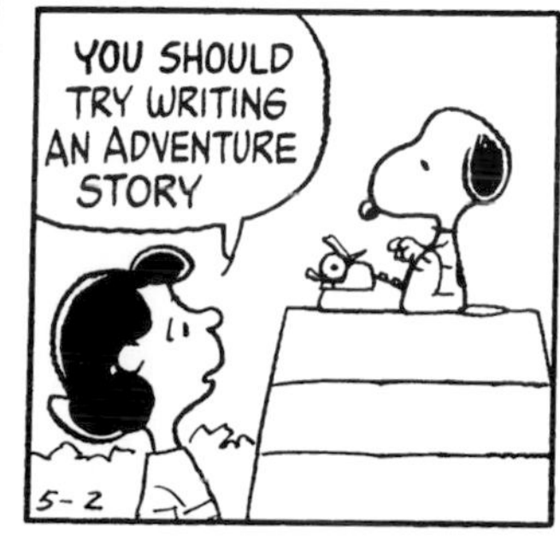
YOU SHOULD TRY WRITING AN ADVENTURE STORY
5-2

TRY WRITING ABOUT A REAL HERO TYPE

He was a dark and stormy knight.
SCHULZ

May 8, 1983

PEANUTS
featuring "Good ol' CharlieBrown"
by SCHULZ
Welcome, MOM!
THIS IS A PERFECT SPOT
I HAVE A FEELING THAT IF WE SIT HERE LONG ENOUGH, WE JUST MIGHT SEE YOUR MOTHER FLY BY... THEN YOU CAN GIVE HER THE FLOWER...
I DON'T SUPPOSE THAT WAS HER, WAS IT ?
NO, THAT'S A 747... SHE WAS NEVER THAT FAT, WAS SHE ? I HOPE NOT...
WHOOPS! THAT WASN'T HER..SOMEONE HIT A VOLLEY OVER THE FENCE...
NOPE..WRONG SPECIES
5-8
JUST A CLOUD
MAYBE I'LL WRITE A SONG.. "MOTHER'S DAY ISN'T MOTHER'S DAY 'TIL YOUR MOTHER FLIES BY"
SIGH
SCHULZ

"Woodstock knows that he is very small and inconsequential indeed. It's a problem we all have. The universe boggles us. In the larger scheme, we suddenly realize, we amount to very little. It's frightening. Only a certain maturity will make us able to cope. The minute we abandon the quest for it we leave ourselves open to tragic results. Woodstock is a lighthearted expression of that idea."

June 20, 1983

OKAY, DOES EACH OF YOU HAVE A CAMERA?

GOOD! WE ARE NOW GOING ON WHAT IS CALLED A PHOTO HIKE

THE IDEA, OF COURSE, IS TO GIVE YOU THE CHANCE TO TAKE SOME BEAUTIFUL AND MAYBE UNUSUAL PICTURES...
6-20

NOT NECESSARILY OF YOURSELVES!
SCHULZ

June 23, 1983

THERE IT IS, GANG..THE PACIFIC OCEAN!

NOW, I WANT TO SEE YOU TAKE A LOT OF PICTURES..THAT'S WHAT WE'RE HERE FOR...
6-23

WHAT ARE YOU TAKING A PICTURE OF, OLIVIER... THE OCEAN? GOOD!

NO, I CAN'T ASK IT TO SMILE
SCHULZ

June 24, 1983

NOW, REMEMBER, WE HAVEN'T COME ALL THE WAY TO "POINT LOBOS" JUST TO TAKE VACATION PICTURES!

I WANT EACH OF YOU TO LOOK AROUND FOR POSSIBLE PHOTOGRAPHS THAT MAY HAVE REAL...

6-24
CLICK!

..ARTISTIC QUALITY!
SCHULZ

June 27, 1983

BEAUTIFUL, ISN'T IT?

MAYBE, WHEN WE GET BACK, YOU CAN SELL SOME OF YOUR PHOTOGRAPHS TO A WILDLIFE MAGAZINE...
6-27

WHAT'S WILDLIFE? YOU'RE WILDLIFE

I'M WHAT YOU CALL SEMI-WILDLIFE
SCHULZ

June 30, 1983

OKAY, GANG, IT'S TIME TO HEAD BACK HOME

WHO'S NOT GOING?

BILL AND HARRIET? WHY AREN'T THEY GOING? THEY'RE GETTING WHAT?
6-30

MARRIED?!!!
SCHULZ

July 1, 1983

BILL AND HARRIET GOT MARRIED
7-1

WE CAME ALL THE WAY TO "POINT LOBOS" TO PHOTOGRAPH THE TREES, THE ROCKS, THE OCEAN...

AND WHAT DO WE GET?

WEDDING PICTURES!
CLICK SNAP
SNAP CLICK!
CLICK!
SCHULZ

July 2, 1983

I TAKE MY TROOPS TO "POINT LOBOS" FOR A PHOTO HIKE, AND WHAT HAPPENS?

BILL AND HARRIET GET MARRIED, AND DECIDE TO STAY...
7-2

ANYWAY, IT WAS A BEAUTIFUL WEDDING... IT HAD TO BE...

I WAS "BEST BEAGLE"!
SCHULZ

July 18, 1983

DON'T TALK TO ME, MARCIE!
WHAT DID I DO, SIR?

YOU GOT A LETTER FROM CHUCK, AND I DIDN'T! AND I WAS THE ONE WHO FELT SORRY FOR YOU WHEN YOU WERE LONELY!
7-18

© 1983 United Feature Syndicate, Inc.

WOULD YOU LIKE TO PUSH ME INTO THE LAKE, SIR?
SCHULZ

July 19, 1983

I CAN'T BELIEVE IT... NOW PEPPERMINT PATTY IS MAD AT ME BECAUSE I DIDN'T ANSWER HER LETTER

I HATE WRITING LETTERS!
7-19

Dear Patty

DON'T GIVE UP... SMUDGE YOUR WAY THROUGH..
SCHULZ

July 20, 1983

HEY, LOOK HERE! I GOT A LETTER FROM CHUCK! HOW ABOUT THAT?!

IT SURE HAS A LOT OF SMUDGES, THOUGH, DOESN'T IT? OL' CHUCK'S NOT MUCH FOR WRITING WITH INK...
7-20

I GOTTA WRITE AN' TELL HIM I'M NOT MAD ANYMORE

MAYBE I SHOULD CALL HIM BY A CUTE NICKNAME..
HOW ABOUT "DEAR SMUDGY"?
SCHULZ

August 8, 1983

IT'S VERY STRANGE...

IT HAPPENS JUST BY LOOKING AT YOU
8-8

WHAT HAPPENS?
SCHULZ

I CAN FEEL A CRITICISM COMING ON

August 27, 1983

IN THE OLD DAYS, VULTURES USED TO SIT ON BRANCHES WAITING FOR VICTIMS...

8-27

IN THE OLD DAYS, THEY HAD STRONGER BRANCHES...
SCHULZ

October 6, 1983

BUGS ARE HOLDING THEIR WORLD SERIES IN MY SUPPER DISH?
10-6

I GUESS I'M JUST IN TIME FOR THE OPENING CEREMONIES...

THE NATIONAL ANTHEM, AND THEN MY FAVORITE PART...

..WHEN THEY RELEASE ALL THE BALLOONS!
SCHULZ

November 29, 1983

11-29

"FLASHBEAGLE"!
SCHULZ

October 16, 1983

PEANUTS
featuring
"Good ol' Charlie Brown"
by SCHULZ
SHE'S GOT TO BE KIDDING!

SHE MUST THINK I'M REALLY DUMB...

HERE WE GO, CHARLIE BROWN...I'LL HOLD THE BALL, AND YOU COME RUNNING UP AND KICK IT...

WHAT YOU REALLY MEAN IS, YOU'LL PULL THE BALL AWAY, AND I'LL LAND ON MY BACK AND KILL MYSELF!

WELL, I HAVE NEWS FOR YOU... NEVER AGAIN! FORGET IT!

WAIT!
I SAID, FORGET IT!!

I'M JUST GLAD YOU'RE THE ONLY PERSON IN THE WORLD WHO THINKS I'M DUMB ENOUGH TO FALL FOR THAT TRICK AGAIN...

10-16
SCHULZ

December 16, 1983

THIS IS WHAT I HAVE TO DO IN THE CHRISTMAS PLAY

WHEN THE SHEEP ARE THROUGH DANCING, I COME OUT AND SAY, "HARK!"
12-16

THEN HAROLD ANGEL STARTS TO SING

HAROLD ANGEL?
IT'S RIGHT HERE IN THE SCRIPT...
SCHULZ

December 20, 1983

I'M ALL SET FOR THE CHRISTMAS PLAY..DO I LOOK LIKE AN ANGEL?

YOU LOOK FINE...ARE YOU GOING TO WALK TO THE AUDITORIUM LIKE THAT?

CAN YOU GET YOUR COAT ON OVER YOUR WINGS?

NO PROBLEM
12-20
SCHULZ

December 21, 1983

SO FAR THIS HAS BEEN A GOOD CHRISTMAS PLAY, CHARLIE BROWN...

WHEN DOES YOUR SISTER COME ON?
12-21

RIGHT AFTER THE DANCING SHEEP...SHE STEPS OUT AND SAYS, "HARK!" AND THEN HAROLD ANGEL SINGS

HAROLD ANGEL?
ALL I KNOW IS WHAT SHE TOLD ME...
SCHULZ

December 22, 1983

THE SHEEP ARE THROUGH DANCING, CHARLIE BROWN.. HERE COMES YOUR SISTER...

HOCKEY STICK!

"HOCKEY STICK"?!?
SCHULZ
12/22

December 24, 1983

I DON'T KNOW...I DIDN'T SEE THE REST OF THE PLAY..AS SOON AS SALLY SAID, "HOCKEY STICK," AND EVERYONE LAUGHED, I LEFT

SHE GETS EVERYTHING MIXED UP...SHE EVEN THOUGHT SOMEONE NAMED "HAROLD ANGEL" WAS GOING TO SING!
12-24

EXCUSE ME, SOMEBODY'S AT THE DOOR...

© 1983 United Feature Syndicate, Inc.
HI, IS SALLY HOME? MY NAME IS HAROLD ANGEL..
SCHULZ

January 13, 1984

DON'T SAY I NEVER DO ANYTHING FOR YOU...

I JUST TOOK YOUR BLANKET OUT OF THE DRYER...

BE CAREFUL, IT'S STILL A LITTLE..
1-13

...WARM!
SCHULZ

January 14, 1984

THEY SAY THAT KIDS IN THE OLD DAYS HAD IT TOUGH...
1-14

WHEN YOUR BLANKET IS STILL HOT FROM BEING IN THE DRYER...

I'M NOT SO SURE

I THINK MAYBE THEY HAD IT EASY
SCHULZ

January 30, 1984

HERE'S THE WORLD WAR I FLYING ACE SITTING IN A SMALL FRENCH CAFÉ...
1-30

HE IS VERY NERVOUS FROM HIS MANY DAYS AT THE FRONT...

HE NEEDS SOMETHING TO CALM HIS NERVES...

DECAFFEINATED ROOT BEER, S'IL VOUS PLAÎT!
SCHULZ

February 1, 1984

THE WORLD WAR I FLYING ACE IS LONELY...

BUT PERHAPS THE BEAUTIFUL FRENCH WAITRESS WILL CARE TO JOIN ME?
2-1

PERHAPS A ROOT BEER AND A LITTLE KISS?

OR MAYBE JUST A ROOT BEER...
SCHULZ

February 9, 1984

I'M NOT GOING TO WORRY ABOUT VALENTINES THIS YEAR...

I NEVER GET ANY VALENTINES ANYWAY, SO WHY SHOULD I WORRY?
2-9

ON THE OTHER HAND, IF SOMEONE DID SEND ME ONE, I'D WANT TO BE THERE WHEN IT ARRIVED...

SCHULZ

February 11, 1984

I WANT TO DRAW A HEART ON A VALENTINE, BUT I DON'T KNOW HOW...
2-11

JUST DRAW HALF OF A HEART

NOW, BEFORE THE INK DRIES, FOLD IT OVER...

SCHULZ

February 13, 1984

WE HAVE A CAR THAT TALKS TO YOU IF YOU DON'T FASTEN YOUR SEAT BELT
2-13

MY DAD HAS A CAMERA THAT TALKS TO YOU IF THE LIGHT ISN'T RIGHT

WE HAVE A MAILBOX THAT TALKS TO YOU IF YOU DON'T GET ANY VALENTINES

"SORRY, KID..THAT'S THE WAY IT GOES!"
SCHULZ

February 14, 1984

RATS!

NOT GETTING ANY VALENTINES IS SAD

THERE'S ONLY ONE THING WORSE..
2-14

GETTING YOUR HEAD CAUGHT IN THE MAILBOX!
SCHULZ

February 27, 1984

WHAT DO THEY CALL THIS, MARCIE? A "YOUNG PEOPLE'S CONCERT"?

HOW DO I KNOW I'M GOING TO LIKE THIS KIND OF MUSIC?

SHH...THE CONDUCTOR IS COMING OUT...WE'RE SUPPOSED TO APPLAUD...
2-27

WHY? HE HASN'T DONE ANYTHING YET
SCHULZ

March 12, 1984

3-12

WHEN YOU'RE PLAYING IN THE OUTFIELD, NEVER BLOW BUBBLE GUM ON A WINDY DAY...
SCHULZ

March 14, 1984

IT'S VERY DIFFICULT TO PITCH WHEN YOU'RE FLOATING AROUND LIKE THAT...

YOU SHOULD KNOW BETTER THAN TO BLOW BUBBLE GUM ON A WINDY DAY!

POP!
3-14

I HAVE A STRANGE TEAM..
KLUNK
SCHULZ

April 9, 1984

WE'RE NEVER GONNA WIN A GAME!
4-9

WE'RE GONNA LOSE EVERY GAME WE PLAY FOR THE REST OF OUR LIVES!

BONK!

SORRY, MANAGER.. THE FUTURE GOT IN MY EYES!
SCHULZ

April 18, 1984

MMM! THERE'S NOTHING THAT SMELLS AS GOOD AS PASTE!

YES, MA'AM, I JUST LOVE THE SMELL OF THIS WHITE PASTE...
4-18

YOU SHOULD PUT A LITTLE BEHIND EACH EAR TONIGHT WHEN YOU GO OUT WITH YOUR BOYFRIEND

JUST A LITTLE ROMANTIC SUGGESTION...
SCHULZ

April 22, 1984

PEANUTS
featuring
"Good ol' CharlieBrown"
by SCHULZ

HE'S GONNA BE SURPRISED

ATTENTION, TROOPS!
4-22

THIS IS A HISTORIC OCCASION..

ONE OF OUR MEMBERS HAS COMPLETED ALL OF HIS TESTS, AND IS NOW ELIGIBLE TO RECEIVE THE "BEAGLE SCOUT" AWARD!

CONRAD, PLEASE STEP FORWARD..

IT GIVES ME GREAT PLEASURE TO PIN THIS BEAUTIFUL BRONZE "BEAGLE SCOUT" AWARD TO THE SIDE OF YOUR HAT...

KLUNK!
SCHULZ

June 9, 1984

I APOLOGIZE FOR WHAT I SAID ON THE PHONE YESTERDAY, CHUCK.. I WAS UPSET...

BUT THINK HOW I FEEL.. THE TEACHER FAILED ME, CHUCK! THAT MEANS I'M A DUMB PERSON!

I KNOW A LOT OF PEOPLE WHO AREN'T AS SMART AS THEY THINK THEY ARE..
6-9
I JUST DON'T WANT TO BE AS DUMB AS I THINK I AM!
SCHULZ

June 15, 1984

LOOK, CHARLES...I GOT A POST CARD FROM PATTY..SHE'S IN PARIS...

Dear Marcie,
The trip over was fun. We have a nice place to stay.
6-15

I'm already doing pretty good with the language.

BONJOUR, KID!
SCHULZ

June 18, 1984

Dear Chuck,
Well, your ol' friend Patty is here in Paris.
6-18

Show Snoopy this picture of me drinking root beer in a sidewalk cafe.

I REMEMBER THAT PLACE..I WAS THERE IN 1918!
SCHULZ

"There is something else here which is worth mentioning, I think, which again it's important towards building personalities and characters, in that Peppermint Patty calls Charlie Brown 'Chuck.' She's the only one in the strip that does that, where Marcie calls him 'Charles.' Everybody else calls him 'Charlie Brown.' Those are the little things. If you have enough of those little things, then I think you take on some kind of depth."

June 20, 1984

Dear Marcie, Here is a picture of me in Paris with the Eiffel Tower in the background.

I don't remember studying about the Eiffel Tower in school, do you? love, Patty

SHE DOESN'T REMEMBER BECAUSE SHE WAS ASLEEP!
SCHULZ
6-20

June 27, 1984

Dear Chuck, Here is a photo of me in front of a World War II pillbox near Honfleur.

I am learning a lot and my French is getting better and better.
6-27

AU REVOIR, KID!
SCHULZ

July 15, 1984

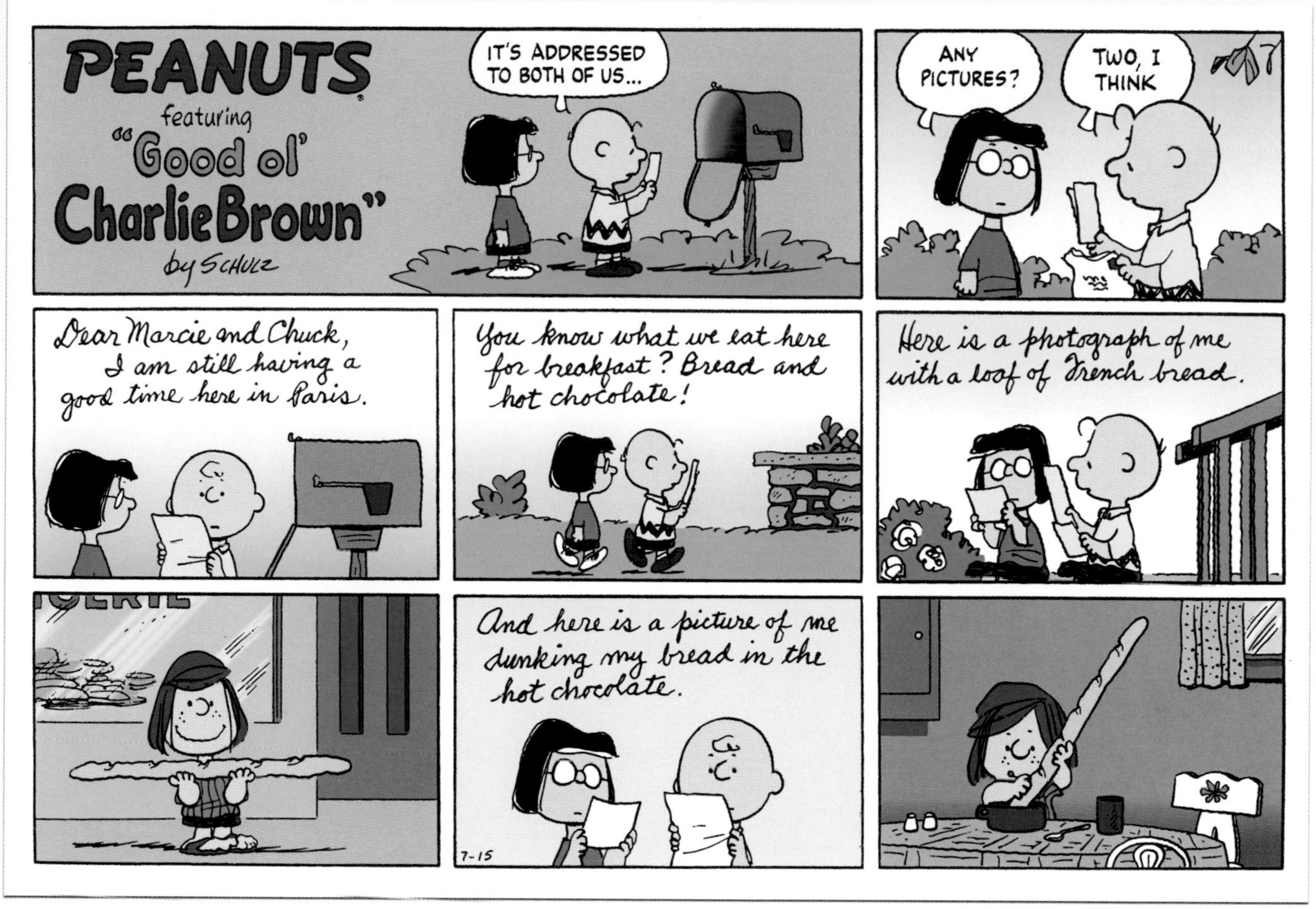

PEANUTS
featuring
"Good ol' Charlie Brown"
by SCHULZ

IT'S ADDRESSED TO BOTH OF US...

ANY PICTURES?

TWO, I THINK

Dear Marcie and Chuck,
I am still having a good time here in Paris.

You know what we eat here for breakfast? Bread and hot chocolate!

Here is a photograph of me with a loaf of French bread.

And here is a picture of me dunking my bread in the hot chocolate.

7-15

August 8, 1984

NICE SHOT
THANK YOU

I HEAR YOU'RE PLAYING IN THE "NATIONAL DISTEMPER TOURNAMENT"

ABSOLUTELY...
8-8

I PLAY IN ANY CHARITY TOURNAMENT FOR A DISEASE I MIGHT GET!
SCHULZ

August 23, 1984

I THINK YOU'RE AFRAID TO BE HAPPY, CHARLIE BROWN

DON'T YOU THINK HAPPINESS WOULD BE GOOD FOR YOU?

I DON'T KNOW...

WHAT ARE THE SIDE EFFECTS?
8/23
SCHULZ

July 22, 1984

PEANUTS
featuring
"Good ol' Charlie Brown"
by SCHULZ
AS LONG AS YOU'RE NOT DOING ANYTHING...
SIGH
HOW ABOUT GETTING ME A DISH OF ICE CREAM?
MINT! MAKE SURE IT'S MINT!!
THANK YOU
7-22
THIS DOESN'T TASTE LIKE MINT..
ALL WE HAD WAS VANILLA...
BUT YOU CAN DO AMAZING THINGS WITH A GREEN FELT TIP PEN
SCHULZ

August 29, 1984

SCHOOL STARTS SOON, FRANKLIN, BUT WE WON'T BE IN THE SAME CLASS THIS TERM...
I'M GONNA MISS YOU, PATRICIA..
I REMEMBER ONCE I THOUGHT I HEARD A JET FLYING OVER OUR SCHOOL..I TURNED AROUND, AND IT WAS YOU SNORING...
8-29
DON'T COUNT ON ME SPEAKING TO YOU AT THE HIGH SCHOOL PROM, FRANKLIN!
SCHULZ

September 4, 1984

PATRICIA? YES, MA'AM..
9-4
THAT'S ME
I'M THE ONE WHO FAILED LAST YEAR
FASTEN YOUR SEAT BELT, MA'AM...HERE I COME AGAIN!
SCHULZ

October 19, 1984

EVERY DAY ABOUT THIS TIME A GIRL DRIVES BY HERE IN A RED PICKUP, AND WAVES TO ME...

I WAVE BACK TO HER, AND GIVE HER A BIG SMILE..

SOMEDAY SHE'LL STOP, AND PICK ME UP AND TAKE ME WITH HER...

HA!
SCHULZ
10-19

October 27, 1984

EVERY DAY I LOOK FORWARD TO SEEING THAT BEAUTIFUL GIRL DRIVE BY HERE IN HER PICKUP...

I'M ALWAYS AFRAID SHE'LL GET TIRED OF WAVING TO ME...
10-27

MAYBE I COULD DO SOMETHING UNUSUAL TO MAKE HER LAUGH...

SCHULZ

November 15, 1984

YES, MA'AM..MY NAME IS "PIGPEN"

OH, YES.. I'VE BEEN IN YOUR CLASS ALL YEAR...
11-15

YOU JUST HAVEN'T NOTICED ME

THE JANITOR KEEPS SWEEPING ME OUT!
SCHULZ

November 16, 1984

PIGPEN, YOU'RE A MESS!

YOU'VE EVEN GOT LEAVES IN YOUR HAIR...

I HAVE? WELL, I WAS IN A HURRY THIS MORNING...
11-16

I FORGOT TO RAKE MY HAIR..
SCHULZ

December 1, 1984

WHEN IT COMES TO RIDING ON THE BACK OF MOM'S BICYCLE, I'M A WHITE KNUCKLE FLIER...

LOOK OUT FOR THE TREE! LOOK OUT FOR THE FENCE!

"JINGLE BELLS (LOOK OUT!) JINGLE (LOOK OUT!) BELLS (LOOK OUT!) JINGLE ALL THE (LOOK OUT!) WAY..."
12-1

SINGING DOESN'T HELP......
SCHULZ

December 12, 1984

SO LONG, MILDRED! GOODBYE, DANNY! TOO BAD, ESTHER!
© 1984 United Feature Syndicate, Inc.

THESE ARE PEOPLE I'M SCRATCHING OFF MY CHRISTMAS CARD LIST

GET LOST, MABEL! THAT'S THE WAY IT GOES, FRED! BYE-BYE, JOE! FORGET YOU, LYDIA!

I'VE NEVER HAD SO MUCH FUN IN ALL MY LIFE!
SCHULZ
12/12

December 13, 1984

I'M REALLY TRIMMING DOWN MY CHRISTMAS CARD LIST THIS YEAR...
12-13

MILDRED, DANNY, ESTHER, MABEL, FRED, JOE, LYDIA, VERNA, EMIL, FLOYD... I CROSSED 'EM ALL OFF!

I'M DOWN TO ONE LAST NAME...

AND THERE GOES JESSIE!!
SCHULZ

December 28, 1984

What I did on my Christmas Vacation. I went outside and looked at the clouds.

They formed beautiful patterns with beautiful colors. I looked at them every morning and every evening.

Which is all I did on my Christmas Vacation.
12-28

And what's wrong with that?
SCHULZ

January 7, 1985

YOU WON, SIR!
WON WHAT?

I JUST HEARD THAT YOUR ESSAY ON WHAT YOU DID DURING CHRISTMAS VACATION WON THE "ALL-CITY SCHOOL ESSAY CONTEST"
1-7-85

YOU WROTE ABOUT LOOKING AT THE CLOUDS, REMEMBER? ANYWAY, YOU WON..CONGRATULATIONS!

DON'T WIPE YOUR TEARS AWAY WITH YOUR FRENCH FRIES, SIR
SCHULZ

January 8, 1985

I HAVE BEEN ASKED TO MAKE THIS IMPORTANT ANNOUNCEMENT

ONE OF OUR CLASSMATES, MISS PATRICIA REICHARDT, HAS JUST WON THE "ALL-CITY ESSAY CONTEST"
1-8-85

HER ESSAY ON WHAT SHE DID DURING HER CHRISTMAS VACATION HAS WON FIRST PRIZE!

HOW DID I WIN? I GOT A "D MINUS"!
SCHULZ

January 9, 1985

EXPLAIN THIS, IF YOU CAN, CHUCK..EVERYONE IN OUR CLASS HAD TO WRITE AN ESSAY ON WHAT WE DID DURING CHRISTMAS VACATION

WHEN I GOT MINE BACK, THE TEACHER HAD GIVEN ME A "D MINUS"... WELL, I'M USED TO THAT, RIGHT, CHUCK? RIGHT!

NOW, GUESS WHAT..ALL THOSE ESSAYS WENT INTO A CITY ESSAY CONTEST, AND I WON! EXPLAIN THAT, CHUCK

1-9-85

NEVER LISTEN TO THE REVIEWERS
SCHULZ

January 10, 1985

THEY WANT ME TO READ MY ESSAY WHEN I GET MY AWARD, MARCIE

I'LL PROBABLY HAVE TO DRESS UP, AND MAYBE EVEN CHANGE MY HAIR STYLE...
1-10-85

SEE IF YOU LIKE IT THIS WAY, SIR..

ONLY IF I WANT TO GO DISGUISED AS A DANDELION
SCHULZ

January 12, 1985

THEY'RE CALLING YOUR NAME, SIR..I THINK THEY WANT YOU TO GO UP AND GET YOUR AWARD...

I'M NERVOUS..COME WITH ME, MARCIE...

1-12-85
PAT
PAT
PAT

PAWS WERE NEVER MADE FOR CLAPPING
SCHULZ

"I think doing stories that last three or four weeks is the best way to capture and hold readers, but I also think you have to have variety because life itself has variety. Some days the strip should be funny because of the drawing—the outlandish facial expression or something. Some days the characters should be shouting, but they shouldn't be shouting every day—some days the strip should be quiet. You've got to mix it up."

January 15, 1985

I HAVE BEEN ASKED TO READ THE ESSAY THAT I WROTE ABOUT MY CHRISTMAS VACATION..

PERHAPS, HOWEVER, A FEW WORDS MIGHT BE IN ORDER HERE TO TELL...

HURRY UP, AND READ IT!!
1-15

MARCIE!
SCHULZ

January 16, 1985

THIS IS THE ESSAY THAT I WROTE ABOUT MY CHRISTMAS VACATION

"I WENT OUTSIDE, AND.."
READ IT FAST, SIR..
1-16

"LOOKED AT THE CLOUDS.. THEY..."
I CAN'T HOLD YOU ANY..

AAUGH!
LONGER!
SCHULZ

January 17, 1985

THIS MORNING WE WANT TO PAY TRIBUTE TO TWO OF OUR CLASSMATES...
1-17

PATRICIA AND MARCIE MADE AN APPEARANCE AT THE TEACHER'S CONVENTION YESTERDAY..

I THINK WE ALL APPRECIATE THE HONOR THEY BROUGHT TO OUR SCHOOL...

UNTIL WE FELL OFF THE STAGE!
SCHULZ

February 10, 1985

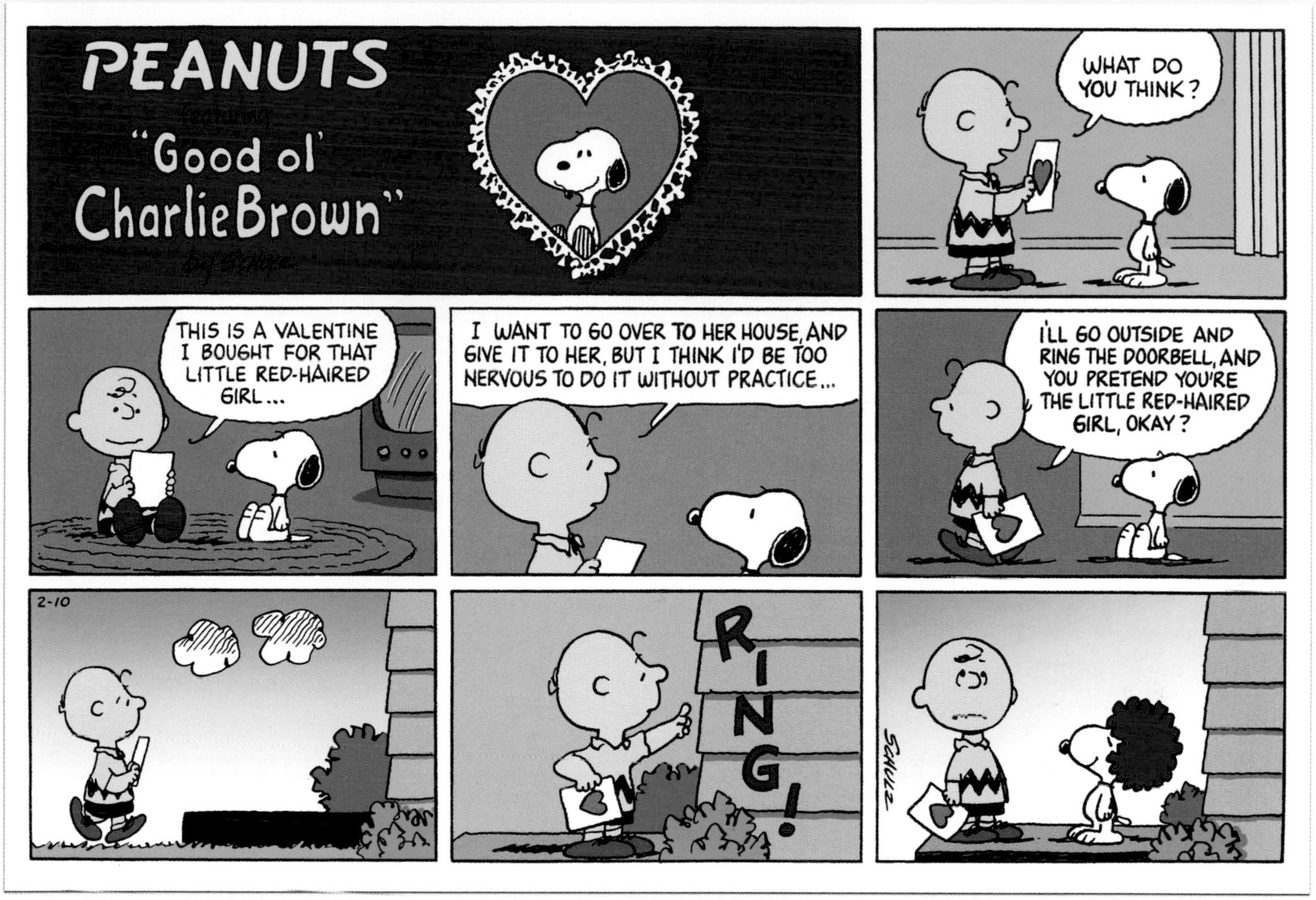

PEANUTS featuring "Good ol' Charlie Brown"

WHAT DO YOU THINK?

THIS IS A VALENTINE I BOUGHT FOR THAT LITTLE RED-HAIRED GIRL...

I WANT TO GO OVER TO HER HOUSE, AND GIVE IT TO HER, BUT I THINK I'D BE TOO NERVOUS TO DO IT WITHOUT PRACTICE...

I'LL GO OUTSIDE AND RING THE DOORBELL, AND YOU PRETEND YOU'RE THE LITTLE RED-HAIRED GIRL, OKAY?

2-10

RING!

SCHULZ

February 18, 1985

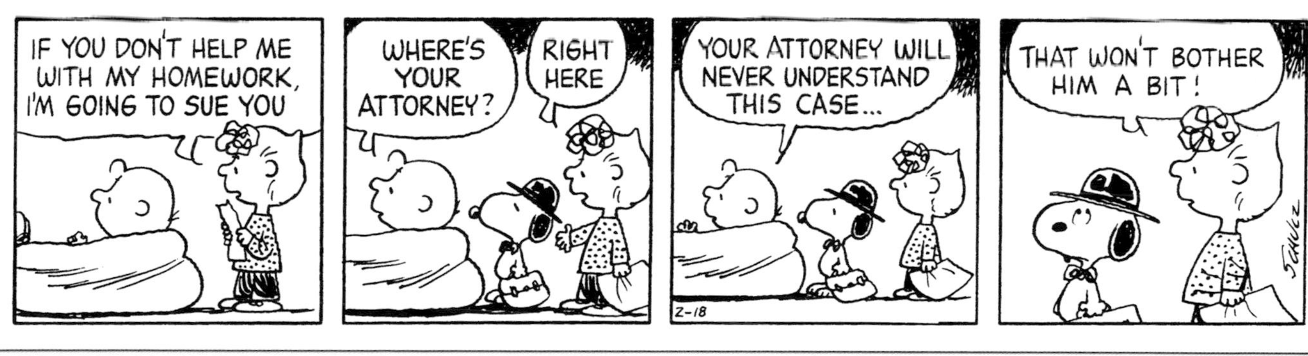
IF YOU DON'T HELP ME WITH MY HOMEWORK, I'M GOING TO SUE YOU
WHERE'S YOUR ATTORNEY?
RIGHT HERE
YOUR ATTORNEY WILL NEVER UNDERSTAND THIS CASE...
2-18
THAT WON'T BOTHER HIM A BIT!
SCHULZ

February 19, 1985

I CAN'T BELIEVE IT... YOU'RE HELPING ME WITH MY HOMEWORK!
IT'S BETTER THAN HAVING YOUR ATTORNEY SUE ME..
I WON'T NEED YOU AFTER ALL, ATTORNEY.. WE'VE DECIDED TO SETTLE OUT OF COURT...
HOW WILL I EVER PAY FOR MY NEW BRIEFCASE?
SCHULZ
2-19

March 5, 1985

EVERY TIME WE COME TO ONE OF THESE CONCERTS, THEY PLAY "PETER AND THE WOLF"

THEY MUST THINK WE DON'T UNDERSTAND ANYTHING ELSE
3/5

DON'T YOU LIKE "PETER AND THE WOLF"?

I DON'T KNOW.. I'VE NEVER UNDERSTOOD IT!
SCHULZ

May 12, 1985

PEANUTS
featuring
"Good ol' CharlieBrown"
by SCHULZ
YOU SIT HERE WITH THE FLOWER, AND IF YOUR MOTHER FLIES OVER, YOU REACH UP AND HAND IT TO HER..MAKE SURE YOU SAY, "HAPPY MOTHER'S DAY"
WE'D BETTER PRACTICE IT ONCE...
I'LL BE YOUR MOTHER, AND I'LL COME FLYING OVER, OKAY?
5-12
HI, SONNY! IT'S ME, YOUR MOM! WHAT A PRETTY FLOWER...
HAND IT TO ME! QUICK!!
BONK
MAYBE SHE'LL JUST COME WALKING BY..
SCHULZ

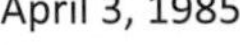
April 3, 1985

ALL MY LIFE I WANTED TO BE AN ONLY CHILD... I HAD A GOOD THING GOING 'TIL YOU CAME..

LITTLE BROTHERS SPOIL EVERYTHING.. LITTLE BROTHERS ARE A BOTHER AND A NUISANCE...
4-3

WHY ARE YOU TELLING ME ALL THIS?

SCHULZ
THERE'S NOTHING GOOD ON TV!

April 20, 1985

I CAN'T BELIEVE IT

THEY CANCELED MY FAVORITE PROGRAM!

SIGH
4-20

I NEVER KNEW LIFE WAS GOING TO BE SO HARD...
SCHULZ

May 10, 1985

I LOVE GOING OVER TO WOODSTOCK'S NEST TO WATCH TV...
5-10

HE'S THE ONLY ONE WHO HAS A SATELLITE DISH..
SCHULZ

June 10, 1985

IT'S RAINING... WE'RE GOING TO CAMP, AND IT'S RAINING!
6-10

I HATE GOING TO CAMP! I ESPECIALLY HATE GOING TO CAMP WHEN IT'S RAINING!

THE FARMERS NEED RAIN
WHAT FOR?

THEIR COWS ARE GOING TO GET ALL WET!
SCHULZ

June 11, 1985

LOOK AT THAT POOR COW STANDING OUT THERE IN THE RAIN...

SOMEDAY THEY'RE GOING TO MAKE A PAIR OF BOOTS OUT OF THAT COW..

I WOULDN'T BUY 'EM...

THEY'D BE ALL WET!
6-11
SCHULZ

June 12, 1985

OUR TENT LEAKED ALL NIGHT.. NOW WE HAVE TO STAND IN THE RAIN FOR BREAKFAST!

MY HAIR IS WET... MY CLOTHES ARE WET... MY SHOES ARE WET...

I EVEN HAVE RAINWATER IN MY MOUTH..
WHY DON'T YOU KEEP YOUR MOUTH CLOSED?

IT WOULDN'T HELP.. I THINK MY HEAD LEAKS...

June 13, 1985

IT'S BEEN RAINING EVER SINCE WE GOT HERE TO CAMP, CHARLIE BROWN...

IT'S KIND OF DEPRESSING, ISN'T IT?

I WONDER HOW ALL THE OTHER CAMPERS ARE TAKING IT...

HERE'S THE WORLD WAR I FLYING ACE STARING GLOOMILY OUT OVER THE RAIN-SOAKED AERODROME

June 21, 1985

YOU'RE GOING TO WHAT?
I'M GOING TO SUE THE CAMP...

I'M GOING TO SUE BECAUSE IT RAINS ALL THE TIME! MY ATTORNEY HAS AGREED TO TAKE THE CASE...

THAT'S NO ATTORNEY.. THAT'S A DOG!

MY LAST CLIENT CALLED ME WORSE THINGS THAN THAT..

June 22, 1985

CAMP'S OVER!! EVERYONE TO THE BUS!

WE'RE GOING HOME! I CAN'T BELIEVE IT...

DID YOU NOTICE SOMETHING?
WHAT'S THAT?

IT STOPPED RAINING..THE SUN JUST CAME OUT..
I CAN'T STAND IT!!

July 10, 1985

ANOTHER TINY TOTS CONCERT, AND LOOK WHAT THEY'RE PLAYING...

"PETER AND THE WOLF"
AGAIN?

MAYBE THIS TIME WE'LL BE LUCKY...
7-10

MAYBE THIS TIME THE WOLF WILL GET HIM!
SCHULZ

August 7, 1985

HE'S FOLLOWING ME, SIR..
WHO IS?

A "PUNKER"

IGNORE HIM..BUT THIS IS A PUBLIC SHOPPING MALL SO IF HE'S BOTHERING YOU, REACH UP, AND PUNCH HIM IN THE NOSE...

8-7
HOW ABOUT REACH DOWN?
SCHULZ

August 20, 1985

WHAT DID YOU DO WITH THE PICTURE OF ME THAT I GAVE YOU?
8-20

I THREW IT AWAY!
WITH YOUR OWN HANDS?

OF COURSE

HE TOUCHED MY PICTURE!
SCHULZ

August 30, 1985

WHEN WE RIDE THE BUS TO SCHOOL NEXT WEEK, I'LL PROBABLY SIT WITH MY SWEET BABBOO..

I'M NOT YOUR SWEET BABBOO, AND I'D CRAWL TO SCHOOL ON MY HANDS AND KNEES BEFORE I'D SIT WITH YOU!
8-30

I'M SURE HE'LL INSIST THAT I SIT BY THE WINDOW...

I'LL INSIST THAT YOU SIT ON THE ROOF!!
SCHULZ

September 20, 1985

It was a dark and stormy night.
9-20

YOU KNOW WHAT'S WRONG WITH YOUR STORIES?

THEY LACK SUBTLETY

It was a sort of dark and kind of stormy night.
SCHULZ

September 27, 1985

I DREAMED ABOUT THAT LITTLE RED HAIRED GIRL AGAIN LAST NIGHT...

NOW, I'LL BE THINKING ABOUT HER ALL DAY, AND BE DEPRESSED...

I THINK I KNOW HOW YOU FEEL, CHARLIE BROWN.. YOU'D LIKE TO CRY, BUT YOU'RE TOO MACHO..
9-27

I **AM** ?!
SCHULZ

September 28, 1985

?
9-28

DO KITES HAVE TO HAVE TAILS?

OF COURSE

HOW ELSE COULD THEY TELL YOU WHEN THEY'RE HAPPY?
SCHULZ

November 21, 1985

WOULD YOU LIKE TO BUY A CHRISTMAS WREATH?
11-21

DO YOU KNOW WHAT YOU'RE DOING?

DON'T YOU REALIZE YOU'RE ADDING TO THE OVERCOMMERCIALIZING OF CHRISTMAS?

NOT 'TIL I SELL ONE!
SCHULZ

December 3, 1985

Dear Santa Claus,
I saw a recent picture of you in a magazine.
12-3

You look fatter than ever.

I know how you usually fly through the air with your reindeer and sleigh.

I'll be surprised this year if you even get off the ground.
SCHULZ

December 12, 1985

MR. SANTA CLAUS ? MY NAME IS SALLY.. I'M CONCERNED ABOUT YOUR WEIGHT...
12-12

WHEN WAS THE LAST TIME YOU HAD A STRESS TEST? HOW IS YOUR CHOLESTEROL?

DO YOU HAVE A CREASE IN YOUR EAR LOBES?

JUST LET ME CHECK THOSE EAR LOBES..
HEY!
SCHULZ

December 13, 1985

DON'T PUSH ME!

JUST BECAUSE YOU'RE SANTA CLAUS, YOU CAN'T THROW ME OUT!
12-13

DON'T PUSH ME! I WAS TRYING TO HELP YOU! YOU'RE TOO FAT!

AND YOU HAVE A CREASE IN YOUR EAR LOBE!!
SCHULZ

December 14, 1985

WHAT'S GOING ON?
12-14

I'M WATCHING THE NEWS..A DEPARTMENT STORE SANTA CLAUS HAD A HEART ATTACK

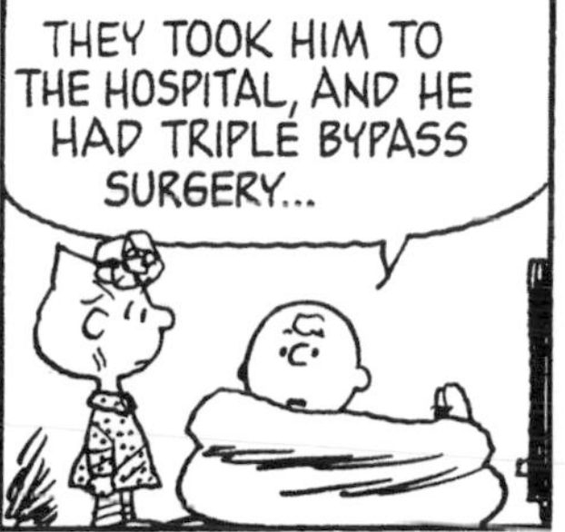
THEY TOOK HIM TO THE HOSPITAL, AND HE HAD TRIPLE BYPASS SURGERY...

THEY SAID THAT JUST BEFORE HIS HEART ATTACK, THERE WAS SOME KIND OF DISTURBANCE BY A LITTLE GIRL AT THE STORE...
SCHULZ

December 22, 1985

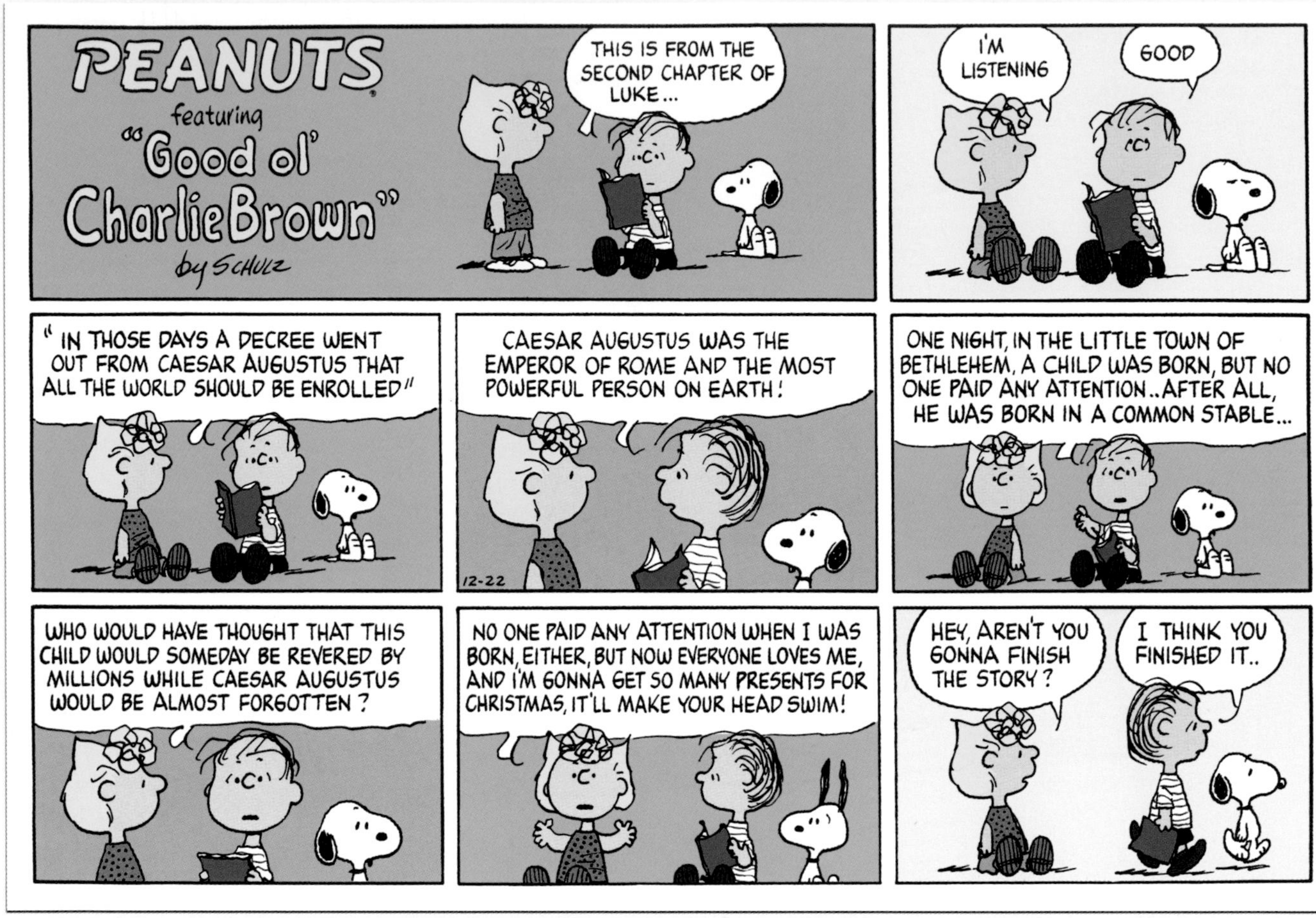

PEANUTS featuring "Good ol' Charlie Brown" by Schulz

THIS IS FROM THE SECOND CHAPTER OF LUKE...

I'M LISTENING

GOOD

" IN THOSE DAYS A DECREE WENT OUT FROM CAESAR AUGUSTUS THAT ALL THE WORLD SHOULD BE ENROLLED"

CAESAR AUGUSTUS WAS THE EMPEROR OF ROME AND THE MOST POWERFUL PERSON ON EARTH!

12-22

ONE NIGHT, IN THE LITTLE TOWN OF BETHLEHEM, A CHILD WAS BORN, BUT NO ONE PAID ANY ATTENTION..AFTER ALL, HE WAS BORN IN A COMMON STABLE...

WHO WOULD HAVE THOUGHT THAT THIS CHILD WOULD SOMEDAY BE REVERED BY MILLIONS WHILE CAESAR AUGUSTUS WOULD BE ALMOST FORGOTTEN ?

NO ONE PAID ANY ATTENTION WHEN I WAS BORN, EITHER, BUT NOW EVERYONE LOVES ME, AND I'M GONNA GET SO MANY PRESENTS FOR CHRISTMAS, IT'LL MAKE YOUR HEAD SWIM!

HEY, AREN'T YOU GONNA FINISH THE STORY ?

I THINK YOU FINISHED IT..

"I'm never grinding an axe; I'm never doing it to teach anybody anything. Very seldom. Maybe if we looked through the scriptures I could point out a few where I might be trying to say something against hypocrisy, I really don't know. It's hard to say overall. It's just that certain phrases pop into my mind and I think that would be funny, so I look up the scriptures or else I remember a scripture and suddenly, I find something comes into my mind, a certain way of using it, that's all."

January 14, 1986

I WONDER WHAT WOULD HAPPEN IF I ASKED THAT LITTLE RED-HAIRED GIRL IF I COULD SIT NEXT TO HER, AND EAT LUNCH...
MAYBE SHE'D TELL ME TO GET LOST, OR THROW A ROCK AT ME OR HIT ME WITH A STICK...
1-14
OR LAUGH IN MY FACE, OR SCREAM FOR HELP OR KICK ME IN THE STOMACH...
I WONDER IF SHE COULD DO ALL THOSE THINGS AT ONCE..
SCHULZ

January 15, 1986

I'M TIRED OF BEING WISHY-WASHY! I'M GONNA WALK RIGHT OVER, AND TALK TO THAT LITTLE RED-HAIRED GIRL!

I'M DOING IT! I'M COMMITTED! NOTHING CAN STOP ME NOW!

ABSOLUTELY NOTHING!
1-15

SCHULZ

January 28, 1986

THESE CATALOGS WITH THEIR MODELS ARE DEPRESSING! EVERYONE IS HANDSOME AND BEAUTIFUL!

LOOK AT THEM IN THEIR NEW SPRING CLOTHES..IT SETS AN IMPOSSIBLE STANDARD FOR US KIDS...

NONE OF US CAN EVER GROW UP TO LOOK THAT GOOD

1-28
I WILL!

February 10, 1986

HERE'S THE WORLD WAR I FLYING ACE HIGH OVER NO MAN'S LAND...

2-10
I SUPPOSE YOU THINK YOU'RE FLYING OVER NO MAN'S LAND, HUH?

WELL, WHAT ABOUT NO WOMAN'S LAND?!

HERE'S THE WORLD WAR I FLYING ACE HIGH OVER NO PERSON'S LAND...
SCHULZ

February 11, 1986

HERE'S THE LONELY WORLD WAR I FLYING ACE SITTING IN A SMALL FRENCH CAFE..

YOUR ROOT BEER, MONSIEUR

I'M IN LOVE! IT'S THE BEGINNING (SIGH) OF ANOTHER TRAGIC ROMANCE...
2-11

I'VE ONLY BEEN IN FRANCE FOUR HOURS, AND ALREADY I'VE HAD SEVEN TRAGIC ROMANCES!
SCHULZ

February 17, 1986

HERE'S THE WORLD WAR I FLYING ACE CONFINED TO BED WITH THE TERRIBLE FLU OF 1918...

THE BEAUTIFUL FRENCH WAITRESS FROM A NEARBY CAFE HAS BEEN TAKING CARE OF ME...

BONJOUR, MONSIEUR.. I HAVE FOR YOU A PIECE OF MAIL...
2-17

HOW NICE... A "GET WELL" CARD FROM THE RED BARON!
SCHULZ

April 17, 1986

GOOD GRIEF! YOU'VE BLOWN THE ROOF OFF YOUR DOGHOUSE!

HOW COULD YOU DO SUCH A THING?

A MILITARY TACTICAL ERROR..
4-17

FROM A DISTANCE IT LOOKED LIKE FORT ZINDERNEUF!
SCHULZ

April 18, 1986

THAT CANNON BALL BLEW THE WHOLE TOP OFF YOUR DOGHOUSE!

BUT THEN WHERE DID IT GO?

I WONDER IF IT HIT ANYTHING ELSE?
4-18

THE DOCTOR IS IN
SCHULZ

April 19, 1986

THAT CANNON BALL DESTROYED YOUR ROOF

THEN IT WENT THROUGH THE TOP OF LUCY'S PSYCHIATRIC BOOTH...
THE DOCTO
IS OUT

I WONDER WHERE IT FINALLY LANDED...

4-19
SCHULZ

June 9, 1986

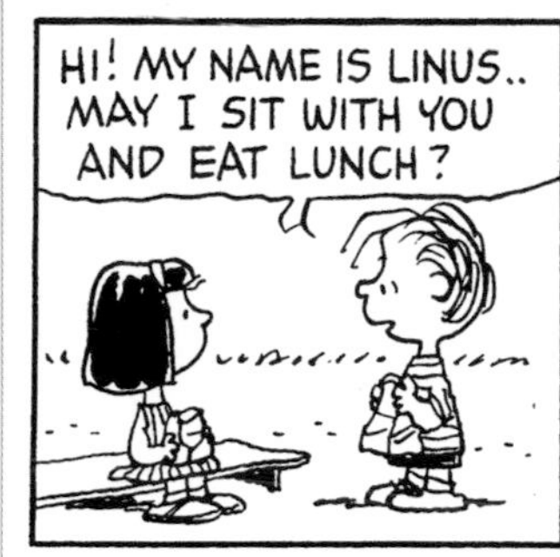
HI! MY NAME IS LINUS.. MAY I SIT WITH YOU AND EAT LUNCH?

I DON'T KNOW..WHEN WERE YOU BORN?
I WAS BORN IN OCTOBER..

I WAS BORN IN DECEMBER

AREN'T YOU KIND OF OLD FOR ME?

"Every thought that I have, and every remembrance, goes into this strip. Once, I was sitting at my desk at the art instruction school—I suppose I was twenty-six—and nothing had been going right lately. I hadn't had any dates of any kind. I was lonely, and this very pretty young girl would come up with some letters to be signed. I'd see her walking around the room, day after day after day. It took me great courage, but I said, 'Would you be interested in going out for dinner and a movie?' and she said, 'Aren't you kind of old for me?' Oh boy, it would have been better if she had just reached over and punched me in the nose."

June 13, 1986

WELL, HI! FANCY MEETING YOU HERE..REMEMBER ME? LINUS VAN PELT?

I'LL HAVE MINT CHOCOLATE CHIP, PLEASE

I'LL HAVE THE SAME, PLEASE...
YOU LIKE MINT CHOCOLATE CHIP? I'M SURPRISED...

MOST OLDER PEOPLE LIKE VANILLA!

June 14, 1986

SO I ORDERED MINT CHOCOLATE CHIP JUST LIKE SHE DID, AND SHE SAID SHE WAS SURPRISED...

SHE SAYS, "MOST OLDER PEOPLE ORDER VANILLA!" WHAT SHE REALLY MEANT WAS SHE THINKS I'M DULL AND BORING!

I'VE ALWAYS LIKED VANILLA

June 17, 1986

MAY I SPEAK TO YOU ABOUT MY FRIEND HERE?

I THINK YOU'RE WRONG ABOUT HIS BEING TOO OLD FOR YOU..

IN MANY WAYS, HE'S STILL QUITE YOUNG..
6-17

I MEAN, YOU SHOULD SEE HIM WITH HIS BLANKET..
AAUGH!
SCHULZ

July 20, 1986

PEANUTS
featuring
"Good ol' CharlieBrown"
by SCHULZ
WATCH IT, BEAGLE! IF YOU TOUCH THIS BLANKET, I'LL DESTROY YOU!
I'LL DESTROY YOU AND ALL YOUR COUSINS, AND THE PLACE WHERE YOU WERE BORN AND ALL THE RECORDS AT THE COURT HOUSE! SMALL CRAFT WARNINGS WILL BE POSTED ALONG BOTH COASTS! I WILL POUNCE ON YOU LIKE THE LAST DAYS OF POMPEII !!
SO BACK OFF!
WHEN I BACK OFF, I BACK OFF!
SCHULZ
7-20

July 1, 1986

HELLO?

NO, I CAN'T... NOT TOMORROW..

YEAH, THE DENTIST..

I HAVE TO GO HAVE MY TEETH CRITICIZED!
SCHULZ
7-1

July 21, 1986

YEAH, MY DAD AND OUR TEACHER THINK MAYBE I NEED A TUTOR

WELL, YOU KNOW, TO HELP ME GET A BETTER START IN SCHOOL THIS YEAR..
7-21

WHOOPS! SOMEONE'S AT THE DOOR... IT'S PROBABLY MY TUTOR...

HI! ARE YOU THE DUMB ONE?
SCHULZ

July 22, 1986

YOU'RE MY NEW TUTOR? HOW'D YOU EVER FIND ME?

WELL, THEY HAVE THESE NUMBERS ON THE FRONT OF HOUSES, SEE, AND...

JOE SARCASM
7-22

YOU'D BETTER COME IN.. IF I HIT YOU OUT HERE, YOU'LL FALL DOWN THE STAIRS!
SCHULZ

July 25, 1986

I CAN'T TALK NOW, MARCIE..CAPTAIN TUTOR IS HERE..

DON'T CALL ME CAPTAIN TUTOR! MY NAME IS MAYNARD!!

WHY DON'T YOU COME ON OVER, MARCIE? YOU SHOULD MEET THIS KID.. HE'S JUST YOUR TYPE.. ..WEIRD!
7-25

SORRY FOR THE INTERRUPTION, CAPTAIN..
MY NAME IS MAYNARD
SCHULZ

July 28, 1986

MARCIE! COME ON IN AND MEET CAPTAIN TUTOR..
MY NAME IS MAYNARD!

COUSIN MAYNARD!
HE'S YOUR COUSIN?

DID YOU KNOW HE'S GETTING PAID TO BE YOUR TUTOR?
HE'S GETTING PAID?!
7-28

HEY!!
SORRY, KID.. I THOUGHT YOU WERE DOING IT OUT OF THE GOODNESS OF YOUR HEART!
SCHULZ

August 29, 1986

MY GRAMPA IS GOING IN FOR A STRESS TEST TODAY

8-29
I HOPE HE DOES WELL

HAVE YOU EVER TAKEN A STRESS TEST?

I LIVE WITH ONE!
WHAT'D HE SAY?
SCHULZ

August 3, 1986

PEANUTS
featuring
"Good ol' CharlieBrown"
by SCHULZ

WHAT DO YOU THINK? SPECTACULAR, HUH?

IT'S RIDICULOUS!
RIDICULOUS?

IT ISN'T AUTHENTIC..
IT ISN'T?

8-3
NOBODY COULD EVER LIVE IN A CASTLE LIKE THAT!

SCHULZ

September 3, 1986

ME? MY TURN? YES, MA'AM

MY NAME IS CHARLES BROWN..MY DAD IS A BARBER...I GUESS MY FAVORITE HOBBIES ARE BASEBALL AND READING

I THOUGHT I DID PRETTY GOOD..WHY DID EVERYONE LAUGH?
9-3

YOU WALKED OUT THE DOOR, AND GAVE YOUR SPEECH IN THE HALLWAY!
SCHULZ

September 4, 1986

GOOD MORNING..I'M NEW HERE IN THIS SCHOOL..I SHALL NOW INTRODUCE MYSELF...

MY NAME IS TAPIOCA PUDDING

WITH MY NAME, MY BLOND HAIR AND MY SMILE, MY DAD SAYS WE CAN MAKE A MILLION DOLLARS..
9-4

MY DAD IS IN LICENSING!
SCHULZ

"I know that syndicates frequently within the last few years have become obsessed with licensing and think that they can create a certain character or a strip that will sell licensed products, then get on television and sell books and all of that. But that is still no way to draw a comic strip. I think there are certain forms of creativity that demand the work of one single person, whether it is a person sitting at a drawing board, a person sitting at a piano, or a person sitting behind the easel painting. And I think good comic strips are drawn by one dedicated person sitting all by himself in a room at a drawing board."

September 15, 1986

I'M SO EXCITED! I THINK I'VE FOUND AN AGENT!

I'M MEETING HIM RIGHT AFTER SCHOOL TODAY.. HERE'S THE CARD HE SENT ME...
9-15

"ACE LICENSING!" SOUNDS IMPRESSIVE...

HERE'S THE WORLD FAMOUS AGENT ON HIS WAY TO SIGN UP ANOTHER CLIENT..
SCHULZ

September 27, 1986

IT SAYS HERE THAT THE WORLD REVOLVES AROUND THE SUN ONCE A YEAR..

THE WORLD REVOLVES AROUND THE SUN?

ARE YOU SURE?

I THOUGHT IT REVOLVED AROUND ME!
SCHULZ
9-27

October 7, 1986

HERE'S THE WORLD WAR I FLYING ACE SEARCHING THE SKIES FOR HIS ENEMY, THE RED BARON..
10-7

DUCKING IN AND OUT OF THE CLOUDS, HE PLAYS A DANGEROUS GAME OF HIDE-AND-SEEK

PEEKABOO, I SEE YOU!

ACTUALLY, WORLD WAR I FLYING ACES VERY SELDOM SAID, "PEEKABOO, I SEE YOU!"
SCHULZ

October 13, 1986

HOW WAS SCHOOL TODAY?
WHO CARES?

I WAS JUST ASKING
IT'S MY NEW PHILOSOPHY... "WHO CARES?"

FROM NOW ON, NOTHING BOTHERS ME
10-13

WHO CARES? WHO CARES? WHO CARES?
SCHULZ

November 23, 1986

PEANUTS
featuring
"Good ol' Charlie Brown"
by SCHULZ
GATE 3
YOU DON'T LIKE ME!
I DON'T CARE! IT'S NOT FAIR!
I WANNA ASK YOU SOMETHING! DO YOU REMEMBER BEFORE WE WERE BORN?
NOT HARDLY
WEREN'T WE UP IN HEAVEN WITH A BUNCH OF OTHER KIDS WAITING TO BE BORN?
THE THEOLOGICAL IMPLICATIONS OF THAT ARE WAY BEYOND ME..
WELL, DO YOU THINK WE EVER ASKED ABOUT BEING BORN?
I DON'T RECALL EVER ASKING ANYONE OR EVEN SEEING ANYONE...
SO YOU'RE SURE WE NEVER ASKED TO BE BORN?
11-23
NO, I DON'T THINK SO
YOU'RE SURE?
I'M POSITIVE
THAT'S WHAT I THOUGHT.. I JUST WANTED TO BE SURE...
© 1986 United Feature Syndicate, Inc.

I DIDN'T ASK TO BE BORN!!
SCHULZ

December 28, 1986

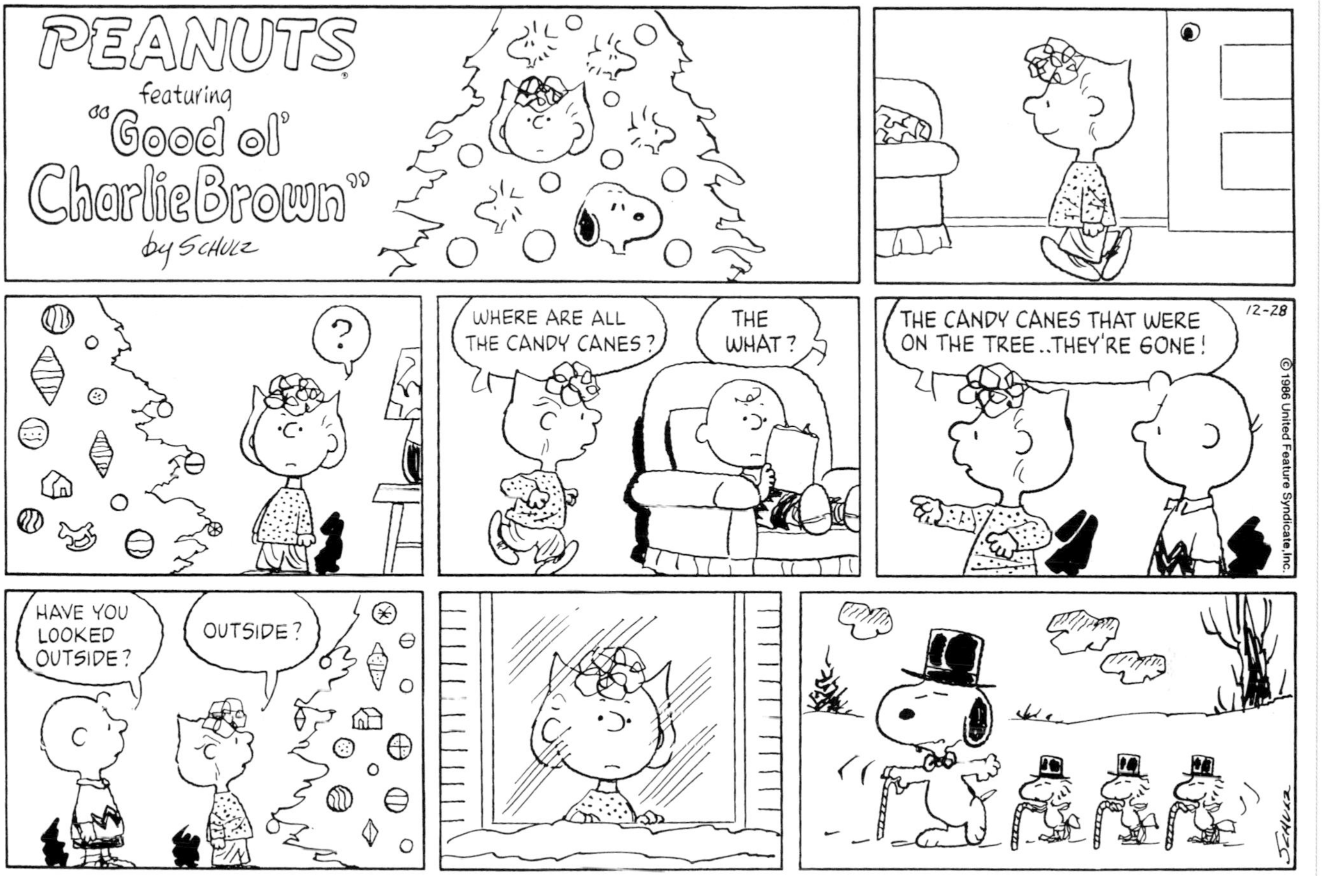

PEANUTS
featuring
"Good ol' Charlie Brown"
by SCHULZ

WHERE ARE ALL THE CANDY CANES?
THE WHAT?
THE CANDY CANES THAT WERE ON THE TREE..THEY'RE GONE!
12-28
© 1986 United Feature Syndicate, Inc.
HAVE YOU LOOKED OUTSIDE?
OUTSIDE?
SCHULZ

December 17, 1986

ANOTHER BIG HOCKEY GAME TODAY..
12-17
SOMEHOW, WE ALWAYS END UP PLAYING ON WOODSTOCK'S HOME ICE
IT WOULDN'T BE SO BAD EXCEPT FOR ONE THING..
HE NEVER LETS ME DRIVE THE ZAMBONI!
SCHULZ

January 6, 1987

Dear Grandma and Grandpa,

They say that grandparents like to spoil their grandchildren.

1-6-87

I'm ready when you are.
SCHULZ

March 8, 1987

PEANUTS
by
SCHULZ
PLEASE WAIT TO BE SEATED
YOU'RE A KITE-EATING TREE, AREN'T YOU?
I HATE KITE-EATING TREES!
YOU'RE JUST WAITING TO GRAB MY NEW RED KITE, AREN'T YOU?
MAYBE I SHOULD HAVE BROUGHT OUT THE BLUE ONE, OR MAYBE THE YELLOW ONE...
3-8
DON'T TELL ME THE TREE DIDN'T LIKE YOUR KITE...
HE WANTS TO SEE A MENU!
SCHULZ

March 12, 1987

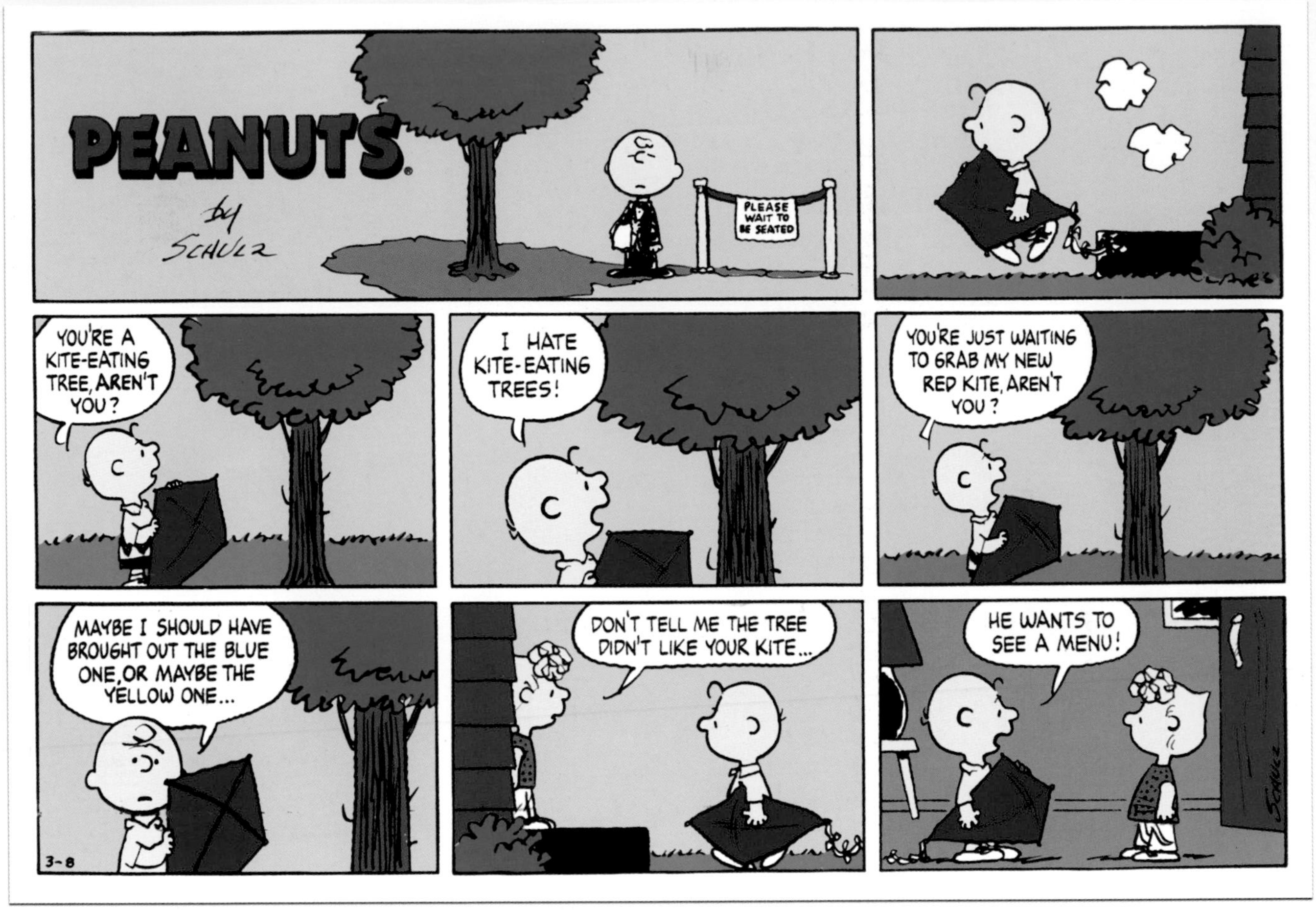

THE GOLF PRO IS MAD AT YOU!
HE SAID TO GET OFF THE GOLF COURSE, AND STOP MARCHING THROUGH ALL THE SAND TRAPS!
3-12
I THOUGHT THIS WAS THE SAHARA..
AND THE CLUBHOUSE ISN'T FORT ZINDERNEUF!
IT ISN'T?
SCHULZ

March 20, 1987

I DID IT! I RAKED EVERY SAND TRAP ON THE GOLF COURSE!
I CAN'T BELIEVE I DID IT! I'VE NEVER WORKED SO HARD IN ALL MY LIFE!
3-20
THERE IT IS, MEN.. FORT ZINDERNEUF!
AAUGH!
WE'RE THE RELIEF COLUMN FROM TOKOTU.. AREN'T YOU GLAD TO SEE US?
SCHULZ

March 25, 1987

OKAY, HERE WE GO.. THE FIRST PITCH OF THE SEASON...
3-25

FOR ME, THIS IS THE MOST EXCITING MOMENT OF THE YEAR...

POW!

WHY, I DON'T KNOW..
SCHULZ

April 30, 1987

4-30

SCHULZ

April 19, 1987

PEANUTS
by
SCHULZ
WHAT ARE YOU DOING?

I'M LOOKING FOR ENLIGHTENMENT
REALLY?
4-19

WELL, I'M PROUD OF YOU! AND AT YOUR AGE, TOO...

I'VE NEVER HEARD OF ANYONE YOUR AGE WHO WAS INTERESTED IN ANY KIND OF SERIOUS THOUGHT!

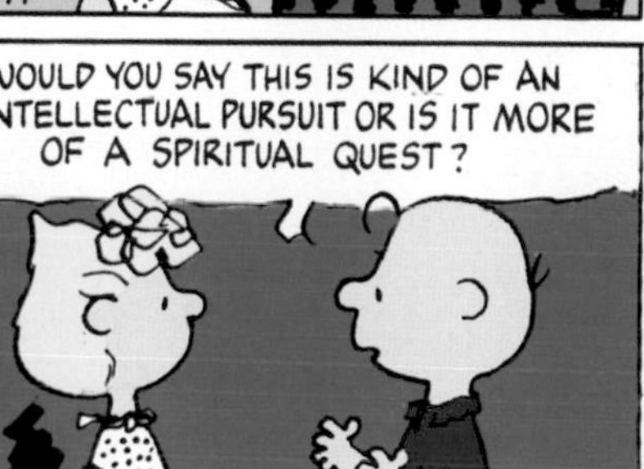
WOULD YOU SAY THIS IS KIND OF AN INTELLECTUAL PURSUIT OR IS IT MORE OF A SPIRITUAL QUEST?

THE BULB IN MY LAMP WENT OUT.. I'M LOOKING FOR ENLIGHTENMENT
SCHULZ

June 27, 1987

WHAT'S YOUR GRAMPA DOING?

HE'S CHOPPING WEEDS WITH A GOLF CLUB..

© 1987 United Feature Syndicate, Inc.
6-27
PROBABLY A NINE-IRON

HAVE YOU EVER SEEN ANYONE SHANK A WEED?
SCHULZ

"I discovered a long time ago that if you take these subjects, whether it's medicine or golf or music or Bill Mauldin, or whatever it is, boy, if you hit somebody's favorite subject, and you treat that subject with dignity and respect and knowledge, they'll be your reader for life."

July 3, 1987

I COULDN'T DECIDE IF I WANTED MARBLE FUDGE, CHOCOLATE, ROCKY ROAD, VANILLA OR BUTTER PECAN..

I FINALLY DECIDED TO TRY MARBLE FUDGE.. THEN I HAD TO CHOOSE BETWEEN A PLAIN CONE OR A SUGAR CONE...
7-3

I DECIDED ON THE SUGAR CONE..SO WHAT HAPPENED? I WENT OUT THE DOOR, AND DROPPED THE WHOLE THING ON THE SIDEWALK!

SCHULZ
DON'T TELL ME MY LIFE ISN'T A SHAKESPEAREAN TRAGEDY..
I WON'T

July 13, 1987

MARCIE AND I ARE ABOUT TO LEAVE FOR CAMP, CHUCK..WE'RE GONNA BE SWIMMING INSTRUCTORS

WE JUST CALLED TO SAY GOODBYE, CHARLES. WE'RE GOING TO MISS YOU.. WE LOVE YOU...
7-13

MARCIE!!

WHO WAS THAT?
I THINK IT WAS A RIGHT NUMBER..
SCHULZ

July 23, 1987

HERE, YOU GOT A LETTER FROM MARCIE..SHE SAYS SHE MISSES YOU...

YOU OPENED MY MAIL?!! YOU READ MY LETTER?!

WELL, WE ALL HAVE REGRETS
REGRETS?

I KNEW IF I DIDN'T READ IT, I'D REGRET IT FOR THE REST OF MY LIFE..
SCHULZ
7-23

August 1, 1987

HI, CHARLES! I JUST GOT BACK..I CALLED YOU SEVERAL TIMES... DID YOU MISS ME?

I JUST POURED MYSELF SOME COLD CEREAL..I DON'T WANT IT TO GET SOGGY...

AAUGH!

8-1
HOW CAN YOU EAT THAT SOGGY LOOKING STUFF?

"These strange little relationships which are taking place all the time are the foundation of the strip. Linus and Snoopy have quite a few struggles fighting over the blanket. Then there's Charlie Brown's struggle with his little sister, Sally. She is pretty dumb, incidentally. She's the dumbest one in the whole strip. She never knows what's going on and that makes it kind of funny."

August 5, 1987

HERE'S THE FIERCE RATTLESNAKE CRAWLING THROUGH THE GRASS...

SLOWLY HE SLITHERS TOWARD HIS PREY...

HE STRIKES!
8-5

JUST WHAT I NEED.. A MOUTHFUL OF FLANNEL
SCHULZ

August 6, 1987

8-6

A REAL RATTLESNAKE RATTLES HIS TAIL BEFORE STRIKING...

FLIP, FLOP, FLIP IS NOT RATTLING!
SCHULZ

August 25, 1987

HEY! WHERE'S EVERYBODY GOING? COME BACK!

IT'S GOING TO CLEAR UP!

THE SUN IS BREAKING THROUGH!
8-25

SORRY, I THOUGHT IT WAS THE SUN..
SCHULZ

November 16, 1987

11-16
REALLY? OKAY, I'LL TELL HIM..

YOUR STUPID DOG IS IN THE EMERGENCY ROOM AT THE HOSPITAL!

GOOD GRIEF! I WONDER WHAT HAPPENED

ARE YOU COMING RIGHT BACK, OR CAN I SWITCH CHANNELS?

November 20, 1987

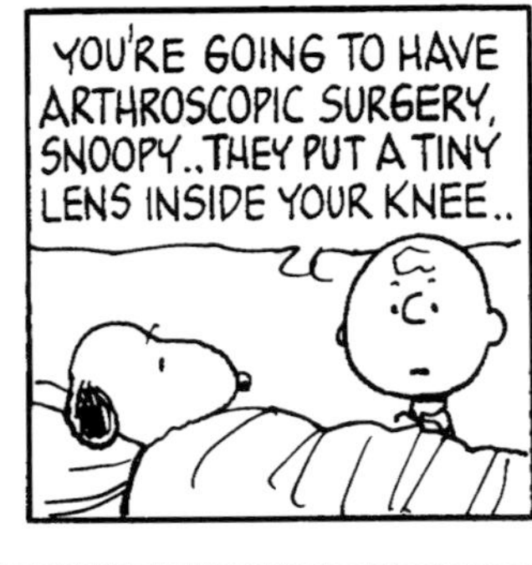
YOU'RE GOING TO HAVE ARTHROSCOPIC SURGERY, SNOOPY..THEY PUT A TINY LENS INSIDE YOUR KNEE..

IT'LL HURT! I WON'T BE ABLE TO STAND IT! THEY WANT TO KILL ME!

THE DOCTOR OPERATES BY LOOKING AT A TV SCREEN..YOU'LL ACTUALLY BE ON VIDEO...
11-20

VIDEO?

November 23, 1987

I FINALLY FOUND OUT HOW YOU HURT YOUR KNEE AT THE ICE ARENA..

I WAS PLAYING HOCKEY..WAYNE GRETZKY TRIPPED ME!

THEY SAID ONE OF THE WAITRESSES IN THE COFFEE SHOP TRIPPED YOU..

SHE LOOKED LIKE WAYNE GRETZKY..
11-23

November 28, 1987

I THINK YOU SHOULD ASK THE NURSE, CHARLES

IT'S YOUR DOG WHO'S HAVING THE SURGERY.. GO AHEAD..ASK HER...
11-28

MA'AM?

DO DOGS HAVE KNEES?

November 30, 1987

WHAT I WANT TO KNOW, MA'AM, IS HOW CAN THEY DO ARTHROSCOPIC KNEE SURGERY ON MY DOG IF DOGS DON'T HAVE KNEES?

YOU DIDN'T KNOW HE WAS A DOG?!

WELL, COULD YOU CALL DOWN TO SURGERY RIGHT AWAY? THANK YOU...
11-30

SHE SAID THEY THOUGHT HE WAS A LITTLE KID WITH A BIG NOSE!
SCHULZ

December 1, 1987

THANK YOU, MA'AM.. WE APPRECIATE IT...

THEY'VE CANCELED SNOOPY'S KNEE SURGERY

DID THEY SAY WHY?
12-1

DOGS DON'T HAVE KNEES!
SCHULZ

December 6, 1987

PEANUTS®
by SCHULZ
I LIKE GETTING LETTERS FROM SPIKE

HE LEADS SUCH AN INTERESTING LIFE

Dear Brother Snoopy,
Well, winter has finally come to the desert.
12-6

Yesterday, it actually started to snow!

I was so excited I decided to build a great big snowman!

But as quickly as the snow started, it stopped.

So, like always, I did the next best thing.
SIGH

I built a tumbleweed man!
SCHULZ

December 21, 1987

HERE.. ONE OF YOUR CHRISTMAS CARDS CAME BACK.. IT SAYS, "NO SUCH ADDRESS"

IT'S THAT GIRL AT SCHOOL! SHE'S GOING TO DRIVE ME CRAZY!!
12-21

WHY DO YOU BOTHER WITH HER?

SHE FASCINATES ME!
SCHULZ

December 23, 1987

I THINK THIS ONE IS FOR YOU..

OH, NO! IT'S A CHRISTMAS CARD FROM LYDIA!
12-23

YOU DIDN'T SEND HER ONE, DID YOU?
I COULDN'T! SHE WOULDN'T EVER TELL ME HER ADDRESS!

I'VE BEEN OUT-CHRISTMASED!!
SCHULZ

December 27, 1987

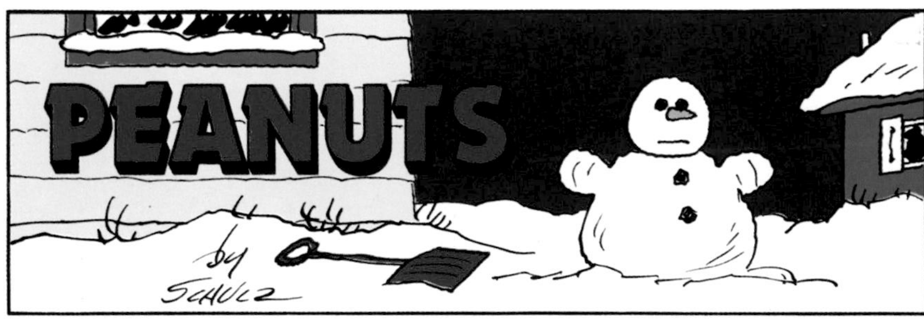
PEANUTS
by SCHULZ

PSST! BIG BROTHER! WAKE UP! THERE'S SOMEONE IN OUR BACK YARD!

THAT'S JUST A SNOWMAN..

WELL, I CAN'T SLEEP WITH HIM STANDING OUT THERE... IT MAKES ME NERVOUS..

BRING ME HIS HEAD SO I'LL KNOW HE'S NOT STILL ALIVE!
GOOD GRIEF!
12-27

WHAT'S GOING ON? I HEAR PEOPLE TALKING...

OKAY, I FEEL BETTER NOW...

WHY DON'T YOU JUST THROW IT BACK OUT INTO THE YARD?

HELLO, DOCTOR? I THINK THERE'S SOMETHING WRONG WITH MY DOG... HE'S TREMBLING ALL OVER..
SCHULZ

January 3, 1988

PEANUTS
by SCHULZ

I DON'T THINK YOU HEARD WHAT I SAID..

WHAT AM I DOING HERE ANYWAY?

YOU NEVER PAY ANY ATTENTION TO ME!

I'LL SHOW YOU!

?

IT'S NONE OF MY BUSINESS, BUT TO ME YOUR MUSIC SOUNDS SORT OF WRINKLED..
SCHULZ
1-3-88

January 5, 1988

THE CONDUCTOR MOUNTS THE PODIUM

HE RAISES HIS BATON..

THE MUSIC BEGINS..

Z
Z
SCHULZ
1-5-88

January 8, 1988

I DECIDED TO COME TO THIS CONCERT PREPARED

I'VE READ ALL ABOUT THE COMPOSERS AND ALL ABOUT THE MUSIC WE'RE GOING TO HEAR..

1-8-88

GOOD FOR YOU, MARCIE

I CAME PREPARED, TOO!
SCHULZ

February 4, 1988

VALENTINE'S DAY IS COMING..BUT AREN'T YOU KIND OF OLD FOR ME?

WHO SAID ANYTHING ABOUT SENDING YOU A VALENTINE?
2-4

I SUPPOSE YOU THINK I'M GONNA GIVE YOU A BIG BOX OF CHOCOLATES WITH "I LOVE LYDIA" ON THE TOP!

TODAY MY NAME IS SAMANTHA
I CAN'T STAND IT!
SCHULZ

February 15, 1988

2-15

NOTHING THAT'S GOING ON IN THE WORLD TODAY IS MY FAULT!

I'LL DRINK TO THAT!
SCHULZ

February 18, 1988

WHEN YOU HIKE IN THE WOODS, YOU HAVE TO BE PREPARED FOR EMERGENCIES...
2-18

THERE'S A SPECIAL CALL WE USE IF WE NEED HELP..

LISTEN CAREFULLY..

MOM!
SCHULZ

February 23, 1988

THERE'S THE HOUSE WHERE THE LITTLE RED HAIRED GIRL LIVES..
2-23

MAYBE IF I STAND HERE LONG ENOUGH, SHE'LL COME OUT...

SHE DOESN'T KNOW THAT I COULD STAND HERE FOR HOURS..

I HAVE TO BECAUSE MY MITTENS ARE FROZEN TO THE TREE!
SCHULZ

February 29, 1988

2-29
RATS! ANOTHER "D-MINUS"!

LIFE HAS ITS SUNSHINE AND ITS RAIN, SIR..ITS DAYS AND ITS NIGHTS..ITS PEAKS AND ITS VALLEYS...

IT'S RAINING TONIGHT IN MY VALLEY!
SCHULZ

March 3, 1988

3-3

SORRY I MISSED THAT ONE, MANAGER..I WAS HOPING I'D CATCH IT...

HOPE GOT IN MY EYES!
SCHULZ

March 18, 1988

3-18

TWO AND A HALF REVOLUTIONS... I USED TO DO BETTER THAN THAT..
SCHULZ

April 2, 1988

YOU USED TO DANCE UP AND DOWN AND ALL AROUND WHEN IT WAS SUPPERTIME..
THERE'S ALWAYS SOMEBODY READY TO REMIND YOU OF THE DUMB THINGS YOU DID WHEN YOU WERE YOUNG..
SCHULZ 4-2

April 16, 1988

4-16
AND THOSE ARE SOME OF THE STORIES WE'LL BE WORKING ON TONIGHT AT ELEVEN..

SCHULZ
I'LL SET MY ALARM

April 28, 1988

DOES MONSIEUR FLYING ACE KNOW THAT NEXT WEEK IS THE BIRTHDAY OF THE RED BARON?

SHE'S RIGHT.. I SHOULD SEND HIM A CARD... SOMETHING SENTIMENTAL..
© 1988 United Feature Syndicate, Inc.
4-28

SCHULZ
LIKE, "HAVE A NICE DAY"

May 10, 1988

"..BUT DAVID WON THE FIGHT WHEN HE HIT GOLIATH IN THE HEAD WITH A STONE..."
WHAT DID GOLIATH'S MOM SAY ABOUT THAT?
5-10
SCHULZ

May 16, 1988

AND IT SAYS THAT NOAH LIVED TO BE NINE HUNDRED AND FIFTY YEARS OLD..
HE COULD HAVE PLAYED ON THE SENIOR TOUR..
5-16
SCHULZ

March 27, 1988

PEANUTS®
by SCHULZ

WELL, HOW WAS THE KITE-FLYING?
I HATE TO ADMIT IT, BUT I JUST SAW SOMETHING THAT MADE ME FEEL REAL GOOD..

May 25, 1988

MY GRAMPA WENT TO HIS HIGH SCHOOL'S FORTIETH REUNION LAST NIGHT..
HE'S ALSO BEEN TO A COLLEGE REUNION AND AN ARMY REUNION...
HE HAS A NEW CAREER.. HE GOES BACK TO THINGS

June 24, 1988

I CAN'T BELIEVE THIS CAMP BROCHURE..WHO'D WANT TO GO THERE?

THEY MAKE YOU SLEEP IN LITTLE TENTS
YOU DON'T LIKE TO CAMP OUT?

NOT ANYMORE..I'M ALL CAMPED OUT..

May 22, 1988

PEANUTS
by Schulz

KEEP AWAY FROM THIS BLANKET, YOU STUPID BEAGLE, OR YOU AND YOUR KIND WILL REGRET IT FOREVER!

MOUNTAINS WILL RISE FROM THE SEA! FIRES WILL RAGE FROM BORDER TO BORDER! FAMINE WILL DESTROY THE FLOCKS AND HERDS!

MIDWIVES WILL DESPAIR, AND THERE WILL BE MUCH WEEPING AND WAILING..

5-22
CLOMP! AAUGH!

I HAD TO DO IT BEFORE HE GOT TO THE LOCUSTS..
SCHULZ

July 4, 1988

YES? TO WHOM DO YOU WISH TO SPEAK?

7-4
THANK YOU... I'LL GET HIM..

SCHULZ
YOUM IS WHOM..

July 6, 1988

YOU KNOW WHAT YOU SHOULD WRITE? YOU SHOULD WRITE A "KISS-AND-TELL" BOOK..
7-6

SMAK

I'M GONNA TELL! I'M GONNA TELL!
SCHULZ

July 20, 1988

IS "TESS OF THE WHO?" ON TV TONIGHT?
"TESS OF THE D'URBERVILLES"

WHATEVER.. I WAS HOPING IT WAS ON TV SO I WOULDN'T HAVE TO READ IT
YOU'RE A REAL STUDENT, AREN'T YOU?
7-20

I HAVE A GREAT FEAR OF BECOMING OVERLY EDUCATED..
SCHULZ

September 1, 1988

HERE'S THE WORLD WAR I FLYING ACE ZOOMING THROUGH THE AIR IN HIS SOPWITH CAMEL..

KNOWING THE WEATHER IS VERY IMPORTANT TO A FLIER...

I HATE CLOUDS..
SCHULZ
9-1

August 14, 1988

PEANUTS
by SCHULZ
DO NOT FEED THE PYTHON

HERE'S THE FIERCE PYTHON HIDING IN A TREE WAITING FOR A VICTIM TO APPEAR..

IF THERE ARE ANY PYTHONS AROUND HERE, THEY'D BETTER COME DOWN OUT OF THIS TREE RIGHT NOW, OR THEY'RE GONNA GET THROWN IN A BOX AND CARRIED OFF TO THE ZOO!
8-14

PYTHONS NEVER KNOW WHAT TO DO WITH THE REST OF THE DAY..
SCHULZ

November 10, 1988

IT WAS COLD LAST NIGHT... I'LL BET ANYTHING MY WATER DISH IS FROZEN..

11-10
I WAS RIGHT..

I COULD HEAR WOODSTOCK DRIVING THE ZAMBONI..

November 11, 1988

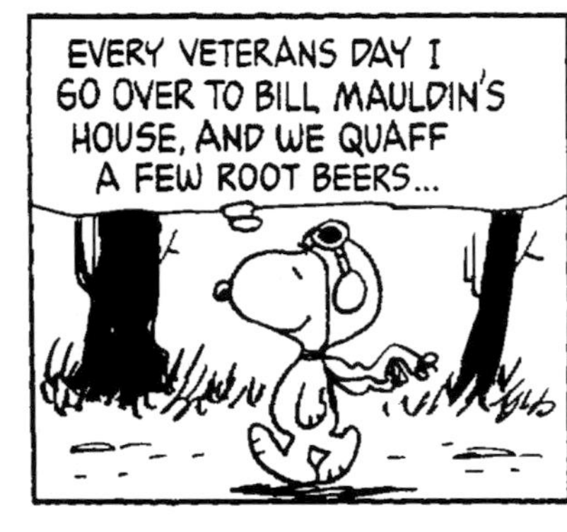
EVERY VETERANS DAY I GO OVER TO BILL MAULDIN'S HOUSE, AND WE QUAFF A FEW ROOT BEERS...

OL' BILL AND I AGREE ON EVERYTHING..

11-11
EXCEPT HE NEVER TAKES ANY OF MY CARTOON IDEAS..
SCHULZ

October 9, 1988

PEANUTS
by SCHULZ
All the Answers
(AND MUCH MUCH MORE)

AM I BOTHERING YOU?
NOT SO FAR

HOW WOULD YOU LIKE TO HAVE SOMEONE LIKE MYSELF REMIND YOU OF ALL YOUR FAULTS?
I WOULDN'T LIKE IT..
SEE? RIGHT THERE IS ONE OF YOUR PROBLEMS..YOU HAVE NO DESIRE TO IMPROVE...

I DON'T NEED YOU TO HELP ME IMPROVE!

AND YOU'RE SO IMPATIENT! YOU GET UPSET SO EASILY..

I DON'T HAVE TO LISTEN TO THIS!

AND YOU THINK EVERYTHING CAN BE SOLVED BY STORMING OUT OF THE ROOM..

10-9

AND YOU ALWAYS FORGET TO TURN OFF THE TV WHEN YOU'RE THROUGH WATCHING IT!
SCHULZ

November 14, 1988

DO PRETTY GIRLS KNOW THAT THEY'RE PRETTY?

11-14
ONLY IF SOMEBODY TELLS THEM..

WELL?
SCHULZ

December 6, 1988

I HEAR YOUR CHRISTMAS PLAY WAS CANCELED
THE SCHOOL BOARD DID US IN..

12-6
I THOUGHT I WROTE A GOOD PLAY, TOO..

MY BEST SCENE WAS WHERE JOSEPH DRIVES HIS FAMILY TO EGYPT IN A '56 THUNDERBIRD..
SCHULZ

December 20, 1988

12-20
SCHULZ

December 24, 1988

EVERY TIME THERE'S A CHRISTMAS PLAY, I END UP BEING A SHEEP..

WATCH OUT FOR THE CURB HERE, SIR..
WHAT?

12-24
SLOUCHING TOWARDS BETHLEHEM, HUH, SIR?
I CAN'T STAND IT!
SCHULZ

January 1, 1989

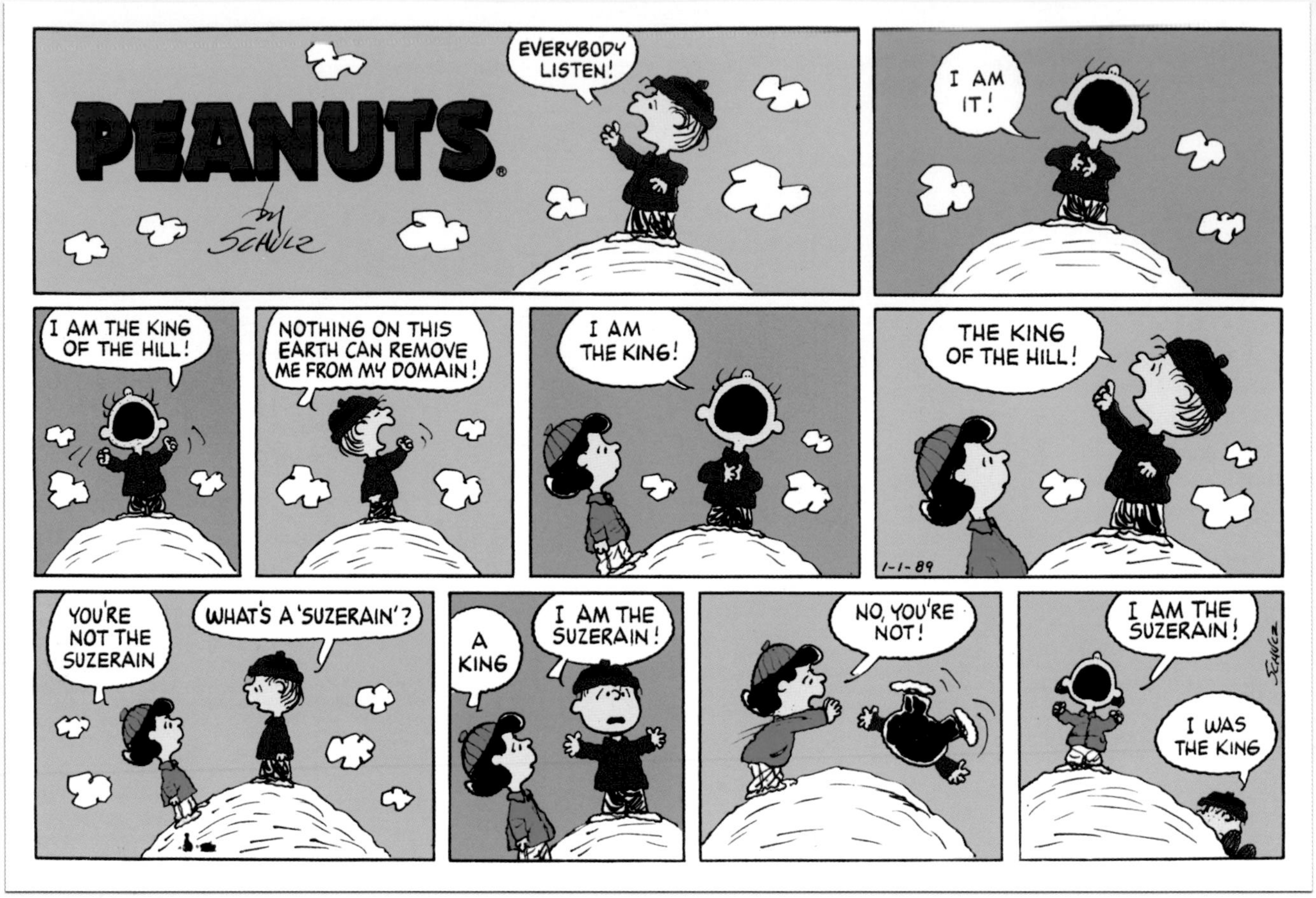

PEANUTS
by SCHULZ
EVERYBODY LISTEN!
I AM IT!
I AM THE KING OF THE HILL!
NOTHING ON THIS EARTH CAN REMOVE ME FROM MY DOMAIN!
I AM THE KING!
THE KING OF THE HILL!
1-1-89
YOU'RE NOT THE SUZERAIN
WHAT'S A 'SUZERAIN'?
A KING
I AM THE SUZERAIN!
NO, YOU'RE NOT!
I AM THE SUZERAIN!
I WAS THE KING
SCHULZ

January 24, 1989—First appearance of Olaf.

HE WON!! OLAF WON!!! YOUR BROTHER WON THE "UGLY DOG" CONTEST!
OLAF! YOU WON!
1-24
RATS!
SCHULZ

January 26, 1989

REMEMBER WHEN WE WERE PUPPIES AT THE DAISY HILL PUPPY FARM? I CAN'T BELIEVE I'VE GROWN UP TO WIN AN "UGLY DOG" CONTEST...
I THINK I'LL HURT MYSELF..
OLAF!
NOT TO WORRY.. I'VE DONE THIS BEFORE..
SCHULZ
1-26

January 15, 1989

PEANUTS
by SCHULZ
1-15
THAT'S NOT SKATING..
THAT'S SLIDING!

YOU DON'T HAVE ANY SKATES ON!
YOU'RE JUST SLIDING ON YOUR
FEET..THAT'S NOT SKATING!

SKATING IS WHEN YOU HAVE
SKATES ON! YOU'RE NOT SKATING
AT ALL! YOU'RE JUST SLIDING!

HOW COULD I HAVE
BEEN SO STUPID?

I THOUGHT I WAS
HAVING FUN..
SCHULZ

March 9, 1989

PSYCHIATRIC
HELP 5¢
HERE'S SORT OF
A SUGGESTION,
"PIGPEN".
THE DOCTOR
IS IN

MAYBE YOU COULD START
BY TRYING TO GO FOR JUST
ONE HOUR WITHOUT GETTING
DIRTY..WHAT WOULD HAPPEN
IF YOU TRIED THAT?

3-9
DO YOU HAVE ANY
IDEA HOW PAINFUL A
MIGRAINE CAN BE?
SCHULZ
THE DOCTOR
IS IN

March 10, 1989

PSYCHIATRIC
HELP 5¢
DO YOU THINK
YOU'RE GOING
TO BE ABLE
TO HELP ME?
THE DOCTOR
IS IN

I DON'T KNOW, "PIGPEN".
WHEN I LOOK AT YOU, ALL
I SEE IS DIRT AND DUST..YOU
DON'T NEED A PSYCHIATRIST...

3-10
YOU NEED AN
ARCHAEOLOGIST!
SCHULZ
THE DOCTOR
IS IN

March 28, 1989

DO YOU THINK PEOPLE EVER REALLY CHANGE?
3-28

SURE, I FEEL I'VE CHANGED A LOT THIS PAST YEAR..
I MEANT FOR THE BETTER!
SCHULZ

October 6, 1989

DID YOU HEAR THE NEWS, MONSIEUR FLYING ACE OF WORLD WAR I ?

THE RED BARON IS COMING HERE TO THE SMALL, QUAINT, CHARMING FRENCH CAFE TO PUNCH YOUR LIGHTS OUT!

HE WOULDN'T HIT SOMEONE WHO IS WEARING GOGGLES, WOULD HE ?
SCHULZ
10-6

June 18, 1989

PEANUTS
by SCHULZ

FOR YOUR DAD, HUH?

THAT'S RIGHT.. FOR FATHER'S DAY..

I JUST FOUND OUT THAT HE'S RETIRED NOW, AND LIVING IN FLORIDA...

THERE WERE EIGHT OF US IN THE LITTER

I KNOW HE'LL APPRECIATE GETTING THIS CARD...

U.S. MAIL

Dear Dad, Happy Father's Day!

AND THEY ALL SIGNED IT!

SCHULZ
6-18

October 29, 1989

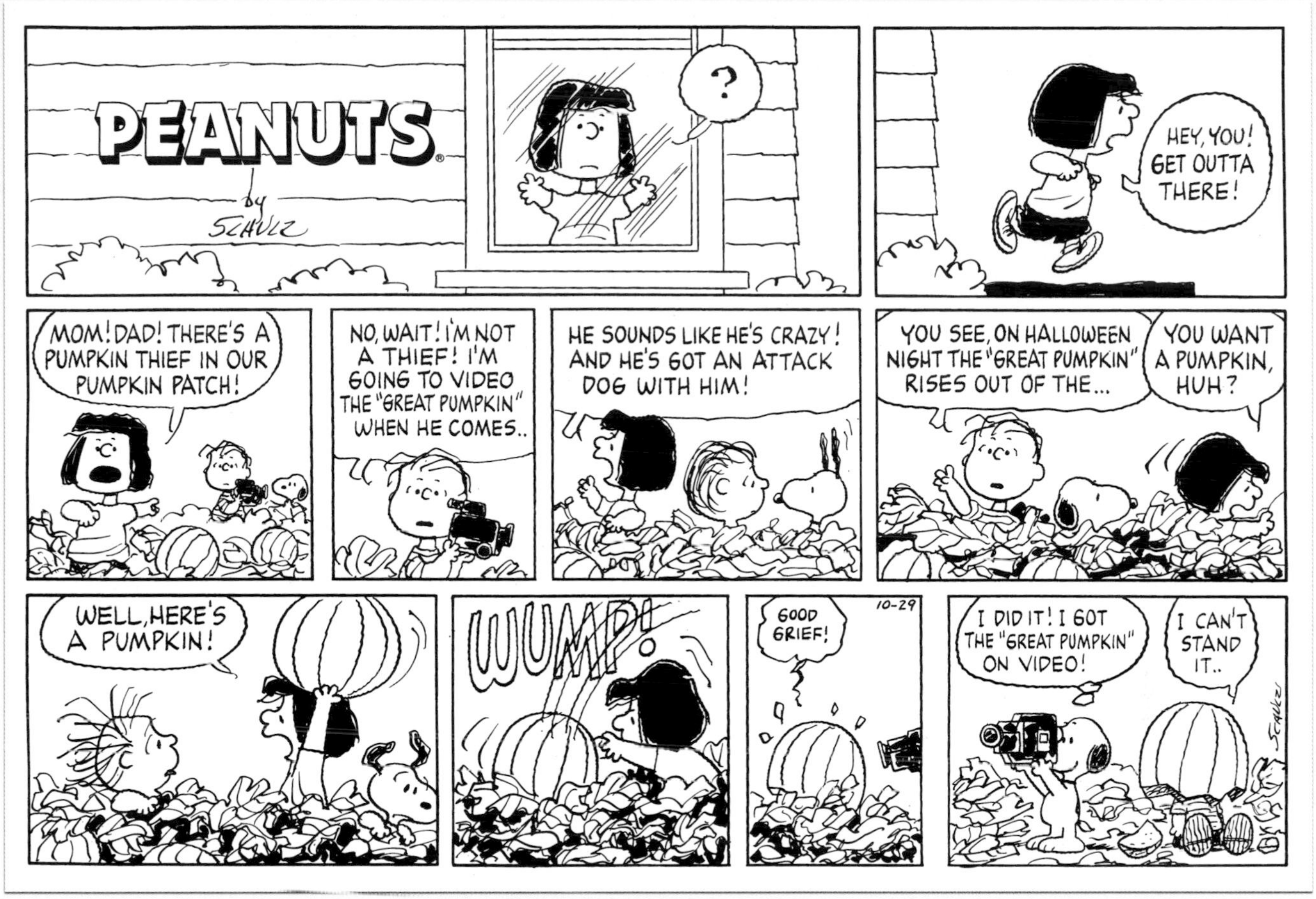

PEANUTS
by SCHULZ
?
HEY, YOU! GET OUTTA THERE!
MOM! DAD! THERE'S A PUMPKIN THIEF IN OUR PUMPKIN PATCH!
NO, WAIT! I'M NOT A THIEF! I'M GOING TO VIDEO THE "GREAT PUMPKIN" WHEN HE COMES..
HE SOUNDS LIKE HE'S CRAZY! AND HE'S GOT AN ATTACK DOG WITH HIM!
YOU SEE, ON HALLOWEEN NIGHT THE "GREAT PUMPKIN" RISES OUT OF THE...
YOU WANT A PUMPKIN, HUH?
WELL, HERE'S A PUMPKIN!
WUMP!
GOOD GRIEF!
10-29
I DID IT! I GOT THE "GREAT PUMPKIN" ON VIDEO!
I CAN'T STAND IT..

October 26, 1989

WHAT WOULD YOU SAY IF I TOLD YOU I WAS GOING TO DEVOTE THE REST OF MY LIFE TO MAKING YOU HAPPY?
WE'LL GO FOR LONG WALKS IN THE WOODS AND ROMP AROUND IN THE YARD...
YOU'LL SIT IN MY LAP, AND I'LL SCRATCH YOUR EARS, AND WE'LL WATCH TV AND I'LL GIVE YOU COOKIES...
WHAT KIND OF COOKIES?
10-26

December 8, 1989

12-8

Celebrate 1990s

"Without knowing it, I could be grinding down, becoming boring or repetitive. So far, I think, I haven't been. I think I've passed the leveling-off period and I'm proud of that. The average comic strip starts off pretty good, then levels off and never changes, never gets better. I think I passed the leveling-off period a long time ago: *Peanuts* moved on and jumped up. And it's simply because I really worked at it."

—Charles M. Schulz

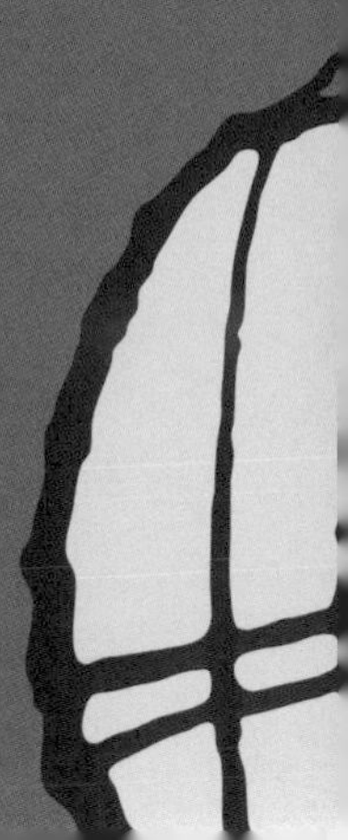

1990–1999

Those comparing the strips Charles Schulz drew in the 1990s with those drawn in the 1950s and 1960s might note some differences. One thing that strikes many readers is that the strips from the 1990s do not seem as sad or angst ridden as strips from the earlier decades. Even Lucy, once known for her crabby, bossy behavior, was no longer as mean spirited or cruel. Charles Schulz remarked in a 1997 interview that *Peanuts* "is much more mild than it used to be."

Another difference that is apparent is in the drawing of the strip. Schulz took great pride in producing the "best pen line" he could make and never considered having anyone assist with drawing or lettering the strip, as many successful cartoonists do. In later years, when his hand began to shake (he was diagnosed by his doctor as having an "essential tremor"), his pen line appears significantly different than it does in the earlier decades. Schulz officially retired from the strip on December 14, 1999.

- Schulz provided details about Peppermint Patty's and Marcie's lives that are largely missing in the development of his other characters. In a multiday story, Marcie confesses to Charlie Brown, "[My parents] want me to get straight A's in school, and do everything perfect! I'm cracking up, Charles." In the October 19, 1990, strip, Peppermint Patty arrives to comfort Marcie and finds that she has fallen into an exhausted sleep. Schulz resists the temptation to provide any pat answers to Marcie's predicament or a happy ending to this multiday story line.

- In the early years of the strip, the kids in *Peanuts* appeared baffled and confused by Snoopy's antics when he was in the grips of one of his alter egos. In the strip's later years, however, the kids are active participants in Snoopy's fantasies, as in the June 10, 1992, strip that finds Sally a passenger on Ace Airlines.

- In a red-letter day for the strip, Charlie Brown finally hits a home run on March 30, 1993. Schulz convincingly portrays Charlie Brown's extravagant delight at this unlikely occurrence.

- Schulz was extremely proud of his military service during World War II and was very grateful to the soldiers who had sacrificed so much during the Allied landing on the Normandy coast on June 6, 1944. On June 6, 1993, the first *Peanuts* strip to commemorate the D-Day landing was published. Schulz created a commemorative D-Day strip for every year between 1993 and 1998, with the exception of 1995.

- On February 14, 1994, Snoopy's last named sibling was introduced in the strip—the fuzzy Andy. Snoopy has seven siblings, although two are never named. The named siblings are Spike, Belle, Marbles, Olaf, and Andy.

- Schulz and his wife, Jean, took ballroom dancing lessons in the 1990s. These lessons provided the germ of an idea that Schulz explored in Snoopy and Charlie Brown's dancing lesson starting with the February 8, 1995, strip.

- Snoopy first appeared as an author on July 12, 1965. Snoopy's role as author provided Schulz an opportunity to include a different type of humor in *Peanuts*. "I can have Snoopy type outrageous puns," Schulz wrote, "the sort of pun that [I] would never draw under ordinary circumstances." Another long-running gag is the callous disregard with which editors view Snoopy's writing. In the October 27, 1995, strip Snoopy finally gets published, if only a book at a time!

- Rerun, having spent the first week of kindergarten hiding under his bed, attended his first day of school on September 11, 1996. Schulz, who found high school to be very difficult, appeared to be deeply compassionate to the trauma that some children face at school.

- For the most part, Schulz avoided controversial social issues, believing that the role of a comic strip is to entertain. On occasion, however, as is the case with the January 16, 1997, strip, Schulz cannot help but comment on some of the more excessive aspects of "political correctness."

- The often-referenced-but-never-seen Little Red-Haired Girl finally appears on May 25, 1998, but only in silhouette!

January 13, 1990

?

"Help! Am stranded in some stupid dog's water dish!
A bug

YOU'RE WELCOME.. BUT I DIDN'T CARE FOR THE PART ABOUT THE STUPID DOG!

"I think that it is very important not to include a lot of extraneous details in the characters themselves, in the drawing of them, or in the background, or all of that. Anything that would interfere with the flow of the dialogue or the idea itself. I would advise someone to go back and read Percy Crosby's Skippy *to see what I'm talking about, rather than my own work. Now, I resent the fact I was forced to draw the world's smallest comic strip at the time, simply because I'm sure the people at United didn't have much faith in it, so my work was reduced almost to the size of four airmail stamps. A lot of my style was developed so that I could accommodate it to those small panels."*

January 23, 1990

I WONDER WHAT I CAN DO TO MAKE THAT LITTLE RED-HAIRED GIRL NOTICE ME..

MAYBE IF I WALK AROUND THE ROOM A BIT...I'LL BET SHE NOTICES ME NOW...

ESPECIALLY AFTER I GET MY SLEEVE CAUGHT IN THE PENCIL SHARPENER..

January 24, 1990

IF THAT LITTLE RED-HAIRED GIRL SEES ME STANDING HERE WITH MY SLEEVE CAUGHT IN THE PENCIL SHARPENER, SHE'LL THINK I'M THE DUMBEST PERSON IN THE WORLD

WHAT I HAVE TO DO IS WRIGGLE OUT OF MY SWEATER BUT STILL LOOK REAL COOL...

January 25, 1990

WHY DO WE HAVE TO STAND IN LINE FOR EVERYTHING?
WHAT'S THE HOLDUP?
PROBABLY AN OVERTURNED VEHICLE
PUSH 'IM OUT O'THERE
WHAT'S TAKING YOU SO LONG, CHARLES?
I LIKE A PENCIL WITH A FINE POINT..
1-25
SCHULZ

January 26, 1990

YOU GOT THE SLEEVE OF YOUR SWEATER CAUGHT IN THE PENCIL SHARPENER?

WELL, WHAT DID YOU DO? HOW DID YOU GET IT OUT?

SCHULZ
1-26

February 9, 1990

EACH FAMILY HAS A CHAIN OF COMMAND, AND DO YOU KNOW WHO'S THE LOWEST ON THAT CHAIN? GUESS!

IT'S THE DOG! THE DOG IS THE LOWEST! DO YOU UNDERSTAND THAT?

I SAID, DO YOU UNDERSTAND THAT?
THEY HATE IT WHEN YOU JUST STARE AT 'EM LIKE THIS..
SCHULZ
2-9

February 20, 1990

SHE'S CUTE, ISN'T SHE?
2-20

CUTE ISN'T EVERYTHING, CHARLIE BROWN...

I FALL IN LOVE WITH ANY GIRL WHO SMELLS LIKE LIBRARY PASTE..
SCHULZ

February 21, 1990

NOTHING IS MORE COMFORTING THAN SITTING WITH YOUR FAITHFUL DOG IN YOUR LAP...
THIS IS MURDER.. MY BACK IS KILLING ME AND ALL FOUR LEGS ARE ASLEEP!
© 1990 United Feature Syndicate, Inc.
2-21
SCHULZ

February 27, 1990

YOU HAVEN'T CALLED US IN A LONG WHILE, CHUCK..DON'T YOU LIKE US ANYMORE?

OR MAYBE YOU NEVER DID LIKE US..IS THAT TRUE, CHUCK? THAT YOU NEVER DID LIKE US? HUH, CHUCK? HUH?
2-27

WE'RE SORRY..THE NUMBER YOU HAVE CALLED IS NO LONGER IN SERVICE..IT WAS A MINUTE AGO, BUT THESE THINGS HAPPEN..
SCHULZ

March 3, 1990

Dear Contributor, We are returning your dumb story

Note that we have not included our return address.

We have moved to a new office,
3-3

and we don't want you to know where we are.
SCHULZ

March 7, 1990

SO IF THE BALL IS HIT TO THE SHORTSTOP, HE FLIPS IT TO THE SECOND BASEMAN WHO THROWS IT TO FIRST FOR THE DOUBLE PLAY!
"DOUBLE PLAY..." SOUNDS LIKE A GOOD NAME FOR A COOKIE..
3-7
SCHULZ

March 4, 1990

PEANUTS
by SCHULZ
CHOMP CHOMP CHOMP
I CAN'T STAND IT
THE WIND SEEMS JUST RIGHT..
I DON'T KNOW WHY I EVEN BOTHER..
THERE'S A KITE-EATING TREE OUT THERE JUST WAITING FOR ME!
THEY'RE ALWAYS REAL HUNGRY AFTER A LONG WINTER...
THEY'RE IMPATIENT, GREEDY AND MERCILESS...
KNOCK KNOCK KNOCK
?
I HATE IT WHEN THEY COME RIGHT UP TO THE FRONT DOOR
3-4
SCHULZ

"The strip is based on memory, really, not on observation."

March 14, 1990

TRUE! FALSE! TRUE! MAYBE! WHO KNOWS? WHY NOT? COULD BE! TRUE AGAIN!
ABSOLUTELY FALSE! A SURE THING! NOW AND THEN! WHO CARES? TRUE AGAIN!
IF THE GOOD LORD IS WILLING, AND THE CREEKS DON'T RISE!
YOU'RE REALLY WEIRD, SIR
3-14
SCHULZ

April 16, 1990

4-16

SCHULZ

April 30, 1990

I DON'T BELIEVE IT..YOU'VE BEEN SELECTED FOR JURY DUTY!

THIS IS RIDICULOUS! DON'T THEY KNOW YOU'RE A DOG?
WHAT'S WRONG WITH THAT?
4-30

OBVIOUSLY, THERE'S BEEN A MISTAKE..
I'LL GO IF THEY GIVE AWAY FREE COOKIES..
SCHULZ

May 2, 1990

YES, MA'AM, I'M CALLING ABOUT MY DOG..APPARENTLY YOU'VE SELECTED HIM FOR JURY DUTY...
ASK HER IF THEY GIVE FREE COOKIES
5-2

NO, MA'AM, I'M NOT CALLING FOR MYSELF...I'M CALLING FOR MY DOG... I THINK THERE'S BEEN A MISTAKE..

PARKING? NO, MA'AM, I'M NOT CALLING ABOUT PARKING.. I'M ...HELLO? HELLO?

YOU DIDN'T ASK HER ABOUT THE COOKIES..

SCHULZ

May 4, 1990

YES, MA'AM, THIS IS MY DOG.. HE WAS TOLD TO REPORT HERE THIS MORNING FOR JURY DUTY

WHY IS HE WEARING GOGGLES?
5-4

PLEASE, MA'AM, DON'T ASK ME TO TRY TO EXPLAIN THAT..
SCHULZ

May 5, 1990

THE LADY SAID FOR YOU TO SIT HERE UNTIL THEY CALL YOUR NAME...

LOOK AT THIS..IT SAYS IF YOU SERVE ON A JURY, THEY PAY YOU FIVE DOLLARS A DAY..

FIVE DOLLARS WILL BUY A LOT OF COOKIES!
SCHULZ
5-5

May 8, 1990

YES, SIR...NO, YOUR HONOR, I'VE NEVER MET A JUDGE BEFORE..

WELL, MY DOG GOT THIS CARD IN THE MAIL SAYING HE HAD BEEN SELECTED FOR JURY DUTY, AND...

THIS IS A NICE ROOM..IT REMINDS ME OF THE TIME I WAS CALLED IN TO ADVISE GENERAL PERSHING...
5-8

May 9, 1990

SO THEN WHAT HAPPENED?
THEN THE JUDGE APOLOGIZED TO US FOR THE MIS-UNDERSTANDING, AND SAID WE WERE GOOD CITIZENS FOR TRYING TO DO WHAT WAS RIGHT..
I WAS ALL SET TO VOTE 'GUILTY'!
5-9

May 19, 1990

MY SHORTSTOP IS ASLEEP...
Z
5-19

MY SECOND BASEMAN IS ASLEEP...
Z

MY RIGHT FIELDER IS ASLEEP...
Z

I'M THE ONLY PERSON I KNOW WHO PITCHES A LULLABY..

September 24, 1990

I'VE DECIDED TO RUN FOR CLASS PRESIDENT

GOOD FOR YOU, "PIGPEN," BUT MAYBE YOU SHOULD SORT OF CLEAN UP A BIT FIRST...
9-24

I HAVE... I TOOK ALL THE OLD CANDY WRAPPERS OUT OF MY POCKETS..

September 25, 1990

DID I TELL YOU? I'VE DECIDED TO RUN FOR CLASS PRESIDENT..

"PIGPEN," YOU'RE SUCH A MESS I WOULDN'T VOTE FOR YOU FOR FROG CATCHER!
9-25

DOGCATCHER
WHATEVER
SCHULZ

September 27, 1990

WHAT KIND OF A PHOTO DID YOU WANT, "PIGPEN"?

WELL, IF IT'S GOING TO BE A CAMPAIGN PHOTO, I FIGURED IT SHOULD HAVE A DOG IN IT...

OKAY, LET'S DO IT..
DON'T BOTHER MAKING ANY EXTRA PRINTS FOR ME..
SCHULZ
9-27

September 28, 1990

AND IF I'M ELECTED CLASS PRESIDENT, I PROMISE TO...

YOU CAN'T BE CLASS PRESIDENT, "PIGPEN"! YOU'RE A MESS, AND YOU HAVE NO DIGNITY!

9-28

SCHULZ

September 29, 1990

9-29
I'M SORRY YOU DIDN'T GET ELECTED CLASS PRESIDENT, "PIGPEN"

I THOUGHT HAVING A CAMPAIGN PHOTO OF ME AND A DOG WOULD DO IT...

NOBODY VOTED FOR ME..THEY ALL VOTED FOR THE DOG!
SCHULZ

September 2, 1990

PEANUTS
by SCHULZ

"TEAL"?

"TEAL" OR "CERULEAN"...WHICH COLOR EXPRESSES WHAT I'M TRYING TO SAY HERE?

DOES "WILD STRAWBERRY" SAY ANYTHING AT ALL?

AND I'M NOT SURE IF "FUCHSIA" MAKES AN EFFORT TO COMMUNICATE..
9-2

WHICH REALLY SPEAKS LOUDER, "TANGERINE" OR "DANDELION"?

IN FACT, DOES "ROYAL PURPLE" SAY WHAT WE...

COLOR THE SKY BLUE AND THE GRASS GREEN!

GET OUT THE "BLACK".. I'LL DO A NIGHT SCENE..
SCHULZ

"If you read the strip, you would know me. Everything I am goes into the strip— all of my fears, my anxieties, and my joys."

October 16, 1990

MY PARENTS ARE DRIVING ME CRAZY, CHARLES! THEY WANT ME TO BE PERFECT..

THEY WANT ME TO GET STRAIGHT A'S IN SCHOOL, AND DO EVERYTHING PERFECT! I'M CRACKING UP, CHARLES..
10/16

I SHOULDN'T EVEN BE HERE..I'M SUPPOSED TO BE READING "IVANHOE"
I DON'T KNOW WHAT TO SAY..

KEEP TALKING WHILE I READ THIS LAST CHAPTER..
SCHULZ

October 17, 1990

SEE HOW MY HANDS SHAKE, CHARLES? IT'S BECAUSE OF ALL THE PRESSURE...

MY PARENTS THINK I SHOULD GET PERFECT GRADES IN EVERYTHING EVERY DAY!
10-17

AND I'M SO TIRED..
WHEN SHE WAKES UP, GIVE HER A COOKIE..
SCHULZ

October 19, 1990

WHERE IS SHE, CHUCK? WHERE'S MARCIE?
SHE'S IN HERE SOUND ASLEEP...

SHE WAS TELLING US HOW MUCH STRESS SHE'S BEEN UNDER LATELY, AND THEN SHE JUST FELL ASLEEP...

POOR MARCIE.. SHE'S TOO HARD ON HERSELF
SHE PROBABLY NEEDS A DOG..
10-19

October 20, 1990

WHERE AM I?
YOU'RE AT MY HOUSE, MARCIE
10-20

I DON'T WANT TO GO HOME.. CAN I STAY HERE? IF I GO HOME, I HAVE TO BE PERFECT...

IF SHE DOESN'T WANT TO BE PERFECT, SHE'S COME TO THE RIGHT PLACE!

October 24, 1990

AS SOON AS I WALK IN THE DOOR, MY MOTHER WILL SAY, "HAVE YOU DONE YOUR HOMEWORK?"

ALL THEY CARE ABOUT IS AM I GETTING STRAIGHT "A'S"?

..JUST SO I CAN GO TO SOME COLLEGE THEY'VE ALREADY PICKED OUT FOR ME...
10-24

AND END UP MARRYING SOME NERD!

October 25, 1990

I'M WORRIED ABOUT POOR MARCIE..HER PARENTS INSIST THAT SHE GET STRAIGHT A'S..

10-25
WE'RE LUCKY...

IT'S KIND OF NICE LIVING IN A C-MINUS HOME

November 27, 1990

IF YOU'RE A REAL SANTA CLAUS, WHERE ARE YOUR REINDEER?

I KNOW WHAT I SHOULD HAVE SAID... I SHOULD HAVE SAID, "I GOT HUNGRY LAST WINTER SO I ATE THEM!"

February 11, 1991

I'M MAKING THIS VALENTINE FOR MY SWEET BABBOO...
I'M NOT YOUR STUPID SWEET BABBOO!!

HE'S MY SWEET BABBOO AND I'M HIS BABBOOETTE..
I'VE NEVER HEARD OF A BABBOOETTE!!

YOU HAVE NOW!!

February 12, 1991

SEE? I MADE THIS VALENTINE FOR MY SWEET BABBOO...
I'M NOT YOUR SWEET BABBOO!!

I SIGNED IT "FROM YOUR SWEET BABBOOETTE"
THERE ISN'T SUCH A THING AS A "BABBOOETTE"

DAVID USED TO CALL BATHSHEBA HIS "SWEET BABBOOETTE"
NO, HE DIDN'T!

OR DID HE?

February 14, 1991

DID YOU GET MY VALENTINE? I SIGNED IT "FROM YOUR SWEET BABBOOETTE"

I'VE NEVER HEARD OF A "BABBOOETTE"

AND IF I EVER GOT A VALENTINE FROM ONE, I'D THROW IT IN THE WASTEBASKET..

MY BROTHER DIDN'T MAKE IT TO SCHOOL TODAY..APPARENTLY SOMEBODY HIT HIM WITH A LUNCH BOX

February 15, 1991

..AND THEN YOUR STUPID SISTER HIT ME WITH HER LUNCH BOX...SANDWICHES FLEW ALL OVER..AND THEN MY ATTORNEY SHOWED UP..

DID HE TAKE THE CASE?
NO, HE ATE ALL THE SANDWICHES!
2-15
SCHULZ

February 16, 1991

MY ATTORNEY AND I ARE HERE TO SUE YOU FOR HITTING ME WITH YOUR LUNCH BOX..

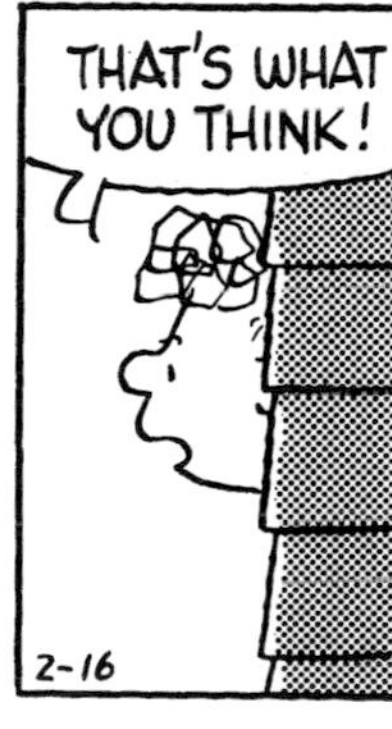
THAT'S WHAT YOU THINK!
2-16

I'VE GOT HIS SUPPER DISH, SEE? IF YOU SUE ME, I'LL THROW IT OVER THE FENCE!

AFTER CAREFUL CONSIDERATION, I'VE DECIDED WE DON'T HAVE A CASE..
SCHULZ

December 2, 1990

PEANUTS
by SCHULZ
AN IGLOO! HOW NICE..
IT'S NOT AN IGLOO? THEN WHAT DO YOU CALL IT?
A BEAGLOO?
12-2
WHY DO YOU CALL IT A BEAGLOO?
NO, I DON'T THINK IT LOOKS LIKE MY NOSE AT ALL..
SCHULZ

March 15, 1991

SOMETIMES I LIE IN BED AT NIGHT, AND I ASK MYSELF, "WHY?"
3-15

THEN A VOICE COMES TO ME THAT SAYS, "WHY, WHAT?"
SCHULZ

April 9, 1991

HERE'S THE WORLD WAR I FLYING ACE RETURNING TO THE AIRDROME IN HIS SOPWITH CAMEL..
4-9

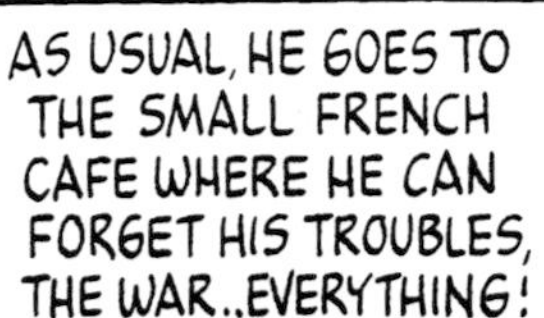
AS USUAL, HE GOES TO THE SMALL FRENCH CAFE WHERE HE CAN FORGET HIS TROUBLES, THE WAR..EVERYTHING!

BON SOIR, MONSIEUR FLYING ACE..WHAT IS YOUR NAME?

I FORGOT
SCHULZ

April 11, 1991

WHAT'S GOING ON HERE?
THIS IS THE FAMOUS FLYING ACE OF WORLD WAR I ...
4-11

HE COMES TO MY SMALL FRENCH CAFE EVERY NIGHT TO FORGET THE WAR..

YOU'RE REALLY WEIRD, MARCIE
SO WHAT ARE YOU, A SPY?
WHAT WOULD HAPPEN IF WE PUT A LITTLE ICE CREAM IN THIS ROOT BEER?
SCHULZ

April 12, 1991

HEY, CHUCK..IT'S EIGHT O'CLOCK... DO YOU KNOW WHERE YOUR DOG IS?

WHAT DO YOU MEAN?

HE'S SITTING IN MARCIE'S KITCHEN DRINKING ROOT BEER, THAT'S WHAT I MEAN!

4-12

HE GOES THERE EVERY NIGHT...WHAT ARE YOU GONNA DO ABOUT IT, CHUCK?
SCHULZ

I CAN'T HEAR YOU..IT'S TOO DARK OUTSIDE

April 13, 1991

BON SOIR, MONSIEUR BRAVE FLYING ACE OF WORLD WAR I ... IT IS GOOD TO SEE YOU AGAIN..

LET ME SERVE THE GALLANT, COURAGEOUS, VALIANT FLYING ACE A ROOT BEER..

4-13
NO STRAW?
SCHULZ

April 15, 1991

MARCIE, DO YOU REALLY THINK YOU SHOULD LET THIS DOG COME OVER EVERY NIGHT FOR ROOT BEER?

WHY NOT, WHAT DO YOU CARE, AND IS IT ANY OF YOUR BUSINESS?!
4-15

THAT WAS A MULTIPLE-CHOICE QUESTION, SIR!

FRENCH WAITRESSES ARE SO EXCITABLE..
SCHULZ

"I really feel good when I have drawn some strips that I think are especially good, that are a little bit different, that have contributed something to the profession, and that are unique in that no one else could have done them at that particular time. To get them all done and look at them and send them off always makes me feel very happy. If I've doubled up that week and gained a week, that also makes me happy. On a very personal note, of course, I'm always happy when I'm with my family, and we're all together doing something that we like to do. I've always said that standing by the side of the rink and watching my girls skate makes me very happy. To see your children accomplish something in their lives is also a wonderful feeling."

April 27, 1991

SCHULZ
4-27

May 12, 1991

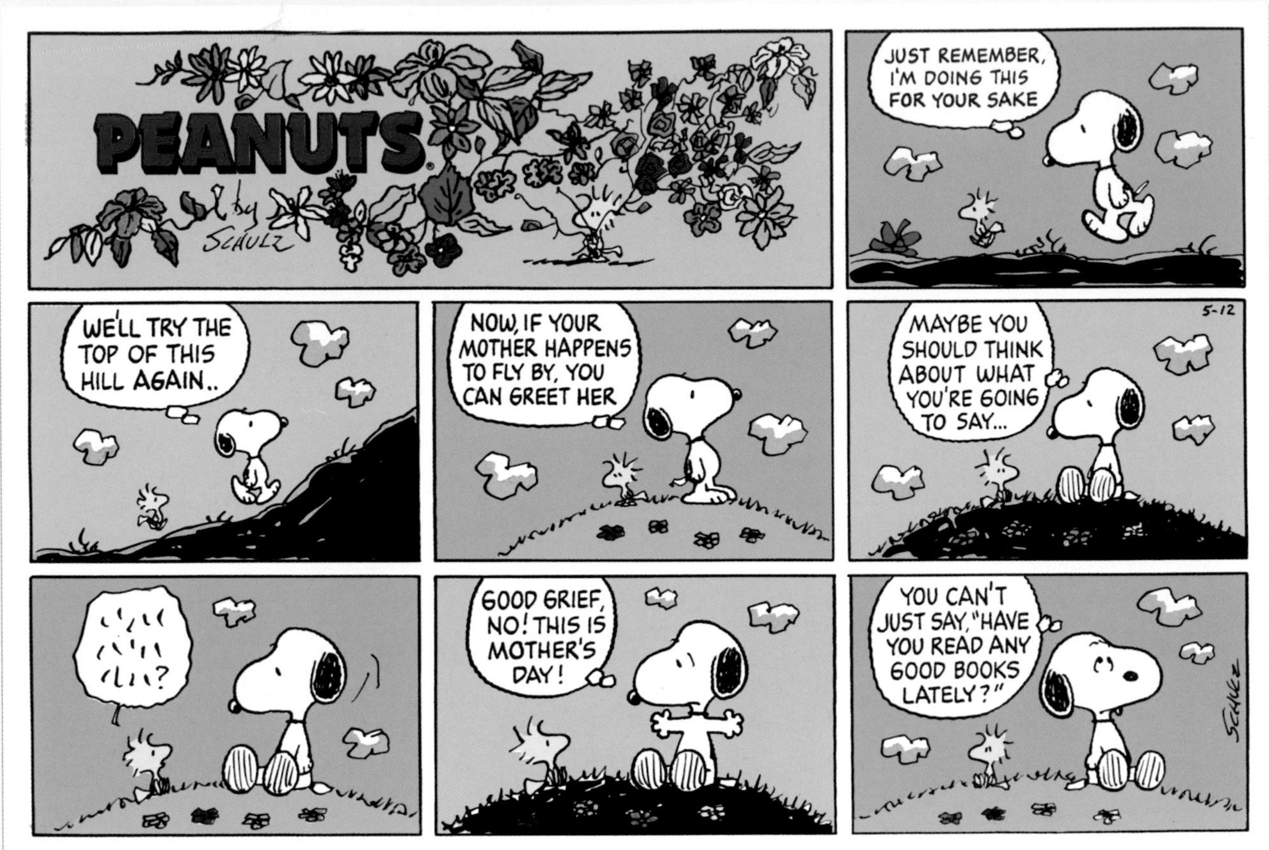
PEANUTS
by SCHULZ
JUST REMEMBER, I'M DOING THIS FOR YOUR SAKE
WE'LL TRY THE TOP OF THIS HILL AGAIN..
NOW, IF YOUR MOTHER HAPPENS TO FLY BY, YOU CAN GREET HER
5-12
MAYBE YOU SHOULD THINK ABOUT WHAT YOU'RE GOING TO SAY...
GOOD GRIEF, NO! THIS IS MOTHER'S DAY!
YOU CAN'T JUST SAY, "HAVE YOU READ ANY GOOD BOOKS LATELY?"
SCHULZ

May 17, 1991

THIS IS MY REPORT ON "THE BROTHERS KARAMAZOV" OF WHICH THERE WERE THREE...
IT REMINDED ME OF A SIMILAR STORY, "THE THREE LITTLE KITTENS" BECAUSE THERE WERE THREE OF THEM ALSO...
5-17
REALLY, MA'AM?
I'M SURPRISED THE SIMILARITY NEVER OCCURRED TO YOU..
SCHULZ

May 28, 1991

GOOD MORNING, GANG... WELCOME TO BIBLE CLASS..
MY NAME IS SALLY, AND BECAUSE I'M BIGGER THAN YOU, I'M GOING TO BE YOUR TEACHER...
5-28
I WAS HOPING WE'D GET A CUTE CHICK..SO WHAT DO WE GET? AN OLD LADY!
SCHULZ

May 29, 1991

GOOD MORNING, CLASS.. MY NAME IS CHARLIE BROWN... WELCOME TO BIBLE SCHOOL..

WILL WE BE ABLE TO ASK QUESTIONS IN THIS CLASS?
ABSOLUTELY! WHAT IS YOUR QUESTION?
5-29

I JUST ASKED IT
SCHULZ

May 31, 1991

TODAY WE'RE GOING TO TALK A LITTLE ABOUT THE SEA OF GALILEE...

GATSBY STOOD BY THE SEA OF GALILEE, AND PICKED OUT THE GREEN LIGHT AT THE END OF DAISY'S DOCK..

5-31

DO YOU LIVE AROUND HERE, KID?
SCHULZ

June 1, 1991

YOU STUPID KID! GATSBY ISN'T IN THE BIBLE!! WHY DO YOU KEEP BRINGING HIM UP?!

GATSBY HAD A MANSION IN JERICHO, AND HE USED TO THROW GREAT BIG PARTIES...
6-1

HE DID NOT! YOU'RE ALL CONFUSED!! YOU'RE RUINING MY CLASS!

YOU'RE NOT VERY NICE.. ARE YOU ON SOME KIND OF MEDICATION?
SCHULZ

June 4, 1991

HOW CAN YOU TEACH SOMEONE WHO THINKS THE GREAT GATSBY WAS IN THE OLD TESTAMENT?

I HEARD YOU KICKED HIM OUT OF YOUR CLASS.. WHAT WAS HIS NAME?

LARRY... WHY?

HE'S THE MINISTER'S SON!
6-4
SCHULZ

June 5, 1991

GOOD MORNING, MA'AM.. I CAME TO APOLOGIZE... I DIDN'T MEAN TO SPOIL YOUR BIBLE CLASS..

ACTUALLY, MA'AM, I'VE FALLEN IN LOVE WITH YOU...
6-5

I'D LIKE TO GIVE YOU SOMETHING THAT HAS ALWAYS MEANT A LOT TO ME...

HOW ROMANTIC
SCHULZ

May 26, 1991

PEANUTS
by SCHULZ
5-26
SCHULZ

July 22, 1991

..AND A THOUSAND YEARS FROM NOW PEOPLE WILL LOOK AT WHAT WE HAVE BUILT HERE TODAY, AND BE TOTALLY AMAZED...
SCHULZ
7-22

August 1, 1991

PSYCHIATRIC HELP 5¢
ONE DAY I FEEL GOOD.. THE NEXT DAY I FEEL BAD..
THE DOCTOR IS IN

I HAVE TOO MANY UPS AND DOWNS...
8-1

I THINK I'M SUSPENDED FROM THE BUNGEE CORD OF LIFE..
THE DOCTOR IS IN
SCHULZ

September 15, 1991

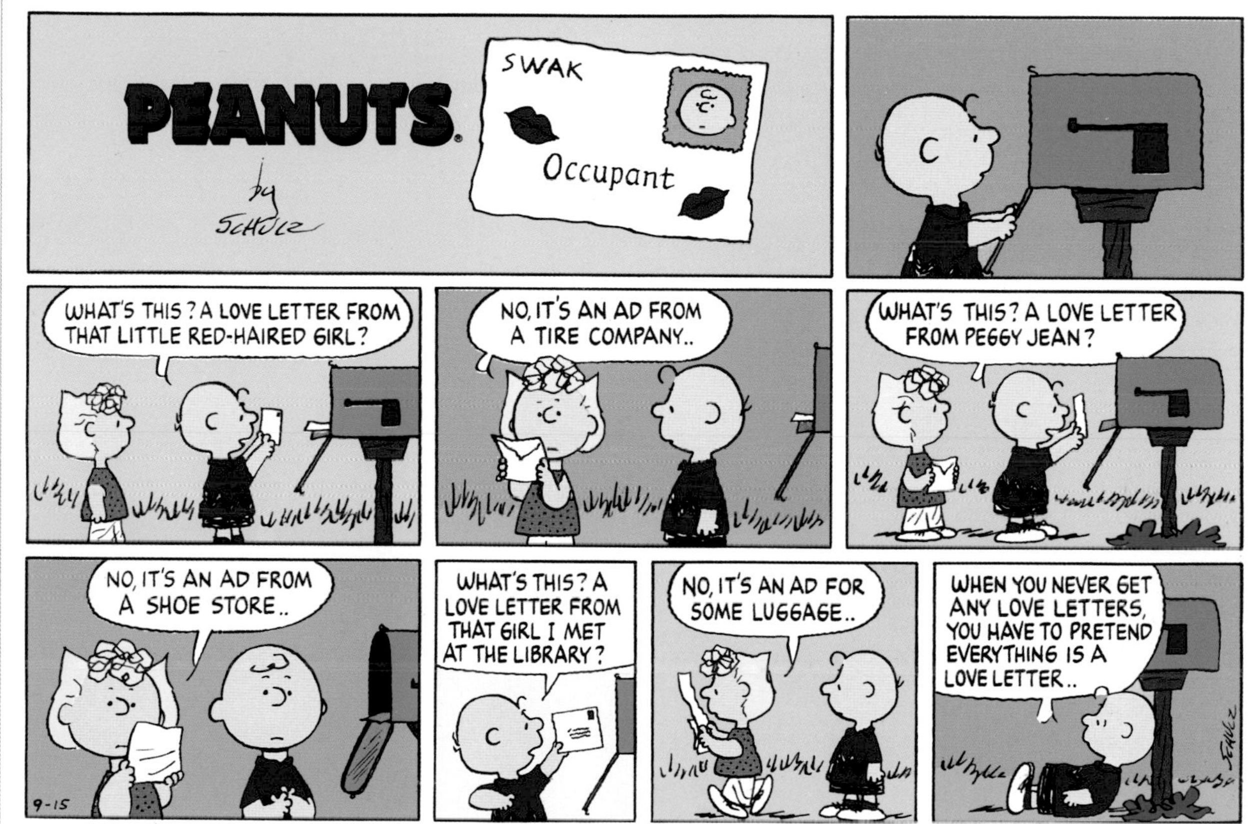
PEANUTS
by SCHULZ
SWAK
Occupant
WHAT'S THIS? A LOVE LETTER FROM THAT LITTLE RED-HAIRED GIRL?
NO, IT'S AN AD FROM A TIRE COMPANY..
WHAT'S THIS? A LOVE LETTER FROM PEGGY JEAN?
NO, IT'S AN AD FROM A SHOE STORE..
9-15
WHAT'S THIS? A LOVE LETTER FROM THAT GIRL I MET AT THE LIBRARY?
NO, IT'S AN AD FOR SOME LUGGAGE..
WHEN YOU NEVER GET ANY LOVE LETTERS, YOU HAVE TO PRETEND EVERYTHING IS A LOVE LETTER..
SCHULZ

September 7, 1991

I NEED HELP WITH MY HOMEWORK..

I'M CONFUSED ABOUT SOMETHING...
9-7

DID COLUMBUS DISCOVER AMERICA IN 24-16-32, OR IS THAT MY LOCKER COMBINATION?
SCHULZ

September 23, 1991

9-23
SCHULZ

September 26, 1991

HAVE YOU DONE YOUR HOMEWORK YET ?
NO, I HAVE A NEW PHILOSOPHY..

I'VE DECIDED TO PUT EVERYTHING OFF UNTIL THE LAST MINUTE, AND TO LEARN EVERYTHING IN LIFE THE HARD WAY..
9-26

GOOD LUCK
THANK YOU.. THAT'S WHAT MY TEACHER SAID
SCHULZ

October 14, 1991

10-14
I LOVE LOOKING AT ANTIQUE DOG DISHES..
SCHULZ

October 23, 1991

I ENTERED THIS CONTEST, SEE... WAIT 'TIL YOU SEE WHAT I WON...

10-23
SCHULZ

November 1, 1991

HALLOWEEN IS OVER, AND THE "GREAT PUMPKIN" DIDN'T SHOW UP AGAIN, DID HE ?

NO, SHE DIDN'T, DID SHE ?

NEVER EVEN OCCURRED TO YOU, DID IT ?

"One of the things I'm most proud of is that we have established a climate of—I don't know what would be the word—of good, clean humor and things which are decent. We've proved that things which are clean and decent can survive. Happiness Is a Warm Puppy *sold more copies than any other book in 1963;* You're a Good Man, Charlie Brown *was one of the biggest hits on Broadway last year and still is; our television shows are watched by more people than most other television shows. Yet all of these things are good and clean and decent. Why? They are just markets for something that people want. People are still clamoring for something like this."*

November 11, 1991

ON VETERANS DAY I ALWAYS GO OVER TO BILL MAULDIN'S, AND QUAFF A FEW ROOT BEERS..

HERE'S TO "WILLIE AND JOE"!

WE SIGH A LOT..

January 13, 1992

WHEN YOU LIVE ON THE DESERT, THERE'S NOTHING MORE EXCITING THAN WATCHING THE SUN GO DOWN..

THEN WHAT ?

January 18, 1992

WHEN I GOT UP THIS MORNING, I THOUGHT, "GEE, WOULDN'T A WAFFLE TASTE GOOD?"
1-18
SCHULZ

February 4, 1992

DO YOU HAVE TO CHEW SO LOUD WHEN YOU EAT?

YOU'RE DRIPPING MILK ALL OVER YOUR SHIRT...

YOU TOOK ALL THE SUGAR AGAIN! YOU NEVER REFILL THE BOWL!

GOOD MORNING..
SCHULZ
2-4

February 2, 1992

PEANUTS
by SCHULZ
I THOUGHT I HEARD A SPLASH
I WONDER WHERE YOU GO TO GIVE UP THE GAME..
IN THE SECOND CHAPTER OF EXODUS, IT SAYS THAT PHARAOH'S DAUGHTER FOUND THE BABY MOSES LYING IN A TINY BASKET BY THE EDGE OF THE RIVER..
I DON'T THINK THIS IS MOSES..
2-2 SCHULZ

February 17, 1992

I COULD HAVE BEEN A SLED DOG, OR MAYBE A PAMPERED PET OF SOME RICH LADY LIVING IN A TOWN HOUSE, OR MAYBE A SHEEP DOG IN AUSTRALIA..
SCHULZ
2-17

February 18, 1992

"INEPT."..... HERE IT IS..." UNFIT, AWKWARD, CLUMSY, OR BUNGLING"
2-18
SCHULZ

February 21, 1992

WELL, I SEE THE SUN IS SHINING, AND THERE'S A NICE BREEZE SO I GUESS IT'S JUST ABOUT THAT TIME AGAIN...
RATS!
SCHULZ
2-21

February 22, 1992

SO WHEN I GOT UP THIS MORNING, MY KITE WAS GONE.. I HOPE WHOEVER TOOK IT CAN FLY IT BETTER THAN I COULD..

2-22
SCHULZ

March 6, 1992

THEY SAY THAT A BALL DROPPED FROM WAIST HEIGHT WILL HIT THE GROUND AT A SPEED OF 9.45 MILES PER HOUR

SO?
3-6

SO, INSTEAD OF PITCHING IT, WHY DON'T YOU JUST DROP IT?
SCHULZ

March 22, 1992

PEANUTS
by SCHULZ
3-22
CLOMP
HA! THOUGHT YOU'D GET THIS BLANKET DIDN'T YOU? BUT I WAS TOO QUICK FOR YOU WASN'T I?
SCHULZ

May 22, 1992

SOMETIMES I LIE AWAKE AT NIGHT, AND I ASK, "WHAT IS THE MEANING OF LIFE?"

THEN A VOICE COMES TO ME THAT SAYS, "I BEFORE E EXCEPT AFTER C!"
5-22
SCHULZ

"I created Beethoven's birthday, I created Linus and his blanket, I created the pursuit of the Red Baron, I created the pulling of the football, I created the Great Pumpkin—all of these, these are the things that make up a comic strip. You can't sit down and say, 'I think I'm gonna draw a comic strip and this will be my main character.' The main character has nothing to do with it. What you really need are the situations and that's where you should start. Nobody wants to start with that. They want to start by thinking up a character which will be a good gimmick and will make good plush toys. That's the wrong direction."

May 17, 1992

PEANUTS
by SCHULZ
HERE'S THE WORLD WAR I FLYING ACE SITTING WITH A YOUNG LASS IN A SMALL CAFE NEAR THE BORDER...
SUDDENLY HE SEES HIS ARCH ENEMY ACROSS THE ROOM.. IT'S THE RED BARON!
HOW MANY TIMES HAVE THEY FACED EACH OTHER IN THE SKY?
NOW, THEY SHALL MEET EYE TO EYE ON THE GROUND!
HOW DISAPPOINTING..
HE SAID HE NEVER GIVES AUTOGRAPHS..
5-17
SCHULZ

June 8, 1992

I'VE DECIDED I AM DEFINITELY NOT GOING TO SUMMER CAMP!
INSTEAD, I'M GOING TO HOLLYWOOD! IT'S MORE MY STYLE..
I HAVE TO LEAVE NOW..I'M FLYING ON "ACE" AIRLINES..
"ACE" AIRLINES?
SCHULZ
6-8

June 9, 1992

IS THIS THE FLIGHT TO HOLLYWOOD?

YOU MUST BE THE BAGGAGE HANDLER, RIGHT?
6-9

DO I GET A CLAIM CHECK?

THE CLAIM CHECK IS BIGGER THAN THE BAGGAGE HANDLER..
SCHULZ

June 10, 1992

WHAT KIND OF AN AIRLINE IS THIS? WHERE'S THE COMPLIMENTARY ORANGE JUICE?

AND ISN'T ANYONE GOING TO WELCOME ME ABOARD?
6-10

SMAK!

I'D RATHER HAVE THE ORANGE JUICE..
SCHULZ

June 11, 1992

WHAT HAPPENS IF THERE'S A LOSS OF CABIN PRESSURE?
6-11

WHERE ARE THE EMERGENCY OXYGEN MASKS?

SCHULZ

June 13, 1992

WHAT ABOUT LUNCH?

I THOUGHT FIRST-CLASS PASSENGERS WERE ALWAYS SERVED A NICE LUNCH..

SCHULZ
6-13

June 16, 1992

IT'S RAINING!

HEY, PILOT, CAN WE FLY IN THE RAIN?
6-16

PILOT?
SCHULZ

June 17, 1992

WE WERE SUPPOSED TO BE FLYING TO HOLLYWOOD!

THEN IT STARTED TO RAIN, AND THE PILOT JUMPED OUT, AND I WAS IN MY OWN BACK YARD!

WHERE'S THAT PILOT?! I'M GONNA POUND HIM!!

AH! BONJOUR, MADEMOISELLE! I AM THE FAMOUS SERGEANT OF THE FOREIGN LEGION...
SCHULZ
6-17

July 8, 1992

I'VE DEVELOPED ANOTHER NEW PHILOSOPHY..REMEMBER, IT USED TO BE, "WHO CARES?"

NOW, IT'S, "WHAT DO I CARE?"

WELL, I'M VERY HAPPY FOR YOU
WHAT DO I CARE?
SCHULZ
7/8

July 9, 1992

WE WERE SUPPOSED TO PLAY BALL TODAY, BUT IT LOOKS LIKE IT MAY RAIN..

WHAT DO I CARE?
7-9

THAT'S MY NEW PHILOSOPHY TO CARRY ME THROUGH LIFE.. "WHAT DO I CARE?"

IT MAY CARRY YOU RIGHT OUT THE BACK DOOR!
SCHULZ

September 8, 1992

WHEN YOU DIE AND GO TO HEAVEN, DO THEY TAKE YOU THERE IN A SCHOOL BUS ?

NO, THEY PICK YOU UP IN A GOLDEN CHARIOT..

9-8
SILVER, IF YOU COME IN SECOND
SCHULZ

September 21, 1992

THIS IS REAL LOVE...
9-21

REAL LOVE IS STANDING BEHIND A TREE SO YOU CAN SEE HER WHEN SHE LEAVES HER HOUSE

OF COURSE, IT CAN SOMETIMES BE EMBARRASSING...

LIKE WHEN YOU DISCOVER YOU'VE BEEN STANDING ON THE WRONG SIDE OF THE TREE..
SCHULZ

"I think I'm speaking to people about things that really affect them. I think I am doing what poetry does in a grander manner, but I'm doing it for the layman. I am identifying things that the average person only feels vaguely. I am defining emotions. A perfect example of this is if somebody says to you, 'Today I feel just like Charlie Brown,' he doesn't have to say any more. You know how he feels."

October 26, 1992

HALLOWEEN IS ALMOST HERE, ISN'T IT ?

I SUPPOSE YOU'LL BE WAITING FOR THE "GREAT GRAPE" TO COME AGAIN, HUH ?
PUMPKIN !
10-26
© 1992 United Feature Syndicate, Inc.

OH, SORRY..I GUESS IT WOULD BE HARD TO CARVE A SCARY FACE ON A GRAPE, WOULDN'T IT ?
I CAN'T STAND IT !
SCHULZ

November 11, 1992

AH, IT MUST BE VETERANS DAY..

I SEE THE FLYING ACE IS ON HIS WAY TO BILL MAULDIN'S HOUSE TO QUAFF A FEW ROOT BEERS

BILL MAULDIN WAS THE GREATEST CARTOONIST OF WORLD WAR II ..
11-11

HE DREW GREAT MUD..
SCHULZ

November 17, 1992

SO HERE I AM ON THE BACK OF MOM'S BICYCLE ON THE WAY TO THE GROCERY STORE..

PEDAL HARD, MOM! HARDER! THAT'S THE WAY!
11-17

LOOK OUT FOR THE LAWN MOWER!

GOOD! WE'RE OUT OF THE GARAGE!
SCHULZ

November 20, 1992

SO I'M IN THE GROCERY STORE WITH MY MOM...
11-20

THIS LADY ASKS ME HOW OLD I AM... I TELL HER I'M A HUNDRED AND FIFTY..

EVERY TIME I RIDE ON THE BACK OF MY MOM'S BICYCLE, I AGE TWENTY YEARS!
SCHULZ

December 4, 1992

12-4
I THINK YOU'RE RIGHT.. ED SULLIVAN WOULD HAVE LOVED THIS
SCHULZ

December 8, 1992

DID BEETHOVEN EVER PLAY "JINGLE BELLS"?
12-8

HE PROBABLY THOUGHT HE WAS TOO GOOD TO PLAY "JINGLE BELLS"

BONK!

IF I HAD BEEN THERE, I WOULD HAVE SAID, "HEY, LUDWIG, PLAY 'JINGLE BELLS'!"
SCHULZ

December 15, 1992

CHRISTMAS IS COMING.. I SHOULD START DOING MY SHOPPING..
12-15

LAST YEAR I EXCHANGED GIFTS WITH A ROCK.. I THINK HE LIKED WHAT I BOUGHT HIM...

HE'S STILL WEARING IT..
SCHULZ

December 16, 1992

12-16
SCHULZ

December 17, 1992

12-17

SCHULZ

December 18, 1992

HERE'S AN INTERESTING ITEM FROM NEEDLES, CALIFORNIA...

SOMEONE SNEAKED INTO THE CHAMBER OF COMMERCE BUILDING LAST NIGHT, AND PLUGGED IN AN EXTENSION CORD

THE CORD LED OUT OF TOWN SOMEWHERE INTO THE DESERT..

EVERYONE IS PUZZLED AS TO WHO OR WHY SOMEONE SHOULD DO SUCH A THING..

12-18
SCHULZ

January 28, 1993

Dear Brother Snoopy, Guess what! It snowed here last night!

I didn't know it snowed in the desert.
1-28

I guess we learn something new every day, don't we?

WHOP!

Like, I didn't know coyotes could throw.
SCHULZ

March 4, 1993

FOR "SHOW AND TELL" THIS MORNING I HAVE A TURTLE WHICH I SAVED WHEN IT WAS TRYING TO CROSS THE ROAD..

IT ISN'T?
3-4

FOR "SHOW AND TELL" THIS MORNING I HAVE A HUBCAP WHICH I SAVED WHEN IT WAS TRYING TO CROSS THE ROAD..
SCHULZ

March 10, 1993

THIS IS A NICE LIBRARY, MA'AM..

I NEED A COUPLE OF BOOKS... DO YOU HAVE "A TALE OF TWO TOWNS" BY CHARLES WHAT'S-HIS-NAME?
3-10

YOU HAVE IT! THIS IS GREAT..
SCHULZ

NOW HOW ABOUT "THE BROTHERS SOMETHING OR OTHER"?

March 16, 1993

I CAN'T PLAY TODAY, MANAGER.. I COULDN'T FIND MY GLOVE..

WOULDN'T IT BE FUNNY IF IT TURNED OUT THAT YOUR GLOVE WAS ON YOUR HEAD AND YOUR CAP ON TOP OF YOUR GLOVE?
3-16

I'LL GO HOME AND LOOK AROUND AGAIN.. IF I CAN'T FIND IT, JUST START WITHOUT ME..
SCHULZ

March 26, 1993

ONE FINGER WILL MEAN YOUR FAST BALL WHICH ISN'T VERY FAST ANYWAY..

TWO FINGERS WILL BE YOUR CURVE WHICH DOESN'T CURVE AT ALL..

THREE FINGERS WILL BE YOUR CHANGE-UP WHICH HASN'T FOOLED ANYONE YET...

FOUR FINGERS WAS FOR A PITCH-OUT, BUT WE WON'T USE THAT ONE
WHY NOT?

EVERYTHING YOU THROW LOOKS LIKE A PITCH-OUT!

March 29, 1993

THIS IS IT, CHARLIE BROWN..LAST INNING.. TWO OUTS... AND YOU'RE UP!

ALL THE PRESSURE IS ON ME, BUT I CAN DO IT! I KNOW I CAN DO IT...

JUST DON'T GET NERVOUS..

HERE, YOU'D BETTER USE A BAT..

March 30, 1993

I HIT A HOME RUN IN THE NINTH INNING, AND WE WON! I WAS THE HERO!!
YOU?!

April 1, 1993

ARE YOU THE KID WHO HIT THE HOME RUN OFF ME YESTERDAY?

WELL, I HOPE YOU'RE SATISFIED! YOU RUINED MY WHOLE LIFE!
YOU CAME CLEAR OVER HERE TO TELL ME THAT?

NO, I WAS JUST KIND OF CURIOUS TO SEE WHERE YOU LIVE..YOU PROBABLY HAVE A DOG, TOO, DON'T YOU?
SORT OF..
WHAT DO YOU MEAN, SORT OF?

April 2, 1993

HEY, KID! WAIT A MINUTE! I DON'T KNOW YOUR NAME!
4-2

ROY HOBBS WAS MY GREAT-GRANDFATHER..WHEN YOU HIT THAT HOME RUN YESTERDAY, YOU RUINED MY LIFE!

I JUST MET THE GREAT-GRANDDAUGHTER OF ROY HOBBS!
I NEVER KNOW WHAT YOU'RE TALKING ABOUT..
SCHULZ

April 5, 1993

WHY DON'T THEY PUT SOME OF THE GREAT OLD COMIC STRIP CHARACTERS ON STAMPS?
4-5

I THINK THAT WOULD BE A FANTASTIC IDEA..

WE COULD HAVE A SPECIAL SERIES STARTING WITH THE "YELLOW KID"

"KID." NOT BIRD!
SCHULZ

"Doing a daily comic strip is like having to write an English theme for homework every day for the rest of your life."

April 12, 1993

WHO WON THE "SPLENDID BOWL" THIS YEAR, SIR?
"SUPER BOWL," MARCIE
4-12

WHATEVER.. WAS IT A GOOD GAME?
YOU'RE NOT MUCH FOR SPORTS, ARE YOU, MARCIE?

I GUESS NOT..BUT SOMETIMES I GET A LITTLE CURIOUS...

DID ANYBODY MAKE A HOLE-IN-ONE?
SCHULZ

April 24, 1993

SOMETIMES I LIE AWAKE AT NIGHT, AND I ASK, "WHY AM I HERE?"

THEN A VOICE SAYS, "WHERE ARE YOU?"

"HERE," I SAY.. "WHERE IS 'HERE'?" SAYS THE VOICE..

"WAVE YOUR HAND SO I CAN SEE YOU"

THE NIGHTS ARE GETTING LONGER..
4-24
SCHULZ

June 6, 1993

PEANUTS.
by Schulz
JUNE 6, 1944, "TO REMEMBER"
Schulz

"It's so easy for us, as generations come and go, to forget what other generations did. It's still disconcerting to talk to younger people and find they have almost no knowledge of what was done. I think there are certain things that must never be forgotten. Perhaps sometimes we do have too many monuments, too many holidays, and things of this kind. But D-Day is not one of them. No, it's one of those days we must not forget."

June 4, 1993

YOU KNOW WHAT I THINK, CHUCK? I THINK YOU GET BETTER GRADES IF YOU'RE CUTE..
I'LL BET MY TEACHER WOULD HAVE GIVEN ME ALL "A'S" IF I LOOKED LIKE THIS..
6-4

I LIKED YOU FINE THE OTHER WAY..
THANK YOU, CHUCK

BOY, THAT HURTS YOUR EYES..
Schulz

July 19, 1993

I KNOW IT'S HOT, MEN, BUT LET'S KEEP GOING..

NOT TOO FAR AHEAD IS AN OASIS WHERE THERE'LL BE LOTS OF WATER...

7-19
Schulz

August 6, 1993

DID YOU KNOW OUR NAME IS IN THE PHONE BOOK?

SEE? THERE'S OUR NAME, OUR ADDRESS AND OUR PHONE NUMBER...
8-6

YOU NEVER TOLD ME WE WERE FAMOUS..
SCHULZ

August 16, 1993

NOW, GET OUT THERE IN RIGHT FIELD, AND CONCENTRATE!

THINK ABOUT WHAT YOU'RE DOING..

KEEP YOUR MIND ON THE GAME..
8-16

KEEP YOUR HEAD OUT OF THE CLOUDS..

SCHULZ

August 29, 1993

PEANUTS
by SCHULZ
8-29
SCHULZ

August 24, 1993

MISS DAVIS IS GOING TO BE SURPRISED WHEN SHE GETS THIS BOOK REPORT..

MISS DAVIS QUIT TEACHING TWO YEARS AGO..SHE GOT MARRIED, AND HAS A NEW BABY

MAYBE I COULD ATTACH A "CONGRATULATIONS" CARD TO THE REPORT..
SCHULZ
8/24

November 1, 1993

HERE'S THE WORLD WAR I FLYING ACE SITTING IN A SMALL FRENCH CAFE.. THE WAR DRAGS ON... HE IS DEPRESSED..

CHARLES, YOUR DOG IS IN OUR KITCHEN AGAIN DRINKING ALL OUR ROOT BEER..

11-1

GENERAL PERSHING SAYS FOR YOU TO GET BACK TO THE AERODROME RIGHT AWAY..

PRESSURE AGAIN FROM HEADQUARTERS, RAIN AND MUD,... DESPAIR...

MOM!
SCHULZ

November 2, 1993

HERE'S THE WORLD WAR I FLYING ACE WALKING BACK TO THE AERODROME..

SUDDENLY HE SEES A LIGHT IN THE WINDOW OF A SMALL SHABBY FARM HOUSE
11-2

HE TAPS GENTLY ON THE DOOR..
BAM! BAM! BAM!!

GO ON HOME, YOU STUPID BEAGLE!

SOMETIMES THE UNIFORM FRIGHTENS THEM..
SCHULZ

November 3, 1993

BEFORE HE GETS BACK TO THE AERODROME, THE FLYING ACE FEELS HE NEEDS ONE MORE ROOT BEER..

HE ENTERS ANOTHER SMALL SEEDY CAFE, AND BECKONS TO THE PLAIN LOOKING WAITRESS...

HEY, CHUCK! YOUR DOG JUST WALKED INTO OUR HOUSE..
11/3

WELL, YEAH, HE SEEMED TO WANT SOMETHING TO DRINK..I GAVE HIM WHAT WE HAD...

PRETTY CHEAP ROOT BEER..
SCHULZ

November 4, 1993

OKAY, FLYING ACE.. YOU'VE HAD ENOUGH... YOU'D BETTER GET GOING..

SMAK!

PATHETIC CREATURE..SHE SEEMED RATHER LONELY..
11-4

November 5, 1993

I WAS PASSING BY THIS QUAINT JOINT, AND HEARD THE TINKLING OF A PIANO..
11-5

PLAY "TIPPERARY" FOR ME, SON.. I FEEL SORT OF DOWN TONIGHT...

November 6, 1993

HI, CHARLES..DID YOUR DOG GET HOME ALL RIGHT?
11-6

SURE, CHARLIE BROWN, HE ALMOST KICKED OUR DOOR DOWN!

HEY, CHUCK, THAT'S A WEIRD DOG YOU'VE GOT THERE!

SO ALL I'M SAYING IS I DON'T WANT HIM LEANING ON MY PIANO..

WHY CAN'T I HAVE A NORMAL DOG LIKE EVERYONE ELSE?
WAS THAT GENERAL PERSHING? TELL HIM I'M ON MY WAY..

November 8, 1993

IT IS DAWN.. HERE'S THE WORLD WAR I FLYING ACE WALKING ONTO THE AERODROME
11-8

HE CLIMBS INTO THE COCKPIT OF HIS SOPWITH CAMEL, AND ADJUSTS THE SUTTON HARNESS...

NOW, THE EARLY MORNING QUIET IS SHATTERED BY THE ROAR OF THE 110 HP LE RHÔNE ENGINE!

SOME PEOPLE HAVE DOGS WHO BARK A LOT, OR DIG HOLES IN THE GARDEN, OR...

November 9, 1993

HERE'S THE WORLD WAR I FLYING ACE SEARCHING THE SKY FOR HIS ENEMY, THE RED BARON..

SUDDENLY, OUT OF NOWHERE, A HAIL OF BULLETS RIPS THE FABRIC OF HIS SOPWITH CAMEL!

WITH UNBELIEVABLE SKILL HE GUIDES THE STRICKEN CRAFT BACK TO THE AERODROME

FEARING A FIERY EXPLOSION, HE LEAPS FROM THE COCKPIT!

WHAT'S A SUPPER DISH DOING ON THE RUNWAY?!
SCHULZ
11-9

November 11, 1993

ON VETERANS DAY I ALWAYS GO OVER TO BILL MAULDIN'S HOUSE TO QUAFF A FEW ROOT BEERS..

BILL KNEW MY HERO, AUDIE MURPHY..
11-11

I'VE TOLD BILL HOW I MET CAPTAIN HARRY TRUMAN IN FRANCE...

BUT BILL NEVER BELIEVES ME..
SCHULZ

October 24, 1993

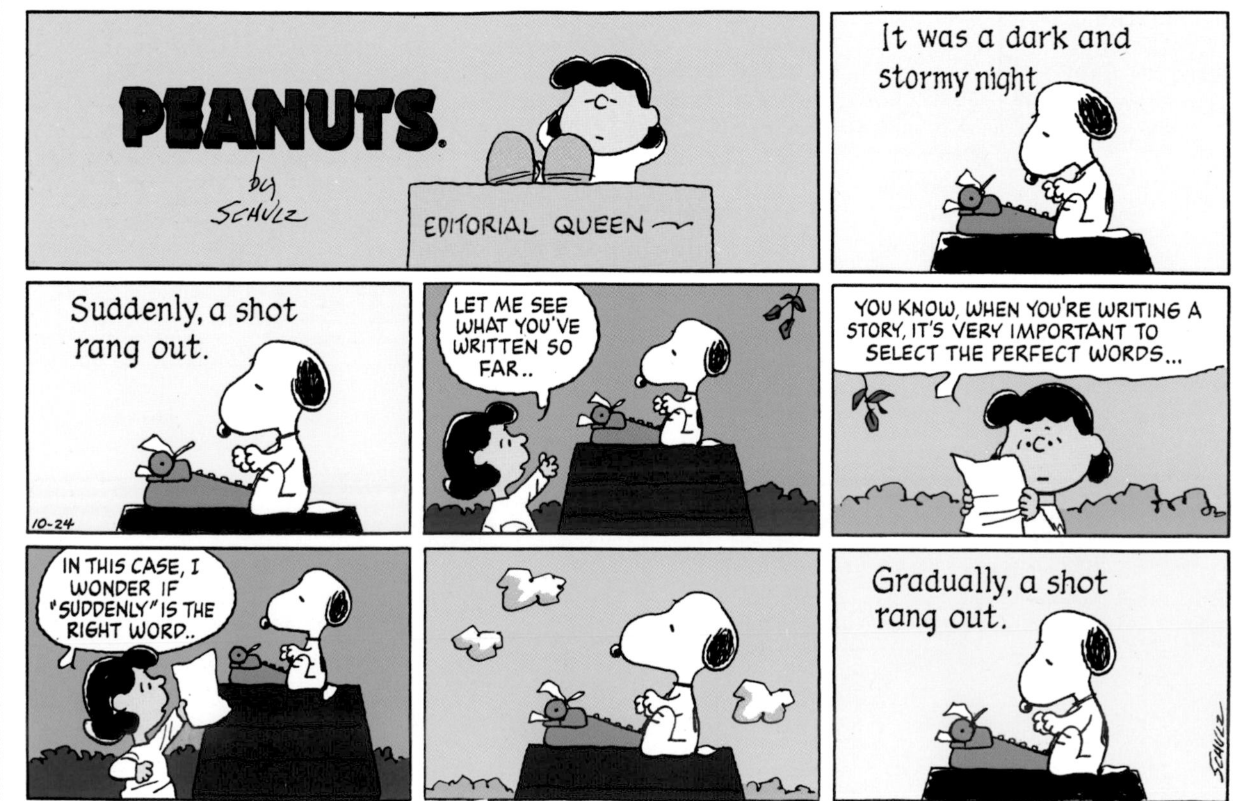
PEANUTS.
by SCHULZ
EDITORIAL QUEEN
It was a dark and stormy night
Suddenly, a shot rang out.
10-24
LET ME SEE WHAT YOU'VE WRITTEN SO FAR..
YOU KNOW, WHEN YOU'RE WRITING A STORY, IT'S VERY IMPORTANT TO SELECT THE PERFECT WORDS...
IN THIS CASE, I WONDER IF "SUDDENLY" IS THE RIGHT WORD..
Gradually, a shot rang out.
SCHULZ

December 5, 1993

PEANUTS
by SCHULZ
..SO WHAT WE'RE TALKING ABOUT HERE IS EMPOWERMENT THROUGH INNER DIALOGUE HOPEFULLY LEADING TO LIFE ENHANCEMENT..
SCHULZ

February 14, 1994—First appearance of Andy.

BIG BROTHER! WAKE UP! YOUR DOG IS IN THE HOSPITAL!
DAD TOOK HIM IN EARLY THIS MORNING!
YES, MA'AM, HIS NAME IS SNOOPY.. VISITORS? HE ALREADY HAS SOME VISITORS?
!
SCHULZ

February 15, 1994

ANDY! SPIKE! OLAF! HOW DID YOU KNOW YOUR BROTHER WAS SICK? HOW DID YOU FIND YOUR WAY HERE?
ANIMALS HAVE AN INSTINCT ABOUT THINGS LIKE THIS..
WE GO BY INSTINCT
A LOT OF IT WAS LUCK..
SCHULZ

February 17, 1994

WAITING ROOM
I HEARD A NURSE SAY OUR BROTHER SNOOPY HAS PNEUMONIA..
HE WAS ALWAYS THE LIVELY ONE IN OUR FAMILY..
2-17
WASN'T HE IN WORLD WAR I?
I THINK HE JUST THOUGHT HE WAS..

YOU KNOW WHAT I ALWAYS WONDERED?
WHERE DID HE GET THE HELMET AND GOGGLES?
SCHULZ

February 18, 1994

IF WE'RE ALL BROTHERS, HOW COME I'M SO FUZZY, YOU'RE SO SKINNY AND OLAF IS SO FAT?
I'M NOT SKINNY.. I'M TRIM!
AND I'M NOT FAT!
2-18
YOU'RE NOT FAT?
I'M ROLY-POLY!
SCHULZ

February 21, 1994

HOW CAN WE KNOW IF OUR BROTHER IS GETTING BETTER IF NO ONE TELLS US ANYTHING?
2-21
I THINK I'LL GO HANG AROUND THE FRONT DESK.. MAYBE I'LL HEAR SOMETHING...
THE NURSE IS HAVING TROUBLE WITH HER BOYFRIEND, AND THE DOCTOR IS GOING TO SWITCH TO A METAL SEVEN-WOOD!
SCHULZ

February 22, 1994

MOM? DAD? GUESS WHAT! SNOOPY IS AWAKE, AND HE'S EATING!
YES! HE'S REALLY ENJOYING HIS LUNCH ...IN FACT, THEY ALL ARE!
2-22
SCHULZ

February 23, 1994

I CAN'T BELIEVE IT.. YOUR BROTHERS HAVE GONE! THEY KNEW YOU WERE FEELING BETTER SO THEY JUST LEFT..
DOGS DON'T SAY, "GOODBYE"

February 24, 1994

MY DOG IS HOME!

February 26, 1994

YOU'VE TIED YOUR OWN SHOES, RERUN! GOOD FOR YOU

NOW, OF COURSE, THERE'S ONE OTHER THING...

THE SOCKS GO ON BEFORE THE SHOES..

April 5, 1994

I WONDER HOW THE COMPOSER COULD WRITE SOMETHING SO BEAUTIFUL..

I WONDER HOW THE VIOLINIST CAN REMEMBER ALL THOSE NOTES..

I WONDER HOW THEY CHANGE THOSE LIGHT BULBS WAY UP THERE IN THE CEILING..

March 20, 1994

PEANUTS
SCHULZ
MY PITCHER'S MOUND LOOKS GREAT..
IT'S GOING TO BE A GOOD SEASON, CHARLIE BROWN!
OUR OL' BACKSTOP SEEMS TO BE IN GOOD SHAPE..
HOW ABOUT THE OUTFIELD?
ALL MOWED, CHARLIE BROWN..IT'S BEAUTIFUL!
AND WE'VE RAKED THE INFIELD SO IT LOOKS BETTER THAN EVER..
3-20
THEN ALL WE HAVE TO WORRY ABOUT IS THE SOUND SYSTEM..
THE SOUND SYSTEM?
THIS YEAR LET'S TRY TO GET THE BALL OVER THE PLATE, YOU BLOCKHEAD!
THE SOUND SYSTEM IS STILL WORKING..
SCHULZ

April 12, 1994

"WHAT'S THAT SUPPOSED TO MEAN?" THAT'S MY NEW PHILOSOPHY!
WHENEVER SOMEONE SAYS SOMETHING TO ME, I JUST SAY, "WHAT'S THAT SUPPOSED TO MEAN?"
4-12
I'M GLAD YOU TOLD ME..NOW I WON'T SAY ANYTHING TO YOU
WHAT'S THAT SUPPOSED TO MEAN?
SCHULZ

"It took almost ten years for Snoopy to get up on his hind legs and walk around like a cartoon dog . . . and probably another ten years for him to think the thoughts that he now does. That's the way comic strips go. There's not a comic strip character that looks today as it did when the strip began. Each day you're trying to draw it the best you can, and you're not even aware of the changes."

June 6, 1994

IT'S D-DAY! HERE'S THE WORLD FAMOUS G.I. CHARGING THROUGH THE SURF AT OMAHA BEACH!
6/6
HEY, CHARLES, YOUR DOG IS OVER HERE RUNNING BACK AND FORTH THROUGH OUR WADING POOL..
SCHULZ

June 7, 1994

D+2! THE WORLD FAMOUS G.I. DIGS A FOXHOLE..
6/7

HEY, CHARLIE BROWN, YOUR DOG IS DIGGING IN OUR BACKYARD!
SCHULZ

June 8, 1994

D+3..THE WORLD FAMOUS G.I. COMES ACROSS AN ABANDONED JEEP
6/8

HEY, CHUCK, WHY IS YOUR DOG SITTING OUT HERE IN A GROCERY CART?
SCHULZ

June 9, 1994

D+4! THE BRAVE INFANTRYMAN HURLS A GRENADE AT THE PILLBOX! THEN ANOTHER..AND ANOTHER!
6/9

WHY DO I HAVE THE FEELING SOMEONE IS THROWING ROCKS AT OUR FRONT DOOR?
SCHULZ

June 10, 1994

Dear Mom, Just a note to tell you I am well. They say we will be home by Christmas. I hope so.
6-10 SCHULZ

June 27, 1994

MY GRAMPA SAYS WHEN HE WAS LITTLE, KIDS USED TO ROLL HOOPS, SHOOT MARBLES AND SPIN TOPS..
AT THE MALL?

June 28, 1994

WE LOST AGAIN!

I CAN'T STAND IT!

FORTUNATELY, THAT'S VERY FUNNY!

July 5, 1994

THE COUNSELOR WANTS YOU TO LEAD IN OUR BREAKFAST PRAYER, SIR

DEAR LORD, THANK YOU FOR THESE PANCAKES..AMEN!

NO ONE CAN ACCUSE YOU OF VAIN REPETITIONS, CAN THEY, SIR?

THE PANCAKES WERE GETTING COLD..

July 23, 1994

SO HERE I AM RIDING ON THE BACK OF MY MOM'S BICYCLE ON THE WAY TO THE DRY CLEANERS..

MOM ALWAYS LIKES TO RETURN THE USED COAT HANGERS

SHE HATES IT WHEN I DO THIS..

July 17, 1994

PEANUTS
IT'S NOT THAT I DON'T APPRECIATE THE HOME I ALREADY HAVE..
BUT..
WHEN YOU'RE A DOG, SOMETIMES IT'S A GOOD IDEA TO SIT IN THE RAIN RIGHT NEXT TO THE CURB..
IT'S ALSO A GOOD IDEA TO LOOK REAL PATHETIC..
MAYBE A RICH LADY IN A BIG LIMOUSINE WILL STOP AND PICK YOU UP..
THEN SHE'LL TAKE YOU HOME TO HER FANCY APARTMENT, WRAP YOU IN A WARM FUZZY TOWEL AND GIVE YOU A PIZZA!
IS THIS HER I SEE COMING? IS SHE THE ONE I'VE BEEN WAITING FOR?
RATS!
7-17

August 1, 1994

IF I WRITE A LOVE NOTE TO THAT LITTLE RED-HAIRED GIRL, WILL YOU DELIVER IT FOR ME?
IF I GET CAPTURED, DO I HAVE TO SWALLOW IT?
8-1

August 2, 1994

I'LL STAY HERE BEHIND THIS TREE, AND YOU TAKE THIS NOTE OVER TO THE LITTLE RED-HAIRED GIRL

8-2

GOOD MORNING, I HAVE A LOVE NOTE FOR YOU FROM MY WEIRD BROTHER..HE THINKS YOU'RE KIND OF CUTE

SHOULD I WAIT FOR AN ANSWER?

August 3, 1994

SHE'S READING YOUR LOVE NOTE!
DID YOU HEAR ME? ARE YOU STILL BEHIND THE TREE? WAVE YOUR HAND!
HE'S STILL THERE.. REALLY? OH, SURE, I UNDERSTAND..

SHE SAID SHE COULDN'T READ YOUR SMUDGY WRITING...

AND WHEN I TOLD HER YOU'RE IN THE SAME CLASS AT SCHOOL, SHE SAID SHE DIDN'T REMEMBER YOU..
I CAN'T STAND IT!

August 4, 1994

MAYBE YOU SHOULD GIVE UP THIS INSANE LOVE AFFAIR.. JUST LET THINGS HAPPEN ..THAT'S WHAT I'VE DONE WITH MY SWEET BABBOO...
I'M NOT YOUR SWEET BABBOO!

August 23, 1994

DON'T BE DISCOURAGED.. I'M NEW AT THIS..

September 5, 1994

SORRY I MISSED THAT FLY BALL, MANAGER..

SO WHAT'S YOUR EXCUSE THIS TIME?

A VAPOR TRAIL GOT IN MY EYES..

September 14, 1994

I NEED HELP WITH THESE SCIENCE QUESTIONS

"WHY DO WE HAVE FINGERNAILS?"
TO KEEP OUR FINGERS FROM FALLING OFF!

HA HA HA HA HA!

9-14
SCHULZ

October 26, 1994

As he turned to leave, he paused, and said,
10-26

"Toodle-oo, Caribou! In a while, Crocodile! Stay loose, Mongoose! It's been neat, Parakeet!"

"Please," she said, "Just leave!"
SCHULZ

September 18, 1994

PEANUTS.
by SCHULZ
MEMORIES

SIGH

WHY DO I LIVE ALL ALONE OUT HERE IN THE DESERT?

I'M GOING TO TELL YOU SOMETHING I'VE NEVER TOLD ANYONE

YEARS AGO WHEN I WAS YOUNG, I WAS OUT WALKING WITH SOME PEOPLE..
9-18

SUDDENLY, A RABBIT RAN ACROSS IN FRONT OF US!

"GET HIM!" SHOUTED THE PEOPLE!

EVEN THOUGH I DIDN'T WANT TO, I DARTED AFTER THE RABBIT!

I WOULDN'T HAVE KNOWN WHAT TO DO EVEN IF I HAD CAUGHT HIM..

THEN IT HAPPENED! THE RABBIT RAN INTO THE ROAD, AND WAS HIT BY A CAR!

I WAS STUNNED! WHY DID I DO IT?! OH, HOW I HATED MYSELF!

AND HOW I HATED THOSE PEOPLE WHO SHOUTED, "GET HIM!"

SO I CAME OUT HERE TO THE DESERT WHERE I COULDN'T HURT ANYTHING AGAIN

I'VE NEVER TOLD THIS TO ANYONE BEFORE..

I GUESS I STILL HAVEN'T..

October 31, 1994

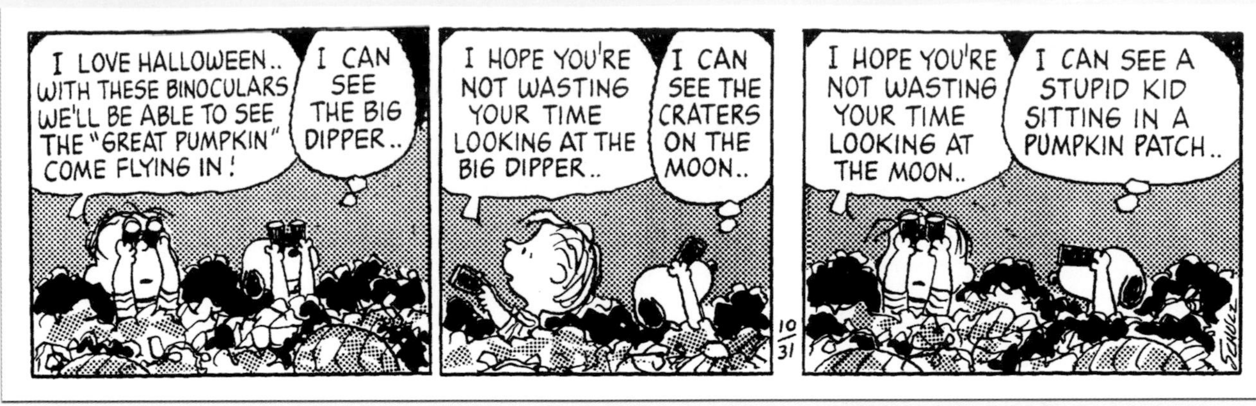
I LOVE HALLOWEEN.. WITH THESE BINOCULARS WE'LL BE ABLE TO SEE THE "GREAT PUMPKIN" COME FLYING IN!
I CAN SEE THE BIG DIPPER..
I HOPE YOU'RE NOT WASTING YOUR TIME LOOKING AT THE BIG DIPPER..
I CAN SEE THE CRATERS ON THE MOON..
I HOPE YOU'RE NOT WASTING YOUR TIME LOOKING AT THE MOON..
I CAN SEE A STUPID KID SITTING IN A PUMPKIN PATCH..
10/31
SCHULZ

November 1, 1994

11-1
SO YOU SAT OUT IN A PUMPKIN PATCH ALL NIGHT LOOKING THROUGH SOME BINOCULARS..
I WAS HOPING I COULD SEE THE "GREAT PUMPKIN" COME FLYING IN..
YOU LOOK BETTER THIS WAY.. YOU LOOK LIKE YOU'RE FAR AWAY...
STUPID DOG!
SCHULZ

November 16, 1994

I'M YOUR YOUNGER BROTHER, AND I DON'T SUCK MY THUMB OR CLING TO A BLANKET FOR SECURITY..
HOORAY FOR YOU
AS THE YEARS GO BY, YOU'LL PROBABLY DEVELOP A REAL RESENTMENT TOWARD ME..
11-16
AND FIND DIFFERENT WAYS TO GET EVEN..
SCHULZ

November 18, 1994

I'M SORRY.. SNOOPY CAN'T GO OUT TO PLAY RIGHT NOW... HE'S READING..
DOGS CAN'T READ..
11-18
WELL, HE'S SITTING IN THERE HOLDING A BOOK..
THERE'S NO WAY IN THE WORLD THAT ANNA KARENINA AND COUNT VRONSKY COULD EVER HAVE BEEN HAPPY..
SCHULZ

January 29, 1995

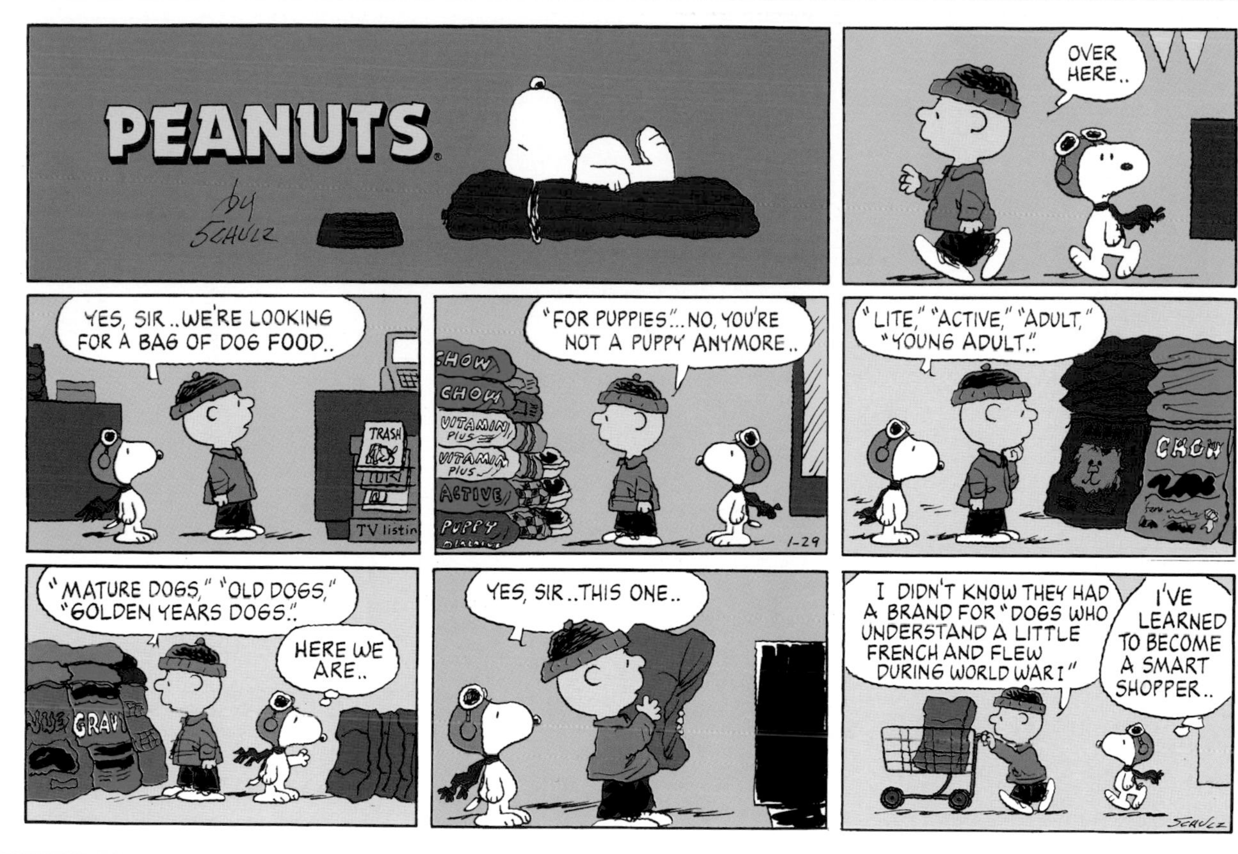
PEANUTS
by SCHULZ
OVER HERE..
YES, SIR..WE'RE LOOKING FOR A BAG OF DOG FOOD..
"FOR PUPPIES"..NO, YOU'RE NOT A PUPPY ANYMORE..
"LITE," "ACTIVE," "ADULT," "YOUNG ADULT."
"MATURE DOGS," "OLD DOGS," "GOLDEN YEARS DOGS."
HERE WE ARE..
YES, SIR..THIS ONE..
I DIDN'T KNOW THEY HAD A BRAND FOR "DOGS WHO UNDERSTAND A LITTLE FRENCH AND FLEW DURING WORLD WAR I"
I'VE LEARNED TO BECOME A SMART SHOPPER..

January 12, 1995

ASK YOUR DOG IF HE WANTS TO COME OUT AND PLAY..
HE'S THINKING ABOUT IT..
HEADS, I GO OUT..TAILS I STAY IN...
TWO OUT OF THREE..HEADS, GO OUT..TAILS, STAY IN... ONE MORE TIME...OKAY, ONE MORE TIME...

January 13, 1995

ALL RIGHT, I'LL ASK HIM..
THAT LITTLE KID WANTS YOU TO COME OUT AND PLAY HOCKEY..

OKAY, WE'LL PLAY THREE TWENTY-MINUTE PERIODS, AND I GET TO DRIVE THE ZAMBONI!

February 12, 1995

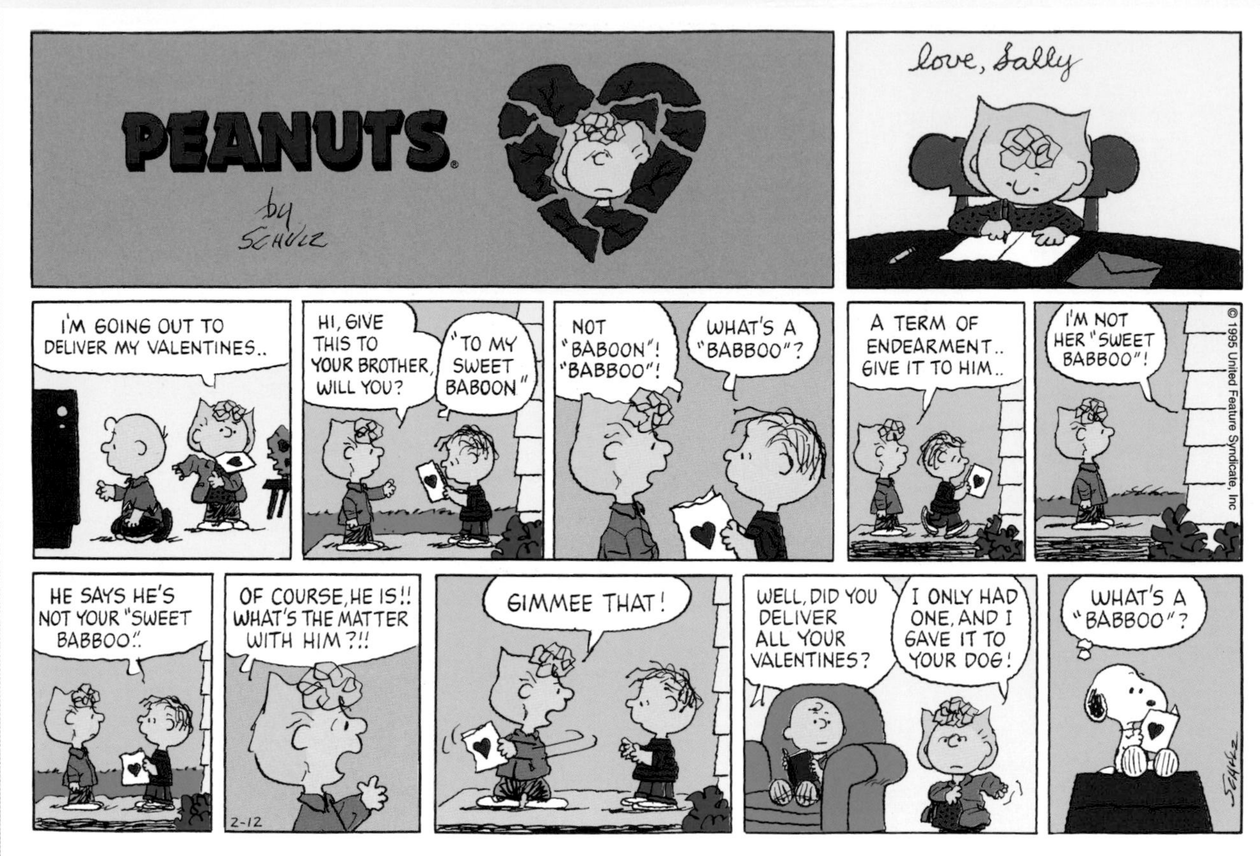
PEANUTS
by SCHULZ
love, Sally
I'M GOING OUT TO DELIVER MY VALENTINES..
HI, GIVE THIS TO YOUR BROTHER, WILL YOU?
"TO MY SWEET BABOON"
NOT "BABOON"! "BABBOO"!
WHAT'S A "BABBOO"?
A TERM OF ENDEARMENT.. GIVE IT TO HIM..
I'M NOT HER "SWEET BABBOO"!
© 1995 United Feature Syndicate, Inc
HE SAYS HE'S NOT YOUR "SWEET BABBOO"..
OF COURSE, HE IS!! WHAT'S THE MATTER WITH HIM?!!
2-12
GIMMEE THAT!
WELL, DID YOU DELIVER ALL YOUR VALENTINES?
I ONLY HAD ONE, AND I GAVE IT TO YOUR DOG!
WHAT'S A "BABBOO"?
SCHULZ

February 8, 1995

YES MA'AM..I WAS TOLD TO SIGN UP FOR DANCE LESSONS BECAUSE I NEED TO BE MORE OUTGOING..
Dance Studio
2-8
MAYBE IF I'M MORE OUTGOING, I WON'T BE SO LONELY..
YES, THAT'S MY DOG... HE'S VERY OUTGOING..

March 7, 1995

THIS IS MY MARBLE COLLECTION.. I HAVE AGGIES, SHOOTERS, IMMIES, MILKIES, BUMBOOZERS, DOBIES AND GLIMMERS..
3-7
WHAT KIND DO YOU HAVE?
ROUND ONES..
SCHULZ

March 9, 1995

PUT THE MARBLE IN YOUR FINGERS LIKE THIS, AND THEN FLIP IT WITH YOUR THUMB..

3-9
RATS!

WHY IS EVERYTHING IN LIFE SO HARD?
SCHULZ

March 10, 1995

I'VE BECOME A MARBLE PLAYING FANATIC!
3-10

THIS SUMMER I'M GOING TO ENTER THE "ROLLEY HOLE" CHAMPIONSHIP IN "STANDING STONE STATE PARK" IN TENNESSEE..

WHEREVER THAT IS..
IT'S NOT ACROSS THE STREET..
SCHULZ

March 26, 1995

PEANUTS
by SCHULZ
HI! IT'S ME AGAIN!
WHAT CAN I DO FOR YOU, RERUN?
ASK YOUR DOG IF HE WANTS TO COME OUT AND PLAY..
TELL HIM WE'LL RUN AROUND IN CIRCLES, AND ROLL ON THE GROUND AND ACT SILLY..
AND THEN, AFTERWARDS, I'LL GIVE HIM A COOKIE..
HA HA HA HA!
HEE HEE HEE!
HA HA HA HA!!
3-26
WHAT HAPPENED? I THOUGHT YOU WERE HAVING FUN..
THE COOKIE HAD COCONUT ON IT!

April 3, 1995

RERUN, WHAT'S THE MATTER?
SOME KID WON ALL MY MARBLES..

YOU'RE JUST A BEGINNER..YOU SHOULDN'T HAVE BEEN PLAYING FOR "KEEPS"
I KNOW.. YOU TOLD ME THAT

HE EVEN WON MY SHOOTER.. ALL I HAVE LEFT IS THIS EMPTY SACK..

I'M SURPRISED HE DIDN'T TAKE THAT, TOO..
HE COULDN'T.. I RAN ALL THE WAY HOME..

April 5, 1995

THERE HE IS! THAT'S THE KID WHO WON ALL MY MARBLES..

WELL, I'LL GO OVER AND TALK TO HIM..
WHY DON'T YOU HIT HIM WITH A STICK?

I JUST WANT TO TELL HIM I THINK HE TOOK ADVANTAGE OF YOU..
IF YOU SNEAKED UP BEHIND HIM, YOU COULD HIT HIM WITH A STICK..

April 7, 1995

HI, KID.. YOU WANNA PLAY MARBLES? C'MON, I'LL SHOW YOU HOW..

IT'S EASY.. WE'LL JUST PLAY FOR FUN..
NO, WE'LL PLAY FOR "KEEPS"

FOR "KEEPS"? YOU MEAN YOU'VE PLAYED BEFORE?

LET'S SAY I DIDN'T JUST ARRIVE ON THE STAGECOACH..

April 8, 1995

YOU SURE YOU WANNA PLAY ME, KID? I'M "JOE AGATE"! I NEVER LOSE!
YOU NEVER LOSE BECAUSE YOU ONLY PLAY BEGINNERS, AND YOU TELL THEM YOU'RE PLAYING FOR FUN UNTIL YOU WIN, AND THEN YOU SAY, "KEEPS!" AND YOU TAKE ALL THEIR MARBLES!!

YOU TRASH TALKIN' ME, KID?
"KNUCKLE DOWN," JOE! THIS IS FOR "KEEPS"!

April 10, 1995

WHAT'S GOING ON?
CHARLIE BROWN IS PLAYING "JOE AGATE" A GAME OF MARBLES..

THEY SAY "JOE AGATE" IS THE BEST PLAYER THIS SIDE OF THE MISSISSIPPI..
4-10

WHICH SIDE OF THE MISSISSIPPI ARE WE ON?
I DON'T HAVE THE SLIGHTEST IDEA..
SCHULZ

April 11, 1995

4-11
PLINK!

PLINK

PLINK!
PLINK!
PLINK!

WHO ARE YOU, KID? WHERE'D YOU LEARN TO SHOOT LIKE THAT?
"COOL THUMB" BROWN..JUST A STRANGER PASSING THROUGH..
SCHULZ

April 12, 1995

HERE YOU GO, RERUN..I WON BACK ALL YOUR MARBLES..
WOW! I CAN'T BELIEVE IT! YOU BEAT "JOE AGATE"!

WILL YOU TEACH ME TO SHOOT LIKE THAT?

NO, RERUN.. I HAVE TO MOVE ON..
4/12

SHANE! SHANE! COME BACK!
I CAN'T STAND IT..
SCHULZ

May 2, 1995

ASK YOUR DOG IF HE WANTS TO COME OUT AND CHASE RABBITS..

I THINK HE'LL DO IT IF YOU DO IT HIS WAY..
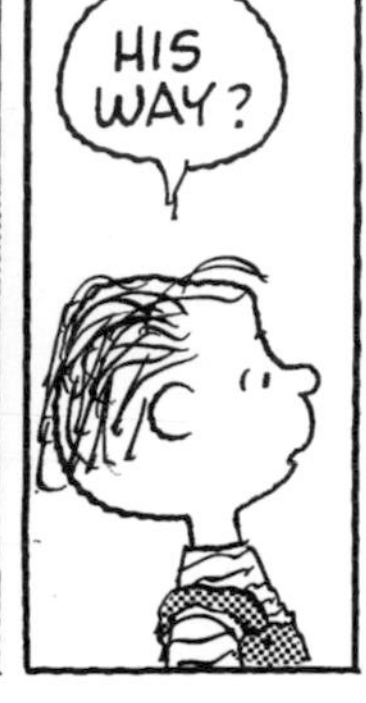
HIS WAY?

5-2
OKAY, DOWN TO THE CORNER AND ACROSS THE FIELD..
SCHULZ

May 9, 1995

MAYBE SOMEDAY YOU CAN EXPLAIN HER TO ME, OKAY?
SCHULZ
5-9

May 30, 1995

WILL YOU HELP ME DRAW A MAP?
WHAT DO YOU NEED A MAP FOR?
I'M THINKING OF RUNNING AWAY FROM HOME SO I'LL PROBABLY NEED A MAP..
5-30
OKAY, WHICH WAY ARE YOU PLANNING TO GO, NORTH OR SOUTH?
HOW SHOULD I KNOW?
JUST PUT DOWN "THIS WAY" AND "THAT WAY"
SCHULZ

June 20, 1995

SOME OF THE GUYS OVER AT THE PLAYGROUND WERE DISCUSSING CRABBY SISTERS
GUESS WHAT.. I WON!
THEY ALL AGREED THAT I HAVE THE CRABBIEST SISTER IN THE NEIGHBORHOOD
I'M A CELEBRITY!
SCHULZ
6-20

June 24, 1995

ARE YOU SURE? ARE YOU POSITIVE?
6-24
WELL, WE CAN'T TELL UNTIL WE TRY IT, CAN WE?
BONK!
OKAY, YOU WERE RIGHT.. I WAS FACING THE WRONG WAY..
SCHULZ

July 5, 1995

ASK YOUR DOG TO COME OUT AND PLAY "CHASE THE STICK"

"THANK YOU FOR YOUR OFFER TO COME OUT AND PLAY..WE ARE BUSY AT THIS TIME, HOWEVER, AND CANNOT ACCEPT YOUR OFFER..WE HOPE YOU WILL BE SUCCESSFUL ELSEWHERE"
7-5

DOGS HAVE REJECTION SLIPS?
SCHULZ

"I introduced the very slight incident. I can remember creating it sitting at the desk, where what would happen in the three panels that I was drawing at that time was a very brief and slight incident. No one had ever done that before in comic strips. Comic strips were the school of 'Well, what are we going to do today?' type—much too drawn out and with a little joke at the end that really was not worth the whole page that it was devoted to. So I changed all of that, and I think very few people realize now, as they look back at my work and compare it, how new what I was doing at that time was. I think I introduced a whole brand-new approach to comic strip humor."

July 12, 1995

7-12
MOLES HAVE VERY WEAK EYES.. THEY DIG TUNNELS JUST UNDER THE GROUND, AND HUNT WORMS AND INSECTS

YOU'RE RIGHT..IT'S A TOUGH WAY TO MAKE A LIVING..
SCHULZ

August 15, 1995

SOMETIMES I LIE AWAKE AT NIGHT, AND I ASK, "WHEN WILL IT ALL END?"
8-15

THEN A VOICE COMES TO ME THAT SAYS, "RIGHT AFTER THE CREDITS!"
SCHULZ

August 28, 1995

I'VE ALWAYS WONDERED HOW YOU DECIDED TO BECOME A DOG..
THAT'S A GOOD QUESTION

I REMEMBER GOING DOWN THE LIST..

8-28
EVERYTHING ELSE WAS TAKEN..
SCHULZ

September 1, 1995

HEY, MARCIE..LET'S GO DO SOME SHOPPING FOR SCHOOL SUPPLIES..

I DID THAT A MONTH AGO, SIR
9-1

SURE, MARCIE..AND I SUPPOSE YOU ALREADY KNOW WHICH COLLEGE YOU'RE GOING TO!

AND I'VE ENROLLED MY THREE KIDS IN PRE-SCHOOL!
SCHULZ

September 6, 1995

I JUST HEARD SOME PEOPLE OVER AT THE CHURCH SINGING "BRINGING IN THE SHEAVES"

I DON'T EVEN KNOW WHAT A SHEAVE IS..
9-6

ME NEITHER, BUT IF I EVER SEE ONE, I'LL BRING IT IN..
SCHULZ

September 7, 1995

YES, MA'AM..I WAS WONDERING IF I MIGHT HAVE A DESK IN THE BACK ROW..
9-7

NO, MA'AM..I UNDERSTAND.. THAT'S LIFE...

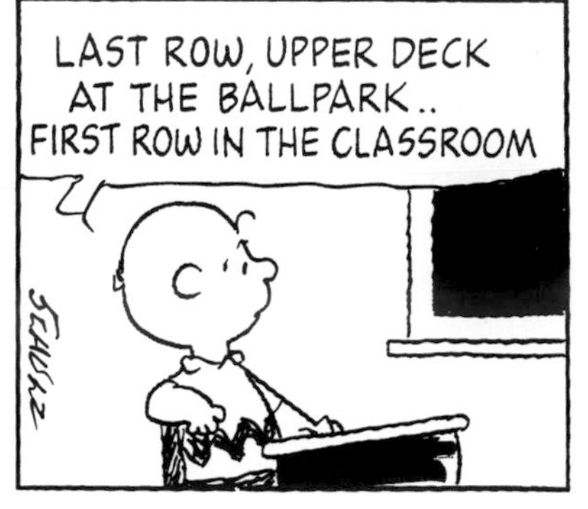

LAST ROW, UPPER DECK AT THE BALLPARK.. FIRST ROW IN THE CLASSROOM
SCHULZ

September 13, 1995

YES, MA'AM..I UNDERSTAND.. YOU WANT MORE THAN JUST THE MATH ANSWER..
9-13

YOU WANT ME TO EXPLAIN **HOW** I GOT THE ANSWER..

I COPIED IT FROM THE KID BEHIND ME..
SCHULZ

October 26, 1995

RERUN, YOU'VE GOT YOUR SHOES ON THE WRONG FEET..

I'M TEACHING THEM A LESSON..

I'M TRYING TO SHOW THEM THEY CAN'T ALWAYS HAVE THEIR OWN WAY..
SCHULZ
10-26

October 27, 1995

Dear Author,
Congratulations! We have decided to publish your novel.

First printing will be one copy.
10-27

If we sell it, we'll print another.
SCHULZ

October 28, 1995

IT'S FROM YOUR PUBLISHER.. THEY PRINTED ONE COPY OF YOUR NOVEL..
10-28

IT SAYS THEY HAVEN'T BEEN ABLE TO SELL IT..

THEY SAY THEY'RE SORRY.. YOUR BOOK IS NOW OUT OF PRINT..
SCHULZ

October 15, 1995

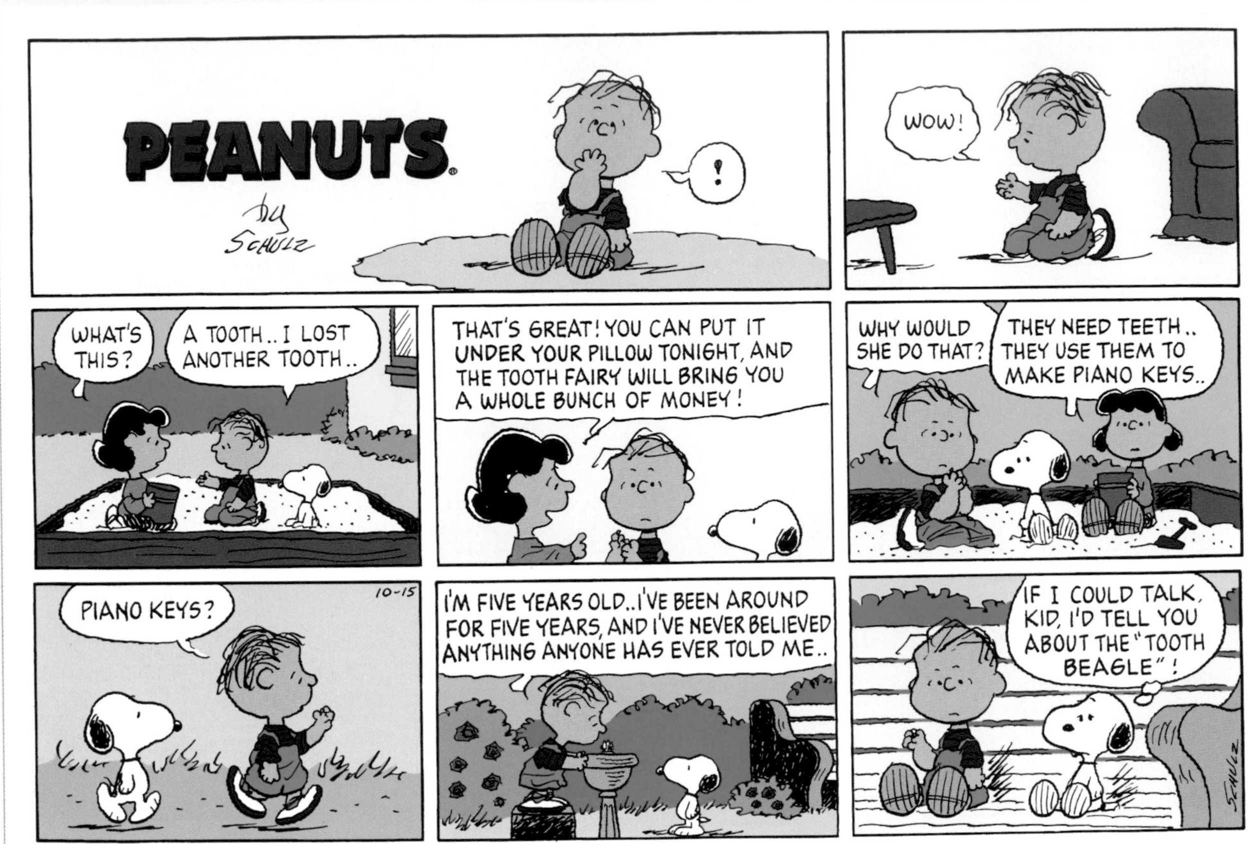
PEANUTS
by Schulz
!
WOW!
WHAT'S THIS?
A TOOTH.. I LOST ANOTHER TOOTH..
THAT'S GREAT! YOU CAN PUT IT UNDER YOUR PILLOW TONIGHT, AND THE TOOTH FAIRY WILL BRING YOU A WHOLE BUNCH OF MONEY!
WHY WOULD SHE DO THAT?
THEY NEED TEETH.. THEY USE THEM TO MAKE PIANO KEYS..
PIANO KEYS?
10-15
I'M FIVE YEARS OLD.. I'VE BEEN AROUND FOR FIVE YEARS, AND I'VE NEVER BELIEVED ANYTHING ANYONE HAS EVER TOLD ME..
IF I COULD TALK, KID, I'D TELL YOU ABOUT THE "TOOTH BEAGLE"!
SCHULZ

November 30, 1995

THERE! I'VE MAILED ALL MY CHRISTMAS CARDS!
I THOUGHT YOU DIDN'T HAVE ANY STAMPS..
11-30
I DREW MY OWN.. I DREW DICK TRACY, AND POPEYE, AND THE YELLOW KID..
THAT'S ILLEGAL
SOMEONE NEED AN ATTORNEY?
SCHULZ

December 1, 1995

ALL MY CHRISTMAS CARDS CAME BACK!
12-1
THAT'S BECAUSE YOU DREW YOUR OWN STAMPS
I COPIED THEM FROM THE NEW CARTOON STAMPS
SHE DREW A BETTER POPEYE THAN THEY DID..
SCHULZ

November 19, 1995

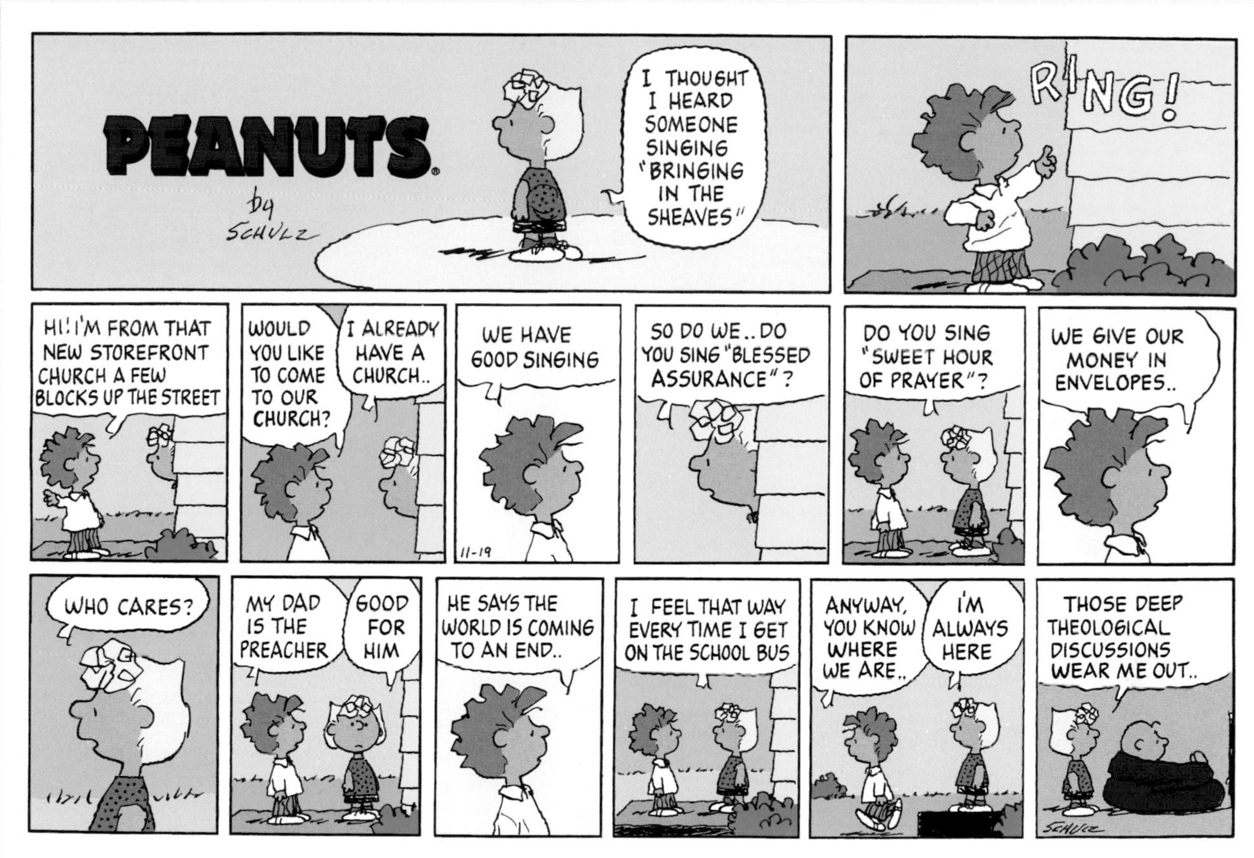
PEANUTS
by SCHULZ
I THOUGHT I HEARD SOMEONE SINGING "BRINGING IN THE SHEAVES"
RING!
HI! I'M FROM THAT NEW STOREFRONT CHURCH A FEW BLOCKS UP THE STREET
WOULD YOU LIKE TO COME TO OUR CHURCH?
I ALREADY HAVE A CHURCH..
WE HAVE GOOD SINGING
11-19
SO DO WE.. DO YOU SING "BLESSED ASSURANCE"?
DO YOU SING "SWEET HOUR OF PRAYER"?
WE GIVE OUR MONEY IN ENVELOPES..
WHO CARES?
MY DAD IS THE PREACHER
GOOD FOR HIM
HE SAYS THE WORLD IS COMING TO AN END..
I FEEL THAT WAY EVERY TIME I GET ON THE SCHOOL BUS
ANYWAY, YOU KNOW WHERE WE ARE..
I'M ALWAYS HERE
THOSE DEEP THEOLOGICAL DISCUSSIONS WEAR ME OUT..
SCHULZ

December 2, 1995

12-2
DO YOU THINK I'LL GET ARRESTED FOR DRAWING MY OWN STAMPS?
WELL, YOU MIGHT START LOOKING FOR A GOOD ATTORNEY..
BEFORE WE BEGIN, YOUR HONOR, MAY WE ASK IF YOU RECEIVED THE CHRISTMAS CARD WE SENT YOU?
SCHULZ

February 21, 1996

I'M WAITING FOR YOUR DOG TO COME OUT, AND PULL ME ON MY SLED..
2-21
HE WANTS TO KNOW IF YOU HAVE A SILVER HARNESS WITH GOLDEN BELLS AND FANCY TASSELS
I'M LUCKY I HAVE A SLED!
SCHULZ

April 12, 1996

EMILY? IS IT REALLY YOU? SURE, I REMEMBER.. FROM DANCE CLASS.. HOW COULD I FORGET?
IT'S PROBABLY A WRONG NUMBER.. JUST HANG UP..
SCHULZ
4/12
THE SWEETHEART BALL? YOU'RE ASKING ME TO GO TO THE SWEETHEART BALL?
IT MUST BE A WRONG NUMBER.. JUST HANG UP..

April 15, 1996

EMILY INVITED YOU TO THE SWEETHEART BALL?
YES! CAN YOU BELIEVE IT?
SORRY, MA'AM.. I WAS THINKING ABOUT SOMETHING ELSE..
SCHULZ
4-15

January 21, 1996

PEANUTS
by SCHULZ
?
WHY ARE YOU STANDING UP THERE, CHARLIE BROWN?
MEMORIES, LINUS..
MY PITCHER'S MOUND MAY BE COVERED WITH SNOW, BUT THE MEMORIES ARE STILL THERE..
1-21
HAPPY TIMES, HUH?
SOME OF MY HAPPIEST MEMORIES
WHAT ABOUT ALL THE GAMES WE LOST?
IT WAS MY RIGHT FIELDER! IT WAS ALWAYS MY RIGHT FIELDER!
I REMEMBER OUR LAST GAME..
SHE DROPPED AN EASY FLY BALL!
THEN THE NEXT BATTER HIT ANOTHER EASY ONE TO RIGHT FIELD, AND SHE DROPPED IT!
THEN SHE MISSED ANOTHER FLY BALL, AND THEN A GROUNDER WENT THROUGH HER, AND THEN SHE DROPPED ANOTHER FLY BALL!
MEMORIES! MEMORIES! MEMORIES!
I THINK I'LL GO BUILD A SNOWMAN..
SCHULZ

April 17, 1996

WELL, WHAT DO YOU THINK?
4-17

MOM! SOMEONE LEFT THE PENGUIN CAGE OPEN AGAIN!
SCHULZ

April 18, 1996

WELL, SNOOPY, WISH ME LUCK.. I'M OFF TO THE SWEETHEART BALL..

I'M SORRY YOU CAN'T COME WITH ME..
4-18

"MAN'S BEST FRIEND," BUT WE NEVER GET INVITED ANYPLACE..
SCHULZ

March 24, 1996

PEANUTS
by SCHULZ

NOW, LISTEN TO ME!

WHAT WE NEED IS CONFIDENCE!

ASK YOURSELF THE QUESTION, "CAN WE WIN?" THEN, SAY, "YES, WE'RE GONNA WIN!"

© 1996 United Feature Syndicate, Inc.

"CAN WE WIN?" "HA! FORGET IT! NO WAY! NOT IN A MILLION YEARS!"
3-24

HEY, MANAGER.. I GOT SOME ANSWERS, BUT I DON'T THINK YOU'RE GONNA LIKE 'EM..

TAKE HER AWAY! SOMEBODY GET HER OUT OF HERE! SHE'S GONNA DRIVE ME CRAZY!!

HEY, MANAGER.. TELL ME AGAIN.. WHAT WAS THE QUESTION?
SCHULZ

April 20, 1996

I CAN'T BELIEVE I'M HERE WITH YOU AT THE SWEETHEART BALL, EMILY..

DO YOU REMEMBER HOW WE MET AT DANCE CLASS?

I STILL ENJOY DANCING WITH YOU, CHARLES..
4/20

"LADIES AND GENTLEMEN, YOUR ATTENTION, PLEASE! DOES ANYONE HERE OWN A SMALL WHITE DOG?"
OH, NO!
SCHULZ

April 22, 1996

"LADIES AND GENTLEMEN, YOUR ATTENTION, PLEASE! DOES ANYONE HERE OWN A SMALL WHITE DOG.."
4-22

"..WITH LONG BLACK EARS.."

"..WHO SEEMS TO BE A SERGEANT IN THE FOREIGN LEGION?"
SCHULZ

April 23, 1996

4-23

NOW LOOK WHAT YOU DID! YOU GOT ME KICKED OUT OF THE SWEETHEART BALL!

I WAS HAVING THE BEST TIME OF MY LIFE! I WAS HAVING FUN!
HOW CAN YOU HAVE FUN IN A PLACE WHERE DOGS AREN'T ALLOWED?
SCHULZ

April 30, 1996

QUICK, MARCIE, I NEED THE ANSWERS TO FIVE, SEVEN, NINE, TEN AND TWELVE..

4-30
I DON'T HAVE THOSE YET, SIR..

WHAT KIND OF A STUDENT ARE YOU, MARCIE?
SCHULZ

May 7, 1996

I CAN'T SLEEP, BIG BROTHER.. WHAT SHOULD I DO?

DON'T DO ANYTHING.. JUST LIE THERE, AND WORRY..

WORRY ABOUT EVERYTHING THAT'S EVER HAPPENED AND EVERYTHING YOU THINK MIGHT HAPPEN..
5-7

THEN WHAT?
SCHULZ

May 8, 1996

I DID WHAT YOU SAID, BIG BROTHER.. I'VE BEEN WORRYING ABOUT EVERYTHING

I EVEN WORRIED ABOUT YOU..

I WORRIED THAT YOU'LL NEVER AMOUNT TO ANYTHING, AND YOU'LL MARRY THE WRONG GIRL AND ALL YOUR KIDS WILL BE STUPID..

WELL, I THINK I'M STARTING TO GET A LITTLE SLEEPY..
5/8

I GUESS I'LL JUST LIE HERE AND WORRY..
SCHULZ

May 5, 1996

PEANUTS
by SCHULZ

THINK ABOUT THIS..

LET'S SAY YOU AND I WERE MARRIED..

AND LET'S SAY YOU ARE A FAMOUS CONCERT PIANIST..

BUT SUDDENLY YOUR CAREER BEGINS TO GO BAD.. NO ONE WANTS YOU ANYMORE..

INSTEAD OF PLAYING IN BEAUTIFUL CONCERT HALLS, YOU'RE FORCED TO PLAY IN SLEAZY JOINTS..
© 1996 United Feature Syndicate, Inc.

AND I HAVE TO GIVE UP MY LUCRATIVE TEACHING CAREER AT THE UNIVERSITY, AND TAKE IN LAUNDRY TO SUPPORT US..
5-5

HOW DO YOU THINK THAT WOULD AFFECT OUR MARRIAGE? LET'S TALK ABOUT THIS..

BONK!

MUSICIANS NEVER WANT TO DISCUSS ANYTHING..
SCHULZ

May 18, 1996

I'M GOING TO HAVE A DOG! SNOOPY'S BROTHER IS COMING FROM THE DESERT, AND HE'S GOING TO BE MY DOG!
YOU'RE CRAZY, RERUN.. MOM WILL NEVER LET YOU HAVE A DOG!
I WONDER IF HE'S THE KIND WHO HOWLS AT THE MOON..
I KNOW SPIKE.. HE'D HOWL AT A NIGHT LIGHT..
SCHULZ 5-18

May 20, 1996

I HATE TO TELL YOU THIS, BUT I'M LEAVING THE DESERT..
5-20
SOME LITTLE KID HAS INVITED ME TO LIVE AT HIS HOUSE..
I'M GOING TO MISS YOU..
SCHULZ

May 21, 1996

WHAT ARE YOU DOING OUT HERE?
WAITING FOR MY NEW DOG..
HOW DO YOU THINK HE'S EVER GOING TO FIND YOU?
DOGS ARE SMART.. THEY CAN FIND THEIR WAY ANYPLACE..THEY ALWAYS KNOW WHERE THEY ARE..
I THINK I LIVE AROUND HERE SOMEPLACE..
SCHULZ
5-21

May 23, 1996

RERUN! YOUR DOG IS HERE!
WHERE?
5-23
SCHULZ

June 30, 1996

PEANUTS
by SCHULZ
WHAT WE NEED IS AN ACTION SHOT..
THAT'S GOOD.. HOLD IT RIGHT THERE!
CLICK
NOW, WHEN IT RUNS IN OUR PAPER, WHAT NAME SHALL WE USE?
YOUR REAL NAME IS TOO COMMON.. YOU NEED A REAL BASEBALL NAME..
HOW ABOUT FLASH, OR SPEED, OR DUSTY?
HOW ABOUT DUKE BROWN? OR BABE BROWN? OR RUSTY, OR SLUGGER, OR KING, OR PEPPER, OR TIGER?
I DON'T KNOW..YOU THINK OF SOMETHING..
HEY, BIG BROTHER! YOUR NAME IS IN THE PAPER WITH YOUR PHOTOGRAPH!
"TAPIOCA" BROWN..
SCHULZ
6-30

May 24, 1996

5-24
YOU KNOW WHAT? I DON'T THINK THAT'S A GOLDEN RETRIEVER..
SCHULZ
© 1996 United Feature Syndicate, Inc.

May 25, 1996

I'M BACK!
5-25

I THINK I MUST HAVE BEEN A DISAPPOINTMENT TO THEM..

BUT I DON'T CARE! THIS IS MY REAL HOME!

SCHULZ

July 9, 1996

MY ARM HURTS.. I'M NOT SURE I CAN PITCH TODAY..

I THINK THROWING ALL THOSE CURVEBALLS PUT TOO MUCH STRAIN ON MY ELBOW..
7-9

THOSE WERE CURVEBALLS ?
SCHULZ

July 11, 1996

HELLO? IS THIS THE DOCTOR'S OFFICE?

WELL, I'VE BEEN HAVING TROUBLE WITH MY ELBOW..
7-11

THE SPORTS MEDICINE PLACE SAID I NEED TO GET A REFERRAL FROM MY PRIMARY CARE PHYSICIAN..

SO MAY I MAKE AN APPOINTMENT?

RIGHT AFTER CHRISTMAS?
SCHULZ

July 13, 1996

WHAT ARE YOU DOING HERE IN THE EMERGENCY ROOM, KID?
I HURT MY ELBOW PITCHING BASEBALL..

I TRIED TO GO TO THE SPORTS MEDICINE PLACE, BUT I COULDN'T GET A REFERRAL FROM MY PRIMARY CARE PHYSICIAN..

THEY ASKED ME THAT, TOO...
7-13

I SAID IT WAS ALBERT SCHWEITZER..
SCHULZ

August 2, 1996

I HAVE A NEW PHILOSOPHY.. "LIFE GOES ON"
GOOD FOR YOU..

SO WHAT'S ON TV?
NOTHING MUCH..
8-2

LIFE GOES ON..
SCHULZ

August 3, 1996

I NOW HAVE THREE PHILOSOPHIES..."LIFE GOES ON," "WHO CARES?" AND "HOW SHOULD I KNOW?"
8-3

PRETTY PROFOUND, HUH?
MAYBE A LITTLE TOO PROFOUND..

WHO CARES? HOW SHOULD I KNOW? LIFE GOES ON!
SCHULZ

"You have to be an egotist to draw comics, just as an actor has to be an egotist. Why else would you think that you are beautiful enough that people would want to see your picture on the screen? Why else would you think the pictures you draw are funny enough that people would want to buy them to show them to other people? This takes a form of egotism. And I don't think there's anything wrong with this. I'll never forget Will Durant's line on the apostle Paul: 'He had to be what he was to do what he did.' And this is the same with all of us. We all have to be what we are in order to do what we are going to do."

August 7, 1996

WHAT IF A BALL IS HIT OVER MY HEAD?

AND WHAT IF I CHASE IT, AND FALL OFF THE EDGE OF THE WORLD AND YOU NEVER SEE ME AGAIN?
8-7

THE WORLD ISN'T FLAT.. THE WORLD IS ROUND LIKE THIS BALL WHICH YOU WOULDN'T KNOW BECAUSE YOU'VE NEVER CAUGHT ONE!

A SENSITIVE PERSON SHOULD NEVER PLAY RIGHT FIELD..
SCHULZ

August 12, 1996

C'MON, MARCIE.. LET'S GO FISHING..

I'LL GO WITH YOU, SIR, BUT I HOPE YOU DON'T CATCH ANYTHING..

I ALWAYS STICK UP FOR THE UNDERFISH..
YOU ARE OVERLY WEIRD, MARCIE..
SCHULZ
8-12

August 13, 1996

LOOK OUT, FISH! HERE SHE COMES!

OH, SURE, MARCIE...
SCARE 'EM ALL AWAY!

JUST LEVELING THE PLAYING FIELD, SIR..
8-13
SCHULZ

August 14, 1996

HEY, FISH! DON'T LET HER FOOL YOU! THERE'S A HOOK ON THE END OF THAT LINE!

BE QUIET, MARCIE..
SHE'S OUT TO GET YOU! RUN WHILE YOU CAN!
8/14

FISH DON'T RUN, MARCIE..
DOG PADDLE!
SCHULZ

September 8, 1996

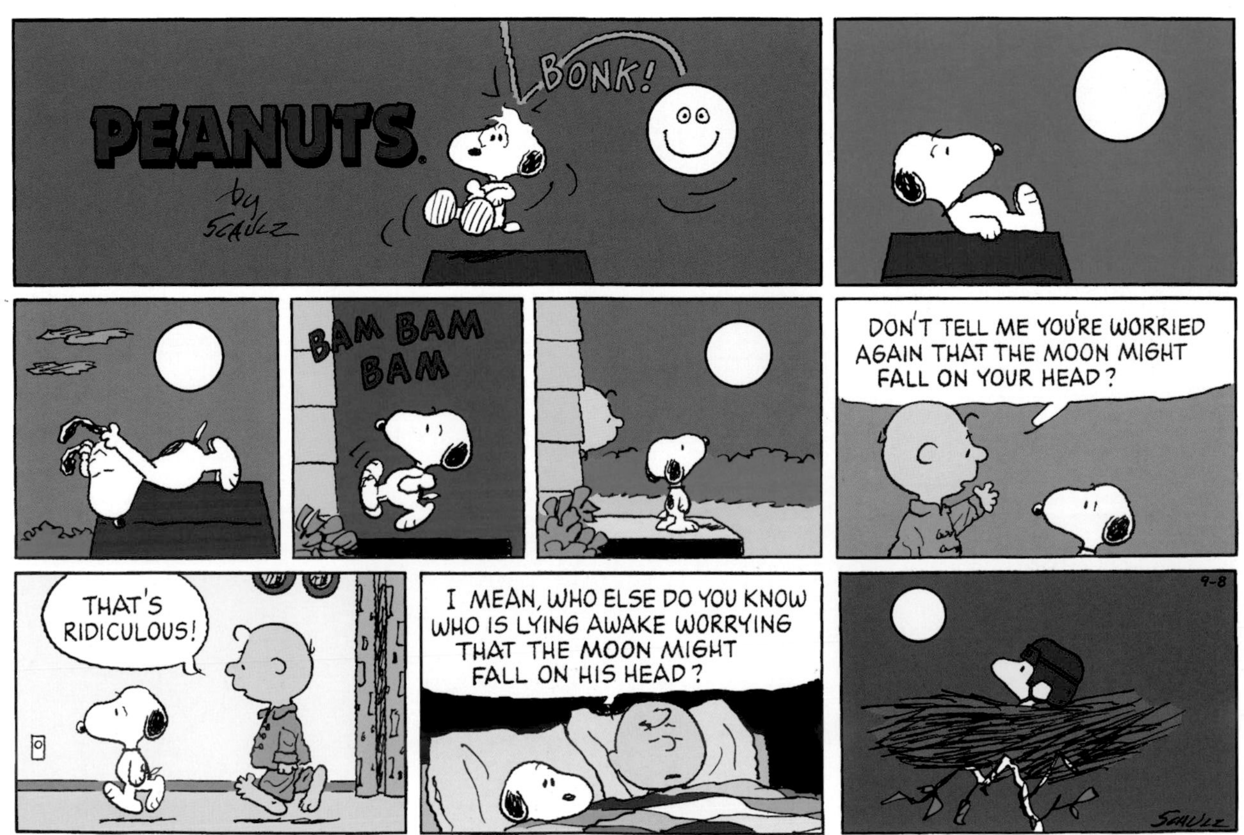
PEANUTS
by SCHULZ
BONK!
BAM BAM BAM
DON'T TELL ME YOU'RE WORRIED AGAIN THAT THE MOON MIGHT FALL ON YOUR HEAD?
THAT'S RIDICULOUS!
I MEAN, WHO ELSE DO YOU KNOW WHO IS LYING AWAKE WORRYING THAT THE MOON MIGHT FALL ON HIS HEAD?
9-8
SCHULZ

October 13, 1996

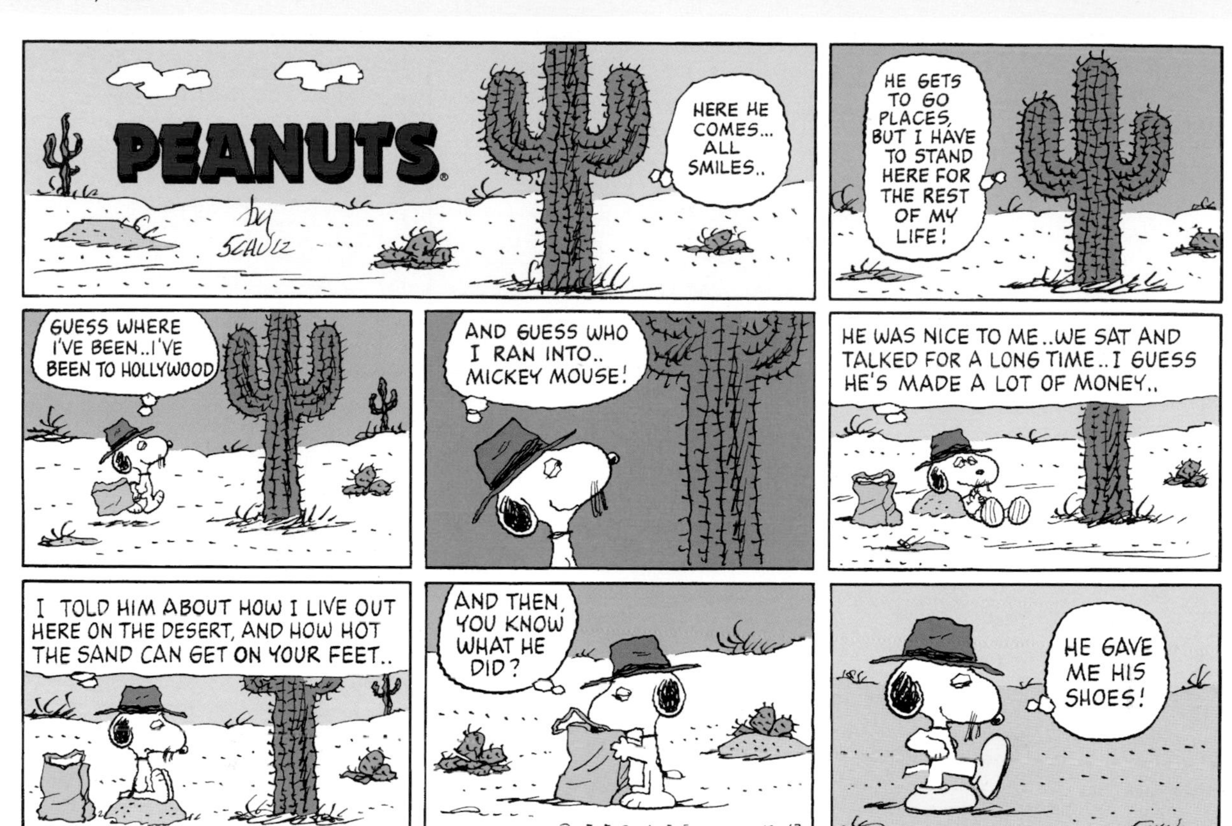
PEANUTS
by SCHULZ
HERE HE COMES... ALL SMILES..
HE GETS TO GO PLACES, BUT I HAVE TO STAND HERE FOR THE REST OF MY LIFE!
GUESS WHERE I'VE BEEN..I'VE BEEN TO HOLLYWOOD
AND GUESS WHO I RAN INTO.. MICKEY MOUSE!
HE WAS NICE TO ME..WE SAT AND TALKED FOR A LONG TIME..I GUESS HE'S MADE A LOT OF MONEY..
I TOLD HIM ABOUT HOW I LIVE OUT HERE ON THE DESERT, AND HOW HOT THE SAND CAN GET ON YOUR FEET..
AND THEN, YOU KNOW WHAT HE DID?
10-13
HE GAVE ME HIS SHOES!
SCHULZ

September 3, 1996

RERUN, IT'S TIME FOR SCHOOL! WHERE ARE YOU?
9-3
I'M NOT GOING! I'M HIDING UNDER MY BED..
YOU'D BETTER COME OUT..WHAT'S DAD GONNA SAY?
HE UNDERSTANDS.. HE SAID WHEN HE WAS LITTLE, HE HID UNDER THE BED FOR THREE DAYS..
SCHULZ

September 9, 1996

I HEARD RERUN DIDN'T START KINDERGARTEN LAST WEEK..
NO, HE HID UNDER THE BED..
I WONDER IF HE'LL TRY IT AGAIN..
MAYBE HE'LL FIND SOMEPLACE ELSE TO HIDE..
9-9
SCHULZ

September 11, 1996

YES, MA'AM..MY NAME IS "RERUN"...I DON'T KNOW..THAT'S WHAT THEY ALL CALL ME..
9-11

YES, I KNOW I SHOULD HAVE BEEN HERE LAST WEEK.. WELL, I'M HERE NOW..

I HOPE WE DON'T HAVE TO READ "WAR AND PEACE" THE FIRST DAY..
SCHULZ

October 28, 1996

10-28
ON HALLOWEEN NIGHT, THE "GREAT PUMPKIN" RISES OUT OF THE PUMPKIN PATCH, AND..
YOU'RE JUST TRYING TO MESS WITH MY MIND, AREN'T YOU?
SCHULZ

October 31, 1996

ARE YOU THE "GREAT PUMPKIN"?
NO, I'M YOUR KID BROTHER WITH A SHEET OVER MY HEAD..

I FORGOT TO CUT OUT THE EYE HOLES SO I HAVE NO IDEA WHERE I'M GOING..
10-31
SCHULZ

January 10, 1997

WHERE WILL IT ALL END?
WHERE WILL WHAT ALL END?

THAT'S MY NEW PHILOSOPHY.."WHERE WILL IT ALL END?"
1-10-97

I'M PROUD OF YOU.. IT SOUNDS LIKE YOU'VE BEEN DOING SOME REAL THINKING..

WHERE WILL IT ALL END?
SCHULZ

January 13, 1997

I'M TIRED OF ALL THIS KINDERGARTEN STUFF..
WHY DON'T WE RUN AWAY TO PARIS?
1-13

IF WE GOT ON A PLANE AT MIDNIGHT, WE COULD BE IN PARIS TOMORROW..

DO YOU HAVE ANY MONEY?
I HAVE FIFTY CENTS..MAYBE WE COULD GET UPGRADED TO BUSINESS CLASS
SCHULZ

January 14, 1997

THERE'S THIS CUTE LITTLE GIRL WHO SITS NEXT TO ME IN KINDERGARTEN..
1-14

I TOLD HER MAYBE SHE AND I COULD GO TO PARIS SOMEDAY..

I DON'T EVEN KNOW WHERE PARIS IS..
SCHULZ

January 16, 1997

YES, SIR, MR. PRINCIPAL... WHO? THE LITTLE GIRL WITH THE BRAIDS? SURE, WE'RE IN THE SAME KINDERGARTEN CLASS..
1-16

DID I ASK HER TO GO TO PARIS?

WELL, SURE, BUT THAT WAS JUST A JOKE..

I MEAN, HOW...
SCHULZ

HARASSMENT?!!

January 18, 1997

THIS LITTLE GIRL IN MY CLASS WAS SORT OF DEPRESSED, SEE, SO I SAID, "WHY DON'T WE RUN AWAY TO PARIS?" IT WAS A JOKE

SHE THOUGHT IT WAS FUNNY SO SHE TOLD HER MOTHER, WHO TOLD OUR TEACHER, WHO TOLD THE PRINCIPAL, AND I GOT FIRED!
1-18

SUSPENDED
I GUESS SO..

HARASSMENT?
STUPIDITY!
SCHULZ

February 1, 1997

THERE I WAS, SOUND ASLEEP.. SUDDENLY, I WAS PLAGUED BY A SELF DOUBT!
2-1

YOU?

YOU'RE PROBABLY RIGHT..
SCHULZ

February 10, 1997

MY PITCHER'S MOUND MAY BE COVERED WITH SNOW, BUT THE MEMORIES ARE STILL HERE..
2-10

FORTY TO NOTHING, TWENTY TO NOTHING, FIFTY-THREE TO NOTHING, SIXTY TO NOTHING..

AND THAT GREAT GAME WHEN YOU GOT HIT ON THE HEAD BY A FLY BALL..
I DON'T REMEMBER THAT..
SCHULZ

March 16, 1997

PEANUTS
by SCHULZ

WHAT WAS THAT YOU WERE PLAYING?

IT'S CALLED "PEANUTS GALLERY"
WHAT IS?

A NEW PIECE COMPOSED BY ELLEN TAAFFE ZWILICH.. WE'RE ALL IN IT!
WHAT DO YOU MEAN, WE'RE ALL IN IT?

IT HAS A GREAT BEGINNING.. "SCHROEDER'S BEETHOVEN FANTASY."

THEN THERE'S "LULLABY FOR LINUS," "SNOOPY DOES THE SAMBA," AND "CHARLIE BROWN'S LAMENT."

THEN THERE'S "LUCY FREAKS OUT" AND "PEPPERMINT PATTY AND MARCIE LEAD THE PARADE"!
3-16

THE WORLD PREMIERE WILL BE AT CARNEGIE HALL..HERE, LOOK AT IT YOURSELF..

MY PART SHOULD BE LONGER..
SCHULZ

February 11, 1997

ARE WE GONNA HAVE A BASEBALL TEAM AGAIN THIS YEAR?

YES, BUT WE WEREN'T GOING TO TELL YOU..

WE WERE ALL HOPING YOU WOULDN'T FIND OUT BECAUSE WE ALL KNOW YOU'RE THE WORST PLAYER IN THE HISTORY OF THE GAME..

PUT ME DOWN FOR RIGHT FIELD
SIGH

February 24, 1997

DO YOU LIKE ME, CHARLES?
DO I WHAT?

"DO I WHAT?" I WALK ALL THE WAY OVER HERE TO ASK YOU A QUESTION, AND ALL YOU CAN SAY IS, "DO I WHAT?"

FORGET IT, CHARLES!
FORGET WHAT?

April 13, 1997

PEANUTS
by SCHULZ

DO YOU NEED ANY HELP?
SURE..THANK YOU..

YOUR JOB WILL BE TO HOLD THE KITE..

DOES MY JOB HAVE A TITLE?

CALL YOURSELF ANYTHING YOU WANT..JUST LET GO OF THE KITE AFTER I START RUNNING..

I CAN BE THE "KITE ASSISTANT."

OR MAYBE "HEAD KITE ASSISTANT." OR EVEN "CHIEF KITE ASSISTANT."

RIP!

HOW ABOUT "EX-KITE ASSISTANT FOURTH CLASS"?
I CAN'T STAND IT! I JUST CAN'T STAND IT!

May 4, 1997

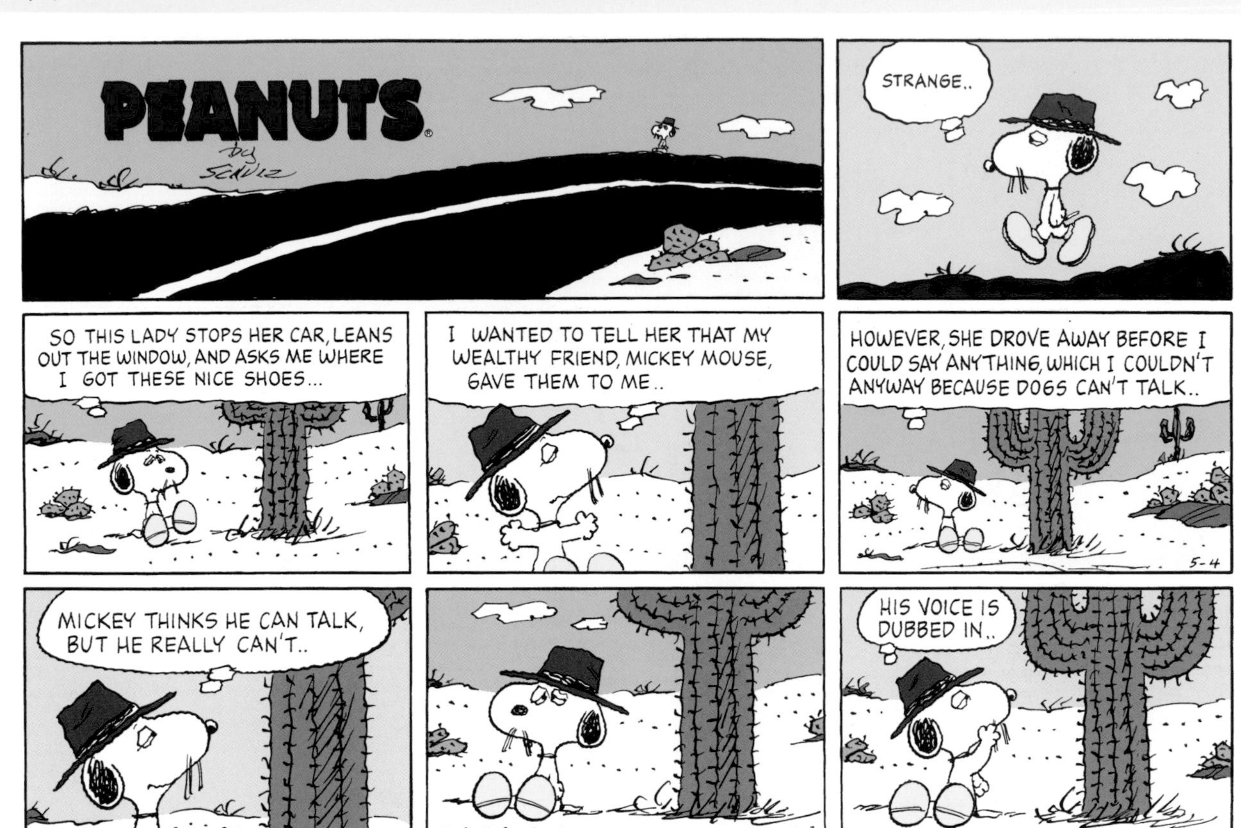
PEANUTS
by SCHULZ
STRANGE..
SO THIS LADY STOPS HER CAR, LEANS OUT THE WINDOW, AND ASKS ME WHERE I GOT THESE NICE SHOES...
I WANTED TO TELL HER THAT MY WEALTHY FRIEND, MICKEY MOUSE, GAVE THEM TO ME..
HOWEVER, SHE DROVE AWAY BEFORE I COULD SAY ANYTHING, WHICH I COULDN'T ANYWAY BECAUSE DOGS CAN'T TALK..
5-4
MICKEY THINKS HE CAN TALK, BUT HE REALLY CAN'T..
HIS VOICE IS DUBBED IN..
SCHULZ

March 11, 1997

I LIKE DOING WATERCOLORS
I HATE IT.. IT'S TOO HARD..
NO, MA'AM.. I HAVEN'T STARTED YET.. I DON'T HAVE ANY WATER..
SCHULZ
3-11
I DRANK IT..

March 18, 1997

"PIGPEN," I DON'T UNDERSTAND YOU..
THIS IS THE FIRST INNING OF OUR FIRST GAME, AND YOU'RE ALREADY COVERED WITH DIRT..
3-18

THIS ISN'T ALL FROM TODAY.. SOME OF IT'S LEFT OVER FROM LAST YEAR..
SCHULZ

May 11, 1997

PEANUTS
by SCHULZ

A YEAR.. MAYBE SIX MONTHS...

SAY WE'VE BEEN MARRIED FOR ABOUT SIX MONTHS...

AND LET'S SAY I'VE MADE A BEAUTIFUL TUNA CASSEROLE FOR DINNER...

YOU WALK INTO THE KITCHEN, AND YOU SAY, "WHAT, TUNA CASSEROLE AGAIN?"

I'D NEVER SAY THAT..
THEN I SAY, "I WORKED HARD MAKING THIS CASSEROLE, BUT ALL YOU CARE ABOUT IS THAT STUPID PIANO!"
5-11

THEN YOU WALK OUT..

SORRY I'M LATE.. I GOT INVOLVED IN A MARITAL DISPUTE..

I NEVER KNOW WHAT ANYONE IS TALKING ABOUT..
SCHULZ

March 19, 1997

DO ME A FAVOR.. GO ASK "PIGPEN" WHY HE DOESN'T WEAR A BASEBALL CAP..

THE MANAGER WANTS TO KNOW WHY YOU DON'T WEAR A CAP..

HE SAID HE DOESN'T WANT TO MUSS UP HIS HAIR..
SCHULZ
3-19

May 13, 1997

NO, THAT'S NOT A STAR.. IT'S A COMET..
5-13

HOW DO I KNOW? IT SAYS SO ON THE SIDE..

HE NEVER BELIEVES ANYTHING I TELL HIM..
SCHULZ

May 15, 1997

YES, MA'AM.. I'M WRITING A STORY..

IT'S ABOUT THIS KID WHO'S IN KINDERGARTEN, AND HOW THE STRESS IS SLOWLY DESTROYING HIM..

EVERY MORNING HE...

MA'AM?
5-15

WELL, I HAVE ANOTHER ONE HERE ABOUT SOME PURPLE BUNNIES..
SCHULZ

"I do think that it is necessary to be reasonably well educated. I think you should read a lot, that you should be well informed about all forms of literature. I think a good knowledge of history is important, and knowledge of the whole world around us. I think knowledge is very important, and to maintain an interest in people, and try to grow as a person yourself."

May 20, 1997

HERE'S THE WORLD FAMOUS PATRIOT SOLDIER STANDING GUARD AT VALLEY FORGE..
5-20

"THESE ARE THE TIMES THAT TRY MEN'S SOULS"

TO PUT IT ANOTHER WAY, "I HOPE I MAKE THE CUT"
SCHULZ

May 21, 1997

HEY, MARCIE.. I UNDERSTAND THERE'S A RUMOR GOING AROUND THAT I MAY BE NAMED "OUTSTANDING STUDENT OF THE YEAR"

THAT'S INTERESTING, SIR.. I HEARD ANOTHER RUMOR THAT THE MOON IS GOING TO FALL OUT OF THE SKY..
5-21

I'M HANGING UP, MARCIE..
SCHULZ

May 22, 1997

MORALE IS LOW AT VALLEY FORGE..
5-22

THE TROOPS ARE HUNGRY.. NOTHING TO EAT BUT FIRECAKE AND WATER..

AND THIS MORNING GENERAL WASHINGTON GAVE US MORE BAD NEWS...

WE'RE ALL OUT OF GRAPE JELLY!
SCHULZ

May 23, 1997

SEE, MARCIE? HERE ARE THE NAMES OF EVERYONE WHO'S UP FOR "OUTSTANDING STUDENT OF THE YEAR"... THERE'S MY NAME, SEE?

I COUNTED THEM, SIR.. YOU'RE FOUR HUNDREDTH ON THE LIST..

FOUR HUNDREDTH AND MOVING UP FAST!
SCHULZ
5-23

May 26, 1997

IT'S ANOTHER COLD DAY AT VALLEY FORGE..I'VE BAKED GENERAL WASHINGTON A PIECE OF FIRECAKE..
5-26

HE SAYS TO ME, "WHERE'S THE GRAPE JELLY?" I TELL HIM WE HAVEN'T HAD GRAPE JELLY FOR SIX WEEKS..

THEN HE SAYS, "CAN'T SOMEONE GO OVER TO THE MALL, AND GET SOME?"

IT WAS TOO HARD TO EXPLAIN
SCHULZ

May 27, 1997

CAN YOU BELIEVE IT, CHUCK? CAN YOU BELIEVE IT?
BELIEVE WHAT?

MARCIE WAS NAMED "OUTSTANDING STUDENT OF THE YEAR"! I THOUGHT I WAS GOING TO WIN!
5-27

I'VE NEVER BEEN SO DEPRESSED IN ALL MY LIFE..
YOU SHOULD HAVE BEEN AT VALLEY FORGE..
SCHULZ

May 31, 1997

I SUPPOSE HAVING A DOG HELPS TO MAKE YOU FEEL BETTER WHEN YOU'RE DEPRESSED, HUH, CHUCK?
I WOULDN'T KNOW..
SAY "GOODBYE" TO VALLEY FORGE, MEN.. WE'RE MOVING OUT!
5-31
SCHULZ

June 17, 1997

MAYBE YOU GUYS SHOULD GO VISIT OUR BROTHER SPIKE IN THE DESERT..HE KNOWS MICKEY MOUSE..

MICKEY MOUSE HAS A LOT OF FRIENDS IN HOLLYWOOD..
6-17

I'LL BET HE COULD GET YOU JOBS AT ONE OF THE STUDIOS.. HOW DOES THAT SOUND?

WHO'S MICKEY MOUSE?
SCHULZ

June 21, 1997

THAT OTHER TEAM IS TRASH-TALKING US, CHARLIE BROWN..

I GOT EVEN WITH THEM, THOUGH...
6-21

I SAID, "YOU GUYS THINK YOU'RE SO GREAT..MOZART WAS WRITING SYMPHONIES WHEN HE WAS YOUR AGE!"

THAT REALLY SHUT 'EM UP..
I'LL BET IT DID..
SCHULZ

June 30, 1997

HEY, CHUCK..WE'RE BACK FROM CAMP! DID YOU LIKE MY LETTER?

I POURED MY HEART INTO THAT LETTER, CHUCK..
6-30

I WANTED YOU TO KNOW THAT EVEN THOUGH WE WERE FAR AWAY, YOU WERE IN OUR THOUGHTS.. KIND OF POETIC, HUH?

ANYWAY, CHUCK..DID YOU LIKE MY LETTER?
WHAT LETTER?
SCHULZ

July 1, 1997

WHAT LETTER?! WHAT DO YOU MEAN, WHAT LETTER?!

I WROTE YOU A LOVE LETTER, CHUCK! I WROTE IT ON PINK STATIONERY!!
7-1

IS THAT WHAT THAT WAS? I THOUGHT IT WAS JUNK MAIL SO I THREW IT AWAY..

AAUGH!
A JUNK MAIL LOVE LETTER! HA HA HA HA!!
SCHULZ

July 7, 1997

I REMEMBER WHEN MICKEY MOUSE GAVE ME THESE NICE YELLOW SHOES...
7-7

I WANTED TO DO SOMETHING FOR HIM IN RETURN TO SHOW MY APPRECIATION...

I OFFERED HIM MY HAT, BUT IT WOULDN'T FIT OVER HIS EARS..
SCHULZ

July 11, 1997

SCHULZ
7-11

July 27, 1997

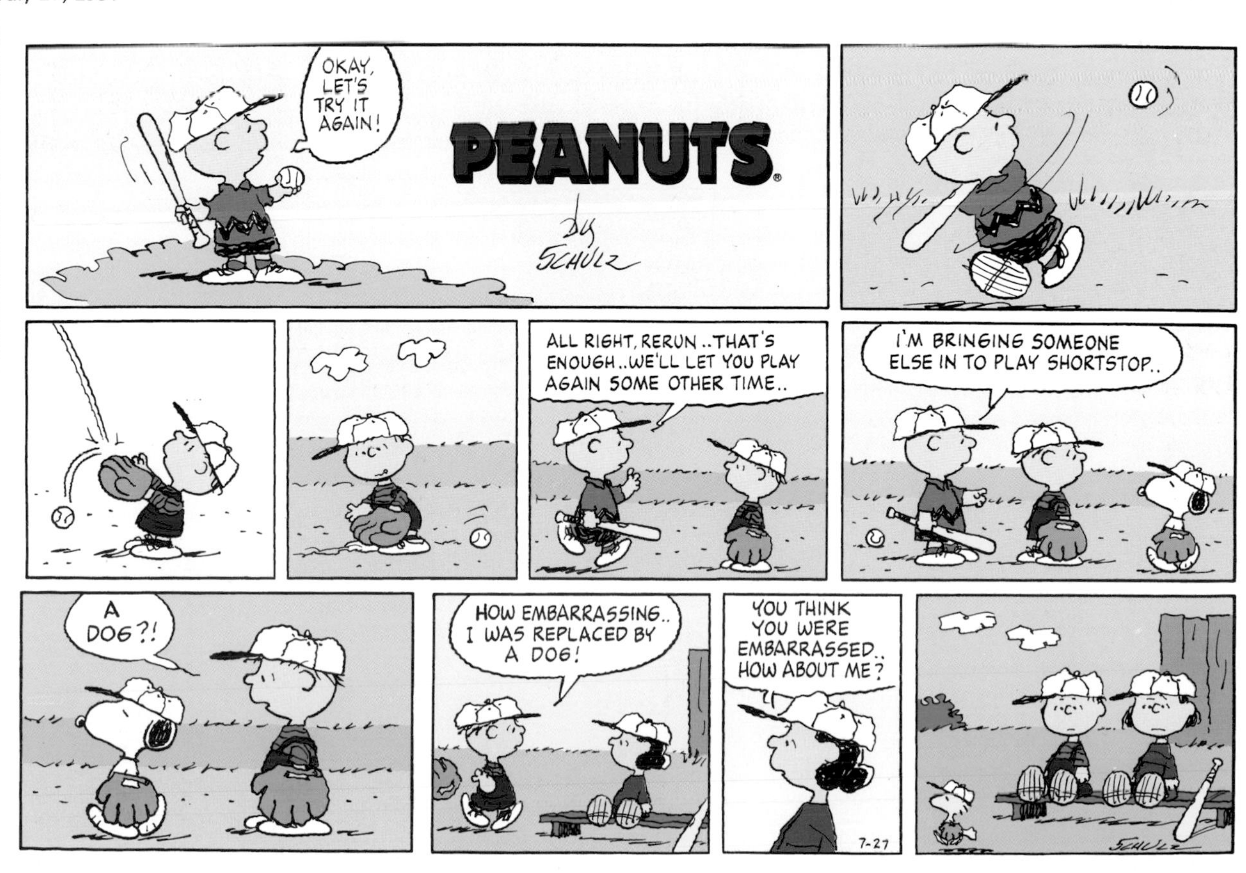
OKAY, LET'S TRY IT AGAIN!
PEANUTS
by SCHULZ
ALL RIGHT, RERUN..THAT'S ENOUGH..WE'LL LET YOU PLAY AGAIN SOME OTHER TIME..
I'M BRINGING SOMEONE ELSE IN TO PLAY SHORTSTOP..
A DOG?!
HOW EMBARRASSING.. I WAS REPLACED BY A DOG!
YOU THINK YOU WERE EMBARRASSED.. HOW ABOUT ME?
7-27
SCHULZ

July 31, 1997

A PIRATE SHIP! I SEE A PIRATE SHIP!
7-31

HERE'S BLACKBEAGLE, THE WORLD FAMOUS PIRATE, LEADING HIS SCURVY BAND ASHORE...

SOMEBODY TELL CONRAD HE'S ONLY SUPPOSED TO WEAR ONE EYE PATCH..
BONK!
SCHULZ

September 12, 1997

As she said, "Goodbye" and ran up the steps, he knew he would never see her again.
9-12

He was heartbroken.

"Oh, well," he thought. "I still have my dog."

Little did he know, his dog had been planning to leave him.
SCHULZ

October 19, 1997

PEANUTS
by SCHULZ
RING!
I THINK IT'S FOR YOU.. SHOULD I HANG UP?
HI, CHUCK.. DO YOU MISS ME?
10-19
DO I WHAT?
MISS ME! DO YOU MISS ME, CHUCK?! WHAT'S THE MATTER WITH YOU? DON'T YOU UNDERSTAND ANYTHING?!
WHO IS THIS?
WHAT DO YOU MEAN, WHO IS THIS?! IT'S ME, CHUCK! WHO DID YOU THINK IT WAS?!!
OH
"OH"? WHAT DOES THAT MEAN? "OH".. IS THAT ALL YOU CAN SAY?!
I'M SORRY.. I WAS THINKING OF SOMETHING ELSE... I HAVE TO FEED MY DOG..
WAIT, CHUCK! DON'T HANG UP! SAY SOMETHING! SAY ANYTHING!
WOOF!
HOW SWEET!
SCHULZ

November 30, 1997

PEANUTS
by SCHULZ
CATCH IT, MARCIE!

YOU KICKED THE FOOTBALL UP INTO THE TREE, SIR..
I KNOW HOW TO GET IT DOWN..

YOU STAND IN FRONT OF THE TREE..I'LL RUN UP AND JUMP ON YOUR SHOULDERS...

MY SHOELACE IS UNTIED AGAIN..
11-30-97

WHAM!

OKAY, SIR..I'M READY WHEN YOU ARE!

WHAT ARE YOU DOING DOWN THERE?
FORGET IT, MARCIE! IF THE BALL WANTS TO STAY IN THE TREE, LET IT STAY..

WE'LL PROBABLY NEVER MAKE IT TO THE SPLENDID BOWL ANYWAY, SIR
SUPER BOWL, MARCIE!
SCHULZ

"I am very proud of the comic strip medium and am never ashamed to admit that I draw a comic strip. I do not regard it as great art, but I have always felt it is certainly on the level with other entertainment mediums which are part of the so-called 'popular arts.' In many ways, I do not think we have realized the potential of the comic strip."

November 10, 1997

THIS IS A BORDER COLLIE, SEE, AND THESE ARE THE SHEEP HE'S GUARDING..

SUDDENLY, A WOLF COMES, SO THE BORDER COLLIE GETS ON THE PHONE, AND CALLS IN AN AIR STRIKE!

WE'RE SUPPOSED TO BE DOING WATER COLORS OF FLOWERS..
IT ALL TAKES PLACE IN A MEADOW..
SCHULZ
11-10

November 13, 1997

Dear Snoopy,
I am still waiting for Andy and Olaf to come here.
11-13

"REMEMBER HOW I TOLD YOU THAT MY WEALTHY FRIEND MICKEY MOUSE LEFT SOME SHOES HERE FOR THEM?"

Bad news! Last night somebody stole them!

"IF YOU SEE A COYOTE WEARING MICKEY MOUSE SHOES, GRAB HIM!"
SCHULZ

February 8, 1998

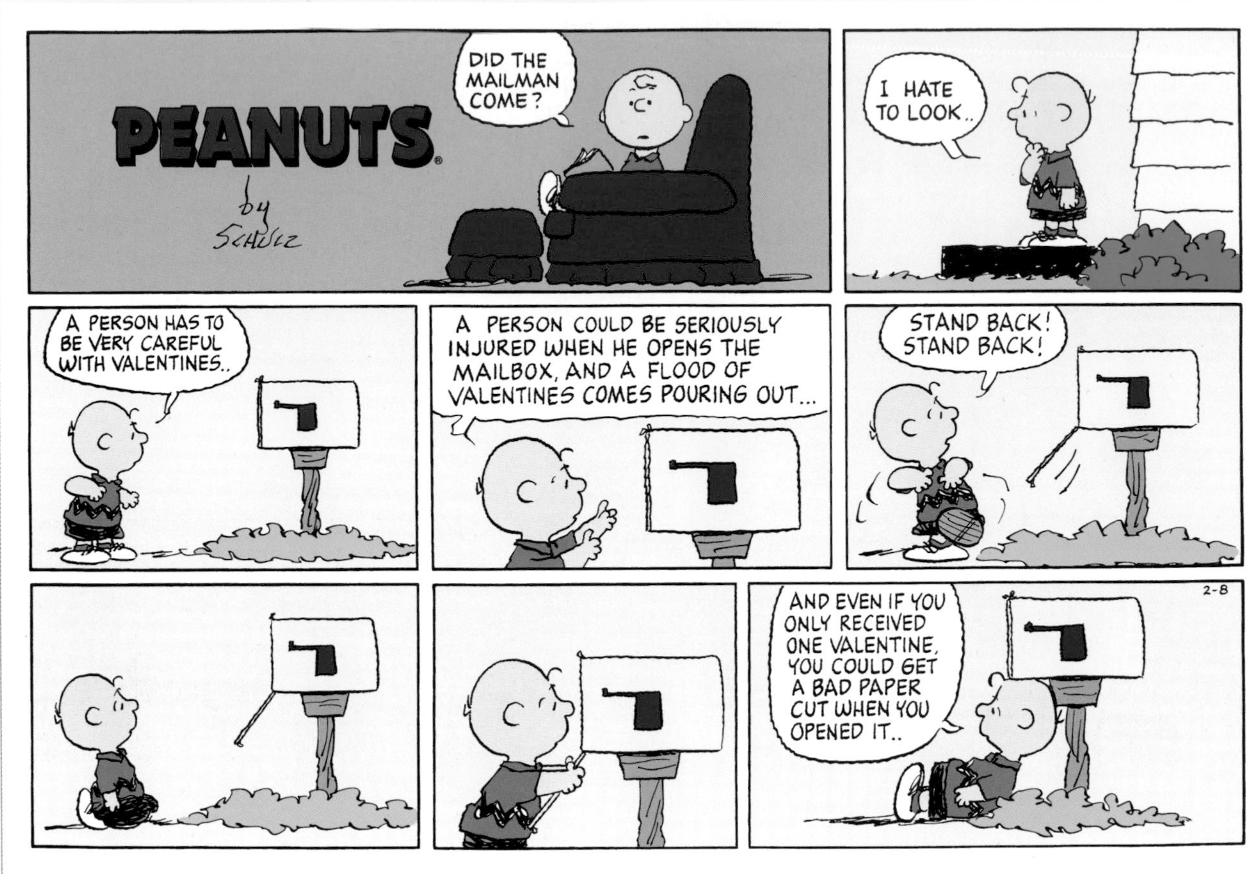
PEANUTS
by Schulz
DID THE MAILMAN COME?
I HATE TO LOOK..
A PERSON HAS TO BE VERY CAREFUL WITH VALENTINES..
A PERSON COULD BE SERIOUSLY INJURED WHEN HE OPENS THE MAILBOX, AND A FLOOD OF VALENTINES COMES POURING OUT...
STAND BACK! STAND BACK!
2-8
AND EVEN IF YOU ONLY RECEIVED ONE VALENTINE, YOU COULD GET A BAD PAPER CUT WHEN YOU OPENED IT..

January 27, 1998

I TOLD YOUR TEACHER WHAT YOU SAID ABOUT HER NEW BOYFRIEND..
SHE SAID YOU WERE RIGHT.. HE'S REALLY STUPID, AND SHE'S NEVER GOING TO SEE HIM AGAIN..
1-27
I COULD RUN THE WHOLE WORLD RIGHT HERE FROM UNDER MY BED!
SCHULZ

January 30, 1998

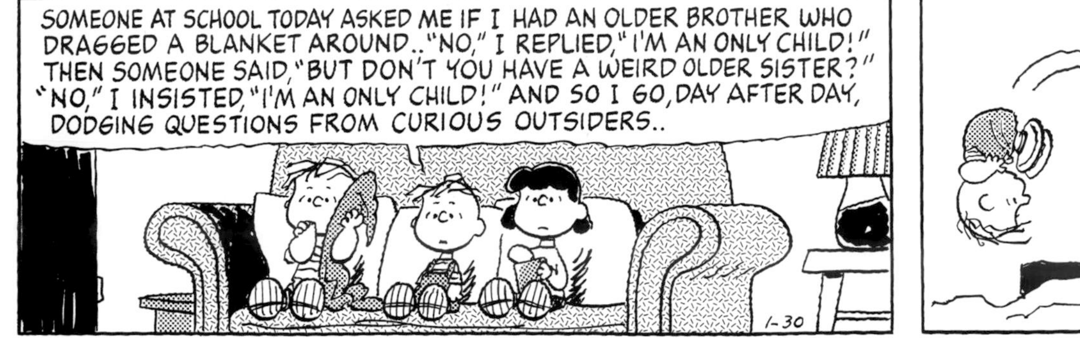
SOMEONE AT SCHOOL TODAY ASKED ME IF I HAD AN OLDER BROTHER WHO DRAGGED A BLANKET AROUND.."NO," I REPLIED,"I'M AN ONLY CHILD!" THEN SOMEONE SAID,"BUT DON'T YOU HAVE A WEIRD OLDER SISTER?" "NO," I INSISTED,"I'M AN ONLY CHILD!" AND SO I GO, DAY AFTER DAY, DODGING QUESTIONS FROM CURIOUS OUTSIDERS..
1-30
SCHULZ

March 12, 1998

I'VE BEEN THINKING OF TAKING A SPECIAL COURSE IN FRENCH..

MAYBE EVEN A LITTLE LATIN AND SOME SPANISH.. WHAT DO YOU THINK ?

"D-MINUS" SPOKEN HERE..
SCHULZ
3-12

March 13, 1998

NO, MA'AM..I DON'T KNOW THE ANSWER..
3-13

ACTUALLY, I DON'T KNOW ANYTHING..

I'M JUST HERE TO DRESS THE SET..
SCHULZ

February 15, 1998

PEANUTS
by
SCHULZ

WELL, HOW DOES OUR BALL FIELD LOOK THIS YEAR, CHARLIE BROWN ?
2-15

I THINK OUR GROUNDSKEEPER IS DOING A GOOD JOB..

THE INFIELD LOOKS GREAT AND THE GRASS IN THE OUTFIELD HAS NEVER LOOKED BETTER..

I THINK IT'S BECAUSE WE HAVE A NEW AUTOMATIC SPRINKLER SYSTEM...

SCHULZ

"I'm afraid that we are slowly being driven out of business . . . we don't have the room in which to work. This is the obvious complaint. Beyond that, there seems to be no room for a lot of experimentation. We seem all to be channeled down the same path, and I don't know what the solution is. I think that if some editor had the great notion to run a comic strip large all the way across the bottom of the paper, or something like that, it would be revolutionary. It just might start everything all over again. But I'm afraid it's just not going to happen."

May 16, 1998

HEY, CHUCK, WHEN WE GO TO THE DANCE, ARE YOU GONNA PICK ME UP IN A LIMO?
OR MAYBE WE SHOULD JUST MEET THERE, HUH, CHARLES?
5-16

MEET WHERE? WHO IS THIS?

IT'S US, CHUCK, YOU BLOCKHEAD!

I THINK YOU'VE GOT THOSE GIRLS ALL CONFUSED, BIG BROTHER..
I FORGOT TO TELL THEM TO SAVE ME THE WALTZ..
SCHULZ

May 18, 1998

I'M FEEDING YOU EARLY BECAUSE I'M GOING TO A DANCE TONIGHT..

I'M HOPING I GET TO DANCE WITH THE LITTLE RED-HAIRED GIRL, AND...
5-18

..AND I DIDN'T KNOW YOU WERE GOING ALONG..
SCHULZ

May 21, 1998

SEE? THERE SHE IS, CHARLIE BROWN..

THERE'S THE LITTLE RED-HAIRED GIRL JUST WAITING FOR YOU TO ASK HER TO DANCE...

I WISH I WERE SOPHISTICATED LIKE GUYS YOU READ ABOUT IN STORIES..
5-21

HERE'S THE SCOTT FITZGERALD HERO STANDING BY THE PUNCH BOWL "TRYING TO LOOK CASUAL AND UNINTERESTED IN THE DANCERS"

"DON'T GIVE IT ANOTHER THOUGHT, OLD SPORT"
SCHULZ

May 22, 1998

I CAN'T BELIEVE I'M DOING THIS..
I'M WALKING TOWARD THE LITTLE RED-HAIRED GIRL..
I'M GOING TO ASK HER TO DANCE..I'M GETTING CLOSER.. I'M ALMOST THERE.. I'M...
CHUCK! WE'VE BEEN LOOKING FOR YOU!
COME ON, CHARLES, THEY'RE PLAYING THE "HOKEY-POKEY"
OH, GOOD GRIEF!
5-22
SCHULZ

May 25, 1998

CHARLIE BROWN! WHERE HAVE YOU BEEN?
I'VE BEEN DOING THE HOKEY-POKEY WITH PATTY AND MARCIE..
LISTEN..THEY'RE PLAYING A FOX TROT..
NOW I CAN ASK THE LITTLE RED HAIRED GIRL TO DANCE..
I THINK SOMEONE IS AHEAD OF YOU..
"DAISY AND GATSBY DANCED..I REMEMBER HIS GRACEFUL CONSERVATIVE FOX TROT"
www.snoopy.com
5-25
SCHULZ

May 27, 1998

SURE, THERE I WAS HAVING A GOOD TIME AT THE DANCE, AND THEN YOU HAD TO GET SICK..
SOMEONE SAID YOU PROBABLY DRANK TOO MUCH PUNCH..
I ATE TOO MUCH.. I DRANK TOO MUCH.. AND I DANCED TOO MUCH...
LET'S DO IT AGAIN TOMORROW NIGHT..
5-27
SCHULZ

May 28, 1998

THE HOKEY-POKEY WASN'T VERY ROMANTIC, CHUCK
I SAVED YOU THE WALTZ, CHARLES, BUT I NEVER SAW YOU..
HOW ABOUT THE LIMO, CHUCK? WE NEVER SAW A LIMO, EITHER..
HOW COME YOU FELL DOWN DOING THE HOKEY-POKEY?
DON'T INVITE US TO ANYMORE DANCES, CHUCK
"MANY A HEART IS BROKEN AFTER THE BALL"
5-28
SCHULZ

June 25, 1998

WHAT A FACE! I'LL NEVER BE BEAUTIFUL..
YOU WILL SOMEDAY, SIR.. ALL OF YOUR FEATURES WILL SETTLE INTO THEIR PROPER SIZES AND PLACES, AND YOU'LL BE BEAUTIFUL
WHAT ABOUT MY HANDS?
SOMEDAY YOU'LL HAVE PRETTY HANDS, SIR..
WHAT ABOUT A CERTAIN FRIEND OF MINE?
SHE'LL BE GORGEOUS!
SCHULZ
6/25

July 2, 1998

HI, CHUCK..JUST THOUGHT I'D CALL AGAIN..
WOOF
7-2
WHAT? NO, JUST CURIOUS AS TO HOW YOU'VE BEEN..
WOOF WOOF WOOF
SCHULZ
YOU'RE STARTING TO REPEAT YOURSELF, CHUCK..

July 11, 1998

I'LL NEVER FORGET THE EXPRESSION ON THE OTHER ATTORNEY'S FACE...
HE SAW I HAD THIS BRAND-NEW YELLOW LEGAL PAD WITH LINES ON IT..
THERE'S A LOT OF JEALOUSY AMONG ATTORNEYS
SCHULZ
7-11

July 14, 1998

I DON'T SUPPOSE YOUR DOG WANTS TO COME OUT AND PLAY..
NO, I DON'T SUPPOSE HE DOES
I SUPPOSE IT WAS A WASTE OF TIME TO ASK..
I SUPPOSE IT WAS
DO YOU SUPPOSE I MIGHT ASK AGAIN TOMORROW?
I SUPPOSE YOU MIGHT
7/14
I SUPPOSE YOU COULD GUESS WHO THAT WAS..
I SUPPOSE I COULD..
SCHULZ

July 21, 1998

SEE? THAT MEANS AN HOUR HAS GONE BY..
7-21

LET'S TURN IT OVER, AND WATCH IT AGAIN..

WOW! LOOK AT THAT! OKAY, NOW WE'LL TURN IT OVER AND WATCH IT AGAIN..

I LEAD A DUMB LIFE!
SCHULZ

August 13, 1998

Dear Pen Pal,
8-13

IF YOUR PEN PAL IS A GIRL, WHY DON'T YOU SAY, "DEAREST PEN PAL" OR "DARLING PEN PAL"?

AND THEN SIGN IT "AFFECTIONATELY YOURS"

ANY OTHER ADVICE?
DON'T SEND A PICTURE
SCHULZ

August 22, 1998

I SUPPOSE YOU REALIZE THAT SCHOOL STARTS AGAIN NEXT MONTH..
I'M READY, KID..
8-22

I COME FROM A FAMILY OF DEDICATED SCHOOL BUILDINGS..

WE'RE A PROUD FAMILY...

OUR OLDER SISTER HAS A NEW CAFETERIA..
SCHULZ

August 29, 1998

SOMETIMES I LIE AWAKE AT NIGHT, AND I ASK, "WHY ISN'T THE WORLD PERFECT?"
8-29

THEN A VOICE COMES TO ME THAT SAYS, "WE ADMIT IT..THERE ARE STILL A FEW KINKS THAT NEED WORKING OUT"
SCHULZ

August 30, 1998

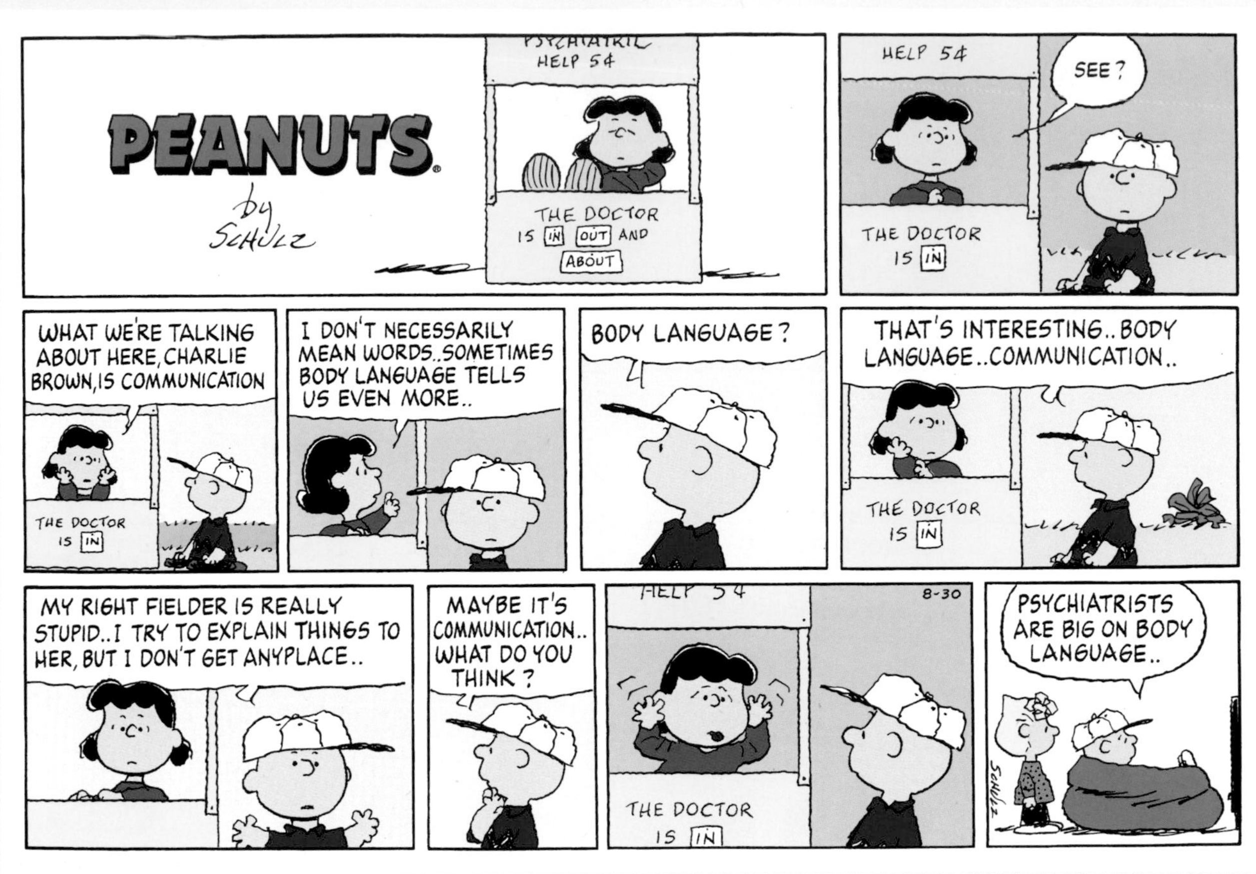
PEANUTS
by SCHULZ
PSYCHIATRIC HELP 5¢
THE DOCTOR IS IN OUT AND ABOUT
HELP 5¢
SEE?
THE DOCTOR IS IN
WHAT WE'RE TALKING ABOUT HERE, CHARLIE BROWN, IS COMMUNICATION
THE DOCTOR IS IN
I DON'T NECESSARILY MEAN WORDS..SOMETIMES BODY LANGUAGE TELLS US EVEN MORE..
BODY LANGUAGE?
THAT'S INTERESTING..BODY LANGUAGE..COMMUNICATION..
THE DOCTOR IS IN
MY RIGHT FIELDER IS REALLY STUPID..I TRY TO EXPLAIN THINGS TO HER, BUT I DON'T GET ANYPLACE..
MAYBE IT'S COMMUNICATION.. WHAT DO YOU THINK?
8-30
THE DOCTOR IS IN
PSYCHIATRISTS ARE BIG ON BODY LANGUAGE..
SCHULZ

August 31, 1998

SCHULZ
8-31

September 4, 1998

HEY, MANAGER.. NEXT YEAR I THINK I'LL PLAY FOR A DIFFERENT TEAM..
9-4
I'M TIRED OF LOSING ALL THE TIME..
I SUPPOSE YOU'RE GOING TO PLAY FOR SOMEONE ELSE, TOO..
I PLAY FOR WHOEVER OWNS THE SUPPER DISH
SCHULZ

September 11, 1998

WHAT ARE THOSE ROUND THINGS?
PEOPLE FACES..
9-11

I'M DRAWING A FOOTBALL STADIUM FILLED WITH SIXTY-THOUSAND FANS..

I ONLY SEE TEN..
PARKING WAS A PROBLEM..
SCHULZ

November 9, 1998

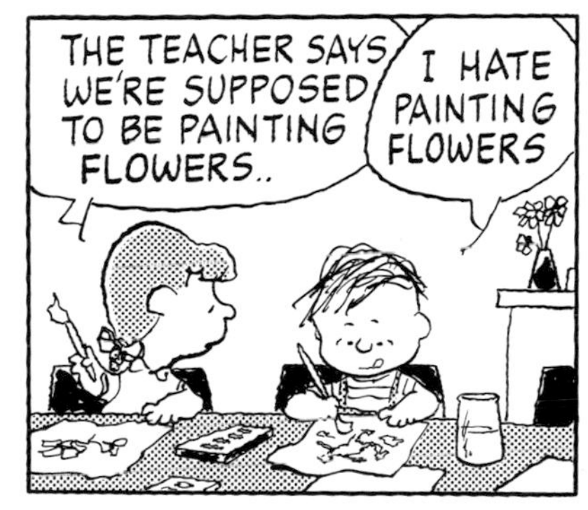
THE TEACHER SAYS WE'RE SUPPOSED TO BE PAINTING FLOWERS..
I HATE PAINTING FLOWERS

I LIKE TO PAINT SUPER HEROES! SEE? MY SUPER HERO FLIES ALL OVER THE UNIVERSE!

THE TEACHER WON'T LIKE IT..
I CALL HIM "SUNFLOWER"
11/9
SCHULZ

"After you achieve a certain stature, of course, then you can go by yourself, and my idea is to draw the best comic strip that I can each day. It is very similar to a person sitting down to play the piano, to playing a Chopin sonata. . . . I'm trying to make each drawing as good as I can and trying to create within the panels a good design. All of this beyond just the fact that it should be funny."

November 11, 1998

I THINK THE NEW REPLACEMENTS ARE GETTING SMALLER ALL THE TIME..
WILLIE AND JOE.. MY HEROES! HAPPY VETERANS DAY, MEN!
SCHULZ and my hero, Bill Mauldin–
11-11

November 16, 1998

NO, I DON'T THINK ANYONE EVER COMES AROUND HERE ANYMORE..

November 24, 1998

"DETAILS AT ELEVEN!" THAT'S MY NEW PHILOSOPHY..

ASK ME WHAT I DID TODAY..
WHAT DID YOU DO TODAY?

DETAILS AT ELEVEN!

December 8, 1998

I THOUGHT I'D PUT BOTH OF OUR NAMES ON OUR CHRISTMAS CARDS THIS YEAR..

IS THAT ALL RIGHT WITH YOU? GOOD..

Merry Christmas from Spike and Joe Cactus

December 29, 1998

Dear Other Grandma,
"OTHER GRANDMA"?

YESTERDAY I WROTE TO ONE GRANDMA.. TODAY I'M WRITING TO MY OTHER GRANDMA..
HOW CAN YOU TELL WHICH IS WHICH?

IT DOESN'T MATTER..ALL GRANDMAS LOOK ALIKE FROM A DISTANCE..

January 20, 1999

HI, SALLY..
IS CHARLIE BROWN THERE?

"WE'LL ALWAYS HAVE MINNEAPOLIS!".. THAT'S MY NEW PHILOSOPHY..
1-20

IT SOUNDS GOOD.. IS CHARLIE BROWN THERE?

"WE'LL ALWAYS HAVE MINNEAPOLIS"

WHO WERE YOU TALKING TO?
PRACTICALLY NOBODY..
SCHULZ

February 9, 1999

2-9

HOW DO YOU GET AN OUTSIDE LINE?
SCHULZ

March 4, 1999

YES, SIR..I'D LIKE TO BUY A NEW KITE..

OH, RED, BLUE, YELLOW... I DON'T CARE..THE COLOR DOESN'T MATTER..
3-4

DO YOU HAVE ONE THAT ISN'T AFRAID OF HEIGHTS?
SCHULZ

March 18, 1999

THEORETICALLY, MY OLDER BROTHER SHOULD BE MY ROLE MODEL..

BUT THAT BLANKET BUSINESS TAKES CARE OF THAT..
3-18

WHICH FORCES ME TO LOOK ELSEWHERE, AND MAYBE ASK THE QUESTION...

CAN THE NEIGHBOR'S DOG BE A ROLE MODEL?
SCHULZ

April 13, 1999

ONE FINGER WILL MEAN A STRAIGHT BALL..TWO FINGERS WILL MEAN ANOTHER STRAIGHT BALL...
4-13

THREE FINGERS WILL MEAN ANOTHER STRAIGHT BALL..
ANYTHING ELSE?

BY THEN IT WON'T MATTER..
SCHULZ

May 23, 1999

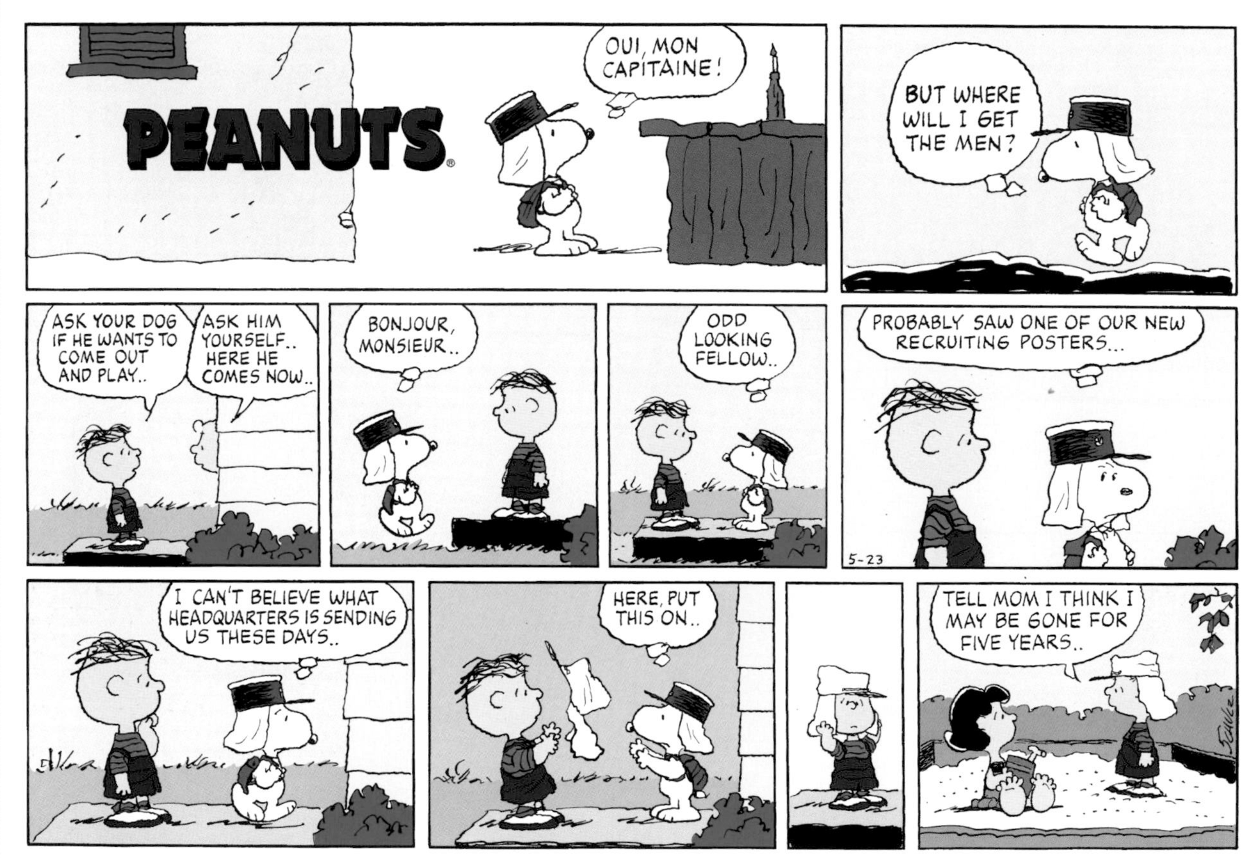
PEANUTS
OUI, MON CAPITAINE!
BUT WHERE WILL I GET THE MEN?
ASK YOUR DOG IF HE WANTS TO COME OUT AND PLAY..
ASK HIM YOURSELF.. HERE HE COMES NOW..
BONJOUR, MONSIEUR..
ODD LOOKING FELLOW..
PROBABLY SAW ONE OF OUR NEW RECRUITING POSTERS...
5-23
I CAN'T BELIEVE WHAT HEADQUARTERS IS SENDING US THESE DAYS..
HERE, PUT THIS ON..
TELL MOM I THINK I MAY BE GONE FOR FIVE YEARS..
SCHULZ

May 17, 1999

YOU MAY NOT REALIZE IT, BUT I FIND THAT YOU'RE VERY INSPIRING..
5-17
I LIKE THE WAY YOU STAND TALL, AND THE WAY YOU SEEM TO BE REACHING FOR THE HEAVENS
IT'S VERY INSPIRING
ON THE OTHER HAND, YOU ALSO LOOK LIKE YOU'RE BEING HELD UP IN A CONVENIENCE STORE..
SCHULZ

May 27, 1999

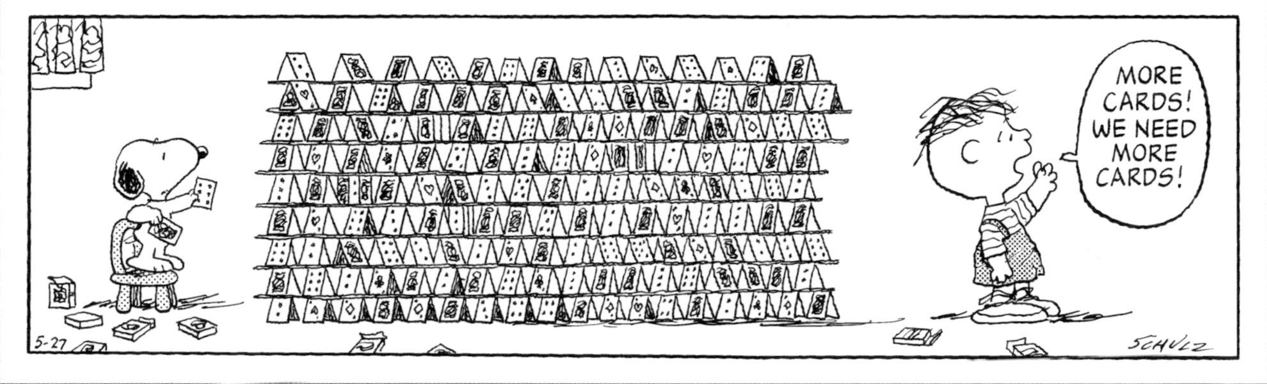
MORE CARDS! WE NEED MORE CARDS!

May 28, 1999

WHOOPS!

"I wanted a strip that was successful, not only commercially, but good artistically so that I would have the respect of fellow craftsmen. I'm pleased that phrases I have coined have become part of the language. And I think Snoopy and Charlie Brown will be remembered."

June 2, 1999

SORRY I MISSED THAT BALL, MANAGER.. THE DANDELIONS GOT IN MY EYES..

WHEN THE SUN REFLECTS OFF THE BRIGHT YELLOW DANDELIONS, I CAN'T SEE THE BALL..

THAT'S THE WORST EXCUSE I'VE EVER HEARD!

BE PATIENT.. I HAVE TWENTY-THREE NEW ONES!

June 23, 1999

LUCY'S ON THE PHONE.. SHE WANTS TO KNOW WHY SHE ALWAYS HAS TO PLAY RIGHT FIELD..

TRADITIONALLY, THE PLAYER WHO IS WEAKEST DEFENSIVELY PLAYS RIGHT FIELD..

HE SAYS THE DUMBEST PLAYER ALWAYS PLAYS RIGHT FIELD..

THIS COULD TURN REALLY UGLY..

June 25, 1999

HEY, MANAGER, I'VE DECIDED IF I HAVE TO PLAY RIGHT FIELD ALL THE TIME, I'D RATHER NOT PLAY AT ALL..

REALLY? WOW! THAT'S GREAT! BOY, WHAT A RELIEF!!

OKAY, I'LL PLAY RIGHT FIELD..
SCHULZ
6-25

June 26, 1999

SO WITH THESE GLASSES I THINK I'LL BE A BETTER OUTFIELDER.. DON'T YOU AGREE?

THE SUN WON'T BE A PROBLEM ANYMORE..YOU'LL APPRECIATE THAT

I'LL CATCH EVERYTHING THAT COMES MY WAY..

NICE TALKING TO YOU, MANAGER..
6-26

I CAN'T STAND IT.. I JUST CAN'T STAND IT..
SCHULZ

July 14, 1999

THAT SOUNDS LIKE A FIRE ENGINE..
SOMETHING MUST BE ON FIRE..
WELL, IT SURE ISN'T OUR PITCHER!
7-14

HA HA HA HA HA HA!

LET HER GET ABOUT TEN FEET AWAY..THEN THROW YOUR GLOVE AT HER..
SCHULZ

July 15, 1999

WE CAME TO WATCH YOUR GAME, CHARLES.. DO WE NEED TICKETS?

NO, YOU CAN SIT OVER THERE BY THE FENCE..

7-15

THESE ARE LOUSY SEATS!
SCHULZ

July 11, 1999

PEANUTS
by SCHULZ
PEGGY JEAN!
BROWNIE CHARLES!
I DIDN'T KNOW YOU WERE HERE AT CAMP.. ACTUALLY, I WAS JUST THINKING ABOUT YOU...
7-11
I WASN'T GOING TO CAMP THIS YEAR, BUT MY BOY FRIEND SAID HE'D BE HERE..
ANYWAY, I PROMISED TO MEET HIM OVER BY THE SOCCER FIELD..
BOY FRIEND?
BUT REMEMBER WHEN..REMEMBER WHEN...
REMEMBER...
SALLY? PUT SNOOPY ON THE PHONE, WILL YOU?
WOOF!
SCHULZ
THANKS.. I NEEDED TO HEAR A FRIENDLY VOICE..

July 17, 1999

IS YOUR GRAMPA STILL PLAYING GOLF?
YES, BUT HE'S GIVEN UP TRYING TO SHOOT HIS AGE.. NOW HE'S TRYING TO SHOOT THE TEMPERATURE..
IT WAS HOT YESTERDAY.. HE SHOT A 102..
7-17
SCHULZ

August 28, 1999

ALL RIGHT, WHO TOOK THE COMIC BOOK THAT WAS ON THIS TABLE?

HERE, I'M SORRY..I DIDN'T KNOW IT WAS YOURS..
8-28

I SUPPOSE YOU READ ALL THE READING OUT OF IT..
SCHULZ

July 18, 1999

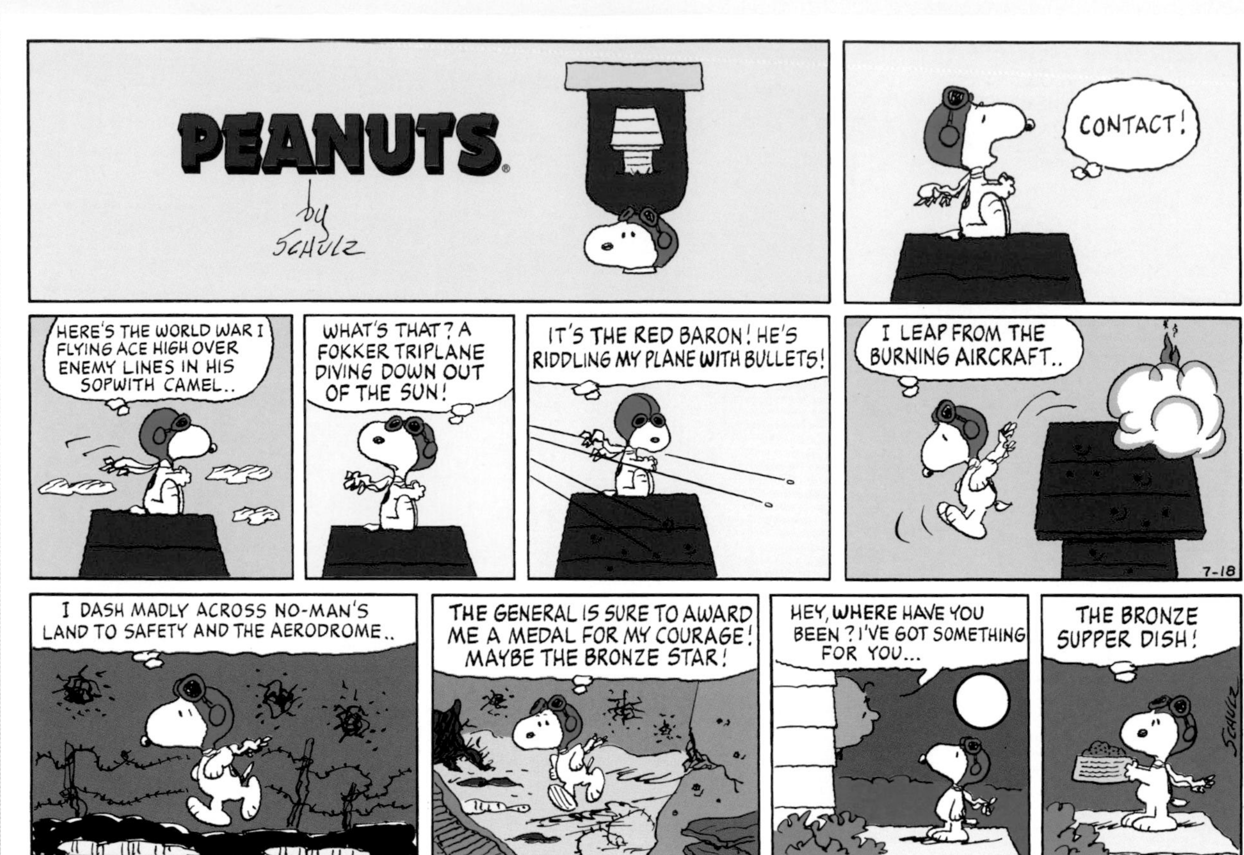

PEANUTS
by SCHULZ
CONTACT!
HERE'S THE WORLD WAR I FLYING ACE HIGH OVER ENEMY LINES IN HIS SOPWITH CAMEL..
WHAT'S THAT? A FOKKER TRIPLANE DIVING DOWN OUT OF THE SUN!
IT'S THE RED BARON! HE'S RIDDLING MY PLANE WITH BULLETS!
I LEAP FROM THE BURNING AIRCRAFT..
7-18
I DASH MADLY ACROSS NO-MAN'S LAND TO SAFETY AND THE AERODROME..
THE GENERAL IS SURE TO AWARD ME A MEDAL FOR MY COURAGE! MAYBE THE BRONZE STAR!
HEY, WHERE HAVE YOU BEEN? I'VE GOT SOMETHING FOR YOU...
THE BRONZE SUPPER DISH!
SCHULZ

September 9, 1999

WE'RE SUPPOSED TO BE PAINTING FLOWERS..
NOT ME
THIS IS TARZAN BEATING UP ON MICKEY MOUSE, AND HERE'S DAFFY DUCK BEATING UP ON TARZAN..
I'M INTO BASEMENT COMICS..
9-9
UNDERGROUND
WHATEVER
SCHULZ

September 13, 1999

THE TEACHER SAYS WE'RE SUPPOSED TO PAINT THESE FLOWERS..
I DON'T PAINT FLOWERS..I DO UNDERGROUND COMIC BOOKS..
SEE? HERE'S A SPACEMAN ON MARS FIGHTING A PURPLE MONSTER..
9-13
WHERE ARE THE WOMEN? I DON'T SEE ANY WOMEN..
THEY HAVE LONG HAIR, RIGHT?
SCHULZ

September 14, 1999

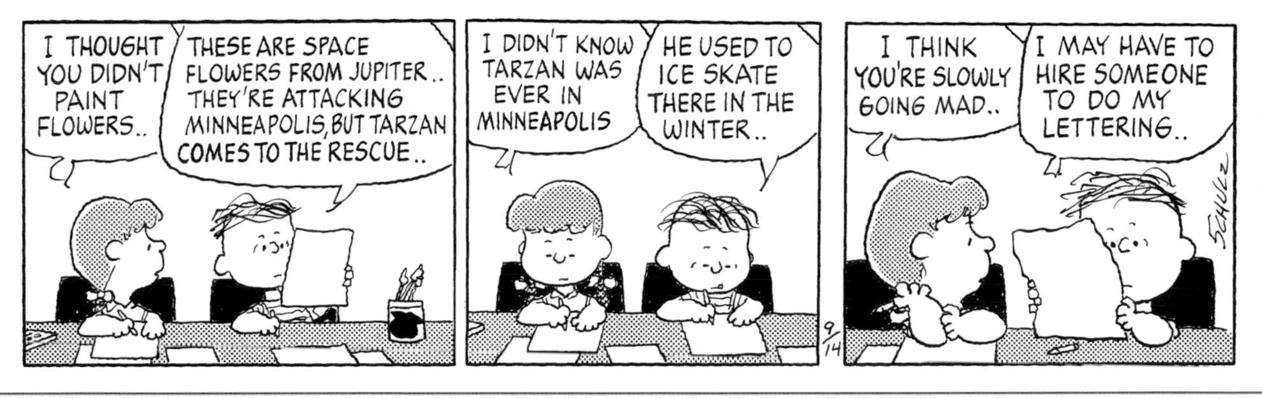
I THOUGHT YOU DIDN'T PAINT FLOWERS..
THESE ARE SPACE FLOWERS FROM JUPITER.. THEY'RE ATTACKING MINNEAPOLIS, BUT TARZAN COMES TO THE RESCUE..
I DIDN'T KNOW TARZAN WAS EVER IN MINNEAPOLIS
HE USED TO ICE SKATE THERE IN THE WINTER..
I THINK YOU'RE SLOWLY GOING MAD..
I MAY HAVE TO HIRE SOMEONE TO DO MY LETTERING..
SCHULZ
9/14

September 15, 1999

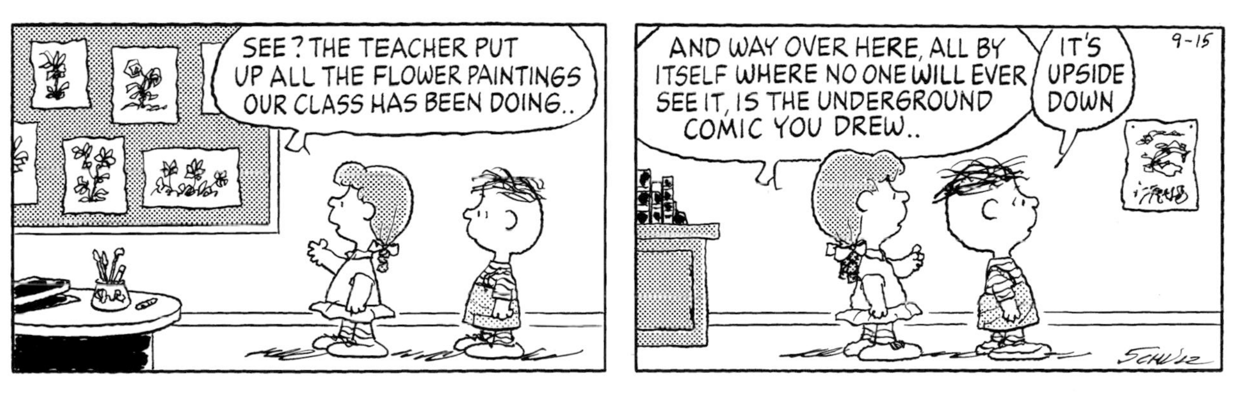
SEE? THE TEACHER PUT UP ALL THE FLOWER PAINTINGS OUR CLASS HAS BEEN DOING..
AND WAY OVER HERE, ALL BY ITSELF WHERE NO ONE WILL EVER SEE IT, IS THE UNDERGROUND COMIC YOU DREW..
IT'S UPSIDE DOWN
9-15
SCHULZ

"I think it's a shame cartooning is so rarely studied in schools. The very books children treasure most are usually snatched away from them in the classroom. But cartooning is a very high form of creativity, one I put above illustration."

August 29, 1999

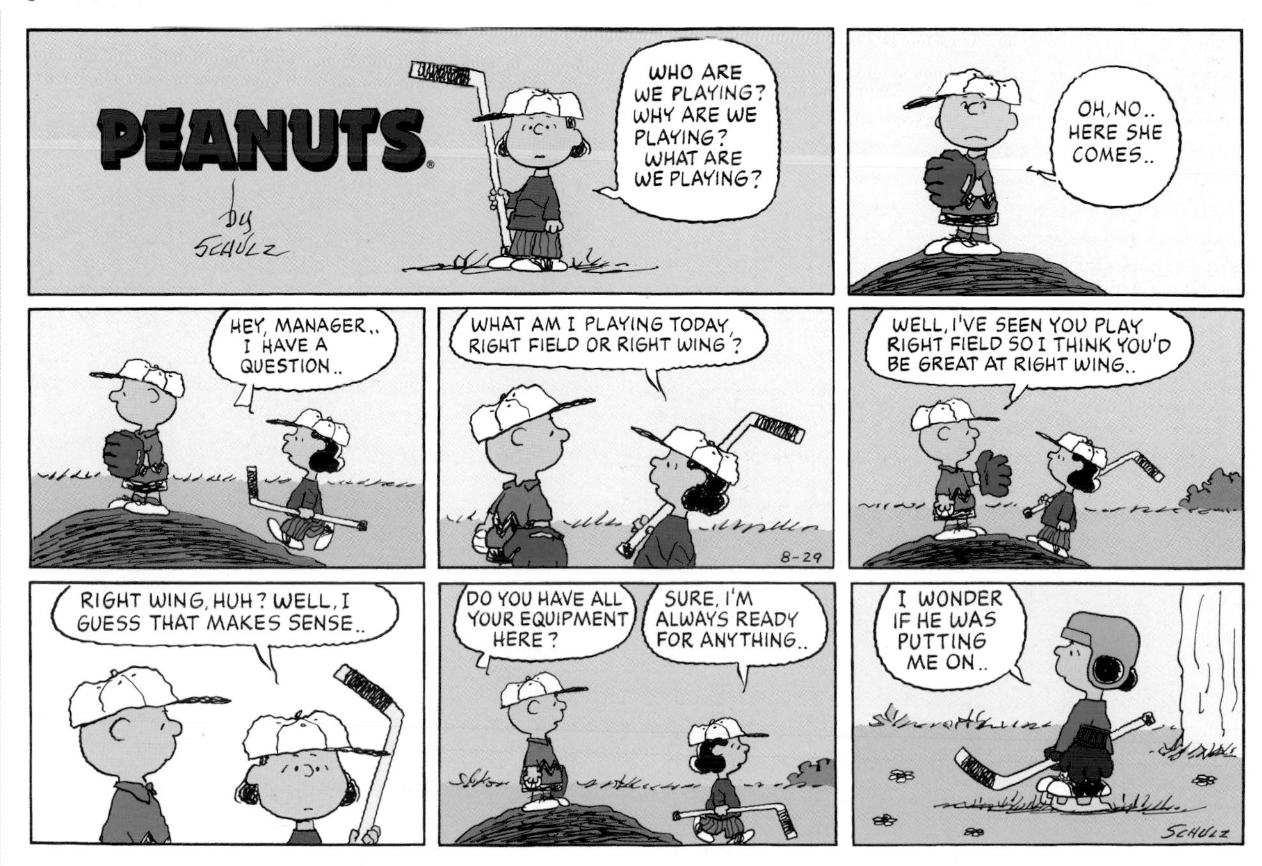
PEANUTS
by SCHULZ
WHO ARE WE PLAYING? WHY ARE WE PLAYING? WHAT ARE WE PLAYING?
OH, NO.. HERE SHE COMES..
HEY, MANAGER.. I HAVE A QUESTION..
WHAT AM I PLAYING TODAY, RIGHT FIELD OR RIGHT WING?
8-29
WELL, I'VE SEEN YOU PLAY RIGHT FIELD SO I THINK YOU'D BE GREAT AT RIGHT WING..
RIGHT WING, HUH? WELL, I GUESS THAT MAKES SENSE..
DO YOU HAVE ALL YOUR EQUIPMENT HERE?
SURE, I'M ALWAYS READY FOR ANYTHING..
I WONDER IF HE WAS PUTTING ME ON..
SCHULZ

September 29, 1999

WHAT'S THAT?
AN UNDERWATER CAMERA..

IT TAKES PICTURES UNDER WATER..

9-29

I DON'T THINK IT'S WORKING..
SCHULZ

October 13, 1999

HOW DOES THIS SOUND? "THE NILE RIVER IS LIKE THE MISSISSIPPI"

"IF YOU'VE SEEN ONE RIVER, YOU'VE SEEN THEM ALL"

"THE NILE RIVER IS ALSO LIKE THE MISSOURI, THE RHINE, THE AMAZON, THE COLORADO, THE VOLGA, THE EUPHRATES, AND THE DANUBE.."
10/13

THIRTY-FIVE, THIRTY-SIX, THIRTY-SEVEN ... WHAT SHE WANTS IS FIVE HUNDRED WORDS..
SCHULZ

October 24, 1999

LUCY!
PEANUTS
BY SCHULZ

LUNCH TIME!

MOM SAYS TO COME IN FOR LUNCH
SO I'LL HOLD THE BALL, CHARLIE BROWN, AND YOU COME RUNNING UP AND KICK IT..
SHE SAYS RIGHT NOW!
OH, GOOD GRIEF!
THAT'S ALL RIGHT.. WE'LL DO IT SOME OTHER TIME..

NO, RERUN CAN TAKE MY PLACE..
ME?
© 1999 United Feature Syndicate, Inc.

THIS TIME I'LL DO IT! THIS TIME I'LL KICK IT.. RERUN WILL NEVER PULL IT AWAY.. HE JUST WOULDN'T..
10-24

SO HERE WE GO!

WHAT HAPPENED? DID YOU PULL THE BALL AWAY? DID HE KICK IT? WHAT HAPPENED?

YOU'LL NEVER KNOW..
AAUGH!
SCHULZ

November 28, 1999

PEANUTS
by SCHULZ
CAFE
TWO ROOT BEERS, S'IL VOUS PLAÎT..
PARDON, MADEMOISELLE..COULD MY BROTHER HAVE A STRAW ?
11-28
ALWAYS THE ROWDY ONE, AREN'T YOU, SPIKE ?
I GOT CARRIED AWAY..
SCHULZ

October 25, 1999

SOMEONE SAID YOU WERE A MESSAGE DOG..
THEY DID?
HERE..THE ADDRESS IS ON THE FRONT..
I WANT IT DELIVERED AS FAST AS POSSIBLE..
10-25

October 26, 1999

10-26
"RETURN TO SENDER"
SCHULZ

October 27, 1999

HEY, CHUCK, GO ASK YOUR DOG WHAT HAPPENED WITH THE MESSAGE HE DELIVERED FOR ME

10-27

SCHULZ

October 28, 1999

WHAT KIND OF A MESSAGE DOG ARE YOU?
10-28

HERE! I WANT THIS DELIVERED RIGHT NOW!

AND DON'T MAKE A PAPER AIRPLANE OUT OF IT!

SCHULZ

November 16, 1999

11-16

HOW WAS SCHOOL TODAY?
I FAILED STORY LISTENING..
SCHULZ

November 19, 1999

11-19
SCHULZ

"The most important thing to remember is to be patient. You can't expect to be a top-notch cartoonist too young, because there simply are no child prodigies among cartoonists. There may be prodigies as far as drawing is concerned, but cartooning is more than just drawing. When it comes to thinking of humorous ideas, you need experience, because seeing the humorous part of life requires having experienced things."

December 3, 1999

NO, I GUESS NOT..IT MAKES YOU LOOK LIKE A SHERIFF..
12-3
SCHULZ

December 4, 1999

OUCH! OW! OOO! OUCH!
12-4
OUCH! OW! OUCH! OUCH!
OUCH! OUCH!
OW! OUCH!
"JOY TO THE WORLD" OUCH!
SCHULZ

December 21, 1999

12-21
HEEL!
SCHULZ

Celebrate 2000

"It's hard for people to comprehend that someone can be born a cartoonist but I believe I was. Why do musicians compose symphonies and poets write poems? Because life would have no meaning for them if they didn't. That's how I feel about drawing cartoons. It's my life."

—Charles M. Schulz

2000

Charles Schulz died at home on February 12, 2000.

- In May 2000, the National Cartoonists Society recognized Charles Schulz for his contribution to the art form by posthumously awarding him the Milton Caniff Lifetime Achievement Award.
- On May 17, 2001, the United States Postal Service issued a first-class postage strip of Snoopy as the World War I Flying Ace.
- Charles Schulz was posthumously awarded the Congressional Medal of Honor by the United States Congress on June 7, 2001.
- The Charles M. Schulz Museum and Research Center opened in Schulz's adopted hometown of Santa Rosa, California, on August 17, 2002.

January 1, 2000

1-1-00
SCHULZ
SUDDENLY THE DOG REALIZED THAT HIS DAD HAD NEVER TAUGHT HIM HOW TO THROW SNOWBALLS..

January 2, 2000

PEANUTS
by SCHULZ
A LITTLE RAIN, A LITTLE MUD... THIS IS WHAT IT'S ALL ABOUT..
HEY, CHUCK, IT'S A GREAT GAME, ISN'T IT?
WE'RE HAVING FUN, AREN'T WE, CHUCK?
IT'S STILL YOUR BALL..
1-2
FOURTH DOWN..
WHAT ARE YOU GONNA DO, CHUCK?
YOU GONNA RUN OR PASS?
EVERYBODY'S GONE HOME, SIR..
YOU SHOULD GO HOME, TOO.. IT'S GETTING DARK..
WE HAD FUN, DIDN'T WE, MARCIE?
YES, SIR..WE HAD FUN..
NOBODY SHOOK HANDS AND SAID, "GOOD GAME"

January 9, 2000

PEANUTS
by SCHULZ
HI, CHARLIE BROWN..
RERUN.. WHAT'S UP?
ASK YOUR DOG IF HE WANTS TO COME OUT AND ROMP IN THE SNOW, AND LAUGH, AND ACT LIKE WE DON'T HAVE THE SENSE WE WERE BORN WITH..
1-9
HAHAHAHA!
HOW COULD IT EVER GET BETTER THAN THIS?
IF YOU WERE A GOLDEN RETRIEVER
SCHULZ

January 16, 2000

PEANUTS
by SCHULZ
ME?
YES, SIR.. WE'LL DO IT..
GENERAL WASHINGTON WANTS TO KNOW IF WE CAN CHOP UP SOME FIREWOOD FOR HIS CABIN..
1-16
YES, SIR.. WOODSTOCK THINKS MAYBE YOU SHOULD JUST TURN UP THE THERMOSTAT..
SCHULZ

January 23, 2000

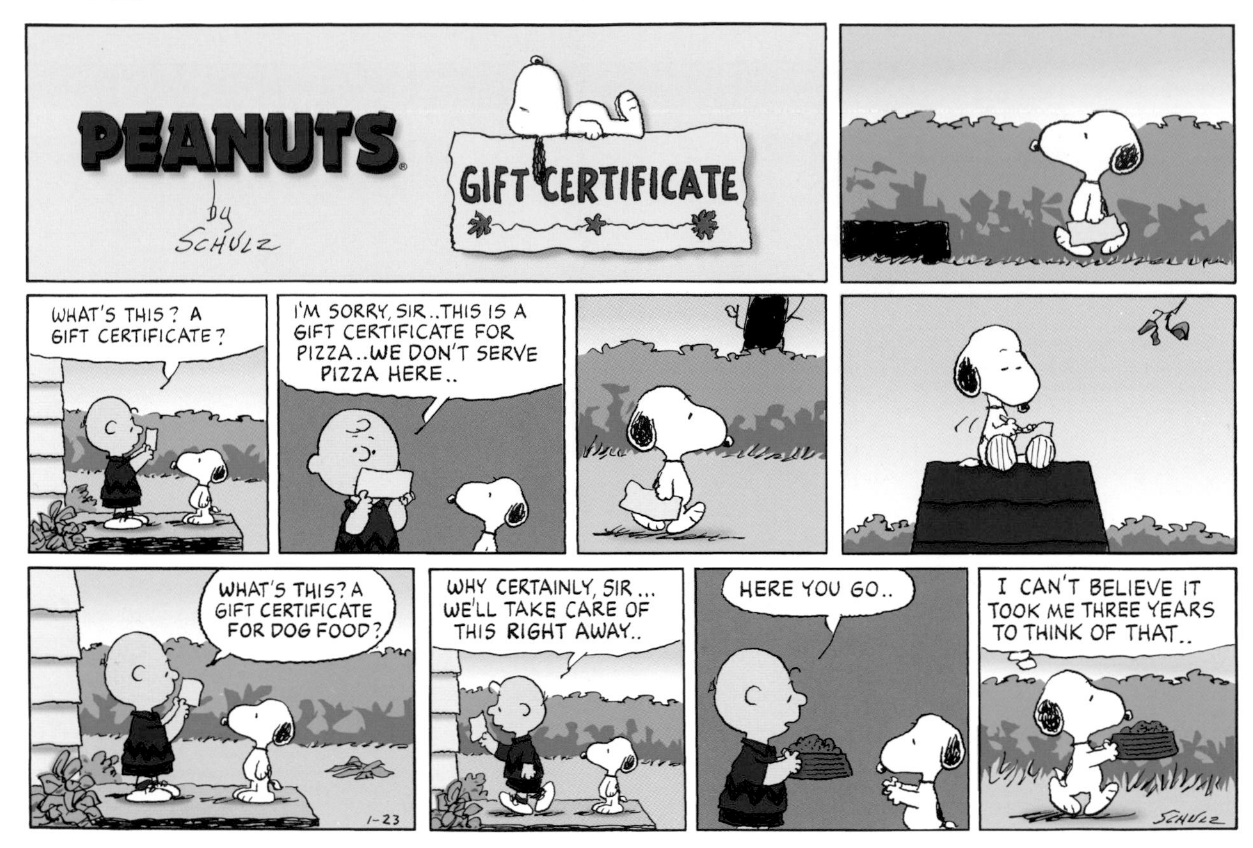

PEANUTS
by SCHULZ
GIFT CERTIFICATE
WHAT'S THIS ? A GIFT CERTIFICATE ?
I'M SORRY, SIR..THIS IS A GIFT CERTIFICATE FOR PIZZA..WE DON'T SERVE PIZZA HERE..
WHAT'S THIS? A GIFT CERTIFICATE FOR DOG FOOD?
WHY CERTAINLY, SIR... WE'LL TAKE CARE OF THIS RIGHT AWAY..
HERE YOU GO..
I CAN'T BELIEVE IT TOOK ME THREE YEARS TO THINK OF THAT..
1-23
SCHULZ

January 30, 2000

PEANUTS
by SCHULZ
MORE ACTION! MORE COLOR!
WE'RE SUPPOSED TO BE PAINTING FLOWERS TODAY
I DON'T DO FLOWERS..I DO UNDERGROUND COMICS..
SEE? HERE'S BILLIE JEAN KING AND DAFFY DUCK THROWING LONG JOHN SILVER OFF THE PIRATE SHIP..
I HAVE BIG PLANS FOR MY WORK..
YES, MA'AM..THESE WILL BE CONSECUTIVELY NUMBERED LIMITED EDITION PRINTS..
EACH PRINT WILL BE SIGNED AND ACCOMPANIED BY A CERTIFICATE OF AUTHENTICATION..
YES, MA'AM.. I UNDERSTAND..
WHAT DID SHE SAY?
SHE SAID TODAY WE'RE PAINTING FLOWERS..
1-30
SCHULZ

February 6, 2000

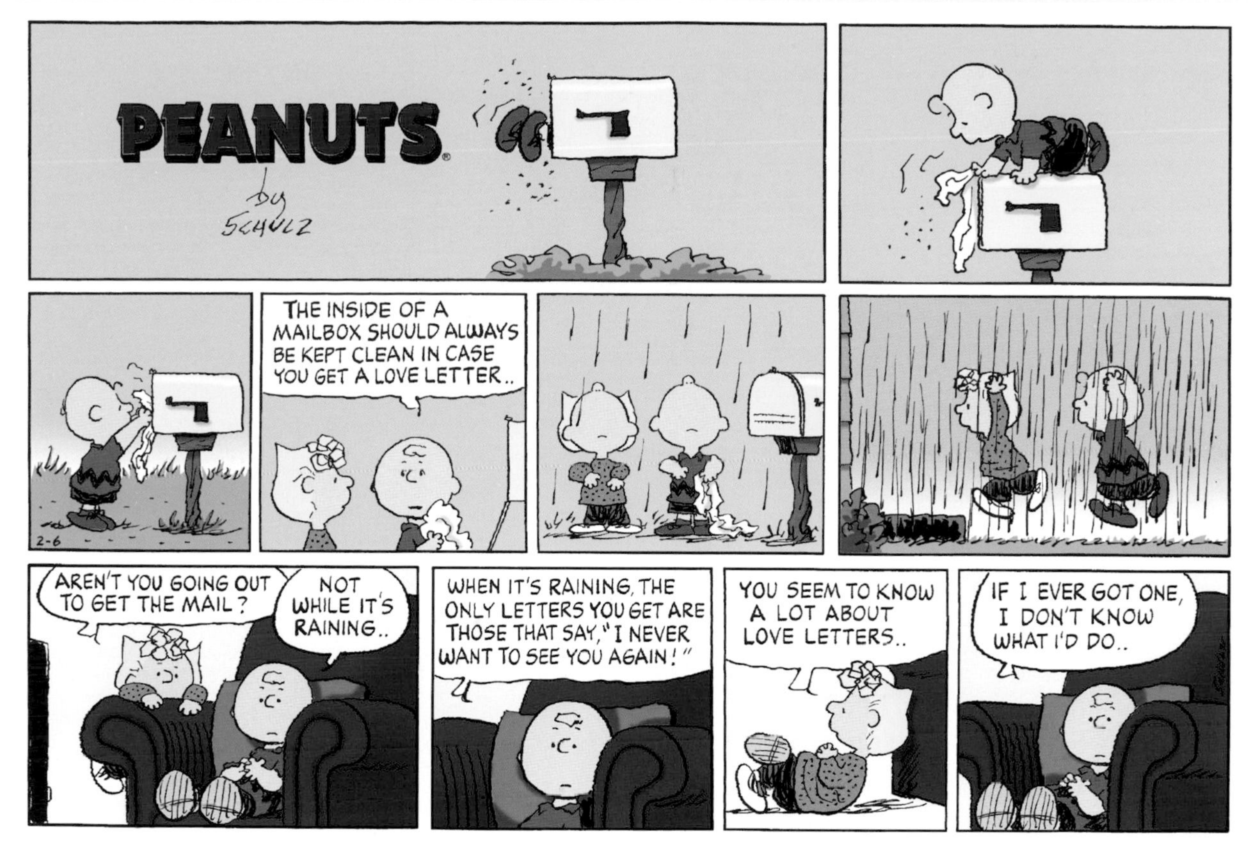
PEANUTS
by SCHULZ
THE INSIDE OF A MAILBOX SHOULD ALWAYS BE KEPT CLEAN IN CASE YOU GET A LOVE LETTER..
AREN'T YOU GOING OUT TO GET THE MAIL?
NOT WHILE IT'S RAINING..
WHEN IT'S RAINING, THE ONLY LETTERS YOU GET ARE THOSE THAT SAY, "I NEVER WANT TO SEE YOU AGAIN!"
YOU SEEM TO KNOW A LOT ABOUT LOVE LETTERS..
IF I EVER GOT ONE, I DON'T KNOW WHAT I'D DO..

"Not many cartoons live into the next generation, and that probably is the best definition of art, isn't it? Does it speak to succeeding generations? Real art—real music, real literature—speaks to succeeding generations."

February 13, 2000

PEANUTS
by SCHULZ
NO, I THINK HE'S WRITING..
Dear Friends...
BONK!
RAINING..
CREDIT ON A D-MINUS?
UNCOMMONLY WEIRD, MARCIE!
PLANS FOR MY WORK..
AAUGH!
CLOMP!
GOOD GRIEF!
PSYCHIATRIC HELP 5¢
THE DOCTOR IS IN
Dear Friends,
I have been fortunate to draw Charlie Brown and his friends for almost 50 years. It has been the fulfillment of my childhood ambition.
Unfortunately, I am no longer able to maintain the schedule demanded by a daily comic strip. My family does not wish Peanuts to be continued by anyone else, therefore I am announcing my retirement.
I have been grateful over the years for the loyalty of our editors and the wonderful support and love expressed to me by fans of the comic strip.
Charlie Brown, Snoopy, Linus, Lucy...how can I ever forget them...
Charles M. Schulz

Sources

p. 2 "*Redbook* Announces a Dialogue Between . . . Jack Lemmon and Charles Schulz," *Redbook,* 1967, volume 130, number 2
p. 5 "A Pleasant Chat with the Creator of *Peanuts*," *Seventeen*, 1977, volume 36, number 12
p. 8 "SOS from the AT&T," *Sports Illustrated*, 1993, volume 78, number 6
p. 9 "Charlie Brown, Snoopy, and Me," *Family Circle*, 1975, volume 87, number 4
p. 13 "You're a Good Man, Charles Schulz," *Designers Illustrated*, 1993, volume 8, number 5
p. 16 "Good Grief! Snoopy's 45," *Baby Boomer Collectibles*, 1995, volume 2, number 7
p. 17 "Charles Schulz Interview," *Nemo*, 1992, number 31
p. 20 "The Man Charlie Brown Made Famous," *PlateWorld*, 1983, volume 5, number 1
p. 24 "Charles Schulz," *Art Product News*, 1984, volume 6, number 3
p. 25 "Charlie Brown, Snoopy, and Me," *Family Circle*, 1975, volume 87, number 4
p. 35 "Comical Capers," *Dog Fancy*, 1998, volume 29, number 2
p. 41 "Celebrating 40 Years of *Peanuts*," *Step-by-Step Graphics*, 1990, volume 6, number 3
p. 42 "Charles Schulz Interview," *Nemo*, 1992, number 31
p. 43 "Charlie Brown, Snoopy, and Me," *Family Circle*, 1975, volume 87, number 4
p. 48 "Good Grief, Charlie Schulz!" *The Saturday Evening Post*, 1964, volume 237, number 16
p. 50 "Charles Schulz Interview," *Nemo*, 1992, number 31
p. 59 "So Long, Snoopy & Co.," *Newsweek*, 2000, volume 134, number 26
p. 66 "Charles Schulz," *Art Product News*, 1984, volume 6, number 3
p. 79 "*Peanuts* with Everything," *Observer Magazine*, August 1983
p. 80 "Charles Schulz Interview," *Nemo*, 1992, number 31
p. 81 "Penthouse Interview: Charles M. Schulz, Creator of *Peanuts*," *Penthouse*, 1971, volume 3, number 2
p. 84 "Charles Schulz Interview," *Nemo*, 1992, number 31
p. 87 "Charles Schulz," *Friends*, 1975, volume 32, number 8
p. 88 "Charles Schulz Interview," *Nemo*, 1992, number 31
p. 93 "The *Peanuts* Man Talks about Children," *Family Circle*, 1968, volume 237, number 16
p. 95 "Good Grief, Charlie Schulz!" *The Saturday Evening Post*, 1964, volume 237, number 16
p. 102 "A Conversation with Charles Schulz," *Psychology Today*, 1968, volume 1, number 8
p. 107 "A Chat with Charles Schulz," *Aspiring Cartoonist*, 1994, volume 1, number 2
p. 110 "Charles Schulz Interview," *Nemo*, 1992, number 31
p. 116 "Good Grief, $150 Million," *Newsweek*, 1971, volume 78, number 26
p. 121 "Good Grief, $150 Million," *Newsweek*, 1971, volume 78, number 26
p. 122 "A Conversation with Charles Schulz," *Psychology Today*, 1968, volume 1, number 8
p. 124 "A License to Create," *Artist's Magazine*, 1996, volume 13, number 26
p. 125 "Charles Schulz Interview," *Nemo*, 1992, number 31
p. 129 "Celebrating 40 Years of *Peanuts*," *Step-by-Step Graphics*, 1990, volume 6, number 3
p. 134 "A Conversation with Charles Schulz," *Psychology Today*, 1968, volume 1, number 8
p. 139 "Penthouse Interview: Charles M. Schulz, Creator of *Peanuts*," *Penthouse*, 1971, volume 3, number 2
p. 143 "Charles Schulz Interview," *Nemo*, 1992, number 31
p. 144 "Good Grief, $150 Million," *Newsweek*, 1971, volume 78, number 26
p. 149 "*Peanuts* with Everything," *Observer Magazine*, August 1983
p. 150 "The Not-So-*Peanuts* World of Charles M. Schulz," *Saturday Review*, 1969, volume 52, number 15
p. 156 "Good Grief, Charlie Schulz!" *The Saturday Evening Post*, 1964, volume 237, number 16
p. 159 "Happiness Is Talking with Charles Schulz," *Views*, April 1970
p. 162 "Happiness Is to Dance with Snoopy and Talk with His Creator," *Youth*, 1968, volume 19, number 6
p. 163 "*Peanuts*: How It All Began," *Liberty*, 1973, volume 1, number 11
p. 168 "Schulz Offers Editors Criticism and Praise," *Editor & Publisher*, 1989, volume 122, number 26
p. 169 "Charlie Brown, Snoopy, and Me," *Family Circle*, 1975, volume 87, number 4
p. 175 "Happiness Is to Dance with Snoopy and Talk with His Creator," *Youth*, 1968, volume 19, number 6
p. 182 "Happiness Is to Dance with Snoopy and Talk with His Creator," *Youth*, 1968, volume 19, number 6
p. 184 "Happiness Is Talking with Charles Schulz," *Views*, April 1970
p. 185 "Four Who Changed the World," *The Sunday Times Magazine,* September 1991
p. 189 "So Long, Snoopy & Co.," *Newsweek*, 2000, volume 134, number 26
p. 195 "Shel Dorf Takes a Trip to Snoopyland," *Comic Book Marketplace*, 2003, volume 3, number 100
p. 203 "The Man Charlie Brown Made Famous," *PlateWorld*, 1983, volume 5, number 1
p. 204 "Book Review: *Peanuts Jubilee*," *Minnesota History*, 1976, volume 45, number 2
p. 207 "The Not-So-*Peanuts* World of Charles M. Schulz," *Saturday Review*, 1969, volume 52, number 15
p. 208 *Charlie Brown and Charles Schulz*, Television Documentary, 1969
p. 219 "A Conversation with Charles Schulz," *Psychology Today*, 1968, volume 1, number 8
p. 223 "Charles Schulz Interview," *Nemo*, 1992, number 31
p. 224 "Good Grief, $150 Million," *Newsweek*, 1971, volume 78, number 26
p. 228 "A Candid Interview with Charles M. Schulz," *Witty World: International Cartoon Magazine*, 1992, number 13
p. 233 "Schulz: Cartoonist, Hockey Player, and Referee," *American Hockey & Arena*, 1980, volume 8, number 3
p. 241 "Charles Schulz's *Peanuts* Philosophy," *TV Guide*, 1972, volume 20, number 44
p. 248 "A Pleasant Chat with the Creator of *Peanuts*," *Seventeen*, 1977, volume 36, number 12
p. 249 "Focus Interview: Charles Schulz on Education," *California English*, 1983, volume 19, number 3
p. 251 "Charles Schulz Interview," *Nemo*, 1992, number 31
p. 255 "Happiness Is Talking with Charles Schulz," *Views*, April 1970
p. 260 "Charlie Brown, Snoopy, and Me," *Family Circle*, 1975, volume 87, number 4
p. 267 "*Peanuts*: How It All Began," *Liberty*, 1973, volume 1, number 11
p. 268 "Snoopy on Tennis, or How to Get Away with 11 Bad Calls in a Row," *Tennis*, 1976, volume 12, number 7
p. 280 "The Goal Interview: Charles Schulz," *Goal: The National Hockey League Magazine*, 1974, volume 2, number 2
p. 285 "What Do You Do with a Dog That Doesn't Talk?" *TV Guide*, 1980, volume 28, number 8
p. 287 "Charles Schulz," *Art Product News*, 1984, volume 6, number 3
p. 294 "What Do You Do with a Dog That Doesn't Talk?" *TV Guide*, 1980, volume 28, number 8
p. 309 "Penthouse Interview: Charles M. Schulz, Creator of *Peanuts*," *Penthouse*, 1971, volume 3, number 2
p. 324 "Thirty Years of Warm Puppies," *American Way*, 1980, volume 13, number 2
p. 327 "A Pleasant Chat with the Creator of *Peanuts*," *Seventeen*, 1977, volume 36, number 12
p. 331 *The Whoopi Goldberg Show*, December 9, 1992
p. 332 "Penthouse Interview: Charles M. Schulz, Creator of *Peanuts*," *Penthouse*, 1971, volume 3, number 2
p. 337 "Focus Interview: Charles Schulz on Education," *California English*, 1983, volume 19, number 3
p. 342 "Security Is Being a Successful Cartoonist," *The Valuator*, Spring 1969
p. 345 "Thirty Years of Warm Puppies," *American Way*, 1980, volume 13, number 2
p. 349 "Publisher's Letter: The Inside Track," *The Runner*, 1986, volume 8, number 5
p. 355 "*Peanuts* with Everything," *Observer Magazine*, August 1983
p. 360 "Charles Schulz," *People Weekly*, 1989, volume 32, number 18
p. 361 "Charles Schulz's *Peanuts* Philosophy," *TV Guide*, 1980, volume 28, number 8
p. 363 "Shel Dorf Takes a Trip to Snoopyland," *Comic Book Marketplace*, 2003, volume 3, number 100
p. 369 "What Do You Do with a Dog That Doesn't Talk?" *TV Guide*, 1980, volume 28, number 8
p. 372 "What Do You Do with a Dog That Doesn't Talk?" *TV Guide*, 1980, volume 28, number 8
p. 382 "Charles Schulz Interview," *Nemo*, 1992, number 31
p. 388 "A Pleasant Chat with the Creator of *Peanuts*," *Seventeen*, 1977, volume 36, number 12
p. 396 "Charles Schulz Interview," *Nemo*, 1992, number 31
p. 399 "Pen Pal," *Mature Outlook*, 1987, volume 4, number 5
p. 403 "A Candid Interview with Charles M. Schulz," *Witty World: International Cartoon Magazine*, 1992, number 13
p. 408 "Pen Pal," *Mature Outlook*, 1987, volume 4, number 5
p. 409 "Security Is Being a Successful Cartoonist," *The Valuator*, Spring 1969
p. 426 "Thirty Years of Warm Puppies," *American Way*, 1980, volume 13, number 2
p. 429 "Thirty Years of Warm Puppies," *American Way*, 1980, volume 13, number 2
p. 432 "A Conversation with Charles Schulz," *Psychology Today*, 1968, volume 1, number 8
p. 436 "Charles Schulz: Drawing on Life," *The Illustrator*, 2000
p. 441 "Charles Schulz," *Art Product News*, 1984, volume 6, number 3
p. 447 "Happiness Is to Dance with Snoopy and Talk with His Creator," *Youth*, 1968, volume 19, number 6
p. 451 "Charles Schulz Interview," *Nemo*, 1992, number 31
p. 454 "Ideas for Living: Interview with Charles Schulz," *Family Circle*, 1983, volume 96, number 3
p. 459 "A Pleasant Chat with the Creator of *Peanuts*," *Seventeen*, 1977, volume 36, number 12
p. 460 "Remembering D-Day," *Soldiers*, 1999, volume 54, number 6
p. 468 "A License to Create," *Artist's Magazine*, 1996, volume 13, number 10
p. 481 "Shel Dorf Takes a Trip to Snoopyland," *Comic Book Marketplace*, 2003, volume 3, number 100
p. 493 "Happiness Is to Dance with Snoopy and Talk with His Creator," *Youth*, 1968, volume 19, number 6
p. 502 "A Chat with Charles Schulz," *Aspiring Cartoonist*, 1994, volume 1, number 2
p. 507 "The Not-So-*Peanuts* World of Charles M. Schulz," *Saturday Review*, 1969, volume 52, number 15
p. 510 "A Chat with Charles Schulz," *Aspiring Cartoonist*, 1994, volume 1, number 2
p. 515 "A Candid Interview with Charles M. Schulz," *Witty World: International Cartoon Magazine*, 1992, number 13
p. 519 "He's Your Dog, Charlie Brown," *Woman's Day*, 1968, volume 31, number 5
p. 523 "*Peanuts* with Everything," *Observer Magazine*, August 1983
p. 527 "A Pleasant Chat with the Creator of *Peanuts*," *Seventeen*, 1977, volume 36, number 12
p. 528 "Charles Schulz," *Friends*, 1975, volume 32, number 8
p. 533 *The Charlie Rose Show*, May 9, 1997